# Visual Basic .NET
# Developer's Handbook

# Visual Basic® .NET Developer's Handbook™

Evangelos Petroutsos
Mark Ridgeway

SYBEX

San Francisco · London

Associate Publisher: Joel Fugazzotto
Acquisitions Editor: Denise Santoro Lincoln
Developmental Editor: Tom Cirtin
Editor: Judy Flynn
Production Editors: Susan Berge, Leslie H. Light
Technical Editor: Greg Guntle
Graphic Illustrator: Tony Jonick
Electronic Publishing Specialists: Rozi Harris, Bill Clark, Interactive Composition Corporation
Proofreaders: Amey Garber, Emily Hsuan, Eric Lach, Dave Nash, Laurie O'Connell, Yariv Rabinovitch, Nancy Riddiough
Indexer: Nancy Guenther
Cover Design: Caryl Gorska, Gorska Design
Cover Photograph: Akira Kaede, PhotoDisc

Library of Congress Card Number: 2002106418

ISBN: 0-7821-2879-3

*To the Joy of my life*
*—Evangelos Petroutsos*

*To the two most important people in my life:*
*my wife, Marian, and our son, Tyler*
*—Mark Ridgeway*

# Acknowledgments

**M**any people contributed to this book, and we would like to thank them all. We'd like to start with the developers who have found useful information in our earlier books. Your comments make us feel even more obligated and committed to producing a solid programming book.

Sybex has been in the business of computer book publishing for over 25 years. We thank them for the opportunity to write a book in one of their most respected series of developers' titles. We read a lot of their books even before we wrote our first article. It's an achievement in and of itself to have that kind of staying power in an industry like ours, and we're proud to be working with Sybex.

Special thanks to the talented people at Sybex—to all of them and to each one individually. We'll start with Denise Lincoln, acquisitions editor, and Tom Cirtin, developmental editor, who have invested a lot of time and effort in this book. They have followed the progress of the book (its ups and downs) and managed to coordinate the entire team. We'd also like to thank technical editor Greg Guntle, for scrutinizing every paragraph and every line of code, and production editors Susan Berge and Leslie Light, who have done more than we can guess to keep this project in order and on schedule.

Thanks also to editor Judy Flynn, electronic publishing specialists Rozi Harris and Bill Clark of Interactive Composition Corporation, indexer Nancy Guenther, and everyone else who added their expertise and talent.

Finally, a big thank you to our respective families for their support and tolerance while we were writing this book.

# Contents at a Glance

# Contents

# Introduction

**W**elcome to .NET, the platform for developing Windows and Internet applications for the next decade. The .NET initiative represents several years of research, and it's Microsoft's vision for a unified framework for building applications that interact with resources over the Internet. Microsoft had to bring together the Windows platform and the Internet. It has attempted to do so in the past, but producing Internet technologies as add-ons to existing technologies wouldn't take the company too far. At some point it became evident that it would have to come up with a new platform to make the most of the Internet, and this is how .NET was born.

Having said that, we must also point out that .NET wasn't designed just for the Internet. It is a platform for building both Windows and web applications. With .NET, you can write better applications for the desktop (applications that may or may not interact with Internet resources), as well as web applications. Despite the hype about the new features of the language, Visual Basic .NET is a better Visual Basic. You can go on using your favorite language to build better applications. The type of applications you'll build with Visual Basic is up to you. You have the tools to harness the best of both worlds (which are merging anyway).

One of the premises of .NET is that it should support any language equally well. There are already many languages that can be used with .NET, but none of them is nearly as popular as Visual Basic and C#. Visual Basic continues to be the most popular language for developing Windows applications, and chances are that it will remain so. Besides, Visual Basic was the language that opened the gate to Windows programming for millions, and many occasional programmers and hobbyists have become professional developers.

Buyers of this book are already familiar with .NET and even more so with Visual Basic—the world's favorite language coupled with the most powerful development environment, a sure winner. The irony is that Microsoft is betting the farm on the .NET initiative, but VB developers haven't embraced it as they did previous versions of the language. Most of them are still reluctant to adopt Visual Basic .NET. No one can really blame the developers; they have good reasons to continue using their old environment. However, there are even better reasons for switching to .NET, and this book is meant to help VB6 developers make the move with the least effort.

What keeps developers from converting to Visual Basic .NET is that the new language is largely incompatible with VB6. For the first time in the history of Visual Basic, you can't open an old project in the new environment and run it. There's a wizard for porting VB6 projects to VB .NET, but the problem is deeper than syntactical differences or the format of the files.

.NET provides new and better techniques for doing the same old things, and you must take advantage of these features. You can exploit the compatibility layer to use the same file I/O techniques as with VB6, but you can't ignore the new techniques for accessing files, namely through streams. You can still call the VB string manipulation functions, but the Framework includes something that's called StringBuilder, which can handle large strings blindingly fast. There are many good reasons to switch to .NET, but developers are still reluctant. So far, it's mostly the professional developers who can appreciate the power of VB .NET and are willing to invest the time to understand the new tools.

Many developers are exploring .NET, but they still miss the features of VB6 that weren't ported to .NET. There are developers who'd rather not have to learn the new file I/O methods of the Framework. They've learned to live with the statements of VB6; they've developed their libraries and don't see why they should switch to streams, which is a totally new method of performing I/O. After all, how many different ways does one need to send data to a file, or read them back from a file? If you take some time to understand streams in the .NET Framework, you'll realize that there's so much more you can do with streams. You can save an entire array to a file with a single statement (and read it back with another statement). We are convinced that any time spent learning to understand the .NET Framework and the new ways of coding the same old tasks is a long-term investment. .NET was designed to address the needs of programming in the next decade; you can't compare it to VB6. Even if VB6 is more than adequate for your current projects, it won't be nearly as adequate a few years down the road.

There's another reason VB6 programmers aren't switching to .NET, and it's basically a misunderstanding. The first component of .NET to be released was ASP.NET, more than two years ago—it was called ASP+ back then. The single most-advertised new feature of .NET was the ability to create Web services. Clearly, Microsoft focused on the new tools for developing distributed, disconnected applications. We won't argue on the usefulness of such features, but we would like to point out that Windows applications are not dead. Corporations are porting their applications to the Web and they're making the most of the new tools. Web services are catching up, and it seems the industry is ready for them. The Web, however, doesn't provide the user experience you can achieve with a Windows application. Even though .NET was designed from the ground up for the Internet, it's also the greatest tool for building Windows applications. It's not just for distributed applications. It's also about better Windows applications and faster data access. Microsoft's marketing focused on the Internet aspect of .NET and people haven't realized yet that VB .NET is the next version of their favorite language and that the .NET Framework is a new application programming interface (API), accessible to the average VB programmer, as opposed to the Win32 API, which was designed for C++ programmers.

Visual Basic .NET addresses the needs of VB developers who have exhausted the capabilities of their favorite language, are tired of exploring the Windows API, or have realized that certain things just can't be done with VB6 (or shouldn't be done with VB6). In this book, we tried to avoid the hype and discuss the parts of the language you will use in your projects, whether they'll be Windows applications or web applications. Sure we discuss Web services and web applications, but our goal is to explain the very nature of .NET. You will find a lot of information on building Windows applications because we believe (and so do most industry analysts) that the future is in client applications that exploit to the maximum the power of the client computer. These applications may interact with remote resources on the Web, but they also take advantage of the platform on which they're executed (be it a Windows 2000 workstation, or a Pocket PC machine). Once you know how to write Windows applications, how to access data with the new tools, and how to make the most of the Framework, you'll find it very easy to apply your knowledge to the Web. We've selected the really important topics in the Framework to discuss in this book and we hope we'll help you develop a solid understanding of the new environment. Instead of light overviews, we decided to discuss the selected topics in detail and give many examples.

The sample projects of this book can be found at the book's pages at www.sybex.com, and we urge you to download the source code. We will provide fixes and updates to the code as they become necessary, and we'll also revise them for the next version of Visual Studio, as soon as a public beta becomes available. Many of the examples are lengthy because real developers face real problems, which can't be addressed with short code segments. In general, the examples in this book are nontrivial, and many of the sample projects can be used as a starting point for building real-world applications.

Some of the topics discussed in this book are totally new to Visual Basic, like multithreaded programming. While most tutorials you will find on this topic demonstrate how easy it is to start a background thread that runs in parallel with the main application, we focus on the potential problems of multithreading. To demonstrate the nature of a multithreaded application, we show how to map the structure of a drive on a TreeView control. Such an elaborate example gives us the opportunity to discuss design decisions and the efficient coding of the application. We take a beginner's approach to topics that are new to VB .NET and a developer's approach when we discuss techniques that are implemented differently in VB .NET and VB6.

## How to Reach the Authors

Despite our best efforts, a book this size is bound to contain errors. Although a printed medium isn't as easy to update as a website, we will spare no effort to fix every problem you report (or we discover) and post revisions and updates at the Sybex website. If you have any problems with the text or the applications in this book, you can contact us directly at pevangelos@yahoo.com and ridge@netcon.net.au. You will reach us easily, because we never sleep at the same time.

# PART I

# Database Programming With .NET

# CHAPTER 1

## Introducing Visual Basic .NET

- Identifying the editions of Visual Studio .NET

- Listing system requirements

- Using the Visual Studio .NET IDE

- Discovering .NET

- Unlocking the new features in Visual Basic .NET

**V**isual Basic .NET represents a significant development over earlier versions of the language. A number of major changes have been introduced to the development environment that represents a quantum shift for developers in the way that application design, development, and deployment is approached.

In this chapter, we will briefly explore these new features as well as the underlying technologies that make them possible.

## Introducing the .NET IDE

One of the most obvious improvements is the new integrated Visual Studio .NET development environment. Previous versions of Visual Studio attempted to bring the various Microsoft languages together under a common umbrella. However, the reality was that each language still worked within its own unique integrated development environment (IDE) and with its own set of debuggers and deployment tools. Developing applications that leveraged the various strengths of each language was achievable but complicated, and it was impossible to build an application by moving seamlessly from one language to another. Using VB to develop rapid application development (RAD) front ends and then supporting them with high-performance Common Object Model (COM) components built using C++ became standard fare for enterprise applications, but it remained an unnecessarily complicated process.

Visual Studio .NET enables you to easily develop applications employing one or more languages. It offers a single IDE and a common set of debugging tools. It seamlessly integrates web development with traditional stand-alone applications. It enables easy scalability within an enterprise environment and grants the developer a powerful and flexible set of tools for creating distributed applications. Figure 1.1 shows the customizable Start Page screen that a developer sees when using Visual Studio .NET for the first time.

The key to this power and flexibility is the .NET Framework and its associated technologies. It is possible to write applications using nothing more than Notepad, a knowledge of Visual Basic .NET (or any of the other languages that are compatible with the .NET Framework), and the relevant command-line compiler(s). However, this represents sheer hard work for even simple applications, and the money invested in purchasing Visual Studio .NET and using its GUI design tools more than represents good value in comparison!

---

**NOTE**    The command-line compiler does still have its uses. There are a few things you can do with this tool that cannot be achieved with the GUI version. In particular, it is very useful for conditional compiling where you might only want to compile certain parts of your code—for example, where you are generating different versions of your application for different flavors of Windows. Refer to Chapter 11, "Debugging and Deploying .NET Applications," for more detail.

**FIGURE 1.1:**

The Visual Studio .NET
Start Page screen

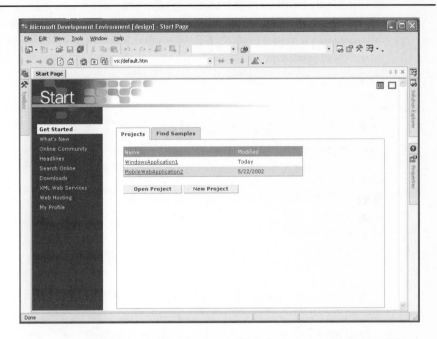

Although this book is principally about Visual Basic .NET, the integrated nature of the new
.NET environment enables you to use a variety of technologies when building your projects.
In fact, to get the very best out of your projects, you need to make use of these other technologies, and in some cases, you have no choice. For example, to use Visual Basic .NET, most
developers will make use of the Visual Studio .NET IDE. Although you can purchase Visual
Basic .NET separately, it is unlikely that many developers will. As mentioned earlier, you can
build your Visual Basic .NET applications directly from a text editor and a command-line
compiler—but again, it is unlikely that many developers will.

For these reasons, throughout the rest of this book, we will assume that you are using the
Visual Studio .NET IDE and have access to the range of technologies that it supports in
addition to the Visual Basic .NET language. Where necessary, we will explore some of
those technologies and their interrelationships with Visual Basic. For example, in the next
chapter we look at working with SQL Server 2000 from within the Visual Studio .NET IDE
and the ease with which you can build multitier applications employing multiple technologies
seamlessly from the same interface.

In this chapter we will cover the basic setup requirements and use of the Visual Studio .NET
IDE. This includes the various editions of the product that are available, the system requirements, and a brief run-through of VS.NET for those new to the environment. Later in the
chapter we will briefly discuss what .NET is all about and take a look at some of its key

elements, such as the way that .NET applications are structured and compiled and how they execute at runtime. We will finish the chapter with a look at the major changes that have been introduced into Visual Basic .NET. We will explore a couple of these areas in more detail, including structured exception handling and the object-oriented (OO) features that have been introduced or changed.

### Identifying the Editions of Visual Studio .NET

Visual Studio .NET comes in four flavors (listed from most to least expensive):

- Enterprise Architect
- Enterprise Developer
- Professional
- Academic

It is also possible to separately purchase the individual languages that make up Visual Studio .NET (currently Visual Basic .NET, Visual C# .NET, and Visual C++ .NET)

All four versions support development for web and Windows environments as well as table and view design for the SQL Server Desktop Engine.

Enterprise Architect and Enterprise Developer offer extended support for developing for platforms such as Windows 2000, SQL Server 2000, and so on. Enterprise Architect then takes this a step further with support for Visio-based database and software modeling and BizTalk Server 2000.

The Academic version is essentially the same as the Professional version (apart from their respective licensing provisions) except that the Academic version ships with some additional tools and documentation specifically targeted at the academic market.

## Listing System Requirements

Hardware requirements to run the .NET Framework are fairly minimal. A client requires something better than a Pentium 90 and 32MB RAM, whereas a server requires a minimum configuration of a Pentium 133 and 128MB RAM. You can run the .NET Framework on anything from Windows 98 or Windows NT Workstation (SP6a) up.

However, Visual Studio .NET is somewhat more demanding on hardware. In practice, we have found that performance is satisfactory on anything faster than 800MHz with at least 256MB RAM. (It is acceptable at 128MB RAM on NT Workstation.) Visual Studio .NET runs reasonably well on a 450MHz machine as long as it has at least 256MB RAM but is very slow on the same machine at 128MB RAM (running Windows 2000 Workstation). In practice, we use at least a 1GHz machine with at least 512MB RAM (XP Pro operating system).

Microsoft recommends a minimum configuration of a Pentium II 450MHz processor, and RAM requirements vary according to the OS (64MB for NT Workstation to 192MB for XP Professional). As mentioned earlier, we have found these a little low (they are minimum configurations). In practice, RAM seems to be the crucial element, and the more the better.

You will also need a fairly lazy 3.5GB of hard drive available (3GB data drive and 500MB system drive—they may be on one and the same drive) to install the thing. Again, the faster the hard drive, the quicker the install will happen. A fast CD drive is also recommended (or even better, a DVD drive, if you can get a DVD release of the media).

You will need Windows 2000, XP, or NT as your operating system. But note that ASP.NET is not available for NT 4 and that you may need to install Internet Information Server (IIS) to be able to test and publish any web-based applications you may build.

However, the best piece of advice we can offer to anybody using Visual Studio .NET is to go out and buy the biggest screen you can afford! And don't be stingy; the IDE likes plenty of real estate. Working at $800 \times 600$ on a 15-inch monitor is highly impractical with the new layout. You really need to be working with a resolution of at least $1024 \times 768$ to get the best out of the development environment.

## Using the Visual Studio .NET IDE

There are many differences between the new Visual Studio .NET development environment and previous versions of Visual Studio or the individual development languages. However, Microsoft has done an excellent job in creating the IDE, and you will find that it is very intuitive and eminently sensible in its design. Most experienced developers will get up to speed with it quickly. In fact, after using it for a while, you will probably be reluctant to return to the old interface to work on any legacy applications. The new IDE for Visual Studio .NET is shown in Figure 1.2.

The interface itself is highly customizable. For example, you can choose between the default tabbed interface or a multiple document interface (MDI) layout. Most of these changes can be implemented through the Tools ➢ Options menu.

Most of the windows are subject to Auto Hide. You can disable Auto Hide for individual windows by clicking the thumbtack symbol in the upper-right corner of the window. It's convenient to disable Auto Hide on most windows and just resize when you need more screen real estate immediately.

A web browser is integrated into the IDE, enabling links to items such as help files to be stored in your Favorites folder (yes, the one you normally use with IE) as well as providing access to web-based resources.

FIGURE 1.2:

The Visual Studio
.NET IDE

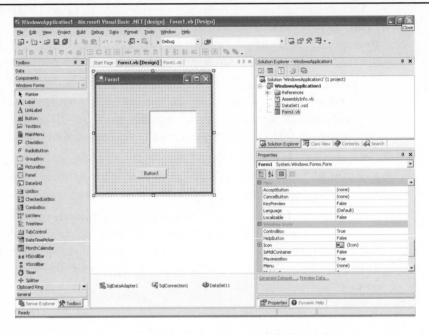

## Getting Started

Clicking the New Project option on the Start Page screen or choosing New ➤ Project from the
File menu opens the New Project dialog box, shown in Figure 1.3.

FIGURE 1.3:

The New Project
dialog box

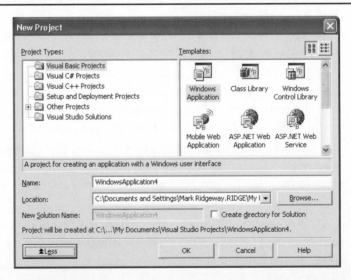

In this dialog box, there is a folder of project types for each language; you can choose the type
of project according to the language you will be using. Once you have chosen your project

(presumably your language is Visual Basic .NET), the project's IDE opens up, as shown in Figure 1.4 for a standard Windows application.

**FIGURE 1.4:**

The IDE for a standard Windows application

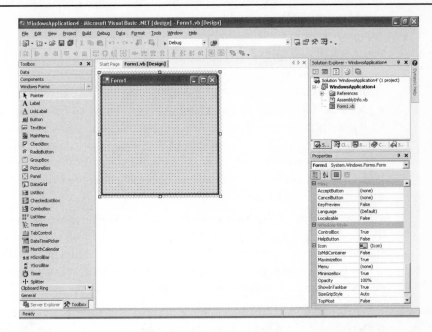

Basic layout is similar to earlier versions of the IDE. The Toolbox with the runtime controls is on the left side of the interface. However, as with all the windows that make up the interface, it is dockable and can be moved to a more suitable location if desired by simply clicking and dragging it. The Toolbox is tabbed with individual tools categorized under headings such as Data and Windows Forms.

A useful addition to the Toolbox is the Clipboard Ring, which can be used to store multiple code snippets as you work. Simply select and copy the code you wish to move to the Ring. Right-clicking the code snippet in the Ring enables you to change the name or delete the item. The item can be reused simply by dragging it from the Ring to your code page.

Additionally, on the left side of the IDE is the Server Explorer (click the tab at the bottom of the Toolbox), which can be used to identify and utilize the various services available on the host computer.

To the right of the IDE is the traditional Properties window; little has changed in the way that it works from previous incarnations except that its default organization is now by categories rather than alphabetical. It also takes up a little more space in Visual Studio .NET than it did previously. The Solution Explorer is above the Properties window. Various other windows, such as the Class View and Help windows, may also be displayed here by clicking their tabs below the Solution Explorer window.

The main central part of the screen is where you can construct your applications using the visual tools and where you can write any necessary code. The IDE allows you to tab between Design view and Code Behind as well as any additional items that you may have opened or placed in your project. Double-clicking a control on your form will take you to the relevant section of code in Code Behind view.

If you were creating a web application, you would also be given the option of tabbing between HTML and Design view (as well as Code Behind). In HTML view, you can make changes and add functionality by directly editing the code that's there. The one drawback of working in HTML view is that a number of the advanced functionality options of the IDE, such as autocomplete and intellisense, are not fully operational. In most cases, it makes sense to separate out your business logic from the design elements and build the business logic in Code Behind view. This way, you can write the program's functionality using "pure" Visual Basic .NET. However, there are some things that can only work if they are written directly into the ASPX page (HTML view).

Help is available as both a searchable facility and in the form of dynamic context-based help. To use the dynamic help, simply select the object you wish to query and the Help window should present you with a range of possible options. Documentation for Visual Studio .NET is very good, and if you have an MSDN subscription (the basic Library subscription is inexpensive), you can include the latest documentation as your help file.

When working in an application, a range of items such as classes, modules, and crystal reports can be added to the project using the Project ➢ Add New Item menu option to expose the Add New Item dialog box (shown in Figure 1.5).

**FIGURE 1.5:**

The Add New Item dialog box

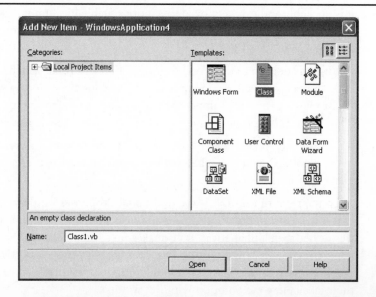

There are plenty of other changes to the Visual Studio .NET IDE. Some are fairly obvious; others aren't. Generally, however, the IDE is intuitive and consistent in design. You can get to know it quite quickly and it shouldn't pose any real difficulties for someone familiar with previous Microsoft design environments.

## Discovering .NET

Microsoft's .NET represents an integrated approach to software development, deployment, and usage. Applications can be built that operate seamlessly across platforms. A single application might be developed to work with mobile wireless devices, desktop clients, embedded systems, and server infrastructure. For example, you could build a single application that uses a bar-code reader to track stock in a warehouse and through the entire invoicing process and then sends delivery instructions to the delivery driver's cell phone.

Understanding the .NET Framework is not essential to writing Visual Basic .NET applications. However, building and deploying quality applications that are fully optimized for their particular environment does require an understanding of how that code will execute at runtime. In this section, we will briefly cover the structure and components of .NET and some of the factors that must be taken into account when designing applications.

The .NET Framework consists of the following:

- The Common Language Runtime (CLR), the platform's execution engine
- The Framework classes
- ASP.NET

### Compiling and Executing in .NET

When you compile code in .NET, you create an *assembly* (containing all the code and metadata relevant to the application) in Microsoft Intermediate Language (MSIL). The assembly is then compiled to machine code by the just-in-time (JIT) compiler as the program is executed. The execution part of the process is managed by the Common Language Runtime (CLR). Type safety is maintained by the Common Type System (CTS). The entire process of compiling and executing a program is referred to as the *managed execution* process.

Individual DLLs or EXE files that form part of an assembly are referred to as *modules*. Typically, an assembly consists of one or more modules and a manifest. The *manifest* contains a list of all files that exist within the assembly as well as information about whether particular files are to be exposed outside the assembly or are only valid within the assembly. It also includes any references necessary for other assemblies or unmanaged DLLs. The assembly itself is published using a combination of Microsoft's Portable Executable (PE) and Common Object File (COFF) formats.

At design time, all the objects belonging to a project are identified using a *namespace*. Objects can be referenced between projects using their respective assembly names and namespaces.

The metadata in the assembly contains information about how the application should be put together. This includes information about every element handled by the runtime.

Code passed to the JIT is checked and verified for type safety and against any security policies that may have been applied at the system admin level. A number of additional safety checks are also carried out to ensure that constituent objects remain isolated from each other and that memory is accessed correctly.

Despite the fact that code is running through an interpreter, performance of the JIT compiler has been optimized to maintain (or even exceed) what you have come to expect from recent versions of Visual Basic (VB).

Code designed to run under the CLR is termed *managed code*. Visual Basic .NET and C# are capable of producing only managed code. However, Microsoft's C++ can still be used to produce unmanaged code (code that can be executed without the intervention of the CLR or the use of MSIL). This is useful in creating COM objects that run as unmanaged DLLs and potentially offers an avenue for developers worried about the potential security risks of exposing their code through the use of MSIL (as long as you are happy with programming everything in C++!).

Figure 1.6 illustrates diagrammatically the managed execution process for .NET applications.

**FIGURE 1.6:**

Diagrammatic representation of the .NET managed execution process

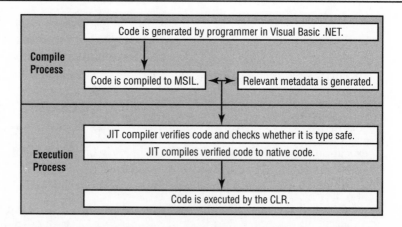

## Advantages and Disadvantages of using MSIL

The use of an Intermediate Language (IL) offers a number of advantages, including the cross-language integration mentioned earlier. Inheritance can also work across languages where new classes are derived from a base class written in another language. It also potentially offers developers the opportunity to run their programs on any platform supporting the CLR (not necessarily just Windows-based platforms). Language interoperability is enabled by the Common Language Specification (CLS), which defines a set of language features to which various languages must conform if they wish to exploit the CLR. This has enabled a number of third-party languages such as Eiffel to be made .NET compatible.

One possible disadvantage of using the IL that has been identified by a number of commentators is that, compared to machine code, code compiled to MSIL is more easily decompiled into a user-readable format, thus posing some security concerns. The process itself is quite simple. The .NET SDK ships with a tool called the MSIL Disassembler (`Ildasm.exe`) that dumps the IL code and any metadata attached to it into a text file. This is intended for use in combination with the MSIL Assembler tool (`Ilasm.exe`) to create test executables for any given MSIL. However, it is also very easy to open the text file and view the code. It's then up to the determination and expertise of the hacker as to how much use they can make out of the exposed code, but it is easier to understand than a whole lot of binary.

These security issues are less of an issue for applications developed in ASP.NET where all the vital code sits securely (well, relatively!) on a server as opposed to desktop applications where the executables have been deployed to individual client machines. We have seen arguments on both sides as to the potential implications and danger for code security, and it still remains to be seen how much of an issue this is likely to be.

## Garbage Collection and Application Security

Garbage collection (GC) is an important area managed by the CLR. The GC provides automatic memory management that clears up stray objects, frees memory, and helps prevent memory leaks. This is a departure from previous versions of VB, where you had to keep track of objects and explicitly remove them as they became unnecessary. However, the GC does not clear objects that have been built using unmanaged code (such as legacy COM objects), nor does it provide for efficient memory management of executing code. These issues still need to be addressed by the developer. It is also possible to exert some direct programmatic control over the garbage collector using the `GC.Collect` method to force a garbage collection, although in most cases, Microsoft recommends that the garbage collector should be left to its own devices.

Application security is another important area managed by the CLR. The assembly structure combined with the CLR enables a security structure that ensures that potentially damaging errors such as buffer overruns do not occur. If a security violation occurs, code execution is halted and the relevant security exceptions are thrown. This not only guards against genuine errors, it also helps protect your code from malicious attempts to infiltrate the .NET runtime.

Particularly if your code is exposed to the public domain, it is a sensible idea to take advantage of the *strong naming* techniques available with .NET. A strong name is uniquely generated from the contents of the assembly. Another form of protection is also available through *digital signing*, involving public key encryption technology.

Additionally, you can set various levels of trust for your assemblies and adjust .NET security at the enterprise, computer, and user level using the Microsoft .NET Framework wizards and the Microsoft .NET Framework Configuration snap-in (found in `Control Panel\Administrative Tools`). When deploying an application in the production environment, it is worth paying close attention to the trust levels being applied because they can be a prime reason for perfectly good development code going all pear-shaped and refusing to work. Figure 1.7 illustrates the .NET Framework Configuration tool.

**FIGURE 1.7:**

.NET Configuration snap-in

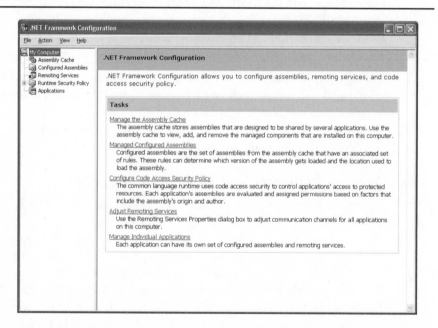

Fully exploring the .NET Framework would take a whole book itself. Developers specializing in this area have a wide range of possibilities open to them, including the opportunity to build their own compilers and .NET-compatible languages. We have only briefly looked at the CLR and how applications compile in this section. Chapter 11, "Debugging and Deploying .NET Applications," explores some of these topics in more detail. Later in this book, in Part IV, "Developing for the Web," we will investigate ASP.NET and the Framework classes as they relate to Visual Basic .NET in more detail.

## Unlocking the New Features in Visual Basic .NET

The following is a brief (and not exhaustive) list of major changes introduced into the VB language under .NET:

- Inclusion of object-oriented features such as inheritance, overloading, overriding, constructors/destructors, shared members, delegates, and interfaces. Visual Basic can now rightfully claim to be a true object-oriented language.

- New data types that include the Char (16 bit to store Unicode characters), Short (16 bit, formerly Integer), and Decimal (96-bit signed integer scaled by a variable power of 10).

- Structured exception handling (introducing the Try…Catch…Finally statement to VB).

- Multithreading, where applications can be set up to run various tasks independently of each other.

- CLS (Common Language Specification) compliance.

Additionally, many legacy keywords such as GoSub and GoTo have been deleted. A number of structural changes, such as removing the ability to declare variables on the fly inside loops and conditional statements, have been made. The Variant data type has been removed and the Integer data type is now 32 bit.

Support for XML Web services and Web Forms has been introduced. You can now happily build websites and high-performance components without having to move outside your favorite language!

Many of the changes introduced (such as the data types) are designed to bring Visual Basic into line with other languages and make it fully CLS compliant, and others are intended to help developers avoid getting into hot water through the use of shortcuts. For example, to load a form, you now need to explicitly instantiate it rather than using the old `frmMyform.Show`.

In other examples, `Option Explicit` is turned on by default and requires a specific statement to turn it off. Thus, you are automatically forced to declare all variables. A new statement, `Option Strict`, has also been introduced to enable strict enforcement of variable types. This prevents implicit type conversions from occurring such as may happen when calculating with numbers held in string variables. This option is turned off by default. Both options can be manipulated in code or globally across the project by setting the project properties. You can access the project properties by right-clicking the project name in the Solution Explorer, selecting Properties, and making the appropriate adjustments in the Build option. The Application Property Pages dialog box is shown in Figure 1.8.

**FIGURE 1.8:**

Setting the project
properties in the
Application Property
Pages dialog box

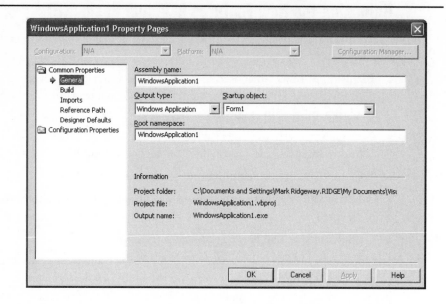

**TIP**   It is a good habit to set Option Explicit and Option Strict to on in the project properties
page. Doing so can help stamp out a lot of those type-related bugs at their source and
before they become a problem. It also enforces good coding practice, which is particularly
important on larger projects involving multiple developers.

Many developers will welcome the inclusion of the new object-oriented features into the
language. Visual Basic has always sat a little in the shade as far as its OO capabilities are concerned.
But no more! You can now hold your head high and overload and instantiate with the best
of them. Another area where developers in "other" languages have been able to hold their
noses a little higher than their VB counterparts has been in the availability of structured exception handling. Exception handling in VB has always been a little clunky at best, but that has
been finally remedied. In the remainder of this chapter, we will explore the new OO and
structured exception handling features of Visual Basic .NET in a little more detail.

## Structured Exception Handling

Structured exception handling (SEH) is really easy to work with, and after using it a few times,
you will wonder how you ever got on without it. The main keywords to come to know and
love are Try, Catch, and Finally. Although we don't always do it in this book (the excuse being
that we try to keep it all nice and simple for demonstration purposes), it is worth developing
the habit of thinking in terms of Try…Catch…Finally blocks when developing your code.
Although it also pays to be a little judicious in your application of exception handling if

performance is absolutely paramount (the process does introduce some overhead), it is also true that in performance terms, a dead application usually runs a poor second to something you didn't try to shave the extra nanosecond off.

A key advantage of working with SEH is that you are forced to consider error handling as an integrated part of your code rather than as the traditional afterthought that the old On Error Goto statements encouraged.

**WARNING**    You can still On Error Goto in Visual Basic .NET, but be warned—at the slightest hint of an unhandled exception in .NET, the CLR will bring your program's execution to a crunching halt.

Essentially, SEH encapsulates whole blocks of code within exception handlers. You instruct the CLR to "Try" the following section of code and anything that comes unstuck is passed to the "Catch" section. You can list multiple "Catches," and each one will be tried sequentially to see if it resolves the exception. You can specify particular actions to occur on specific errors caught using the syntax for the Catch keyword combined with its When clause. An exception not covered by a specific Catch clause will be passed up the stack and managed by the default handler (one hopes!).

The Finally block consists of code to be executed once the SEH protected code has been executed and any exceptions dealt with. The Finally statement is optional except where a Catch statement hasn't been included. (You must always have at least one Catch or a Finally within the Try...End Try block.)

The following listings demonstrate how this might work using the classic "divide-by-zero" error. Listing 1.1 shows a very simple calculator with two text fields as input boxes. The calculator is designed to calculate a fraction and report the answer in a label control when activated by clicking Button1. Entering a zero into Textbox2 will generate an unhandled exception and the program's execution will abort.

**Listing 1.1        Basic Code to Generate a Divide-by-Zero Error**

```
Private Sub Form1_Load(ByVal sender As System.Object,_
ByVal e As System.EventArgs) Handles MyBase.Load
        Label1.Text = ""
        Label2.Text = ""
        TextBox1.Text = ""
        TextBox2.Text = ""
    End Sub

Private Sub Button1_Click(ByVal sender As System.Object,_
ByVal e As System.EventArgs) Handles Button1.Click
        Dim a, b, c As Integer
```

```
        a = TextBox1.Text
        b = TextBox2.Text
        c = a / b
        Label2.Text = c
End Sub
```

In Listing 1.2, we show only the code for Button1 and show you how a simple Try...Catch block may be introduced.

**Listing 1.2        Simple SEH to Manage Divide-by-Zero Error**

```
Private Sub Button1_Click(ByVal sender As System.Object,_
  ByVal e As System.EventArgs) Handles Button1.Click
        Dim a, b, c As Integer
        a = TextBox1.Text
        b = TextBox2.Text

        Try
            c = a / b
        Catch
        End Try

        Label2.Text = c
End Sub
```

In Listing 1.2, we use a generic Catch to pick up any possible errors and to pass them to the default exception handlers. We could include a note to tell us that something has gone wrong by an inclusion into the Catch statement, as illustrated by the following snippet:

```
Try
    c = a / b
Catch
    Label1.Text = "Something came unstuck!"
End Try
```

Notice that an unhandled exception is thrown if we do not specify a value for variables *a* or *b* in the text boxes. We can manage this by extending the Try statement to cover the declarative part of the code, as illustrated in the following snippet:

```
Try
        a = TextBox1.Text
        b = TextBox2.Text
        c = a / b
Catch
        Label1.Text = "b needs to be > 0!"
End Try
```

We can also be quite specific about which error to trap by using the When clause. The following code snippet detects whether the *a* value has been left blank or if the *b* value has been set to zero. Note that the Catch clause is only activated if an exception is thrown. Thus, we can assign *a* to zero without generating the error text because no actual exception is thrown. It is only when *a* is left blank that it is given a nominal zero value and the exception is thrown:

```
Try
        a = TextBox1.Text
        b = TextBox2.Text
        c = a / b
Catch When a = 0
            Label1.Text = "a requires a value"
Catch When b = 0
            Label1.Text = "b needs to be > 0"
End Try
```

Additionally, we can specify the error caught and report it directly as follows:

```
Try
        a = TextBox1.Text
        b = TextBox2.Text
        c = a / b
Catch example As Exception When a = 0
            Label1.Text = example.ToString
Catch example As Exception When b = 0
            Label1.Text = example.ToString
End Try
```

We use *example* as a variable that holds the value of the exception thrown. We can also specify the type of class filter to apply. (In this example, we have simply specified the class Exception, but we can be a lot more specific when it is appropriate). We can test the exception handling by running the calculator and either leaving the *a* value blank or inserting zero into the *b* value. We could also have reported the actual content of the thrown exception messages in message boxes.

Last, we can set the Finally block in our exception handler. The completed code should look like Listing 1.3. We have included the message boxes in this code.

**Listing 1.3        Completed Code for Structured Exception Handler Example**

```
Private Sub Form1_Load(ByVal sender As System.Object,_
  ByVal e As System.EventArgs) Handles MyBase.Load
        Label1.Text = ""
        Label2.Text = ""
        TextBox1.Text = ""
        TextBox2.Text = ""
    End Sub
```

```
Private Sub Button1_Click(ByVal sender As System.Object,_
 ByVal e As System.EventArgs) Handles Button1.Click
        Dim a, b, c As Integer
        Try
            a = TextBox1.Text
            b = TextBox2.Text
            c = a / b

        Catch example As Exception When a = 0
            Label1.Text = "a requires a value"
            MsgBox(example.ToString)
        Catch example As Exception When b = 0
            Label1.Text = "b needs to be > 0"
            MsgBox(example.ToString)
        Finally
            Label2.Text = c

        End Try
    End Sub
```

Although this is a fairly trivial example, it does highlight a number of things you need to consider when setting up your exception handling. First, you need to consider how much of your code needs to be "protected." If we had declared our variables as floats (using Single or Double), we would have needed to protect only the code that reads the values of the text boxes, because dividing by zero with these types does not throw an exception but returns an answer of infinity. Second, using the current setup, we need to trap the *a* exception first. If we coded them around the other way and threw an exception when reading the TextBox1 value into *a*, control would be passed straight to the Catch statements and *b* would be assigned an arbitrary value of 0 (irrespective of the actual value entered into TextBox2). This would result in the exception code for *b* being executed when in fact it was the *a* value that originally caused the error condition.

Also worth noting is that this code would not compile if we had set Option Strict to True. We would need to carry out type conversions (using the Convert.To... syntax), as illustrated in the following snippet. Note that we have also declared the variables as Single and made the appropriate changes to the exception handler:

```
Dim a, b, c As Single

Try
        a = Convert.ToSingle(TextBox1.Text)
        b = Convert.ToSingle(TextBox2.Text)

Catch
        Label1.Text = "Please enter a value"

Finally
```

```
        c = a / b
        Label2.Text = Convert.ToString(c)

End Try
```

As you can see, working with SEH is basically quite straightforward, but it does mean developing a different mind-set from what you may have used in the past. You now need to think in terms of how errors are likely to impact your code as you design the code rather than applying error management at the end of the process.

## Object-Oriented Features

Visual Basic has acquired or expanded on the following object-oriented features in its .NET incarnation:

- Inheritance

- Overloading

- Overriding

- Shared members

- Interfaces

- Delegates

- Constructors and destructors

These features enable Visual Basic .NET to be finally regarded as a fully mature object-oriented programming language. In quickly exploring these features, we are assuming that you already have more than a passing acquaintance with OO techniques and that we can dispense with the usual introduction to OO programming.

### Inheritance

With Visual Basic .NET, developers can define base classes from which new classes can be derived. This has always been a fundamental feature of OO programming. The derived classes not only inherit the methods and properties of the base class, they also have the capacity to extend them and/or to override the existing methods with new ones. All Visual Basic classes are inheritable by default unless otherwise indicated with the *NonInheritable* modifier keyword. Another modifier that may be applied is the *MustInherit* keyword, which specifies that a particular class is a base class only and cannot be used to directly generate instances.

Despite Microsoft's focus on implementing true OO ability in the language, Visual Basic .NET does not support inheritance from multiple classes. Derived classes are able to have only one base class, but they can implement multiple interfaces, which Microsoft believes (in its documentation) largely gets around this limitation.

## Overloading

Overloading enables particular methods, properties, or procedures to be defined in a class that may share the same name but use different data types. This in turn enables multiple implementations of a single procedure that can handle a broad range of data types. From a user's perspective, the class has a single, very versatile procedure that can handle many different types of data. Listing 1.4 illustrates how this works.

**Listing 1.4      Example Class Demonstrating Overloading**

```
Public Class _MyClass

    Overloads Function MyFunction(ByVal a As String,_
ByVal b As String)
        MyFunction = "String Result =" & _
Convert.ToString(Convert.ToInt16(a) + Convert.ToInt16(b))
    End Function

    Overloads Function MyFunction(ByVal a As Integer,_
ByVal b As Integer)
        MyFunction = "Integer Result =" & (a + b)
    End Function


End Class
```

This example adds together a couple of numbers irrespective of whether they have been entered as integers or strings. From the perspective of the user, the function called (MyFunction) is identical, even though two implementations of the function have been described in the class.

You can test this example by opening a new project in Visual Studio .NET, adding a new class (MyClass), and copying in the code from Listing 1.4. Go to the Design view for Form1 and add a Button and a Label control to the form. Double-click the button and add the code from Listing 1.5 to Code Behind.

**TIP**      If using the new Visual Studio .NET IDE is foreign territory to you, read the section in this chapter titled "Using the Visual Studio .NET IDE" before attempting this example.

**Listing 1.5      Code to Call MyClass Example**

```
Private Sub Button1_Click(ByVal sender As System.Object,_
  ByVal e As System.EventArgs) Handles Button1.Click
```

```
        Dim a As Integer = 4
        Dim b As Integer = 8
        'Dim a As String = "4"
        'Dim b As String = "8"
        Dim TestClass As New _MyClass()
        Label1.Text = TestClass.MyFunction(a, b)

    End Sub
```

The code can be tested by remming out either the first or second two variable declarations (in this example, the string declarations have been remmed out) and testing the result by clicking the button. In this example, the result would read "Integer Result = 12." If the integer declarations had been remmed out, the result should read "String Result = 12."

Note that the Overloads keyword is optional, but if it is used once for a particular member, it must be used be used for every overloaded implementation of that member.

## Overriding

Overriding enables you to modify properties and methods in your derived classes that have been inherited from base classes. It makes use of the Overrides keyword and is dependent on the particular member in the base class being tagged with the Overridable keyword. Properties and methods are tagged as NotOverridable by default. Additionally, when overriding, your overridden members must have the same number of arguments as the inherited members. You can also call the original implementation of the member in the base class by specifying MyBase before the method name.

You can use the class created in Listing 1.4 for an example. The following code snippet demonstrates the modified version of MyClass with the Overridable keyword (we have also removed the overloaded functions):

```
Public Class _MyClass

    Overridable Function MyFunction(ByVal a As String,_
ByVal b As String)
        MyFunction = "String Result =" & _
Convert.ToString(Convert.ToInt16(a) + Convert.ToInt16(b))
    End Function

End Class
```

You can then derive a class (MyDerivedClass) that inherits from MyClass and overrides MyFunction to multiply your input values (rather than adding them):

```
Public Class _MyDerivedClass

    Inherits _MyClass

    Overrides Function MyFunction(ByVal a As String,_
```

```
ByVal b As String)
    MyFunction = "String Result =" & _
Convert.ToString(Convert.ToInt16(a) * Convert.ToInt16(b))
  End Function

End Class
```

Note that you need to specify which class your derived class inherits from (using the Inherits keyword) and you apply the Overrides keyword to MyFunction to change it. You could also have made use of the original base function if it had been appropriate—for example, if you wished to append an additional comment to the original calculation:

```
Public Class _MyDerivedClass
    Inherits _MyClass
    Overrides Function MyFunction(ByVal a As String, _
  ByVal b As String)
    MyFunction = MyBase.MyFunction(a,b) & _
" from MyDerivedClass"
    End Function

End Class
```

Using MyBase.MyFunction(a,b), you can call the original calculation as it was implemented in the parent class.

## Shared Members

Members of a class that are shared by all instances are known as *shared members*, although they may be more familiar to C++ and Java programmers as *static members*. Effectively, they behave as global variables that can only be accessed from instances of a class. A shared variable that is modified in one instance of a class will be modified in all other instances. Shared methods, on the other hand, are not associated with any particular instance of a class and can be called directly from the class without actually instantiating an object. This is an exception to the rule that you must create an instance of a class before you can make use of any of its members.

The following code snippet demonstrates how to create a shared field and method:

```
Public Class _MyClass

    Public Shared MySharedValue as Double

    Public Shared Sub MySharedMethod()
       Very clever and highly sophisticated code goes here!
    End Sub

End Class
```

To make use of the shared values, you create an instance of _MyClass (such as _MyDerived-Class) and work with the value using the following notation:

```
_MyDerivedClass.MySharedValue
```

You can call the shared method without creating an instance simply by using this notation:

```
_MyClass.MySharedMethod()
```

## Interfaces

Interfaces define a set of properties and methods but do not provide any implementation. They are defined using the Interface statement, and although implemented by classes, they are quite separate from them. Interfaces are implemented using the Implements keyword.

When a class implements an interface, it must use every aspect of that interface exactly as it is defined. Once an interface is defined and published, it cannot be changed. This way, the interface provides a consistent tool that isn't likely to break existing code through changes down the track.

Visual Basic .NET developers can now create their own interface using the Interface and End Interface statements.

## Delegates

Delegates are objects that can call methods and procedures from other objects. They are very useful in multithreaded applications, and they can be used to call functionality from another object at runtime rather then having to inherit the functionality at design time.

## Constructors and Destructors

Objects are created and destroyed in Visual Basic .NET using the Sub New (constructor) and Sub Finalize (destructor) procedures. Unless explicitly called, Visual Basic .NET implicitly creates a Sub New constructor at runtime. This code always runs before any other code within a class.

If you wish to explicitly release an object, you can use the Sub Finalize method to prompt the CLR to call the Finalize method before disposing of an object. The Finalize method needs to be overridden to contain the code that you wish to be executed on cleanup (such as file closures, data writes, etc.). This can result in some performance overhead, and Microsoft recommends that the process be used judiciously. Obviously, there is a lot more to the process than we have documented here, but a full discussion is really beyond the scope of this book. Remember that the cleanup of orphaned and unused objects is now largely automated with the garbage collection by the CLR.

Additionally there is a second destructor, Dispose, that can be called at any time from the IDisposable interface to release resources immediately. This is useful for managing resources not handled by the CLR such as database connections.

It is also still possible to assign Nothing to object variables, but Microsoft recommends that this is normally not a good idea under the new garbage collection system in .NET.

## Summary

As you can see, Visual Basic .NET is far more than just an incremental increase over VB6. In many respects, it represents a radical departure from many of the things that we have come to take for granted in the language over the years. However, once you get over the initial surprise, the changes are fairly easy to become accustomed to. The learning curve is not quite as steep as some might have feared they would be. Many of the new features, such as the OO capability, represent aspects that developers have been clamoring for, for years.

The Visual Studio .NET interface is very easy to use, and its highly customizable interface is sure to appeal to many developers who have been waiting for the opportunity to specify exactly how their workspace should look and operate.

There is a lot more to many of these topics than we have covered here. Some will be dealt with later in this book, but others, such as developing with the .NET Framework, are beyond the scope of what we look at in this book. However, they serve to illustrate just how integrated the new .NET environment has become. To successfully develop in .NET, it is no longer sufficient to have a have a fairly narrow focus on a single language. Developers need to think in terms of web applications, distributed applications, data access, server technology, and yes, the .NET Framework and more. The beauty of .NET is that it enables you to essentially develop across all these areas using your favorite language (Visual Basic, of course), whereas in the past, you would have to learn a range of other languages and technologies if you wished to use any of this stuff.

An important example of this cross-technology approach is in the use of SQL Server 2000. Database development is an important part of the armory of any modern developer, and Microsoft has created strong links between the Visual Studio development environment and the company's enterprise database platform. In the next chapter, we will be looking at how you can use the Visual Database Tools in Visual Studio .NET to interact directly with SQL Server 2000 from the Visual Studio IDE. We will also look at how you can make use of SQLXML and Visual Basic .NET to construct and consume an XML Web service directly from SQL Server 2000.

# CHAPTER 2

## Working with SQL Server 2000 and Visual Studio .NET

- Overview of SQL Server 2000

- Recommended updates for SQL Server 2000

- Working with SQL Server 2000 from Visual Studio .NET

- Using XML support for SQL Server 2000 to build and consume an XML Web service

**C**reating and supporting database-driven applications is very much the bread and butter for many developers. Most developers, irrespective of their preferred development language, have experience across at least a couple of different DBMS packages and have some knowledge and understanding of database development. Microsoft has continued to cater to the requirements of database developers with the .NET Framework.

Visual Studio .NET provides a rich set of database connection and communication tools with its ADO.NET technology, and it also provides a comprehensive set of database development tools with its Visual Database Tools. Additionally, Microsoft has tightly interconnected its enterprise-level database technology (SQL Server 2000) with the .NET Framework and Visual Studio .NET in particular. Later, in Chapter 3, "ADO.NET: An Architectural Overview," and Chapter 4, "Working with the DataSet," ADO.NET technology will be covered in much more detail.

In this chapter, we will look at the Visual Database Tools and how they can be used in conjunction with Visual Basic .NET to build database-driven applications entirely from within the Visual Studio .NET integrated development environment (IDE). We will also see how some of the new XML features available for use with SQL Server 2000 can be used to create and consume an XML Web service that provides data connectivity and management between a SQL Server 2000 database and a Visual Basic front end.

## Overview of SQL Server 2000

SQL Server 2000 is the latest incarnation of Microsoft's enterprise-level database management system (DBMS). It has been out for a couple of years now and has a number of service packs and updates available. (At the time this book was being written, Service Pack 2, the Web Services Toolkit, and SQLXML 3 SP1 were among the recommended updates.)

For users of earlier versions of SQL Server (in particular, SQL Server 7), SQL Server 2000 represents a progressive development rather than a radical departure, and in addition to keeping up with ongoing developments in other Microsoft products (.NET in particular), it introduces a number of features and enhancements in response to the needs of developers and users.

Throughout the remainder of the book, SQL Server 2000 will be mainly used as the back end for database-driven applications. From a developer's perspective, this has the advantage of offering the following benefits:

- Seamless integration between Visual Studio .NET and SQL Server 2000
- Highly optimized data connections via ADO.NET for maximum performance
- Visual Database Tools within Visual Studio .NET for creating and managing SQL Server 2000 databases

If you are unfamiliar with SQL Server 2000, the appendix, "Getting Started with SQL Server 2000," provides a primer to help get you going.

The next section of this chapter covers a number of recommended updates for SQL Server 2000, including those required for the examples we will use later in the chapter.

## Recommended Updates

The following updates for SQL Server 2000 can be downloaded from the Microsoft website (at http://msdn.microsoft.com/downloads).

- SQL Server 2000 Service Pack 2
- SQL Server 2000 Web Services Toolkit
- SQLXML 3 Service Pack 1
- SQL Server 2000 Driver for JDBC

The following sections describe these updates.

**NOTE**     Additional resources and support can be obtained from the SQL Server section of the Microsoft website: www.microsoft.com/sql/default.asp.

### SQL Server 2000 Service Pack 2

Service Pack 2 consists of three parts: the Database Components SP2, Analysis Services SP2, and the Desktop Engine SP2. The Desktop Engine SP2 provides updates for an instance of the SQL Server 2000 Desktop Engine (MSDE 2000) and is available on CD as a separate service pack (the SQL Server 2000 Desktop Engine Service Pack 2).

The full SP2 package addresses all issues and updates covered by SP1. It is available on CD but can also be downloaded from the Microsoft site (at a fairly bulky 115MB!). If you choose the download option, the three elements of the service pack are available as individual downloads and can be installed separately.

### SQL Server 2000 Web Services Toolkit

The Web Services Toolkit follows on from the previous updates aimed at enhancing SQL Server's XML support, which included the Web Release 1 and Web Release 2 kits. The download is 12.3MB in size.

The current toolkit introduces Microsoft's third version of XML support for SQL Server; SQLXML 3. It also includes sample code, white papers, and the necessary tools for building

Web services and supporting web-based applications with SQL Server 2000. Additionally, it includes features introduced in the earlier Web Release 1 and 2 kits (so there is no need to install these as well). It also provides enhanced .NET interoperability along with additional support for working with Visual Basic .NET and SQLXML.

### SQLXML 3 Service Pack 1

This is a recommended update for the Web Services Toolkit that fixes a number of problems identified with the original release of SQLXML 3. It also includes some security and performance enhancements but requires you to uninstall SQLXML 3 before installing the service pack. It is a 2.7MB download. (It can also be used to install SQLXML 3 into your version of SQL Server 2000 without all the bells and whistles of the Web Services Toolkit.)

### SQL Server 2000 Driver for JDBC

This is a 2.1MB download that provides support for the Java enterprise environment.

## Working with SQL Server 2000 from Visual Studio .NET

Although database applications can be built directly within the SQL Server 2000 environment, the Visual Studio .NET IDE contains a set of database design tools that can be used to build applications using SQL Server 2000. In this section, we will take a look at these tools and do a quick walk-through to build a simple database-driven application.

WARNING     When working with web-based applications created in ASP.NET, you will need to grant them explicit access to the relevant databases. You can do this by modifying the access permissions for the ASP.NET user from Logins under the Security node in Enterprise Manager.

### Visual Database Tools

The Visual Database Tools (in Visual Studio .NET) consist of the following:

- Server Explorer
- Database Designer
- Table Designer
- SQL Editor
- Query and View Designer

The Server Explorer is normally found with the Toolbox on the left side of the IDE. Alternatively, it can be accessed via the View menu. The Server Explorer usually contains two nodes. The first contains a list of any data connections previously created on the computer, and the second lists any servers currently available, as shown in Figure 2.1.

**FIGURE 2.1:**

The Visual Studio IDE with the Server Explorer

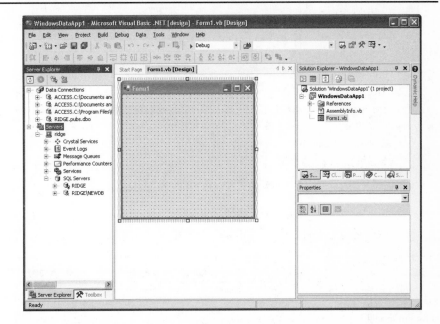

The Database Designer is only available in the Enterprise editions of Visual Studio .NET. It provides a graphical interface that can be used to modify database tables, relationships, and other properties. The Database Designer can be accessed by selecting the particular database in question from the Server node in Server Explorer, right-clicking the Database Diagrams option, and selecting New Diagram from the menu. In Figure 2.2, the Database Designer is applied to the pubs database and shows the relationship between the roysched and titles tables. The various database objects can be managed from the Database Designer by right-clicking them and choosing appropriate options from the context menus.

To access the Table Designer to create a new table, right-click the Tables node under the node for the relevant database and select New Table. An existing table can be edited by right-clicking the table listing in question and choosing Design Table. Figure 2.3 illustrates the Table Designer loaded with the authors table from the pubs database.

The Database Designer
shown with tables from
the pubs database

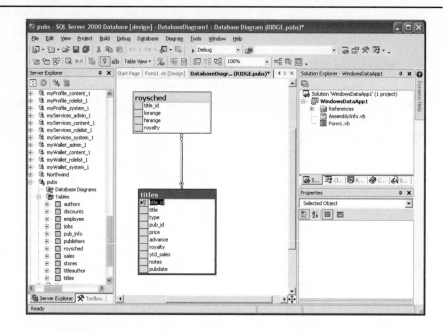

The Table Designer with
the authors table from
pubs database

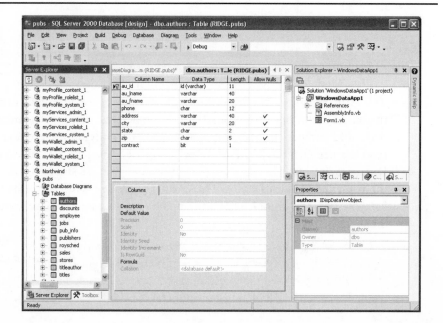

The SQL Editor is useful for creating functions and stored procedures. It can be accessed from the relevant database node in Server Explorer by right-clicking either Functions or Stored Procedures and choosing the appropriate menu option (such as New Stored Procedure). A basic template is provided. Figure 2.4 shows the SQL Editor with the basic template set to create a new stored procedure for the pubs database.

**FIGURE 2.4:**

The SQL Editor with the template for creating a new stored procedure

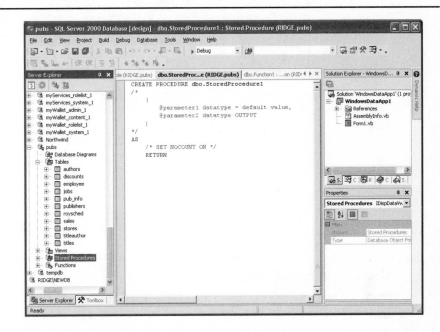

The Query and View Designer is used to help you create the Transact-SQL (T-SQL) statements for use in your functions and stored procedures. For example, if you wish to build a SELECT statement for a new stored procedure, type **SELECT** into the relevant part of the stored procedure. A thin blue line should appear forming a box around your SELECT keyword. Right-click the SELECT somewhere in the box and choose Insert SQL from the context menu. This opens the Designer, which can then be used to build your SELECT statement. The Designer can also be used to modify blocks of statements previously created in the SQL Editor. The blocks are also indicated by a thin line around them. The Designer can be accessed by right-clicking the contents of the block and selecting either Design SQL Block (to edit) or Insert SQL where appropriate. Figure 2.5 shows the Designer in Edit mode for the byroyalty stored procedure for the pubs database.

The Query and View Designer for creating and editing blocks of T-SQL statements

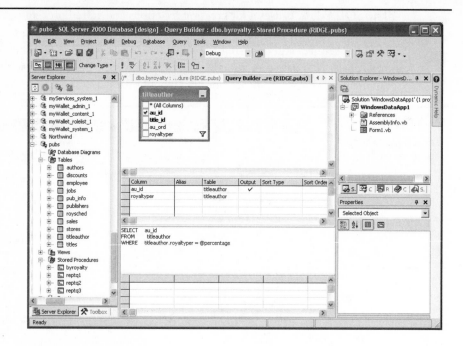

## Creating a Simple Application

In this example, we will use Visual Studio .NET and the Visual Database Tools to build a simple database to hold some data and then access this data from a Windows form. The application will be designed to hold a list of customer names for a restaurant and match the customers against their preferred menu type. We will use two tables, Clients and Menu, shown here with their associated fields.

| Field | Data Type |
| --- | --- |
| client_id | int |
| client_firstname | char |
| client_surname | char |
| client_menu_id | int |

| Field | Data Type |
|-------|-----------|
| menu_id | int |
| menu_type | char |

The steps to build the application are as follows:

1. Open Visual Studio .NET and create a new Windows application (in Visual Basic .NET). The application in this example is named WindowsDataApp1.

2. In the Server Explorer, right-click the Data Connections node and choose Create New SQL Server Database. Enter the appropriate details into the Create Database dialog box, as shown in Figure 2.6.

**FIGURE 2.6:**

The Create Database dialog box

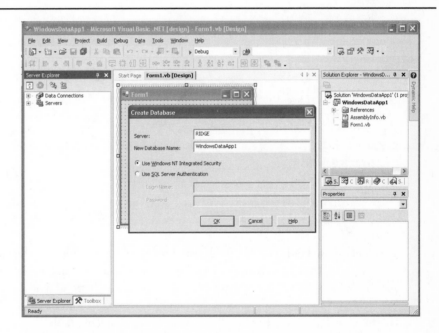

3. You will need to know the name of your SQL Server instance. In this case, we have given the database the same name as the application. Click OK. A node representing your newly created database and its connection appears under the Data Connections node.

4. Expand the node for the WindowsDataApp1 database and right-click the Tables node. Select New Table from the menu. Your screen should now look something like Figure 2.7.

The WindowsDataApp1
database open in the
Table Designer

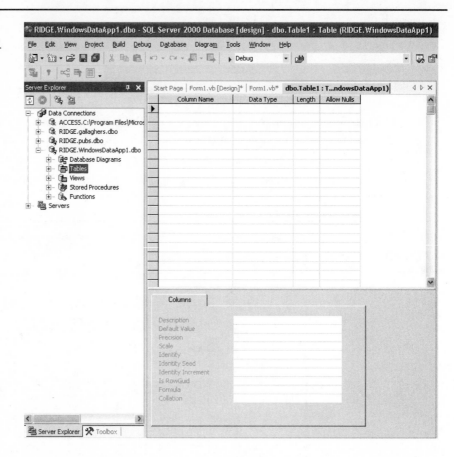

5. Set up the table with the fields listed for the Clients table. Set the client_id field as the
   primary key (right-click the gray box to the left of the field name). In the Columns properties box, set the Identity property to Yes for the client_id field. Uncheck the Allow Nulls
   column for the client_menu_id field. Save the table and name it Clients in the Choose
   Name dialog box. Figure 2.8 illustrates the completed table.

6. Repeat the process to set up the Menu table. Set the menu_id field as the primary key for
   this table. Set its Identity property to Yes.

**FIGURE 2.8:**

The completed
Clients table for the
WindowsDataApp1
application

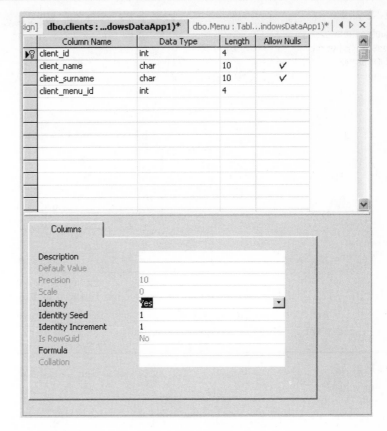

Next we will create a relationship between the two tables:

1. Right-click anywhere in the Table Designer for the Clients table and choose Relationships. Click New. Set the primary key table to Menu and the foreign key table to Clients. Set the primary key column to menu_id and the foreign key column to client_menu_id. Click Close and then save your work. Figure 2.9 illustrates how the relationship should appear.

**NOTE**     A Save Warning dialog box may appear asking you if you wish to continue saving the tables to your database. Click Yes. You can disable further occurrences of this dialog box.

**FIGURE 2.9:**

Establishing the relationship between the Clients and Menu tables

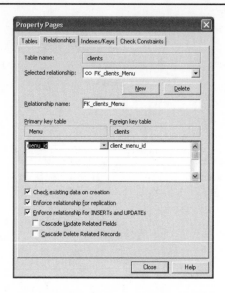

2. You can add data to the tables by right-clicking them and selecting Retrieve Data from Table. Start with the Menu table and insert the sample data illustrated in Figure 2.10. Note that the menu_id values are auto-generated.

**FIGURE 2.10:**

Sample data in the Menu table

| menu_id | menu_type |
|---|---|
| 1 | French |
| 2 | Italian |
| 3 | Chinese |

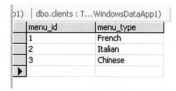

3. Insert the data into the Clients table as illustrated in Figure 2.11.

**FIGURE 2.11:**

Sample data in the Clients table

| client_id | client_name | client_surname | client_menu_id |
|---|---|---|---|
| 1 | Fred | Bloggs | 1 |
| 2 | Mary | Jones | 2 |
| 3 | Chris | Smith | 3 |

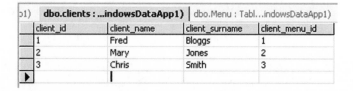

In the next few steps, we will create a simple user-defined function to perform a calculation on some values we will add to the database and then build a simple stored procedure to update the values in the database with these calculations.

1. Add two additional fields to the Menu table titled menu_cost and menu_tax. Set their data types to Money. You will enter some arbitrary values into the menu_cost field as the cost of the respective menus and then use the function to calculate the tax on these values (at 10%). We have added 50, 60, and 70 as the three menu_cost items.

2. Under the WindowsDataApp1 database node in the Server Explorer, right-click the Functions node and select New Scalar-Valued Function. The SQL Editor opens along with an appropriate template. Copy the code from Listing 2.1 into the template. Save the function as Function1.

3. To create the stored procedure, right-click the Stored Procedures node under the database in Server Explorer and select New Stored Procedure. Copy the code from Listing 2.2 into the Stored Procedure template.

**Listing 2.1        Code for user_defined Function in WindowsDataApp1**

```
ALTER FUNCTION dbo.Function1
   (

   @menu_cost money = 0

   )
RETURNS money
AS
   BEGIN

   RETURN (@menu_cost/10)

   END
```

**Listing 2.2        Code for user_defined Stored Procedure in WindowsDataApp1**

```
ALTER PROCEDURE dbo.StoredProcedure1 As

   UPDATE    Menu
   SET       menu_tax = dbo.Function1(menu.menu_cost)

   RETURN
```

**NOTE**    Notice that the UPDATE statement is surrounded by a blue box. Right-clicking in this box gives you access to the Query and View Designer (by selecting Design SQL Block), which could have been used to graphically build this statement.

Save the stored procedure as StoredProcedure1. Make sure that you have closed the Retrieve Data from Table window for the Menu table. Right-click the node for StoredProcedure1 (in

Server Explorer) and select Run Stored Procedure. (Alternatively, many of these commands can be executed from the Database drop-down menu in Visual Studio .NET.) The Data Output window for the stored procedure should appear at the bottom of the IDE. If everything is normal, open up the Data view of the Menu table and you should see the calculated tax amounts in the menu_tax column.

We will now set up a Windows form to view the data:

1. Tab the Server Explorer back to the Toolbox. Add a DataGrid control to Form1. You can play with the formatting a bit. The DataGrid comes with a selection of formats that are accessed via the AutoFormat option below the Properties box on the right side of the IDE.

**NOTE**    Note that the process of creating a database connection and accessing data through it may seem a little strange to developers unfamiliar with the .NET environment. We will be covering these processes in far more detail in Chapters 3, 4, and 5 of this book ("ADO.NET: An Architectural Overview," "Working with the DataSet," and "Building Data-Driven Windows Applications," respectively).

2. Select the Data option in the Toolbox and drag a SqlDataAdapter to your form. This automatically opens the Data Adapter Configuration Wizard. Click Next and choose the WindowsDataApp1.dbo connection from the Choose Your Data Connection screen (shown in Figure 2.12).

**FIGURE 2.12:**

The Choose Your Data Connection screen

3. Click Next. In the Choose a Query Type screen, choose the Use SQL Statements option as shown in Figure 2.13. Click Next.

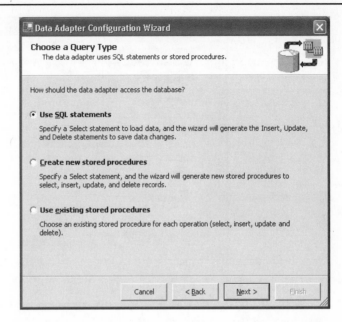

4. The Generate the SQL Statements screen appears (Figure 2.14). Click the Query Builder button to open the Query Builder dialog box (Figure 2.15). This dialog box can be used to visually construct your SQL statements.

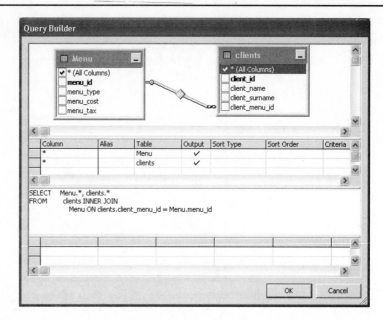

5. The Query Builder dialog box initially opens with an Add Table dialog that you can use to add relevant tables to the Query Builder. Click Close once you have added the tables, views, or functions necessary for your SQL. In this example (as can be seen in Figure 2.15), we'll add both the Clients and Menu tables to the Builder. Once they're added, select all columns from the two tables.

6. Click OK to return to the Generate the SQL Statements screen. It should now have a copy of the generated SQL statement in its main window. Because we are using multiple tables, we will need access to the Advanced Options dialog box from here. In the Advanced Options dialog box, uncheck the Generate Insert, Update and Delete Statements option (refer to Figure 2.16). These statements cannot be automatically generated for a SELECT statement that has columns from multiple tables.

7. Click OK and then click through to the end of the wizard, which should hopefully report that everything has worked fine. At the bottom of your form designer in the Visual Studio .NET IDE, you should now see both SqlDataAdapter1 and SqlConnection1 objects. Right-click the SqlDataAdapter1 object and choose Generate Dataset using the default DataSet1 name. This will create an instance of DataSet11 on the Designer window with the other data objects. You can then preview your data by right-clicking SqlDataAdapter1 again and choosing Preview Data. This will open the Data Adapter Preview dialog box, shown in Figure 2.17. Clicking the Fill Dataset button in the upper-left corner of this box loads the data from the database.

**NOTE**     The precise appearance of the data layout in the screen shown in Figure 2.17 may vary depending on the order in which you added items within the Query Builder.

**FIGURE 2.16:**

The Advanced Options
dialog box

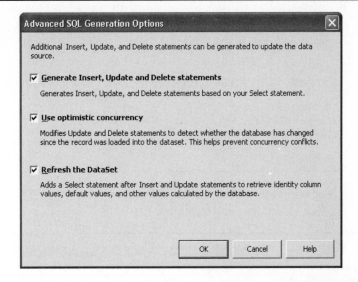

**FIGURE 2.17:**

The Data Adapter
Preview dialog box

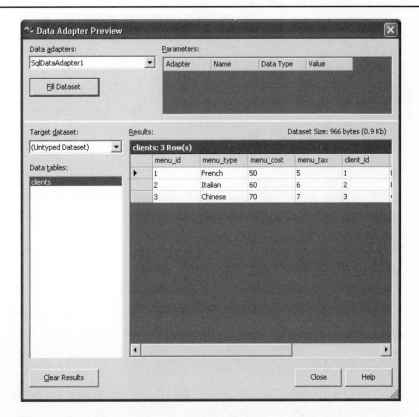

8. Select the DataGrid control on your form and set its DataSource property to DataSet11 .clients. We also set the Auto Format property to Colorful4. Double-click Form1 and add the line of code from Listing 2.3 to the form's Load event.

---

**Listing 2.3**     **Load Event Code for Form1 in WindowsDataApp1 Application**

```
Private Sub Form1_Load(ByVal sender As _
  System.Object, ByVal e As System.EventArgs) _
  Handles MyBase.Load
          SqlDataAdapter1.Fill(DataSet11)
End Sub
```

---

The completed application should appear as in Figure 2.18. Running the application should produce something similar to Figure 2.19.

**FIGURE 2.18:**

The completed WindowsDataApp1 application in Design view

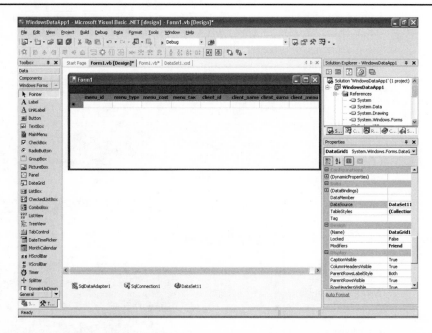

WindowsDataApp1 might be pretty simple as far as computer applications go, but it does illustrate how quickly and easily you can set up database front ends using Visual Studio .NET. Additionally, you have seen how you can do a large part of your database creation and manipulation from within the Visual Studio .NET IDE, including sophisticated tasks such as creating user-defined functions and stored procedures. Although we haven't looked at it here, you can also debug your stored procedures from within the Visual Studio environment.

In the next section, we will look at the process of setting up a simple XML Web service using SQL Server 2000 and Visual Studio .NET.

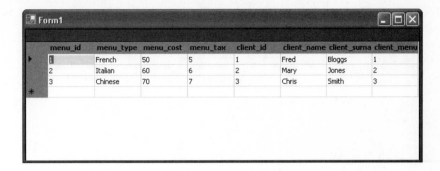

| | menu_id | menu_type | menu_cost | menu_tax | client_id | client_name | client_surna | client_menu |
|---|---|---|---|---|---|---|---|---|
| ▶ | 1 | French | 50 | 5 | 1 | Fred | Bloggs | 1 |
| | 2 | Italian | 60 | 6 | 2 | Mary | Jones | 2 |
| | 3 | Chinese | 70 | 7 | 3 | Chris | Smith | 3 |
| * | | | | | | | | |

# Using XML Support for SQL Server 2000 to Build an XML Web Service

Before we begin this section, make sure that you have downloaded and installed SQLXML 3 (from the SQLXML 3 SP1) from Microsoft. Additionally, we will be using the Configure IIS Support MMC from SQLXML 3 rather than the IIS configuration utility that shipped originally with SQL Server 2000. You can access the SQLXML 3 version of the utility from the SQLXML 3 section of the Start menu items.

If you currently have virtual directories set up with earlier versions of SQLXML, they can continue to function with the earlier DLLs (the different versions of SQLXML are capable of running together), or you can upgrade the virtual directory to SQLXML 3 by employing the upgrade option from the Properties dialog box for that virtual directory accessed via the IIS configuration utility for SQLXML 3.

In this section, we will show you how to both query your SQL Server via your Internet browser using a URL and set up and consume an XML Web service designed to execute a stored procedure on SQL Server 2000. We will make use of the pubs database.

## Setting Up

All of the files necessary for carrying out the various tasks on SQL Server 2000 need to be accessible through a specially configured virtual directory.

Create a new directory somewhere convenient. For this example, we have set up the directory in My Directory and named it Pubs (as this will be the database we will be accessing).

Inside the Pubs directory, create four subdirectories: Templates, WebServices, Schemas, and Objects. You will be making use of only the Templates and WebServices directories for this example. To configure the virtual directory, carry out the following steps:

1. Open the Configure IIS Support snap-in from the SQLXML 3 Start menu; the snap-in is shown in Figure 2.20.

**FIGURE 2.20:**

The IIS Virtual Directory Management for SQLXML 3 snap-in

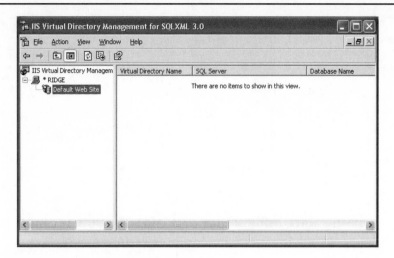

2. Right-click Default Web Site in the left pane and select New ➤ Virtual Directory. The New Virtual Directory Properties dialog box opens.

3. In the first (General) screen, set the name of the virtual directory and the path to the Pubs directory we created earlier. We also named the virtual directory Pubs, as shown in Figure 2.21.

**FIGURE 2.21:**

Setting the name of and the path to the virtual directory in the New Virtual Directory Properties dialog box

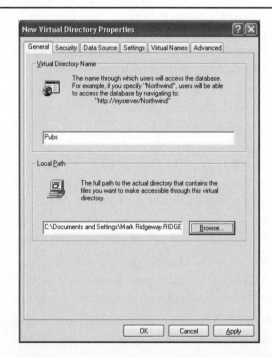

4. Click the Security tab and choose your preferred authentication method. (We used Windows integrated authentication.)

5. Click the Data Source tab and choose your server (local in our case) and database (pubs).

6. For the Settings tab, select the Allow sql=..., Allow Template Queries, and Allow POST options, as shown in Figure 2.22.)

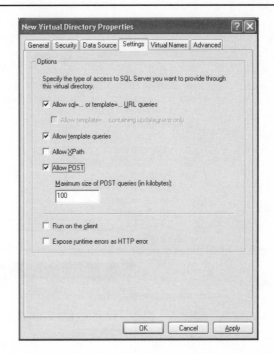

7. Click the Virtual Names tab. You need to set the properties for your `Templates` and `WebServices` subdirectories. Choose the <New virtual name> option in the left pane of the dialog box to create a new virtual name. For the `Templates` directory, we used the highly original virtual name of Templates and chose Template from the Type drop-down menu, as shown in Figure 2.23. Identify its path in the Path box. Save the settings. Repeat this process for the `WebServices` directory, except choose Soap from the Type drop-down menu. Name the Web service WebService1 and set the domain to whatever local domain you are using (a default value for this will have been posted). Figure 2.24 illustrates the settings for the `WebServices` directory.

8. Click OK to exit the dialog box.

**FIGURE 2.23:**

Virtual name settings for the Templates directory

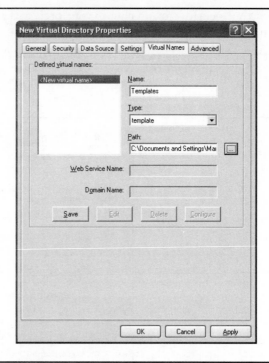

**FIGURE 2.24:**

Virtual Name settings for the WebServices directory

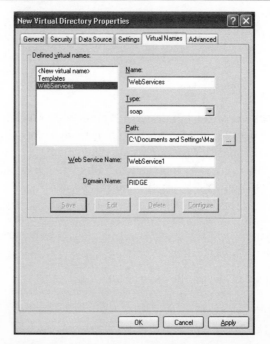

The IIS Virtual Directory Management console should now have an entry for Pubs as shown in Figure 2.25.

**FIGURE 2.25:**

The IIS Virtual Directory Management console with the completed Pubs entry

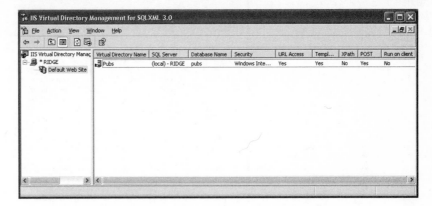

Now that you have set up your virtual directories, let's do something with them.

## Querying SQL Server via a URL

In this project, we will create a simple XML template containing an SQL-based query and use it to return the names of the authors stored in the authors table of the pubs database.

Open up Notepad (or your favorite text/code editor) and copy the code from Listing 2.4. Save the file as authors.xml in your Templates subdirectory, remembering to use the Save As and All Files (under Save as Type) options in Notepad.

---

**Listing 2.4**        *authors.xml*

```
<ROOT xmlns:sql="urn:schemas-microsoft-com:xml-sql">
  <sql:query client-side-xml="0">
    SELECT au_fname, au_lname
    FROM authors
    FOR XML AUTO
  </sql:query>
</ROOT>
```

---

Once you have set up your template, open up Internet Explorer and type the following URL into the browser: **http://localhost/Pubs/templates/authors.xml**.

We can access Pubs via localhost as the Pubs directory has been registered as a virtual directory in IIS. This should return the list of author's names from the pubs database, as illustrated in Figure 2.26.

**FIGURE 2.26:**

Authors' names returned in IE by an XML query of the pubs database

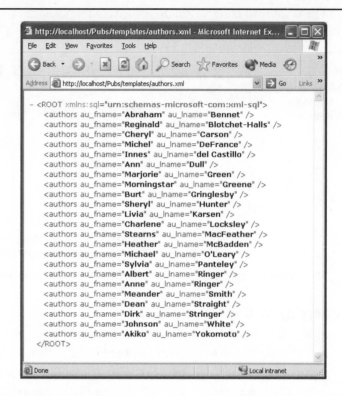

## Building an SQLXML Web Service

You need to do two things here: create the actual XML Web service and then establish a client to consume it.

The first thing to do is create a stored procedure in the pubs database that returns all the authors' names and surnames (similar to the template in Listing 2.4). Open up the SQL Server Enterprise Manager and expand the Databases node to reveal the pubs database. Expand the pubs node to reveal Stored Procedures. Right-click Stored Procedures and select New Stored Procedure. Copy the code from Listing 2.5 as illustrated in Figure 2.27. Save the stored procedure as allauthors.

**Listing 2.5    Code for the Authors Stored Procedure in the Pubs Database**

```
CREATE PROCEDURE allauthors
 AS

SELECT au_fname, au_lname
     FROM authors

GO
```

**FIGURE 2.27:**

The Stored Procedures
Dialog box

Next, we will begin creating the Web service:

1. From the IIS Virtual Directory Management for SQLXML 3 snap-in, double-click the Pubs entry to bring up the Properties dialog box. (This is effectively the same dialog box as the New Virtual Directory Properties dialog box that you worked with earlier.)

2. Click the Virtual Names tab and select the WebServices virtual name. Click the Configure button to bring up the SOAP Virtual Name Configuration dialog box, shown in Figure 2.28 (notice that the dialog box in this figure has already been configured).

3. Within the SOAP Virtual Name Configuration dialog box, make sure that the type is set to SP (stored procedures) and select the relevant stored procedure using the browse (…) button. (In this case, we choose the allauthors stored procedure.) Keep the output as XML objects (in the Row Formatting section). Click Save and exit the dialog boxes.

You have now created your XML Web service (a very simple process indeed). You can also set up a method mapping to the authors template that we created earlier. Click the New Method Mapping option, set the type to Template, and browse to the template's location. (Remember to save the mapping.) When you consume the WebService1, both methods would be available for you to work with on the client. Additionally, you can add more stored procedures or other templates (or UDFs, User Defined Functions) in the same manner and consume them as additional methods. You can also alter the output to either a single DataSet or DataSet objects.

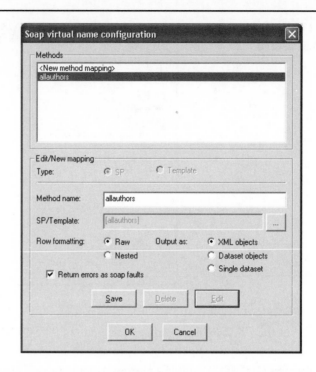

Once the XML Web service is created, two files are generated in the `WebServices` directory that we set up earlier. These are the `WebService1.ssc` and the `WebService1.wsdl` files. You can check the existence and viability of the XML Web service by calling it through Internet Explorer using the following URL (Notice the slightly different syntax with the use of a "?"):

```
http://localhost/Pubs/WebServices?wsdl
```

To consume the Web service, we will need to build a client application. This can be done very simply with the following steps:

1.  Open up Visual Studio .NET and create a new Windows application (WindowsDataApp2).

2.  Add a reference to the XML Web service you created by choosing Add Web Reference from the Project menu. Type the following URL into the address bar:

```
http://localhost/Pubs/WebServices?wsdl
```

3.  Figure 2.29 illustrates how the Add Web Reference dialog box should look after entering the URL. Click the Add Reference button and exit the dialog box.

4.  Set up a ListBox control and a Button control on Form1. Change the Text property of the button to read "List Authors." Figure 2.30 illustrates the completed form and controls.

**FIGURE 2.29:**

The Add Web Reference dialog box

**FIGURE 2.30:**

The completed Form1 for the WindowsDataApp2 project

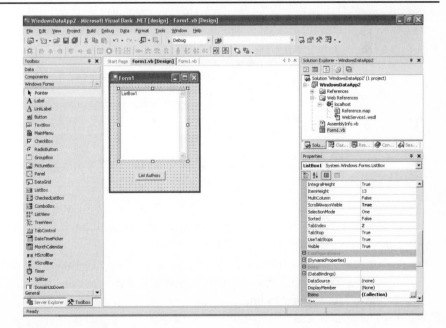

5. Double-click the button to enter Code Behind. Copy the code from Listing 2.6 into the Click event for the button.

**Listing 2.6**      **Click Event Code for the List Authors Button**

```
Private Sub Button1_Click(ByVal sender As _
System.Object, ByVal e As System.EventArgs) _
Handles Button1.Click
        Dim myService As localhost.WebService1 _
= New localhost.WebService1()
        Dim xmldata As New Object()
        Dim i, n As Integer
        Dim data As System.Xml.XmlElement
        Dim ErrorMessage As localhost.SqlMessage

        myService.Credentials = _
System.Net.CredentialCache.DefaultCredentials
        xmldata = myService.allauthors()

        For i = 0 To UBound(xmldata)

            Select Case xmldata(i).GetType().ToString
                Case "System.Xml.XmlElement"
                    data = xmldata(i)
                    For n = 0 To _
                        data.ChildNodes.Count - 1
ListBox1.Items.Add(data.ChildNodes.ItemOf_
(n).FirstChild.InnerText & " " & _
data.ChildNodes.ItemOf(n).LastChild.InnerText)
                    Next
                Case "WSclient.localhost.SqlMessage"
                    ErrorMessage = xmldata(i)
                    ListBox1.Items.Add(ErrorMessage.Message)
            End Select
        Next

    End Sub
```

This code calls the stored procedure via the Web service. The return value is an object array that must be then cast into either an XMLElement or SQLMessage type. The XMLElement objects include the data we are hoping to access, and the SQLMessage can carry any error messages may need to be reported back to us.

Because we used Windows authentication when we set up the XML Web service, we also need to include the `myService.Credentials = System.Net.CredentialCache` `.DefaultCredentials` line.

The outside loop checks through the returned XML to identify what parts of the response are data and what parts are error messages (as picked up by the Case statements). The nested loop is used to strip away any additional markup information from the data itself. The names and surnames are then displayed in the ListBox as illustrated in Figure 2.31.

**FIGURE 2.31:**

The completed WindowsDataApp2 displaying the information retrieved from the allauthors SQLXML Web service

## Summary

In this chapter, we covered a range of topics that we could have easily spent a lot more time with. Database-driven applications are very much the bread and butter for many developers, and the main purpose of this chapter was to create a familiarity with a number of technologies that are commonly used when developing with Visual Basic .NET.

In particular, it is important to understand the close relationship that Microsoft is building between SQL Server technologies and its development platforms. You can now build the front end, the middle tier, and the database all without leaving the Visual Studio .NET IDE. The connection objects with SQL Server 2000 have been optimized to deliver maximum performance, and applications built using .NET technologies can work seamlessly with a SQL Server back end.

In future chapters in this book, we will revisit a number of these topics in more detail. In the next chapter, we will be investigating ADO.NET in far more depth. It is important to spend some time familiarizing yourself with the structure of ADO.NET and its various objects because it behaves very differently from what most of us have previously come to expect from ADO.

# CHAPTER 3

# ADO.NET: An Architectural Overview

- The connected and disconnected layers of ADO.NET

- Using the DataReader

- The visual data tools

- Populating and editing DataSets

- Update operations with DataSets

- Optimistic concurrency

**M**odern applications are not limited to local area networks; they reach out to the Internet, utilize resources on remote servers, and interact with clients on other networks. Applications running on different operating systems need to exchange data on demand and update the underlying databases. To address the data access needs of modern applications, Microsoft has introduced ADO.NET, which is the evolution of ActiveX Data Object (ADO). It is an enormous step in the evolution of Microsoft's data access components, because ADO.NET bears very little resemblance to the old ADO you're probably familiar with.

The main characteristic of ADO.NET is that the data on the client is totally disconnected from the database server. The idea is to retrieve some data from the server, copy it to the client, and work with it locally. ADO.NET provides the DataSet object for storing the data at the client. Even if the database server is running on a machine on the same local area network, the data at the client is totally disconnected from the database. Any changes you make to your data are not reflected in the database. Of course, you can connect to the server and update the data source as needed.

Another important aspect of ADO.NET is that it uses XML in its core and you can access the same data either as relational data or as hierarchical data (an XML document). You can persist the data in XML format, pass the XML file to other clients, or receive data from other clients in XML format. We're going to look at some of the XML-related features of ADO.NET in Chapter 4, "Working with the DataSet," as well as in Chapter 19, "Using XML and Visual Basic .NET," but the emphasis in this book is on the relational view of the data—related tables made up of rows.

This chapter is an overview of ADO.NET. We can't discuss the differences between ADO and ADO.NET because there are hardly any similarities. The experience you've acquired while programming ADO with VB6 will help you understand ADO.NET, but we can't explain the architecture of ADO.NET by comparing it to ADO. Their object models are widely different. This chapter provides an overview of the object model of ADO.NET and demonstrates many of the common data access operations through examples. The emphasis in this chapter is on the visual tools, but we'll also look at the code generated by the various wizards. Chapter 4 focuses on the main object in the ADO.NET architecture, the DataSet.

## A Disconnected Architecture for Data Access

The most prominent characteristic of ADO.NET is its disconnected architecture: unlike its predecessors, ADO.NET is designed on the premise that client applications will connect to the server to request some data, store it to the client where they can process it, and then connect again to the server to submit the changes. The client need not maintain a connection to the database during the course of the application. Connections are established as needed to send or receive data and then closed immediately. Actually, connections are not established all the time; ADO.NET maintains a pool of connections, and each time a client needs a connection, it's assigned one of the pool's connections.

However, you need not worry about maintaining the pool of connections; it's maintained automatically. There's one aspect of programming with ADO.NET that you must pay attention to at all times: Every time you open a connection explicitly, you must also close it explicitly. If not, the system won't know that you're done with the connection and it won't return it to the pool. In many cases, you don't even have to worry about closing the connection because it's established and released automatically (this happens when you use a DataAdapter to access your data).

This architecture is suitable for the world of disconnected, distributed applications. An application of this type may contact multiple servers to retrieve data and submit changes and new data. The remote servers may submit the data in a variety of ways, including Web services, which is one of the hottest new technologies introduced with .NET and is discussed in detail later in this book. A Web service is in essence a function on a machine that acts as a web server and any other computer on the web can call it as if it were calling a function. The process is a bit more involved, but the idea is to call a function that resides on a remote machine just as you request a web page: through a URL. If the function accepts arguments, they're passed along with the URL, which is how you submit data to a web application today. The results are encoded in XML format and passed back to the client. A Web service can return a scalar result (an integer or a string), but it may also return an entire DataSet (a collection of tables).

Applications of this type are by nature distributed. Some of the processing takes place on the client computer and the rest takes place on several remote servers. They're also disconnected, because no computer architecture and software tools could guarantee a connection to all the remote servers while the client application is running. Instead, the client application establishes a connection to the server, gets all the data it will (or may) need for a while, and then closes the connection to the server. Users can work with the data locally and request connections to remote servers when they're ready to send updates or retrieve additional data. If no connection can be established at the time, the changes can be persisted locally and submitted to the data source whenever a connection becomes available. A distributed application can't rely on constant connections to one or more remote servers, so it's no surprise that the data access mechanism has to be based on a disconnected architecture.

The second major characteristic of ADO.NET is its XML integration: the data retrieved from the database and moved to the client can be viewed either relationally (through the ADO.NET objects) or hierarchically, through an XmlDocument object. The reason for this is to support the distributed nature of the applications. If the data needs to be transferred from machine to machine, sometimes between machines with different operating systems and databases, it has to be encoded in a way that can be easily understood by all components.

Microsoft has chosen the XML format, which has been gaining momentum in the last few years. The XML specifications are decided upon by an independent committee, and all the major players in the field follow these specifications. Just as HTML emerged as an absolute standard for the Web, XML will become (if it hasn't already) a standard for exchanging data.

XML as a data exchange protocol started gaining momentum in the days of ADO. ADO Recordsets could be persisted in XML format and used to exchange data between dissimilar computers. XML is at the core of ADO.NET, and the two views of the data are synchronized at all times. You can edit the DataSet and view the changes in the corresponding XML document and vice versa. You can also retrieve data from SQL Server 2000 directly in XML format and submit data (new or edited rows) in XML format.

If you know nothing about XML, you don't need to learn anything in order to build data-driven applications. You can work with traditional relational tools (such as SQL statements) and consider XML as another proprietary protocol for persisting relational data. So far, we've been manipulating relational data with SQL statements and none of us knows how SQL Server stores its data. Eventually, the same will become true for XML. All we need is a language to manipulate XML data and we may never have to look at (let alone edit) an XML document. XQuery is such a language, but it's brand new and it's too early to say whether XQuery will become the query language for XML documents. Eventually, XML will become transparent to the application developer, but this won't happen in the next few years, so some exposure to XML will help you as a developer.

We could do the same with Remote Data Objects (RDO) and ADO, couldn't we? It's true, but ADO was based on a connected architecture (it assumed a connection to the server). Disconnected features were added as an afterthought to these architectures. ADO.NET was designed with this goal in mind and provides an object model that addresses the needs of distributed applications—the type of applications that take advantage of the Web and can be scaled from a local network with a few dozen users to thousands of geographically dispersed users.

The data is stored at the client in an object called DataSet, which contains one or more tables and their relations. As you will see, working with the DataSet is similar to working with a miniature database at the client. The DataSet contains one or more tables, enforces referential integrity between them, maintains different versions of the data (the original data that was read from the database and the edited data), and can be persisted in XML format. This means that you can edit a disconnected DataSet, persist it to a file on the client computer, reload it, edit it again, and submit it to the data source whenever you're ready. You can also undo some or all of the changes made to the DataSet because the DataSet maintains not only the current values, but also the original field values read from the database.

## The Two Layers of ADO.NET

The two major components of ADO.NET are the data provider and the DataSet. The data provider is not really an object, it's a collective name for several objects that perform similar actions and/or work with one another. The objects of the data provider communicate with the database: they are responsible for querying the database and passing data from the client to the database and vice versa. The DataSet is where the data is stored at the client's side. The DataSet object is where all the action takes place at the client and it's loosely equivalent to the Recordset of the ADO. However, it's a much richer object and it has a different structure. By "loosely equivalent," we mean that it's the object where data is stored at the client, but the similarities end here. The most important difference between Recordset and DataSet objects is that the DataSet object is always disconnected. The DataSet contains a copy (snapshot) of the requested data, and it's in no way connected to the database. The changes you make to your data remain in the DataSet and can even be persisted to a local file at the client. When you want to update the underlying tables, you must submit the changes to the data source.

As shown in Figure 3.1, the data provider is the connected layer of ADO.NET, whereas the DataSet is the disconnected layer. The data provider is the layer on top of the database and abstracts the communication between the client application and the database. As such, it's optimized for a specific database. ADO.NET provides two data providers, one for SQL Server and another one for OLE DB–compliant databases, such as Access. The Connection class, for example, is an abstract class from which two other classes derive: the SqlConnection class (for connecting to SQL Server databases) and the OledbConnection class (for connecting to OLE DB–compliant databases). All the classes of the connected layer come in two flavors, one for SQL Server and another one for OLE DB databases. Their names differ in the prefix, which is either *Sql* or *Oledb*. It's quite likely that a third class, optimized for Oracle databases, will become available in the near future.

**FIGURE 3.1:**

The connected and disconnected layers of ADO.NET

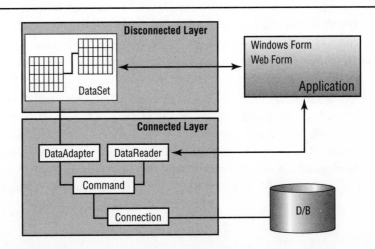

The classes that make up the data provider are explained next. We describe the abstract classes here, even though you can't use them directly. All the information we'll present in the following sections applies to both classes that derive from the corresponding abstract class—either the SQL or the OLE DB version of the class.

### The Connection Class

Use a Connection object to establish a connection to the data source. The connection is opened right before you submit a query to the database and closed as soon as you get the results back. If you use the DataAdapter object to populate a DataSet object, the connection is managed automatically for you by the DataAdapter and you don't have to open or close the connection explicitly. If you use the DataReader to read the data, you must close the connection explicitly.

The client application requires a single Connection object for each database. Most applications work with a single database and all the data flowing into and out of the database go through the same Connection object.

The Connection object is also used to perform transactions against the database. Each transaction must be initiated and ended on the same Connection object, which must remain open for the duration of the transaction.

### The Command Class

Command objects are used to execute commands against the data source. These commands can be SQL statements or stored procedures. You can use the same Command object to execute any number of commands against the database in the course of the application. You can execute selection queries, which usually return a set of rows, or action queries, which return a single integer value that's the number of rows affected by the query. Depending on the type of query you want to execute, the Command object provides a number of different methods: ExecuteNonQuery (for executing action queries), ExecuteReader (for executing queries that return a set of rows), ExecuteScalar (for executing commands that return a single value), and ExecuteXmlReader (for executing commands that return a set of rows in XML format).

If the command requires one or more parameters, you specify the values of the parameters through the Parameters property of the Command object. The Parameters property is a collection with one element per query parameter. If you use a DataAdapter object to access the data source, the Parameters collection is created automatically and you need only specify the values of the parameters. If you set up Command objects in your code, you must create the Parameters collection with the appropriate statements and then assign a value to each parameter.

## The DataReader Class

The DataReader object is a stream with the data you've retrieved from the data source with the Command object. Use this stream to read the rows returned by a query, just as you'd use a Stream object to read the contents of a file. The DataReader class is a read-only, forward-only stream and you can't use it to update the data source. You use it to read the fields of the rows and store them to a custom structure in the client application or populate a multiline control like the ListView control. Notice that you can't populate a DataSet object with the DataReader class. If you want to load data into a DataSet object, you must use a DataAdapter object.

## The DataAdapter Class

The DataAdapter object is an intermediary between the DataSet object and the data source. The DataSet object must be populated through a DataAdapter—you can't use the Command object or the DataReader object to populate the DataSet. The DataAdapter knows how to populate the DataSet and how to commit the changes made to the DataSet back to the data source. In a way, the DataAdapter is your application's gateway to the database tables and the DataSet is the local data store. Note that each table in the DataSet has its own DataAdapter, which knows how to move data into and out of a single table of the DataSet. Each table in the DataSet, however, may contain columns from various database tables.

Figure 3.2 shows the objects of the data provider. The DataAdapter uses several Command objects to submit queries to the database through the Connection object and retrieve the result set. Behind the scenes, the DataAdapter sets up a number of Command objects and uses DataReader objects to read the data returned by the query. The IDE provides a wizard that allows you to set up DataAdapters visually. You can also set up DataAdapter objects from within your code, but you'll have to write quite a bit of code.

**FIGURE 3.2:**

The classes that make up the data provider's layer

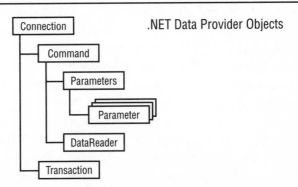

.NET Data Provider Objects

### The DataSet Class

This is the most important class in ADO.NET, because this is where you store the data on the client and also where all the processing takes place. The DataSet is a local storage for your data and it has no idea where the data came from (it's data-source agnostic). Its structure is similar to the structure of a database: it contains one or more tables and, optionally, relations between the tables. You can edit any row of any table, add new rows to any table and delete existing rows. If the tables are related, the DataSet can also enforce primary/foreign key relations. Figure 3.3 outlines the objects that make up a DataSet.

**FIGURE 3.3:**

The DataSet object's architecture

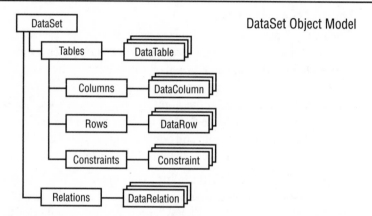

DataSet Object Model

The DataSet is an object that can store relational data no matter where the data originates. You can create a DataSet by using tables from different databases, importing XML files, and even adding tables to it from within your code. All the data you need for a specific task can be combined into a single DataSet, which remains disconnected for the course of the application. When you're finished editing the data in the DataSet, you can submit the changes to their data source(s). You can even create a DataSet in code and use relational tools to manipulate the data. This type of DataSet can't be stored to a database, but you can persist it to a local file and reload the data from this file in a later session.

The tables of the DataSet are objects of the DataTable type, and they correspond largely to the tables of the database. However, a DataTable object rarely contains an entire database table. It usually contains selected rows and selected columns. Consider, for example, a DataSet with the Products and Categories tables. The Products DataTable object in the DataSet may contain a few columns (product names, prices, and category IDs) of the underlying table and only a subset of the rows of the underlying table (the products of a specific supplier). The Categories table may contain category IDs and names only. Depending on the nature of the application, you may also limit the number of rows in the Categories DataTable to the categories contained in the selected products.

Relations between tables are represented in a DataSet with DataRelation objects, and you must add the relations manually to the DataSet, either with the DataSet's editor at design time or through code at runtime. Notice that you can add multiple tables in their entirety to the client's DataSet (like the Products and Categories tables of the Northwind database), but the relations won't be picked up from the database automatically. All relations must be established explicitly.

In the following sections, we'll explore the classes presented so far through simple code examples. All the examples of this chapter can be found in the ADOTests project, and each section's example is implemented with one of the buttons of the ADOTests project, whose interface is shown in Figure 3.4.

**WARNING**  As you go through the examples of this chapter, don't forget to change the settings of the connection (our settings may not work with your setup).

**FIGURE 3.4:**

The ADOTests project demonstrates most of the code samples of this chapter.

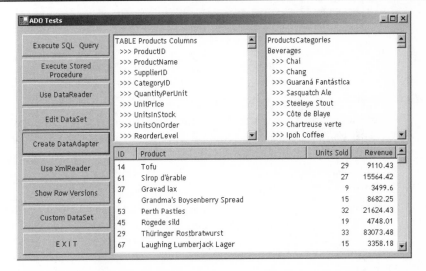

Once you develop a basic understanding of these objects and their role in contacting databases and manipulating their contents, you'll be able to make the most of the visual tools. The visual tools are nothing but user-friendly interfaces for accessing the functionality of these objects. They do a fine job of hiding the programming details of the basic data access objects, but we felt that most developers feel more comfortable with code rather than visual tools. Only when you understand the underlying principles and programming techniques will you be able to make the most of the visual tools and tweak the code they produce.

## Establishing a Connection

Your first task is to establish a connection to the database. To do so, you must create an SqlConnection or an OledbConnection object, set its ConnectionString property, and then open it with the Open method. When you no longer need the connection, call its Close method to close it. You should try to open the connection as late as possible (just before executing a command) and close it as early as possible (right after getting the data and before processing it). Do not even consider establishing a connection when the program starts and releasing it when the program ends. Maintaining connections is an expensive process, and it becomes especially expensive with web applications. ADO.NET maintains a pool of connections and reuses them to accommodate all the clients with the least number of connections.

The ConnectionString property provides all the information necessary to establish a connection to the data source. The following statements set up an SqlConnection object for the Northwind database:

```
Dim CN As SqlClient.SqlConnection
CN.ConnectionString = _
      "initial catalog=Northwind;persist" & _
      "security info=False;" & _
      "data source = .; " & _
      "user id=USERNAME;password=USERPASSWORD; " & _
      "workstation id=POWERTOOLKIT;packet size=4096"
```

You must replace the name of the workstation id attribute with the name of your computer and supply the proper settings for the user id and password attributes. *Change these settings to match your installation.* The initial catalog attribute is the name of the database you want to open in the current instance of SQL Server, and you need not change it. At the very least, you must change the user ID and password in the previous connection string. The default user ID and password (account sa with a blank password) will work on many systems, but this doesn't mean it's a recommended practice. The data source attribute is the instance of SQL Server you want to access. The period indicates the local host (the instance of SQL Server running on the current machine). Replace the period with the name of the machine on which SQL Server is running on a local area network.

The simplest method of setting up a Connection object is to add a connection to a specific database with the Data Links window (described later in this chapter) and then drop this connection to every form that needs access to the specific database. The connection string property will be created automatically for you, and you can copy it from the Property Browser window and reuse it in your code.

The format of the connection string shown earlier contains the user's name and password. It's fairly safe to use a connection string like that in the middle tier, but you shouldn't embed crucial information to the client application's code. The password is stored in the executable file as plain text, and anyone who has access to this file can read it (this file resides on every client machine that uses the application). The middle tier components usually reside on an application server, which has stricter security settings.

If you want to connect to a database directly from within the client application, as we do in this chapter, you should let Windows authenticate the user. To use Windows authentication, specify the Integrated Security option, as shown in the following ConnectionString setting:

```
Integrated Security=SSPI;Initial Catalog=Northwind;
Data Source=localhost
```

This connection string doesn't embed sensitive information, such as passwords, in the application's code. Once users have been authenticated by Windows, you can grant them access to the database as well.

## Executing Commands and Stored Procedures

In this section, you'll learn how to set up Command objects to execute queries against a database, and the code we'll present in this section is quite common in programming database front ends. Our first example updates the Products table of the Northwind database; it increases the prices of the products from a specific supplier by executing the following action query against the database:

```
UPDATE    Products
SET       UnitPrice = UnitPrice * 1.12
WHERE     SupplierID = 4
```

The code shown here is implemented with the Execute SQL Query button in the ADOTests project. First, we must establish a connection to the database with the Connection object, as explained in the previous section. Then you must create a new SqlCommand object and set its Connection property to the Connection object you have just created:

```
Dim CMD As New SqlClient.SqlCommand()
CMD.Connection = CN
```

The next step is to specify the command to be executed against the data source with the SqlCommand object's CommandText and CommandType properties. The CommandText property accepts the text of the SQL query, or the name of the stored procedure, to be executed against the database. The CommandType property determines the type of the command and its value is one of the members of the CommandType enumeration: StoredProcedure, TableDirect, and Text. The CommandType.Text setting applies to SQL statements, and the CommandType .StoredProcedure setting applies to stored procedures. Use the Command.Type.TableDirect setting if you're specifying a table's name (a practice that's not common, or recommended, with ADO.NET). The following statements prepare the *CMD* object to execute the SQL statement that updates the prices of selected rows in the Products table:

```
CMD.CommandText = "UPDATE Products SET " & _
          "UnitPrice = UnitPrice * 2 WHERE SupplierID = 4"
CMD.CommandType = CommandType.Text
```

Finally, you can execute the command by opening the connection and calling the SqlCommand object's ExecuteNonQuery method. This method accepts no arguments and returns the number of rows affected by the query:

```
CN.Open()
Dim rows As Integer
rows = CMD.ExecuteNonQuery()
CN.Close()
MsgBox("The query affected " & rows.ToString & " rows")
```

After executing the command, we close the connection to the database (there's no reason to wait for the user to acknowledge the message box before closing the connection). The ExecuteNonQuery method executes an action query and returns the number of rows affected by the command. There are other methods that execute selection queries against the database and return the qualifying rows.

Let's edit the code of the last example so that it calls a stored procedure instead of a SQL statement. First, you must attach to the database a stored procedure that increases the prices of the products from a specific supplier. The actual increase percentage and the ID of the supplier are passed to the stored procedure as parameters. Here's the stored procedure's code:

```
CREATE PROCEDURE HikePrice
@percent decimal,
@supplierID int
AS
UPDATE      Products
SET         UnitPrice = UnitPrice * (1+@percent)
WHERE       SupplierID = @supplierID
GO
```

First you must attach the HikePrices stored procedure to the database. To do so, right-click the Stored Procedures node under the Northwind database in Server Explorer, and from the context menu select New Stored Procedure. Then you can execute the stored procedure by calling the ExecuteNonQuery method of the SqlCommand object. The code is similar to the one we used earlier to execute an SQL statement against the database except for the settings of the CommandText and CommandType properties. In addition, you must set up two Parameter objects, through which you'll pass the values of the two input parameters to the stored procedure. Each parameter is represented by a Parameter object, which is attached to the Parameters collection of the SqlCommand object. The code that raises the price of a number of products by calling the HikePrices stored procedure is shown in Listing 3.1.

**Listing 3.1    Executing a Stored Procedure with Parameters**

```
Dim CN As New SqlClient.SqlConnection()
CN.ConnectionString = "initial catalog=Northwind;" & _
            "persist security info=False;" & _
            "user id=sa;workstation id=POWERTOOLKIT;" & _
            "packet size=4096"
Dim CMD As New SqlClient.SqlCommand()
CMD.Connection = CN
CMD.CommandText = "HikePrice"
CMD.CommandType = CommandType.StoredProcedure
CMD.Parameters.Add(New _
            SqlClient.SqlParameter("@percent", -0.2))
CMD.Parameters.Add(New _
            SqlClient.SqlParameter("@supplierID", 4))
CN.Open()
Dim rows As Integer
rows = CMD.ExecuteNonQuery()
CN.Close()
MsgBox(rows.ToString & " rows updated")
```

Each Parameter object has a name, which is the name of the corresponding argument in the stored procedure, a type and a value. The data type is determined by the parameter's value when you create a Parameter object in its constructor.

Executing action queries against a database is straightforward with the Command object. More often than not, however, you need to retrieve data from the database with selection queries. Some action queries also return the updated row(s). The data returned by a selection query is read through the DataReader object or stored in a DataSet object. Using the DataReader object is the fastest method of reading data off the server. It provides read-only, forward-only access to the stream returned by the server. The DataSet is an elaborate object for storing data. It allows the editing of its data and it can update the data source too. The DataSet object is very flexible but not as fast in reading data. The difference between the two, however, is that the DataSet is a data store whereas the DataReader can't store data; it's used to read the data returned by the query, similar to a Stream object.

## SQL Injection

Executing stored procedures, instead of queries built on the fly from within your code, requires many more statements. Whenever possible, code your queries as stored procedures and call them by name, as shown earlier. Do not build SQL statements on the fly, especially if they involve user-supplied arguments. There are two very good reasons for using stored procedures: They execute faster because they reside in the database; they're compiled once and are ready to be executed. SQL statements must be compiled every time you submit them to the database.

*Continued on next page*

There's a much better reason for using stored procedures, or parameterized SQL statements. More often than not, SQL statements contain user-supplied arguments, which are coded into the statement itself. Let's say your program allows users to specify the name of a customer and then it builds a SQL statement that contains the text entered by the user as part of the WHERE clause, where `txtCustName` is the name of a TextBox control on your form:

```
cmd = _
    "SELECT * FROM Customers WHERE CustomerName LIKE '" & _
    txtCustName.Text & "%'"
```

If the user supplies the string "Alfred", the following statement will be executed against the database:

```
SELECT * FROM Customers
WHERE CustomerName LIKE 'Alfred%'
```

So far, so good. But what if a user injects additional statements in the parameter? Suppose the user knew that the database contains a table called Products (a very reasonable guess) and entered the following string in the txtCustName control:

```
zzz';drop table Products--
```

What SQL statement would your code submit to the database? Take a close look at the following statement:

```
SELECT * FROM Customers
WHERE CustomerName LIKE 'zzz';drop table Products--%'
```

This is a batch query made up of two individual queries: a selection query followed by an action query. The action query removes a table from the database! Even if the user doesn't know the names of the tables, there are system tables that have the same names in all installations of SQL Server.

The technique we just described is called *SQL injection*, and you should make sure that the users of your application can't use your user interface and client code as a Trojan horse to execute their own queries against the database. The safest method of avoiding SQL injection is to use stored procedures and pass the appropriate parameter values. The stored procedure is precompiled and the parameters passed by the user can't alter the procedure's execution plan. If you're building SQL statements on the fly in existing code, you can add code to remove "dangerous" statements like DELETE, DROP, and UPDATE or remove the batch separator (;) from any user-supplied string. It's recommended, however, that you avoid building SQL statements on the fly in your code—especially if they involve user-supplied arguments—and that you instead implement the same operations as stored procedures.

An added protection is to ask the database administrator to create groups of users with restricted rights. A data entry operator shouldn't have the right to drop a table from the database, but you'll be surprised by the number of installations that use the sa account for all tasks.

## Retrieving Data with the DataReader

The next example demonstrates how to use the DataReader object to retrieve a set of rows from the database and display their fields. The rows are the result of a selection query, and they may come from a single table or multiple joined tables. This time we'll use a fairly complicated query that retrieves the names of all products along with each product's total number of units sold and total revenues generated. Here's the GetSalesFigures stored procedure that retrieves the desired information from the Northwind database:

```
CREATE PROCEDURE GetSalesFigures
AS
SELECT    Products.ProductName,
          COUNT([Order Details].OrderID),
          CAST(SUM([Order Details].UnitPrice*Quantity*
          (1-Discount)) AS DECIMAL(12,2))
FROM      Products INNER JOIN [Order Details]
          ON Products.ProductID=[Order Details].ProductID
GROUP BY Products.ProductName, Products.ProductID
GO
```

Attach the stored procedure as described in the previous section. You can also execute it from within the IDE to make sure it's correct and returns the desired rows. To execute the stored procedure in the IDE, expand the appropriate connection in the Server Explorer, locate the stored procedure, and right-click its name. From the context menu, select Run to execute it. The results of the query will appear in the Output window. If the stored procedure accepts any parameters, the Run Stored Procedure dialog box will appear, where you can specify the appropriate parameter values.

Then switch to Visual Studio and add the statements of Listing 3.2 in a button's Click event handler (this is the Use DataReader button of the ADOTests project). These statements execute the stored procedure with the Command object's ExecuteReader method, which returns the result of the query through a DataReader object. The DataReader is a forward-only, read-only stream that contains the rows retrieved from the database. To iterate through the rows of the DataStream object, use its Read method and the Item property to read the value of each field.

**Listing 3.2**     **Using the SqlDataReader Object**

```
Private Sub bttnReader_Click(ByVal sender As System.Object,_
                        ByVal e As System.EventArgs) _
                        Handles bttnReader.Click
    Dim CN As New SqlClient.SqlConnection()
    CN.ConnectionString = _
          "Integrated Security=SSPI;Persist Security " & _
          "Info=False;Initial Catalog=Northwind; " & _
```

```
                    "Data Source=.;Packet Size=4096; " & _
                    "Workstation ID=POWERTOOLKIT"
        Dim CMD As New SqlClient.SqlCommand()
        CMD.Connection = CN
        CMD.CommandText = "GetSalesFigures"
        CMD.CommandType = CommandType.StoredProcedure

        Dim SqlIn As SqlClient.SqlDataReader
        CN.Open()
        SqlIn = CMD.ExecuteReader
        Dim LI As ListViewItem
        ListView1.Items.Clear()
        While SqlIn.Read
            LI = New ListViewItem()
    LI.Text = SqlIn.Item("ProductID")
            LI.SubItems.Add(SqlIn.Item("ProductName"))
            LI.SubItems.Add(SqlIn.Item("UnitsSold"))
            LI.SubItems.Add(SqlIn.Item("Revenue"))
            ListView1.Items.Add(LI)
        End While
        SqlIn.Close()
        CN.Close()
    End Sub
```

**WARNING** As with the other samples in this chapter, you must edit the ConnectionString property. The Data Source attribute is the name of the machine on which SQL Server is running (the sample code assumes that SQL Server runs on the same machine as the client application). You can also create a new connection with the visual tools, as explained in the previous chapter, and then copy the ConnectionString property's value generated by the wizard from the Property Browser and paste it into your code. Don't forget to attach the GetSalesFigures stored procedure to the database.

After you're done using the DataReader, you must close both the DataReader and the Connection objects. The sample code displays the fields of each row on a ListView control, but you can store them to an array, populate a structure with the appropriate fields, and so on. Notice that the DataReader object's Read method doesn't return a row or any field values. It moves the current position to the next row and returns True if there is a current row. If you attempt to read past the last row, the Read method will return False and the loop will terminate. To access the fields of the current row, use the Item property. Each field's value in the current row can be accessed either by the field's name (as shown in the sample code) or by an index value. Indexing with field names makes the code easier to read, but for fastest execution, you should use numeric indices (numeric indices don't involve lookups). The indexing of the columns in each row is zero based.

So far, you've seen how to use the Command object to query the database and how to retrieve data with the DataReader. Using the DataReader is the fastest method of moving data from the server to the client, but it doesn't maintain a copy of the data. It's your responsibility to store the data to a structure, and you use the DataReader to populate a control or to process data serially. The code in Listing 3.2 uses the rows retrieved by the query to populate a ListView control. The DataReader is used frequently in middle-tier code to read rows from the database and create objects, which are then passed to the client. You'll see how to apply this technique in Chapter 5, "Building Data-Driven Windows Applications."

Note that there's no DataWriter object. To commit changes to the data source, you must build and execute the appropriate Command objects. If you need to retrieve data for presentation purposes only, use the DataReader object. If you want to be able to edit the data at the client, you can use the DataAdapter object to populate a DataSet, as discussed in the following section.

## Populating DataSets with DataAdapters

Most client applications need to retrieve data, store them locally, process them, and then submit the changes to the server. It is possible to use the Command and DataReader objects to process the data on the client, but ADO.NET offers two more objects that simplify the processing of data at the client. These objects are the DataAdapter object and the DataSet object. Most data-driven applications aren't limited to a single table. They process rows of several related tables and they need a convenient data storage mechanism at the client. This is exactly what the DataSet object does: it stores related data in one or more tables and allows you to conveniently access any field of any row of any table.

To appreciate the function of DataSets and DataAdapters in developing data-driven applications with ADO.NET, consider the operations you want to perform against a database in a typical application. You begin by selecting rows from one or more tables and bringing them to the client. These are the rows selected by the client application based on some criteria provided by the user on the client application's form (a range of dates, a customer name, and so on). Rows are selected by executing the appropriate SELECT statement(s) against the database. A very basic rule in designing interfaces for data-driven applications is that you shouldn't move more data than necessary to the client. Never download an entire table; use a WHERE clause, or the TOP clause if necessary, to limit the number of rows to be downloaded to the client.

The data is moved to the client, where it must be stored somewhere. The object that accepts the data at the client is the DataSet object. More often than not, you select data from multiple tables. You rarely retrieve a few rows from the Products table, for example. You also need to select corresponding rows from the Suppliers table, as well as the corresponding rows from the Categories tables. Each row in the Products table contains two integers, which represent the ID of the product's supplier and the ID of the category, and these two values are quite meaningless for the end user. You must also retrieve the matching rows from the two other tables so that you can display the supplier's name and address and the category's name instead of its ID.

So, the idea is to select one or more rows from a table and the matching rows from their related tables. Moreover, you may not need all the columns of these two tables, just the columns you're going to work with. If you plan to update the data source, you should always copy the key field of each table to the DataSet.

The DataSet object stores the rows of each table in a DataTable object. The rows of the Products table will be stored in the Products DataTable object, the rows of the Categories table will be stored in the Categories DataTable object, and so on. Furthermore, the Data-Tables of the DataSet will be related to one another just like the underlying tables in the database. In short, the DataSet is a segment of the database, and you can work with its tables as if it were a local database. Figure 3.5 outlines the architecture of the DataAdapter object. The DataAdapter object retrieves data from the databases with the SelectCommand object and populates a client DataSet. The data is edited in the DataSet, and when you call its Update method, the DataAdapter uses the other three objects to update the underlying data source. The DeleteCommand object knows how to remove the deleted rows from the corresponding table, the UpdateCommand knows how to update the edited rows, and the InsertCommand knows how to add new rows to the appropriate table.

**FIGURE 3.5:**

The architecture of the DataAdapter object

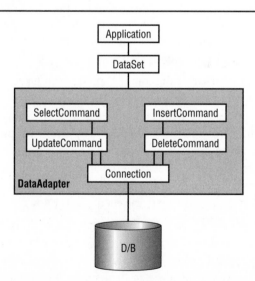

In short, each DataTable in the DataSet is associated with a DataAdapter object that knows how to retrieve rows from the database and populate its corresponding table with them. It also knows how to submit to the database the changes made to its table.

Each DataTable object has a Rows collection, which represents the table's rows, and each Row object has an Items collection, which represents the fields of the row. You can edit the data in the DataSet from within your client application's code at will as long as you don't violate the primary and foreign key constraints. You can change the values of existing fields, add new rows to any table, and delete existing rows. All the action takes place at the client, and changes are committed to the database's tables only after you call the DataAdapter object's Update method. You'll see how to edit a DataSet later in this chapter as well as in the following chapter, where we'll discuss the DataSet object in more detail.

But how does the DataAdapter know how to update the underlying tables? It simply uses INSERT, UPDATE, and DELETE statements, or stored procedures, as you would do from within your own code. It's your responsibility to specify the SQL statements, but there are wizards to assist you in designing the queries. The DataAdapter's job is almost trivial: it calls the INSERT statement for adding new rows to the underlying table, the UPDATE statement for updating edited rows, and the DELETE statement for deleting rows.

DataSets are used almost exclusively with DataAdapters, and we're going to look at the process of configuring DataAdapters and populating the corresponding DataSets in the following section. The IDE provides visual tools to generate DataSets with point-and-click operations, and we'll explore the visual data tools first. Later in this chapter, we're going to look at the code generated by the wizard, and as you will see, writing code to configure the DataAdapter and generate the DataSet is a straightforward process.

## The Visual Data Tools

Visual Studio .NET comes with several wizards for building data-driven applications. In this section, we're going to build a DataSet, the Products DataSet, with three tables: the Products, Suppliers, and Categories tables. We'll create a DataSet with three tables and we'll copy the rows of the three tables into the corresponding DataTable object of the DataSet. Once the data is in the DataSet, we'll be able to edit it and submit it back to the data source at any time. We'll use the visual tools to create a connection to the database, specify the data we want to retrieve. and populate the DataSet. To demonstrate the process of building DataSets and using them in your code, we'll build the DataAdapters application. Let's start by creating a new Connection object to connect to a specific database.

### Adding a Connection Object

Start a new Windows Application project, open the Server Explorer, and under the Data Connection node, look for a connection to the Northwind database. Unless you've built one already, you'll have to follow these steps to add a connection to the Northwind database:

1. Right-click the Data Connections item, and from the context menu, select Add Connection. You'll see the Data Link Properties dialog box, shown in Figure 3.6. The dialog box will be initially empty and you'll have to specify the properties of the connection to the Northwind database.

**FIGURE 3.6:**

The Data Link Properties dialog box

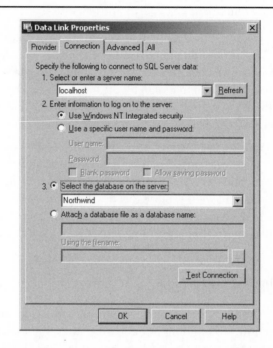

2. Switch to the Provider tab. The Microsoft OLE DB Provider for SQL Server is preselected for you. If you're working with Access, select the Microsoft Jet 4.0 OLE DB Provider.

3. On the Connection tab, select the name of the server you want to connect. If you're using a stand-alone machine, you won't see any items in the first drop-down list. The local server (the instance of SQL Server running on your machine) is the default server. Then select the Northwind database in the second drop-down list on the dialog box and click the Test Connection button. If all goes well, you'll see a message box with the message "Test connection succeeded." If you see another message, make sure SQL Server is running and that the username and password you specified are correct.

The newly created connection to the Northwind database will be named WorkstationName .Northwind.dbo, where WorkstationName is the name of the computer on which SQL Server is running (your machine's name for the local server). If you expand the connection by clicking the plus sign in front of its name, you'll see the following items:

**Database Diagrams**    This node contains the names of all diagrams in the database. Double-click a diagram's name to view it, or right-click the Database Diagrams items, and from the context menu, select New Diagram to create a new diagram. Creating a new database diagram in the IDE is identical to creating a diagram in SQL Server's Enterprise Manager.

**Tables**    This node contains the names of all tables in the database, including the system tables. Double-click a table's name to see its rows in a grid on the design surface. This grid is editable, and you can edit existing rows or add new ones to any table. You can also change the specifications of an existing table or add a new one with the Design Table and New Table commands of the context menu.

**Views**    A view is a selection query. If you're using a specific statement to retrieve some rows from one or more tables in your database, you can store the SQL statement as a view. Every time you open this view, the corresponding SQL statement is executed against the database and the qualifying rows are returned. Think of views as virtual tables made up by combining columns of existing tables. You can create a new view or edit an existing view through the appropriate commands of the Views item's context menu. You can also retrieve the rows of a view by double-clicking its name.

**Stored Procedures**    A stored procedure is a T-SQL script that can be executed against the database. In addition to SQL statements, stored procedures contain control flow statements as well as other statements unique to SQL Server. In general, stored procedures are flexible SQL statements that can also process rows before returning them to the client. Every SQL statement can be implemented as a stored procedure and called by name (as opposed to passing an SQL statement to the database).

**Functions**    Functions are similar to stored procedures, but they can't be called from external applications. Any task that may be reused by several stored procedures should be implemented as a function.

These are also the main categories of objects you use in managing databases with SQL Server's Enterprise Manager. Expand the Tables node and drop the Products table onto the form's design surface. This action will add two new items to the Components tray: an SqlConnection1 object that represents the connection to the database, and an SqlData-Adapter1 object that enables your application to talk to the database. If you look at the properties of the SqlConnection object, you'll see that the appropriate connection string has been generated automatically. This is the easiest method of creating connection strings for the Connection objects you configure in your code (copy the setting of the ConnectionString property generated by the wizard and use it in your code).

The next step is the configuration of the DataAdapter object. The default DataAdapter selects all rows and all columns of the corresponding table. The DataAdapter can be configured with visual tools, or from within your code. In the following section, we'll look at the process of configuring a DataAdapter with the visual tools, and later in this chapter, you'll see how the same operations can be carried out programmatically.

## Configuring DataAdapters

The DataAdapter's job is to select rows from one or more tables as well as submit any changes made to the local tables back to the database. To carry out its basic operations, the DataAdapter needs to know the SQL statements or the names of the stored procedures that will perform these tasks. It can also supply the appropriate parameters and execute the commands against the database. To see the process of configuring a DataAdapter in action, drop one of the database's tables from the Server Explorer onto the design surface. For our example, we'll drop the Products table of the Northwind database (the sample application of this section is the DataAdapters project). A new SqlConnection object will be created, as well as a new SqlDataAdapter object. The two objects will be named SqlConnection1 and SqlDataAdapter1. It's a good idea to rename the DataAdapter object (there's only one Connection object for the project, so the default name isn't going to be any problem). Rename the DataAdapter object *DAProducts*.

Select the *DAProducts* DataAdapter's icon in the components tray with the mouse and then locate the Configure Data Adapter hyperlink at the bottom of the Property Browser. Alternatively, you can select the DataAdapter in the components tray and select the Configure Data Adapter command from the Data menu. A wizard will start, and its first screen is a welcome screen. Click Next to see the Choose Your Data Connection screen, where you're prompted to select the Connection object. The wizard proposes the existing connection, but you can create a new one by clicking the New Connection button. The process of creating a new connection is identical to the one described in the preceding section. Click Next again to see the Choose a Query Type window, which is shown in Figure 3.7. This window prompts you to choose the type of command that will be used to access the database. You can specify an SQL statement or a query. If the stored procedure exists already, select the Use Existing Stored Procedures option. Depending on your selection, the wizard will take you through the steps of creating the appropriate SQL statements or stored procedures.

Select the Use SQL Statements option and click Next to see the Generate the SQL Statements screen, shown in Figure 3.8. We'll look at the process of designing SQL statements, but the same principles apply to designing stored procedures. In the text box in the Generate the SQL Statements screen, you can enter a SELECT statement that retrieves the desired rows and the desired columns of the Products table. In general, we rarely retrieve all the rows of a table, unless it's a relatively small table we need to access constantly from within our client application. In a real application, you'd never retrieve all the products, but you can retrieve all category names, because the Categories table is much smaller than the Products table and you need to access the categories all the time.

FIGURE 3.7:

The Choose a
Query Type window
of the DataAdapter
Configuration wizard

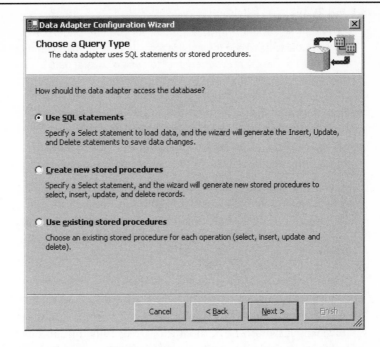

FIGURE 3.8:

The Generate the SQL
Statements screen
of the DataAdapter
Configuration wizard

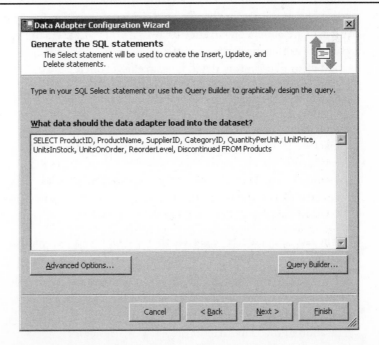

---

**NOTE**    The names of the categories are usually displayed on a ListBox or ComboBox control so that the user can select one with the mouse. As you can understand, it's not just the size of a table but also its role in the application's interface that determines how many of its rows will be moved to the client. You're going to design several data-bound applications in Chapter 5.

If you click the Query Builder button on this screen of the wizard, the Query Builder window will pop up and you can specify the SELECT statement with point-and-click operations. The Advanced Options button leads to a dialog box in which you can specify a few additional options for the SQL statements that the wizard will build for you. The Advanced SQL Generation Options dialog box, shown in Figure 3.9, has the following options:

**Generate Insert, Update and Delete Statements**    This option is checked by default, which means that the wizard will generate statements to update the data source as well. Clear this check box if you want to retrieve data from the data source for presentation purposes only and don't need to update the underlying tables. When this option is cleared, the INSERT, UPDATE, and DELETE statements will not be generated.

**Use Optimistic Concurrency**    This option affects the statements for updating the data source (the UPDATE and DELETE statements). Optimistic concurrency means that it's rather unlikely that two or more users will attempt to edit the same row at the same time. If this happens, only one of them will successfully update the underlying tables. When the other users submit their changes to the database, the corresponding SQL statements will detect that the row has been edited since it was read and they will not update it again. If you don't care about concurrency (that is, if you want users to overwrite changes made by other users without any special handling), clear this option. We'll discuss optimistic concurrency and its implications in detail later in this chapter.

**Refresh the DataSet**    After the data source is updated, the DataSet's data at the client is identical to that of the data source. If some of the tables, however, contain identity fields, their values won't be necessarily the same. Identity fields are assigned a unique value by the DataSet as new rows are added, but they obtain their final values when the corresponding rows are written to the database table(s). To make sure that the DataSet contains the correct identity values, you can refresh the DataSet—in other words, read again the rows that were updated and copy them into the DataSet, overwriting the existing values. We'll have a lot to say about handling identity columns in the following chapter.

The last option determines whether the DataSet will read back from the database the rows it updates and it's usually a good practice to read the modified rows back from the database.

After you've specified the SELECT statement and, optionally, the advanced options, click Next to see the final screen of the wizard, which informs you that the SQL statements for retrieving and updating rows have been generated. Click the Finish button to finalize the configuration of the DataAdapter object.

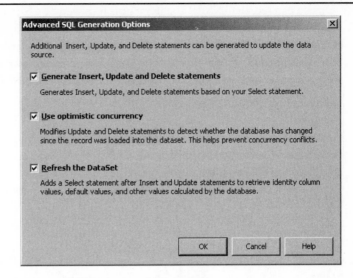

On this last screen, the wizard will inform you that all the statements were generated successfully. If the SELECT statement you specified contains totals, or combines multiple tables with joins, the DataAdapter won't be able to generate the appropriate UPDATE, INSERT, and DELETE statements to update the underlying data source. The appropriate messages will appear on the last screen of the wizard.

## The DataAdapter's Command Objects

Select the DataAdapter on the form and examine its properties in the Property Browser. You'll see that this component exposes four Command properties: the SelectCommand, Insert-Command, UpdateCommand, and DeleteCommand properties. These properties are objects that contain all the information needed to manipulate the underlying table. Although you specified the text of only the SELECT statement, the wizard generated the other SQL statements as well. Expand the members of the InsertCommand property and locate the CommandText member. This is the text of the SQL statement that adds new rows to the table:

```
INSERT INTO Products(ProductName, SupplierID, CategoryID,
            QuantityPerUnit, UnitPrice, UnitsInStock,
            UnitsOnOrder, ReorderLevel, Discontinued)
VALUES      (@ProductName, @SupplierID, @CategoryID,
            @QuantityPerUnit, @UnitPrice, @UnitsInStock,
            @UnitsOnOrder, @ReorderLevel, @Discontinued);
SELECT      ProductID, ProductName, SupplierID, CategoryID,
            QuantityPerUnit, UnitPrice, UnitsInStock,
            UnitsOnOrder, ReorderLevel, Discontinued
FROM        Products
WHERE       (ProductID = @@IDENTITY)
```

As you can see, the INSERT statement is followed by a SELECT statement, which returns the newly added row. This is a confirmation of the insertion operation, and the new row will be updated in the DataSet as it's returned by the SELECT statement. If you clear the option Refresh the DataSet in the Advanced SQL Generation Options dialog box, the wizard will skip the generation of the SELECT statement following the INSERT statement.

The lengthy statement generated by the wizard uses a number of parameters, which are supplied by the DataAdapter when the statement is executed. The types of the parameters are the same as the types of the corresponding fields. You can access the Parameters collection of each Command object and review the properties of the various parameters by clicking the button next to the Parameters property in the Property Browser. When you do, the SqlParameter Collection Editor dialog box, shown in Figure 3.10, will appear. As you have guessed, it's possible to specify the text of each Command property and set up the appropriate Parameters collection from within your code. However, it's much more convenient to use the visual data tools and let the wizard build the statements for you.

**FIGURE 3.10:**

Using the SqlParameter Collection Editor dialog box to set up the parameters of the DataAdapter's Command objects

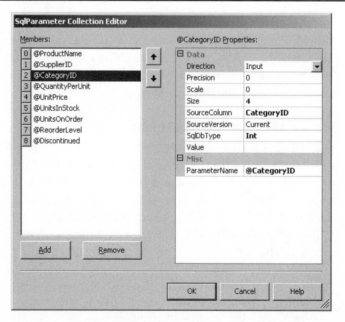

The other properties of the various Command objects are trivial. The Connection property is a Connection object representing the DataAdapter's connection to the database, the CommandType indicates the type of the command (SQL statement or stored procedure), and the CommandTimeout property is the time-out period in seconds. The UpdateRowSource property determines how the DataAdapter uses the result of the command to update the row being edited. Its settings are the members of the UpdateRowSource enumeration: None (the result of the command, if any, is ignored), FirstReturnedRecord (the row submitted to the data source is replaced by the first record of the result set returned by the command), OutputParameters (the fields of the row submitted to the data source are set to the output parameters returned by the command), and Both (it's a combination of the last two settings).

The main advantage of using the DataAdapter Configuration Wizard is that it creates the appropriate INSERT, UPDATE, and DELETE statements for you. It would be difficult to get these statements right (you have to look up the name and data type of each parameter and set the proper order of the parameters). The DataAdapter Configuration Wizard will generate correct statements (or stored procedures), which you can tweak through the properties of the DataAdapter object.

In our simple example, the DataAdapter retrieves all the rows of the Products table. This is highly unusual (and undesirable) for typical business applications. The Products table may contain a very large number of rows. You don't want to download enormous amounts of data to the client, for two reasons: First, you don't want to increase network traffic by moving large DataSets between the server and the clients. The second reason is even more important from a programmer's point of view. Large DataSets usually translate into a large number of changes. When you attempt to update the data source, there will be many conflicts you will have to handle from within your code. In the following chapter, we'll discuss techniques to limit the number of rows in the DataSet and move only the rows needed by the application at the time.

## Creating and Configuring the DataSet

Once the DataAdapter has been configured, you can create the DataSet, where the data will reside at the client. At design time, you create the structure of the DataSet object, and you populate the DataSet at runtime, as needed. The information required to design the DataSet is already available (it's stored in the DataAdapter's properties) and the DataSet will be configured for you automatically. Open the Data menu and select Generate Dataset (or click the Generate DataSet hyperlink below the Property Browser).

The dialog box shown in Figure 3.11 will appear; you can use it to specify the name of the DataSet and the table(s) you want to add to it. The wizard proposes the name DataSet1 and the Products table. Notice that next to each table's name appears the name of the corresponding DataAdapter object in parentheses. Set the DataSet's name to Products, make sure the option Add This Dataset to the Designer is checked, and click OK.

A new item will be placed in the Solution Explorer and it will be named after the specified DataSet name (Products.xsd, in our example). This item is an XML file that contains the schema of the DataSet (XSD stands for XML Schema Definition). In addition, the Products1 item will be added to the components tray. Products1 is an instance of the Products.xsd class and actually contains the data. You can edit the schema either visually or directly in XML. Because we're more comfortable using visual tools than using XML Schema Definition statements, we'll use the built-in tools to view and edit the schema.

**FIGURE 3.11:**

The Generate Dataset
dialog box

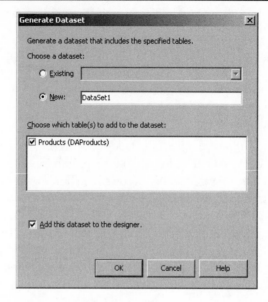

However, keep in mind that you'll never have to edit the schema generated by the wizard—if you do, the application won't run properly. You may wish to copy the schema definition and use it for other purposes, but you won't have to change the definitions of the tables and their columns.

### Establishing Relations in the DataSet

This is a good point at which to add a few more tables to the DataSet. We rarely use DataSets made up of a single table, or of multiple unrelated tables, because the tables in the database are not islands of isolated data. Tables are usually related to other tables, and we need the related rows as well. Let's add the Suppliers and Categories tables to the existing DataSet.

Drag the tables Suppliers and Categories from the Server Explorer and drop them onto the design surface. For each table, a new DataAdapter object will appear in the components tray. Rename it and configure it as discussed earlier. You don't want to download all the information about categories and suppliers to the client. All you really need are the ID and name of each category and each supplier. The SELECT statements for the two tables are as follows:

```
SELECT CategoryID, CategoryName FROM Categories
SELECT SupplierID, CompanyName FROM Suppliers
```

Then add the new tables to the existing DataSet. From the Data menu, select Generate Dataset, and in the Generate Dataset dialog box, click the names of all three tables. The wizard will suggest the name of the existing DataSet, the Products DataSet. So far, you've created a DataSet with three tables but no relations between the tables. You can use the DataSet as is, but it's always good practice to establish relations between its tables, just like the actual relations in the database. The DataSet will enforce referential integrity and won't let you violate it by mistake. If you don't specify any relations, it will be possible to add products and specify any values for their CategoryID and SupplierID fields. Of course, these rows won't be added to the database when you attempt to update it, but why allow users to enter invalid data in the DataSet?

Double-click the `Products.xsd` file in the Solution Explorer to open it in Design mode, as shown in Figure 3.12. What you see is similar to a database diagram (it will look like a diagram as soon as you add the relations), but from an XML designer's point of view. The boxes represent the DataSet's tables (which are mapped to XML elements). There are no relations between the tables initially.

**FIGURE 3.12:**

Editing the DataSet's schema

Move the pointer over the Toolbox, and when the Toolbox expands, you'll see a set of objects that you can add to the XML schema of the DataSet. You will find information on creating XML schemas in the following chapter, but this book is about manipulating relational data, not about XML. The element icon corresponds to a new table and the attribute icon corresponds to a new column. You can use these tools to modify an existing schema or to create a new schema from scratch. The single object you must add to the schema manually is the Relation object. Select the Relation item and drop an instance of it on one of the related tables. The Edit Relation dialog box will appear, as shown in Figure 3.13.

Start by specifying a meaningful name for your relation. Then select the two tables involved in the relation from the Parent Element and Child Element drop-down lists. In the Key Fields and Foreign Key Fields boxes, you can select the fields involved in the relation (expand the corresponding list and select the desired field name). The Categories and Products tables are related through the CategoryID field. The Cateogories.CategoryID field is the primary key field in the Categories table and the Products.CategoryID field is the foreign key in the

Products table. At the bottom of the window there are three controls for setting the rules to be applied when updating the corresponding tables. These rules are discussed in the section "Common Update Problems" later in this chapter.

**FIGURE 3.13:**

The Edit Relation dialog box is where you specify the properties of a relation.

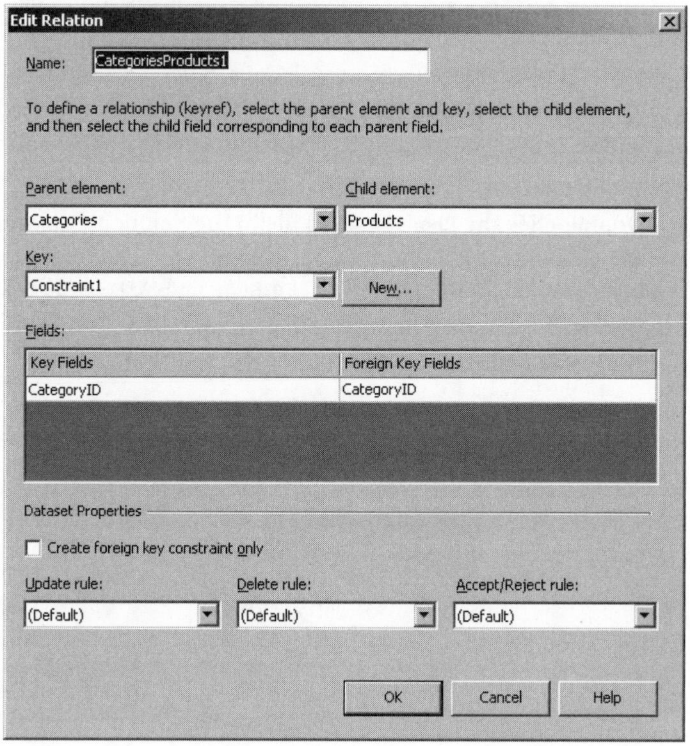

In short, they determine how the DataSet should handle changes in the primary key of a relation (what to do about the related rows in the child tables when a primary key in the parent table changes). The default value for the UpdateRule property is Cascade, which means that the foreign key in related rows of the child tables will change automatically.

You can add as many relations as you need to the DataSet's XML Schema. At the bottom of the Schema Designer there are two tabs: the DataSet tab, which is selected by default, and the XML tab. The two tabs display the same schema in two different views. The XML tab shows the schema in XML view. If you understand XML, you can edit the DataSet's schema in either tab and see how the visual changes affect the XML description of the schema or how editing the XML description of the schema updates its pictorial representation.

Our schema contains two relations: the CategoriesProducts relation (based on the CategoryID field of the Categories and Products tables) and the SuppliersProducts relation (based on the SupplierID field of the Suppliers and Products tables). Once the two relations have been added, the definition of the DataSet is complete and you can use it in your code.

## Populating the DataSet

DataSets are not populated automatically when you start the application. You must call the corresponding DataAdapter object's Fill method, passing as arguments the names of the DataSet and corresponding table. To populate the three tables of the Products DataSet, insert the following commands in a button's Click event handler or in the form's Load event handler:

```
Products1.Clear()
DACategories.Fill(Products1, "Categories")
DASuppliers.Fill(Products1, "Suppliers")
DAProducts.Fill(Products1, "Products")
```

The Fill method of the DataAdapter object accepts two arguments, which are the name of a DataSet and the name of a table in the DataSet. Each DataAdapter is associated with a specific table, and this is the table you must specify with the Fill method's arguments.

If you insert the statements that populate the DataSet into the form's Load event handler, there's no need to clear the Products DataSet. If you place them in another event's handler, which may be invoked more than once in the course of the application, you must clear the DataSet. If not, the same data will be appended to the existing data in the DataSet. Of course, because most tables have a primary key, you'll get an error message to the effect that you can't use a duplicate key (the program is attempting to add a row with same primary key as an existing one). If you haven't established any relations between the tables of the DataSet, you can load them in any order.

**TIP**   We can't stress enough the importance of the order in which you populate the DataTables of the DataSet. First you must populate the tables with the primary keys (the parent tables) and then the tables with foreign keys (the child tables). If you attempt to populate the Products table before the other two, you'll get an error message to the effect that one or more rows violate referential integrity. This error message says simply that the first row of the Products table has a CategoryID and a SupplierID field, but they have no matching rows in the other two tables because the tables are empty.

OK, we've populated the DataSet and we can now explore its contents, edit its rows (or add new ones), and submit the changes to the database. Later in this chapter, you'll see how to build DataAdapters and their matching DataSets in code, without the benefit of the visual tools.

## Viewing and Editing the DataSet

You're now ready to use the DataSet in your client application's code. What this means is that you must write an application that presents the DataSet's tables to the user, accepts user input, and submits the changes to the data source. This is your real programming job and it's not simple.

We'll discuss how to build functional user interfaces for data-driven applications in Chapter 5, but right now we need a quick method of displaying the data from within the client application's code, allowing the user to edit the data, and submitting the changes to the database.

One of the most advanced, and most convenient, Windows controls is the DataGrid control, which is basically a grid control that can be bound to a DataSet. It knows how to handle related tables and allows you to view the child rows of each row in a parent table. It also allows you to edit the rows of any table. Place an instance of the DataGrid control on the form, anchor it on all four edges of the form, locate its DataSource property in the Property Browser, and set it to the name of the DataSet, Products1. Then run the application (it's the DataAdapters project in the book's support pages at www.sybex.com).

Assuming that you've added the statements to populate the DataSet in the Load Data button's Click event handler, start the project and click the Load Data button. Nothing will happen on the DataGrid control initially except that a small plus symbol will appear on the grid. If you click this symbol, a list with the names of the tables in the DataSet will appear, as shown in Figure 3.14. The table names are hyperlinks, and you can click any one of them to select it. Once you click a table's name, the table's rows will appear on the grid, as shown in Figure 3.15.

**FIGURE 3.14:**

The DataGrid control is bound to the DataSet and waits for the user to select one of the tables.

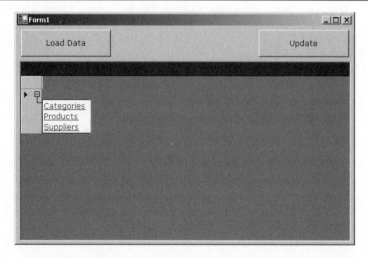

Each row of the Categories table in Figure 3.15 has a plus symbol in front of it, indicating that each category has a number of child rows in another table, the Products table. If you click this symbol, you'll see a list with the related tables. The Categories table is related to the Products table, so you see the name of the CategoriesProducts relation, as shown in Figure 3.15. Click the name of the relation and the grid will be populated with the matching rows of the Products table, as shown in Figure 3.16.

**FIGURE 3.15:**

Once a table has been selected, its rows are displayed on the grid.

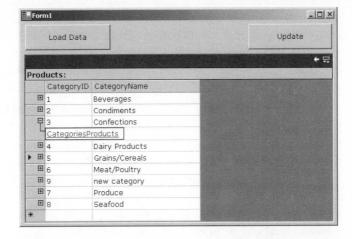

**FIGURE 3.16:**

Viewing the matching rows of the selected category

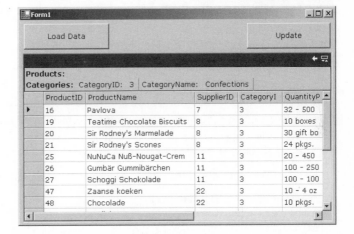

In the dark stripe at the top of the DataGrid control, there's a Back arrow. Click this icon to return to the parent row. Below this stripe you see a section that describes where you are in the DataSet. You're viewing the rows of the Products table that belong to the category Confections (CategoryID = 3). If you don't want to view this information, click the rightmost button on the dark stripe of the control. The top name on this section of the form is the name of the DataSet and underneath it you see the name of the related table you have selected.

As you can see, the DataGrid control is ideal for displaying related tables. It allows you to view any table, select a row in any table, and view the matching rows in any of the related tables. You'll notice in the data shown in Figure 3.16 that the DataGrid control doesn't map the IDs to a more meaningful field of the related table (like the category's name). However, you're allowed to edit the cells and enter new rows or delete existing ones. The DataGrid control is an excellent tool for putting together a quick interface to view a DataSet, but it's a developer's tool. You can build user interfaces based on the DataGrid control, but not easily. Most front-end applications simply aren't suited for this control. The DataGrid doesn't capture keystrokes and it can't display ComboBox controls with the rows of related tables in its grid.

Any changes you make to the DataSet (either through the DataGrid control or from within your code) are local to the client, where the DataSet resides. To commit any changes made to the DataSet to the database, you must call the appropriate DataAdapter object's Update method, passing the name of the appropriate DataSet as argument. If the client application is truly disconnected, you can call the Update only when a connection to the data source is available. The same is true if you're using a slow connection over the Internet. At that time, all the changes will be submitted to the client. If you're developing an application that will be used on a local area network, you can call the Update method more frequently. You can update the underlying tables in the DataSet every time the user edits a row in one of the DataSet's tables if you wish. As a rule, the less frequently you update the data source, the more conflicts are likely to occur.

Each DataAdapter can commit the changes made to a specific DataTable object of the DataSet. As with the Fill method, it's important to update the underlying tables in the correct order. If the user hasn't edited the Categories table, you may be able to submit the changes made to the Products table first. If you attempt to commit the changes in the Products table before you commit the changes in any other table and one or more products refer to a new category, the update operation will fail as soon as it runs into a product that refers to a category that hasn't been added yet to the Categories table.

The following statements show how to commit the changes made to the Products DataSet:

```
DACategories.Update(Products1)
DASuppliers.Update(Products1)
DAProducts.Update(Products1)
```

This is the simplest implementation of the Update button on the main form of the DataAdapters project. As you will see, the code is anything but perfect, and it works only if the user made changes that don't violate any of the database's constraints. If a product has a negative price, the update operation of the Products table will fail. Likewise, if another user removed one of the lines you edited in the DataSet, the DataAdapter's Update method will fail because it won't find a row to update.

If you call the Update method of the various DataAdapters in the wrong order, even more subtle errors may occur. Let's say you've added a new category and a new product that refers to the ID of the new category. Another user adds a new row to the Categories table. If you attempt to submit the changes in the Products table first, the new row will refer to the new category added by the other user and not to the new category you've added to the Categories table. Updating rows with identity fields is one of the most important issues regarding the DataAdapter, and you'll find more information on this topic in the following chapter.

The Update method of the DataAdapter object isn't very efficient either. It creates the appropriate SQL statements for every row and submits them to SQL Server for execution. As you will see in the following chapter, you can retrieve the rows with changes (you can retrieve rows that were modified, added, or deleted) and submit only a small section of the DataSet to the database. This is the recommended technique for updating the database, but it requires some extra code.

## Common Update Problems

In this section, we'll look at a few common problems that occur when changes to a local DataSet are submitted to the underlying data source and how the DataAdapter handles them. Add a new row to the Categories table and name it New Category. If you haven't edited the Categories table, the new row will be assigned an ID value of 9 because there are eight rows in the database's table. Then switch to the Products table and change any row's CategoryID field to the ID of the newly added row in the Categories table. Everything looks fine on the DataGrid control. If you expand the new category, you'll see that it contains a single product.

Now start SQL Server Enterprise Manager, open the Categories table, and add a new category. Because the DataSet is disconnected, the new category will be assigned the value 9 as well. The database is not aware of any changes made to the local DataSets, neither does it notify the DataSet about any changes in the database itself.

If you switch to the DataAdapters application and click the Update button to submit the changes to the data source, the following will happen: The row you've added to the Categories table through the client application will be assigned a new value, which will be 10. This is the identity value assigned to the new row by the database and it will never change again. The CategoryID field of the matching row in the Products table will change from 9 (the temporary category ID) to 10 (the final ID). As you can see, the DataSet propagated the changes in the parent table to the matching row(s) of the child table.

If you want to know why the DataSet cascades changes in the parent table(s) to the child table(s), double-click the Products.xsd file in the Solution Explorer. When the DataSet's Schema Designer appears, select the relation between the Categories and Products tables, and from the context menu, select Edit Relation. The Edit Relation dialog box will appear, as explained earlier in this section (see Figure 3.13).

When you define a relation's properties in the Edit Relation dialog box, you can specify the Update, Delete, and Accept/Reject rules. The Update rule determines how the DataSet will handle changes in the parent tables. Likewise, the Delete rule determines how the DataSet will handle deletions in the parent table, and the Accept/Reject rules take effect when you call the DataSet's AcceptChanges or RejectChanges methods. These two methods accept or reject the changes made to the DataSet since the last time they were called or the last time the DataSet was committed to the database; they are discussed in the following chapter.

The settings of the various rules are `Default`, `None`, `Cascade`, `SetNull`, and `SetDefault`. The most common setting for the Update rule is `Cascade`: when the primary key is modified, the new value is plugged into the foreign key field of all related columns. This is also the default value of the rule. The `None` setting means that no special action should be taken, and the `SetNull` and `SetDefault` rules set the foreign key field to null or its default value, respectively. The Accept/Reject rule can have one of these three settings only: `Default`, `None`, `Cascade`. Notice that the `Cascade` setting of the Delete rule doesn't modify a key value; instead, it removes the related rows from their tables.

If you edit a product and specify a category ID that doesn't exist, the following message will appear in a message box as soon as you move to another row:

```
ForeignKeyConstraint CategoriesProducts requires the child key values (13) to
exist in the parent table. Do you want to correct the value?
```

The DataSet will not accept a row that violates referential integrity and will not allow you to switch to another row unless you correct the value. If you click the No button in the dialog box with the error message, the field in error will be restored to its previous, valid value. If you don't specify a value for a field that can't accept a null value, the DataSet will warn you with another message.

---

**TIP**   The ProductName field of the same table is not nullable, and you'd expect that by not setting it to a value an exception would be thrown. To set this field to a null value, select it and press Control+0 (the digit zero). As soon as you leave the current row, a message box with a warning will appear, and you must either correct the field's value or let the DataSet restore it to its last valid value. If you clear the cell with the product's name, however, nothing will happen. A zero-length string ("") is not a null value and you won't see the warning. If you want to set a field to null, you must enter Control+0 and not simply clear the corresponding cell. This is also true for numeric fields (the numeric value zero is not the same as null).

---

As you can see, the DataSet will catch certain errors, but not all of them. The error handling is provided by the DataSet and not by the DataGrid control. The DataGrid control is simply a mechanism for displaying the contents of the DataSet. The UnitPrice field of the Products table must have a positive value. This is a constraint specified in the design of the database and it's not enforced by the DataSet. The current implementation of the DataSet can only enforce referential integrity and non-nullable values. While editing the Products table on the Data-Grid control, you can specify a negative value for a product. As far as the DataSet goes, this is a valid value because the DataSet can't enforce arbitrary constraints. This type of error will be caught by the database itself when your code calls the Update method to submit the changes to the data source (unless, of course, you perform an exhaustive validation from within your client application's code before submitting the changes to the data source).

Let's see how the DataAdapter handles errors raised by the database. Set a product's price to a negative value and then click the Update button on the form. The following exception will be thrown:

```
UPDATE statement conflicted with COLUMN CHECK constraint
'CK_Products_UnitPrice'. The conflict occurred in database
'Northwind', table 'Products', column 'UnitPrice'.
```

This message is explicit for a developer, but not for a final user. You should catch all update errors from within your code and display friendlier messages to the user. A side effect of this exception is that it terminates the process of updating the data source.

**TIP**     One of the most important properties of the DataAdapter object is the ContinueUpdate-OnError property, whose default setting is False. By default, the DataAdapter object terminates the update process as soon as it encounters the first error. This is an odd behavior because it doesn't undo any changes already made to the data source. In most cases, we set this property to True so that the DataAdapter will update all the rows that are not in error. The rows in error are marked in the DataSet, and you can process them separately. For example, you can create a new DataSet that contains only the rows in error. If you're using a DataGrid control to display the DataSet, the rows in error are marked with an exclamation mark in red in the leftmost column.

## Handling Update Errors

In this section, we'll explore a more robust method of updating the data source. To update the data source, you should set the ContinueUpdateOnError property to True, call the Update method of each DataAdapter, and then iterate through the rows returned by the Update method and handle the errors. You can find out the error in each row by reading its RowError property, which is a string with a description of the error.

The most important aspect of handling update errors is how you handle a large number of errors. In most applications, when you can assume a constant link to the data source, you can update each row as soon as the user edits it. If the operation fails, you can display a message and restore the row to its original form. The user can edit its fields again and this time supply values that will not cause the update operation to fail. Of course, you will not use a DataGrid to display the tables. Instead, you should build a user interface with common Windows controls

(TextBox, CheckBox, ComboBox, and so on). You should also provide the usual Edit, Add, and Delete buttons so that the user can initiate an action by clicking one of the these buttons and terminate it by clicking the OK or Cancel button. When the OK button is clicked, your code must call the Update method of the appropriate DataAdapter or create the appropriate Command objects and execute them against the database. The topic of building Windows data-driven applications is covered in Chapter 5. Here, we're using the DataGrid control to demonstrate the basics of handling disconnected DataSets without the overhead and complexity of building elaborate user interfaces. We're not suggesting that you can't build user interfaces based on the DataGrid control, but this control doesn't provide all the flexibility you need for a real application.

So, how do you handle update errors with disconnected DataSets? This isn't a simple topic, and we can't offer you guidelines that apply to all cases. One approach is to create a new DataSet with the rows in error and let users edit it further. The DataGrid control displays an error icon next to each row in error. If you hover the pointer over this icon, you'll see a description of the error that caused the update operation to fail. Listing 3.3 shows the revised code behind the Update button.

---

**Listing 3.3        Handling Update Errors**

```
Private Sub bttnUpdate_Click( _
                  ByVal sender As System.Object, _
                  ByVal e As System.EventArgs) _
                  Handles bttnUpdate.Click
    Dim rows As Integer
    ' Update the Categories table
    rows = DACategories.Update(Products1)
    If rows > 0 Then MsgBox("Updated successfully " & _
            rows.ToString & " rows in the Products table")
    Dim DRow As DataRow
    Dim errDescription As String
    If Products1.Suppliers.HasErrors Then
        For Each DRow In Products1.Categories.GetErrors
            errDescription = errDescription & _
                  "ERROR WHILE UPDATING CATEGORY " & _
                  Drow.Item("CategoryID") & " - " & _
                  Drow.Item("CategoryName") & vbCrLf & _
                  DRow.RowError & vbCrLf
        Next
        MsgBox(errDescription)
    End If
    ' Update the Suppliers table
    rows = DASuppliers.Update(Products1)
    If rows > 0 Then MsgBox("Updated successfully " & _
            rows.ToString & " rows in the Suppliers table")
```

```
        errDescription = ""
        If Products1.Suppliers.HasErrors Then
            For Each DRow In Products1.Suppliers.GetErrors
                errDescription = errDescription & _
                        "ERROR WHILE UPDATING SUPPLIER " & _
                        DRow.Item("SupplierID") & " - " & _
                        DRow.Item("CompanyName") & vbCrLf & _
                        DRow.RowError & vbCrLf
            Next
            MsgBox(errDescription)
        End If
        ' Update the Products table
        rows = DAProducts.Update(Products1)
        errDescription = ""
        If rows > 0 Then MsgBox("Updated successfully " & _
                rows.ToString & " rows in the Products table")
        If Products1.Products.HasErrors Then
            For Each DRow In Products1.Products.GetErrors
                errDescription = errDescription & _
                        "ERROR WHILE UPDATING PRODUCT " & _
                        DRow.Item("ProductID") & " - " & _
                        DRow.Item("ProductName") & vbCrLf & _
                        DRow.RowError & vbCrLf & vbCrLf
            Next
            MsgBox(errDescription)
        End If
    End Sub
```

The code in Listing 3.3 calls the Update method for each DataAdapter and retrieves the number of rows affected by each call. Ideally, this should be the number of edited rows. If one or more rows are in error, the numeric value returned by the Update method will be less than the number of edited rows. The DataAdapter marks the rows in error in the DataSet, and you can retrieve these rows with the GetErrors method of the appropriate DataTable object. The following statement retrieves all rows of the Products table that are in error:

```
Products1.Products.GetErrors
```

The HasErrors property of the DataTable object returns True if the specific table contains errors. If so, the code calls the GetErrors method to retrieve the rows in error.

The GetErrors method returns an array of DataRow objects, and you can iterate through the rows in error with a For Each…Next loop, as shown in Listing 3.3. The error for the current row is given by the RowError property of the corresponding DataRow object, and the code displays the value of this property (the error's description) along with the ID and name of the category/supplier/product in error. After editing the Products1 DataSet and injecting a few errors, we received the following warnings from the application (the error messages returned by SQL Server are shown in italic):

```
ERROR WHILE UPDATING PRODUCT 64 - Wimmers gute Semmelknödel
UPDATE statement conflicted with COLUMN CHECK constraint
'CK_UnitsOnOrder'. The conflict occurred in database
'Northwind', table 'Products', column 'UnitsOnOrder'.

ERROR WHILE UPDATING PRODUCT 65 - Louisiana Fiery Hot Pepper Sauce
UPDATE statement conflicted with COLUMN CHECK constraint
'CK_UnitsInStock'. The conflict occurred in database
'Northwind', table 'Products', column 'UnitsInStock'.

ERROR WHILE UPDATING PRODUCT 74 - Longlife Tofu
UPDATE statement conflicted with COLUMN CHECK constraint
'CK_Products_UnitPrice'. The conflict occurred in database
'Northwind', table 'Products', column 'UnitPrice'.

ERROR WHILE UPDATING PRODUCT 75 - Rhönbräu Klosterbier
UPDATE statement conflicted with COLUMN CHECK constraint
'CK_Products_UnitPrice'. The conflict occurred in database
'Northwind', table 'Products', column 'UnitPrice'.
```

What good is it to display the errors returned by the database on a message box? The user needs specific information about each row that failed to update its data source and a chance to edit it. Depending on the application's interface, you can provide more robust and user-friendlier mechanisms to revise the edits. The DataGrid control displays an icon in front of each row in error, as shown in Figure 3.17, and users can read the description of the corresponding error by hovering the pointer of the icon. Once they know what caused the operation to fail, they should be able to correct the error.

**FIGURE 3.17:**

The DataGrid control displays an icon in front of each row in error after an update operation.

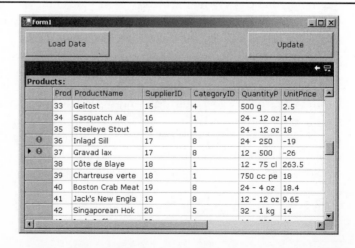

You can also set the RowError property from within your code to a more meaningful description. As mentioned already, the DataGrid is not the perfect control for editing a DataSet with multiple related rows. Our suggestion is to build a friendlier interface using regular Windows controls. The DataGrid is more of a developer's tool than an end user's tool.

**NOTE**    If you set the RowError property of the *DRow* objects in the code in Listing 3.3, nothing will happen. The GetErrors method returns an array of DataRows, not a set of pointers to the actual rows of the DataSet. You must set the RowError property of the actual row in the DataSet, not the RowError property of its copy.

It goes without saying that you should validate the data as best as you can before submitting it to the database. You already know that certain columns in the products table can't be negative (the UnitPrice column, as well as the UnitsOnOrder column). Even if you're not aware that these constraints exist in the database, it won't take you long to figure it out. There's no reason to submit data with trivial errors to the database. Your goal should be the validation of the data at the client; let the database catch only the errors that can't be foreseen (like an attempt to edit a row that has been deleted in the meantime by another user).

## Implementing Optimistic Concurrency

In this section, we're going to look at the code generated by the wizard for the DataAdapter's Command objects. Adding new rows is fairly straightforward, as long as these actions don't violate any referential integrity and non-null constraints. These errors are actually caught by the DataSet object itself, and you can't add to the DataSet rows that violate referential integrity (assuming that you have added the appropriate relations to the DataSet, of course). All other errors will be caught by the database, which will not complete the execution of the appropriate SQL statement. Such errors may include an attempt to update a row that has been removed from the table by another user. The most common update errors are those that can't be caught at the client before the changes are submitted. However, some of the rows may fail to update the underlying table(s) in the DataSet. These rows will be marked in the DataSet and you'll be able to handle them from within your code.

Editing and deleting rows is a bit more complicated. To identify the row to be updated or deleted, we usually specify the row's primary key in the SQL statement. To ensure the integrity of the data, the DataAdapter uses the values of all the fields read from the table. The DataSet object doesn't overwrite the values read from the table when you edit a row. Instead, it maintains a copy of the original row as well as a copy of the edited row. The UPDATE statement generated by the DataAdapter uses the original field values to identify the row to be edited. The same is true for the DELETE statement.

Let's say you've used the following SELECT statement to retrieve a few rows from the Products table:

```
SELECT  ProductID, ProductName, SupplierID,
        CategoryID, UnitPrice
FROM    Products
WHERE   CategoryID = 6
```

The UPDATE statement generated by the DataAdapter wizard for the previous SELECT statement is shown next:

```
UPDATE  Products
SET     ProductName = @ProductName,
        SupplierID = @SupplierID, CategoryID = @CategoryID,
        UnitPrice = @UnitPrice
WHERE   (ProductID = @Original_ProductID) AND
        (CategoryID = @Original_CategoryID OR
        @Original_CategoryID IS NULL AND CategoryID IS NULL)
        AND (ProductName = @Original_ProductName)
        AND (SupplierID = @Original_SupplierID OR
        @Original_SupplierID IS NULL AND SupplierID IS NULL)
        AND (UnitPrice = @Original_UnitPrice OR
        @Original_UnitPrice IS NULL AND UnitPrice IS NULL);
SELECT  ProductID, ProductName, SupplierID,
        CategoryID, UnitPrice
FROM    Products
WHERE   (ProductID = @ProductID)
```

This is lengthy statement indeed and it uses quite a few parameters, which are supplied by the DataAdapter object prior to the command's execution. The parameters named `@original_xxx` are replaced with the original field values, and the parameters `@xxx` are replaced by the new field values (after the editing). So, this statement attempts to locate a row whose fields match the original values read by the SELECT statement. If such a row exists, its fields are replaced. The SELECT statement following the UPDATE statement retrieves the updated row and returns it to the client. This is a confirmation of the operation, and the client application reads back the updated row. The DELETE statement is similar: it attempts to locate a row whose field values match the original values read from the database.

The SQL statements used by the DataAdapter are not slow because they involve all the fields of the row to be updated. One of the fields is the primary key field, which means that SQL Server can locate the row you're about to update instantly. Then it simply compares the remaining fields of this row to the values supplied in the statement's WHERE clause.

Why all the IS NULL clauses in the statement? If a field in the table is null and the application didn't change it, the original and current values are not equal. SQL Server doesn't perform comparisons with null values, and that's why the statement must handle this case separately. This is an interesting technique to keep in mind when you perform comparisons in your SQL statements. Two fields are equal if they have the same non-null value or if they're both null. You can't count on SQL Server to compare a null value with anything else, even another null value. Null values can't be compared to anything, and you must add the appropriate clauses in the statement yourself.

The lengthy statements generated by the DataAdapter implement the so-called *optimistic concurrency*. If all the fields read by the SELECT statement haven't changed values when you attempt to update them, this means that no other user has edited the row and you can safely overwrite it. If one or more of the fields you've read into the DataSet has changed value in the database, then some other user has edited the row between the time your client application read the data and the time it's attempting to update their values.

Optimistic concurrency is based on the premise that it's rather unlikely for two or more users to attempt to edit the same row at the same time. A very reasonable assumption, but an assumption nevertheless. When you run into a row that has been edited by another user since it was read, the UPDATE statement fails and your application must take proper action (notify the user, undo the edits, and so on). In many situations you can use a *last-write-wins* scenario, which means that all users commit the changes they made to the database even if some of the rows have been edited since they were read.

You can turn off optimistic concurrency, in which case the DataAdapter will generate the following statement:

```
UPDATE    Products
SET       ProductName = @ProductName,
          SupplierID = @SupplierID, CategoryID = @CategoryID,
          UnitPrice = @UnitPrice
WHERE     (ProductID = @Original_ProductID);
SELECT    ProductID, ProductName, SupplierID,
          CategoryID, UnitPrice
FROM      Products
WHERE     (ProductID = @ProductID)
```

When optimistic concurrency is turned off, the changes you've made to the DataSet are committed to the database regardless of whether the row has been edited in the meantime or not. To turn off optimistic concurrency, clear the option Use Optimistic Concurrency in the Advanced SQL Generation Options dialog box (shown in Figure 3.9).

The opposite of optimistic concurrency is *pessimistic concurrency*. However, turning off optimistic concurrency doesn't automatically enable pessimistic concurrency. When you disable optimistic concurrency, you simply ignore the concurrency issue and allow users to commit their changes to the database.

With pessimistic concurrency, you lock the row and don't allow other users to edit it while you're editing it. ADO.NET doesn't support pessimistic concurrency by default because you just can't afford to lock a large number of rows for as long as they're being edited at the client. Pessimistic concurrency isn't suited for a disconnected architecture like ADO.NET. However, there are situations in which you may wish to implement pessimistic concurrency, and you can do so with a little extra code.

To implement pessimistic concurrency with ADO.NET, you must initiate a transaction, edit one or more rows, commit the changes, and then close the transaction. We'll discuss transactions in detail in the following chapter, and we'll show you an example of implementing pessimistic concurrency. The idea is that the rows you're editing remain locked while they're being edited and no one else can open them. This is a fairly expensive operation, and you should use it only if it's really necessary. A row that takes part in a transaction can't be edited by any process other than the one that initiated the transaction. In other words, you can edit the row from within a transaction, but other processes (including another instance of the same application) can't access it. Typical transactions involve a small number of operations, and they complete within a fraction of a second. No one really notices, because when an application requests a row currently involved in a transaction, SQL Server waits for the transaction to complete and then returns the requested row.

Fortunately, pessimistic concurrency isn't necessary for most applications. You may have to use it in banking systems or airline reservation systems, but not with typical business applications. In most situations, we don't even implement optimistic concurrency; we just commit the changes to the database. Consider a program that maintains a database of products or customers. User A reads a row at 10.02:32. User B reads the same row at 10:03.01. There's a copy of the same row in the two DataSets on two client computers. Both users edit the copy of the row and user B sends the changes back to the server at 10:05.40. At 10.05:43, user A decides to submit their changes to the database. If optimistic concurrency is in effect, the update operation will fail because the row has changed since it was read in the DataSet of the client application running on user's A computer. Yet why should the operation fail? It's quite likely that both users made valid changes to the row, and one user beat the other by 3 seconds in sending the changes back to the database. If both users were trying to make a reservation, these 3 seconds would make all the difference in the world. But most applications deal with customers, products, invoices, and so on. If two users attempt to change the phone number of a customer or the price of a product, chances are that they're both sending the same data to the database. The last-write-wins scenario is quite common in business applications because it doesn't lead to "impossible" situations (like assigning the same seat to two different passengers).

Consider for a moment an application that maintains a database of books. When you edit a book, you should edit the table with the book's data as well as the tables that connect the book to its authors and its topics from within a transaction. If not, you're taking the risk of updating the books table with the data submitted by one user and updating the authors (or topics) of the same book with the data submitted by another user. If you update all the tables involved from within a single transaction, the last transaction will win. Otherwise, you may commit to the database the changes user A made to the table with the books and the changes user B made to the table with the book's authors. It's not catastrophic, but you'll have a very hard time figuring out what happened to the database when frustrated users report this "bizarre" behavior.

## Building a DataAdapter in Code

If you select one of the DataAdapters in the DataAdapters project and look up its properties in the Property Browser, you'll see that the DataAdapter exposes the following properties: DeleteCommand, InsertCommand, SelectCommand, and UpdateCommand. These properties are objects that know how to delete, insert, select, and update rows in their respective tables. Their CommandText property is a long SQL statement, and they also expose a number of parameters. As you know, you'll have to type a lot of code (the SQL statement itself and the parameters), but it's fairly straightforward to build DataAdapter objects in your code. Setting up the Command properties of a DataAdapter is no different than setting up Command objects to execute a query against a database, as explained at the beginning of this chapter.

Listing 3.4 shows how to create a DataAdapter in code and use it to populate multiple tables. It's not the brightest idea to use the same DataAdapter for multiple tables, but because we're only reading (and not updating) data, we thought we'd better demonstrate the process of building and using a DataAdapter in code by using it to populate several tables. The code shown in Listing 3.4 is the event handler of the Create DataAdapter button of the ADOTests project.

**Listing 3.4**      **Building and Using DataAdapters in Code**

```
Private Sub bttnCustomAdapter_Click(_
                ByVal sender As System.Object, _
                ByVal e As System.EventArgs) _
                Handles bttnCustomAdapter.Click
   Dim CN As New SqlClient.SqlConnection()

   CN.ConnectionString = "initial catalog=Northwind; " & _
       "persist security info=False;user id=sa; " & _
       "workstation id=POWERTOOLKIT;packet size=4096"
   CN.Open()

   Dim CMDstring As String = "SELECT * FROM Products"
   Dim DA As New SqlClient.SqlDataAdapter(CMDstring, CN)
```

```
      Dim DS As New DataSet()
      DA.Fill(DS, "Products")

      CMDstring = "SELECT * FROM Categories"
      DA = New SqlClient.SqlDataAdapter(CMDstring, CN)
      DA.Fill(DS, "Categories")

      CMDstring = "SELECT * FROM Suppliers"
      DA = New SqlClient.SqlDataAdapter(CMDstring, CN)
      DA.Fill(DS, "Suppliers")
      CN.Close()
End Sub
```

The simplest form of the SqlDataAdapter object's constructor is the following, which accepts two arguments—the SELECT statement to be executed against the database to select rows and a Connection object:

```
Dim DA As New SqlClient.SqlDataAdapter(CMDstring, CN)
```

CN is a properly initialized Connection object and CMDString a String variable that holds the command to be executed against the database. Once the DataAdapter object has been created, you can call its Fill method to move the data retrieved by the SQL statement into a local DataSet.

Notice that the DS DataSet is created as we add tables to it with the Fill method. We didn't have to configure the DataSet at design time—it's created automatically for us at runtime.

The DA DataAdapter can't be used to update the data source because we haven't configured any of its Command properties, except for the SelectCommand. You'll also notice that the tables are populated in the "wrong order." We're able to populate the Products table before the Categories table because we haven't established any relations between the DataSet's tables at design time. It's possible to add the proper relations to your DataSet from within your code. To do so, create the appropriate DataRelation objects and append them to the DataSet's Relations collection. The statements in Listing 3.5 show how to establish relations between the tables of the DataSet.

**Listing 3.5**     **Adding Relations between a DataSet's Tables**

```
Dim DRProductsCategories As DataRelation
DRProductsCategories = _
        New DataRelation("ProductsCategories", _
        DS.Tables("Categories").Columns("CategoryID"), _
        DS.Tables("Products").Columns("CategoryID"))

Dim DRProductsSuppliers As DataRelation
    DRProductsSuppliers = New _
```

```
    DataRelation("ProductsSuppliers", _
    DS.Tables("Suppliers").Columns("SupplierID"), _
    DS.Tables("Products").Columns("SupplierID"))
DS.Relations.Add(DRProductsCategories)
DS.Relations.Add(DRProductsSuppliers)
```

A DataRelation object is specified in terms of the two tables involved in the relation (the parent and child tables) and the keys that relate the two tables (the primary key of the parent table and the foreign key in the child table). One of the simplest forms of the overloaded constructor of the DataRelation object accepts three arguments: the name of the relation, the primary key column, and the foreign key column. The parent and child tables can be determined by the primary and foreign columns, and you need not specify them explicitly. If a relation involves multiple fields, the second and third arguments of the DataRelation object's constructor are two arrays of DataColumn objects, which hold the columns involved in the relation.

## Summary

This concludes our overview of ADO.NET. By now, you should have a good idea of how ADO.NET works and what its disconnected architecture means. You already know how to connect to a database, execute commands against it, and retrieve selected rows from one or more tables. You also know how to configure DataAdapters and use them to populate DataSets and how to submit changes to the data source.

Most of the code on the presentation tier manipulates the contents of the DataSet, and this is the topic of the following chapter, in which we'll look at the object model of the DataSet class in more detail. In the following chapter we'll get into the details of manipulating DataSets at the client, updating the underlying tables in the database, and handling update errors. After discussing the DataSet and how to manipulate it programmatically, we're going to explore the topic of building data-driven Windows applications, in Chapter 5.

# CHAPTER 4

## Working with the DataSet

- The structure of the DataSet

- Editing and filtering the DataSet

- Update operations

- Persisting DataSets

- Transactions in ADO.NET

In Chapter 3, you learned how to design and populate DataSets and how to bind them to the DataGrid control. The DataGrid control offers a relational view of the DataSet's tables and allows you to navigate from parent to child rows as well as edit the rows. In this chapter, we're going to look at the DataSet's object model, demonstrate the members for accessing its contents, and explore its structure programmatically. You'll learn how to edit the DataSet from within your code, how to handle identity columns, how to execute multiple commands in transactional mode, and other interesting techniques. We'll also discuss the XML-related features of ADO.NET and you'll learn how to persist DataSets in XML format and exchange them with remote systems.

We're also going to take a close look at how the DataSet maintains the original and current versions of its rows and how you can extract the edited rows (modified, inserted, and deleted rows) into a new DataTable and submit to the data source only the rows that were changed. Calling the DataAdapter object's Update method, as we did in the preceding chapter, is an inefficient way to update large DataSets because it submits all the rows of the corresponding table. You'll learn how to isolate the modified rows and submit them separately to the data source.

## The Structure of the DataSet Object

The DataSet is at the core of ADO.NET; it's where the data resides at the client. It provides many members you can use to manipulate its contents, it exists independently of a data source, and it resembles a small database that lives at the client. In short, the DataSet is an in-memory database.

The DataSet is made up of DataTable objects, which represent tables. DataTables are related to one another with DataRelation objects, which represent relations between tables. Each DataTable object is made up of DataColumn and DataRow objects. Any constraints on the columns are expressed with Constraint objects. The column constraints, however, are not picked automatically from the database. You have to specify them from within your code. The DataColumn objects represent the table's columns (the structure of the table), and DataRow objects represent the table's rows (the data of the table). Figure 4.1 shows the object model of the DataSet, and these are the objects we'll discuss in this section.

Let's start by exploring the basic components of the DataSet, its DataTables. The DataTables, as well as their relations, are created when you generate the DataSet and populated automatically when you call the DataAdapter's Fill method. As you will see later in this chapter, it's possible to create a DataSet entirely in your code by creating and adding tables and the relations between them.

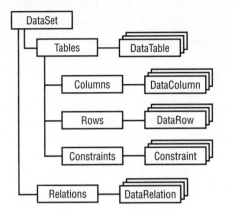

DataSet Object Model

## Accessing a DataSet's Tables

The DataSet contains one or more DataTable objects, one for each table. Each table is associated with a specific DataAdapter, which knows how to populate the table and, optionally, how to submit changes to the data source. The DataTables are members of the Tables collection of the DataSet object. The number of DataTable objects is given by the expression `DataSet.Tables.Count`.

The DataSet's tables can be accessed either by name or by an index. The order of the tables in the DataSet is the same as the order in which they were added to the DataSet (the order in which you called the Fill method of the corresponding DataAdapter object). The indices of the tables are in the range from 0 to `DataSet.Tables.Count - 1`. It's safer to access tables by name because the risk of accessing the wrong table is eliminated, but using table names means additional lookups. Assuming that the first table in the DataSet is the Customers table, the following two expressions are equivalent:

```
DS.Tables("Customers")
DS.Tables(0)
```

If the DataSet was created at design time (which is usually the case), the DataSet object itself exposes the names of its tables as properties. The previous expression is equivalent to this:

```
DS.Customers
```

This DataSet is called *strongly typed*, because it knows the names of the tables and the names of their columns at design time and exposes them as properties. The expression `DS.Customers` represents a DataTable object, which contains the rows of the Customers table.

To iterate through all the tables in the DataSet, use a loop like the following. In each iteration, the variable *iTable* represents another table in the DataSet:

```
Dim iTable As DataTable
For Each iTable In DS.Tables
    ' process table iTable
Next
```

The basic properties of a DataTable object are the TableName property (the name of the table), the Columns collection (which is made up of DataColumn objects, one for each column in the DataTable), and the Rows collection (which represents the rows of the DataTable). The Tables and Columns collections can be accessed both by name and by an index value, but the Rows collection can be accessed by an index (a numeric value) only. This index value is the row's order in its DataTable, and it's the same as the order in which the rows were retrieved from the data source.

## Accessing a DataTable's Columns

The columns of a table are exposed as properties of the DataTable class, and you can access them through the Columns property of the DataTable object. The Columns property is a collection, and it has as many members as there are columns in the corresponding table. Each member is of the DataColumn type. To access all the columns of a specific table, use a loop like the following. With each iteration, the *iCol* variable represents another column in the table:

```
Dim iCol As DataColumn
For Each iCol In DS.Tables(0).Columns
'   process DataColumn iCol
Next
```

If the DataSet is typed, you can access the table columns by name. The expressions `DS.Customers.CustomerIDColumn` and `DS.Customers.CompanyNameColumn` represent the first two columns of the Customers table. These expressions are of the DataColumn type, and they expose properties that describe the corresponding columns. The basic properties of the DataColumn object include the ColumnName property (the column's name), the DataType property (the column's data type), the DefaultValue property (the column's default value), and many more. You usually don't manipulate the properties of a DataTable object's columns, unless you create a new DataSet in code (a topic that's discussed in the section "Creating a DataSet in Code" later in this chapter).

Finally, you can customize a DataSet by adding a few extra columns that do not exist in the database. For example, you can create a DataSet that contains a single table with all the products in the database. Then you add a new column for entering quantities to the table with the products, populate the DataSet (the quantity column will be initialized to zero), and send the DataSet to a remote customer who will fill in the quantities. Any application that can handle

DataSets (or an application that can edit XML documents) can be used at the remote client to prepare the order and then return the original DataSet with the appropriate quantities. To enter the order in your database, you must set up the appropriate Command objects, because you must add the appropriate rows to the Orders and Order Details tables. You'll see how you can create new orders in the last section of this chapter.

The Columns collection exposes the Add method, which accepts as argument a DataColumn object and adds it to the Columns collection. The DataColumn object exposes many properties that allow you to specify the column (its name, data type, whether it's nullable, and so on). The new column is added to the DataSet, but it's not mapped to a column of the underlying table.

### Accessing a DataTable's Rows

The rows of a DataTable object are accessed through the Rows collection. The expression `DS.Tables(i).Rows` returns a collection of DataRow objects, one for each row in the corresponding table. The number of rows in a table is given by either of the following expressions (assuming that the first table in the DataSet is the Customers table):

```
DS.Tables(0).Rows.Count
DS.Customers.Rows.Count
```

To access a specific row, supply the appropriate index:

```
DS.Tables(i).Rows(j)
```

This expression returns a specific row in the table as a DataRow object. The DataRow object's basic properties include the Item property (it returns or sets the value of a field specified by its index), the ItemArray property (it returns or sets all the fields of the row in an array), the HasErrors property (a Boolean value indicating whether the row contains invalid data), and more. The DataRow object also exposes methods like the Delete method, which marks the row as deleted in the DataSet. Deleted rows are not physically removed from the DataSet unless you call the AcceptChanges method. You can call the RejectChanges method at any time to restore deleted rows (as well as cancel any edits).

The following loop goes through the fields of the row represented by the iRow object:

```
Dim iFld As Integer
For iFld = 0 To iTable.Columns.Count - 1
    ConsoleWriteLine(iRow.Item(iFld).ToString)
Next
```

**TIP**     The concept of the current row, which was a key concept in working with ADO, does not exist in ADO.NET. All the rows are copied to the client, and you can access any row by its index.

### The *ExploreDataSet()* Subroutine

The ExploreDataSet() subroutine, which we used in the ADOTests project of the last chapter but didn't discuss its code, accepts as argument a DataSet object and displays the names of its tables and each table's columns on a ListBox control. Then it iterates through the Tables collection, and this time it displays the fields of each row in the table. Listing 4.1 shows the code of the ExploreDataSet() subroutine, which exercises the basic members of the DataSet object.

**Listing 4.1    The *ExploreDataSet()* Subroutine**

```
Private Sub ExploreDataSet(ByVal DS As DataSet)
    Dim iTable As DataTable
    ListBox1.Items.Clear()
    For Each iTable In DS.Tables
        ListBox1.Items.Add("TABLE " & _
                    iTable.TableName & " Columns")
        Dim iCol As DataColumn
        For Each iCol In iTable.Columns
            ListBox1.Items.Add("   >>> " & iCol.ColumnName)
        Next
    Next

    For Each iTable In DS.Tables
        ListBox1.Items.Add("TABLE " & _
                    iTable.TableName & " Rows")
        Dim iRow As DataRow
        For Each iRow In iTable.Rows
            Dim iFld As Integer
            For iFld = 0 To iTable.Columns.Count - 1
                ListBox1.Items.Add( _
                    iRow.Table.Columns(iFld).ColumnName & _
                    " : " & iRow.Item(iFld).ToString)
            Next
        Next
    Next
End Sub
```

The subroutine iterates through the items of the Tables collection twice. The first time it displays the structure of each table (the names of the table's columns) on the ListBox1 control. During the second iteration, it displays the data in each table on the ListBox2 control. A segment of the output produced by the code in Listing 4.1 is shown next. We've set the headers in bold to stand out in the text.

```
TABLE Products Columns
   >>> ProductID
   >>> ProductName
   >>> SupplierID
 ...
```

```
TABLE Categories Columns
  >>> CategoryID
  >>> CategoryName
...
TABLE Suppliers Columns
  >>> SupplierID
  >>> CompanyName
...
TABLE Products Rows
ProductID : 1
ProductName : Chai
SupplierID : 1
CategoryID : 1
...
ProductID : 2
ProductName : Chang
SupplierID : 1
CategoryID : 1
...
```

The ExploreDataSet() subroutine is used by the code of the Create DataAdapter button on the form of the ADOTests project. This button creates a DataSet with the Products, Categories, and Suppliers tables in code and then calls the ExploreDataSet() subroutine to display the structure and contents of the three tables on a ListBox control. Then it establishes relations between the tables and calls the ExploreAddRelations() subroutine, which displays related parent and child rows. We'll discuss the ExploreAllRelations() subroutine's code in the following section.

## Manipulating a DataSet's Relations

The DataTable objects in a DataSet are not related to one another automatically. As we discussed in the previous chapter, relations must be established at design time or with the appropriate code at runtime. Once the relations are in place, you can easily navigate from one table's rows to the related rows in other tables. Relations are represented by DataRelation objects, and all the relations in a DataSet are members of the DataSet's Relations collection. The basic members of the DataRelation class are the Name property (the relation's name) and the ParentColumns and ChildColumns properties. The last two properties are collections, and they contain the relation's parent and child columns, respectively. Tables are usually related to one another through a single column, but relations that involve multiple columns are not uncommon. The ChildTable and ParentTable properties are of the DataTable type, and they represent the relation's parent and child tables, respectively.

To create a new relation between two tables, use the following form of the Relation object's overloaded constructor:

```
Dim DR As New DataRelation(RelationName, _
        parentTable.parentColumn, childTable.childColumn)
```

The first argument is a string with the relation's name. The following two arguments are two DataColumn objects. For complex relations that are based on multiple columns, use another overloaded form that accepts two arrays of DataColumn objects as arguments, in addition to the relation's name, of course.

To relate the Products and Supplier tables, pass the SupplierID column of the Suppliers table as the second argument and the SupplierID of the Products table as the third argument. The first argument of the constructor is just a name, and it need not be the same as the relation's name in the database. The following statements create a new relation between the Suppliers and Products tables:

```
Dim DR As DataRelation
DR = New DataRelation("SuppliersProducts", _
            Suppliers.SupplierID, Products.SupplierID)
```

**The *ExploreRelations* Subroutine**

Another of the subroutines we used in the ADOTests project of the previous chapter is the ExploreRelations() subroutine, whose code is shown in Listing 4.2. The subroutine accepts as argument a DataSet object and displays the parent and child rows of the SuppliersProducts and CategoriesProducts relations. First, it displays all the rows in the Categories table, and under each category, it displays the names of the related products (the products that belong to this category). Then it does the same with the Suppliers and the related products. The Explore-Relations() subroutine is of little practical use because it assumes knowledge of the relations. We'll discuss the code of Listing 4.2 to demonstrate the basics of iterating the DataSet's tables through its relations. We'll also present the code of the ExploreAllRelations() subroutine, which iterates through the relations of an arbitrary DataSet.

**Listing 4.2**        **The *ExploreRelations* Subroutine**

```
Private Sub ExploreRelations(ByVal DS As DataSet)
    ListBox2.Items.Clear()
    Console.WriteLine("Suppliers - Products")
    Dim parentRow As DataRow
    For Each parentRow In DS.Tables("Suppliers").Rows
        ListBox2.Items.Add( _
                    parentRow.Item("CompanyName"))
        Dim childRow As DataRow
```

```
        For Each childRow In _
                parentRow.GetChildRows("ProductsSuppliers")
            ListBox2.Items.Add("  >>> " & _
                    childRow.Item("ProductName"))
        Next
    Next

    ListBox2.Items.Add("Suppliers - Categories")

    For Each parentRow In DS.Tables("Categories").Rows
        ListBox2.Items.Add( _
                    parentRow.Item("CategoryName"))
        Dim childRow As DataRow
        For Each childRow In _
                parentRow.GetChildRows("ProductsCategories")
            ListBox2.Items.Add("  >>> " & _
                            childRow.Item("ProductName"))
        Next
    Next
End Sub
```

To retrieve the related rows of a parent row, call the parent row's GetChildRows method. The related tables and the set of related rows are determined by a specific relation, which is passed as argument to the method. To retrieve the products that belong to a specific category, call the GetChildRows method of the corresponding row of the Categories table, passing as argument the name of the CategoriesProducts relation.

The related rows are returned as an array of DataRow objects, and the code iterates through the elements of this array and prints a field that identifies the row (the product name, in our example). Similarly, you can use the GetParentRow method to retrieve the current row's parent row. If the relation is of the many-to-many type, you can use the GetParentRows method to retrieve all matching rows. Normally, we call the GetChildRows to retrieve the related rows with a specific foreign key and the GetParentRow to retrieve a single parent row. If the *supplierRow* variable represents a row in the Suppliers table, you can retrieve all the rows of the Products table that are related to the specific row of the Suppliers table with the following statement:

```
supplierRow.GetChildRows("SuppliersProducts")
```

Likewise, you can retrieve the matching category and supplier of a row in the Products table with the following statements, where *productRow* is a row of the Products table:

```
productRow.GetParent("SuppliersProducts")
productRow.GetParent("CategoriesProducts")
```

No trip to the database is involved; the requested rows exist in the DataSet and are returned as an array. When we request a row's child rows, we usually iterate through the array and process them with a loop like the following:

```
Dim childRow As DataRow
For Each childRow In _
            parentRow.GetChildRows("ProductsSuppliers")
    ' process childRow
Next
```

Each element of the array returned by the GetChildRows method is a DataRow object, and you can access its fields with the Item property. `childRow.Item(0)` is the first field in the row, `childRow.Item(1)` is the second field, and so on. You can also access the elements of the Item collection by name (`childRow.Item("ProductID")`, `childRow.Item("ProductName")`, and so on).

The first For Each … Next loop in Listing 4.2 iterates through the rows of the Suppliers table. An inner loop retrieves the child rows of the current supplier from the Products table and displays the ProductName field under the current supplier.

Another similar loop iterates through the Categories table and displays each category's child rows in the Products table. The (partial) output generated by the `ExploreRelations()` sub-routine is shown here:

```
CategoriesProducts
Meat/Poultry
   >>> Mishi Kobe Niku
   >>> Alice Mutton
   >>> Thuringer Rostbratwurst
   >>> Perth Pasties
   >>> Tourtiere
   >>> Pate chinois
Produce
   >>> Uncle Bob's Organic Dried Pears
   >>> Tofu
   >>> Rossle Sauerkraut
   >>> Manjimup Dried Apples
   >>> Longlife Tofu
```

### The *ExploreAllRelations()* Subroutine

A more flexible subroutine for navigating through the rows of related tables is the `Explore-AllRelations()` subroutine, which is shown in Listing 4.3. This subroutine goes through all the relations in the DataSet. For each relation, it iterates through the rows of the parent table and prints the related rows in the child table under each row of the parent table. The code prints the second field of each row on the second ListBox control, because this field happens to be a string (a category's name or a product's name). The first field is usually an ID, which is pretty meaningless information for the user. You can edit the code so that it prints any combination of fields.

---

**Listing 4.3**   **The *ExploreAllRelations()* Subroutine**

```
Private Sub ExploreAllRelations(ByVal DS As DataSet)
    ListBox2.Items.Clear()
    Dim parentRow As DataRow
    Dim R As DataRelation
    For Each R In DS.Relations
        ListBox2.Items.Add(R.RelationName)
        For Each parentRow In _
                DS.Tables(R.ParentTable.TableName).Rows
            ListBox2.Items.Add(parentRow.Item(1))
            Dim childRow As DataRow
            For Each childRow In parentRow.GetChildRows(R)
                ListBox2.Items.Add("  >>> " & _
                        childRow.Item(1))
            Next
        Next
    Next
End Sub
```

---

## Editing the DataSet

In Chapter 3, you saw how easy it is to edit the DataSet by binding it to a DataGrid control. DataSets can also be edited programmatically with simple statements that set field values. To edit an existing row, assign the new value to each field you want to change. Let's say that the first table in the DataSet is the Customers table and you want to change the phone number of the first customer. The following expression changes the Phone field of the first row of the first table:

```
DS.Tables(0).Rows(0).Item("Phone") = "(333) 444.5678"
```

You can take advantage of the fact that the DataSet is strongly typed and use the following statement, which is equivalent:

```
DS.Customers(0).Phone = "(333) 333.3333"
```

Using the table and column names exposed by the DataSet, you can write shorter, easier-to-read statements. DS is a DataSet variable that contains the three tables.

When you change the value of a field from within your code, you should make sure that it is of the proper type. New values are usually entered by the user on the application's visible interface, and you should validate these values as best as you can before submitting them to the database. Data that violate the constraints specified in the design of the database will not be committed to the database anyway, but you shouldn't wait until submitting the changes to the database to catch the errors. The sooner you notify users about incorrect data, the easier it is for them to fix their mistakes.

To delete a row, call the Delete method of the DataRow object. The following statement will delete the third row in the first table of the DS DataSet:

```
DS.Tables(0).Rows(2).Delete
```

Alternatively, you can use this statement for a strongly typed DataSet:

```
DS.Categories.Rows(2).Delete
```

The number of rows in the table won't be reduced because the row is marked for deletion, but it's not actually removed from its table. The row will be removed when you call the AcceptChanges method, which you should do only after you update the data source. If you're using a DataAdapter to update the data source, you need not call the AcceptChanges method (the Update method reads back the rows committed to the data source, which is equivalent to accepting the changes with the AcceptChanges method).

Another similarly named method of the DataRow object is the Remove method, which physically removes a row from the DataSet. The removed rows will not update the data source; they simply disappear from the DataSet. The Remove method isn't really a data-editing method, it's a method for DataSet housekeeping. Let's say you've written an application to edit a large number of rows and the application updates the data source every so often. After calling the Update method, you can remove from the DataSet the rows that successfully updated the data source. The Remove method isn't used very frequently in typical applications.

**NOTE**　The Remove and Delete methods of the DataRow object are totally different. The Delete method marks a row as deleted but doesn't remove it from the table. The table's row count doesn't change. You can undo the deletion of a row by calling the RejectChanges method on that row. The Remove method removes a row from the DataSet and the DataSet will not send a query for the specific row to the data source. In addition, you cannot undo the removal of a row from its DataTable with the RejectChanges method.

To add a new row to a table, use the Add method of the table's Rows collection. The Add method accepts a DataRow object as argument and appends it to a DataSet table. To create a new DataRow object, use the NewRow property of the DataTable object, which returns a DataRow object. The following statements append a new row to the Products table:

```
Dim ProductRow As DataRow
ProductRow = DS.Tables("Products").NewRow
ProductRow("ProductName") = "New Product's Name"
ProductRow("CategoryID") = 3
ProductRow("SupplierID") = 12
ProductRow("UnitPrice") = 9.95
DS.Products.Rows.Add(ProductRow)
```

The first executable statement creates a new DataRow object by calling the Products table's NewRow method. The following statements set the columns of the new row, and the last statement appends it to the Products table.

The *ProductRow* variable in the last code segment is of the DataRow type, which is a generic type representing table rows. This is the type of the object returned by the NewRow method of the DataTable object. Because the DataSet is strongly typed, you can create variables that represent the rows of specific tables, and they expose the table's columns as properties. The following statements add a new row to the Products table using the strongly typed notation:

```
Dim ProdRow As Products.ProductsRow
ProdRow = Products1.Products.NewProductsRow
ProdRow.ProductName = "New Product's Name"
ProdRow.CategoryID = 3
ProdRow.SupplierID = 12
ProdRow.UnitPrice = 9.95
Products1.Products.Rows.Add(ProdRow)
```

The ProdRow variable represents a row of the Products table, and it's not totally empty: its fields have their default values as they were specified in the table's schema.

Each DataTable object exposes a member to represent a new row for the corresponding table. The NewProductsRow method returns an object that represents a new row of the Products table. This object is of the Products.ProductsRow type and not the generic DataRow type. The code sets the values of the new row's fields and then adds it to the Rows collection of the Products table. Likewise, the Categories DataTable exposes the NewCategoriesRow method, which is of the Products.CategoryRow type and represents a new row of the Categories table.

---

**NOTE**   If you want to know how the DataSet gets the information about the types of its contents, you should look at the code generated by the wizard for the DataSet. Select the Products .xsd item in the Solution Explorer and then click the Show All Files button. A new file (which is normally hidden) will appear below the Products.xsd file in the Solution Explorer. Double-click the Products.vb file to open it in Design mode and you can see the code of the classes that implement the various components of the DataSet. You shouldn't edit this file, but you can examine it to understand a little better how typed DataSets are implemented. If this file were totally hidden from you (or if it were encoded in a proprietary format), typed DataSets would look like magic. The wizard generated the code that you could have written for a large project to streamline the most common operations. It generated a bunch of classes that represent the DataTables and their DataColumns and DataRows.

The changes you make to the DataSet are local to the client and do not affect the data source in any way. To commit the changes to the data source, you must call the appropriate DataAdapter object's Update method or set up the appropriate Command objects and execute them against the database. We'll discuss the topic of submitting to the database the changes made to the DataSet, but first let's look at a few more tools for manipulating the contents of the DataSet.

# Sorting, Filtering, and Searching Rows

The rows in each DataTable object of the DataSet are in the order in which you read them out of the data source (the order in which the DataAdapter object returned the rows to the DataSet). Quite often we need to sort the rows of the DataTable, or even select a subset of its rows. None of these operations justifies a trip to the database, and the DataSet provides the necessary tools to sort and filter its rows at the client. There are two techniques to sort and filter a DataSet. The first technique is to call the Select method of the DataTable object and specify the appropriate filtering and sorting criteria. The second technique is to create a DataView on a DataTable specifying the same criteria. The DataView is basically another DataTable with selected rows of the original DataTable. SQL Server programmers use views routinely to simplify many programming tasks. Unfortunately, the DataSet doesn't support SQL statements. If it did, it would be truly an in-memory database.

## The Select Method

The simplest method of sorting and/or filtering the rows of a DataTable is to use the Select method, which returns an array of rows. They're the filtered and/or sorted rows of the DataTable object to which the method is applied. The Select method has many overloaded forms, which accept up to three arguments: a filtering expression, a sorting expression, and a member of the DataRowState enumeration, which determines the subset of the rows on which the method will act depending on their state. The simplest form of the Select method accepts no arguments and returns all the rows in the table. The form that uses all three arguments is as follows:

```
Dim selRows() as DataRow
selRows = DT.Select(filter, sort, state)
```

The first two arguments are similar to the filtering and sorting expressions you use with an SQL statement. The following filter expression extracts the customers from Germany:

```
"Country = 'Germany'"
```

The following sort expression sorts the rows according to the customer name, city, and country. Customers from the same country are clustered together and ordered according to their cities. Customers within the same city are ordered according to their names:

```
"Country, City, CompanyName"
```

To reverse the default sort order, supply the DESC qualifier after the sort expression:

```
"Country, City, CompanyName DESC"
```

The last argument allows you to select rows according to their state in the DataTable. To retrieve only the rows that were added to the DataTable since it was populated (or since the AcceptChanges method was last called), use the following expression:

```
selRows = DT.Select("", "", DataViewRowState.Added)
```

The overloaded forms of the Select method are reminiscent of methods that accept optional arguments in VB6. There's no overloaded form that accepts a member of the DataViewRowState enumeration only. However, you can retrieve all the rows in a specific state by specifying two empty strings in the place of the filter and sort arguments.

The DataViewRowState enumeration is not the same as the DataRowState enumeration. The DataViewRowState exposes members that allow you to read various row combinations based on the type of editing performed in the DataSet. Table 4.1 shows the members of the DataViewRowState enumeration.

**TABLE 4.1:** The DataViewRowState Enumeration

| Member | Description |
| --- | --- |
| Added | Returns the rows that were added to the DataTable. |
| CurrentRows | Returns all current rows (including the ones that were not changed). Only deleted and removed rows are omitted. |
| Deleted | Returns the deleted rows. |
| ModifiedCurrent | Returns the current version of the rows that were modified. |
| ModifiedOriginal | Returns the original version of the rows that were modified. |
| OriginalRows | Returns the original version of all rows, including the rows that were deleted. |
| Unchanged | Returns the rows that weren't changed. |

The following statement retrieves the original versions of the rows that were deleted from the DT DataTable:

```
DT.Select("","", DataViewRowState.Deleted)
```

To retrieve the original versions of the rows that represent customers from the U.K. and were edited, use the following expression:

```
DT.Select("Country = 'UK'","", _
          DataRowViewState.ModifiedOriginal)
```

Note that the Select method doesn't return a new DataTable object, just an array of DataRow objects. Using array of DataRow objects is not always the most convenient method of accessing your data. It's trivial to iterate through a small array of DataRow objects and process them, but most of the time, you will need the convenience and the functionality of a DataTable. You can create a new DataTable in your code and use the DataTable object's Import method to import the elements of the array returned by the Select method to populate a new table. If the original DataSet contains multiple tables, chances are that you will select rows from multiple tables. It is possible to create a new DataSet with multiple tables and dump the rows returned by the Select method to the tables of the new DataSet. To do so, use the Merge method of the DataSet object, which merges two DataSets. If one of the DataSets is empty, then the data of the second DataSet will be copied into the original one. The Merge method accepts an argument with the data to be merged, and this argument can be another DataSet, a DataTable, or simply an array of DataRow objects, like the one returned by the Select method. Let's write some code to extract the current versions of the modified rows in all tables of the Products DataSet and dump them into a new DataSet.

In the section "Editing the DataSet" earlier in this chapter, we showed the code to edit the Products, Categories, and Suppliers tables of the Products DataSet. If you insert the following code before the statements that call the Update method to commit the changes to the data source, you will create another DataSet that contains the current versions of the rows that were edited in all three tables:

```
Dim DSEdits As New DataSet()
DSEdits.Merge(Products1.Tables(0).Select("", "", _
              DataViewRowState.ModifiedCurrent))
DSEdits.Merge(Products1.Tables(1).Select("", "", _
              DataViewRowState.ModifiedCurrent))
DSEdits.Merge(Products1.Tables(2).Select("", "", _
              DataViewRowState.ModifiedCurrent))
```

These statements will create a new DataSet, the DSEdits DataSet, which contains three tables populated with the rows returned by the three calls to the Select method. The order of the tables in the DataSet's Tables collection is the same as the order in which the Merge statements were executed, and the names of the tables are Table0, Table1, and Table2. Use the TableName property to specify more meaningful names for the three tables.

The three tables contain the rows of the original tables that have been modified. The field values of all three tables are the current values of the matching rows in the tables of the Products1 DataSet. Also notice that the current and original versions of all rows in the DSEdits DataSet are the same. The DSEdits DataSet hasn't been edited yet. If you edit it, it will maintain its original and current versions as usual.

Now add a few statements to print out the contents of the new DataSet:

```
Console.WriteLine("The DSEdits DataSet contains " & _
         DSEdits.Tables.Count.ToString & " tables")
```

```
Dim itable As Integer
For itable = 0 To DSEdits.Tables.Count - 1
    Console.WriteLine("Table " & itable.ToString & _
                      " contains the following rows")
    Dim irow As Integer
    For irow = 0 To DSEdits.Tables(0).Rows.Count - 1
        Dim icol As Integer
        For icol = 0 To DSEdits.Tables(0).Columns.Count - 1
            Console.Write(_
                    DSEdits.Tables(itable)._
                    Rows(irow).Item(icol) & vbTab)
        Next
        Console.WriteLine()
    Next
Next
```

When these statements are executed, the following lines will be printed on the Output window (we've set the headers in bold to stand out):

**The DSEdits DataSet contains 3 tables**
**Table 0 contains the following rows**
3   CONFECTIONS NEW      Desserts, candies, and sweet breads
**Table 1 contains the following rows**
11 QUESO CABRALES    5
**Table 2 contains the following rows**
1  EXOTIC LIQUIDS   Charlotte Cooper

If you change the third argument to the Select method from `ModifiedCurrent` to `Added`, the following output will be produced:

**The DSEdits DataSet contains 2 tables**
**Table 0 contains the following rows**
91 New Product      12     3     9.95
**Table 1 contains the following rows**
59 New Company  New Contact   New Contact's Title    New Address

The filter argument of the Select method may contain many of the SQL keywords you use in building selection queries. You can combine multiple fields with the usual Boolean and arithmetic operations or concatenate fields with the + operator:

```
UnitPrice * (1 - Discount)
CompanyName + '(' + ContactName + ' - ' + ContactTitle + ')'
```

The LIKE operator can also be used to specify general search patterns. The wildcard characters % and * are equivalent in the context of ADO.NET expressions. The following expression locates rows in the Customers table with company names that begin with the string "FISH" followed by any other string and whose Country field is either "UK" or "England".

```
CompanyName LIKE 'FISH%' AND
        (Country = 'UK' OR Country = 'England'
```

The last SQL keyword you can use in building expressions is the IN keyword. In addition, you can use the following functions:

**Convert(expression, type)**   Converts the specified expression into the specified .NET type.

**Len(string)**   Returns the length of the string argument.

**IsNull(field, nullExpression)**   Returns the value of the field specified with the first argument if it's not null or the nullExpression if the field is null.

**Iff(expression, TrueValue, FalseValue)**   Evaluates the expression, and if its value is True, it returns the TrueValue argument, if not it returns the FalseValue argument.

**SubString(string, start, length)**   Returns length characters from the string argument, starting at location start.

## Using Views

Another technique for sorting and filtering rows is to create a view on one or more the tables. The DataView object is similar to a table in the sense that it's made up of columns and rows. You can even edit a view with the same methods you'd use to edit the DataTable on which it's based, and all the changes in the DataView are reflected in the corresponding DataTable object. Unlike the DataTable object, the DataView exposes a few properties that determine what types of changes can be applied to it. They're the AllowNew, AllowDelete, and AllowEdit properties. These properties are all Boolean values that determine whether the corresponding operations are allowed.

To create a new view on a table, you must first create a new DataView object and then set its RowFilter, Sort, and RowState properties. These three properties are equivalent to the three arguments of the Select method. The RowFilter property is set to a filtering expression, the Sort property is set to a sorting expression, and the RowState property can be set to one of the members of the DataViewRowState enumeration (see Table 4.1). The following statements create a DataView object and populate it with the rows added to the Products table since it was populated by the DataAdapter (or since the AcceptChanges method was called for the last time):

```
Dim ProductsView As New DataView(DsProducts1.Products)
ProductsView.RowStateFilter = DataViewRowState.Added
```

To display the rows of the ProductsView view, you can bind it to a DataGrid control. The ADOViews project creates a DataSet with the Products, Categories, and Suppliers tables and then edits a few rows of the Products table. The current versions of the DataSet's rows are displayed on the top DataGrid control on the form, as shown in Figure 4.2. The lower DataGrid displays a view with selected rows; which rows are displayed depends on which of the radio buttons at the top of the form is checked. Every time you click another radio button, the lower DataGrid is repopulated.

**FIGURE 4.2:**

The ADOViews project demonstrates the use of DataViews.

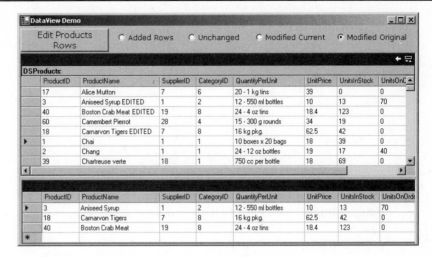

The code behind the Edit Products Rows button is rather trivial, and you've seen before code that edits a DataSet's tables. The StateChanged() subroutine handles the CheckedChanged event of all radio buttons on the form, and its code is shown in Listing 4.4.

**Listing 4.4      Creating a View and Binding It to a DataGrid Control**

```
Private Sub StatedChanged(ByVal sender As System.Object, _
               ByVal e As System.EventArgs) _
               Handles rdAdded.CheckedChanged, _
               rdModifiedCurrent.CheckedChanged, _
               rdModifiedOriginal.CheckedChanged, _
               rdUnchanged.CheckedChanged

    Dim ProductsView As New DataView(DsProducts1.Products)

    If rdAdded.Checked Then
        ProductsView.RowStateFilter = _
                    DataViewRowState.Added
    End If
    If rdModifiedCurrent.Checked Then
        ProductsView.RowStateFilter = _
                    DataViewRowState.ModifiedCurrent
    End If
    If rdModifiedOriginal.Checked Then
        ProductsView.RowStateFilter = _
                    DataViewRowState.ModifiedOriginal
    End If
    If rdUnchanged.Checked Then
        ProductsView.RowStateFilter = _
                    DataViewRowState.Unchanged
```

```
      End If
      DataGrid2.DataSource = ProductsView
   End Sub
```

The code creates a new DataView object with a specific subset of the rows in the Products table. The selection of the rows is based on their state (whether they were added to the DataSet, edited, and so on).

## Finding Rows by ID

You can also search for a specific row by its primary key with the Find method of the Rows collection. The Find method accepts as argument the value of the primary key you're looking for and returns a DataRow object, which represents the matching row. The argument of the Find method is of the Object type because the primary key column's data type isn't known at design time. If the Find method fails, it returns Nothing. The Find method applies only to untyped DataSets.

Strongly typed DataTable objects expose a Find*xxx* method, where *xxx* is the name of the primary key column. The Products1.Products DataTable object exposes the FindByProductID method, which accepts as argument an integer value (the ID of the desired row). The primary key is unique, so the Find (or the Find*xxx* method) returns a single row (or no row at all). The Find*xxx* method is a member of the class that implements the typed DataSet and its code is generated by the wizard. This code can be found in a VB file with the same name as the DataSet. To view this file in the Solution Explorer, you must enable the Show All Files button. It's actually quite interesting to see the implementation of the Find*xxx* method (the implementation of the FindByCategroyID method of the Products DataSet is shown next):

```
Public Function FindByCategoryID( _
            ByVal CategoryID As Integer) As CategoriesRow
   Return CType(Me.Rows.Find(New Object() _
                  {CategoryID}),CategoriesRow)
End Function
```

Its code simply calls the Find method of the Rows collection, passing to it as argument the value that was passed as argument to the Find*xxx* method. Notice that the argument is first cast to the Object type.

**TIP**    The Find methods will not locate deleted rows, even though they remain in the DataSet. To locate a deleted row by its primary key, use the Select method, specify a filter expression like ProductID=xx, and set the last argument to the Select method to DataViewRowState .Deleted. This expression will return a single row, which you can process in your code— for example, you can call the RejectChanges method of the object returned by the Find method to restore a deleted row.

You will see how the Find*xxx* method of the Rows collection is used in an application in the following chapter, in the presentation of the Customers project. The Customers project is a Windows application that allows the user to edit the Customers table, view the changes made so far, and undo selected changes (insertions, deletions, modifications) at will.

## Creating a DataSet in Code

A DataSet exists independently of a data source. In other words, you don't need to connect to a database to create and use a DataSet object in your code. In Chapter 3, you learned how to create the schema of the DataSet with visual tools and populate it through a GUI. It is possible to create a DataSet entirely in code. You may have to create your own DataSet in code if you want to use the functionality of the DataSet object without the overhead of a database. For example, you may wish to generate and update a set of related tables that is small and doesn't justify the maintenance of an actual database. You can still use a DataSet to store your data and persist the DataSet's data to a local disk file in XML format, even if there's no underlying database for the data. You may have to create a DataSet in code and populate it with data from an XML file, which is sent to your application by a remote system. The disconnected architecture of the DataSet allows you to take advantage of its relational features and use it as a small database without the overhead of creating and maintaining a database.

To demonstrate the process of generating a DataSet in code, we're going to build a DataSet with two related tables, the Employees and Projects tables. Each project has a manager, who is an employee. The sample code can be found in the ADOTests project, behind the "Custom DataSet" button.

To create a DataSet in code, you start by declaring a DataSet object:

```
Dim DS As New DataSet
```

The next step is to add one or more tables to the DataSet and then one or more columns to each table. Tables are represented by DataTable objects and table columns are represented by DataColumn objects. The statements in Listing 4.5 create a new DataTable object, add a few columns to it, and then attach the DataTable object to the DataSet's Tables collection.

---

**Listing 4.5**      **Creating a DataSet in Code**

```
Dim Tbl1 As New DataTable()
Tbl1.TableName = "Employees"
Dim Col As New DataColumn()
Col.ColumnName = "ID"
Col.DataType = GetType(System.Int64)
Col.AutoIncrement = True
Tbl1.Columns.Add(Col)
Col = New DataColumn()
Col.ColumnName = "Name"
```

```
Col.DataType = GetType(System.String)
Col.MaxLength = 100
Tbl1.Columns.Add(Col)
Col = New DataColumn()
Col.ColumnName = "DOB"
Col.DataType = GetType(System.DateTime)
Tbl1.Columns.Add(Col)
Col = New DataColumn()
Col.ColumnName = "Salary"
Col.DataType = GetType(System.Decimal)
Tbl1.Columns.Add(Col)
DS.Tables.Add(Tbl1)
```

The first table in the DataSet is called Employees and it has four columns, with the names and types shown here:

| Column Name | Type | Size |
| --- | --- | --- |
| ID | Long Integer | AutoIncrement |
| Name | String | 100 |
| DOB | DateTime | |
| Salary | Decimal | |

The ID column is an AutoIncrement column and the DataSet will automatically assign a value to it. The DOB (Date of Birth) and Salary columns have fixed sizes that are determined by the data type and you need not specify their size.

The basic properties of the DataColumn object are the ColumnName property, the DataType property, and the MaxLength property. You can set other properties as well, such as the AllowDBNull property (a Boolean value that determines whether the column can be null and its default value is True) and the DefaultValue property (the column's default value). If you don't specify a default value, the column's value for new rows will be null. The basic properties of the DataTable object are the Columns collection (the table's columns) and the PrimaryKey property (an array of columns that form the table's primary key). In our case, the ID column is the table's primary key and we'll use it later to build relations.

The second table in the DataSet is the Projects table, which holds data about the company's current projects. Each project has a name (column ProjectName), a manager who's a person and is specified by their ID, and a budget. Here are the statements that create the second DataTable object and add it to the DataSet:

```
Dim Tbl2 As New DataTable()
Tbl2.TableName = "Projects"
Col = New DataColumn()
Col.ColumnName = "ProjectName"
```

```
Col.DataType = GetType(System.String)
Col.MaxLength = 100
Tbl2.Columns.Add(Col)
Col = New DataColumn()
Col.ColumnName = "ManagerID"
Col.DataType = GetType(System.Int64)
Tbl2.Columns.Add(Col)
Col = New DataColumn()
Col.ColumnName = "Budget"
Col.DataType = GetType(System.Decimal)
Tbl2.Columns.Add(Col)
DS.Tables.Add(Tbl2)
```

Once the tables have been added to the DataSet, you can create relations between them. First, you must specify the primary key for each table involved in a relation. To do so, create an array of DataColumn objects with the columns that make up the table's primary key (this is usually an array with a single element) and then assign this array to the PrimaryKey property of the DataTable object. The following statements specify the primary keys for the two tables:

```
Dim Tbl1Keys() As DataColumn = {Tbl1.Columns(0)}
Tbl1.PrimaryKey = Tbl1Keys
Dim Tbl2Keys() As DataColumn = {Tbl2.Columns(0)}
Tbl2.PrimaryKey = Tbl2Keys
```

After specifying the tables' primary keys, you can establish relations between them. For this example, we'll create a relation between Projects and Employees based on the ID column of the Employee table and the ManagerID field of the Projects table:

```
DS.Relations.Add("PMRelation", _
          Tbl1.Columns("ID"), Tbl2.Columns("ManagerID"))
```

Notice that we kept the references to the two DataTable objects (variables *Tbl1* and *Tbl2*) and you can reuse them in your code to define the relation. You could have also created the relation between the projects and their managers by referencing the actual tables in the DataSet because the appropriate DataTable objects have been added to the DataSet:

```
DS.Relations.Add("PMRelation", _
          DS.Tables("Employees").Columns("ID"), _
          DS.Tables("Projects").Columns("ManagerID"))
```

You've created the structure of the DataSet. The next step is to add data to it. (See Figure 4.3.) To add new rows to your tables, you can create instances of the DataRow object, assign values to their columns, and attach the DataRow objects to the appropriate DataTable object of the DataSet. The following statement adds a new row to the Employees table:

```
Dim Row1 As DataRow
Row1 = DS.Tables(0).NewRow
Row1.Item(0) = 132
Row1.Item(1) = "Name1"
DS.Tables(0).Rows.Add(Row1)
```

Likewise, you can create rows for the Projects table:

```
Dim Row2 As DataRow
Row2 = DS.Tables(1).NewRow
Row2.Item(0) = "Project Grace"
Row2.Item(1) = 132
Row2.Item(2) = 485000
DS.Tables(1).Rows.Add(Row2)
```

To view the contents of the DataSet, you'll bind the DataSet to a DataGrid control. Because the structure of the DataSet isn't available at design time, you can't bind it to the DataGrid control at design time. Insert the following statement at the end of the "Custom DataSet" button's Click event handler:

```
DataGrid1.DataSource = DS
```

**FIGURE 4.3:**

The CustomDataSet project demonstrates how to generate and populate a DataSet in code.

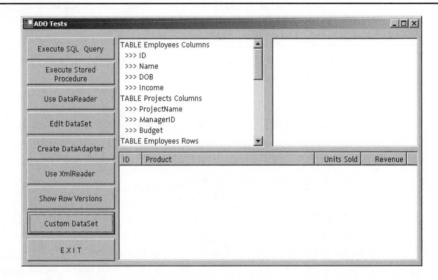

As you may have noticed, the DataSet we created in our code exhibits a slightly different behavior than the previous ones we created manually at design time. This DataSet doesn't expose the names of the tables as properties. In other words, you can't use an expression like the following to address the first table in the DataSet:

```
DS.Employees
```

Instead, you must use the Tables collection and specify the desired table either by name or by its index. This expression specifies it by name:

```
DS.Tables("Employees")
```

This expression specifies it by index:

```
DS.Tables(0)
```

This type of DataSet is not strongly typed. The names of the tables that make up the DataSet (and the names of the columns of each DataTable object) are not known at design time, and the IDE can't display their names in the IntelliSense box. This means that you must get the names of the tables, or their indices, right as you write your code or else runtime exceptions will be thrown. DataSets that are set up at design time are called strongly typed, and their syntax helps generate more robust and readable code.

There's another implication when specifying tables in a DataSet that's not strongly typed. Although table names make the code easier to read, they require a lookup. Using indices will make your code harder to read, but it will run faster because no lookup is necessary. An expression like the following requires two lookups, one for the table name and another one for the column name:

```
DS.Tables("Employees").Rows(iRow).Items("ManagerTitle")
```

If this statement appears in a loop that's repeated for hundreds or thousands of values of the *iRow* variable, the performance penalty is no longer negligible.

## DataSets and XML

Once a DataSet has been populated, you can create an XmlDataDocument object that contains the same data in XML format. The DataSet and XmlDataDocument objects are synchronized and you can manipulate your data through either object. The DataSet provides a relational view of the data, and the XmlDataDocument provides a hierarchical view of the same data.

Why is XML such an important part of ADO.NET and why has Microsoft chosen to support this format in their languages, database and data access tools? ADO.NET is a disconnected architecture; its primary goal is to provide a mechanism for storing related data at the client and methods to update the underlying tables in the database. To make this architecture even more useful in a distributed environment, the DataSet should also support a universal format for exchanging data with other sources, and this universal format couldn't be anything else but XML.

Microsoft is using XML as a universal data exchange format in other products as well. The most characteristic example is SQL Server. SQL Server 2000 is being updated constantly with new XML-related features. As you may know, it is possible to request that the results of a query be returned in XML format. You will find more information about SQL Server's XML support in Chapter 2, "Working with SQL Server 2000 and Visual Studio .NET." The goal is to make XML the universal format for passing data between applications and operating systems.

XML is more than a format for exchanging data; it's also a format for describing data. In essence, XML has been so successful because it describes not only the data, but its structure as well. This makes it an ideal format for describing the structure of the DataSet, where the data will reside at the client. Different database management systems may use different data types and describe the relations between their tables differently. The definition of the data in their tables can be translated into XML (this part of the file is called the *schema* and it describes the structure of the data that will be stored in the file). Once the schema is in place, the file can be loaded with data. It's also possible to populate an XML file without a schema. There are tools that can infer the schema from the data. The schema of such a file may not match exactly the schema of the data source, but you can use it to populate another DataSet or the underlying database tables.

Figure 4.4 shows the relation between the DataSet and its two data sources: a database and an XML document. The DataSet can be populated from either source, and it can be persisted to either data source. For example, you can populate a DataSet with data from a database, edit it, and then save it to a local file. You can reload the DataSet from the XML file, edit it again, and submit it to the data source to update the underlying tables. The XML file can be sent to another system, edited by another application, and then returned to your application.

**FIGURE 4.4:**

The DataSet can be loaded from, and persisted to, either a database or an XML file.

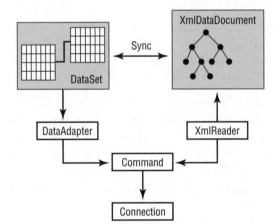

The best thing about ADO.NET's support for XML is that you don't need to know much about XML in order to use it in your code. The goal is to make XML transparent to the application developer, but we're not there yet. XML may very well become a mechanism for storing data, and with the adoption of a query mechanism for its data, XML may become a "universal" database for structured, and even unstructured, data. Actually, XML can already be used as a client data store and manipulated with the relational tools of the DataSet.

In the following sections, we're going to explore the most basic XML-related features of the DataSet, which will help you understand a little better the nature of the DataSet. We're not going to discuss the structure of XML documents or how to create valid, well-formed XML documents. We'll discuss XML-related topics that don't require a thorough understanding of XML, starting with the methods that persist a DataSet in XML format.

## Persisting a DataSet

Converting a DataSet's contents to XML format and persisting them to a file is trivial. The WriteXml method of the DataSet object generates the XML description of the DataSet's schema and/or data and writes it to a file or a Stream object. The simplest form of the WriteXml method is as follows, where *XMLFileName* is the path to file to which the XML data will be written:

```
DS.WriteXml(XMLFileName)
```

Open the ADOTests project and add the following statement in the Edit DataSet button's Click event handler, right after the statements that populate the DataSet:

```
Products1.WriteXml("c:\OriginalDataset.xml")
```

This statement will persist the DataSet's initial state (the data read from the database) to an XML file. Run the program, click the Edit DataSet button, and then open the XML file by double-clicking its name (the code places the file in the root folder so that you can locate it easily). The file will open in Internet Explorer. Listing 4.6 shows what it looks like.

---

**Listing 4.6      The XML View of a Typical DataSet**

```xml
<?xml version="1.0" standalone="yes" ?>
  <Products xmlns="http://www.tempuri.org/Products.xsd">
  <Categories>
  <CategoryID>1</CategoryID>
  <CategoryName>Beverages</CategoryName>
  <Description>Soft drinks, coffees, teas, beers, and ales</Description>
  </Categories>
  <Categories>
  <CategoryID>2</CategoryID>
  <CategoryName>Condiments</CategoryName>
  <Description>Sweet and savory sauces, relishes, spreads,
   and seasonings</Description>
  </Categories>
...
  <Products>
  <ProductID>1</ProductID>
  <ProductName>Chai</ProductName>
  <SupplierID>1</SupplierID>
  <CategoryID>1</CategoryID>
  <UnitPrice>18</UnitPrice>
  </Products>
  <Products>
```

```
<ProductID>2</ProductID>
<ProductName>Chang</ProductName>
<SupplierID>1</SupplierID>
<CategoryID>1</CategoryID>
<UnitPrice>19</UnitPrice>
</Products>
...
<Suppliers>
<SupplierID>1</SupplierID>
<CompanyName>EXOTIC LIQUIDS</CompanyName>
<ContactName>Charlotte Cooper</ContactName>
<ContactTitle>Purchasing Manager</ContactTitle>
<Address>49 Gilbert St.</Address>
<City>London</City>
<PostalCode>EC1 4SD</PostalCode>
<Country>UK</Country>
<Phone>(171) 555-2222</Phone>
</Suppliers>
<Suppliers>
<SupplierID>2</SupplierID>
<CompanyName>New Orleans Cajun Delights</CompanyName>
<ContactName>Shelley Burke</ContactName>
<ContactTitle>Order Administrator</ContactTitle>
<Address>P.O. Box 78934</Address>
<City>New Orleans</City>
<Region>LA</Region>
<PostalCode>70117</PostalCode>
<Country>USA</Country>
<Phone>(100) 555-4822</Phone>
<HomePage>#CAJUN.HTM#</HomePage>
</Suppliers>
...
</Products>
```

## Controlling the Structure of the XML File

Listing 4.6 is a valid XML file that contains no schema information and it's *flat* (all its nodes are listed on the same level). Each row is mapped to an XML element and each field of the row is mapped to a subelement. The opposite of a flat XML document is a *nested* document, in which child rows are child elements of their parent elements. The default XML description of the data generated by the DataSet may not be what you need. You can control the format of the XML file by setting a few properties. Let's start by converting the IDs from XML elements to XML attributes. The ProductID field is inserted into the file as an element:

```
<ProductID>1</ProductID>
```

You can turn that into an attribute of the Products table, so that each product will be saved to the file as follows:

```
<Products ProductID="17">
<ProductName>Alice Mutton</ProductName>
```

```
<SupplierID>7</SupplierID>
<CategoryID>6</CategoryID>
<UnitPrice>39</UnitPrice>
</Products>
```

To specify that a column be saved as attribute rather than as an element in the XML file, set the ColumnMapping of the appropriate column to `MappingType.Attribute`, as shown in the following statements:

```
Products1.Products.ProductIDColumn.ColumnMapping = _
                    MappingType.Attribute
Products1.Suppliers.SupplierIDColumn.ColumnMapping = _
                    MappingType.Attribute
Products1.Categories.CategoryIDColumn.ColumnMapping = _
                    MappingType.Attribute
```

The MappingType enumeration has a few more members, which are `Element`, `Hidden`, and `SimpleContent`. The statements that affect the generation of the XML code should be executed before calling the WriteXml method.

You can also create nested XML files, where the rows of child tables appear under the matching rows of their parent table. To generate nested XML files, set the Nested property of the appropriate relation to True, as in the following statement:

```
Products1.Relations("CategoriesProducts").Nested = True
```

If you insert this statement before the call to the WriteXml method, the products will be listed in the XML file under their respective categories. Here's a small section of the XML file with the products nested under their categories:

```
<Categories CategoryID="1">
  <CategoryName>Beverages</CategoryName>
  <Description>Soft drinks, coffees, teas, beers,
              and ales</Description>
    <Products ProductID="1">
      <ProductName>Chai</ProductName>
      <SupplierID>1</SupplierID>
      <CategoryID>1</CategoryID>
      <UnitPrice>18</UnitPrice>
    </Products>
    <Products ProductID="2">
      <ProductName>Chang</ProductName>
      <SupplierID>1</SupplierID>
      <CategoryID>1</CategoryID>
      <UnitPrice>19</UnitPrice>
    </Products>
    <Products ProductID="24">
      <ProductName>Guaraná Fantástica</ProductName>
```

```
    <SupplierID>10</SupplierID>
    <CategoryID>1</CategoryID>
    <UnitPrice>4.5</UnitPrice>
</Products>
```

When you create nested relations, you can't nest the same child table under two parent tables. The Products table is the child table in both relations of the schema (the CategoriesProducts and SuppliersProducts relations). However, when you generate the XML file, you must choose the table under which you want the products to appear. You can list the products under either parent table but not under both tables.

## Creating and Using XML Schemas

The main advantage of XML over other universal data exchange formats is that XML isn't just about data; it also describes the structure of the data and their relations, if any. The XML examples you've seen so far in this chapter contain data. XML as a data-exchange format is straightforward. Each data item is embedded in a special delimiter (an XML tag). In this section, we're going to create a new DataSet by specifying its schema. We're not going to write XML code to describe the schema of the DataSet; we'll use the visual tools of the IDE, but you can look at the XML code they will generate. You can also specify the XML schema in code, if you are up to it. This process is straightforward in principle, but it's tedious and very difficult to get the schema right without a visual tool.

The DataSet will not be associated with any data source; it will exist on its own. We'll also provide a simple user interface for populating and persisting the DataSet. The form of the sample project (the XMLDataSet project) is shown in Figure 4.5.

**FIGURE 4.5:**

Binding a DataGrid to a custom DataSet

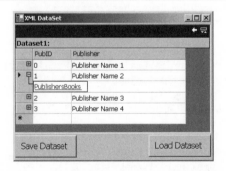

Start a new Windows application and rename it XMLDataSet. Right-click the project's name in the Solution Explorer and select Add ➤ Add New Item from the context menu. When the Add New Item dialog box appears, click the DataSet Template and accept the default name, Dataset1.xsd (or enter another name). A new item will be added to the project, the Dataset1.xsd item. Double-click the new item's name in the Solution Explorer to open it in Design mode.

Initially, you will see an empty design surface, because the DataSet has no schema. We'll create a very simple schema for storing books and publishers. You already know how to do this with SQL Server's Enterprise Manager, but now you'll use the XML tools of the IDE. The process is very similar.

Open the Toolbox, select the Element item, and drop two instances of it onto the design surface. The two elements correspond to the DataSet's tables. Rename one of the elements Books and the other one Publishers. Then select the boxes below the first element's name, enter the names of the columns, and select each column's type from the drop-down list next to it. The columns are subelements of their corresponding elements. The following table shows the names of the columns and their types for the Books element:

| Column | Type |
| --- | --- |
| BookID | Int |
| Title | String |
| PubID | Int |

This table shows the names of the columns and their types for the Publishers element:

| Column | Type |
| --- | --- |
| PubID | Int |
| Publisher | String |

Obviously, when we'll build a DataSet based on this schema, the Books table will store book data and the Publishers table will store publisher data. The two tables will be related to one another through the PubID field. To establish the relation, select the Relation item from the Toolbox and drop an instance of it onto the Publishers element and you'll see the Edit Relation dialog box. Set up the relation's properties (this dialog box was discussed in the previous chapter) and close the dialog box. The complete schema should look like the one shown in Figure 4.6.

**FIGURE 4.6:**

Creating a simple XML schema from scratch

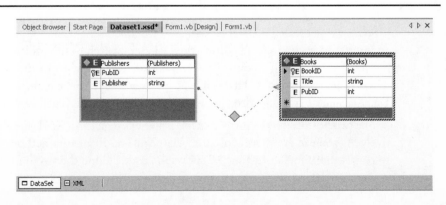

If you click the XML tab on the Designer, you'll see the XML description of the schema you just created. Readers familiar with XML can edit the schema, but it's much simpler to edit the schema with the visual tools of the Designer.

What you see on the Designer is the schema of a DataSet. To create an actual DataSet based on this schema, open the Toolbox, and from the Data tab, select the DataSet component and drop it on the form. To see the regular Toolbox, you must first switch to the project's form because the current Toolbox contains the components you can place on the DataSet's Schema Designer. The Add DataSet dialog box will appear (see Figure 4.7), prompting you to select one of the existing DataSets. These are the typed DataSets, because their schema is known at design time. Because the DataSet1 is the only typed DataSet in the project, its name is also suggested. Click OK to close the dialog box and create the DataSet.

**FIGURE 4.7:**

The Add DataSet
dialog box

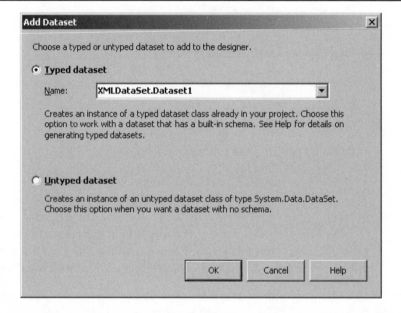

So far we've created a DataSet with a well-defined schema and no data. We'll now create an interface for viewing and editing the DataSet. Switch to the project's form and place an instance of the DataGrid control and two buttons on it (it will look like the form in Figure 4.5). Then locate the control's DataSource property and set it to the name of the DataSet (select the DataSet's name from the drop-down list with the available typed DataSet names).

The two buttons on the form save the DataSet's data to an XML file and load it back respectively. As you can guess, we'll use the WriteXml and ReadXml methods of the DataSet object to persist the DataSet. Listing 4.7 shows the code behind the two buttons.

---

**Listing 4.7**         **Persisting a DataSet to an XML File**

```
Private Sub bttnSave_Click(ByVal sender As System.Object, _
                           ByVal e As System.EventArgs) _
                           Handles bttnSave.Click
    Dataset11.WriteXml("c:\Books.xml")
End Sub

Private Sub bttnLoad_Click(ByVal sender As System.Object, _
                           ByVal e As System.EventArgs) _
                           Handles bttnLoad.Click
    Dataset11.Clear()
    Dataset11.ReadXml("c:\books.xml")
End Sub
```

---

Run the application, add some data to the DataGrid control, and save the edited data by clicking the Save button. You can load the saved data in a later session, edit it further, and persist it again to a local file. As you can see, it's quite possible to use the functionality of DataSets in your code without associating them with a data source. If you need to exchange data frequently with a remote system (be it a Windows system or not), you can even agree on the schema and then use it to exchange DataSets by transmitting the XML file. The remote system may not even use DataSets; as long as it can understand (or produce) XML files, you can easily share data with the remote system.

You can also open the XML generated by the XMLDataSet application and edit it with Notepad or XML Notepad (a text editor optimized for editing XML files, which you can download from http://msdn.microsoft.com). To download the XML Notepad go to this site and search for "XML Notepad." If the data doesn't violate the schema, you can open the edited file with the XMLDataSet application and view your edits on the DataGrid control.

If you want to share a schema with another application running on a remote computer, use the WriteXmlSchema method. The remote application should be able to create XML files based on this schema, and your application can load them into a DataSet for further processing. The remote computer need not be a Windows system. Any application that understands XML and can generate XML data files that comply with the specified schema will be able to exchange data with your Windows application.

For a complete exposition of schemas, see *XML Schemas* by Chelsea Valentine, Lucinda Dykes, and Ed Tittel (Sybex, 2002).

## DataSets Exposed

In this section, we're going to take a closer look to the DataSet object and explore how it maintains its data. As you already know, the DataSet contains the original data as well as information about the changes made to its data by the client application. As a result, you can undo any change at any time. The DataSet maintains two versions of each row in each table: the current version and the original version. The *current version* of the row contains the current values of the row's fields (the field values after editing). The *original version* of the row contains the values read from the database. When you're implementing optimistic concurrency, both versions of the row are used to build the appropriate SQL statements to update the underlying tables, as explained in the previous chapter. Every time you edit a line, a current version of that line is created (or updated), and the original one remains unchanged. When you add a line, a current version without a matching original version is created. The opposite is true for deleted lines: they have no current version, but there's a matching original version of the deleted row.

The versions of the rows are maintained automatically by the DataSet, but you can manipulate them to an extent through the AcceptChanges and RejectChanges methods. These two methods accept and reject the changes, respectively. The AcceptChanges method overwrites the original version of each row with the current version and physically removes the deleted rows from the DataSet. This method, in effect, makes a new DataSet, as if it were just read from the data source. However, the DataSet's rows will no longer match the rows of the underlying table in the database. Notice that after accepting the changes in your DataSet, you can no longer count on optimistic concurrency to update the underlying data source.

The RejectChanges method does the opposite: it copies the original version of each row to the current version and physically removes the new lines. In effect, it resets the DataSet to the state it was in when it was first read from the database or the last time you called the AcceptChanges method. You can use the RejectChanges method to undo all the changes in the DataSet or to selectively undo the changes in specific tables, or even specific rows. Both the AcceptChanges and RejectChanges methods apply to DataSet, DataTable, and DataRow objects, so you can accept the changes, or undo them, at any level.

## Accepting and Rejecting Changes

We'd like to point out here that you should be careful when calling the AcceptChanges method. If you don't understand the implications, you shouldn't call it at all, because you may discard information that's necessary to update the data source. The only time you can safely call the AcceptChanges method is after successfully updating the data source and only if the DataSet contains no errors. The AcceptChanges method will modify the DataSet and you'll end up with a new DataSet that reflects the current state of the underlying table(s) in the database. You'd get the same DataSet if you repopulate it after a successful update operation, with one exception: any rows added to the table(s) by other users that might qualify for your DataSet will be copied to the DataSet. If you call the AcceptChanges method, these rows will not be copied into the DataSet, obviously.

Let's say you've created a DataSet with two tables that contain all the customers and suppliers from Germany. You edit the two tables, update the underlying tables with the Update method, and then call the AcceptChanges method. The rows in the DataSet's tables are the same as the rows in the underlying tables. If another user added another German supplier, however, this row will be missing from the application's DataSet. To include the new row, you must repopulate the DataSet after committing the changes to the data source.

So, is there a good reason to call the AcceptChanges method? In general, you should avoid this method. Theoretically, you can synchronize a DataSet at the client with the underlying table without a trip to the server. But as we just demonstrated, the synchronization isn't perfect. The single argument in favor of the AcceptChanges method is that the DataSet may be too large and populating it frequently can cause delays and increase network traffic. It's a valid argument, but more often than not an excessively large DataSet indicates serious design flaws. The DataSet is convenient for storing and manipulating data at the client, but it's not a license to download a large portion of the database to the client. DataSets shouldn't be very large. Don't download the entire Customers table to the client every time the user needs to look up a phone number or change an address. Smaller DataSets are easier to update, and you can afford to update them frequently. On the other hand, if you're using large DataSets, chances are that you'll postpone updating them. The more changes in the DataSet, the more update problems you will run into.

---

**WARNING**     The AcceptChanges method doesn't update the data source. Instead, it marks the changes as submitted. The RejectChanges method, on the other hand, cancels all changes made to the DataSet and brings it back to the state it was in when you created it or the last time you called the AcceptChanges method.

If your application needs to send a copy of the DataSet to a remote computer, you can call the AcceptChanges method to reduce the size of the document that will be transferred. Besides, the information about the changes in the DataSet is of no practical value to the remote computer if it can't access the database where the data originated.

## Row Versions

Rows have two more versions, the default version and the proposed version. The *default version* contains the default values of the fields in a row as they're defined in the data source. The *proposed version* is a temporary one, and it's available between the time you start editing a row and the time you're done editing it. We use this version in certain events to validate the fields' values, as you'll see in the following chapter.

To summarize, a DataRow can have one of the versions shown in Table 4.2 at any one time.

**TABLE 4.2:** The DataRowVersion Enumeration

| Member | Description |
|---|---|
| Current | This version consists of the current values of the fields in the DataSet. As soon as you edit a row, its current version is no longer the same as the original version. |
| Default | This version consists of the default values of the fields as specified in the design of the database. The default version of a row doesn't change. |
| Original | This version consists of the original values of the fields as they were read from the database. |
| Proposed | This version consists of the proposed values of the fields. |

Row versions can't be manipulated directly; they're maintained by the DataSet, and you can only read a specific version of a row if it exists. If you attempt to read a version that doesn't exist, an exception will be thrown. Make sure a specific version exists before you attempt to read it. Never try to read the original version of a row that was added to the DataSet because new rows have no original version, only a current version. To read a specific version of a field's value, use an overloaded form of the Row.Item property, which accepts two arguments: the usual index of the field and a member of the DataRowVersion enumeration specifying the version you want to read. The following statements return the original values of the first and second fields of the DataRow represented by the *DR* variable:

```
DR.Item(0, DataRowVersion.Original).ToString
DR.Item(1, DataRowVersion.Original).ToString
```

To retrieve the current versions of the same two rows, use the following statements:

```
DR.Item(0, DataRowVersion.Current).ToString
DR.Item(1, DataRowVersion.Current).ToString
```

## Row States

In addition to a version, rows have a state too. The RowState property of the DataRow object indicates the state of a specific row and its value is one of the members of the DataRowState enumeration, listed in Table 4.3.

**TABLE 4.3:** The DataRowState Enumeration

| Member | Description |
|---|---|
| Added | The row has been added to a table since the table was read or since the last time the AcceptChanges method was called. This row has a current version but no original version. |

*Continued on next page*

**TABLE 4.3 CONTINUED:** The DataRowState Enumeration

| Member | Description |
|---|---|
| Deleted | The row was deleted. Deleted rows remain in the DataSet and have an original version but no current version. |
| Detached | This is the state of a DataRow that has been created but hasn't been added to the DataRow collection of a table yet. |
| Modified | The row has been edited since it was read or since the last time the AcceptChanges method was called. |
| Unchanged | The row hasn't been edited since it was read or since the AcceptChanges was last called. |

If a row's RowState property is DataRowState.Modified, it means that the row has been edited and therefore it has both an original and a current version. If the RowState property is DataRowState.Added, the corresponding row has only a current version but no original version.

This is a good point at which to experiment a little with the versions of a DataSet's rows. Open the ADOTests projects and add a new button, the Edit DataSet button (its name is bttnDatasetChanges). Add the following statements to populate the Products1 DataSet and then call the WriteXml method to persist the DataSet to an XML file:

```
DASuppliers.Fill(Products1, "Suppliers")
DACategories.Fill(Products1, "Categories")
DAProducts.Fill(Products1, "Products")
Products1.WriteXml("c:\OriginalDataset.xml")
```

If you double-click the name of the file OriginalDataset.xml, it will open in Internet Explorer and you'll see all the products and their categories and suppliers. The following is a short segment of the OriginalDataset.xml file:

```
<?xml version="1.0" standalone="yes"?>
<Products xmlns="http://www.tempuri.org/Products.xsd">
  <Categories>
    <CategoryID>1</CategoryID>
    <CategoryName>Beverages</CategoryName>
    <Description>Soft drinks, coffees,
                         teas, beers, and ales
            </Description>
  </Categories>
  <Categories>
    <CategoryID>2</CategoryID>
    <CategoryName>Condiments</CategoryName>
    <Description>Sweet and savory sauces, relishes,
            spreads, and seasonings
    </Description>
  </Categories>
  ...
```

```
<Products>
  <ProductID>30</ProductID>
  <ProductName>Nord-Ost Matjeshering</ProductName>
  <SupplierID>13</SupplierID>
  <CategoryID>8</CategoryID>
  <UnitPrice>25.89</UnitPrice>
</Products>
<Products>
  <ProductID>31</ProductID>
  <ProductName>Gorgonzola Telino</ProductName>
  <SupplierID>14</SupplierID>
  <CategoryID>4</CategoryID>
  <UnitPrice>12.5</UnitPrice>
</Products>
  ...
<Suppliers>
  <SupplierID>1</SupplierID>
  <CompanyName>Exotic Liquids</CompanyName>
  <ContactName>Charlotte Cooper</ContactName>
  <ContactTitle>Purchasing Manager</ContactTitle>
  <Address>49 Gilbert St.</Address>
  <City>London</City>
  <PostalCode>EC1 4SD</PostalCode>
  <Country>UK</Country>
  <Phone>(171) 555-2222</Phone>
</Suppliers>
<Suppliers>
  <SupplierID>2</SupplierID>
  <CompanyName>New Orleans Cajun Delights</CompanyName>
  <ContactName>Shelley Burke</ContactName>
  <ContactTitle>Order Administrator</ContactTitle>
  <Address>P.O. Box 78934</Address>
  <City>New Orleans</City>
  <Region>LA</Region>
  <PostalCode>70117</PostalCode>
  <Country>USA</Country>
  <Phone>(100) 555-4822</Phone>
  <HomePage>#CAJUN.HTM#</HomePage>
</Suppliers>
```

The three tables in the DataSet are not related because we haven't established any relations. However, the information exists in the XML document and you can find each product's category or supplier by retrieving the appropriate element of the XML document. If you're familiar with the System.Xml class of the .NET Framework, you can manipulate the XML document you generated with the WriteXml method. However, as a developer, you're accustomed to using the relational rather the hierarchical view of the data, and in this chapter we'll focus on the members of the DataSet object.

Next, enter a few statements to edit selected rows of all three tables. These statements are shown in Listing 4.8.

**Listing 4.8          Editing the DataSet's Tables**

```
Dim newName As String
newName = InputBox("Enter a new company name " & _
            "for the first supplier", "Data Editing", _
            Products1.Suppliers.Rows(0).Item _
                ("CompanyName").ToString.ToUpper)
Products1.Suppliers(0).CompanyName = newName
newName = InputBox("Enter a new name for the " & _
            "following product ", "DataSet Editing", _
            Products1.Products.Rows(10).Item _
                ("ProductName").ToString.ToUpper)
Products1.Products(10).ProductName = newName
Products1.Products(11).UnitPrice = _
                Products1.Products(11).UnitPrice + 2
newName = InputBox("Enter a new name for " & _
            "the following category ", "DataSet Editing", _
            Products1.Categories.Rows(2).Item _
                ("CategoryName").ToString.ToUpper)
Products1.Categories(2).CategoryName = newName

Dim SupplierRow As DataRow = Products1.Suppliers.NewRow
SupplierRow("CompanyName") = "New Company"
SupplierRow("ContactName") = "New Contact"
SupplierRow("ContactTitle") = "New Contact's Title"
SupplierRow("Address") = "New Address"
SupplierRow("City") = "New City"
SupplierRow("Country") = "New Country"
SupplierRow("Phone") = "555.1111"
Products1.Suppliers.Rows.Add(SupplierRow)
```

The code prompts the user to enter a new name for the first supplier and it suggests the same name in uppercase letters (so that you can easily undo the edits to the database). It also changes the ProductName field of the 11th row in the Products table as well as the price of the 12th row in the Products table. Then it changes the name of the 3rd row in the Categories table (again, it prompts the user with the current setting in uppercase letters). Finally, it creates a new supplier and adds it to the Suppliers DataTable.

If you execute these statements, the DataSet will be updated, but the underlying tables won't be. Let's save the DataSet to an XML file and explore its contents. The following statement calls the WriteXml method to write the contents of the DataSet to another XML file, the EditedDataset.xml file. Notice the second argument to the WriteXml method; it instructs the method to save not only the current values but also the differences between the original and edited values:

```
Products1.WriteXml("c:\EditedDataset.xml", _
                   System.Data.XmlWriteMode.DiffGram)
```

The row that corresponds to the Confections category in the Categories table was saved as follows:

```
<Categories diffgr:id="Categories3" msdata:rowOrder="2"
            diffgr:hasChanges="modified">
    <CategoryID>3</CategoryID>
    <CategoryName>CONFECTIONS</CategoryName>
    <Description>Desserts, candies, and
                 sweet breads</Description>
</Categories>
```

The category's name was changed to uppercase (or whatever string you supplied when the program prompted you to enter a new name for the category). Notice that this element is marked with the modified keyword. Near the end of the XML file, you'll see a section called diffgram, which contains the following elements:

```
<diffgr:before>
  <Categories diffgr:id="Categories3" msdata:rowOrder="2"
              xmlns="http://www.tempuri.org/Products.xsd">
    <CategoryID>3</CategoryID>
    <CategoryName>Confections</CategoryName>
    <Description>Desserts, candies,
                 and sweet breads</Description>
  </Categories>
  <Products diffgr:id="Products11" msdata:rowOrder="10"
            xmlns=http://www.tempuri.org/Products.xsd">
    <ProductID>11</ProductID>
    <ProductName>Queso Cabrales</ProductName>
    <SupplierID>5</SupplierID>
    <CategoryID>4</CategoryID>
    <UnitPrice>21</UnitPrice>
  </Products>
  <Products diffgr:id="Products12" msdata:rowOrder="11"
            xmlns="http://www.tempuri.org/Products.xsd">
    <ProductID>12</ProductID>
    <ProductName>Queso Manchego La Pastora</ProductName>
    <SupplierID>5</SupplierID>
    <CategoryID>4</CategoryID>
    <UnitPrice>50</UnitPrice>
  </Products>
  <Suppliers diffgr:id="Suppliers1" msdata:rowOrder="0"
             xmlns="http://www.tempuri.org/Products.xsd">
```

```
        <SupplierID>1</SupplierID>
        <CompanyName>Exotic Liquids</CompanyName>
        <ContactName>Charlotte Cooper</ContactName>
        <ContactTitle>Purchasing Manager</ContactTitle>
        <Address>49 Gilbert St.</Address>
        <City>London</City>
        <PostalCode>EC1 4SD</PostalCode>
        <Country>UK</Country>
        <Phone>(171) 555-2222</Phone>
    </Suppliers>
    </diffgr:before>
 </diffgr:diffgram>
```

These are the original versions of the rows we've edited; they're marked with the `before` attribute. The first element is the original version of the Confections category. As you can see, the DataSet maintains information about the current and original versions of its tables' rows and uses this information to update the underlying tables in the database. If you locate the new row we added to the Suppliers table, you'll see that it's marked as inserted:

```
<Suppliers diffgr:id="Suppliers30" msdata:rowOrder="29"
diffgr:hasChanges="inserted">
    <SupplierID>30</SupplierID>
    <CompanyName>New Company</CompanyName>
    <ContactName>New Contact</ContactName>
    <ContactTitle>New Contact's Title</ContactTitle>
    <Address>New Address</Address>
    <City>New City</City>
    <Country>New Country</Country>
    <Phone>1111111</Phone>
</Suppliers>
```

The DataSet knows how to retrieve the current and original versions of each row as well as how to locate deleted and inserted lines. All the information is in the XML document that describes the DataSet. Of course, the data is not stored in the DataSet in XML format. It's stored in a proprietary format, but the DataSet can easily convert it to an XmlDataDocument. As a developer, you can access the data and perform all kinds of operations on it through the members of the `System.XmlDataDocument` class. However, you need not get deep into XML in order to understand the structure of DataSets and how to manipulate them. As a developer, you're accustomed to the relational view of the data and the DataSet provides numerous methods for manipulating its contents.

Not only can you persist a DataSet to an XML document, you can also re-create the original DataSet from the XML document. The ReadXml method of the DataSet reads an XML file and creates a DataSet based on the schema described by the file. If no schema information is present, the DataSet will infer the schema from the data.

## Viewing Row Versions and States

To demonstrate the topics discussed so far, we'll open the edited DataSet we just persisted to the EditedDataSet.xml file, extract the modified rows of the three tables, and then print their versions. We'll print the current and original versions of each of the edited rows.

Add another button to the ADOTests project's main form, the Show Row Versions button, and then enter the statements of Listing 4.9 to the button's Click event handler. The code in this event handler reads the edited DataSet persisted by the Edit DataSet button. Then it retrieves the changes in each table with the GetChanges method. Notice that the argument passed to the GetChanges method requests the new, deleted, and edited rows. The modified rows of each table are returned into a new DataTable: the EditedProducts DataTable for the modified rows of the Products table, the EditedCategories DataTable for the modified rows of the Categories table, and so on.

---

**Listing 4.9**     **Printing the Versions of the Modified Rows**

```
Private Sub bttnVersions_Click( _
                ByVal sender As System.Object, _
                ByVal e As System.EventArgs) _
                Handles bttnVersions.Click

Products1.ReadXml("c:\EditedDataset.xml")

Dim EditedProducts As DataTable = _
        Products1.Tables("Products").GetChanges( _
                    DataRowState.Added Or _
                    DataRowState.Deleted Or _
                    DataRowState.Modified)
Dim EditedCategories As DataTable = _
        Products1.Tables("Categories").GetChanges( _
                    DataRowState.Added Or _
                    DataRowState.Deleted Or _
                    DataRowState.Modified)
Dim EditedSuppliers As DataTable = _
        Products1.Tables("Suppliers").GetChanges( _
                    DataRowState.Added Or _
                    DataRowState.Deleted Or _
                    DataRowState.Modified)
Console.WriteLine("There are " & _
            EditedProducts.Rows.Count.ToString & _
            " edited rows in the Products table")
Dim i As Integer
For i = 0 To EditedProducts.Rows.Count - 1
    Console.WriteLine( _
                EditedProducts.Rows(i).RowState.ToString)
    Console.Write("    ORIGINAL ROW   ")
    ShowOriginalValues(EditedProducts.Rows(i))
    Console.WriteLine()
```

```
        Console.Write("      EDITED ROW    ")
        ShowCurrentValues(EditedProducts.Rows(i))
    Next
        Console.WriteLine("There are " & _
                    EditedCategories.Rows.Count.ToString & _
                    " edited rows in the Categories table")
    For i = 0 To EditedCategories.Rows.Count - 1
        Console.WriteLine( _
                    EditedCategories.Rows(i).RowState.ToString)
        Console.Write("     ORIGINAL ROW    ")
        ShowOriginalValues(EditedCategories.Rows(i))
        Console.WriteLine()
        Console.Write("      EDITED ROW    ")
        ShowCurrentValues(EditedCategories.Rows(i))
        Console.WriteLine()
    Next

    Console.WriteLine("There are " & _
                EditedSuppliers.Rows.Count.ToString & _
                " edited rows in the Suppliers table")
    For i = 0 To EditedSuppliers.Rows.Count - 1
        Console.WriteLine( _
                    EditedSuppliers.Rows(i).RowState.ToString)
        Console.Write("     ORIGINAL ROW    ")
        ShowOriginalValues(EditedSuppliers.Rows(i))
        Console.WriteLine()
        Console.Write("      EDITED ROW    ")
        ShowCurrentValues(EditedSuppliers.Rows(i))
        Console.WriteLine()
    Next
```

The argument of the GetChanges method is a member of the DataRowState enumeration and it specifies what type of changes we're interested in. (The members of the DataRowState enumeration are shown in Table 4.3.) In our sample code, we retrieve the inserted, edited, and deleted rows, so the argument to the GetChanges method combines three members with the OR operator.

The three For…Next loops iterate through the rows of each one of the DataTable objects with the modified rows, print the type of change (whether the row was edited, inserted, or deleted), and then print the row's original and current versions. The ShowOriginalValues() and ShowCurrentValues() subroutines accept a DataRow as argument and print the corresponding values of the row's fields (see Listing 4.10).

**Listing 4.10**     **The *ShowOriginalValues()* and *ShowCurrentValues()* Subroutines**

```
Private Sub ShowOriginalValues(ByVal DR As DataRow)
    If DR.HasVersion(DataRowVersion.Original) Then
        Dim i As Integer
```

```
        For i = 0 To DR.Table.Columns.Count - 1
            Console.Write( _
                    "[" & DR.Item(i, _
                    DataRowVersion.Original).ToString & "]")
        Next
    End If
End Sub

Private Sub ShowCurrentValues(ByVal DR As DataRow)
    If DR.HasVersion(DataRowVersion.Current) Then
        Dim i As Integer
        For i = 0 To DR.Table.Columns.Count - 1
            Console.Write( _
                    "[" & DR.Item(i, _
                    DataRowVersion.Current).ToString & "]")
        Next
    End If
End Sub
```

Notice that the code makes sure that a specific row version exists before attempting to access it. If a row has no current or original version, the code skips it. If you attempt to access the original version of a row that was added to its DataTable or the current version of a row that was deleted, a runtime exception will be thrown.

Here's what the output generated by the Show Row Versions button looks like. We have aligned the various field values manually, set some lines in bold, and have omitted several of the fields to make the output appear nicer on the printed page:

```
There are 4 edited rows in the Products table
Modified
    ORIGINAL ROW    [11][Queso Cabrales][5][4][21]
    EDITED ROW      [11][QUESO CABRALES][5][4][21]
Modified
    ORIGINAL ROW    [12][Queso Manchego La Pastora][5][4][70]
    EDITED ROW      [12][Queso Manchego La Pastora][5][4][72]
Deleted
    ORIGINAL ROW    [79][New Product][47][3][9.95]
    EDITED ROW
Added
    ORIGINAL ROW
    EDITED ROW      [84][New Product][12][3][9.95]

There is 1 edited row in the Categories table
Modified
    ORIGINAL ROW    [3][Confections]
                    [Desserts, candies, and sweet breads]
    EDITED ROW      [3][CONFECTIONS NEW]
                    [Desserts, candies, and sweet breads]
```

```
There are 2 edited rows in the Suppliers table
Modified
   ORIGINAL ROW    [1][Exotic Liquids]
                   [Charlotte Cooper][Purchasing Manager]
                   [49 Gilbert St.][London][]
                   [EC1 4SD][UK][(171) 555-2222][][]
   EDITED ROW      [1][EXOTIC LIQUIDS]
                   [Charlotte Cooper][Purchasing Manager]
                   [49 Gilbert St.][London][]
                   [EC1 4SD][UK][(171) 555-2222][][]
Added
   ORIGINAL ROW
   EDITED ROW      [53][New Company][New Contact]
                   [New Contact's Title][New Address]
                   [New City][][][New Country][123456789][][]
```

As you can see, the DataSet maintains the original values of the rows read from the database along with the current values. It also knows which rows were edited, which rows were added to each DataTable, and which rows were deleted from each DataTable. This information is crucial for implementing optimistic concurrency, as discussed in the previous chapter. If you want to remove a row from a DataTable and not maintain any information about it, use the Remove method.

## Updating the Data Source

To update the data source (in other words, commit the changes made to the DataSet to the underlying database tables), you must execute the appropriate UPDATE, INSERT, and DELETE statements through a Command object. But how do you know which rows have changed and in what ways? First, you must figure out which rows have been edited, which rows were added, and which rows were deleted. Then you can execute the appropriate statement for each one or call the appropriate stored procedure.

If you have used data adapters to populate your DataSet, you can call each DataAdapter object's Update method. This method will commit the changes to the database and will report any errors. The DataAdapter object's Update method is almost trivial. Each table in the DataSet has its associated DataAdapter object, and all you have to do is call each DataAdapter object's Update method, passing the name of the DataSet that contains the corresponding table as argument. The order in which the tables are updated can be crucial, just as the order in which you load the DataSet is. If you've edited a few rows in all tables, you can probably update the tables in any order. If you've added new rows, however, you must update first the tables with the primary keys, then the tables with the foreign keys.

As long as the rows don't violate the constraints of the database, the changes will be committed to the database. If some rows fail to update the database, you can retrieve them with the GetErrors method and handle them individually. The DataTable object provides the HasErrors property, which returns a Boolean value, indicating whether the specific table contains rows in error. To retrieve the rows in error, you can use the GetErrors method, which returns an array of DataRow objects: the table's rows that are in error. Once you've created an array with the rows in error, you can extract information about each error by examining the DataRow object's RowError property. This property is a string with the description of the error.

You can also set the RowError property from within your code. After you do so, the corresponding DataTable and DataSet objects' HasErrors property is automatically set to True. Normally, we don't set the RowError property from within our code when we use DataAdapters. This property is set automatically when we attempt to commit the changes to the data source. If you don't use DataAdapters object to update the data source, then you'll have to set this property from within your code.

The last issue concerning updates is how to handle the errors. It all depends on the nature of the application. In many situations, it suffices to turn off optimistic concurrency and use the last-write-wins scenario. Even so, some rows may fail to update the data source. If a user removes from its table one of the rows in the client DataSet, the DataAdapter will not find a row to update. A row with the same key doesn't exist in the DataSet and there's nothing to update. When this happens, you should probably warn the user and give them a chance to add the row. You can remove this row from the DataSet with the Remove method and a new row with the same field values (except for the unique ID field, of course) to the DataSet. The DataAdapter will detect the presence of a new row in the DataSet and insert it in the appropriate table. Alternatively, you can set up a Command object to insert the row in its table as a new row. You must also remove it from the DataSet because the DataAdapter will keep attempting to update the underlying table.

To see how the DataAdapter handles optimistic concurrency, experiment a little with editing a DataSet. Run the ADOTests project and click the Edit DataSet button. While the program prompts you to enter the new value of the Exotic Liquids category, switch to SQL Server Enterprise Manager, open the Categories table, and change the category's name to Confections NEW. This is equivalent to changing the database from within another instance of the same application or another client application. The data read into the DataSet is no longer the same as the data in the Categories table and the update operation should fail. Switch to the ADOTests project, accept the new value of the category, and proceed.

When the Update method of the DACategories is executed, the following exception will be raised:

```
Concurrency violation: the UpdateCommand affected 0 records.
```

If you want to implement the last-write-wins scenario with this project, you must reconfigure the data adapters as follows. Select each of the DataAdapter objects on the form and click the Configure Data Adapter link in the Property Browser. When the Data Adapter Configuration Wizard appears, click Next several times to get to the Generate the SQL Statements screen. On this screen, click the Advanced Options button and you'll see the Advanced SQL Generation Options dialog box. On this dialog box, clear the Use Optimistic Concurrency box. This action tells the wizard to generate different UPDATE and DELETE statements that identify the row to be edited (or deleted) by its primary key only. The UPDATE statement that implements optimistic concurrency is as follows:

```
UPDATE    Categories SET CategoryName = @CategoryName,
          Description = @Description
WHERE     (CategoryID = @Original_CategoryID) AND
          (CategoryName = @Original_CategoryName);
SELECT    CategoryID, CategoryName, Description _
FROM      Categories
WHERE     (CategoryID = @CategoryID)
```

Here is the same statement without optimistic concurrency:

```
UPDATE    Categories SET CategoryName = @CategoryName,
          Description = @Description
WHERE     (CategoryID = @Original_CategoryID)
SELECT    CategoryID, CategoryName, Description
FROM      Categories
WHERE     (CategoryID = @CategoryID)
```

The last option on the Advanced SQL Generation Options dialog box controls the generation of the SELECT statement following the UPDATE and INSERT statements. If you clear this option, the SELECT statement will be omitted. Refreshing the DataSet is generally a good idea because it allows your client application to retrieve identity values. The ProductID column in the Products table, for example, is an identity column: it gets a value every time a new row is inserted, and this value can't be specified by the client application. When a new row is added to the Products table in the DataSet, a new identity value is assigned to the ProductID field automatically, but this value may already be taken when the data is submitted to the server. SQL Server will assign to each new row a new identity value, which may not be the same as the value assigned by the DataSet. The SELECT statement reads the version of the row that was saved to the DataTable, and you can use this value in your code for establishing foreign key relations.

When a primary key value changes, you must make sure that all related rows are also updated to reflect the changes. You can do so by setting the UpdateRule of all relationships in your DataSet to UpdateRule.Cascade. This rule causes the DataSet to propagate the changes made to the primary key to the matching rows of the related tables. Related rows will retain their relations and the database's integrity won't be violated when you submit the changes to the database.

To summarize, when updating the data source by submitting one or more tables with the DataTable object's Update method, you may run into two types of problems. The simpler update problems are those that you can prevent with proper validation. A negative price or a new supplier without a company name are examples of errors that can be caught at the client. If you apply proper validation using all the constraints of the database, it's possible to eliminate problems of this type.

There's another category of update problems, which you can't prevent from within your code. If one instance of your client application attempts to update a row that has been removed by another instance of the same application, the update operation will fail. The update operation will also fail if another user has removed one of the categories used by one or more product rows in the DataSet. These problems can't be caught at the client. Only the database will detect them and then raise the appropriate error.

To handle these problems, you'll most likely have to interact with the user. You can minimize these problems by being very careful about the rights of the various users or the operations they can perform. Not every client application should be able to delete rows. Write an auxiliary maintenance application (which will most likely run at midnight) that cleans up the tables in your database. Instead of allowing many users to delete rows from the Categories tables, write a small utility that detects categories that are not referenced by any product (orphaned rows) and deletes them.

What if a user has edited a product that was removed from the database by another user in the meantime? This product isn't referenced by any orders (otherwise, no one would be able to remove it). So, it's safe to reject the update operation if the underlying row is missing. The worst thing that can happen is that a user may have to reenter the same product. Just display a warning to the effect that the program couldn't update the specific row and continue.

However, there's a fine point in updating rows with identity columns. The DataSet assigns new values to identity columns as new rows are inserted into its tables. An identity column, however, gets its final value when it's inserted into its underlying table. If other users have added new rows to the corresponding tables, then the values assigned by the DataSet will conflict with the values in the database. There are a couple of techniques for addressing these potential conflicts and we discuss them in the following section.

## Handling Identity Columns

In this section, we're going to discuss updates of rows that contain identity columns. Let's consider what happens to the DataSet when we add a new row to the Suppliers DataTable. The new supplier's ID will be 30 (there are already 29 suppliers in the table and the new row's ID will take the next available integer value). Some other user may add a new supplier to the database before our application had a chance to commit the new row to the database. The new row's ID field in the Suppliers table will become 30, but our application has no way of knowing that the ID has already been taken. The DataAdapter will attempt to insert a new row with a primary key that exists already in the Suppliers table. The result is a runtime exception. SQL Server will return an error to the effect that the uniqueness of the primary key has been violated.

This type of error isn't that uncommon in data-driven applications that are used by many clients. There are even more subtle errors. Even if you manage to commit the new supplier to the data source with the proper ID (whatever ID value is assigned to the row by the database), what if this value is used as a foreign key to another table? You'd have to edit the related row before committing it to the data source. If you enforce the relationship between the two tables and set the relationship's Update rule to `Cascade`, the DataSet will update the related rows when the primary key is changed.

To handle the insertion of rows with identity fields, Microsoft recommends the following technique. If you've built the DataSet in your code, you must set the identity column's AutoIncrement property to True. If the DataSet was designed with the visual database tools, the column's AutoIncrement property is already True. The two basic properties of an identity column are the AutoIncrementSeed and AutoIncrementStep and their default values are 1. Set these two properties to –1 from within your code, or in the Property Browser. The identity column of the first row in the table will have a value of –1, the same column of the second row will have a value of –2, and so on.

These negative values won't be stored in the database because the definition of the identity column in the data source is different. It most likely starts at 1 and it has a positive increment. As soon as the rows with the negative identity values are submitted to the data source, the identity columns will be assigned a proper unique value.

## The IdentityUpdates Project

Let's experiment with the insertion of identity columns to see how well this technique works. We'll build a simple application, IdentityUpdates, to insert new orders to the Northwind database. An order (invoice) involves two tables: the Orders table, which holds the order's header (one row per order), and the Order Details table, which holds the order's details (one or more rows per order). An order's rows in the Order Details table are identified by the OrderID field, which points to the primary key of the Orders table. The OrderID column in the Orders table is the primary key and it's an identity column. To add a new order to the client DataSet, we first create a new row for the Orders table. And for each product ordered, we must create a new row in the Order Details table. We'll use the OrderID field of the row added to the Orders table as the foreign key of the Order Details table. The entire order will be created in a DataSet at the client's side and then we'll submit the changes to the data source.

To build the IdentityUpdates sample application, start a new project and place three buttons on it, as shown in Figure 4.8. The Add Order button adds a new order to the local DataSet, which will be submitted later to the database. The Show New Orders button shows the orders you've created so far in the Output window, and the Commit Orders button commits the new orders to the database.

**FIGURE 4.8:**

The IdentityUpdates
project adds new orders
to the Northwind
database.

The orders will be stored to a local DataSet. To create the application's DataSet, drop the tables Products, Customers, Orders, and Order Details on the form. The Customers and Products tables are needed for the order's header and detail lines. You'll populate these two tables and keep them at the client because all invoices will make use of these two tables. The other two tables, Orders and Order Details, will be initially empty and will be populated by the application as the user creates new orders by clicking the New Order button. Then configure the following DataAdapter objects:

**DAProducts**   Selects all the rows of the Products table. This DataAdapter doesn't update the data source.

**DACustomers**   Selects all the rows of the Customers table. This DataAdapter doesn't update the data source.

**DAOrders**   Selects the rows of the Orders table. This DataAdapter will not populate any table in the DataSet. You need only the structure of the Orders table to add new rows to it. This DataAdapter updates the data source by inserting new rows in the Orders table.

**DADetails**   Selects the rows of the Order Details table. This DataAdapter will not populate any table in the DataSet. You need only the structure of the Order Details table to add new rows to it. This DataAdapter updates the data source by inserting new rows to the Order Details table.

Once the DataAdapters are in place, you can create a new DataSet (it's named `DataSet1` in the sample project) and add the appropriate relationships between its tables. You can open the IdentityUpdates project to see the structure of the DataSet and its relations.

When the form is loaded, populate the Customers and Products tables with the following statements:

```
Private Sub Form1_Load(ByVal sender As Object, _
                       ByVal e As System.EventArgs) _
                       Handles MyBase.Load
    DAProducts.Fill(DataSet11, "Products")
    DACustomers.Fill(DataSet11, "Customers")
End Sub
```

The other two tables aren't populated—no reason to download any of the existing orders to create a new one. The Orders table contains an identity column, the OrderID column. This column is used to relate the Orders table to the Order Details table.

The code that creates a new invoice is the Add Order button's Click event handler, and it's shown in Listing 4.11. First, it creates a new row for the Orders table (the order's header) and assigns a random customer ID by retrieving the CustomerID field of a row of the Customers table. The row is selected randomly and the *rnd* variable is declared at the form's level with the following statement:

```
Dim rnd As New System.Random()
```

Then the code creates the order's detail lines. Each order has a random number of detail lines (a value between 2 and 10). Each detail line refers to a product selected randomly from the Products table. We select a random row from the Products table and assign its ProductID field to the ProductID field of the variable that represents a new row of the Order Details table (the *DetailRow* variable). The quantity for each product is also set to a random integer value from 3 to 30.

---

**Listing 4.11**     **Adding a New Order to the Client DataSet**

```
Private Sub bttnNewOrder_Click( _
                       ByVal sender As System.Object, _
                       ByVal e As System.EventArgs) _
                       Handles bttnNewOrder.Click
    DataSet11.Orders.OrderIDColumn.AutoIncrement = True
    DataSet11.Orders.OrderIDColumn.AutoIncrementSeed = -1
    DataSet11.Orders.OrderIDColumn.AutoIncrementStep = -1
    DataSet11.Relations("OrdersOrderDetails")._
             ChildKeyConstraint.UpdateRule = Rule.Cascade
    Dim cmd As SqlClient.SqlCommand
    Dim OrderRow As DataSet1.OrdersRow
    OrderRow = DataSet11.Orders.NewOrdersRow
```

```
    Dim custRow As Integer = _
            rnd.Next(0, DataSet11.Customers.Rows.Count - 1)
    OrderRow.CustomerID = _
        DataSet11.Customers.Rows(custRow).Item("CustomerID")
    DataSet11.Orders.Rows.Add(OrderRow)

    Dim DetailRow As DataSet1.Order_DetailsRow
    Dim lines As Integer
    For lines = 0 To rnd.Next(2, 10)
        DetailRow = _
                DataSet11.Order_Details.NewOrder_DetailsRow
        Dim prodRow As Integer = _
            rnd.Next(0, DataSet11.Products.Rows.Count - 1)
        DetailRow.OrderID = OrderRow.OrderID
        DetailRow.ProductID = _
                    DataSet11.Products.Rows(prodRow)._
                    Item("ProductID")
        DetailRow.Quantity = rnd.Next(3, 30)
        DetailRow.UnitPrice = _
                DataSet11.Products.Rows(prodRow). _
                Item("UnitPrice")
        DetailRow.Discount = rnd.Next(0, 30) / 100
        Try
            DataSet11.Order_Details.Rows.Add(DetailRow)
        Catch exc As Exception
            MsgBox(exc.Message)
        End Try
    Next
End Sub
```

The first few statements configure the properties of the identity column as described, and then we set the Update rule for the OrdersOrderDetails relation. This is the default value of the UpdateRule property, but we've inserted the statement in our code because it's crucial for the operation of the application. By setting the relation's UpdateRule to `Rule.Cascade`, we're telling the DataSet to cascade any changes made to the primary key column to all related rows of the Order Details table. When we commit a new row to the Orders table, the new order gets its final ID. This ID is then propagated to the order's detail rows.

You may wonder why we configure the DataSet every time a new order is added and not when the form is loaded. If you commit the first batch of orders, the DataSet will be populated with the final version of these orders. The properties of the identity column will be reset and you won't be able to commit another set of orders to the database. After committing one or more orders to the database, we must clear the DataSet. The new orders have no reason to remain in our DataSet; if the user needs to see one of these orders, we must retrieve it from the database. If you don't clear the DataSet, any new orders you add after committing the first batch to the database may fail to update the underlying tables, because the Orders table's identity field will no longer be negative.

Why do we need the exception handler around the statements that add the new row to the Order Details DataTable? The Order Details table in the Northwind database includes a unique constraint based on the OrderID and ProductID columns. In other words, no two rows of the same order should refer to the same product. Because we create the product IDs randomly, there's a good chance we may generate the same product ID twice for the same order. When this happens, the exception handler prevents the insertion of a row with same product ID as an existing row.

The code behind the Show New Orders button iterates through the rows of the Orders table and prints all orders, followed by their details. The code of the Show New Rows buttons is shown in Listing 4.12.

**Listing 4.12    Showing the New Orders and Their Details**

```
Private Sub bttnShowRows_Click( _
        ByVal sender As System.Object, _
        ByVal e As System.EventArgs) _
        Handles bttnShowRows.Click
    Dim orderRow As DataSet1.OrdersRow, _
        detailRow As DataSet1.Order_DetailsRow
    For Each orderRow In DataSet11.Orders.Rows
        Console.WriteLine(" ORDER " & _
                        orderRow.Item("OrderID"))
        Console.WriteLine("     PLACED BY " & _
            DataSet11.Customers.FindByCustomerID( _
            orderRow.Item("CustomerID")).CompanyName)
        For Each detailRow In _
            orderRow.GetChildRows("OrdersOrderDetails")
            Console.Write(vbTab & "ITEM # " & _
                        detailRow.Item("ProductID"))
            Console.Write(vbTab & "QTY     " & _
                        detailRow.Item("Quantity"))
            Console.WriteLine(vbTab & "PRICE   " & _
                        detailRow.Item("UnitPrice"))
        Next
    Next
End Sub
```

The output produced by the bttnShowRows() subroutine looks like this:

```
ORDER -1
PLACED BY Rattlesnake Canyon Grocery
    ITEM # 17    Alice Mutton      QTY    25    PRICE  39
    ITEM # 57    Ravioli Angelo    QTY    13    PRICE  19.5
    ITEM # 50    Valkoinen suklaa  QTY    13    PRICE  16.25
```

```
ORDER -2
PLACED BY Berglunds snabbkop
     ITEM # 1          Chai              QTY    3     PRICE  18
     ITEM # 47         Zaanse koeken     QTY    22    PRICE  9.5
     ITEM # 34         Sasquatch Ale     QTY    14    PRICE  14
     ITEM # 31         Gorgonzola Telino QTY    3     PRICE  12.5
     ITEM # 69         Gudbrandsdalsost  QTY    18    PRICE  36
     ITEM # 73         Rod Kaviar        QTY    28    PRICE  15
```

You can add as many orders to the client DataSet as you wish. Their initial IDs are negative, but the orders will be assigned their final IDs when they're submitted to the database. This is a truly disconnected application and will update the data source at will. You can even add the code to persist the DataSet to an XML file and reload the data during several sessions. A proper application should persist the DataSet automatically after adding a new order so that no work will be lost, in the occasion of a power outage or a computer crash (even if the crash was caused by your application). To commit the new orders to the database, we need only call the Update method of the DAOrders and DADetails DataAdapter objects, in that order. Listing 4.13 shows the code behind the Commit Orders button.

**Listing 4.13**     **Submitting a Number of New Orders to the Data Source**

```
Private Sub bttnCommit_Click( _
                ByVal sender As System.Object, _
                ByVal e As System.EventArgs) _
                Handles bttnCommit.Click
    DAOrders.Update(DataSet11)
    DADetails.Update(DataSet11)
    DataSet11.Order_Details.Clear()
    DataSet11.Orders.Clear()
End Sub
```

The code is straightforward except for the statements that remove the rows that were added successfully to the underlying tables from the DataSet. We remove these rows by clearing the DataSet because they have no reason to remain in our DataSet any longer. This is an application for adding new orders to the Northwind database, not an application for browsing existing orders. You should comment out the statement that clears the DataSet and then run the application. You will be able to add new orders and commit them to the database. Then switch to the Enterprise Manager and add a new order manually. Just add a new row to the Orders table by supplying a valid customer ID and another row to the Order Details table by supplying a valid product ID, a price, and a quantity. This order will be assigned an ID automatically by the database. If you switch back to the application and attempt to add a new order, this time a runtime exception will occur. After adding the first order, the OrderID field of the new row will be set to its final value (the one created by the database). When you attempt to commit another order, its ID will conflict with the ID of the row you added manually to the

Orders table. To avoid this problem, clear the DataSet and reset the AutoIncrementSeed and AutoIncrementStep properties from within your code.

Most developers will configure a Command object to insert new rows to a table rather than rely on a trick (changing the properties of an identity column). This part of ADO.NET just doesn't look quite right to us, so we'll suggest an even more robust technique for inserting new rows with identity columns to the data source in the last section of this chapter.

After adding the new orders to the database with the Commit Orders button, you can switch to SQL Server's Enterprise Manager to see that the orders were assigned unique IDs. You can even insert new orders manually before committing the rows of the DataSet1 DataSet to the database. To do so, add a few orders to the local DataSet through the application's interface. Then switch to the Enterprise Manager and add a few new rows; just add a header with a CustomerID and a single detail line for the order. Then switch back to the IdentityUpdates application and commit the orders to the database.

Before ending this section, we'd like to point out a very important point about handling identity columns. You shouldn't forget to set the properties of the identity column after each update. If not, the UPDATE statement will reread the same rows from the database and will also reset the properties of the identity columns. As a result, the second time you attempt to commit new orders to the database, the update operation will fail.

Another problem with this technique is that the application may need to actually print the ID of the order. A salesperson taking orders on the go will most likely have to print a copy of the order for the customer. The printout should obviously include an ID for identification purposes. But the temporary ID is neither unique nor convenient. An ID is a positive value (and usually a large positive value). A good solution to this problem is to add an extra column and set it to a unique value. A GUID (globally unique identifier) column is a good choice. Or you can concatenate the ID of the salesperson and the absolute value of the order's temporary ID to create a unique identifier for the order. This column will be used to identify orders by their temporary ID (the only piece of information you can pass to the client when the order is taken), but it will not be used in any relations.

The technique we just presented here works for massive updates. However, there are situations in which the update of the database can't take place with batch procedures. The invoice is a typical example. The IdentityUpdates project will happily add an invoice, even if few of its lines fail to update the database. As you probably know, invoices must be entered as transactions: if a single detail line fails, then the entire invoice must fail. Usually, we can't take an order for 10 products and deliver half of them, at least not without consulting with the customer, making it clear that certain products are out of stock (or discontinued) and, in essence, acquiring a new order from the customer. This brings us to a very important topic in database programming, the topic of transactions. In the following section, we'll explore transactions in ADO.NET and we'll build another version of the IdentityUpdates project, this time using transactions.

## Transactions in ADO.NET

One of the most important topics in database programming is the process of updating multiple tables from within a transaction. Any nontrivial database application involves operations that update multiple tables at once. If one of these updates fails, then the entire operation must fail. When you enter an invoice, for example, you must add the invoice header to the Orders table and the invoice's detail lines to the Order Details table. You will write code that inserts a new row in the Orders table and a number of rows in the Order Details table, but you must make sure that all of these actions complete successfully. If one of the insertions fails, then you must undo any changes made so far because you can't record a partial invoice.

When you code multiple operations that must either succeed or fail, you use a *transaction*, which is an operation supported by the data source. It would be extremely difficult to implement transactions in your code, but fortunately, you don't have to do anything short of specifying the beginning and the end of the transaction. While the transaction is processed, the rows involved are locked momentarily and other applications can't even read them. If another application requests a row involved in a transaction, SQL Server will simply wait for the transaction to complete and then read the row. It's crucial, therefore, that transactions complete as soon as possible.

There are other examples of transactions, such as transferring funds from one account to another. Clearly, you can't have an incomplete money transfer transaction (subtract money from one account but not add it to another). The topic of transactions is fundamental in database programming, and fortunately, it has already been solved for you. As you will see, it's quite straightforward to implement a transaction in ADO.NET. The following pseudo-code outlines the process of a typical transaction:

```
' Create a Connection object
Dim CN As New SqlClient.SqlConnection()
CN.Open()
' Initiate a Transaction object
Dim TRN As SqlClient.SqlTransaction
TRN = CN.BeginTransaction()
Try
    ' Set up one or more Command objects
    Dim CMD As New SqlClient.SqlCommand()
    CMD.Connection = CN
    CMD.CommandText = . . .
    CMD.CommandType = . . .
    ' Execute command in the context
    ' of the Transaction object
```

```
    CMD.Connection = CN
    CMD.Transaction = TRN
    CMD.ExecuteNonQuery
    ' Execute additional commands in the
    ' context of the same transaction
    TRN.Commit
Catch exc As Exception
    ' Handle errors
    TRN.Rollback
End Try
```

The code starts by establishing a connection to the database. This connection will be used to carry out the transaction, which involves the following steps:

1. Create a Transaction object by calling the BeginTransaction method of a Connection object.

2. Use the same Connection object to execute the commands that update the data source.

3. Set the Transaction property of each of the Command objects you want to execute in the context of the transaction to the Transaction object you created in step 1.

4. Terminate the transaction by calling the Commit method (if all the steps were carried out successfully) or the RollBack method (if one of the steps failed). The RollBack method restores the changes made so far to the data source.

Let's look at a few examples and explore how ADO.NET and SQL Server handle transactions.

### The ADOTransactions Project

In this section, we'll build an application to demonstrate how to update the data source through transactions. Our first transaction will be a very simple one: we'll change the UnitsOnOrder field of two rows in the Products table. We'll use a transaction to make sure that both rows are changed. If one of them can't change value for any reason, the other one shouldn't change either. Create a new project, the ADOTransactions project; then place a button on the form and insert the code in Listing 4.14 in its Click event handler.

---

**Listing 4.14**        **Implementing a Simple Transaction**

```
Private Sub bttnTransaction1_Click( _
                        ByVal sender As System.Object,_
                        ByVal e As System.EventArgs) _
                        Handles Button1.Click
    Dim CN As New SqlClient.SqlConnection()
    CN.ConnectionString = "data source=.; " & _
        "initial catalog=Northwind;integrated " & _
        "security=SSPI;persist security" & _
```

```
                 "info=False;workstation id=POWERTOOLKIT; " & _
              "packet size=4096"
      Dim CMD1 As New SqlClient.SqlCommand()
      Dim CMD2 As New SqlClient.SqlCommand()
      CMD1.CommandText = _
                    "UPDATE Products SET UnitsOnOrder=8 " & _
                    "WHERE ProductID=33"
      CMD1.CommandType = CommandType.Text
      CMD1.Connection = CN
      CMD2.CommandText = _
                    "UPDATE Products SET UnitsOnOrder=9 " & _
                    "WHERE ProductID=34"
      CMD2.CommandType = CommandType.Text
      CMD2.Connection = CN
      CN.Open()
      Dim TRN As SqlClient.SqlTransaction = _
                  CN.BeginTransaction()
      CMD1.Transaction = TRN
      CMD1.ExecuteNonQuery()
      MsgBox("First command executed")
      CMD2.Transaction = TRN
      CMD2.ExecuteNonQuery()
      MsgBox("Second command executed")
      Dim reply As MsgBoxResult
      reply = MsgBox("Commit the transaction?", _
                    MsgBoxStyle.YesNo)
      If reply = MsgBoxResult.Yes Then
          TRN.Commit()
      Else
          TRN.Rollback()
      End If
  End Sub
```

This event handler executes two commands against the database and both commands change the value of the UnitsOnOrder field of two different rows (the rows with IDs of 33 and 34). The code starts by initiating a transaction with the BeginTransaction method of the Connection object. The transaction will be terminated with a call to the Transaction object's Commit method (which will commit the changes to the data source) or the Rollback method (which will abort the transaction and restore the fields to their values prior to the execution of the transaction).

Not every command you execute through the specific Connection object needs to be part of the transaction. To execute a command in the context of a Transaction object, set the corresponding Command object's Transaction property to the Transaction object returned by the BeginTransaction method. In other words, you need not create a new Connection object to carry out a transaction. Instead, some of the commands you'll execute through an existing Connection object can be executed in the context of a transaction.

The code displays a message box after the execution of each command to report the progress of the transaction. Your code should never ever interact with the user during a transaction. We've inserted these statements in our code to simulate an artificial delay so that we can switch to another application in the middle of the transaction and see how SQL Server handles transactions.

To determine whether the transaction will be committed or rolled back, the sample code prompts the user with a message box. Notice that a single call to the Commit or RollBack method will commit or roll back the effects of all the commands executed in the context of the specific transaction. Let's verify it.

Click the Execute Transaction button. When the first message box appears, switch to the Query Analyzer and execute the following query:

```
USE Northwind
SELECT * FROM Products WHERE ProductID=33
```

If you attempt to read a row involved in a transaction, SQL Server will not respond. The row is locked and SQL Server waits for the lock to be released. However, as long as you keep the transaction open (by keeping the dialog box open), the lock isn't released and SQL Server doesn't even time out. Click the OK button on the message box and then the OK button on the second message box, which is displayed after the second step of the transaction. Then another message box will ask you whether you want to commit or roll back the transaction. Click No. This will abort the transaction and the UnitsOnOrder fields of the two rows won't change value. Then switch back to the SQL Analyzer and examine the two rows. Nothing has happened and the two rows still have their original values.

Click the Execute Transaction button again and accept the transaction this time. If you switch to the SQL Analyzer and retrieve the two rows, you'll see that their UnitsOnOrder fields have changed value.

**TIP**     Transactions should complete as soon as possible so that the locks on the involved rows will not last for more than a few milliseconds. Never interact with the user from within a transaction, and don't execute in the transaction's block any code that can be executed outside the transaction.

If you execute the program again and repeat the steps outlined here, you'll realize that the row isn't locked while the transaction takes place. SQL Server doesn't place unnecessary locks on the rows involved in a transaction. If a row hasn't changed, there's no reason for it to be locked. Changed rows, on the other hand, are locked and here's why: While a transaction is executing, SQL Server doesn't know the values of the fields of the row. If the transaction completes successfully, the new values will replace the old ones. If not, the row's fields will be restored to their original values. In the middle of the transaction, the row is undefined. SQL

Server keeps both the old and new versions of the rows involved in the transaction, and if they're different, it waits until the end of the transaction to finalize the rows.

Our sample code sets the UnitsOnOrder field to a new value. The first time you execute the application, the UnitsOnOrder field for the specified row is changed and the row is locked. If you execute the program again, the field's value won't change (it will be set to the same value) and it's not locked. Its new value is the same as the original value, so SQL Server does not lock this row. That's why you can read it in the middle of the transaction. If you change the UPDATE statement to something like the following, the transaction will always lock the row that corresponds to the product with ID = 33:

```
UPDATE    Products SET UnitsOnOrder = UnitsOnOrder + 1 _
WHERE     ProductID=33
```

However, this isn't why we use transactions. Transactions are used to make sure that even if only one of the updates fails, the entire transaction will fail and the database will not be left in an invalid state. The Northwind database contains quite a few constraints, one of them being the UnitsOnOrder field constraint, whose definition is as follows:

```
([UnitsOnOrder] >= 0)
```

To see (or edit) this constraint, open the Products table in Design mode and click the Manage Constraints button at the top of the dialog box. The Properties dialog box will appear and you must switch to the Constraints tab. Select the CK_UnitsOnOrder constraint and the constraint's expression will appear on the dialog box. If you attempt to set this field to a negative value, the update operation will fail. If this operation is part of a transaction, then the entire transaction will fail as well. If you change the code of Listing 4.14 and set the value of the UnitsOnOrder field to a negative value, a runtime exception will occur.

Let's add a second button to the form and enter the code in Listing 4.15 in its event handler. The code is almost identical to the code in Listing 4.14 except that it always attempts to commit the changes. This is how we typically use transactions in our code. The entire transaction takes place in a structured exception handler, which will catch any errors. Should an error occur during the transaction, the entire transaction is rolled back in the exception handler's Catch clause.

---

**Listing 4.15**     **Coding a Typical Transaction**

```
Private Sub Button2_Click(ByVal sender As System.Object, _
                    ByVal e As System.EventArgs) _
                    Handles Button2.Click
    Dim CN As New SqlClient.SqlConnection()
    CN.ConnectionString = "data source=.; " & _
        "initial catalog=Northwind;integrated " & _
        "security=SSPI;persist security" & _
```

```
               "info=False;workstation id=POWERTOOLKIT; " & _
               "packet size=4096"
Dim CMD1 As New SqlClient.SqlCommand()
Dim CMD2 As New SqlClient.SqlCommand()
CMD1.CommandText = _
            "UPDATE Products " & _
            " SET UnitsOnOrder=88 WHERE ProductID=33"
CMD1.CommandType = CommandType.Text
CMD1.Connection = CN
CMD2.CommandText = _
            "UPDATE Products " & _
            " SET UnitsOnOrder=-99 WHERE ProductID=34"
CMD2.CommandType = CommandType.Text
CMD2.Connection = CN
CN.Open()
Dim TRN As SqlClient.SqlTransaction = _
                   CN.BeginTransaction()
CMD1.Transaction = TRN
Try
    CMD1.ExecuteNonQuery()
    CMD2.Transaction = TRN
    CMD2.ExecuteNonQuery()
    TRN.Commit()
    MsgBox("Transaction committed successfully")
Catch ex As Exception
    TRN.Rollback()
    MsgBox("Transaction failed" & _
           vbCrLf & ex.Message)
End Try
End Sub
```

If you run the application and click the Execute Transaction (2) button, the following message will be displayed on a message box:

```
UPDATE statement conflicted with COLUMN CHECK constraint
   'CK_UnitsOnOrder'. The conflict occurred in database
   'Northwind', table 'Products', column 'UnitsOnOrder'.
The statement has been terminated.
```

The updates take place in a structured exception handler so that if one of them fails, the Catch clause of the exception handler will be executed. In this clause, the code rolls back the transaction and displays the description of the error that prevented the transaction from completing successfully. The exception handler will catch any errors, even errors that are not related to the database operations.

## Executing Transactions with the DataAdapter

You need not set up Command objects for your transactions. You can use the Command objects of the DataAdapter object to execute transactions against the database. To execute an

UPDATE, INSERT, or DELETE statement in the context of a transaction, set the appropriate Command object's Transaction property to a Transaction object with a statement like the following:

```
DAProducts.UpdateCommand.Transaction = TRN
```

As you recall, the DataAdapter will attempt to update as many rows as possible, assuming that the UpdateOnError property is set to True. If you don't want to update a few rows only, you should set this property to False and execute the Update command in the context of a transaction. If one of the rows fails to update the data source, the entire transaction will be rolled back and even rows that successfully updated the data source will be restored to their previous values.

Transactions are commonly used to update a parent row along with its child rows. This means that you must first create a Transaction object, update the parent row on its own and then its child rows, and finally, close the transaction. You'll see how you can use the DataAdapter object to perform transactions against a database in the following section.

To summarize, the Transaction object is associated with a Connection object, and it's applied to one or more Command objects (either a Command object configured manually or the InsertCommand, UpdateCommand, and DeleteCommand objects of a DataAdapter object). The Command object exposes the Transaction property, which you must set to a Transaction object you have already created. The commands of the transaction must be executed in a structured exception handler, which will commit the updates with the Commit method. If an exception is thrown, the RollBack method must be called in the Catch clause of the exception handler to undo any changes made to the database so far.

### The IdentityTransaction Project

In the last section of this chapter, we'll explore another technique for adding rows with identity columns, this time using transactions. The application we'll build to demonstrate this technique, the IdentityTransactions project, is an adaptation of the IdentityUpdates project of the previous section. We'll create the same DataSet and use the same code to add new orders. However, we'll use transactions to submit the new orders to the database. If for any reason the order's header isn't committed successfully, then the entire order will be rejected. Likewise, if a single detail line fails to update the underlying table, the entire order will be rejected. We use transactions to ensure that only valid orders are committed to the data source.

The code that populates the Customers and Products tables from within the form's Load event handler is identical to the equivalent code of the IdentityUpdates project. The same is true for the code that creates the new orders, and we'll not repeat it here.

The code that commits the orders to the database is quite different. Where the IdentityUpdates project updates the rows of the Orders table first and then the Order Details table, the code of the new project goes through each order in the DataSet, inserts a new row in the Orders table, and then inserts the related rows in the Order Details table. The insertions of the new rows for each order take place from within a transaction, and each new order is either inserted in its entirety or it's aborted. The complete code behind the Commit Orders button is shown in Listing 4.16.

**Listing 4.16**       **Committing Invoices through Transactions**

```
Private Sub bttnCommit_Click(ByVal sender As System.Object,_
               ByVal e As System.EventArgs) _
               Handles bttnCommit.Click
    Dim orderRow As DataSet1.OrdersRow, _
        detailRow As DataSet1.Order_DetailsRow
    Dim orderRows(0) As DataRow
    Dim DetailRows() As DataRow
    Dim tran As SqlClient.SqlTransaction
    SqlConnection1.Open()
    For Each orderRow In DataSet11.Orders.Rows
        tran = SqlConnection1.BeginTransaction
        DAOrders.InsertCommand.Transaction = tran
        DAOrderDetails.InsertCommand.Transaction = tran
        Try
            orderRows(0) = orderRow
            DAOrders.Update(orderRows)
            DetailRows = _
                orderRow.GetChildRows("OrdersOrderDetails")
            DAOrderDetails.Update(DetailRows)
            tran.Commit()
        Catch exc As Exception
            MsgBox(exc.Message)
            tran.Rollback()
        End Try
    Next
    SqlConnection1.Close()
End Sub
```

Here's how the code works. First, it creates the two arrays, the `OrderRows` and `DetailRows` arrays. These two arrays will hold the order's header and the order's detail rows, respectively. To commit the new orders in the context of a transaction, we can't commit all the headers and then all the details. Instead, we must commit the header and the details of each order.

To commit each order separately, we must use an overloaded form of the Update method, which accepts as argument an array with the rows to be updated. For each order (that is, in each transaction), we call this form of the Update method of the `DAOrders` and `DAOrderDetails` DataAdapter objects. The Update methods either succeed, in which case we commit the transaction, or fail, in which case we roll back the transaction. To retrieve the rows that correspond to the current order, we call the GetChildRows method of the *OrderRow* variable that represents the current order in the Order table.

What do you think will happen if we attempt to update the database twice by clicking the Commit Orders button more than once? Do so and then open the Orders table. No matter how many times you click this button, no new rows will be added to either table. The reason for this behavior is that after the new rows have been committed to the database, their original values match the current values. Therefore, the DataAdapter doesn't submit any data to the database. When you call its Update method, the DataAdapter sees no changes in the DataSet and doesn't do anything.

Let's see what will happen if we reset the UpdateRule to None. Change the UpdateRule in the property pages of the OrdersOrderDetails relation (open the DataSet in Design view by double-clicking the item Dataset1.xsd in the Solution Explorer window, right-click the box that represents the relation between the Orders and Order Details tables, and from the context menu, select Edit Relation). Run the program, add a new invoice to the client DataSet, and then attempt to commit it to the database by clicking the Commit Orders button. The following exception will occur as soon as the code attempts to change the ID of the order's header:

```
Cannot make this change because constraints are enforced on
    relation OrdersOrderDetails, and changing this value will
    strand child rows.
```

What this means practically is that the database itself is protecting you from mistakes. You should always enforce crucial relations in your database design, so that even when an application attempts to violate them, the database will reject any changes that will place the database's integrity at risk. By the way, the default UpdateRule is Cascade, so you won't notice any changes if you change it from Cascade to Default.

Some readers may approach this topic very safely: why not insert the order's header as early as possible in the Order table, retrieve the ID assigned by the database, and then use it with all the detail rows? The only time you shouldn't do this is when the client application doesn't have constant access to the database. In a truly disconnected application, users should be able to add invoices to the disconnected DataSet and synch it with the database when a connection becomes available. Of course, most applications run on local area networks and they can connect to the server at any time.

## Summary

This chapter concludes our overview of ADO.NET and the members of the DataSet object, which is the single most important class of ADO.NET class. You know how to connect to a database, how to execute commands against it, and how to retrieve data with selection queries and store them to a DataSet. You also learned how to manipulate the DataSet at the client: how to edit its rows, insert new rows, and delete existing ones. You also know how to submit the changes back to the database and how to get information about the rows that failed to update the data source.

The most practical topics covered in this chapter are the handling of rows with identity fields, the filtering of a DataTable's rows, and the execution of multiple updates from within a transaction. The DataSet class (and its subordinate classes) provide many members for manipulating its tables and their rows. The DataSet can store data in related tables, just as the database can. After editing the data in the DataSet, you can commit the changes to the database either individually or in batches.

So far, you learned to perform these operations through your code. You have all the information you need to start developing front-end applications that interact with the user on one end and the database on the other end. However, there are tools that simplify the design of data-driven applications. In the following chapter, we'll explore the topics of building data-driven Windows applications and binding Windows controls to DataSets. We're going to build a few typical data-driven Windows applications, and you will see how the objects of ADO.NET can be used with the common Windows controls to design functional user interfaces for your database.

In the following chapter we're going to put all this information together to build a few practical data-bound Windows applications. We're going to explore the topic of data binding, but we'll also build functional user interfaces using non-bound controls. Two of the more advanced Windows controls, the TreeView and ListView controls, can't be bound to a data source, but you'll see how to build elaborate Windows interfaces using these two controls with data.

# CHAPTER 5

# Building Data-Driven Windows Applications

- Data binding and data-bound controls

- The BindingManagerBase class

- Building data-driven Windows interfaces

- Navigating through related tables

- Three-tier, data-driven applications

In the last two chapters, we discussed the architecture of ADO.NET and its object model. You already know how to access databases, copy data from the database into DataSet objects at the client, edit them, and submit the changes back to the database. You also learned how to handle update errors, to some extent. In this chapter, we'll build practical data-driven applications that update the underlying tables in the database and handle update errors.

As you already know, you can query and update the data source either through the DataAdapter or through Command objects, which can be set up at design time or configured at runtime from within your code. You have all the information you need to develop data-driven Windows applications. All you really need is a form with various controls and a few buttons to perform the basic operations. You can set the controls' values to the fields of one or more tables in the DataSet, allow the user to edit the controls, and then submit the edited data back to the database.

However, there's more to developing data-driven applications. As you probably know, most of the Windows controls can be bound to a data source. When a control is bound to a field in the data source (a DataSet), every time the field in the DataSet changes value, the control's value is also changed to reflect the field's current value. When the control's contents are edited, the changes are committed to the DataSet. In effect, data binding maps a control's Text property to a field. You can map other properties besides the Text property, but it's not very common. In this chapter, we're going to explore the topic of data binding, and you'll see when to use data binding and when to use regular Windows controls in your interface.

**TIP**    This chapter's projects are practical and contain quite a bit of code, and their interfaces are not trivial. Instead of designing the forms yourself and entering all the code manually, we recommend that you download them from the book's section at the www.sybex.com.

## Data Binding

Data binding is a mechanism that associates a control with a specific column of a specific Data-Table in a DataSet. When a control is bound to a field, the field's value is displayed automatically on the control. As you move through the rows of the DataTable, the control's value changes to reflect the value of the bound field in the current row. If the control's text is edited, either by the user or from within the application's code, the new value replaces the column's value in the DataSet. A data-bound control is in effect a window for viewing and editing a specific column in the DataTable.

Different controls allow you to bind different properties. In most cases, you bind the Text property, but there are other properties you can bind to a data source, such as the Tag property. To set the data-bound properties of a control, expand its DataBindings section in the Property Browser and set it to the appropriate field. In the DataBindings section of the

Property Browser, you will see the names of the properties that can be bound to data. To set a property, expand the list of available values and select the appropriate field. You will notice that the names of the properties listed in the DataBindings are not unique; you will see a Text and a Tag property in the DataBindings section and two more properties by the same name further down in the Property Browser. In the DataBindings section, you bind the values of these properties to a data field. The properties by the same name that appear outside the DataBindings section can be set to static values as usual.

Some of the Windows controls aren't bound to a single row, but to a set of rows. The ListBox control, for example, can be populated with the rows of a table and display a specific column. You will see later in this chapter how to bind the Windows controls that can display multiple rows (basically, the ListBox and ComboBox controls). These controls are used almost exclusively as lookup tools on data entry forms. It's possible to populate a ComboBox control with the rows of the Categories table and bind the control's editing area to the CategoryID field of the Products table. As a result, every time you move to another row in the Products table, the current product's category name will appear on the control. To change the category of the current row, you simply select another category name (and not an ID) on the control.

Data binding is not new to ADO.NET. Data binding was available with earlier versions of ADO, but it has never been a real developer's tool. The major disadvantage of data binding in ADO was that it worked best with server-side cursors. It required a connection to a database, and any changes to the data made through the application's interface were instantly committed to the database. DataSets in ADO.NET are disconnected data stores, and any changes you make to their data are not submitted automatically to the database.

## The BindingContext Object

Binding controls to selected fields of a table in the DataSet is rather trivial and requires no code. To make the most of data binding, however, you have to be able to manipulate data-bound controls from within your code, and this can be done with the help of the BindingContext object. This object is a property of the Form object and it's of the BindingManagerBase type. The BindingManagerBase class's members manage all the objects bound to the same data source. To access this object, call the BindingContext property of the form and specify as arguments the name of a DataSet and the name of a table in this DataSet (basically, the data source of a binding). The BindingManagerBase object that will be returned handles the binding between all the controls on the form and the specific data source. If a form contains the DSCustomers DataSet, which in turn contains the Customers table, you can use the following statements to retrieve the BindingManagerBase object that handles all controls on the form that are bound to the rows of the Customers table:

```
Dim BC As BindingManagerBase
BC = Me.BindingContext(DsCustomers1, "Customers")
```

The BC object handles the binding of the controls that are bound to the Customers table of the DSCustomers DataSet. Its members allow you to interact with the data source of the bound controls. For example, you can read its Position property to find out the position of the current row in the table, or you can set this property to move to a specific row. To find out the order of the current row in the table, use one of the following expressions:

```
BC.Position
Me.BindingContext(DSCustomers1, "Customers").Position
```

When you move to another row in the DataTable by setting the value of the Position property, the changes made to the current row are saved in the DataSet. If you want to cancel an edit operation on the current row, you can call the BindingManagerBase object's CancelEdit method.

**NOTE**    In Chapter 3, we mentioned that the concept of the current row doesn't apply to ADO.NET. This isn't quite true, because the Position property of the BindingContext object implies a current row. You can think of the row pointed to by the Position property as the current row in the DataTable. However, you can access any row in the DataTable regardless of the value of the Position property. In ADO, you couldn't access any row beyond the current row, and the concept of the current row was central in programming ADO Recordsets.

The basic members of the BindingManagerBase class are listed in Tables 5.1, 5.2, and 5.3.

**TABLE 5.1:** The Basic Properties of the BindingManagerBase Class

| Properties | Description |
| --- | --- |
| Count | The number of rows in the data source, which is the number of rows managed by the BindingManagerBase object. This property is the same as the number of rows in the corresponding table (property Rows.Count). |
| Position | The number of the row that the controls on the form are bound to. This is the current row in the data source of the BindingManagerBase object. |

**TABLE 5.2:** The Basic Methods of the BindingManagerBase Class

| Methods | Description |
| --- | --- |
| AddNew | Adds a new row to the data source and moves to the new row. This means that the new row's fields are automatically displayed on the bound controls and you can start editing the new row. |
| CancelCurrentEdit | Cancels the current edit operation and restores the current row (the row identified by the Position property) to its original values. |
| EndCurrentEdit | Ends the current edit operation and commits the edits to the DataSet. |

*Continued on next page*

**TABLE 5.2 CONTINUED:**  The Basic Methods of the BindingManagerBase Class

| Methods | Description |
|---|---|
| RemoveAt | Removes the row at the position specified by its argument, which is an integer value. |
| SuspendBinding | Suspends temporarily the data binding for the form. |
| ResumeBinding | Resumes the data binding for the form. |

**TABLE 5.3:**  The Basic Events of the BindingManagerBase Class

| Events | Description |
|---|---|
| CurrentChanged | This event is fired when the bound value changes. |
| PositionChanged | This event is fired when the Position property changes value. |

It's important to understand that the CurrentChanged event isn't fired only when a data-bound control is edited. If you move to another row by setting the Position property, the data-bound value will also change and the CurrentChanged event will be fired in addition to the Position-Changed event.

Through the BindingContext property, you can implement all the basic navigation and editing operations, as we'll demonstrate in the sample projects of the following sections.

## DataTable Events

When you bind the controls on the form to a DataSet, you can program certain events raised by its DataTable objects. These events are caused by changes in the contents of the data-bound controls and they're listed in Table 5.4. We use these events to validate the data entered by the user in the data-bound controls on the form.

**TABLE 5.4:**  The Data Update Events of the DataTable Object

| Event | Description |
|---|---|
| ColumnChanging | A field value is being changed. The event passes to its handler as arguments the row, the column, and the field's proposed value. |
| ColumnChanged | A field value has been changed. The event passes to its handler as arguments the row, the column, and the field's proposed value. |
| RowChanging | The changes in the bound row are about to be committed to the DataSet. If you called the BeginEdit before making changes, the RowChanging event is raised only when you call the EndEdit method. The event passes to its handler the row that's about to be committed to the DataSet and a value indicating the action that caused the event. |

*Continued on next page*

**TABLE 5.4 CONTINUED:** The Data Update Events of the DataTable Object

| Event | Description |
|-------|-------------|
| RowChanged | A row in the DataSet has been changed. The event passes to its handler the row that has been changed and a value indicating the action that caused the event. |
| RowDeleting | A row in the DataSet is about to be deleted. This event passes to its handler the row to be deleted. |
| RowDeleted | A row in the DataSet has been deleted. The event passes to its handler the row that was deleted. |

To program the data update events of a DataTable object, you must first create the appropriate delegate and then associate it with an event. Here are the signatures of the data update events:

```
Private Shared Sub Column_Changing( _
        sender As Object, e As DataColumnChangeEventArgs)
End Sub

Private Shared Sub Column_Changed( _
        sender As Object, e As DataColumnChangeEventArgs)
End Sub
Private Shared Sub Row_Changing( _
        sender As Object, e As DataRowChangeEventArgs)
End Sub

Private Shared Sub Row_Changed(_
        sender As Object, e As DataRowChangeEventArgs)
End Sub

Private Shared Sub Row_Deleting( _
        sender As Object, e As DataRowChangeEventArgs)
End Sub

Private Shared Sub Row_Deleted(_
        sender As Object, e As DataRowChangeEventArgs)
End Sub
```

To create a handler for one of the DataTable's events, write a function with the same signature as shown here and then associate it with the appropriate event with a statement like the following:

```
AddHandler DsProducts1.Products.ColumnChanging,
            New DataColumnChangeEventHandler _
            (AddressOf ColumnChanging)
```

The AddHandler statement must appear in the form's Load event handler, usually after the code that populates the form's DataSet.

In the event handler's code, you can examine the fields of the row that caused the event and act accordingly. Among the properties exposed by the second argument of the handler are the following:

**Row**  A DataRow object that represents the row being changed. Use this property in the Changing events to retrieve the row's original values.

**Column**  A DataColumn object that represents the column being changed.

**ProposedValue**  The value of the column being changed. You can read the column's new value or change its value by setting this property.

The following handler validates the UnitPrice and ProductName fields of the Products table. The UnitPrice column must be a non-negative value, and the ProductName column can't be null. The code examines the name of the column that was changed and then validates its value:

```
Private Shared Sub ColumnChanging(ByVal sender As Object,_
                    ByVal e As DataColumnChangeEventArgs)
    If e.Column.ColumnName = "UnitPrice" Then
        If CDec(e.ProposedValue) < 0 Then
            MsgBox("Price can't be negative!")
' The exception prevents the completion of the handler
' and the focus remains at the control with the problem
            Throw New Exception("Invalid price")
        End If
    End If
    If e.Column.ColumnName = "ProductName" Then
        If e.ProposedValue = "" Then
            MsgBox("Please specify a product name!")
            Throw New Exception("Invalid product name")
        End If
    End If
End Sub
```

The message informs the user about the error and the exception prevents the update of the DataSet. The field in error is restored to its original value automatically. Let's see how data binding is used in building practical applications, starting with a simple application for editing the Northwind database's customers.

## The Customers Project

To demonstrate the functionality of the BindingContext property, we're going to build a simple application for editing the Customers table. It's the Customers project and its main form is shown in Figure 5.1. The form shown in the figure allows you to browse the rows of the

Customers table and edit the current row. The navigational model isn't especially functional, but we'll return to this topic shortly.

**FIGURE 5.1:**

A simple data entry and browsing project

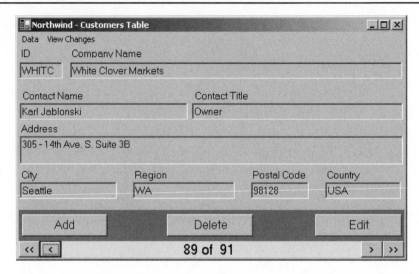

The form contains a number of data-bound controls which display the fields of the current customer. To move to another customer, click the navigational buttons at the bottom on the form. To edit or delete an existing customer, click the Edit or Delete button, respectively. To add a new customer, click the Add button. The Data menu contains commands to commit to the database the changes made to the local DataSet. The View Changes menu contains commands to retrieve the modified rows in the DataSet (edited, deleted, added). As you will see, you can undo any or all the changes made to the DataSet before submitting it to the database.

Start a new project, name it Customers, and place on its form the controls shown in Figure 5.1. Then drop the Customers table on the form to create a Connection object to the database (the SqlConnection1 object) and a DataAdapter for querying the Customers table. Rename the DataAdapter to DACustomers and configure it with the following SELECT statement:

```
SELECT   CustomerID, CompanyName, ContactName,
         ContactTitle, Address, City, Region,
         PostalCode, Country, Phone, Fax
FROM     Customers
ORDER BY CompanyName
```

We aren't going to use all the fields in our sample application, so you can either adjust the default SELECT statement generated by the wizard or add more controls on the form to edit all the fields (which is probably what you should do). After configuring the DataAdapter, create a new DataSet with the Data ➢ Generate DataSet command. Change the name of the DataSet to `DSCustomers` and add the Customers table to it.

Now that you've created the data source for the form, you can bind the various controls on the form to the DataSet. Select the TextBox control that corresponds to the CompanyName field (the txtCompany control in the sample application), and in the Property Browser, open the DataBindings section. The TextBox control has two properties that can be bound to a data source: the Text and Tag properties. If you expand the Text property, you'll see a list of all the tables in the DSCustomers1 DataSet. You can expand any table, see its columns, and select one of them to bind the control to. For our application, set the txtCompany control's Text property to the `Customers.CompanyName` field of the DSCustomers1 DataSet. Notice that this is the Text property of the DataBindings section, not the usual Text property of the control. If you locate the regular Text property of the control, you will see the symbol of a database (a yellow cylinder) next to it. This symbol indicates that the Text property of the control is bound to a field and you can't set its value in the Property Browser.

The rest of the controls should be bound to the corresponding columns of the Customers table. Our application is quite trivial, but a real application may involve multiple DataSets, and each DataSet may contain multiple DataTables. The values of the data-bound properties can be selected on a drop-down list. All you have to do is select the appropriate column of the appropriate table in one of the project's DataSets.

When the form is loaded, the DataSet is populated with the following statement:

```
DACustomers.Fill(DsCustomers1, "Customers")
```

The code also calls the `ShowEditButtons()` subroutine, which displays the editing buttons and locks the controls on the form. All the controls that display data have their ReadOnly property set to True while the user is browsing the Customers table because you don't want users to be able to edit a row at any time. They must click the appropriate editing button (see Figure 5.1), and only then will the application unlock the controls and allow the user to edit their contents.

When the Add and Edit buttons are clicked, the code hides the editing buttons and displays the usual OK and Cancel buttons. In addition, the navigational buttons are disabled. The user must end the current operation by clicking either the OK or the Cancel button. When the OK and Cancel buttons are clicked, the reverse actions take place. The `HideEditButtons()` and `ShowEditButtons()` subroutines hide and display the editing buttons on the form. We'll show you the code of the `HideEditButtons()` subroutine only here:

```
Private Sub HideEditButtons()
    bttnOK.Visible = True
    bttnCancel.Visible = True
    bttnAdd.Visible = False
```

```
        bttnDelete.Visible = False
        bttnEdit.Visible = False
        mnuData.Enabled = False
        mnuUndo.Enabled = False
        bttnFirst.Enabled = False
        bttnPrevious.Enabled = False
        bttnNext.Enabled = False
        bttnLast.Enabled = False
        UnlockControls()
    End Sub
```

The ShowEditButtons() subroutine toggles the values of the Visible and Enabled properties and calls the LockControls() subroutine to unlock the data-bound controls. As you can guess, the LockControls() and UnlockControls() subroutines toggle the ReadOnly properties of the various controls.

The navigational section of the form consists of four Button controls and a Label control. The Label displays the current row in the DataTable (the row you're viewing at the time) and the total number of rows in the table. The order of the current row in the Customers table is given by the following property:

```
    Me.BindingContext(DsCustomers1, "Customers").Position
```

You can write a subroutine that updates the Text property of the Label control and call it from within any event handler that changes the current row (the event handlers of the navigational buttons, for example).

There's an even better technique—namely to program the PositionChanged event of the form's BindingManagerBase class. Add a new event handler and associate it with the Position-Changed event using two statements like the following:

```
    formBindingManager = _
                Me.BindingContext(DsCustomers1, "Customers")
    AddHandler formBindingManager.PositionChanged, _
            AddressOf PositionChanged
```

These statements usually appear in the form's Load event handler, following the statements that populate the DataTable(s). The PositionChanged subroutine is executed every time we move to another row in the corresponding DataTable, and its implementation is fairly straightforward:

```
    Me.Label1.Text = _
            (((Me.BindingContext _
            (DsCustomers1, "Customers").Position + 1).ToString + _
            " of " & Me.BindingContext_
            (DsCustomers1, "Customers").Count.ToString)
```

We add one to the value returned by the Position property because the Position property is zero-indexed (the first row's position in its DataTable is zero).

## Navigating through the Rows

You can use the Position method of the BindingContext object to read or set the current row in the DataTable. For small data sources, you can put on the form four buttons that correspond to the four basic navigational operations: move to first row, move to last row, move to previous row, move to next row. The code that implements the four navigational methods is shown in Listing 5.1.

**Listing 5.1**         **Implementing Navigational Buttons**

```
Private Sub BttnFirst_Click(ByVal sender As System.Object, _
                            ByVal e As System.EventArgs) _
                            Handles BttnFirst.Click
    Me.BindingContext(DsCustomers1, _
                    "Customers").Position = 0
End Sub

Private Sub bttnLast_Click(ByVal sender As System.Object, _
                            ByVal e As System.EventArgs) _
                            Handles bttnLast.Click
    Me.BindingContext(DsCustomers1, "Customers").Position= _
                            Me.BindingContext(DsCustomers1, _
                            "Customers").Count
End Sub

Private Sub bttnNext_Click(ByVal sender As System.Object, _
                            ByVal e As System.EventArgs) _
                            Handles bttnNext.Click
If Me.BindingContext(DsCustomers1, "Customers").Position _
                    < Me.BindingContext(DsCustomers1, _
                    "Customers").Count Then
        Me.BindingContext(DsCustomers1, _
                    "Customers").Position = _
                    Me.BindingContext(DsCustomers1, _
                    "Customers").Position + 1
    End If
End Sub

Private Sub bttnPrevious_Click( _
                            ByVal sender As System.Object, _
                            ByVal e As System.EventArgs) _
                            Handles bttnPrevious.Click
    If Me.BindingContext(DsCustomers1, _
                    "Customers").Position >= 0 Then
        Me.BindingContext(DsCustomers1, _
                    "Customers").Position = _
                    Me.BindingContext(DsCustomers1, _
                    "Customers").Position - 1
    End If
End Sub
```

The code in the Next and Previous event handlers examines the position of the current row and doesn't advance beyond the first or last row. This is how you implement a simple navigational model to move through the rows of a table in a linear fashion.

### Editing the Current Row

To edit the current row, the user can start editing the various controls on the form. As soon as the user moves to another row, the edited fields will be committed to the local DataSet. However, this isn't a very safe technique. To make a better interface, add three buttons to the form and name them Edit, Add, and Delete. To initiate an edit operation, the user must click the Edit button, which unlocks the various controls on the form. The controls are normally locked so that the user can't edit the DataSet by mistake. The Add button adds a new row to the Data-Table and the Delete button deletes the current row. An edit operation is terminated when the user clicks the OK or Cancel button, which are visible only while the form is in Edit mode.

The usual editing operations can be performed with the methods of the BindingManager-Base object returned by the form's BindingContext property. The AddNew method of the BindingManagerBase object adds a new row to the data source, and it's all you really need to implement a New button on your user interface. However, if the user is in the middle of an edit operation, you must end the operation with a call to the EndCurrentEdit method before adding a new row to the data source:

```
Private Sub bttnAdd_Click(ByVal sender As System.Object, _
                    ByVal e As System.EventArgs) _
                    Handles bttnAdd.Click
    Me.BindingContext(DsCustomers1, _
                "Customers").EndCurrentEdit()
    Me.BindingContext(DsCustomers1, "Customers").AddNew()
    HideEditButtons()
End Sub
```

The call to the EndCurrentEdit method isn't needed here because our interface prevents the user from adding a new row while editing another. If you were building a different interface, however, you'd have to call this method to end the current operation before calling the Add-New method to add a new row to the table.

The Edit button is really trivial. It simply hides the navigational buttons and makes all data-bound controls on the form editable by calling the HideEditButtons() subroutine. While the current row is being edited, users can't switch to any other row with the navigational buttons. The user can either abort the operation with the Cancel button, or accept the changes with the OK button.

The Delete button's implementation is also simple. This button's Click event handler calls the BindingManagerBase object's RemoveAt method. This method requires that you pass as argument the position of the row to be removed, which you can retrieve with the Position property:

```
If (Me.BindingContext(DSCustomers1, _
            "Customers").Count > 0) Then
    Me.BindingContext(DSCustomers1, _
                "Customers").RemoveAt( _
                Me.BindingContext(DSCustomers1, _
                "Customers").Position)
End If
```

The Cancel button on the form cancels the edits and restores the current row to its original state. The code behind the Cancel button calls the CancelEdit method to reject the editing of the bound controls:

```
Private Sub bttnCancel_Click( _
            ByVal sender As System.Object, _
            ByVal e As System.EventArgs) _
            Handles bttnCancel.Click
    Me.BindingContext(DsCustomers1, _
            "Customers").CancelCurrentEdit()
    ShowEditButtons()
End Sub
```

Finally, the OK button's code ends the current operation by calling the EndCurrentEdit method. This method commits the edited values to the DataSet. Should an error occur, a structured exception handler rejects the edits by calling the CancelCurrentEdit method:

```
Private Sub bttnOK_Click(ByVal sender As System.Object, _
                    ByVal e As System.EventArgs) _
                    Handles bttnOK.Click
    Try
        Me.BindingContext(DsCustomers1, _
                    "Customers").EndCurrentEdit()
    Catch exc As Exception
        MsgBox(exc.Message)
        Me.BindingContext(DsCustomers1, _
                    "Customers").CancelCurrentEdit()
    End Try
    ShowEditButtons()
End Sub
```

As you can see, the BindingContext property exposes all the basic functionality you really need to build a functional user interface for viewing and editing a table.

You can run the application now and check out its navigational and data editing features. You can edit any of the existing rows, delete a row, and add new rows to the Customers table. The changes are local to the DSCustomers1 DataSet, and you must commit them to the database by calling the DataAdapter's Update method. You shouldn't be able to delete any of the rows in the Customers table because they all have related rows in the Orders table. The relation between the Customers and Orders tables is enforced, and SQL Server won't let you delete a row from the Customers table as long as there are rows in the Orders table that reference the row that's about to be deleted. The DataSet, however, resides on the client. It contains only the Customers table and no relation to enforce. It will allow you to delete any row, but deleted rows in the DataSet will not result in the deletion of the corresponding rows in the Customers table when you call the Update method. Other types of updates may also fail, and the application should be able to handle these errors.

## Updating the Data Source

We must also provide the means to update the Customers table in the database. This is a disconnected application: we allow users to make as many changes as they wish to the local DataSet and we apply all the changes to the database at once. As you can understand, our application should be able to deal with all kinds of update errors. If we were submitting the changes as soon as the user edits a row, we'd have to deal with errors in a single row. Should an error occur, we could simply display a message and let the user edit the row again. In a disconnected application, however, it's possible to have many rows in error. Obviously, we can't abort all the edits and ask users to repeat the edits.

To submit the edits to the database and handle the update errors, we'll add two menus to our application: the Data menu and the View Changes menu. The Data menu contains commands to submit the changes to the database as well as refresh the DataSet by repopulating it from the database. The View Changes menu allows you to view the modified, edited, and deleted rows and undo selected changes. The two menus of the form contain the following commands:

**Data menu**   The Data menu contains a few commands for manipulating the entire DataSet:

> **Undo All Changes**   Rejects all the changes made to the DataSet and restores it to the state it was in when it was populated initially or when the changes were submitted to the database for the last time.

> **Refresh Data**   Refreshes the DataSet by populating it from the database. Any new rows added or deleted or any changes made to the Customers table by other users will be reflected in the DataSet (as opposed to simply rejecting the changes made by the user).

> **Submit Changes**   Submits to the database all the changes made to the DataSet so far. Not all changes may be committed to the database, however.

> **Exit**   Terminates the application

**View Changes menu**   This menu contains commands to select rows according to their state (added, deleted, and modified rows) and displays them on a dialog box. The user can undo the changes in selected rows. This menu contains the following commands:

**View Added Rows**   Displays the rows that have been added to the DataSet but not yet committed to the database.

**View Deleted Rows**   Displays the rows that have been deleted from the DataSet but not yet removed from the corresponding table(s) in the database.

**View Edited Rows**   Displays the rows that have been edited but not yet committed to the database.

**View Update Errors**   Displays the rows that contain errors after an update operation. All the rows that failed to update successfully the Customers table in the database are marked by the DataSet. The program retrieves these rows and displays them along with the description of the error that caused the update operation to fail.

The Submit Changes command submits all changes to the database by calling the DataAdapter's Update method. The Update method accepts as argument the data source to be updated. After submitting the changes to the database, the code examines the DataTable's HasErrors property, and if it's True, the code displays a message to the user. The message is quite generic, but the user can view the errors with the View Changes ➢ View Update Errors command. If the DataTable contains no errors, which means that all the changes in the DataSet were committed to the database successfully, the code calls the DataTable's AcceptChanges method. Listing 5.2 shows the code of the Data ➢ Submit Changes command.

---

**Listing 5.2**       **Committing to the Database the Changes in the Customers Table**

```
Private Sub mnuAccept_Click( _
                ByVal sender As System.Object, _
                ByVal e As System.EventArgs) _
                Handles mnuAccept.Click
    DACustomers.Update(DsCustomers1, "Customers")
    If DsCustomers1.Customers.HasErrors Then
        MsgBox("The Update operation failed for one " & _
               "or more rows. Select Update Errors " & _
               "to view the rows in error")
    Else
        DsCustomers1.AcceptChanges()
    End If
End Sub
```

---

The DACustomers DataAdapter's ContinueUpdateOnError property should be set to True so that the DataAdapter won't stop updating the database on the first error it encounters.

Another technique to update the data source is to retrieve the rows that have been changed with the GetChanges method and call the Update method for each one. If the changes made to a row in the DataSet are applied to the database successfully, then you can call the AcceptChanges method on that row. This technique works best in large DataSets with a few changed rows.

To undo the changes in the local DataSet, the Data ➤ Undo All Changes command calls the DataSet's RejectChanges method. This command undoes all the changes made to the DataSet since it was read or since the last time it updated its data source. The Data ➤ Refresh Data command clears the DataSet and populates it by reading the entire table from the database, as shown in Listing 5.3.

**Listing 5.3**       **Refreshing the Client DataSet**

```
Private Sub mnuRefresh_Click( _
              ByVal sender As System.Object, _
              ByVal e As System.EventArgs) _
              Handles mnuRefresh.Click
    DsCustomers1.Clear()
    DACustomers.Fill(DsCustomers1, "Customers")
End Sub
```

When the user selects one of the commands of the View Changes menu, the statements in Listing 5.4 are executed. These statements create a new DataTable object with the rows that have been changed. To retrieve them, the code calls the GetChanges method of the Customers DataTable, passing as argument one of the members of the DataRowState enumeration. The exact member depends on the menu command that was clicked. To retrieve the rows that have been added to the DataTable but not yet committed to the database, the code creates the DT DataTable with the following statement:

```
DT = DsCustomers1.Customers.GetChanges( _
              System.Data.DataRowState.Added)
```

Once the DataTable with the added rows has been created, the program displays its rows on a CheckListBox control on an auxiliary form, which is shown in Figure 5.2. The rows are added to the control's Items collection. To display a meaningful value on the control, we set the control's DisplayMember property to the name of the CompanyName column. The user can select one or more rows and undo their changes by clicking the Undo Changes button on the form.

To store the edited rows to the DT DataTable, we pass to the GetChanges method the constant DataRowState.Modified. For the deleted rows, we call the GetChanges method with the DataRowState.Deleted argument. After selecting the appropriate rows, the code populates the CheckedListBox control on the auxiliary form and displays it.

**FIGURE 5.2:**

Viewing the changed rows
of the Customers table
and undoing the changes
on selected rows

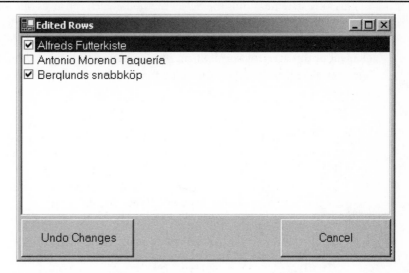

The auxiliary form in Figure 5.2 is displayed modally—we don't want the user to be able to edit additional rows (or add new ones) while viewing the changed rows. Upon return, the code goes through the selected rows and calls the RejectChanges method with a loop like the following:

```
For Each DRow In auxFrm.CheckedListBox1.CheckedItems
    ' reject changes made to DRow
Next
```

Notice that you can't undo the changes in the DT DataTable. You must locate the selected rows in the original DataSet and call their RejectChanges method. To locate the corresponding rows in the DSCustomers1 DataSet, we use the FindByCustomerID method, passing as argument the customer's ID (this value is retrieved from the selected row on the CheckedList-Box control). The following statement rejects the changes for added and modified rows; DRow is a DataRow variable that represents one of the rows selected on the auxiliary form:

```
DsCustomers1.Customers.FindByCustomerID( _
    DRow.Item("CustomerID")).RejectChanges()
```

This technique, however, won't work with deleted rows. The FindByCustomerID method can't locate deleted rows, so we had to locate the selected row with the Select method. We also had to use the overloaded form of the Select method that allows you to specify the state of the row you want to read. Here's the statement that rejects the deletion of a specific row represented by the DRow variable:

```
DsCustomers1.Customers.Select("CustomerID='" & _
        DRow.Item("CustomerID") & "'", "", _
        System.Data.DataViewRowState.Deleted) _
        (0).RejectChanges()
```

This long statement calls the Select method, which retrieves one or more rows based on the specified filter. The specific filter we use will return a single row (the CustomerID field is unique in the table), but still as the first element of an array of DataRow objects. We retrieve the first element of this array by specifying a zero index and then we call its RejectChanges method. The complete listing of the subroutine that handles the first three commands of the View Changes menu is shown in Listing 5.4.

**Listing 5.4          Viewing and Undoing the Changes Made to a DataTable**

```
Private Sub mnuUndo_Click(ByVal sender As System.Object, _
                          ByVal e As System.EventArgs) _
                          Handles mnuUndoAdded.Click, _
                          mnuUndoEdited.Click, _
                          mnuUndoDeleted.Click
    Dim auxFrm As New Form2()

    Dim DT As DataTable
    If CType(sender, MenuItem).Text = _
                                "Show Added Rows" Then
            DT = DsCustomers1.Customers.GetChanges( _
                    System.Data.DataRowState.Added)
        If Not DT Is Nothing Then
            auxFrm.Text = "Added Rows"
        Else
            MsgBox("There are no new rows to " & _
                "the Customers table!")
            auxFrm = Nothing
            Exit Sub
        End If
    End If

    If CType(sender, MenuItem).Text = _
                                "Show Deleted Rows" Then
        DT = DsCustomers1.Customers.GetChanges( _
                System.Data.DataRowState.Deleted)
        If Not DT Is Nothing Then
            DT.RejectChanges()
            auxFrm.Text = "Deleted Rows"
        Else
            MsgBox("There are no deleted rows " & _
                "in the Customers table")
            auxFrm = Nothing
            Exit Sub
        End If
    End If

    If CType(sender, MenuItem).Text = _
                                "Show Edited Rows" Then
```

```
        DT = DsCustomers1.Customers.GetChanges( _
                    System.Data.DataRowState.Modified)
        If Not DT Is Nothing Then
            auxFrm.Text = "Edited Rows"
        Else
            MsgBox("There are no edited rows " & _
                    "in the Customers table")
            auxFrm = Nothing
            Exit Sub
        End If
    End If

    Dim DRow As DataRow
    auxFrm.CheckedListBox1.DisplayMember = "CompanyName"
    For Each DRow In DT.Rows
        auxFrm.CheckedListBox1.Items.Add(DRow)
    Next
    Dim reply As DialogResult
    reply = auxFrm.ShowDialog()
    If reply = DialogResult.Cancel Then
        auxFrm = Nothing
        Exit Sub
    End If
    ' undo selected changes by calling RejectChanges
    For Each DRow In auxFrm.CheckedListBox1.CheckedItems
        If auxFrm.Text = "Deleted Rows" Then
            DsCustomers1.Customers.Select("CustomerID='" & _
                    DRow.Item("CustomerID") & "'", "", _
                    System.Data.DataViewRowState.Deleted) _
                    (0).RejectChanges()
        Else
            DsCustomers1.Customers.FindByCustomerID( _
                    DRow.Item("CustomerID")).RejectChanges()
        End If
    Next
    auxFrm = Nothing
End Sub
```

When you select the Submit Changes command of the Data menu to update the Customers table in the database, some of the rows in the Customers table may not be updated successfully. These rows are marked by the DataSet as being in error, and you can retrieve them with the GetErrors method. This is exactly what the View Update Errors command does. It retrieves the rows in error and displays them on the same auxiliary form. You can build a more elaborate interface that displays the rows in error along with a description of the error that prevented each specific row from updating its data source.

The GetErrors method doesn't return a DataTable object, but an array of DataRow objects. The program goes through the elements of the array returned by the GetErrors method, and for each row in error, it prints the CustomerID and CompanyName columns to identify the row followed by a description of the error. To test this command, run the application and delete a few rows. Then submit the changes to the database with the Submit Changes command. This command will most likely fail to update because all the customers of the Northwind database are referenced by one or more orders. Although these rows are deleted in the DataSet, when you attempt to update the underlying table, SQL Server will raise an error. The DataSet will mark these rows in the Customers DataTable as being in error and you can select the View Changes ➢ View Update Errors command to view them. This command retrieves the update errors and displays them on the same auxiliary form we used to display the changed rows. Listing 5.5 shows the code that implements the View Update Errors command of the View Changes menu.

**Listing 5.5**          **Displaying the Update Errors**

```
Private Sub mnuUpdateErrors_Click( _
            ByVal sender As System.Object, _
            ByVal e As System.EventArgs) _
            Handles mnuUpdateErrors.Click
    Dim RowsInError() As DataRow
    RowsInError = DsCustomers1.Customers.GetErrors()
    If RowsInError.Length = 0 Then
        MsgBox("There are no errors in the Customers table")
        Exit Sub
    End If
    Dim DRow As DataRow
    Dim auxFrm As New Form2()
    For Each DRow In RowsInError
        If DRow.RowState = DataRowState.Deleted Then
            auxFrm.CheckedListBox1.Items.Add( _
                DRow.Item("CustomerID", _
                DataRowVersion.Original) & " : " & _
                DRow.Item("CompanyName", _
                DataRowVersion.Original) & " [" & _
                DRow.RowError & "]")
        Else
            auxFrm.CheckedListBox1.Items.Add( _
                DRow.Item("CustomerID", _
                DataRowVersion.Current) & " : " & _
                DRow.Item("CompanyName", _
                DataRowVersion.Current) & " [" & _
                DRow.RowError & "]")
        End If
    Next
    auxFrm.bttnUndo.Enabled = False
    auxFrm.ShowDialog()
    auxFrm = Nothing
End Sub
```

Notice that the code handles the deleted rows differently than it handles added and modified rows. As you recall from the previous chapter, deleted rows have no current version, and we can only display their original version.

The auxiliary form doesn't give the user the option the undo the changes in any of the DataSet's rows that failed to update the corresponding rows in the database, but you can add the appropriate code to undo the changes in the rows selected on this auxiliary form. As long as the DataSet contains update errors, the AcceptChanges method isn't called and the user can view all the rows in error and fix them. You can provide a different interface for handling update errors, but the process won't be substantially different than the one we describe in this example. For example, you can display the ID of the rows that failed to apply the changes to the data source along with a description of the error on a ListBox control and let the user select a row on this control by double-clicking an item.

The most serious drawback of the Customers application is its navigational model. This navigational model doesn't allow you to jump to a specific row of the Customers table at will. You have to click the Next or Previous buttons repeatedly until you hit the desired row. Inexplicably, this is the navigational model used in many examples in the documentation and it's the navigational model used by the Data Form Wizard. The Data Form is a regular form you can add to your project to display and edit a DataSet. As soon as you add this component to your project, a wizard collects information interactively and creates the form. We are not going to discuss the Data Form Wizard in this book because it's not a developer's tool. It's a very simple tool that creates a crude interface and code without the necessary error handling statements.

## A Better Navigational Model

There are two navigational models developers use most often. The classical, time-honored method is to prompt the user to specify one or more search criteria on a separate form. The qualifying rows are displayed on a ListBox or ListView control, and the user can select with the mouse the desired row (or initiate another search). To help the user identify the desired row, you can display multiple columns (such as a customer's name, phone number, and e-mail address). You can also allow the user to specify multiple criteria and combine them with the OR/AND logical operators.

The second navigational method is to display a sorted list of strings that identify the rows of the table (customer names, product names, and so on). This method can't be used if you have to display many rows because the list will grow too long. Even with tables that contain several hundred rows, this navigational model is far more functional than the next/previous model we used in the preceding example.

In our next example, we'll use a combination of the two navigational models to locate a product row. The advantage of this method is you need not download very large tables to the

client and users won't be spending their time scrolling a list up and down. We'll provide a
TextBox control, in which the user can enter the first few characters of the product name.
When the Enter key is pressed, the program retrieves the matching rows from the Products
table and displays their names on a ListBox control. The user can then locate the desired row
in a small list. The navigational model we'll present in the following section can be used with
tables of any size.

### The Products Project

Our next example, the Products application, is an application for editing the Products table.
We've chosen the Products table this time because its rows are related to the rows of the
Categories and Suppliers tables and you'll see how to handle matching rows of related
tables. Instead of displaying IDs, we're going to display the rows of the Categories and
Suppliers tables on two ComboBox controls so that users can select the values of these
two fields by name. As the user navigates through the selected rows of the Products table, the
values on the two ComboBox controls reflect the category and supplier of the current product.

**FIGURE 5.3:**

Browsing and editing
products with the
Products application

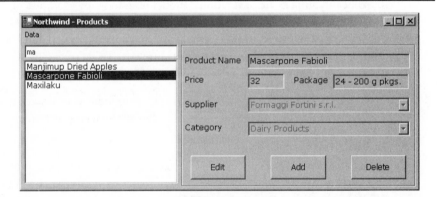

The Products project doesn't maintain the changes in a local DataSet like the Customers
project. The majority of the small- and medium-scale applications don't use a truly disconnected architecture. The clients are on the same local network as the database server, and
they can access the database at any time. The Products project submits the changes to the
database as soon as they occur. It still uses ADO.NET to access the database, and it sees any
changes made to the database by other users. Any changes made to the data by the user
of the application are committed immediately to the database, and other users can see them
as well.

Another advantage offered by this architecture is that you don't have to worry about multiple
updates and handling update errors. Each changed row (edited, added, or deleted row) is

submitted immediately to the database, and if it fails to update the underlying table, you only have to deal with the current row. You can display a message to the user, give them a chance to edit it further, or restore the row to its original state. In general, it's a lot easier to handle errors in a single row than it is to handle them in multiple rows. In short, the Customers project is a disconnected application, whereas the Products projects is a connected application. They both use the same data access mechanism, but the Products projects doesn't store the rows of the table being edited in a local DataSet.

We'll start with an overview of the application's interface and then we'll explore its code. To locate the desired product row, the user can enter a few characters in the TextBox control at the upper-left corner of the form and press Enter. The program will populate the ListBox control below the TextBox control with the names of the rows that match the user-supplied criteria (products with names that contain the specified characters).

As the user scrolls through the items of the ListBox control with the arrow keys, the fields of the selected row are displayed on the various data-bound controls in the right pane of the form. These controls have their ReadOnly property set to True so that the current row can't be edited at any time. To edit the currently selected row, the user must click the Edit button. The ReadOnly property of the controls is reset to False and the ListBox control is disabled so that no other row can be selected while a row is being edited. The user must end the edit operation by clicking the OK or Cancel button as usual.

### Selecting Products by Name
To select the rows of the Products table that match the user-specified search argument, we need the following parameterized SQL statement (you can also write a stored procedure that accepts a single parameter):

```
SELECT ProductID, ProductName, SupplierID, CategoryID,
       QuantityPerUnit, UnitPrice, UnitsInStock,
       UnitsOnOrder, ReorderLevel, Discontinued
FROM   Products
WHERE  (ProductName LIKE @productName + '%')
```

This is the CommandText property of the SelectCommand object of the DAProducts Data-Adapter. Drop the Products table on the Designer, rename the DataAdapter1 object that will be created automatically to DAProducts, and then set its CommandText property to the previous SQL statement. The statements for the DataAdapter's InsertCommand, Update-Command, and DeleteCommand properties will be generated automatically.

Generate the DSProducts DataSet with the Data ➢ Generate DataSet command. An instance of the new DataSet, the DSProducts1 object, will be added to the project. Then drop the Categories and Suppliers tables on the Designer. Rename the two DataAdapters DACategories and DASuppliers respectively and clear the option Generate Insert, Update and Delete Statements on the Advanced Options tab. As you configure the two DataAdapters for the Categories and Suppliers tables, edit the default SELECT statement so that it retrieves only the name and ID of each row in the two tables. The rows of these two tables will be used to look up category and supplier names, and we will not update their data source. Then add the two tables to the `DSProducts1` DataSet.

Because the three tables we use in our project are related in the database and the database enforces their relations, we must also establish the same relations in our DataSet and request that the DataSet enforce them. The interface itself makes it impossible for users to specify an invalid category or supplier for a product, but it's always a good idea to establish in the DataSet the same relations that are in the definition of the database. Double-click the `DSProducts` item in the Solution Explorer, and when the DataSet Designer appears, establish the relations between the Categories/Products and Suppliers/Products tables.

### Designing a Data-Bound Form

Your next step is to design the form of the application by placing on it the controls you see on the form in Figure 5.3. The controls in the right pane are bound to the corresponding fields of the DataSet's tables. To bind the controls to their matching fields, set their properties as shown in the following list. The names of the controls match the names of the fields they're bound to, and you can map easily the names in the first column in the list to the controls on the form:

| Control Name | Property | Setting |
|---|---|---|
| txtProductName | Text | `Products1 - Products.ProductName` |
| txtPrice | Text | `Products1 - Products.UnitPrice` |
| txtPackage | Text | `Products1 - Products.QuantityPerUnit` |
| cmbSupplier | DataSource | `Products1 - Suppliers` |
|  | DisplayMember | `CompanyName` |
|  | ValueMember | `SupplierID` |
|  | SelectedValue | `Products1 - Products.SupplierID` |
| cmbCategory | DataSource | `Products1 - Categories` |
|  | DisplayMember | `CategoryName` |
|  | ValueMember | `CategoryID` |
|  | SelectedValue | `Products1 - Products.CategoryID` |

Binding the TextBox controls to their data source is quite trivial. Notice that the Text property of the TextBox that's bound to the appropriate column of the data source is the Text property in DataBindings section of the Property Browser. Binding the two ComboBox controls is a bit involved. First, you must specify the data source from which the control's items will be read. For the cmbSupplier control, set the DataSource property to the name of the Suppliers table and the DisplayMember property to the name of the column you want to display, which is the CompanyName column. If you run the application at this point, the cmbSupplier control will be populated with the rows of the Suppliers table, but as you navigate through the rows of the Products table, the value on the cmbSupplier control won't change to reflect the supplier of the selected product.

You must now associate the item selected on the control to the supplier of the selected product. To do so, set the ValueMember property to the name of the column that relates the Suppliers table to the Products table. This is the SupplierID field of the Suppliers table. Then set the control's SelectedValue property to the name of the related column in the Products table. This is the SupplierID field of the Products table. Every time you select another row in the Products table, its SupplierID field will be passed to the cmbSupplier ComboBox control. The control's SelectedValue property will be set to the same value, and this action will cause the current product's supplier name to be selected in the Combo-Box control.

### Coding the Products Application

When the form is loaded for the first time, we populate the Category and Suppliers tables in the DataSet. The code to do so is shown in Listing 5.6. These two tables will not change in the course of the application; they will simply provide the items for the two ComboBox controls on the form.

**Listing 5.6**       **Filling the Categories and Suppliers Tables**

```
Private Sub Form1_Load(ByVal sender As System.Object, _
                       ByVal e As System.EventArgs) _
                       Handles MyBase.Load
    DACategories.Fill(DsProducts1, "Categories")
    DASuppliers.Fill(DsProducts1, "Suppliers")
    AddHandler DsProducts1.Products.ColumnChanging, _
                   New DataColumnChangeEventHandler( _
                           AddressOf ColumnChanging)
    AddHandler DsProducts1.Products.RowChanged, _
                   New DataRowChangeEventHandler( _
                           AddressOf RowChanged)
End Sub
```

You can ignore the two last two statements in this event handler for now. We'll discuss them shortly.

The Fill method of the DAProducts DataAdapter is called when the user presses Enter in the TextBox control to populate the Products table of the DataSet with the qualifying rows (see Listing 5.7).

**Listing 5.7    Selecting Rows from the Products Table**

```
Private Sub TextBox1_KeyUp(ByVal sender As Object, _
        ByVal e As System.Windows.Forms.KeyEventArgs) _
        Handles TextBox1.KeyUp
    If e.KeyData = Keys.Enter Then
        DAProducts.SelectCommand.Parameters( _
                 "@productName").Value = TextBox1.Text
        DsProducts1.Products.Clear()
        DAProducts.Fill(DsProducts1, "Products")
        ListBox1.Focus()
    End If
End Sub
```

Every time a new item is selected in the ListBox control, the corresponding row's fields are displayed on the controls in the right pane of the form.

When the Edit button is clicked, the code hides the Edit/Add/Delete buttons on the form, shows the OK/Cancel buttons, unlocks the controls for editing, and places the selected row in Edit mode. Notice that this time we don't use the DataBindings property in this project. Instead, we use the DataRow object's methods to control the editing operations. The BeginEdit method, shown in Listing 5.8, initiates the editing of the current row.

**Listing 5.8    Initiating the Editing of the Current Row of the Products Table**

```
Private Sub bttnEdit_Click(ByVal sender As System.Object, _
                    ByVal e As System.EventArgs) _
                    Handles bttnEdit.Click
    If ListBox1.SelectedIndex = -1 Then
        MsgBox("Please populate the list and " & _
               "select a product to edit!")
        Exit Sub
    End If
    HideEditButtons()
    editing = True
    CType(ListBox1.SelectedItem, DataRowView).BeginEdit()
    txtProductName.Focus()
End Sub
```

The *editing* variable is a Boolean one, and it's declared at the form level. It's set to True to indicate that the current operation is an edit operation. We need to distinguish between edit and add operations, because the OK button will handle both the editing of an existing row and the insertion of a new row.

To add a new row, call the DataSet's NewProductsRow method. This method returns a ProductsRow object, which represents a new row of the Products table. The code adds the new row to the Products table, but first it sets its Discontinued field. This field must be set to a valid value before the new row can be committed to the database. Because this field doesn't appear on the form and can't be edited, we set it to False (a setting that makes sense for a new row). Listing 5.9 shows the implementation of the Add button.

**Listing 5.9          Adding a New Row to the Products Table**

```
Private Sub bttnAdd_Click(ByVal sender As System.Object, _
                          ByVal e As System.EventArgs) _
                          Handles bttnAdd.Click
    HideEditButtons()
    editing = False
Dim productRow As DSProducts.ProductsRow
    productRow = DsProducts1.Products.NewProductsRow
    productRow.Discontinued = False
    DsProducts1.Products.Clear()
    DsProducts1.EnforceConstraints = False
    DsProducts1.Products.AddProductsRow(productRow)
    txtProductName.Focus()
End Sub
```

Notice that the code sets the EnforceConstraints property to False. By default, the DataSet enforces the constraints on its tables. One of the constraints in the Products table is that the ProductName field can't be null. This means that the new row can't be added to the Products table as is. One method to get around this problem is to disable the constraints temporarily and restore them when the user decides to commit the new row. Another method of getting around this problem is to set the new row's ProductName field to an empty string, which isn't the same as a null value.

**Submitting the Changes to the Database**

To commit the changes (either a new row or an edited one) to the database, the OK button's Click event handler executes the statements shown in Listing 5.10.

**Listing 5.10          Committing an Edited/Changed Row to the Database**

```
Private Sub bttnOK_Click(ByVal sender As System.Object, _
                         ByVal e As System.EventArgs) _
                         Handles bttnOK.Click
```

```
If editing Then
        CType(ListBox1.SelectedItem, _
                    DataRowView).EndEdit()
        If DsProducts1.HasChanges Then
                DAProducts.Update( _
                DsProducts1.Products.GetChanges( _
                DataRowState.Modified))
            If DsProducts1.Products.HasErrors Then
                MsgBox("The row failed to update the " & _
                        "Products table")
            End If
        End If
    Else
        DAProducts.Update(DsProducts1.Products)
        If DsProducts1.Products.HasErrors Then
            MsgBox("The row failed to update the" & _
                    "Products table")
        End If
    End If
    DsProducts1.EnforceConstraints = True
    DsProducts1.Products.AcceptChanges()
    ShowEditButtons()
End Sub
```

The same code commits a row to the database whether it's a new row or an edited one. The program submits the changes to the database, not just to the local DataSet. This isn't a truly disconnected application, and the changes are submitted to the database as soon as they occur so that other users can see them. The application also sees the changes made to the tables by other users as soon as they happen.

To commit the changes to the database, the code uses an overloaded form of the Update method, which accepts as argument an array of DataRow objects. We pass as argument to the Update method the array returned by the DataTable's GetChanges method. As a reminder, the GetChanges method returns an array with the rows that were changed. In our application, the GetChanges method will always return a single row, which is the modified row (for an edit operation) or the new row (for an add operation). If the Update method succeeds, the code also accepts the changes in the local DataSet so that the same row will no longer be marked as modified in the DataSet.

The Cancel button's code, shown in Listing 5.11, must either cancel the current edit operation or remove the line that was added to the table. If the user is canceling an edit operation, the program calls the CancelEdit method of the current row. If the user is canceling an add operation, the program removes the new row from the DataSet's Products table. There's only one row in the DataTable, so the code removes the very first row in it.

---

**Listing 5.11    Canceling an Edit/Add Operation**

```
Private Sub bttnCancel_Click(ByVal sender As System.Object,_
                             ByVal e As System.EventArgs) _
                             Handles bttnCancel.Click
    If editing Then
        CType(ListBox1.SelectedItem, _
                    DataRowView).CancelEdit()
    Else
        DsProducts1.Products.Rows(0).Delete()
        ClearFields()
    End If
    ShowEditButtons()
    ListBox1.Enabled = True
    TextBox1.ReadOnly = False
    Dim selIndex As Integer = ListBox1.SelectedIndex
    ListBox1.SelectedIndex = -1
    ListBox1.SelectedIndex = selIndex
    DsProducts1.EnforceConstraints = False
End Sub
```

---

## Viewing Related Tables

Many of the data-driven applications you'll write will simply display data and allow the user to navigate through the matching rows of multiple related tables. A typical application of this type allows users to select a customer and view the customer's orders and each order's details. These applications are not as demanding as applications that allow users to edit the data, but they're not trivial either. You already know how to use the DataGrid control to build an interface for viewing multiple related tables. This control, however, isn't the best choice for building functional user interfaces. You can use any of the available Windows controls to build very functional applications that enable users to navigate through the rows of related tables.

In this section, we're going to show you two applications that display related tables using some of the more advanced Windows controls. The ViewCustomerOrders project, whose main form is shown in Figure 5.4, displays the customers grouped by country on a TreeView control. You can expand country nodes to locate a customer. Every time you select a customer name, the customer's orders are displayed on the top ListView control in the right pane of the form. You can select any order on this control to see the order's details on the bottom ListView control. Notice that each customer's total is displayed next to the customer's name and each order's total is displayed along with each order. These values are not stored anywhere in the database. You have to write the appropriate statements to calculate the totals as you retrieve the rows from the database.

The ViewCustomerOrders project's main form displays customers, orders, and order details.

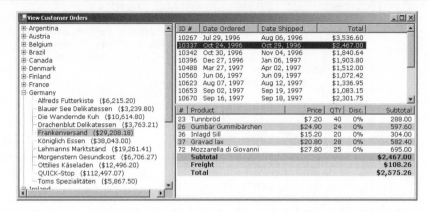

Notice also the formatting of the items of the ListView control with each order's detail lines. This is another good reason to avoid the DataGrid control, which doesn't allow you to format its rows differently (at least, the current version of the control). The ViewCustomerOrders is a typical example of a functional interface build with non-data-bound Windows controls.

The second application is the ViewProducts application, whose main form is shown in Figure 5.5. This application uses the ListView control as an alternate TreeView control. A drawback of the TreeView control is that it doesn't provide columns. The ViewProducts application displays the categories as items. When the plus symbol in front of each category's name is clicked, the category is expanded and the matching products are displayed on separate columns under the category name. The unique feature of this application is that it displays the master rows (which are the categories) and the detail rows (which are the products) in the same view of the control. The DataGrid control can display either the parent or the child rows, but not both, on the same view.

The ViewProducts project's main form displays the products under the selected category.

Each category collapses as soon as another one is expanded. You can also click a product name to see the product's units in stock and units on order as well as the total number of units sold for each product.

## DataSets vs. Queries

Both programs share a very important feature: the data is not loaded all at once. In a real production environment, you can't afford to download enormous tables to the client so that users may see a few of the rows (even though the DataSet makes it very convenient to download related tables to the client). The table with the orders can grow extremely large, and so can the table with the products. Sometimes, the number of rows is not the only limitation. The View-Products application retrieves not only product names, but also totals (the number of items sold so far). The calculation of the totals for a few thousand products represents a significant burden on SQL Server, especially if the products appear in many orders. There's no reason to calculate totals for thousands of products if the user isn't going to look at more than a few dozen (at best) rows.

Instead of downloading a whole load of data to the client, the two applications use stored procedures to retrieve the requested data on demand. Even though the DataSet is an ideal tool for storing data at the client and many developers will be tempted to get at once all the data they may need in the course of the application, it's not a good idea to move more data than necessary to the client. Here's what will, most likely, happen in an application like this: The developer will download an entire table to the client and test the application. The application will perform very well with a single user and a few small tables, and it will be deployed on many clients. As more and more users are added and as the tables grow, the application will become less and less responsive, and eventually it will become quite sluggish. We've seen this happen time and again and we can give you some practical advice here.

At first, you must always test your code with real data, even if you have to create large tables with fake data. Fortunately, this won't be the case frequently. Most corporations already have volumes of data, which you will eventually have to port to another database. Start by porting the data and populating the new database so that you can test your code with real data as you develop the application.

You should always try to minimize the amount of data you move to the client. We usually try to avoid the number of trips to the database by retrieving as much data as possible at once, but there's always a trade-off between the amount of data you're willing to download to the client in a single trip and the number of trips you're willing to make to the database. There are no hard rules as to the number of rows you should retrieve from the database or how often you should make a trip to the database and request new data. In general, you shouldn't bring too many rows that the user is not likely to see. In other words, you shouldn't download to the client an entire table because the user won't see all the rows. Let the user specify selection criteria and then move the matching rows to the client. Users may specify very general selection criteria, which will result in enormous DataSets. You can still limit the selection with the help of the TOP keyword or by retrieving the count of the matching rows and displaying a warning if this value exceeds a threshold.

Of course, there are two exceptions to this rule. If the application is truly disconnected, you'll have to copy a large number of rows to the client. If you're writing an application that allows salespersons to take orders on the go, you must obviously copy the entire table with the products to the client. The second exception concerns auxiliary tables that are used frequently in the course of an application. A table with category names or a table with zip codes should probably be read once and used by various parts of the application.

Let's return to the two sample projects and examine their code, starting with the View-CustomerOrders project.

### The ViewCustomerOrders Project

Start a new project, name it ViewCustomersOrders, and place the controls you see in Figure 5.4 on the project's main form: a TreeView control and two ListView controls. The form uses a Panel control and two Splitter controls so that the three panes can be resized in any way that suits the user. The View property of the two ListView controls must be set to Details and you must populate the Columns collection of the two controls with the appropriate headers.

We'll start by creating the proper Connection and DataAdapter objects. Drop the Customers tables onto the form to create the SqlConnection1 and SqlDataAdapter1 objects. Rename SqlDataAdapter1 Customers. The Customers DataAdapter will retrieve all the customers along with the total revenue generated by each customer. Specify the following SELECT statement and do not generate the statements for updating the data source. The SELECT statement contains totals, so the wizard won't be able to generate any statements to update the underlying tables anyway:

```
SELECT      Customers.CustomerID, Customers.CompanyName,
            Customers.Country,
            SUM(([Order Details].UnitPrice *
                [Order Details].Quantity) *
                (1 - [Order Details].Discount))
            AS CustomerTotal
FROM        Customers LEFT OUTER JOIN
            Orders ON Customers.CustomerID =
            Orders.CustomerID LEFT OUTER JOIN
            [Order Details] ON
            [Order Details].OrderID = Orders.OrderID
```

```
GROUP BY    Customers.Country, Customers.CompanyName,
            Customers.CustomerID
ORDER BY    Customers.Country, Customers.CompanyName
```

This statement will return the rows of the Customers table grouped by country. Each row contains the customer's ID and name as well as the total of all orders placed by the customer. Next, create a new DataSet with the Data ➣ Generate DataSet command and name it AllCustomers. The AllCustomers DataSet contains a single table, the Customers table. The Customers DataAdapter will be used in the form's Load event handler to fill the AllCustomers DataSet.

We need two more DataAdapters, one to retrieve the orders of the selected customer, and another one to retrieve the selected order's detail lines. These rows will be downloaded to the client on demand. Drop the Orders table from the Solution Explorer onto the form and rename the DataAdapter object that will be created into CustomerOrders. The following statement retrieves the orders of a specific customer (specified by their ID). Use this SELECT statement to configure the CustomerOrders DataAdapter. Again, you don't need to generate any INSERT, UPDATE, and DELETE statements for this DataAdapter:

```
SELECT      Orders.OrderID,
            ROUND(SUM([Order Details].UnitPrice *
            (1 - [Order Details].Discount) *
            [Order Details].Quantity), 2) AS Total,
            Orders.OrderDate, Orders.ShippedDate,
            Orders.Freight
FROM        [Order Details] INNER JOIN Orders ON
            [Order Details].OrderID = Orders.OrderID
WHERE       (Orders.CustomerID = @custID)
GROUP BY    Orders.OrderID, Orders.OrderDate,
            Orders.ShippedDate, Orders.Freight
```

After configuring the CustomerOrders DataAdapter, create the CustomerOrders DataSet and add to it the Orders table. This DataSet will be populated every time a new customer is selected and will be used to populate the upper ListView control.

We need yet another DataAdapter to retrieve the details of the selected order. Drop the Order Details table on the form and rename the new DataSet OrderDetails. The Select-Command object of the OrderDetails DataAdapter in the project retrieves the detail lines of a specific order; it is shown here:

```
SELECT      [Order Details].OrderID,
            [Order Details].ProductID,
            [Order Details].UnitPrice,
            [Order Details].Quantity,
            [Order Details].Discount, Products.ProductName
FROM        [Order Details] INNER JOIN Products ON
            [Order Details].ProductID = Products.ProductID
WHERE       [Order Details].OrderID = @orderID
```

The @orderID parameter will be supplied by the program prior to calling the OrderDetails DataAdapter's Fill method. Create the OrderDetails DataSet and add the Order Details table to it.

When the form is loaded, the TreeView control will be populated with the names of the countries and the names of the corresponding customers under each country. The code that populates the TreeView control iterates through the AllCustomers1.Customers table's rows and adds customer names, along with their totals, to the control. If the current customer's country is the same as the country of the previously added customer, the code adds a new customer node under the current country node. If not, it adds a new country node and the customer's name under the newly created country code. Listing 5.12 shows the code that's executed when the form is loaded.

**Listing 5.12**          **Populating the TreeView Control with the Customers Table's Rows**

```
Private Sub Form1_Load(ByVal sender As System.Object, _
                       ByVal e As System.EventArgs) _
                       Handles MyBase.Load
    customers.Fill(AllCustomers1)
    Dim iRow As Integer
    Dim countryNode, customerNode As TreeNode
    countryNode = New TreeNode()
    countryNode.Text = _
            AllCustomers1.Tables("Customers"). _
            Rows(0).Item("Country")
    TreeView1.Nodes.Add(countryNode)
    For iRow = 0 To AllCustomers1.Tables( _
                    "Customers").Rows.Count - 1
        Dim currentRow As DataRow = _
                        AllCustomers1.Tables( _
                        "Customers").Rows(iRow)
        If countryNode.Text <> _
                currentRow.Item("Country") Then
            countryNode = New TreeNode()
            countryNode.Text = currentRow.Item("Country")
            TreeView1.Nodes.Add(countryNode)
        End If
        customerNode = New TreeNode()
        If TypeOf (currentRow.Item("CustomerTotal")) _
                    Is System.DBNull Then
            customerNode.Text = _
                    currentRow.Item("CompanyName")
        Else
            customerNode.Text = _
                    currentRow.Item("CompanyName") & _
                    "  (" & Format(currentRow.Item _
                    ("CustomerTotal"), "$#,###.00") & ")"
        End If
```

```
        customerNode.Tag = currentRow.Item("CustomerID")
        countryNode.Nodes.Add(customerNode)
    Next
End Sub
```

Notice that the Tag property of the nodes that correspond to customers is set to the corresponding customer's ID. This will allow us later to quickly read the ID of the selected customer and retrieve the customer's order from the database when the user selects a customer on the control. The Tag property of the country nodes isn't set.

Now we must program the TreeView control's AfterSelect event so that every time the user selects another node, the corresponding customer's orders are retrieved from the database and displayed on the top ListView control in the right pane of the form. The code in Listing 5.13 is executed every time the user selects another customer on the TreeView control.

**Listing 5.13      Retrieving and Displaying the Selected Customer's Orders**

```
Private Sub TreeView1_AfterSelect( _
      ByVal sender As System.Object, _
      ByVal e As System.Windows.Forms.TreeViewEventArgs) _
      Handles TreeView1.AfterSelect
    If e.Node.Tag Is Nothing Then Exit Sub
    CustomerOrders1.Clear()
    CustomerOrders.SelectCommand. _
              Parameters("@custID").Value = _
              e.Node.Tag.ToString
    CustomerOrders.Fill(CustomerOrders1)
    Dim iRow As Integer
    ListView1.Items.Clear()
    For iRow = 0 To CustomerOrders1.Tables(0).Rows.Count - 1
        Dim currentRow As DataRow = _
              CustomerOrders1.Tables(0).Rows(iRow)
        ListView1.Items.Add( _
                  currentRow.Item("OrderID").ToString)
        If currentRow.Item("OrderDate") Is DBNull.Value Then
            ListView1.Items(iRow).SubItems.Add("")
        Else
            ListView1.Items(iRow).SubItems.Add( _
                  Format(currentRow.Item("OrderDate"), _
                  "MMM dd, yyyy"))
        End If
        If currentRow.Item("ShippedDate") Is _
                              DBNull.Value Then
            ListView1.Items(iRow).SubItems.Add("")
        Else
            ListView1.Items(iRow).SubItems.Add( _
                  Format(currentRow.Item("ShippedDate"), _
                  "MMM dd, yyyy"))
```

```
        End If
        If currentRow.Item("Total") Is DBNull.Value Then
            ListView1.Items(iRow).SubItems.Add("0")
        Else
            ListView1.Items(iRow).SubItems.Add( _
                    Format(currentRow.Item("Total"), _
                    "$#,###.00"))
        End If
        If currentRow.Item("Freight") Is DBNull.Value Then
            ListView1.Items(iRow).SubItems.Add("0")
        Else
            ListView1.Items(iRow).SubItems.Add( _
                    currentRow.Item("Freight"))
        End If
    Next
    ' SELECT THE FIRST ITEM IN THE COLLECTION
    If ListView1.Items.Count > 0 Then _
                    ListView1.Items(0).Selected = True
End Sub
```

The code fills the `CustomerOrders` DataSet with the rows of the Orders table that correspond to the selected customers. Then it iterates through the rows of the Customers table and adds a new item to the ListView control for each customer. The subitems are added one at a time, and they correspond to selected columns of the Orders table.

When an order's row in the upper ListView control is clicked, the program executes another command against the database to retrieve the selected order's detail lines. The selection of an order is signaled by the SelectedIndexChanged event of the ListView1 control. In this event's handler, we extract the ID of the selected row (the order's ID is stored in the first column of the control, which is not visible) and pass it as argument to the SelectCommand object of the `OrderDetails` DataAdapter. Then we call the DataAdapter's Fill method to populate the first table in the OrderDetails DataSet with the rows of the Order Details table that refer to the selected order. Finally, the code iterates through the rows of the `OrderDetails.Tables(0)` table and adds a new item to the lower ListView control for each row. Listing 5.14 shows the statements that retrieve the detail lines of the selected row and display them on the ListView control.

**Listing 5.14**       **Retrieving and Displaying the Selected Order's Details**

```
Private Sub ListView1_SelectedIndexChanged( _
            ByVal sender As System.Object, _
            ByVal e As System.EventArgs) _
            Handles ListView1.SelectedIndexChanged
    If ListView1.SelectedItems.Count > 0 Then
        Dim LineTotal, OrderSubtotal As Decimal
        Dim orderID As Integer
        orderID = CInt(ListView1.SelectedItems(0). _
                SubItems(0).Text)
```

```
OrderDetails1.Clear()
OrderDetails.SelectCommand. _
          Parameters("@orderID").Value = orderID
OrderDetails.Fill(OrderDetails1)
Dim iRow As Integer
ListView2.Items.Clear()
For iRow = 0 To _
          OrderDetails1.Tables(0).Rows.Count - 1
    Dim currentRow As DataRow = _
          OrderDetails1.Tables(0).Rows(iRow)
    ListView2.Items.Add( _
          currentRow.Item("ProductID").ToString)
    If currentRow.Item("ProductName") Is _
                                   Nothing Then
        ListView2.Items(iRow).SubItems.Add(" ")
    Else
        ListView2.Items(iRow).SubItems.Add( _
          currentRow.Item("ProductName"))
    End If
    If currentRow.Item("UnitPrice") Is Nothing Then
        ListView2.Items(iRow).SubItems.Add("*")
    Else
        ListView2.Items(iRow).SubItems.Add( _
          Format(currentRow.Item("UnitPrice"), _
              "$#,###.00"))
    End If
    If currentRow.Item("Quantity") Is Nothing Then
        ListView2.Items(iRow).SubItems.Add("*")
    Else
        ListView2.Items(iRow).SubItems.Add( _
          Format(currentRow.Item("Quantity"), _
              "###"))
    End If
    If currentRow.Item("Discount") Is Nothing Then
        ListView2.Items(iRow).SubItems.Add("0")
    Else
        ListView2.Items(iRow).SubItems.Add( _
          Format(currentRow.Item("Discount") _
              * 100, "##0\%"))
    End If
    LineTotal = _
    CDec((1 - currentRow.Item("Discount")) * _
              currentRow.Item("UnitPrice") * _
              currentRow.Item("Quantity"))
    ListView2.Items(iRow).SubItems.Add( _
              Format(LineTotal, "#,###.00"))
    OrderSubtotal = OrderSubtotal + LineTotal
    If iRow Mod 2 Then
        ListView2.Items(iRow).BackColor = _
                              Color.Gainsboro
    End If
Next
```

```
                    ' Add a new item to display the order total
                    ' The first cell is empty
                    ListView2.Items.Add("")
                    ListView2.Items(iRow).SubItems.Add("Subtotal")
                    ListView2.Items(iRow).SubItems.Add("")
                    ListView2.Items(iRow).SubItems.Add("")
                    ListView2.Items(iRow).SubItems.Add("")
                    ListView2.Items(iRow).SubItems.Add( _
                            Format(OrderSubtotal, "$#,###.00#"))
                    ' display the row with subtotal in bold
                    ListView2.Items(iRow).Font = _
                            New Font("Verdana", 9, FontStyle.Bold)
                    ListView2.Items(iRow).BackColor = Color.Thistle
                    ' Add a new item to display freight
                    ListView2.Items.Add("")
                    Dim OrderFreight As Decimal = _
                            CDec(ListView1.SelectedItems(0). _
                            SubItems(4).Text)
                    ListView2.Items(iRow + 1).SubItems.Add("Freight")
                    ListView2.Items(iRow + 1).SubItems.Add("")
                    ListView2.Items(iRow + 1).SubItems.Add("")
                    ListView2.Items(iRow + 1).SubItems.Add("")
                    ListView2.Items(iRow + 1).SubItems.Add( _
                            Format(OrderFreight, "$#,###.00#"))
                    ' display the row with freight in bold
                    ListView2.Items(iRow + 1).Font = _
                            New Font("Verdana", 9, FontStyle.Bold)
                    ListView2.Items(iRow + 1).BackColor = _
                            Color.PaleTurquoise
                    ' Finally, add a new item to display the grand total
                    ' The first cell is empty, as usual
                    ListView2.Items.Add("")
                    Dim OrderTotal As Decimal = _
                            OrderSubtotal + OrderFreight
                    ListView2.Items(iRow + 2).SubItems.Add("Total")
                    ListView2.Items(iRow + 2).SubItems.Add("")
                    ListView2.Items(iRow + 2).SubItems.Add("")
                    ListView2.Items(iRow + 2).SubItems.Add("")
                    ListView2.Items(iRow + 2).SubItems.Add( _
                            Format(OrderTotal, "$#,###.00#"))
                    ' display the row with total in bold
                    ListView2.Items(iRow + 2).Font = _
                            New Font("Verdana", 10, FontStyle.Bold)
                    ListView2.Items(iRow + 2).BackColor = _
                                    Color.Moccasin
        End If
End Sub
```

The code in Listing 5.14 is lengthy, but it's easy to follow. After adding to the lower ListView control the items that correspond to the detail lines of a specific order, it adds a few more items for displaying the totals. Most of the subitems in the rows with the totals are empty, and each of these rows is formatted differently. The ListView control allows you to set a different font and background color for each row, and we exploit this feature of the control to generate a grid with custom formatting (something you can't do with the DataGrid control). The ListView control isn't data-bound, which explains why we had to write so much code to populate it. Populating a DataGrid, on the other hand, doesn't require any code at all.

In this project, we made the assumption that the Customers table isn't very large and we can download it in its entirety to the client. If you don't want to download all the rows to the client, you can display only the countries on a ComboBox or ListBox control. Every time the user selects a country, you can download the customers from that specific country. You can select customers based on different criteria, such as the name, the contact's name, and so on.

The interface we propose in this project doesn't store any information about orders to the client. This means that a customer's orders may be downloaded several times in the course of the application if the user selects to view the same customer more than once. This may happen while you test the application, but real users won't request the same information more than once. If they return to view a customer for a second time, they probably need the most up-to-date information, and it makes sense to retrieve the information from the database again rather than display information stored in the local client.

### The ViewProducts Project

The ViewProducts project is more of an exercise in coding the ListView control than coding a traditional data-bound form. The application's main form is covered mostly by a ListView control, which behaves a lot like a TreeView control. It displays parent rows (the categories) and child rows (the products under each category). To expand a category and view the products under it, the user can click anywhere on the corresponding row. The plus symbol in front of the category name, which turns into a minus symbol when the category is expanded, indicates that the current category contains child rows and can be expanded. Notice that you can expand only one category at a time. Every time you expand a new category, the currently expanded category is automatically collapsed.

The ViewProducts project uses two DataAdapters, one to retrieve the rows of the Categories tables and another one to retrieve the products under a specific category. The DACategories DataAdapter is based on the following SELECT statement:

```
SELECT CategoryID, CategoryName FROM Categories
```

The DAProducts DataAdapter is based on a parameterized query that retrieves the rows of the Products table based on their CategoryID column:

```
SELECT     ProductID, ProductName,
           UnitPrice, UnitsInStock
```

```
FROM       Products
WHERE      (CategoryID = @category)
ORDER BY   ProductName
```

None of the two DataAdapters updates the database; they only select rows with their respective SelectCommand properties. After configuring the two DataAdapters, you can create two DataSets, one for each DataAdapter. The DataSet that corresponds to the DACategories DataAdapter is called DSCategories and it contains all the rows from the Categories table. The other one, the DSProducts DataSet, corresponds to the DAProducts table and it contains the selected rows from the Products table.

We also need a mechanism to display the details of the selected product on the controls to the right of the ListView control. These details are the units in stock, units on order, and units sold. This information is retrieved from the database with a stored procedure, the GetProduct-Units stored procedure. The GetProductUnits stored procedure retrieves the details about a specific product, whose ID is passed as argument:

```
ALTER PROCEDURE GetProductUnits
@productID AS int
AS
SELECT Products.ProductID, Products.ProductName,
       Products.UnitsInStock, UnitsOnOrder,
       SUM([order details].quantity) AS UnitsSold
FROM   products INNER JOIN [order details]
       ON products.productid=[order details].productid
WHERE  Products.ProductID=@productID
GROUP BY   Products.ProductID, Products.ProductName,
           Products.UnitsInStock, UnitsOnOrder
```

The GetProductUnits stored procedure returns a single row with the selected product's ID and name, the units on order, and the total number of units sold. The last value is computed as the sum of the quantities of all rows in the Order Details table that reference the specific product. To use it, you must first attach it to the database. Right-click the Stored Procedures entry of the Northwind database in Server Explorer, select New Stored Procedure from the context menu, and enter the last SQL statement shown here.

To execute this stored procedure from within your code, you must set up a Command object. Drop the GetProductUnits stored procedure from Server Explorer onto the form and a new SqlCommand object will be created. Its Connection object will be set to SqlConnection1, its CommandText property will be set to the name of the stored procedure, and its Command-Type property will be set to CommandType.StoredProcedure.

A Parameters collection will also be set up for the Command object. If you click the button with the ellipsis next to the Parameters entry of the Property Browser, you will see the two parameters of the stored procedure. The return value (all stored procedures have a return value) and the `@productID` parameter. To execute this Command object, you must set up the `@productID` parameter and then call its ExecuteReader method.

When the form is loaded, the Categories DataTable of the DataSet is filled with the rows of the Categories table. The code, shown in Listing 5.15, iterates through the rows of this table and displays them on the second column of the ListView control. In the first column it displays a plus symbol to indicate that the item can be expanded. Each item's Tag property is set to the ID of the corresponding category. We'll use this information to retrieve the matching products when the user clicks a category's name (or the plus symbol in front of its name) to expand the selected category.

**Listing 5.15      Displaying the Categories on a ListView Control**

```
Private Sub bttnLoad_Click(ByVal sender As System.Object, _
                        ByVal e As System.EventArgs) _
                        Handles bttnLoad.Click
    ListView1.Items.Clear()
    DsCategories1.Clear()
    ' Set an hourglass cursor while filling
    ' the Categories table and populating the grid
    Me.Cursor = Cursors.WaitCursor
    DACategories.Fill(DsCategories1, "Categories")
    Dim treeFont As New Font("Verdana", 10, FontStyle.Bold)
    ListView1.Columns(3).TextAlign = _
                        HorizontalAlignment.Right
    Dim row As Integer
    Dim LItem As ListViewItem
    Dim lSubItem As ListViewItem.ListViewSubItem
    For row = 0 To DsCategories1.Tables(0).Rows.Count - 1
        LItem = New ListViewItem()
        LItem.Font = treeFont
        LItem.Text = "+"
        LItem.Tag = _
                DsCategories1.Tables("Categories"). _
                Rows(row).Item("CategoryID")
        lSubItem = New ListViewItem.ListViewSubItem()
        lSubItem.Text = _
                DsCategories1.Tables(0). _
                Rows(row).Item(1).ToString
        LItem.SubItems.Add(lSubItem)
        ListView1.Items.Add(LItem)
    Next
    ' Reset cursor back to default shape
    Me.Cursor = Cursors.Default
End Sub
```

When the user selects an item on the ListView control, the code must decipher whether the selected item is a category name or a product name. If it's a product name, it executes the cmdSelectedProduct Command against the database and displays the values returned by the query on the corresponding TextBoxes. If the selected item is a category name (the code examines the selected item's Text property and if it's a plus symbol, it knows that a category name was clicked), it removes all the items that don't have the plus symbol in front of them (in effect, it collapses the currently expanded category) and then expands the selected category. It does so by retrieving the selected category's products with the DAProducts DataAdapter and inserting them into the ListView control under the selected category.

The selection of a product is handled from within the control's Click event handler, which calls the HandleItemSelection() subroutine. This subroutine, shown in Listing 5.16, extracts the ID of the selected category and passes it as a parameter to the SelectCommand object of the DAProducts DataAdapter. The DataAdapter is then used to populate the DSProducts1 DataSet. The For...Next loop iterates through the rows of the Products table in the DSProducts1 DataSet and inserts a new item in the ListView control for each row. The new items are inserted right below the selected category.

**Listing 5.16     The *HandleItemSelection()* Subroutine**

```
Sub HandleItemSelection()
    If ListView1.FocusedItem.Text = "+" Then
        Dim i As Integer
        For i = ListView1.Items.Count - 1 To 0 Step -1
            If ListView1.Items(i).Text = "" Then
                ListView1.Items.RemoveAt(i)
            ElseIf ListView1.Items(i).Text = "-" Then
                ListView1.Items(i).Text = "+"
            End If
        Next
        ClearTextFields()
        Dim LItem As ListViewItem
        Dim categoryID As Integer = _
                    CInt(ListView1.SelectedItems(0).Tag)
        DAProducts.SelectCommand. _
                Parameters("@category").Value = categoryID
        DsProducts1.Clear()
        Me.Cursor = Cursors.WaitCursor
        DAProducts.Fill(DsProducts1, "Products")
        Me.Cursor = Cursors.Default
        Dim row As Integer
        Dim productRow As DataRow
        Dim currentIndex As Integer = _
                ListView1.SelectedIndices(0)
        For row = 0 To _
            DsProducts1.Tables("Products").Rows.Count - 1
            productRow = _
                    DsProducts1.Tables("Products").Rows(row)
            LItem = New ListViewItem()
```

```
                LItem.Tag = productRow.Item("ProductID")
                LItem.SubItems.Add("")
                LItem.SubItems.Add( _
                        productRow.Item("ProductName").ToString)
                LItem.SubItems.Add( _
                        Format(productRow.Item("UnitPrice"), _
                                "$#,##0.00"))
                        currentIndex += 1
                ListView1.Items.Insert(currentIndex, LItem)
            Next
            ListView1.SelectedItems(0).Text = "-"
        ElseIf ListView1.FocusedItem.Text = "-" Then
            Dim selectedItem As Integer = _
                        ListView1.SelectedIndices(0)
            Dim itm As Integer = selectedItem + 1
            While ListView1.Items(itm).Text = ""
                ListView1.Items(itm).Remove()
            End While
            ListView1.SelectedItems(0).Text = "+"
            ClearTextFields()
        End If
    End Sub
```

The selection of an item that corresponds to a product is handled in the control's Selected-IndexChanged event handler, which is shown in Listing 5.17. If the selected row is not a category, then the user has selected a product row. The code executes the cmdSelectedProducts object's SelectCommand, passing the ID of the selected product as argument. This command should return a single row. If not, an error occurred. Most likely the product row has been removed from the table since the category's products were last read (a very unlikely error). If all goes well, the code reads the fields of the single row returned by the command and displays them on the appropriate controls on the form.

**Listing 5.17        Handling the Selection of a Product**

```
Private Sub ListView1_SelectedIndexChanged( _
                ByVal sender As System.Object, _
                ByVal e As System.EventArgs) _
                Handles ListView1.SelectedIndexChanged
    If ListView1.SelectedIndices.Count = 0 Then Exit Sub
    If ListView1.FocusedItem.Text <> "+" And _
            ListView1.FocusedItem.Text <> "-" Then
        cmdSelectedProduct.Parameters _
                ("@productID").Value = _
                CInt(ListView1.FocusedItem.Tag)
        SqlConnection1.Open()
        Dim sqlReader As System.Data.SqlClient.SqlDataReader
        sqlReader = cmdSelectedProduct.ExecuteReader()
```

```
        If sqlReader.Read Then
            txtSelProduct.Text = _
                    sqlReader.Item("ProductName").ToString
            txtStock.Text = _
                    sqlReader.Item("UnitsInStock").ToString
            txtOrder.Text = _
                    sqlReader.Item("UnitsOnOrder").ToString
            txtSold.Text = _
                    sqlReader.Item("UnitsSold").ToString
        Else
            MsgBox("The selected product has been " & _
                    "removed from the table")
        End If
        SqlConnection1.Close()
    End If
End Sub
```

The code of the various event handlers of the ViewProducts project is fairly lengthy and most of it handles the ListView control's items and their appearance. Nevertheless, it demonstrates how to use non-bound Windows controls to create a functional user interface for viewing data.

## The Three Tiers of a Data-Bound Application

Data-driven Windows applications fall into two major categories: client/server applications and multitier applications. A client/server application consists of two layers: the client application and the database. These two layers are also known as the *tiers* of the application, and they're called the presentation tier and the data tier. The *presentation tier* is the application that interacts with the user and submits queries to the database. When the user edits one or more rows through the client application, these changes are submitted to the database with the appropriate code. You can keep the changes to the local DataSet and submit them in batches to the database, or you can submit each row as soon as it's edited. The *data tier* is the database. You can interact with the database through SQL statements, or you can build stored procedures that perform the queries against the database and call these stored procedures to query the database. The examples we looked at so far were client/server applications. The client application, which is the presentation tier, talks directly to the database. Of course, you need not write any code for the data tier because SQL Server knows how to store and query its data. You may have to attach to the database some stored procedures that perform common operations, but this is all the code you may need to write for the data tier. Your effort as a programmer is in the implementation of the client application.

One of the problems with the client/server architecture is the organization of the code. When you work as a project manager and you allow the developers to embed the data access code in the client application, you have to rely on all developers to fully understand the structure of the database. If you decide to change the structure of the database a little, or if the corporation decides to change the method for calculating discounts or commissions, many developers will have to revise their code.

A better technique for building robust, maintainable applications is to insert a new layer of code between the client and the server. This layer includes what is known as *business logic*. The method for calculating discounts belongs to the business logic: the clients will submit an invoice to this layer, which is responsible for calculating the discount and returning it to the client application. If you change the method for calculating the discount, you'll only have to change the code in a single place and the client applications will see the new method.

This is a new tier that sits between the presentation and data tier, and it's implemented as a custom class that exposes properties and methods. Developers working on the presentation tier (the client application) don't need to understand how the database is structured or how to commit an order through a transaction. They simply call a function, say the AddInvoice function, passing the invoice's header and detail lines as arguments. Developers use objects that represent the entities they manipulate with their code and their task is greatly simplified.

The client application and the middle tier communicate by passing objects that represent the physical entities they manipulate (customers, products, orders, and so on). The client application manipulates the properties of an object and calls its methods to act on these objects. The Customer object, for example, should expose the columns of the Customers table as properties. The expressions Customer.CompanyName and Customer.Address represent basic attributes of the customer. After setting up a new Customer object, you can call its Save method to add a new row to the Customers table. You can also change the properties of an existing customer and then call the Update method to submit the changes to the database. As you will see in the example in this section, the developers working on the presentation tier access the middle tier and never execute commands directly against the database. The middle tier is their "door" to the database, and you can protect the database by adding layers upon layers of validation code in the middle tier.

Another problem with the client/server architecture is that client/server applications don't *scale* very well. As more and more users are added to a database, you'll have to deal with performance issues: the application becomes less and less responsive. When a client/server application becomes less responsive, there are two things you can do. The first solution is to upgrade the hardware. A faster server will extend your application's life. You can even add processors to the machine on which SQL Server runs. This is known as *scaling up the application:* you beef up the hardware to prolong the life of your application.

Applications, however, can't be scaled up for too long. Scaling up an application is a viable technique for client applications that run on a local area network and for which the number of users is under control. But what if your application is accessed from the Web? What if your application turns out to be quite popular and more and more users in the organization want to run it? You may reach a point at which you'll have to *scale out* your application, which means that you'll have to add more database servers and use replication to keep them synchronized. You'll also deploy some form of balance-loading software to determine which server will service each request (obviously, the server with the smallest load at the time). An application that scales out must be implemented in three tiers. The presentation tier runs on the client and it contains the code necessary to interact with the user. The middle tier can run on one or more application servers. As more users are added, you can add a second and possibly more application servers and each application server can contact one or more database servers. As you can see, the three-tier architecture can be scaled to support far more users than the client/ server architecture could ever support.

You will hear again and again that the client/server application doesn't scale well and large applications should be implemented with a three-tier architecture. This is quite true, but it doesn't apply to small-scale business applications. Not all applications (or even most applications) written today are designed to be indefinitely scaled. In our view, the separation of the code according to its role in the application is the most important characteristic of the multitier architecture. If you decide to write a middle tier for your application, even if you don't deploy it on an application server (as we will do in the example of this section), you will have to understand the problem you're called to solve, model the process with the appropriate objects, and then use these objects in your code. The design of the components of the middle tier will force you to reflect on the process itself and understand it in depth.

The design of the middle tier takes substantial time and effort. Once you have implemented the middle tier, however, your job will become considerably easier. In large projects, the middle tier is a practical necessity. You will implement in the middle-tier all the business logic and the middle tier will become a solid foundation for the client application. The same components will be used by all the parts of the client application as well as by different client applications. You may start with a client application that runs on Windows workstations. If you decide to port parts of the application to the Web, you can build a web application that uses the same middle-tier components. A component that accepts orders and commits them to the database can be used to take orders with a Windows client application as well as with a web application. The client applications may be totally different, but the same middle tier components are reused.

At a later time, you may decide to build a client application that runs on Pocket PCs. Although you won't be able to use any of the client application's code, you will be able to reuse the middle tier as is. After all, no matter what platform the client application is running on and what type of interface it uses to interact with the user, it performs the same operations against the database.

There are other benefits to the multitier architecture. If you deploy the middle tier on an application server, you can post changes to a single computer and all clients will see the new code. For example, you can change the code that calculates customer credit limits or discount categories for groups of customers. In a client/server application you'd have to deploy the revised client application to all the workstations. With a three-tier application, you need only install the revised component on the application server and all clients will use the new version of the component.

You will find more information on building multitiered applications in Chapter 7, "The Business Tier." In the same chapter, you'll learn how to use Web services to implement the business tier. In the following section, we'll focus on the principles of breaking a data-driven application into two tiers, the application tier and the business tier. Our goal is to show you how to isolate the different operations and implement them separately. Both tiers in our application reside in the same solution, so the application's tiers are logical rather than physical tiers.

## The NonBound Products Project

To demonstrate the process of designing three-tiered applications, we'll build another version of the Products application. This is the Products NonBound project. Its interface, shown in Figure 5.6, is the same as the interface of the Products project, but this time we'll implement all the data-related operations in a class. This class is the application's third tier and it communicates with the database on one end and with the application on the other end.

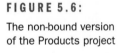

**FIGURE 5.6:**

The non-bound version of the Products project

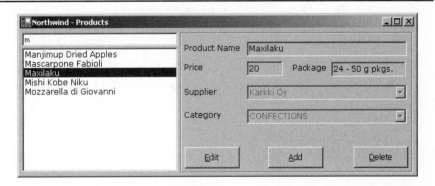

Copy the `Products` folder to a new location and rename it `Products NonBound`. We'll use the same interface as the Products project, so we can reuse the Product project's form. The only difference in the visual interface between the two applications is that the non-bound version of the project doesn't have a menu with the commands for viewing the edited rows, undoing selected changes, and committing the changes to the database. The changes are submitted to the database as soon as the user clicks the OK or the Delete button.

We won't reuse much of the original application's code, so you can delete all the code. Actually, we used the existing code as our guide, but we had to rewrite most of it. The middle tier is made up of objects that represent the entities you manipulate in your application. Ours is a very simple application that manipulates a single object that represents products. The properties of this object are the columns of the Products table (the product's name, the product's price, and so on). In addition, our class should expose methods that perform the basic operations like retrieving a specific product by its ID (or a set of products by name), adding new products to the database, and updating and deleting existing products. In effect, all the operations we performed against the database from within the Products application's code will now be coded as methods of the new class. The front end of the application will never execute any commands against the database directly. It will simply pass requests to the middle and the methods of the middle tier will access the database. The presentation tier should be able to create an object that represents a product, set its properties, and then call a method to add the new product to the database:

```
Dim Prod As New Product
Prod.Name = "new product's name"
Prod.Price = 12.95
Prod.SupplierID = 2
Prod.CategoryID = 8
Prod.Discontinued = 0
Prod.AddProduct()
```

As you can see from this short segment of code, the implementation of the presentation tier is greatly simplified with the introduction of the middle tier. The presentation tier's code doesn't know anything about the structure of the database, and it doesn't execute any statements against the database. It simply handles an object that represents a physical entity. Another object could represent customers, another one could represent orders, and so on.

The new application is running on a client machine on the same local network as SQL Server. As a result, the application's code can submit to the database any changes to the DataSet as soon as they occur.

### The Project's Middle Tier

In the middle tier, we must implement a class that represents a product. Add a new Class item to the project and name it ClassProducts.vb. This class implements a Product object and exposes properties that correspond to the columns of the Products table (we'll also add methods to the class shortly). Listing 5.18 includes the definitions of the properties of our Product class.

**Listing 5.18**   **The Properties of the Product Class**

```
Public Class Product
    Private _ProductID As Long
    Private _ProductName As String = ""
```

```
Private _ProductPrice As Decimal = 0
Private _ProductPackage As String = ""
Private _ProductSupplierID As Integer = 0
Private _ProductCategoryID As Integer = 0
Private _lastError As String

Public Property ProductID() As Long
    Get
        Return _ProductID
    End Get
    Set(ByVal Value As Long)
        _ProductID = Value
    End Set
End Property

Public Property ProductName() As String
    Get
        Return _ProductName
    End Get
    Set(ByVal Value As String)
        If Value.Trim <> "" Then
            _ProductName = Value
         End If
    End Set
End Property

Public Property ProductPrice() As Decimal
    Get
        Return _ProductPrice
    End Get
    Set(ByVal Value As Decimal)
        If Value > 0 Then
            _ProductPrice = Value
        End If
    End Set
End Property

Public Property ProductPackage() As String
    Get
        Return _ProductPackage
    End Get
    Set(ByVal Value As String)
        If Value.Trim <> "" Then
            _ProductPackage = Value
        End If
    End Set
End Property

Public Property ProductSupplierID() As Integer
    Get
        Return _ProductSupplierID
```

```
            End Get
        Set(ByVal Value As Integer)
            If Value > 0 Then
                _ProductSupplierID = Value
            End If
        End Set
    End Property

    Public Property ProductCategoryID() As Integer
        Get
            Return _ProductCategoryID
        End Get
        Set(ByVal Value As Integer)
            If Value > 0 Then
                _ProductCategoryID = Value
            End If
        End Set
    End Property
End Class
```

The class maintains the values of each product's fields in private variables and exposes them as properties. Our middle tier component will create instances of the Product class and assign to the properties of these objects the field values of a specific row in the Products table. Before we can use the Products class in our presentation tier (the VB application), we must add to the class a few methods to retrieve selected rows and update the underlying tables in the database.

The _lastError private variable is used to store the description of the most recent error. If an update operation fails, we set this variable to the description of the error. The client application can retrieve the error's description with the GetLastError method.

**The Methods to Retrieve Rows**

The next step is to implement the basic data-related operations of the application as methods. These methods must also be inserted in the Product class, a partial listing of which is shown in Listing 5.19. The first method is the GetProductsName method, which accepts a string as argument and returns the matching rows from the Products table. We'll use this method to populate the ListBox control. Listing 5.19 shows the implementation of the GetProductsBy-Name method, which returns the qualifying rows of the Products table in an ArrayList. The method doesn't return all the columns, only the ones that have a matching property in the Product class.

---

**Listing 5.19**    **The GetProductsByName Method**

```
Public Shared Function GetProductsByName( _
            ByVal prodName As String) As ArrayList
    Dim sqlConnectionString As String = _
```

```
                    "data source=.;initial catalog=Northwind; " & _
                    "integrated security=SSPI;" & _
                    "persist security info=False; " & _
                    "workstation id=POWERTOOLKIT;packet size=4096"
        Dim CN As New SqlClient.SqlConnection()
        CN.ConnectionString = sqlConnectionString

        Dim CMD As New SqlClient.SqlCommand()
        CMD.CommandText = "SELECT ProductID, ProductName, " & _
                "ISNULL(SupplierID, -1) AS SupplierID, " & _
                "ISNULL(CategoryID, -1) AS CategoryID, " & _
                "ISNULL(QuantityPerUnit, '') AS Package, " & _
                "ISNULL(UnitPrice , 0) AS Price " & _
                "FROM Products " & _
                " WHERE (ProductName LIKE @productName + '%')"
        CMD.Parameters.Add( _
                    New SqlClient.SqlParameter("@productname", _
                        prodName))
        CN.Open()
        CMD.Connection = CN
        Dim Reader As SqlClient.SqlDataReader
        Reader = CMD.ExecuteReader()
        Dim Products As New ArrayList()
        While Reader.Read
            Dim P As New Product()
            P.ProductID = Reader.Item("ProductID")
            P.ProductName = Reader.Item("ProductName")
            P.ProductPackage = Reader.Item("Package")
            P.ProductPrice = Reader.Item("Price")
            P.ProductSupplierID = Reader.Item("SupplierID")
            P.ProductCategoryID = Reader.Item("CategoryID")
            Products.Add(P)
        End While
        CN.Close()
        Return Products
    End Function
```

The GetProductsByName method is a shared one. This means that you don't have to create an instance of the class in order to call it. In this class, we'll use both shared and nonshared methods. For more information on shared methods, see the discussion of custom classes in Chapter 12, "Authoring Custom Components."

After constructing the appropriate SQL statement, the code calls the CMD Command object's ExecuteReader method. The While loop iterates through all the rows returned by the query, creates a new Product object for each row, sets the object's properties, and appends the object to the Products ArrayList. At the end, the code returns the ArrayList with Product objects.

Notice that the SELECT statement uses the ISNULL function to return meaningful values for the null fields. If you don't handle the null values in the query, you must insert multiple If statements in the loop that populates the properties of the Product object to catch the null values (one If statement for each property). If you attempt to assign the value of a null field to a property of the P object, an exception will be thrown. It's faster (and safer) to handle nulls in the statement that retrieves the data. This technique can be used only if the client tier doesn't have to distinguish between empty strings (or zero numeric values) and nulls. A field that contains a zero-length string is not Null. In most business applications, however, Nulls are represented in the presentation tier as empty strings (and zeros for numeric strings).

We also need to be able to retrieve products by their ID. The GetProductByID does exactly that, and it's similar to the GetProductsByName method. The difference is that it accepts the ID of the desired product (an integer value) as argument and returns a Product object instead of an ArrayList. The implementation of the GetProductByID method is shown in Listing 5.20 (we've omitted some lengthy statements, like the statement that sets the ConnectionString).

**Listing 5.20**     **The GetProductByID Method**

```
Public Shared Function GetProductByID( _
                    ByVal prodID As Long) As Product
    Dim sqlConnectionString As String = . . .
    Dim CN As New SqlClient.SqlConnection()
    CN.ConnectionString = sqlConnectionString

    Dim CMD As New SqlClient.SqlCommand()
    CMD.CommandText = "SELECT ProductID, ProductName, " & _
            "ISNULL(SupplierID, -1) AS SupplierID, " & _
            "ISNULL(CategoryID, -1) AS CategoryID, " & _
            "ISNULL(QuantityPerUnit, '') AS Package, " & _
            "ISNULL(UnitPrice , 0) AS Price " & _
            "FROM Products " & _
            " WHERE (ProductID = @productID)"
    CMD.Parameters.Add(_
        New SqlClient.SqlParameter("@productID", prodID))
    CN.Open()
    CMD.Connection = CN
    Dim Reader As SqlClient.SqlDataReader
    Reader = CMD.ExecuteReader()
    Dim P As New Product()
    While Reader.Read
        P.ProductID = Reader.Item("ProductID")
        P.ProductName = Reader.Item("ProductName")
        P.ProductPackage = Reader.Item("Package")
        P.ProductPrice = Reader.Item("Price")
```

```
        P.ProductSupplierID = Reader.Item("SupplierID")
        P.ProductCategoryID = Reader.Item("CategoryID")
    End While
    CN.Close()
    Return P
End Function
```

## The Methods to Update the Data Source

Finally, we need three more methods for adding a new product to the database, updating an existing product, and deleting an existing product. They're the AddProduct, UpdateProduct, and DeleteProduct methods. Unlike the methods that query the database, these three methods are implemented as instance methods: they act on the current instance of the Product object. The DeleteProduct method accepts as argument the ID of the product to be deleted, so it could be implemented as a shared method. As you will see, all the methods set the _lastError_ variable to the description of the error (should an error occur) and therefore can't be implemented as shared methods. Shared methods will not be able to access the _lastError local variable.

We didn't implement optimistic concurrency in our code, but you can edit it to add optimistic concurrency to the application. You must revise the UPDATE statement (or create a DataAdapter object and copy the UPDATE statement generated by the wizard and reuse it) and pass to the method an instance of the Product object that represents the product before editing. Listing 5.21 shows the implementation of the UpdateProduct method.

**Listing 5.21      The UpdateProduct Method**

```
Public Function UpdateProduct(_
            ByVal thisProduct As Product) As Boolean
    Dim sqlConnectionString As String = . . .
    Dim CN As New SqlClient.SqlConnection()
    CN.ConnectionString = sqlConnectionString

    Dim CMD As New SqlClient.SqlCommand()
    CMD.CommandText = _
        "UPDATE Products " & _
        "SET ProductName=@ProductName, " & _
        "QuantityPerUnit = @ProductPackage, " & _
        "UnitPrice = @ProductPrice, " & _
        "CategoryID=@ProductCategoryID, " & _
        "SupplierID = @ProductSupplierID " & _
        " WHERE ProductID = @productID"
    CMD.Parameters.Add( _
        New SqlClient.SqlParameter("@ProductID", _
            thisProduct.ProductID))
    CMD.Parameters.Add( _
        New SqlClient.SqlParameter("@ProductPrice", _
            thisProduct.ProductPrice))
```

```
        CMD.Parameters.Add( _
              New SqlClient.SqlParameter("@ProductName", _
                  thisProduct.ProductName))
        CMD.Parameters.Add( _
              New SqlClient.SqlParameter("@ProductPackage", _
                  thisProduct.ProductPackage))
        CMD.Parameters.Add( _
              New SqlClient.SqlParameter("@ProductCategoryID", _
                  thisProduct.ProductCategoryID))
        CMD.Parameters.Add( _
              New SqlClient.SqlParameter("@ProductSupplierID", _
                  thisProduct.ProductSupplierID))
        CN.Open()
        CMD.Connection = CN
        _lastError = ""
        Try
              CMD.ExecuteNonQuery()
        Catch exc As Exception
            _lastError = exc.Message
              CN.Close()
              Return False
        End Try
        CN.Close()
        Return True
    End Function
```

The AddProduct method, which is shown in Listing 5.22, is an instance method. You must first instantiate a Product object and then call its AddProduct method to commit it to the database. The calling application should execute a few statements like the following to add a new row to the Products table:

```
Dim editedProduct As New ClassProducts.Product()
editedProduct.ProductName = txtProductName.Text.Trim
editedProduct.ProductPackage = txtPackage.Text.Trim
editedProduct.ProductSupplierID = cmbSupplier.SelectedValue
editedProduct.ProductCategoryID = cmbCategory.SelectedValue
editedProduct = editedProduct.AddProduct
```

**Listing 5.22     The AddProduct Method**

```
Public Function AddProduct() As Product
    Dim sqlConnectionString As String = . . .
    Dim CN As New SqlClient.SqlConnection()
    CN.ConnectionString = sqlConnectionString

    Dim CMD As New SqlClient.SqlCommand()
    CMD.CommandText = _
```

```
                    "INSERT Products (ProductName, " & _
                    "QuantityPerUnit, UnitPrice, " & _
                    "CategoryID, SupplierID, Discontinued) " & _
                    "VALUES (@name, @package, @price, "
        If _ProductCategoryID = -1 Then
            CMD.CommandText = CMD.CommandText & " NULL, "
        Else
            CMD.CommandText = CMD.CommandText & " @categoryID, "
        End If
        If _ProductSupplierID = -1 Then
            CMD.CommandText = CMD.CommandText & " NULL, "
        Else
            CMD.CommandText = CMD.CommandText & " @supplierID, "
        End If
        CMD.CommandText = CMD.CommandText & _
                        " 1); SELECT SCOPE_IDENTITY()"
        CMD.Parameters.Add(New _
                    SqlClient.SqlParameter("@name", _
                            _ProductName))
        CMD.Parameters.Add(New _
                    SqlClient.SqlParameter("@package", _
                            _ProductPackage))
        CMD.Parameters.Add(New _
                    SqlClient.SqlParameter("@price", _
                            _ProductPrice))
        CMD.Parameters.Add(New _
                    SqlClient.SqlParameter("@categoryID", _
                            _ProductCategoryID))
        CMD.Parameters.Add(New _
                    SqlClient.SqlParameter("@supplierID", _
                            _ProductSupplierID))
        CN.Open()
        CMD.Connection = CN

        Dim newID As Integer = CMD.ExecuteScalar
        _lastError = ""
        Try
            newID = CMD.ExecuteScalar()
        Catch exc As Exception
            newID = -1
            _lastError = exc.Message
        Finally
            CN.Close()
        End Try
        If newID >= 0 Then
            Return GetProductByID(newID)
        Else
            Return Nothing
        End If
    End Function
```

Notice how the code builds the INSERT statement gradually. If the parameter is an empty string, the code converts it to null. The empty string is not the same as null, but in this application we can safely assume that fields not set to a specific value are null.

Then the code appends the proper Parameter object to the command's Parameters collection, sets its value, and finally, executes the command against the database with the ExecuteScalar method. The statement that inserts the new row returns the ID of the newly added row as its return value. At the end, the code attempts to read the product with this ID by calling the GetProductByID method if the INSERT statement returned a positive ID (this is the ID of newly inserted product). If the insertion operation failed, the INSERT statement returns –1 and the AddProduct method returns a Nothing value.

The DeleteProduct method is also an instance method. It could have implemented as a shared method, but the shared method doesn't have access to the _*lastError* variable. You can delete a row from the Products table by calling this method and passing the ID of the product to be removed as argument. Once the ID of the row to be deleted is known, you can call the DeleteProduct method with a statement like the following, where the *prodID* variable has been assigned the ID of the row to be deleted:

```
Prod.DeleteProduct(prodID)
```

The implementation of the DeleteProduct method is shown in Listing 5.23. This method attempts to delete the specified row and returns True if the row was deleted successfully, False otherwise.

**Listing 5.23      The DeleteProduct Method**

```
Public Function DeleteProduct(ByVal ProdID As Long) As Boolean
    Dim sqlConnectionString As String = . . .
    Dim CN As New SqlClient.SqlConnection()
    CN.ConnectionString = sqlConnectionString

    Dim CMD As New SqlClient.SqlCommand()
    CMD.CommandText = _
            "DELETE Products WHERE ProductID = @ProductID"
    CMD.Parameters.Add( _
            New SqlClient.SqlParameter("@ProductID", ProdID))
    CN.Open()
    CMD.Connection = CN
    _lastError = ""
    Try
        CMD.ExecuteNonQuery()
    Catch exc As Exception
        CN.Close()
        _lastError = exc.Message
        Return False
```

```
        End Try
        CN.Close()
        Return True
    End Function
```

The last method in the Class is the GetLastError method, which returns a string that describes the last error. The client's code can call the GetLastError method to find out why the last operation failed. If the DeleteProduct method returns False, which means that the deletion operation failed, you can call the GetLastError method to find out why the operation failed—most likely because the row has related rows in other tables. If the AddProduct method doesn't return a Product object that represents the newly added product, you can call the GetLastError method to find out what caused the INSERT statement to fail. The implementation of the GetLastError method is quite trivial:

```
Public ReadOnly Property GetLastError() As String
    Get
        Return _lastError
    End Get
End Property
```

All the properties and methods we discussed in this section should appear within a new class definition, the ClassProducts class:

```
Public Class ClassProducts
    Public Class Product
    . . .
    End Class
    'method definitions
End Class
```

Open the ClassProducts file and examine the code of the class that implements the application's middle tier. It's straightforward code that implements a custom class with properties and methods.

## The Presentation Tier

With the middle tier's code in place, we can now implement the presentation tier. When the form is first loaded, we populate a DataSet with two tables, the Categories and Suppliers tables. These two tables don't contain too many rows, and it makes good sense to download them in their entirety to the client DataSet once. They'll be used over and over again, so we can create a DataSet to store them at the client. Besides, when the user adds a new product, they should be able to select one of the available suppliers and categories from a ComboBox. Set up the DACategories and DASuppliers DataAdapters, create the DSProducts DataSet, and populate it with the following statements:

```
Private Sub Form1_Load(ByVal sender As System.Object, _
                    ByVal e As System.EventArgs) _
                    Handles MyBase.Load
```

```
        DACategories.Fill(DsProducts1, "Categories")
        DASuppliers.Fill(DsProducts1, "Suppliers")
    End Sub
```

The Categories and Suppliers tables of the DataSet will be used to populate the two Combo-Box controls on the form. We can easily bind the two controls to the corresponding tables of the DataSet by setting a few properties. The data binding properties of the cmbSupplier Control are as follows:

| Property Name | Setting |
|---|---|
| DataSource | DSProducts1.Suppliers |
| DisplayMember | CompanyName |
| ValueMember | SupplierID |
| SelectedItem | DSProducts1 - Products.SupplierID |
| SelectedValue | DSProducts1 - Products.SupplierID |

Here are the settings for the data binding properties of the cmbCategory Control:

| Property Name | Setting |
|---|---|
| DataSource | DSProducts1.Category |
| DisplayMember | CategoryName |
| ValueMember | CategoryID |
| SelectedItem | DSProducts1 - Products.CategoryID |
| SelectedValue | DSProducts1 - Products.CategoryID |

When the user presses Enter in the top TextBox control to retrieve a few products by name, the code calls the GetProductsByName method to retrieve the matching rows of the Products table. The method accepts as argument the string entered by the user on the Text-Box control and returns an ArrayList with the matching products, which are then used to populate the ListBox control. Listing 5.24 shows the revised code of the TextBox control's KeyUp event handler.

---

**Listing 5.24**    **Retrieving Products by Name**

```
Private Sub TextBox1_KeyUp(ByVal sender As Object, _
            ByVal e As System.Windows.Forms.KeyEventArgs) _
            Handles TextBox1.KeyUp
```

```
      If e.KeyData = Keys.Enter Then
          Dim objProducts As New ClassProducts()
          Dim selProducts As ArrayList = _
                  objProducts.Product.GetProductsByName( _
                  TextBox1.Text.Trim)
          Dim Prod As ClassProducts.Product
          ListBox1.Items.Clear()
          ListBox1.DisplayMember = "ProductName"
          For Each Prod In selProducts
              ListBox1.Items.Add(Prod)
          Next
          If ListBox1.Items.Count > 0 Then
              ListBox1.Focus()
          End If
      End If
  End Sub
```

The event handler adds a Product object for each matching product to the ListBox control and sets the control's DisplayMember property to the ProductName property of the Product object so that the list displays product names.

Every time the user selects another product on the list, the code in the control's Selected-IndexChanged event handler displays the selected product's fields on the various TextBox controls by calling the ShowProduct() subroutine. This subroutine accepts as argument a Product object and displays its properties on the appropriate controls. Listing 5.25 shows the ListBox control's SelectedIndexChanged event handler and the ShowProduct() subroutine.

**Listing 5.25**      **Displaying the Fields of the Selected Product**

```
Private Sub ListBox1_SelectedIndexChanged( _
                ByVal sender As System.Object, _
                ByVal e As System.EventArgs) _
                Handles ListBox1.SelectedIndexChanged
    If ListBox1.SelectedIndex = -1 Then Exit Sub
    Dim P As ClassProducts.Product = _
CType(ListBox1.SelectedItem, _
                    ClassProducts.Product)
    ShowProduct(P)
End Sub

    Sub ShowProduct(ByVal P As ClassProducts.Product)
        ClearFields()
        txtProductName.Text = P.ProductName
        txtPrice.Text = P.ProductPrice
        txtPackage.Text = P.ProductPackage
        cmbSupplier.SelectedValue = P.ProductSupplierID
        cmbCategory.SelectedValue = P.ProductCategoryID
    End Sub
```

Notice how the code selects the appropriate item in the Supplier and Category ComboBox controls. These two controls are data bound, and you must set their SelectedValue property to the unique key of the rows stored in the control's Items collection.

The code behind the editing buttons (the Add, Edit, and Delete buttons) is straightforward. The Add button clears the controls on the right pane of the form so that the user can enter the field values of the new product. When the user clicks the OK button, the program will pick up the values of these controls, create a new Product object, and pass it to the AddProduct method. The Edit button simply unlocks the controls, and the Delete method calls the DeleteProduct method, passing the ID of the selected product as argument. Listing 5.26 shows the implementation of the three editing buttons.

**Listing 5.26      The Implementation of the Data Editing Buttons**

```
Private Sub bttnEdit_Click(ByVal sender As System.Object, _
                           ByVal e As System.EventArgs) _
                           Handles bttnEdit.Click
    If ListBox1.SelectedIndex = -1 Then
        MsgBox("Please populate the list and select a " & _
               "product to edit!")
        Exit Sub
    End If
    HideEditButtons()
    editing = True
    txtProductName.Focus()
End Sub

Private Sub bttnAdd_Click(ByVal sender As System.Object, _
                          ByVal e As System.EventArgs) _
                          Handles bttnAdd.Click
    HideEditButtons()
    ClearFields()
    editing = False
    txtProductName.Focus()
End Sub

Private Sub bttnDelete_Click( _
                    ByVal sender As System.Object, _
                    ByVal e As System.EventArgs) _
                    Handles bttnDelete.Click
    Dim Prod As ClassProducts
    If Not Prod.Product.DeleteProduct( _
                    CType(ListBox1.SelectedItem, _
                    ClassProducts.Product).ProductID) Then
        MsgBox("Failed to delete selected row!")
    Else
        ListBox1.Items.RemoveAt(ListBox1.SelectedIndex)
    End If
End Sub
```

Notice that the Delete button's code removes the selected item on the ListBox control in addition to deleting the row (unless the DeleteProduct method fails to remove the specified row from the database).

The code behind the Cancel button displays the fields of the selected product regardless of the type of operation that's being canceled. If the user has canceled an edit operation, the program reads the current Product object from the ListBox control and displays it. This object represents the original product as it was read from the database. When the user is canceling an Add operation, the program picks the currently selected product from the ListBox control and displays it. In effect, it displays the product that the user was viewing before the Add button was clicked. Listing 5.27 shows the code behind the Cancel button.

**Listing 5.27        Canceling an Edit or Add Operation**

```
Private Sub bttnCancel_Click( _
                ByVal sender As System.Object, _
                ByVal e As System.EventArgs) _
                Handles bttnCancel.Click
    If editing Then
        ShowProduct(CType(ListBox1.SelectedItem, _
                        ClassProducts.Product))
    Else
        ClearFields()
        If ListBox1.SelectedIndex >= 0 Then
            ShowProduct(CType(ListBox1.SelectedItem, _
                        ClassProducts.Product))
        End If
    End If
    ShowEditButtons()
    ListBox1.Enabled = True
End Sub
```

The OK button commits an edit or add operation by calling the UpdateProduct or the AddProduct method, respectively. The code examines the value of the *editing* variable, which is declared at the form's level, and performs different actions depending on whether the OK button terminates an edit or add operation.

To commit an edited row, the code creates a new instance of the Product class, the *edited-Product* variable, sets its properties to the field values as specified by the user on the form, and then calls the UpdateProduct method. Notice that the ID of the edited row doesn't change (it's picked from the ListBox). After successfully updating the data source, the code removes the corresponding item from the ListBox control (the user may have changed the name of product). The code then calls the GetProductByID() method to retrieve the newly added row from the database and adds it to the ListBox control.

To commit an add operation, the code sets the properties of the *editedProduct* variable and calls the AddProduct method. If the row was added successfully, the code adds it to the ListBox control as well. The new product's name may be quite different from the names of the other products in the ListBox control. In other words, we insert the added or edited product to the ListBox control even if it doesn't belong to the result of the query that initially populated the ListBox control. This isn't much of a problem. If the user is adding products, the new products will all appear on the ListBox control and the user will be able to select and edit any of these rows. Listing 5.28 shows the code behind the OK button, which commits edited and new rows to the database.

**Listing 5.28**    **Committing an Edit or Add Operation**

```
Private Sub bttnOK_Click(ByVal sender As System.Object, _
                    ByVal e As System.EventArgs) _
                    Handles bttnOK.Click
    Dim P As ClassProducts
    If editing Then
        Dim editedProduct As New ClassProducts.Product()
        Dim CurrentID As Long = _
                    CType(ListBox1.SelectedItem, _
                    ClassProducts.Product).ProductID
        editedProduct.ProductID = CurrentID
        editedProduct.ProductName = _
                    txtProductName.Text.Trim
        editedProduct.ProductPrice = _
                    CDec(txtPrice.Text.Trim)
        editedProduct.ProductPackage = _
                    txtPackage.Text.Trim
        editedProduct.ProductCategoryID = _
                    cmbCategory.SelectedValue
        editedProduct.ProductSupplierID = _
                    cmbSupplier.SelectedValue
        If editedProduct.UpdateProduct() Then
            Dim prod As ClassProducts.Product = _
                    P.Product.GetProductByID(CurrentID)
            Dim idx As Integer = ListBox1.SelectedIndex
            ListBox1.Enabled = True
            ListBox1.Items.RemoveAt(idx)
            ListBox1.Items.Insert(idx, prod)
            ListBox1.SelectedIndex = idx
            ShowProduct(prod)
        Else
            MsgBox("Update operation failed" & _
                    editedProduct.GetLastError)
            ShowProduct(ListBox1.SelectedItem)
        End If
    Else
```

```
        Dim addedProduct As New ClassProducts.Product()
        Dim newProduct As ClassProducts.Product
        addedProduct.ProductName = txtProductName.Text.Trim
        addedProduct.ProductPackage = _
                    txtPackage.Text.Trim
        addedProduct.ProductPrice = _
                    CDec(txtPrice.Text.Trim)
        addedProduct.ProductSupplierID = _
                    cmbSupplier.SelectedValue
        addedProduct.ProductCategoryID = _
                    cmbCategory.SelectedValue
        newProduct = addedProduct.AddProduct
        If Not newProduct Is Nothing Then
            ListBox1.SelectedIndex = _
                        ListBox1.Items.Add(addedProduct)
            ListBox1.DisplayMember = "ProductName"
        Else
            MsgBox("Insertion failed!" & _
                        addedProduct.GetLastError)
            Exit Sub
        End If
    End If
    ShowEditButtons()
End Sub
```

As you have noticed, the application uses the ListBox control as a client data store. The selected rows are added to the ListBox control, which acts as a navigational tool as well as a data store. This control maintains the original versions of the selected rows, and you can use them to implement optimistic concurrency. However, we don't store DataRow objects to the ListBox control; we add instances of the Product object, which are not bound to any control, so we're free to manipulate them from within our code. If you examine the project's code, you'll realize that the presentation tier handles simple objects and doesn't know (or care) where and how the data is stored.

## Summary

This chapter completes our discussion of ADO.NET. We have discussed the components of ADO.NET and shown you how to set up DataAdapters and DataSets with the visual tools as well as how to manipulate these objects from within your code. ADO.NET was designed to address the needs of disconnected applications and it allows you to update multiple rows in any of the DataTables of the DataSet. The changes can be submitted to the database at any time. However, not all changes will be successfully applied to the underlying tables, and one of the most important programming tasks is to handle the update errors. The rows that failed to update the underlying tables in the databases are marked as being in error in the DataSet. You can extract the error that prevented each row in the DataSet to update the database. You can also extract the column error(s) in each row in error. Your task is to build a proper interface that will allow users to further edit the DataSet.

We have shown you how to retrieve the rows in error after an update operation. You can create a new DataSet with the rows in error and allow the user to further edit these rows through the same interface. It's crucial to inform users about update errors and not let them think that their changes have been committed to the database.

You also saw the code that retrieves the rows that have changed and how to undo the changes in specific rows. You can use the information and the code presented in this chapter to build functional interfaces for your data-driven Windows applications.

# CHAPTER 6

# Building Data-Driven Web Applications

- Working with ASPX pages

- The data adapters and ASP.NET

- Data-binding in ASP.NET

- Building a sample front end

Increasingly, developers are being called upon these days to design their applications with a web-based front end that can be viewed through a browser. This is happening in response to a greater need for accessing applications over a distributed network, a need to access applications from a variety of clients, and an increase in the number of applications with a distributed nature being built today. In the latter case, because web-based technologies are being used both to lay down the architecture and to build the application, giving the application a web-based front end is an easy and natural progression.

It is also undeniable that web-based technologies have progressed to the point that rich client interfaces can be built just as easily and with the same degree of power as their Windows-based counterparts. Java has flourished largely on its capability to introduce a powerful and flexible development and delivery environment for web-based applications. In Microsoft's case, we have seen a rapid growth in recent years of technologies capable of addressing n-tier application development and building interactive web-based applications. The .NET technologies in particular have advanced this process to the point where it is now a seamless exercise that can be carried out from within the Visual Studio .NET IDE.

ASP.NET ships with a set of rich controls for creating interactive websites and web-based applications. It's essential task that most of these modern websites applications have the capability to communicate with some form of back-end database. This may be either directly or via a middle tier in the form of an XML Web service or COM object (which may or may not be inside a SOAP wrapper). Although the DataGrid, DataList, and Repeater controls are the principal data-bound controls that ship with ASP.NET, we can work with most of the other controls in the Toolbox to access and manipulate data.

Later on, in Chapter 18, "The Data-Bound Web Controls," we will explore the DataGrid, DataList, and Repeater controls in more detail. In this chapter, we will be focusing on data binding as it applies to all the relevant web controls, and we will show you how you can work with these controls to produce rich interactive front ends for your applications.

## Working with ASPX Pages

Before we launch into any sort of investigation of building application front ends with ASP.NET, it is worth covering a few of the basics of working with ASPX pages and how they differ from standard Windows applications. (In the .NET world, the `.aspx` extension replaces the `.asp` file extension.) We will look at the structure of .NET-based web applications and how they relate to the IDE in Visual Studio .NET in a lot more detail in Chapter 15, "Developing Web Applications with ASP.NET." For the moment, we will show you where to enter code and how to preview your applications.

The IDE for web applications is virtually identical to that for standard Windows applications. You access it by choosing ASP.NET Web Application from the New Project menu in Visual Studio .NET. You have the option of choosing which language you wish to initially develop your web project in. (Of course, we are going to choose Visual Basic.) Figure 6.1 shows the New Project dialog box for web applications.

**FIGURE 6.1:**

The New Project dialog box for web applications

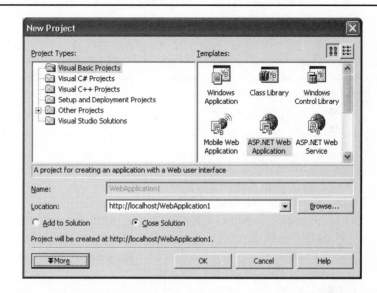

At this screen, you can also choose the location for the project (the project is actually named by setting or changing its location path). WebApplication1 is usually the first default name offered. If you use the default names, it helps to keep track of how many web applications you've created so you don't have to enter WebApplication1, WebApplication2, and so on until you come to the next unused name.

Once the new project is open, the main difference between the interface for building a web application and the interface for building a standard Windows application is that the Form Designer for web applications has two views: Design and HTML. You can use Design view to see and work with the graphical version of the controls and HTML view to work with the actual code that describes the web page (including the controls). HTML view is a bit of a misnomer, though, because these pages are created as ASPX pages.

You will also notice that the contents of the Toolbox have changed as well. You now have a choice of controls from both the Web Forms and the HTML palettes. The Web Form controls consist of the set of server-side controls that will be principally used to create interactive applications. The HTML controls are essentially client-side controls that mimic many of the traditional HTML elements, such as tables and horizontal rules.

**NOTE**    It is possible to use HTML controls as server-side components by right-clicking them and choosing the Run as Server Control option from the context menu. However, if you are going to do this, in most cases it makes sense to use the equivalent Web Forms control.

Although most of the tools look superficially similar to their desktop application counterparts, there are many web-specific methods and properties included. For example, the color palettes all include a web-safe color set.

Dropping controls onto the page in Design view and altering their properties in the Properties dialog box will produce corresponding changes to the code in HTML view. Altering code in HTML view, such as adding controls or manipulating their properties, will produce corresponding changes in the graphical Design view and property settings.

You can also do most of your coding directly onto the ASPX form in Design view. This includes not only your design aspects, but all your business logic as well. It is possible to build an entire project without going near Code Behind or ever having to press the build sequence keystroke (Ctrl+Shift+B). However, it makes sense to separate your business logic from the design aspects and add a little bit of code security because the IL (Intermediate Language) of something written in Code Behind is a touch more difficult to read than the markup on an ASPX page (written in HTML view). Additionally, many of the autocomplete and intellisense options that help keep us on the straight and narrow are not available when working in HTML view. However, there are some things that can only be coded in the HTML view, so it pays to be familiar with working in both areas.

When you view your applications, they open in a web browser. (This has ramifications from a debugging perspective, which we will look at later in Chapter 11, "Debugging and Deploying .NET Applications.") You can choose the default browser to use for viewing your applications. This is available via the Browse With option under the File menu. Figure 6.2 shows the Browse With dialog box.

**FIGURE 6.2:**

The Browse With dialog box for setting browser options for Web Forms

Additionally, you can view your pages directly in the browser (without going through the compile routine) by selecting the View in Browser option from the File menu. You can also select the page a Web Form opens with in the application by right-clicking an individual Web Form in the Solution Explorer and choosing the Set as Start Page option.

You can add existing HTML pages to a project and work with them as ASPX pages simply by changing their file extension to .aspx and copying them into the web directory that holds the rest of the project. The files can then be included in the project by using the Add Existing Item option from the Project menu. (Note that you may need to close and reopen the Visual Studio .NET IDE to see the added files in the web directory.)

**TIP**    You can also edit an HTML page directly in Visual Studio .NET by simply dragging and dropping it onto the Start Page screen and switching to HTML view.

## The Data Adapters and ASP.NET

As with desktop-style applications, you can access your source database using either SqlDataAdapter or OleDbDataAdapter, together with their associated Command and Connection objects. You can then perform data operations using the DataSet or DataReader objects. Because the performance of web-based applications can be paramount (and subject to a whole lot of factors already beyond our control), it pays to optimize as much of the execution process as you can. Therefore, it is usually a good idea to use SQL Server with its associated connection objects because they have already been tuned to give the best performance possible.

**TIP**    For maximum performance, it is worth using stored procedures within SQL Server to process data rather than handling data-processing externally with SQL statements from the calling application.

It also often pays to use the DataReader object as opposed to the DataSet whenever you can. However, if you use the DataReader object, you'll be trading flexibility for performance. The DataSet remains the most powerful tool for manipulating your data without having to write reams of code.

## Data Binding in ASP.NET

You can data-bind most of the web controls and use them to display and/or manipulate data in some way. You can manipulate data before binding it to a control, and the

`DataBinder.Eval` method enables you to easily format the data as you wish when displaying it in the control.

## The Data Form Wizard

By far the easiest way of creating a form with controls that can access and manipulate data is to use the Data Form Wizard. You will first need to create a new ASP.NET web application in Visual Studio .NET. Then from the Project menu, select the Add New Item option. Select the Data Form Wizard as shown in Figure 6.3. In this example, we will be setting up a master/detail form between the titles and sales tables in the pubs database.

**FIGURE 6.3:**

The Data Form Wizard selected in the Add New Item dialog box

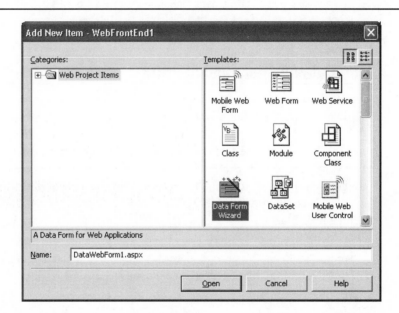

Once the Data Form Wizard opens, it offers a fairly self-explanatory setup routine that gives you the choice of using an existing DataSet or creating a new one, as shown in Figure 6.4.

At the next screen, you are asked which connection you wish to use. In this case, we established a connection to the pubs database. Click Next and the Choose Tables or Views screen, shown in Figure 6.5, appears. You use this screen to select from the database the tables or views that you wish to use as your data source (sales and titles in this instance).

FIGURE 6.4:

FIGURE 6.4:

Choosing a DataSet
from the Data Form
Wizard

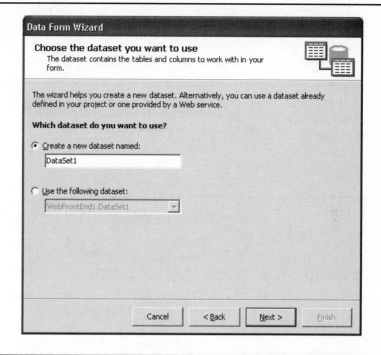

FIGURE 6.5:

Using the Choose Tables
or Views screen in the
Data Form Wizard

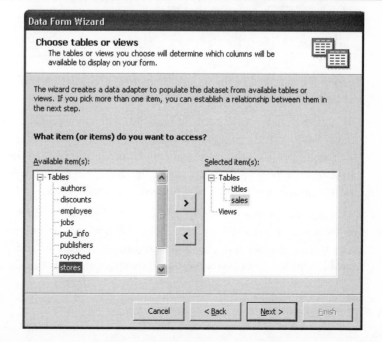

The next screen (Figure 6.6) enables you to set up any relationships between the tables that you might want featured in your form (for example, when setting up a master-detail form). After establishing a relationship, click the arrow button to move it to the Relations box and save it. This way you can set up multiple relationships to use.

**FIGURE 6.6:**

Creating relationships in the Data Form Wizard

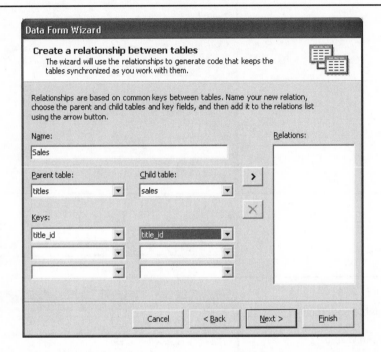

In the final screen of the wizard (Figure 6.7), you are given the chance to determine which tables and columns to display on the form.

Exit the Data Form Wizard. You will see that a new form has been created in your project, DataWebForm1. If you right-click on this form in the Solution Explorer, set it as the start page for the project from the context menu. Compile and run the project and you should have a master/detail form setup similar to Figure 6.8. Note that we have made a couple of cosmetic changes to the master DataGrid properties in this example.

Click the Load button to display the master form and click any of the Show Detail buttons to display the relevant information. In its default form, the display is a little rough around the edges, but it is easily modified into something presentable and it represents a very fast and flexible solution to a common task when developing web-based applications.

**FIGURE 6.7:**

Choosing tables and
columns to display in
the Data Form Wizard

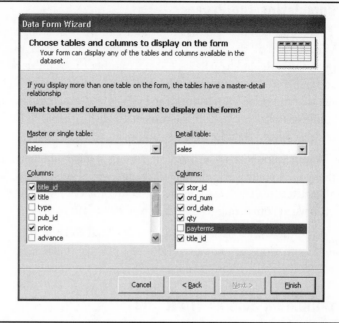

**FIGURE 6.8:**

DataWebForm1
at runtime

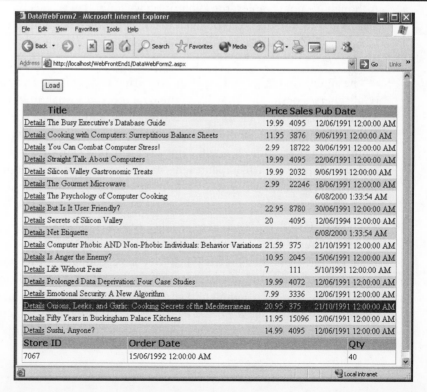

## Completing the Process

There are a number of things to be aware of when building applications with the Data Form Wizard. Not all the code is complete. If you double-click the Load button at design time and open Code Behind, you will see that a number of "to do" tasks have been commented into the autogenerated code. In particular, you need to add error management code (although you will see that the basic framework of the structured exception handling has already been set up). Additionally, if you had set the project up with an existing DataSet, you would need to add the code to fill the DataSet in Code Behind.

Another potential issue, if you are aiming at maximum performance from your applications, is that you can only work with a DataSet and would need to recode everything if you wished to use a DataReader. The wizard seems to set up only OleDbDataAdapters and not SqlDataAdapters, even when connecting to a SQL Server 2000 database.

Last, the wizard basically only sets up DataGrid controls, which, although perfectly fine in many situations, are not always the best control to use for particular tasks.

## Building a Sample Front End

Although it's not complex, the application we'll build in this section illustrates a number of factors and techniques that you need to consider when building a web-based front end. (In Chapter 15, we will look at working with the various Web Forms controls in a lot more detail.)

The application is a simple two-tier ordering facility for a mythical catering company (Gallaghers Gourmet). We will use the data tools in Visual Studio .NET to create a SQL Server 2000 database, set up some relationships, and populate the database with data. We will then create a simple Web Form to interact with this data and a second form to confirm the interaction. We will demonstrate data access via a DataSet and a DataReader, and we will perform table updates by running an SQL statement directly against the database connection. We will also data-bind web controls other than the standard data-bound controls.

The website will be designed to enable customers of Gallaghers to order a drink and meal package. They need to enter their delivery details into the site as well as make selections for the meal and drink they prefer. Once they have made their selections, there needs to be some form of validation of customer details (in this case, we will check to see that all necessary fields have been completed) and the opportunity for customers to either confirm or cancel the order. When the order has been confirmed, the customer is transferred to a confirmation page indicating that the order has been processed and displaying the details of the order. You'll see how to navigate between pages in ASP.NET and how information can be transferred between pages. We will also use an example of a session variable to hold relevant information in the first page.

   This example is meant to be a demonstration only. Its sole purpose is to illustrate a number of basic techniques associated with building web-based front ends in a practical context. Many aspects of it have not been done fully or well. (In other words, don't try this at home!) Later on, in Chapter 16, "Programming Web Forms," we will revisit the same example as a more coherent and complete application.

## Creating the Database

Open a new web project in Visual Studio .NET. We named the project DemoWebFrontEnd1. The back-end database will be a fairly simple relational database with three tables: menu, drinks, and orders. The menu and drinks tables will hold details about these two categories of products sold by Gallaghers, and the orders table will hold the details of each particular order that customers make through the website. Essentially, the drinks and menu tables will be read-only tables, but new records, each representing a customer order, need to be created from the orders table. We used SQL Server 2000 for these examples, but the database could just as easily be built using SQL Server 7 or Microsoft Access. To set up the database, follow these steps:

1. Select the Server Explorer tab from the Toolbox side of the IDE and expand the Servers node to expose your databases. Right-click the database node (this will have the name that you have given it—ours is called RIDGE) and select New Database.

2. In the Create Database dialog box (Figure 6.9), name the database (Gallaghers) and choose your preferred method of authentication.

**FIGURE 6.9:**

The Create Database dialog box

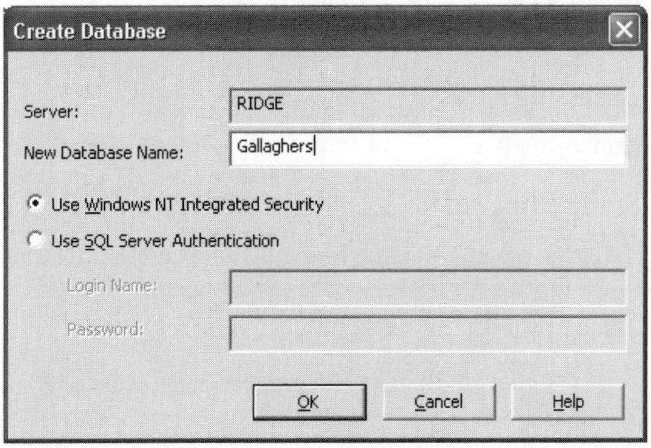

3. Expand the newly created Gallaghers node in the Server Explorer (under your SQL Server databases). Right-click the Tables node and choose the New Table option. We will begin by creating the menu table. Here is the field setup:

| Column Name | Data Type | Length | Allow Nulls |
|---|---|---|---|
| menu_id | int | 4 | |
| menu_item | varchar | 50 | Yes |
| menu_price | money | 8 | Yes |
| menu_instock | bit | 1 | Yes |

4. Set the menu_id field as the primary key and set this field's Identity property to Yes.
5. Save this table and name it menu. Figure 6.10 illustrates some sample data to insert into this table.

**FIGURE 6.10:**

Sample data for the menu table in the Gallaghers database

'ebForm2.aspx.vb **dbo.menu : Tab...DGE.gallaghers)** dbo.menu : Table (RIDGE

| menu_id | menu_item | menu_price | menu_instock |
|---|---|---|---|
| 1 | Ploughman's Lunch | 5.2 | 1 |
| 2 | Hot grill | 7.5 | 1 |
| 3 | Fruit Platter | 6.2 | 1 |
| 4 | Gourmet Sandwiches | 5.5 | 1 |
| 5 | Proud's Pie | 3.6 | 0 |

6. Right-click the Tables node in Server Explorer and choose the New Table option again. We will now create the Drinks table. Here is the field setup for this table:

| Column Name | Data Type | Length | Allow Nulls |
|---|---|---|---|
| drinks_id | int | 4 | |
| drinks_item | varchar | 60 | Yes |
| drinks_price | money | 8 | Yes |
| drinks_instock | bit | 1 | Yes |

7. Set the drinks_id field as the primary key and set this field's Identity property to Yes.
8. Save this table and name it drinks. Figure 6.11 illustrates some sample data to insert into this table.

Sample data for the
drinks table in the
Gallaghers database

| drinks_id | drinks_item | drinks_price | drinks_instock |
|-----------|-------------|--------------|----------------|
| 1 | Cola | 1 | 1 |
| 2 | Orange | 1 | 1 |
| 3 | Fruit Juice | 1 | 1 |
| 4 | Soda | 1 | 1 |
| 5 | Mineral Water | 1 | 1 |

*(dbo.menu : Table (RIDGE.gallaghers)   **dbo.drinks : T...DGE.gallaghers)**)*

9. Create another new table. This will be the orders table. Here is the field setup for this table:

| Column Name | Data Type | Length | Allow Nulls |
|-------------|-----------|--------|-------------|
| order_id | int | 4 | |
| menu_itemID | int | 4 | Yes |
| drinks_itemID | int | 4 | Yes |
| order_name | varchar | 50 | Yes |
| order_street | varchar | 50 | Yes |
| order_town | varchar | 50 | Yes |
| order_telephone | varchar | 50 | Yes |
| order_processed | bit | 1 | Yes |

10. Set the order_id field as the primary key and this field's Identity property to Yes. Additionally, set the default value of the order_processed field to 0. We will not add any data to this table at this point.

11. From the Server Explorer, right-click the Database Diagrams node in Gallaghers and select New Diagram. Add the three tables just created to the diagram and right-click the drinks table. Choose the Relationships option. Create a relationship between the drinks and orders tables using drinks_id from drinks in the primary key table and drinks_itemID from the orders table in the foreign key table. It is probably also worth checking the Cascade Update Related Fields box. Figure 6.12 shows the completed Relationships tab. Click Close to save the relationship and exit the dialog box.

12. Right-click the menu table in the database diagram and chose the Relationships option. Create a relationship between the menu and orders tables using menu_id from the menu table in the primary key table and menu_itemID from the orders table in the foreign key table. Again, check the Cascade Update Related Fields box. Figure 6.13 shows the completed tab. Save and exit the dialog.

**FIGURE 6.12:**

The Relationships tab for the drinks and orders tables

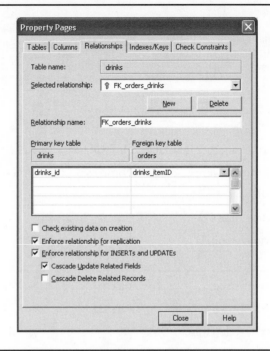

**FIGURE 6.13:**

The Relationships tab for the menu and orders tables

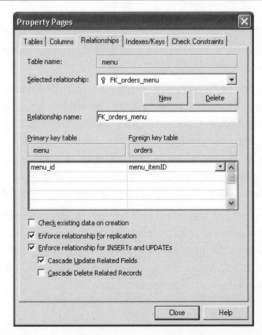

**13.** Save the database diagram as GallaghersDiagram1. The completed diagram is shown in Figure 6.14.

---

**FIGURE 6.14:**

GallaghersDiagram1

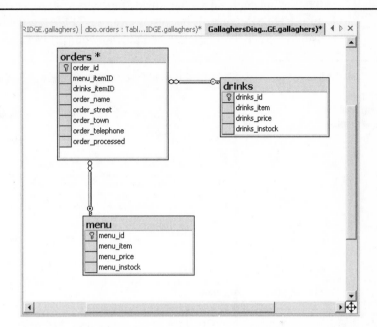

**14.** You will now have an array of open database items in the design surface in Visual Studio .NET. You can choose to leave them there, but we usually find that this workspace can become unnecessarily cluttered, making it difficult to navigate between the stuff we need to use. Clicking the Close check box (in the upper-right corner of the Design surface, not the IDE) will close the window in the active tab.

The database is built, and we are ready to create the web-based front end.

## Building WebForm1

The object of this process is to come up with something similar to the web page illustrated in Figure 6.15.

Return to the Design view for WebForm1. We will be adding a number of controls to the form both from the Web Forms Toolbox and the HTML Toolbox. Follow these steps:

**1.** Begin by dragging a Label and ImageButton control from the Web Forms Toolbox to WebForm1. Set the Font (bold and size XXLarge), ForeColor (Firebrick), and Text (Gallaghers Gourmet) properties of the Label1 control to create the Gallaghers Gourmet heading. For the logo, we used a clip-art image from Microsoft Office and dropped it into the root web directory for this application (C:\Inetpub\wwwroot\DemoWebFrontEnd1, if you are using the defaults). Then point the ImageURL property of the ImageButton control to the image. It might have made more sense in this case to use the Image control from the HTML controls because we can set HTML attributes such as alt. It is worth considering such alternatives when putting your project together.

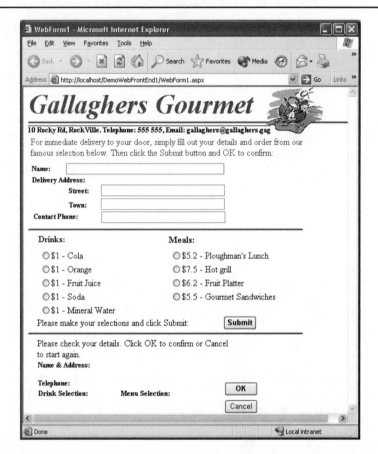

2. From the HTML toolbox, create a horizontal rule (HR) under the heading. We used the following property settings: width is 600px, size is 3, and color is #cc0000 (from the web palette). Under this place a Label control (Label2) from the Web Controls. Set the Font: Size property to X-Small and the Bold property to True. Create some dummy contact details for the company. At this point, play with the relative placement and order of the controls using the Order command from the Format menu to get things looking just right.

3. Under the heading information, place another Label control (Label3) with some instructions on using the site in the Text property. If you find it awkward to type in the rather limited space in the Property window, switch to HTML view and type directly into the tags for that control. (It's still not great, but a little easier if you have text extending beyond one or two words.)

4. Place four TextBox controls (TextBox1, TextBox2, etc.) on the form with corresponding labels: Name (Label4), Delivery Address (Label5), Street (Label6), Town (Label7), and Contact Phone (Label8). There are five labels for four TextBox controls because one, Delivery Address, will act as a heading for the Street and Town text boxes. The only properties we set here were to delete any text from the Text property of the TextBoxes and set their font size to X-Small (to accommodate everything on the form).

5. To the right of each of the TextBoxes place a RequiredField Validator control. Set the ControlToValidate property of each of the validation controls to its corresponding TextBox. In their ErrorMessage properties, add the messages as can be seen in Figure 6.16. Complete this section of the form by placing another horizontal rule (from the HTML controls) with a width of 500px (set the color to #cc0000 and the size to 3).

**FIGURE 6.16:**

The personal details entry section of WebForm1

The next step is to provide the menu choices for the customer. In this example, we will data-bind the Drinks list to a DataSet and leave the Menu list unbound (at design time), populating it via a DataReader at runtime. This will provide examples of two methods of manipulating data with these list controls. Follow these steps:

1. Place two Label controls on the Web Form with their Text properties set to Drinks (Label10) and Meals (Label9). Below these controls, add two RadioButtonList controls. (RadioButtonList1 for Drinks and RadioButtonList2 for Menu). We will programmatically populate these controls at runtime. Although the DataGrid, DataList, and Repeater controls are the principal data-bound controls, the RadioButtonList and CheckBoxList controls are two types of DataList controls and, apart from some obvious individual differences, share most of the properties and behaviors of the DataList control.

**NOTE**     In a real-world application, you also need to consider a number of display issues when using list controls. The obvious one is how big will you permit the list to grow. In this example, we have limited space to work in because the confirmation section of the application appears below the drinks and meals section. We could easily solve the problem of the lists flowing into the next section by placing the confirmation section onto a separate form or by placing the lists inside a table that can grow to accommodate them. We can also limit the amount of data displayed in the list or use the display properties of the list to enable it to adapt to the amount of data to be displayed within the space available. The properties involved here are the RepeatColumns, RepeatDirection, and RepeatLayout properties.

2. Drag a SqlDataAdapter to your Web Form (SqlDataAdapter1). This should open the Data Adapter Configuration Wizard. (You can also access the wizard from the context menu by right-clicking the SqlDataAdapter.) Establish a connection to the Gallaghers database, choose the Use SQL Statements option from the Choose a Query Type screen (later on we'll use this screen to set up a stored procedure in SQL Server to access our data). From the Generate the SQL Statements screen, set up the following SQL SELECT statement (either by typing it directly or using the Query Builder):

```
SELECT drinks_id, drinks_item, drinks_price, drinks_instock FROM drinks
```

3. Choose Advanced Options and uncheck the Generate Insert, Update and Delete Statements option (we will not be using them). Click through to the end and exit the wizard.

4. Right-click the SqlDataAdapter1 and choose the Generate Dataset option. This should create an instance of DataSet11, which will be displayed at the bottom of the design surface.

5. Set the DataSource property for the Drinks RadioButtonList (RadioButtonList1) to DataSet11, the DataMember property to drinks, the DataTextField to drinks_item, and the DataValueField to drinks_id. You can also use the DataTextFormatString to apply some formatting to the way data is rendered in this control. Given that we have set all of our drink prices to $1, we can easily display this in the control along with the individual drinks by adding the following to the property:

```
$1 - {0}
```

6. Place a Label control (Label13) at the bottom of this section (leave an appropriate amount of space for your radio button lists to "grow") with some instructions on what to do next along with a Button control (Button1) with its text property set to Submit.

7. Add two RequiredFieldValidator controls (5 and 6) to the Web Form with their ControlToValidate properties set to each of the RadioButtonLists and an appropriate error message set in each. (We placed these controls in the top of the section, above the radio button lists and next to the respective title label controls.)

8. As with the previous section, complete this section with a horizontal rule. Figure 6.17 shows how the section should look at design time.

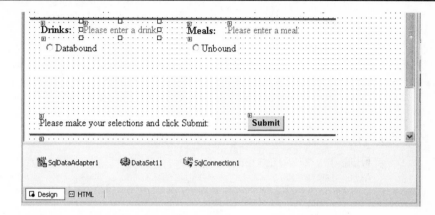

The last section of this Web Form provides a confirmation of the order details entered and the opportunity to cancel or confirm the order:

1. Insert a Label control (Label11) to display the instructions to confirm or cancel the order. Set up six Label controls to hold the data entered earlier in the application (Label12 to hold the name, Label14 for the street, Label15 for the town, Label16 to hold the telephone number, Label17 to hold the drink selection, and Label18 to hold the menu selection). Set up four additional Label controls to act as headers for the information displayed (Label19 will be Name & Address, Label20 will be Telephone, Label21 will be Drink Selection, and Label22 will be menu selection). Lay out the Label controls and make any necessary changes to the Font properties to aid with presentation.

2. Add two Button controls to this section. Set the Text properties of the buttons to OK (Button2) and Cancel (Button3), respectively. Figure 6.18 illustrates how this section should look.

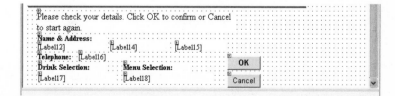

Listing 6.1 gives the full code for the ASPX page created for WebForm1. This is the code that you can access through HTML view.

**Listing 6.1**     **Full ASPX Code for WebForm1 of Gallaghers Application**

```
<%@ Page Language="vb" AutoEventWireup="false" _
Codebehind="WebForm1.aspx.vb" _
Inherits="DemoWebFrontEnd1.WebForm1"%>
<!DOCTYPE HTML PUBLIC "-//W3C//DTD HTML 4.0 _
Transitional//EN">
<HTML>
  <HEAD>
     <title>WebForm1</title>
     <meta content="Microsoft Visual Studio.NET 7.0" _
name="GENERATOR">
        <meta content="Visual Basic 7.0" _
name="CODE_LANGUAGE">
     <meta content="JavaScript" _
name="vs_defaultClientScript">
     <meta _
content="http://schemas.microsoft.com/intellisense/_
ie5" name="vs_targetSchema">
  </HEAD>
  <body bgColor="#ffffff" MS_POSITIONING="GridLayout">
     <form id="Form1" method="post" runat="server">
        <HR style="Z-INDEX: 120; LEFT: 9px; _
POSITION: absolute; TOP: 61px" width="600" _
color="#cc0000" SIZE="3" noShade>
           <asp:label id="Label23" style="Z-INDEX: _
134; LEFT: 179px; POSITION: absolute; TOP: 531px" _
runat="server" Height="9px" Font-Bold="True" _
Font-Size="X-Small" Width="122px">Menu _
Selection:</asp:label>
           <asp:label id="Label22" style="Z-INDEX: _
135; LEFT: 27px; POSITION: absolute; TOP: 531px" _
runat="server" Height="9px" Font-Bold="True" _
Font-Size="X-Small" Width="122px">Drink _
Selection:</asp:label>
<asp:label id="Label20" _
style="Z-INDEX: 133; LEFT: 26px; POSITION: _
absolute; TOP: 513px" runat="server" Height="9px" _
Font-Bold="True" Font-Size="X-Small" _
Width="61px">Telephone:</asp:label>
<asp:label id="Label19" style="Z-INDEX: 132; LEFT: _
26px; POSITION: absolute; TOP: 481px" _
runat="server" Height="9px" Font-Bold="True" _
Font-Size="X-Small" Width="122px">Name & _
Address:</asp:label>
<asp:label id="Label18" style="Z-INDEX: 131; _
LEFT: 179px; POSITION: absolute; TOP: 550px" _
runat="server" Height="9px" Font-Size="X-Small" _
Width="163px"></asp:label>
<asp:label id="Label17" style="Z-INDEX: _
130; LEFT: 27px; POSITION: absolute; TOP: 550px" _
runat="server" Height="9px" Font-Size="X-Small" _
Width="134px"></asp:label>
```

```
<asp:label id="Label16" style="Z-INDEX: 129; _
 LEFT: 99px; POSITION: absolute; TOP: 513px" _
 runat="server" Height="9px" Font-Size="X-Small" _
 Width="88px"></asp:label>
<asp:label id="Label15" style="Z-INDEX: 128; _
 LEFT: 272px; POSITION: absolute; TOP: 496px" _
 runat="server" Height="9px" Font-Size="X-Small" _
 Width="89px"></asp:label>
<asp:label id="Label14" style="Z-INDEX: 127; _
 LEFT: 155px; POSITION: absolute; TOP: 496px" _
 runat="server" Height="9px" Font-Size="X-Small" _
 Width="105px"></asp:label>
<asp:button id="Button3" style="Z-INDEX: 118; _
 LEFT: 367px; POSITION: absolute; TOP: 550px" _
 runat="server" Width="60px" Text="Cancel"> _
</asp:button>
<asp:label id="Label2" style="Z-INDEX: 121; _
 LEFT: 8px; POSITION: absolute; TOP: 68px" _
 runat="server" Height="23px" Font-Bold="True" _
 Font-Size="X-Small" Width="516px" _
 Font-Overline="True">10 Rocky Rd, RockVille. _
   Telephone: 555 555,  Email: _
gallaghers@gallaghers.gag</asp:label>
<asp:label id="Label1" style="Z-INDEX: 102; _
 LEFT: 9px; POSITION: absolute; TOP: 4px" _
 runat="server" Height="64px" Font-Bold="True" _
 Font-Size="XX-Large" Width="441px" _
 Font-Italic="True" ForeColor="Firebrick">_
Gallaghers Gourmet</asp:label>
<asp:imagebutton id="ImageButton1" style="Z-INDEX: _
 122; LEFT: 441px; POSITION: absolute; TOP: 0px" _
 runat="server" Height="83px" Width="105px" _
 ImageUrl="file:///C:\Inetpub\wwwroot\_
DemoWebFrontEnd1\FD00306_.WMF"></asp:imagebutton>
<asp:label id="Label3" style="Z-INDEX: 103; LEFT: _
 13px; POSITION: absolute; TOP: 87px" _
 runat="server" Height="23px" Width="523px" _
 ForeColor="Firebrick">For immediate delivery to your _
door, simply fill out your details and order from _
our famous selection below. Then click the Submit _
button and OK to confirm:</asp:label>
<asp:label id="Label4" style="Z-INDEX: 104; LEFT: _
 15px; POSITION: absolute; TOP: 136px" _
 runat="server" Height="24px" Font-Bold="True" _
 Font-Size="X-Small" Width="49px">Name:</asp:label>
<asp:textbox id="TextBox1" style="Z-INDEX: 105; _
 LEFT: 79px; POSITION: absolute; TOP: 134px" _
 runat="server" Height="20px" Font-Size="X-Small" _
 Width="287px"></asp:textbox>
<asp:label id="Label5" style="Z-INDEX: 106; LEFT: _
 16px; POSITION: absolute; TOP: 156px" _
 runat="server" Height="26px" Font-Bold="True" _
 Font-Size="X-Small" Width="157px">Delivery _
Address:</asp:label>
```

```
<asp:label id="Label6" style="Z-INDEX: 107; LEFT: _
83px; POSITION: absolute; TOP: 175px" _
runat="server" Height="25px" Font-Bold="True" _
Font-Size="X-Small" Width="55px">Street:</asp:label>
<asp:label id="Label7" style="Z-INDEX: 108; LEFT: _
84px; POSITION: absolute; TOP: 200px" _
runat="server" Height="20px" Font-Bold="True" _
Font-Size="X-Small" Width="69px">Town:</asp:label>
<asp:textbox id="TextBox2" style="Z-INDEX: 109; _
LEFT: 143px; POSITION: absolute; TOP: 172px" _
runat="server" Height="20px" Font-Size="X-Small" _
Width="224px"></asp:textbox>
<asp:textbox id="TextBox3" style="Z-INDEX: 110; _
LEFT: 143px; POSITION: absolute; TOP: 196px" _
runat="server" Height="20px" Font-Size="X-Small" _
Width="224px"></asp:textbox>
<asp:label id="Label8" style="Z-INDEX: 111; LEFT: _
18px; POSITION: absolute; TOP: 220px" _
runat="server" Height="26px" Font-Bold="True" _
Font-Size="X-Small" Width="107px">Contact _
Phone:</asp:label><asp:textbox id="TextBox4" _
style="Z-INDEX: 112; LEFT: 144px; POSITION: _
absolute; TOP: 219px" runat="server" Height="20px" _
Font-Size="X-Small" Width="224px"></asp:textbox>
<asp:label id="Label9" style="Z-INDEX: 113; LEFT: _
265px; POSITION: absolute; TOP: 259px" _
runat="server" Height="26px" Font-Bold="True" _
Width="57px">Meals:</asp:label>
<asp:label id="Label10" style="Z-INDEX: 114; LEFT: _
27px; POSITION: absolute; TOP: 258px" _
runat="server" Font-Bold="True">Drinks:</asp:label>
<asp:label id="Label11" style="Z-INDEX: 115; LEFT: _
25px; POSITION: absolute; TOP: 441px" _
runat="server" Height="15px" Width="352px">_
Please check your details. Click OK to confirm or _
Cancel to start again.</asp:label>
        <HR style="Z-INDEX: 101; LEFT: 9px; _
POSITION: absolute; TOP: 249px" width="500" _
color="#cc0000" noShade SIZE="3">
        <HR style="Z-INDEX: 116; LEFT: 9px; _
POSITION: absolute; TOP: 432px; HEIGHT: 3px" _
width="500" color="#cc0000" noShade SIZE="1">
        <asp:button id="Button1" _
style="Z-INDEX: 124; LEFT: 365px; POSITION: _
absolute; TOP: 403px" runat="server" _
Font-Bold="True" Width="60px" _
Text="Submit"></asp:button>
<asp:button id="Button2" style="Z-INDEX: 117; _
LEFT: 367px; POSITION: absolute; TOP: 519px" _
runat="server" Font-Bold="True" Width="60px" _
Text="OK"></asp:button>
<asp:label id="Label12" style="Z-INDEX: 119; _
LEFT: 26px; POSITION: absolute; TOP: 496px" _
runat="server" Height="9px" Font-Size="X-Small" _
```

```
 Width="122px"></asp:label>
<asp:label id="Label13" style="Z-INDEX: 123; _
 LEFT: 25px; POSITION: absolute; TOP: 405px" _
 runat="server" Height="25px" Width="284px">_
Please make your selections and click_
 Submit:</asp:label>
<asp:radiobuttonlist id=RadioButtonList1 _
 style="Z-INDEX: 125; LEFT: 28px; POSITION: _
 absolute; TOP: 283px" runat="server" _
 DataTextFormatString="$1 - {0}" _
 DataTextField="drinks_item" _
 DataValueField="drinks_id" _
 DataMember="drinks" DataSource="<%# DataSet11 %>" > _
</asp:radiobuttonlist>
<asp:radiobuttonlist id="RadioButtonList2" _
 style="Z-INDEX: 126; LEFT: 266px; POSITION: _
 absolute; TOP: 283px" runat="server"> _
</asp:radiobuttonlist>
        <asp:RequiredFieldValidator _
 id="RequiredFieldValidator1" style="Z-INDEX: 136; _
 LEFT: 378px; POSITION: absolute; TOP: 135px" _
 runat="server" Width="143px" _
 ErrorMessage="Please enter your name" _
ControlToValidate="TextBox1">_
</asp:RequiredFieldValidator>
        <asp:RequiredFieldValidator _
id="RequiredFieldValidator2" style="Z-INDEX: _
 137; LEFT: 379px; POSITION: absolute; TOP: _
 173px" runat="server" Width="147px" _
ErrorMessage="Please enter your street" _
 ControlToValidate="TextBox2">_
</asp:RequiredFieldValidator>
        <asp:RequiredFieldValidator _
 id="RequiredFieldValidator3" style="Z-INDEX: 138; _
 LEFT: 379px; POSITION: absolute; TOP: 199px" _
 runat="server" Width="143px" _
 ErrorMessage="Please enter your town" _
 ControlToValidate="TextBox3">_
</asp:RequiredFieldValidator>
        <asp:RequiredFieldValidator _
 id="RequiredFieldValidator4" style="Z-INDEX: _
 139; LEFT: 379px; POSITION: absolute; TOP: 223px" _
 runat="server" Width="206px" _
 ErrorMessage="Please enter your phone number" _
 ControlToValidate="TextBox4">_
</asp:RequiredFieldValidator>
        <asp:RequiredFieldValidator _
 id="RequiredFieldValidator5" style="Z-INDEX: 140; _
 LEFT: 96px; POSITION: absolute; TOP: 258px" _
 runat="server" ErrorMessage="Please enter a _
 drink" ControlToValidate="RadioButtonList1">_
</asp:RequiredFieldValidator>
        <asp:RequiredFieldValidator _
 id="RequiredFieldValidator6" style="Z-INDEX: 141; _
```

```
    LEFT: 331px; POSITION: absolute; TOP: 258px" _
    runat="server" ErrorMessage="Please enter a meal" _
    ControlToValidate="RadioButtonList2">_
</asp:RequiredFieldValidator></form>
        </body>
    </HTML>
```

At this point, click the Start arrow on the menu (or press the F5 key) to test the Web Form. We haven't yet built any real functionality into it and the lists will stay empty, but you can check the layout of the form and the functionality of the RequiredFieldValidators by clicking the Submit button.

## Building WebForm2

WebForm2 is a simple confirmation form that we will use to confirm that the order has been placed and to display some of the order details back to the user. Figure 6.19 illustrates how this form should look.

**FIGURE 6.19:**

The completed WebForm2 of the Gallaghers application

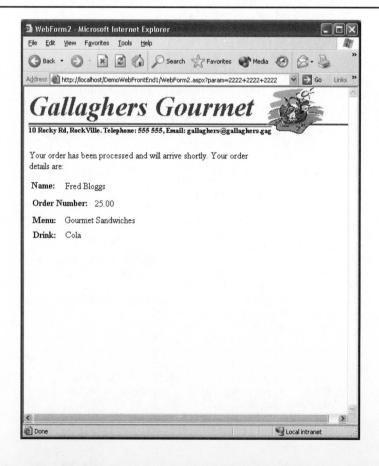

We begin by creating a new Web Form and completing the following steps:

1. From the Project menu, select Add Web Form and confirm the addition in the Add New Item dialog box.

2. Open the new Web Form in Design view and copy and paste the header Label controls (and Image Button) from WebForm1 to the new Web Form (WebForm2).

3. Set up a Label control (Label3) on the form with some text that acknowledges the order and when it is likely to be delivered. Add eight more Label controls. Use four to display key order details: Label5 for the name, Label7 for the order number, Label9 for the menu selection, and Label11 for the drink selection. Use the other four Label controls as text headers for the data display labels (Name, Order Number, Menu, and Drink).

4. Add a SqlDataAdapter to the form. Establish the connection to the Gallaghers database. In this example, we will set up a stored procedure to return the data we are after and we will use the facility in the Data Adapter Configuration Wizard to create and access stored procedures back in the parent database. At the Choose a Query Type screen of the wizard, select the Create New Stored Procedures option. This opens up a version of the Query Builder that is very similar to what we have used before (see Figure 6.20).

**FIGURE 6.20:**

Creating a stored procedure in the Data Adapter Configuration Wizard

5. For this example, we will create a SELECT statement that returns the order number, name, and order details based on the customer's telephone number as the search criteria

(and we will also check to see if the order has been flagged as processed already). Using the phone number as the search criteria is a little flaky for a real-world application, but in this instance, it saves us from writing a lot of code to overcome the shortcuts we are about to take.

Listing 6.2 gives the SELECT statement for use in the stored procedure.

---

**Listing 6.2**     **SELECT Statement for Use with Stored Procedure in Gallaghers Application**

```
SELECT orders.order_id, orders.order_name, _
 orders.menu_itemID, menu.menu_item, _
 menu.menu_id, drinks.drinks_id, _
 drinks.drinks_item, orders.order_telephone, _
 orders.order_processed FROM orders INNER _
 JOIN menu ON orders.menu_itemID = _
 menu.menu_id INNER JOIN drinks ON _
 orders.drinks_itemID = drinks.drinks_id _
 WHERE (orders.order_telephone = @order_telephone) _
 AND (orders.order_processed = 0)
```

---

In this example, we will also make use of Advanced Options dialog box to uncheck the Generate Insert, Update and Delete Statements option (we won't be using them). The next screen (the Create Stored Procedures screen) is shown in Figure 6.21. On this screen, you have the opportunity to name your stored procedures and either continually build them manually or have the wizard complete the process for you. We named the stored procedure SelectCurrentOrder. Click through the rest of the screens and exit the wizard. If you want to make sure your stored procedure has been created correctly, you can either view it via Server Explorer in Visual Studio .NET or open up Enterprise Manager for SQL Server and view it from there for the Gallagher database (check its syntax, get it to run, etc.).

This is a simple example but it illustrates the tight interrelationship that now exists between Visual Studio and SQL Server. It also shows how easily once sophisticated tasks can now be performed.

Once you have set up the stored procedure, continue with the following steps:

1. Right-click the SqlDataAdapter1 and select Generate Dataset from the menu. Create DataSet21.

2. The next step is to data-bind the Label controls. Select the Label that will hold the name data and click the ellipsis that appears when you click in the Databindings segment of the Property window. This exposes the DataBindings dialog box for this control (shown in Figure 6.22).

**FIGURE 6.21:**

The Create Stored
Procedures screen
of the Data Adapter
Configuration Wizard

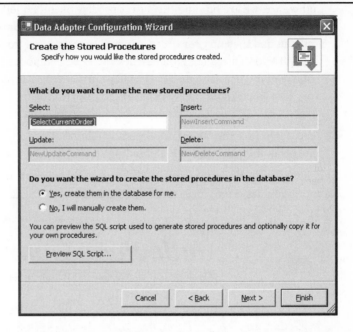

**FIGURE 6.22:**

The DataBindings dialog
box for a Label control

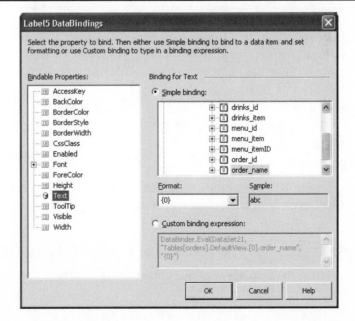

3. In this case, we are binding the Text property of the Label control. Make sure that this is selected in the Bindable Properties window. In the Simple Binding window, expand the nodes until you find the entry for order_name. (DataSet21 ➢ Orders ➢ DefaultView ➢ Default-View.[0] ➢ order_name). Double-click the expanded nodes to confirm the expression; you should end up with something in the Custom Binding Expression window (grayed out) that looks like `DataBinder.Eval(DataSet21, "Tables[orders].DefaultView.[0].order_name", "{0}")`. Select {0} from the Format drop-down menu.

4. Repeat step 3 for the other Label controls (choosing the appropriate fields relevant to those controls in their respective Databindings dialog boxes).

Figure 6.23 illustrates how this Web Form should appear in Design view.

**FIGURE 6.23:**

The completed WebForm2 in design View

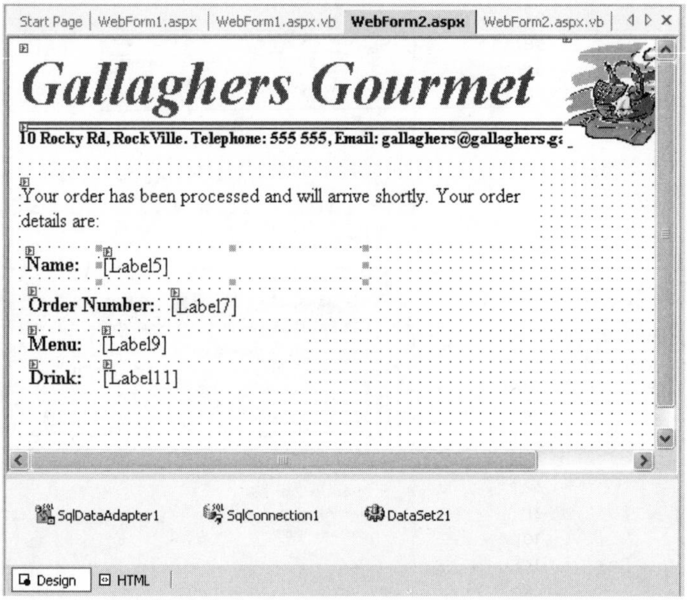

Listing 6.3 contains the full ASPX code for WebForm2. You will notice that the databinder expressions for the Label controls is also included in this code.

**Listing 6.3** **Full ASPX code for WebForm2 of the Gallaghers Application**

```
<%@ Page Language="vb" AutoEventWireup="false" _
 Codebehind="WebForm2.aspx.vb" _
 Inherits="DemoWebFrontEnd1.WebForm2"%>
<!DOCTYPE HTML PUBLIC "-//W3C//DTD HTML 4.0 _
```

```
Transitional//EN">
<HTML>
    <HEAD>
        <title>WebForm2</title>
        <meta name="GENERATOR" content="Microsoft Visual _
Studio.NET 7.0">
        <meta name="CODE_LANGUAGE" content="Visual Basic _
7.0">
        <meta name="vs_defaultClientScript" _
content="JavaScript">
        <meta name="vs_targetSchema" _
content="http://schemas.microsoft.com/intellisense/ie5">
    </HEAD>
    <body MS_POSITIONING="GridLayout">
        <form id="Form1" method="post" runat="server">
            <asp:label id="Label1" style="Z-INDEX: 101; _
LEFT: 8px; POSITION: absolute; TOP: 8px" _
runat="server" Font-Italic="True" _
ForeColor="Firebrick" Font-Bold="True" _
Height="64px" Font-Size="XX-Large" _
Width="441px">Gallaghers Gourmet</asp:label>
            <asp:Label id="Label3" style="Z-INDEX: _
105; LEFT: 9px; POSITION: absolute; TOP: 111px" _
runat="server" Height="48px" Width="414px">_
Your order has been processed and will arrive shortly. _
Your order details are:</asp:Label>
            <asp:imagebutton id="ImageButton1" _
style="Z-INDEX: 104; LEFT: 441px; POSITION: absolute; _
TOP: 0px" runat="server" Height="83px" Width="105px" _
ImageUrl="file:///C:\Inetpub\wwwroot\_
DemoWebFrontEnd1\FD00306_.WMF"></asp:imagebutton>
            <asp:label id="Label2" style="Z-INDEX: _
103; LEFT: 8px; POSITION: absolute; TOP: 69px" _
runat="server" Font-Bold="True" Height="23px" _
Font-Size="X-Small" Width="516px" _
Font-Overline="True">10 Rocky Rd, RockVille. _
  Telephone: 555 555,  Email: _
gallaghers@gallaghers.gag</asp:label>
            <HR style="Z-INDEX: 102; LEFT: 8px; _
POSITION: absolute; TOP: 64px" width="600" _
color="#cc0000" SIZE="3">
            <asp:Label id="Label4" style="Z-INDEX: _
106; LEFT: 13px; POSITION: absolute; TOP: 164px" _
runat="server" Width="56px" _
Font-Bold="True">Name:</asp:Label>
            <asp:Label id=Label5 style="Z-INDEX: _
107; LEFT: 76px; POSITION: absolute; TOP: 165px" _
runat="server" Width="204px" Text='<%# _
DataBinder.Eval(DataSet21, "Tables[orders].DefaultView.[0].order_name", _
"{0}") %>'>
            </asp:Label>
            <asp:Label id="Label6" style="Z-INDEX: _
```

```
108; LEFT: 15px; POSITION: absolute; TOP: _
195px" runat="server" Width="104px" Height="21px" _
Font-Bold="True">Order Number:</asp:Label>
        <asp:Label id=Label7 style="Z-INDEX: _
109; LEFT: 130px; POSITION: absolute; TOP: _
196px" runat="server" Width="161px" _
Text='<%# DataBinder.Eval(DataSet21, _
"Tables[orders].DefaultView.[0].order_id", "{0:N}") %>'>
        </asp:Label>
        <asp:Label id="Label8" style="Z-INDEX: _
110; LEFT: 15px; POSITION: absolute; TOP: 225px" _
runat="server" Width="50px" _
Font-Bold="True">Menu:</asp:Label>
        <asp:Label id=Label9 style="Z-INDEX: _
111; LEFT: 75px; POSITION: absolute; TOP: 225px" _
runat="server" Width="164px" Text='<%# _
DataBinder.Eval(DataSet21, _
"Tables[orders].DefaultView.[0].menu_item", "{0}") %>'>
        </asp:Label>
        <asp:Label id="Label10" style="Z-INDEX: _
112; LEFT: 16px; POSITION: absolute; TOP: 251px" _
runat="server" Width="49px" _
Font-Bold="True">Drink:</asp:Label>
        <asp:Label id=Label11 style="Z-INDEX: _
113; LEFT: 76px; POSITION: absolute; TOP: 251px" _
runat="server" Width="160px" Text='<%# _
DataBinder.Eval(DataSet21, _
"Tables[orders].DefaultView.[0].drinks_item", "{0}") _
%>'>
        </asp:Label>
    </form>
  </body>
</HTML>
```

The next step is to build the Code Behind for the application.

## Code Behind for WebForm1

From the Design view of the WebForm1, double-click the Web Form to enter Code Behind. Listing 6.4 gives the code for the Page_Load event that we will use to populate the two RadioButtonList controls.

| Listing 6.4 | Code for the Page_Load Event of WebForm1 of the Gallaghers Application |
|---|---|

```
Private Sub Page_Load(ByVal sender As System.Object, _
  ByVal e As System.EventArgs) Handles MyBase.Load
```

```
        If Not IsPostBack Then

            'Fill CheckBoxList1 from DataSet
            SqlDataAdapter1.Fill(DataSet11)
            RadioButtonList1.DataBind()

            'Use DataReader to fill CheckboxList2
            'Use custom Command object
            Dim MySqlDbCommand As New _
  SqlClient.SqlCommand()
            MySqlDbCommand.CommandText = "SELECT menu.* _
  FROM menu where menu_instock = 1"
            MySqlDbCommand.Connection = SqlConnection1
            SqlConnection1.Open()
            Dim sqlRead As SqlClient.SqlDataReader
            sqlRead = MySqlDbCommand.ExecuteReader
            While sqlRead.Read
                RadioButtonList2.Items.Add(New _
  ListItem("$" & sqlRead.Item("menu_price") & " - " & _
  sqlRead.Item("menu_item"), sqlRead.Item("menu_id")))
            End While
            SqlConnection1.Close()

        End If

    End Sub
```

We test for the IsPostBack condition to ensure that we only populate the controls once in the application/user lifecycle. As you can see, it is a lot easier to populate a control from a DataSet than with a DataReader (in terms of the amount of code). The first two lines of the routine are used to populate the drinks list from the dataset:

```
SqlDataAdapter1.Fill(DataSet11)
RadioButtonList1.DataBind()
```

We then used the menu list as an example of how you can carry out a similar task using the DataReader. In this case, we are also modifying the output to include both price and item details in the radio button list. This is handled by the following line of code:

```
RadioButtonList2.Items.Add(New ListItem("$" & _
  sqlRead.Item("menu_price") & " - " & _
  sqlRead.Item("menu_item"), sqlRead.Item("menu_id")))
```

Our SELECT statement is designed to filter only those items that are marked as in stock:

```
MySqlDbCommand.CommandText = "SELECT menu.* FROM menu where menu_instock = 1"
```

If we had created a second SqlDataAdapter using a SELECT statement similar to the preceding one, we could have used the autogenerated SELECT statement with our DataReader.

Consider, for example, the following code snippet:

```
'Use Command object from SqlDataAdapter2
SqlConnection1.Open()
Dim sqlRead As SqlClient.SqlDataReader
sqlRead = SqlSelectCommand2.ExecuteReader

While sqlRead.Read
            RadioButtonList2.Items.Add(sqlRead.Item_
("menu_item"))
End While
SqlConnection1.Close()
```

In this case, the SqlSelectCommand2 is the autogenerated statement from the SqlData-Adapter.

Listing 6.5 illustrates the code for the Submit button, which copies the items entered and selected by the customer into the verification section at the bottom of the form. It also enables the RequiredFieldValidation controls to do their bit. If any of the fields are incomplete, the relevant error message is shown before any further code execution takes place. In a production application, you would probably also have the OK button disabled until everything has been validated. Most of the code for the Submit button is straightforward with the exception that we have taken the opportunity to demonstrate setting up a session variable here. In this case, the *"phonenum"* variable is used to hold the user's telephone number. In ASP.NET, you can declare a session variable and assign it a value in the following fashion:

```
Session("mySessionVariable") = Value of Session Variable
```

**Listing 6.5      Click Event Code for the Submit Button**

```
Private Sub Button1_Click(ByVal sender As _
  System.Object, ByVal e As System.EventArgs) Handles _
  Button1.Click

        Label12.Text = TextBox1.Text
        Label14.Text = TextBox2.Text
        Label15.Text = TextBox3.Text
        Label16.Text = TextBox4.Text
        Label17.Text = RadioButtonList1.SelectedItem.Text
        Label18.Text = RadioButtonList2.SelectedItem.Text
        Session("phonenum") = TextBox4.Text
    End Sub
```

In Listing 6.6, you see the code for the OK button that creates the new record representing the customer's order in the Gallaghers database (orders table). It then transfers the user to the confirmation page using the Response.Redirect object with the user's telephone number encoded in the URL for WebPage2.

---

**Listing 6.6**        **Code for Click Event of OK Button**

```
Private Sub Button2_Click(ByVal sender As _
System.Object, ByVal e As System.EventArgs) Handles _
Button2.Click
        Dim menu_choice As Int16 = _
RadioButtonList2.SelectedItem.Value
        Dim drink_choice As Int16 = _
RadioButtonList1.SelectedItem.Value

        Dim MySqlDbInsertCommand As New _
SqlClient.SqlCommand()
        MySqlDbInsertCommand.CommandText = "INSERT _
into orders (menu_itemID, drinks_itemID, order_name, _
order_street, order_town, order_telephone) VALUES _
( " & menu_choice & ", " & drink_choice & ", '" & _
TextBox1.Text & "', '" & TextBox2.Text & "' , '" & _
TextBox3.Text & "' , '" & TextBox4.Text & "' )"

        MySqlDbInsertCommand.Connection = SqlConnection1
        SqlConnection1.Open()
        MySqlDbInsertCommand.ExecuteNonQuery
        SqlConnection1.Close()

        Dim Parameter As String
        Parameter = "param=" & Server.UrlEncode_
(Session("phonenum"))
        Response.Redirect("WebForm2.aspx?" & Parameter)

End Sub
```

---

In this code we have set up an SQL INSERT statement to create a new record based on the data that has been entered. When you execute the INSERT command, you have the choice of using ExecuteNonQuery (which returns the number of rows affected) or ExecuteScalar (returns the value of the first row in the first column affected). The two variables declared at the top of the routine, *menu_choice* and *drink_choice*, illustrate how you can read a selected value out of the RadioButtonList control using the .SelectedItem.Value properties. To navigate to WebForm2, we encode the value of the session variable (*phonenum*) created earlier, and add it to the URL for WebForm2, which we call using Response.Redirect.

The final code for this Web Form is the Click event for the Cancel button. This simply clears all the entries that the user has made. It's shown in Listing 6.7.

**Listing 6.7** **Click Event for the Cancel Button in WebForm2**

```
Private Sub Button3_Click(ByVal sender As _
  System.Object, ByVal e As System.EventArgs) _
  Handles Button3.Click
        TextBox1.Text = TextBox1.Text.Empty
        TextBox2.Text = TextBox2.Text.Empty
        TextBox3.Text = TextBox3.Text.Empty
        TextBox4.Text = TextBox4.Text.Empty
        Label12.Text = Label12.Text.Empty
        Label14.Text = Label14.Text.Empty
        Label15.Text = Label15.Text.Empty
        Label16.Text = Label16.Text.Empty
        Label17.Text = Label17.Text.Empty
        Label18.Text = Label18.Text.Empty
        RadioButtonList1.ClearSelection()
        RadioButtonList2.ClearSelection()

End Sub
```

Next we will look at the code for WebForm2.

## Code Behind for WebForm2

Open up WebForm2 in Design view and double-click the form to enter Code Behind. We
need only to create a Page_Load event for this form. Listing 6.8 illustrates this code.

**Listing 6.8** **Code Behind for WebForm2 of Gallaghers Application**

```
Private Sub Page_Load(ByVal sender As _
  System.Object, ByVal e As System.EventArgs) _
  Handles MyBase.Load

        SqlDataAdapter1.SelectCommand.Parameters_
("@order_telephone").Value = Request.QueryString("param")
        SqlDataAdapter1.Fill(DataSet21)
        Label5.DataBind()
        Label7.DataBind()
        Label9.DataBind()
        Label11.DataBind()

End Sub
```

In this event, we data-bind each of the relevant Label controls and feed the telephone number
brought over from WebForm1 in as our parameter for the stored procedure enacted by

SqlDataAdapter1. This is handled by the following line of code:

```
SqlDataAdapter1.SelectCommand.Parameters_
("@order_telephone").Value = Request.QueryString("param")
```

Save and compile the application by clicking the Start arrow on the toolbar (or pressing F5).

## Running the Application

Test the application by running some sample orders through it. Not completing all the fields or choosing a meal or drink should result in the appropriate error message appearing. Figure 6.24 shows where some of these messages have been activated. Figure 6.25 shows the same order, completed and about to be confirmed. Figure 6.26 illustrates WebForm2 confirming the order.

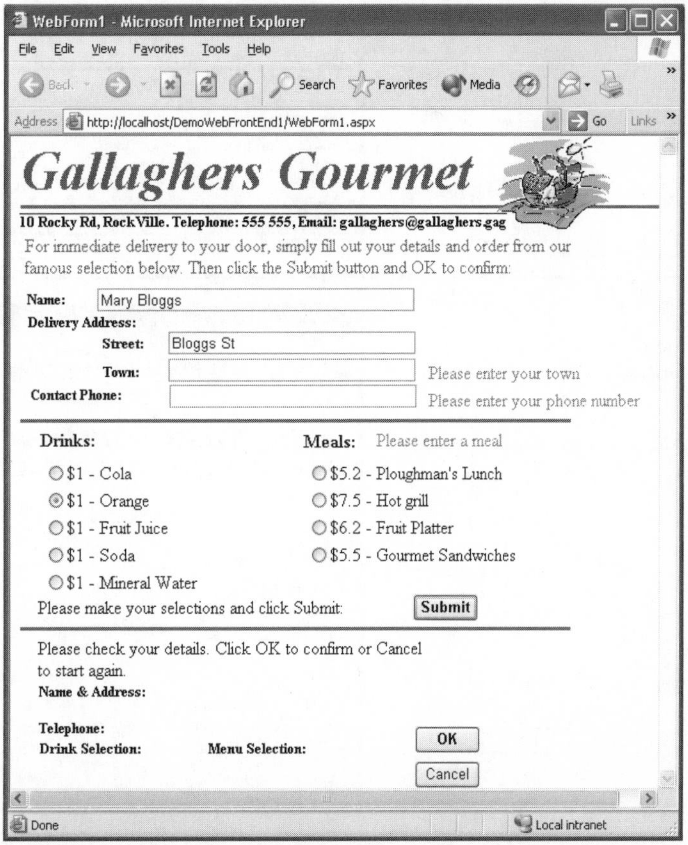

**FIGURE 6.24:**

The Gallaghers application with error messages

**FIGURE 6.25:**

A complete order
entered into the
Gallaghers application

**FIGURE 6.26:**

Confirmation of an
order in WebForm2

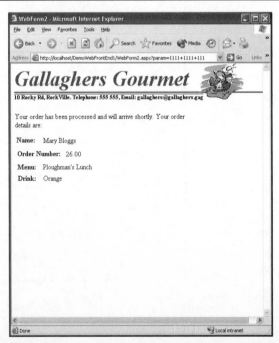

## Summary

The Gallaghers application clearly demonstrates the ease with which you can build web-based front ends with the .NET technologies. Essentially, you can build the entire application from a back-end database, middle-tier components, and the user interface without leaving Visual Studio.

Although this application is only a demonstration exercise, you can see how quickly and easily you can carry out tasks that once would have required a great deal of code and specialized knowledge. Data access from web applications is simplicity itself, and fully interactive pages that utilize server-side technologies can be put together in only a few moments. Using .NET technology means that you no longer have to look at building a web-based front end as a separate part of the application creation process. In Chapter 15 and Chapter 16, we will explore the various controls available with Web Forms in a lot more detail. In Chapter 18, we will specifically look at the DataGrid, DataList, and Repeater controls.

The next chapter covers the design and development of n-tier applications using Visual Basic .NET.

# CHAPTER 7

## The Business Tier

- Introducing n-tier applications

- When do you use an n-tier approach?

- An example of a distributed n-tier approach

- Building the n-tier project

I n this chapter, we will be examining the structure of a modern distributed application and the technology available to create such an application. In particular, we will be focusing on the so-called middle tier, or business logic layer, of the modern n-tier structure, and we will look at the resources available in .NET to build and support these services. Naturally, in this book, we will be doing this from the perspective of the Visual Basic developer.

Later in this chapter, we will build a simple n-tier application using COM+ and an XML Web service in the business tier. We will build our managed components using both Visual Basic .NET and C++. (You may be wondering why we are using C++ in a VB book. This is a simple example that is easy to build and is used to illustrate how non-VB components can be utilized within VB projects.) Although we create and consume a simple XML Web service in this chapter, later in this book (in Chapter 20), we will explore how to create and consume XML Web services in a lot more detail. Microsoft has been enthusiastically pushing XML Web services as an integral part of the .NET initiative, but COM+ remains a key technology within .NET and has the advantages of having stood the test of time and being familiar to many developers.

## Introducing N-Tier Applications

An important aspect of modern application design is the ability to separate the various aspects of the application into separate and distinct layers. For many years, a popular implementation model was the two-tier application, and a typical example would consist of a back-end database with a front-end interface. Traditional two-tier systems combined all their business logic with the presentation layer, and this resulted in a range of problems, particularly when it came to scaling and/or updating the application.

Modern applications often consist of more than a simple database-interface combination, and they usually have some form of intermediate logic layer that provides an additional level for data manipulation before it is passed onto the presentation layer. We call such an application a three-tier (or n-tier) application.

Generally, an n-tier application is divided into three main layers:

- Presentation layer
- Business logic layer(s)
- Data service layer

We use the term *n-tier* because the middle layer, in particular, may consist of a number of separate components. The main advantage of this model is that business logic can be reused, scaled, and updated without getting caught up with the user-interface code. Work can also be carried out on user interfaces without interfering with the actual business logic of the application.

Typically, prior to .NET, three-tier applications were built using some form of back-end database (such as SQL Server), middle-tier components written in C++, and a front end built using a RAD (Rapid Application Development) tool such as VB (see Figure 7.1). Middle-tier components were developed in C++ mainly to maximize performance because C++ is a compiled language, whereas Visual Basic (earlier versions) is interpreted in nature. Despite the fact that later versions of VB closed the performance gap on C++, the preference has generally been to continue building middle-tier components using C++ and technologies such as COM and COM+. COM technology enabled the creation of software components that can be reused and provide services to one or more applications.

**FIGURE 7.1:**

A traditional n-tier application

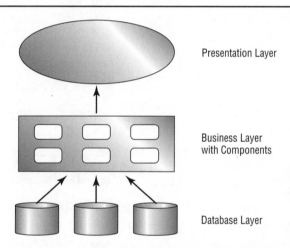

Presentation Layer

Business Layer with Components

Database Layer

Within the Microsoft development environment (initially DCOM and then later COM+), component technology enabled the development of distributed applications in which the various layers are able to exist in physically separate locations and communicate with each other over a network. The development of the Internet has ramped up the concept of a distributed applications to a new level with the possibility of an application built from components scattered across various computers located in different parts of the world. Additionally, the creation of web-based front ends has enabled a cross-platform approach to distributed applications.

However, there have been a number of stumbling blocks to the goal of developing truly platform-independent components that can provide support for widely distributed applications. These include the various ways that different platforms read and interact with data and security considerations such as firewalls that do unhelpful things such as block ports required for access by components. Another issue for developers was that earlier editions of COM required the developer to perform a lot of the background "plumbing" in order for the object to interact with the application(s) as desired.

COM technology has steadily improved (in particular, with the introduction of COM+), but the introduction of .NET has altered the playing field significantly. We still have COM+ and we still have C++, but we can now introduce XML Web services as a player into our middle layer, as shown in Figure 7.2.

**FIGURE 7.2:**

Using XML Web services in an n-tier application

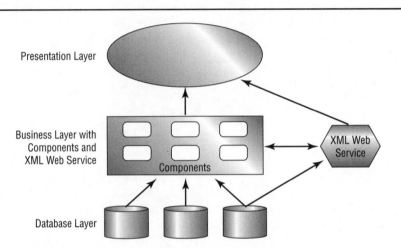

The beauty of using XML is that it provides a universal language that can be understood across platforms and applications. This enables you to package up data from one application and send it to another without the need for developing some form of understanding between the two applications as to how they represent their data. Additionally, you can send this stuff via port 80, which is normally left open as the standard TCP/IP port for the Internet.

XML Web services create a potential business model in which a developer can create a generic XML Web service that provides a particular service over the Internet, which in turn can be purchased or leased in some way for use by a variety of consumer applications. A simple example of this may be an XML Web service that provides a "thought for the day" service. Consumers of the service would be able to use it to insert a relevant homily into their application or website. There are some obvious drawbacks to such a model, such as how do you guarantee the ongoing viability of a third-party service used within an application, but certainly XML Web services are a very easy and effective way to generate and execute middle-tier business logic from within the .NET environment.

g COM components can still be utilized in a number of ways. You can
give them an XML wrapper and effectively make them behave as XML
n call them directly using the COM Interop Services. You can also
nsume components using COM+ services. These can be created using
nt languages such as Visual Basic .NET. Such a .NET component is
nent. You can also continue to build unmanaged components using C++.

g with Visual Studio .NET is that you can develop all aspects of your
within the one IDE. You can use the database development tools to
0 database, right down to its stored procedures (see Chapter 6, "Building
ications"), you can create your middle-tier components using a variety of
ges, and you can generate your front end(s) across a number of formats.
bile Internet Toolkit, which is discussed in Chapter 22, "Targeting
an produce a user interface that will run on virtually anything.) Figure 7.3
rn n-tier distributed application might be constructed.

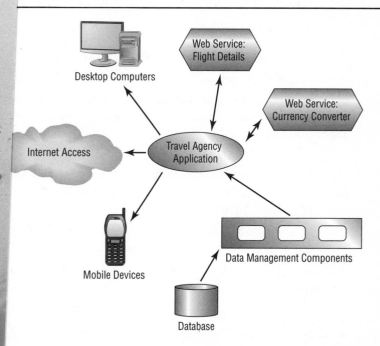

is mean for you and your shiny new Visual Studio .NET. There are a
is an impact:

le to separate an application across a number of layers or tiers.

a decision as to what technology(s) to use for your middle-tier components.
ML Web services and/or COM+.

- You need to decide which language is appropriate for each of your middle-tier components.
- You need to think about how you are going to interact with your application. You may end up with multiple interfaces for different devices, users, and scenarios.
- You also need to consider your choice of developmental and delivery technology for your user interface(s).

Although there are a number of decisions that need to be made, they really all fall into what should be a natural part of the application's development process, which is the design phase. Good planning and appropriate forethought should be an essential part of any project's life cycle, and this is particularly true for enterprise-level applications.

In the past, Visual Basic's RAD features have enabled the design process to often become one with the development process. Under the pressures of time, budget, and so on, the design aspect has been downplayed. Certainly for many small projects, this is not an issue, but developers will find that if they particularly want to take advantage of VB .NET's new OO features, they will need to spend a lot more time with the design phase of the project.

## When Do You Use an N-Tier Approach?

Building an n-tier application used to be a very deliberate undertaking that was made by an organization only after some very careful consideration of the costs involved and the resources involved. People with specialist skills in areas such as COM and C++ were required to work on the project.

However, .NET allows you now to use an n-tier approach almost as a natural part of your programming toolbox. Even small applications can be easily and economically built using this model, and the range of benefits that used to only flow from economies of scale can now be achieved with everyday projects.

ASP.NET projects offer a virtually natural n-tier structure by the easy separation of the presentation layer into the ASPX page and the business logic into Code Behind.

Before you begin to build your project, sit back and take a long, hard look at it. Ask yourself the following questions:

- Is this application of such a scale that it immediately lends itself to an n-tier approach?
- If the answer to Q1 is no, what are the future expansion and/or upgrading requirements of the application?
- What elements of the project can be expressed uniquely and which elements have a natural affinity for each other?

- Are there aspects of the project that you have previously built components for or for which you know that components exist?
- Which parts of the project constitute the user interface?
- What, if any, are the data centers for the project?
- What constitutes the business logic of the project and can this be organized in distinct, logical, and functional islands of code?

The first two questions are really the most important. For simple data processing applications, an n-tier approach may be seen as serious overkill, and in many cases it will be. It is then necessary to consider the likelihood of this application requiring any scalability or modification in the future. An n-tier approach enables you to easily scale or upgrade a project down the track. More important for many projects, it enables someone else to easily modify and maintain the application.

The remaining questions enable you to explore the granularity of your project—or how well it can be expressed as an n-tier application. In reality, this is not a hard task. Any program that involves some form of database access almost automatically presents itself as a two-tier application: datacenter and presentation/business logic layer. To then build it as a three-tier application, it is simply a case of separating any of the data-processing code out of the presentation layer and giving this its own separate layer.

In the next section, we will look at a sample project and how such a project may be structured as a distributed n-tier application.

## An Example of a Distributed N-Tier Approach

Consider the hypothetical situation of Wilson's Luxury Houseboats. Wilson's hires out houseboats on Lake Isabitdeep in the scenic hinterland of Outyonder. One of the services that Wilson's provides on its houseboats is an onboard computer equipped with wireless network access. Wilson's own intranet provides a series of services to its houseboats such as updated weather reports, maps, recommended fishing spots, lists of specials at the various lakeside venues, and so on. The computer also provides information back to Wilson's on the running condition of the boat—its location, fuel and water supplies, current mechanical condition, and so forth.

Unfortunately, this whole computer application is still largely at the stage of "a very good idea," and the development team has been charged with the task of turning it into reality. At the moment, the system consists of the condition reports from the boats back to Wilson's. These are built as a collection of COM components that process information from various sensors on the boat (including its navigation equipment) and then send this information back to a database on the mainland that can be accessed for status reports on the condition of each boat. Figure 7.4 illustrates the current system.

**FIGURE 7.4:**

The current Wilson's system

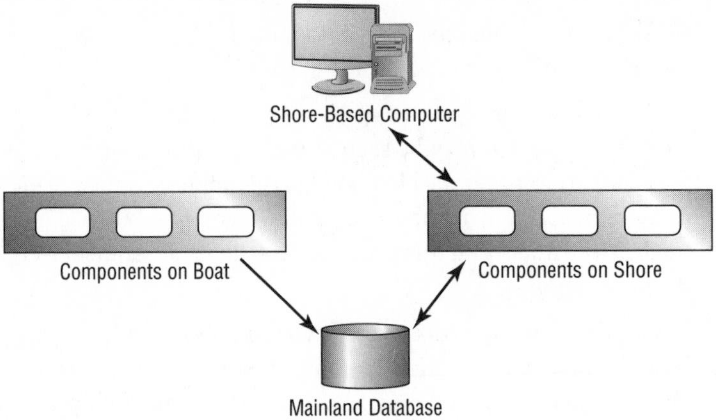

An additional resource that can be utilized is made available from the local TV station, which bundles its weather reports as an XML Web service for use by local boat people and authorities.

Essentially, we need to build a system that provides a browser front end on the houseboat to database services on the mainland. These services might also include the boat's running condition as well as the tourist and navigational information envisaged by Wilson's. We could create a desktop front end to administer the database on the mainland and make use of the XML Web service from the TV station in the business logic layer. We could also develop additional components of our own to manage requests for information on fishing spots and various tourist incentives. These components might also be in the form of XML Web services that could then be used by other members of the local community in promoting the local area. This is particularly relevant with the fishing spots data because Wilson's relies on reports from locals to keep this information up-to-date. (Tourism is an essential part of the Lake Isabitdeep economy.) Additionally, we could bundle this information through a mobile front end or even as part of a Short Message Service (SMS) solution that holiday makers could access over their cell phones. Figure 7.5 shows how the revised Wilson's application might be structured.

Naturally, there will be much more work in creating such an application than what we have discussed here. However, this illustrates how we can begin the process of structuring a distributed n-tier application.

Next we will look at some practical examples of building middle tier components.

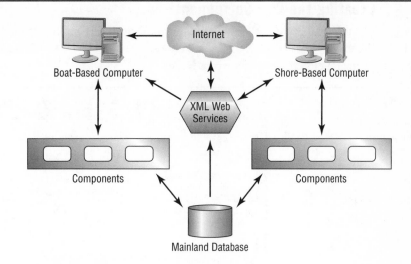

## Building the N-Tier Project

In this example, we will build a simple project that reads a table from the pubs database. We will use a managed component built in Visual Basic .NET to handle the data access. Additionally, we will create a managed component in C++ to perform a simple calculation—in this case, adding 10 percent—which can be used to manipulate some of the data from the table. A simple XML Web service will also be introduced to provide the current time on the web server. The user interface will consist of a simple Windows form.

The structure of the application is illustrated in Figure 7.6. We'll use the titles table out of the pubs database.

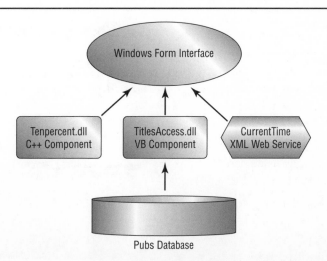

## Creating the C++ Component

Open Visual Studio .NET and create a new project. From the New Project dialog box, open the Visual C++ Projects folder and choose the Managed C++ Class Library option. Name the project Tenpercent, as shown in Figure 7.7.

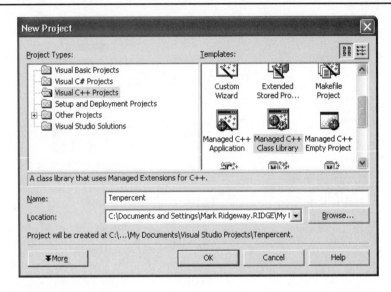

Then complete the following steps:

1. In the Solution Explorer part of the IDE (right side), switch to Class view and expand the Tenpercent node. Right-click the Class1 node that appears beneath it (shown in Figure 7.8), and from the context menu, choose Add ➢ Add Function.

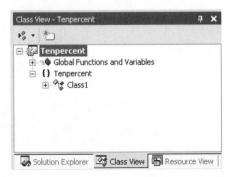

2. Choosing the Add Function option will open the Add Member Function Wizard. This provides a civilized, although not quite "hands-on" mechanism for writing code in C++. In the Add Member Function Wizard, set the following:

Function Name: Calculate_percent

Return Type: double

Parameter Type: double

Parameter Name: price

3. Click the Add button to add the member function. Figure 7.9 illustrates how the wizard should look at this stage. Click Finish to exit the wizard.

**FIGURE 7.9:**

The completed Add Member Function Wizard

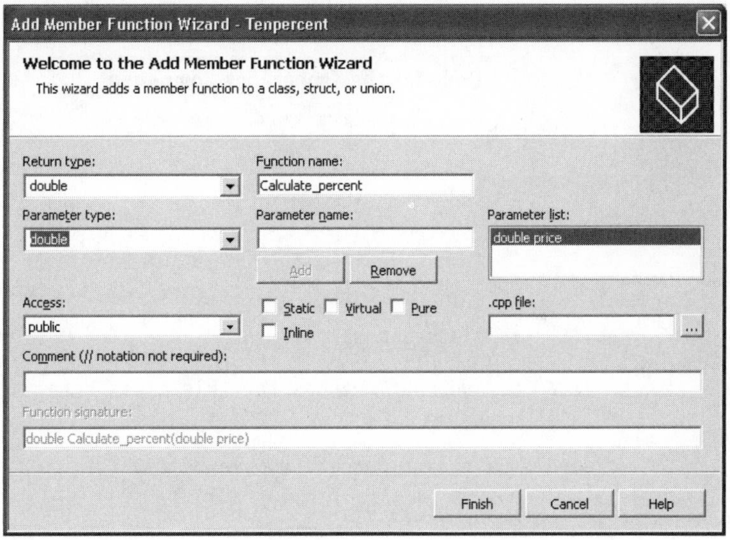

The following code should appear on the screen:

```
// Tenpercent.h

#pragma once

using namespace System;

namespace Tenpercent
{
    public __gc class Class1
```

```
        {
        // TODO: Add your methods for this class here.
    public:

        double Calculate_percent(double price)
        {
            return 0;
        }
    };
}
```

**4.** Modify the `return 0;` statement to read as follows:

```
return price * 1.1;
```

The complete code should now look like it does in Listing 7.1.

**Listing 7.1**      **Code for the Tenpercent Component**

```
// Tenpercent.h

#pragma once

using namespace System;

namespace Tenpercent
{
    public __gc class Class1
    {
        // TODO: Add your methods for this class here.
    public:

        double Calculate_percent(double price)
        {
            return price * 1.1;
        }
    };
}
```

Save the project and compile it using the Build Solution command from the Build menu. Then exit the project. The next step is to build the Visual Basic .NET component.

## Creating the VB Component

Open up Visual Studio .NET and select the New Project option. From the `Visual Basic Projects` folder choose Class Library. Name it TitlesAccess as shown in Figure 7.10.

**FIGURE 7.10:**

Creating the TitlesAccess
class library

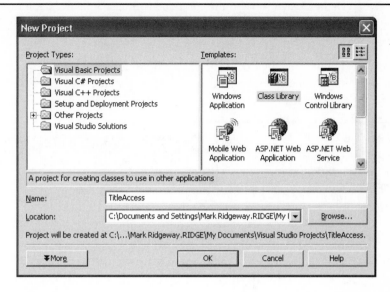

Complete the following steps:

1. From the Project menu, select Add Component and name the component Component1, as shown in Figure 7.11.

**FIGURE 7.11:**

Creating Component1
in TitlesAccess

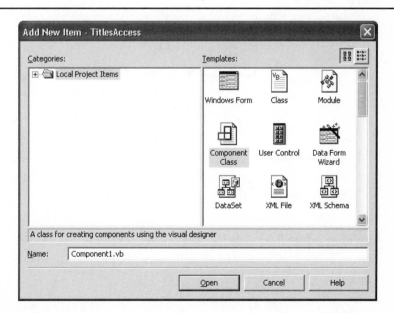

2. In the Design view for the component, drag a SqlDataAdapter to the designer and configure it with a connection to the pubs database and the following SQL statement:

```
SELECT title_id, title, price FROM titles
```

Figure 7.12 illustrates the Query Builder dialog box for setting up this statement. Leave the advanced options checked in order to create the INSERT, UPDATE, and DELETE statements.

**FIGURE 7.12:**

The Query Builder dialog box for the pubs SELECT statement

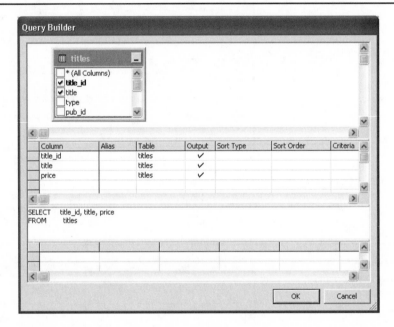

3. In Design view for the component, right-click the SqlDataAdapter1 object and choose the Generate Dataset option. Do not check the Add This Dataset to the Designer check box. This will create DataSet1. Double-click the designer to switch to Code Behind.

4. Underneath the node that reads "Component Designer generated code" (but inside the class declaration), add the code from Listing 7.2 to create the GetTitles method, which will retrieve all the titles from the pubs database.

**Listing 7.2**      **Code for the GetTitles Method**

```
Public Function GetTitles() As DataSet1
        Dim titles As New DataSet1()
        SqlDataAdapter1.Fill(titles)
        Return titles
End Function
```

Save the component and compile it using the Build Solution option from the Build menu.

## Creating the XML Web Service

The object here is to create a simple XML Web service and consume it in our n-tier application. (In Chapter 20, we will explore how XML Web services work in more detail.) Microsoft has made this an essentially easy process (as they have with the other components), and we can use a very simple "paint-by-number" approach to achieving practical outcomes with very sophisticated technology.

The XML Web service that we will build here is a really trivial example, but it clearly demonstrates the main steps in the creation and consumption process.

The first step is to open a new project in Visual Studio .NET and choose ASP.NET Web Service from the Visual Basic Projects folder (refer Figure 7.13). In this case, name the XML Web service CurrentTime.

**NOTE**    You will need to have IIS installed and functioning on your computer to enable this XML Web service to work. XML Web services are delivered from a web server.

**FIGURE 7.13:**

Creating a new XML Web service in Visual Basic .NET

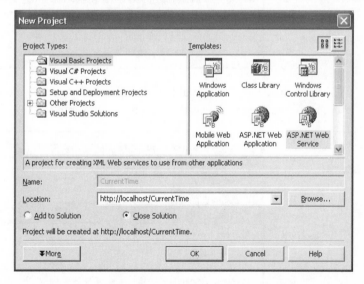

Continue building the XML Web service by completing the following steps:

1. Double-click the design surface to switch to Code view.

2. Code view opens with a sample framework for a "Hello World" demonstration application. We will modify this into our current time application. Underneath the "Hello World" sample, but inside the Service1 class framework, add the code from Listing 7.3.

**Listing 7.3**      **Code for Service1 in the CurrentTime XML Web Service**

```
<WebMethod()> Public Function cTime() As String
        cTime = Now().ToString("t")
    End Function
```

To test the XML Web service, press F5 or click the Start arrow. This opens Service1 in your default browser window, along with a link to its cTime method and some recommendations about default namespaces (see Figure 7.14). The cTime method simply returns the current time as a string from the web server clock. The "t" format defines an hours/minutes presentation.

**FIGURE 7.14:**

Service1 in Internet Explorer

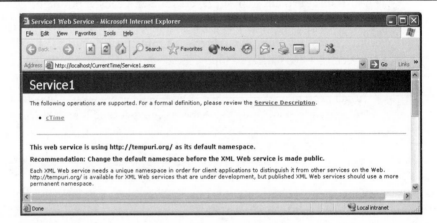

Clicking the cTime link should open cTime in Internet Explorer. As shown in Figure 7.15, there is an Invoke button to call the method and some additional information about SOAP.

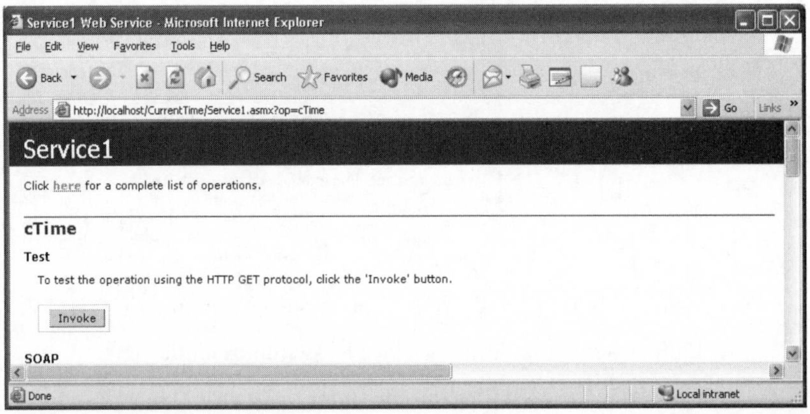

**FIGURE 7.15:**

cTime in Internet Explorer

Clicking the Invoke button calls the cTime method and opens a new instance of the web browser with the returned value from cTime along with some XML. Figure 7.16 illustrates how this should look.

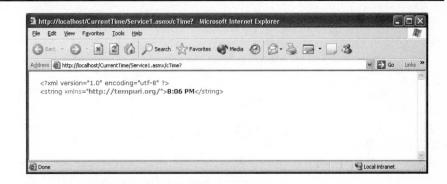

## Building the Presentation Layer

Finally, we need to create the Windows form to consume our components. From the New Project menu in Visual Studio .NET, select the Windows Application option from the Visual Basic Projects folder. Name the project nTierProject. The following steps describe how to set up the user interface:

1. Once the project has opened, we begin by setting references to the components. From the Solution Explorer, right-click the nTierProject node and select the Add Reference option from the context menu. This opens the Add Reference dialog box.

2. Click the Browse button to locate the Tenpercent and TitlesAccess components. If you have followed the defaults, these should be in your Visual Studio Projects directory, which is normally located in the My Documents directory. The file that you need for the Tenpercent reference is Tenpercent.dll, and it's normally found in the Debug folder in the Tenpercent directory. The file that you need for TitlesAccess is TitlesAccess.dll, and it can be found in the bin subdirectory of the TitlesAccess directory. Figure 7.17 illustrates these in the Add Reference dialog box. Click OK to add the references to the project.

3. You can confirm the addition of the components by expanding the References node under nTierProject in the Solution Explorer. You should be able to see references to Tenpercent and TitlesAccess.

4. We add the XML Web services by using the Add Web Reference option. Right-click the nTierProject node in Solution Explorer and choose Add Web Reference from the context menu. This opens the Add Web Reference dialog box, which can be a little impenetrable unless you know the specific address of the service you are after or unless there are really good discovery mechanisms on the machine from which you are planning to access them. Figure 7.18 shows this dialog box.

**FIGURE 7.17:**

The Add Reference
Dialog box with
the C++ and VB
managed components

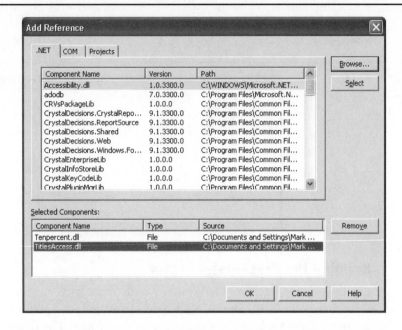

**FIGURE 7.18:**

The Add Web Reference
dialog box

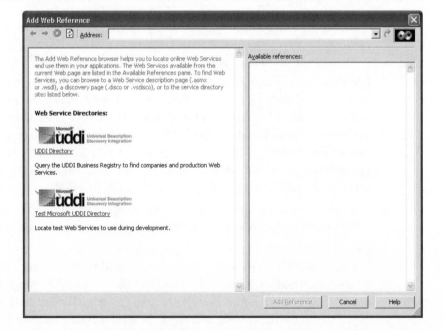

5. Type the URL of Service1 from the CurrentTime XML Web service. If you followed the defaults, this should be `http://localhost/CurrentTime/Service1.asmx`. Figure 7.19 illustrates how this service should be displayed in the Add Web Reference dialog box. If you wish, you can take a look at the contract, documentation, or service description, but all you really have to do at this point is click the Add Reference button at the bottom of the dialog box. You will notice that a reference to Service1 is now created under localhost in the Web References node in Solution Explorer. By adding the references to the components in this fashion, we are able to use the full autocomplete and syntax checking facilities available in the Visual Studio .NET code editor.

**FIGURE 7.19:**

The CurrentTime XML
Web service displayed in
the Add Web Reference
dialog

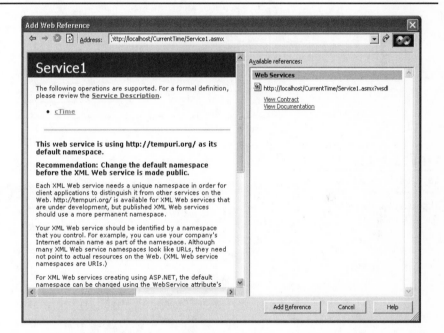

6. Drag a DataSet object to Form1 from the Data controls (Toolbox). This opens the Add Dataset dialog box. From the Typed Dataset drop-down menu, choose Referenced Datasets and then choose TitlesAccess.DataSet1 (see Figure 7.20). Click OK. This creates an instance of DataSet1 (DataSet11) at the bottom of the Design view window.

7. On Form1 set up a DataGrid control, three Command Button controls and seven Label controls. Three of the Labels simply provide additional captions for the Button controls. Label1 holds the value for the adjusted price (and Label2 provides a caption for it), and Label4 holds the value returned by the XML Web service (Label3 is its caption). Figure 7.21 illustrates how we set up the form. We made some additional cosmetic changes in increasing font sizes to 10 point and some of the Label text properties to Bold. With Labels 1 and 4, we set the background color to white to make them visible in Figure 7.21.

**FIGURE 7.20:**

The Add Dataset
dialog box

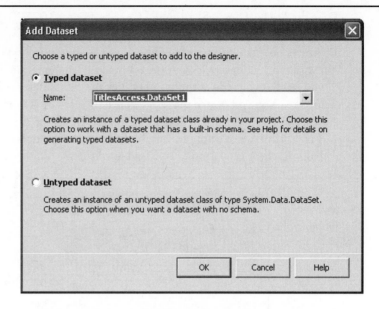

**FIGURE 7.21:**

Layout of the controls
for Form1 in the
nTierProject

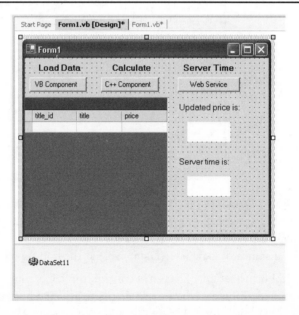

**8.** Set the DataSource property of DataGrid1 to DataSet11.titles. Set the Text properties of Buttons 1, 2, and 3 to VB Component, C++ Component, and Web Service, respectively.

9.  Double-click Button1 to enter Code Behind. We will use Button1 to call the VB component and load the data from the titles table into the DataGrid. Listing 7.4 has the code for Button1. The first line creates an instance of the Component1 component. The second line merges the data returned from the GetTitles method into the DataSet11.

**Listing 7.4**      **Code to Call VB Component TitlesAccess.Component1 from the nTierProject**

```
Private Sub Button1_Click(ByVal sender As System.Object,_
 ByVal e As System.EventArgs) Handles Button1.Click

        Dim titles As New TitlesAccess.Component1()
        DataSet11.Merge(titles.GetTitles)

End Sub
```

10. In Code Behind, add the code from Listing 7.5 to the code for the Button2 click event. This calls the C++ component we created earlier (Tenpercent.Class1) and employs its Calculate_percent method to produce an adjusted value of the price of the publication selected in the DataGrid. We have made use of structured exception handling (the Try…Catch statement) to trap some of the more obvious exceptions, such as a null value in price or clicking Button2 before the DataGrid has been filled.

**Listing 7.5**      **Code to Call C++ Component Tenpercent.Class1 from the nTierProject**

```
Private Sub Button2_Click(ByVal sender As System.Object,_
 ByVal e As System.EventArgs) Handles Button2.Click
        Dim percent As New Tenpercent.Class1()
        Dim price As Double
        Dim newprice As Double
        Dim n As Integer
        Try
            n = DataGrid1.CurrentRowIndex
            price = DataGrid1.Item(n, 2)
            newprice = percent.Calculate_percent(price)
            Label1.Text = FormatCurrency(newprice)
        Catch
            Label1.Text = "Invalid price"
        End Try
End Sub
```

Additionally, you could place an Imports Tenpercent statement at the top of the code editor for Form1, above the class declaration. This enables you to work directly with the component type without using the library name. For example, you would now use Dim percent As New Class1() in the first line of Listing 7.5.

You can do the same with the VB component, placing an Imports TitlesAccess statement at the top of the code editor and using Component1 directly in your code. However, if you are to do this, you need to choose a more sensible name than Class1 when creating your C++ component because it is a name that could easily become ambiguous across different class libraries. (It does in this case, if you did not delete the default Class1 template from the TitlesAccess class library.)

If you do end up with ambiguous component names in your application, it can be easily resolved by including the library name in the declaration, as we originally did in Listing 7.5.

Listing 7.6 demonstrates how to consume the XML Web service that we created. We create an instance of Service1 (time) in the first line and in the second line call the cTime method. We write this code into the click event of Button3.

**Listing 7.6    Code to Call XML Web Service CurrentTime from the nTierproject**

```
Private Sub Button3_Click(ByVal sender As System.Object,_
ByVal e As System.EventArgs) Handles Button3.Click
        Dim time As New localhost.Service1()
        Label4.Text = time.cTime
End Sub
```

This completes the project. Save, compile, and run the application. Figure 7.22 illustrates how the application should look on startup. Click the VB Component button to load the list of publications into the DataGrid, as illustrated in Figure 7.23.

**FIGURE 7.22:**

The nTierproject at startup

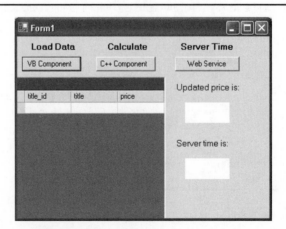

Select a record from the DataGrid and click the C++ Component button to post the revised price value, as shown in Figure 7.24. Figure 7.25 shows the application after the Web Service button has been clicked.

**FIGURE 7.23:**

Calling the VB
component in the
nTierProject

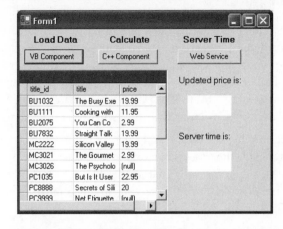

**FIGURE 7.24:**

Calling the C++
Component in the
nTierProject

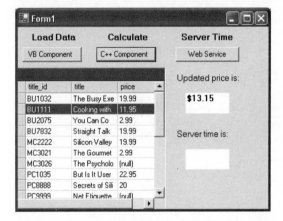

**FIGURE 7.25:**

Calling the XML
Web service in the
nTierProject

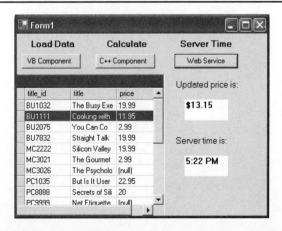

## Summary

This simple project illustrates how you can easily create and consume middle-tier objects in distributed applications. In particular, you saw how simply and quickly you can put these multiple-layer applications together. In the past, the sheer complexity of building and consuming a middle-tier component was sufficient to make them impractical for use in basic applications. However, with COM+, XML Web services, and Visual Studio .NET, you can now easily and affordably apply n-tier architecture wherever and whenever it suits.

Not only has the .NET architecture helped with creating business tier components, it has also made the process of working with the other tiers far easier and more integrated. It has opened the door for easily creating flexible and powerful web-based front ends to your applications and provides tools for creating and manipulating enterprise-level databases from within the Visual Studio .NET IDE.

This completes the section on database programming with .NET. The next section focuses on creating and deploying desktop applications with Visual Basic .NET. In the next chapter, we will be looking in more detail at building and working with Windows forms.

# PART II

# Windows Forms Projects

# CHAPTER 8

# Developing Windows Forms

- The Windows Form Designer

- The Controls collection

- Multiple form applications

- Menus

- MDI applications

T his chapter is an overview of the new features of the Windows Form Designer introduced with .NET. We're assuming you know how to design simple interfaces by placing Windows controls on a form. In this chapter, we'll focus on the new features of the Windows Form Designer and the tools for designing more functional forms with less effort.

The first two tools are the Anchor and Dock properties, which allow you to anchor and dock your controls on the form. With the appropriate settings for these two controls, you can design forms that can be easily resized at runtime and maintain the relative locations and sizes of their controls.

This chapter focuses on the new features of Visual Basic .NET and the things that are done differently. For example, handling one form from within another form's code isn't as simple as it used to be; you can't use the name of the form followed by the name of a control to access the controls on another form. Multiple Document Interface (MDI) applications are supported in .NET, but the design approach is a little different. The process of designing menus has also been enhanced in Visual Basic .NET. Menus are implemented with two new controls, the MainMenu and ContextMenu controls, and you can easily manipulate your menus from within your code.

The goal of this chapter is to show you how to take advantage of the new features of the IDE, as well as to point out the differences between the VB .NET and previous versions. The changes are not drastic, but many things are done differently now. Many programmers will attempt to apply their previous knowledge to VB .NET and find that some of the techniques they've mastered in the past won't work. Even worse, some techniques may work, but there may be better ones for the job.

## The Windows Form Designer

One of the major new components of Visual Basic .NET is the Windows Form Designer. For starters, the Designer is used by all .NET languages; it's not a VB-specific environment. Designing forms with the Windows Form Designer has become a very simple process. Many of the tasks that required substantial code in the past are now easily accomplished with point-and-click operations. The basic features of the Designer that relate to form design are discussed in the following sections.

### Anchoring and Docking

The Anchor and Dock properties are the basic tools for designing forms that can be easily resized at runtime and that can maintain the relative sizes and locations of their controls. Each control can be anchored to any of the four edges of the form by setting its Anchor property appropriately. (In previous versions of Visual Basic, all controls were anchored to the left and upper sides of the form.) When a control is anchored to a single edge, it's repositioned as the form is resized, so that the distance between the anchored side of the control and the corresponding edge of the form remains the same. If a control is anchored to two opposite sides of the forms, its size changes as the form is resized. When you anchor a TextBox control to the top and bottom sides of the form, its size will change as the form is resized, so that the gaps above the control (the distance between the top of the control and the top of the form), as well as the gap below the control, will remain fixed. Finally, if you anchor all four sides of the control, the control will be resized so that it will always be visible in its entirety. Of course, you must make sure that the form isn't resized below a certain threshold, and you'll see shortly how this is done.

The settings of the Anchor property are the members of the AnchorStyles enumeration: Bottom, Left, None, Right, and Top. When you open the Anchor property of a control in the Properties window, you will see a small window with a small button and four pegs, one on each side (see Figure 8.1). The button is the control you're anchoring, and the four pegs are the control's anchors to the four sides of the form. To anchor the control on one or more sides, click the corresponding peg(s). The pegs on the anchored sides should be gray, and the remaining pegs should be white.

**FIGURE 8.1:**

Setting a control's Anchor property in the Properties window

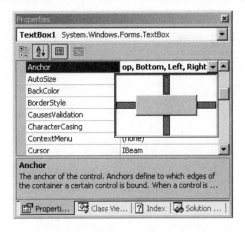

**NOTE**   You'll find all the code from this chapter on www.sybex.com. Search for the book by its ISBN, 2879, or its title, *Visual Basic .NET Developer's Handbook.* You can download the code from the download link.

The Anchor project contains a single form that demonstrates the functionality you can add to your forms by setting the Anchor and Dock properties of the controls on the form. Figure 8.2 shows this form in two totally different sizes. The controls maintain their relative positions and some of them are resized in the process. The TextBox control is anchored to all four sides of the form. The TextBox control is the main control on the form, and it must be resized along with the form. If not, users will end up with a TextBox control larger than the form itself (in which case, entering text will become awkward) or with a small text box on a large form.

**FIGURE 8.2:**

Resizing a form with anchored controls

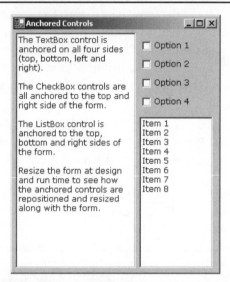

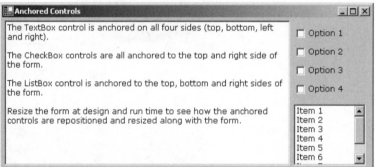

The four check boxes are anchored to the top and right. They will remain at the top-right corner of the form at all times. The last control, the ListBox control, is anchored to the top, bottom, and right. It will remain in the lower-right side of the form, always below the check boxes. As the form is resized, its height will change to fill the area below the check boxes. Open the project and resize the form to see how its controls will remain visible at all times and that they will not interfere with one another. The check boxes have a fixed size—there's no reason to change the size of these controls. The list has a fixed width, but its height changes to reveal (or hide) some of the items. The text box, finally, takes up all the remaining space on the form because this is the control that should be able to accommodate any amount of information.

Docking is an even more powerful technique that enables controls to take up a section of the form and automatically be resized with the form. You can think of docking as anchoring a control to the edges of all four sides of the form. Docking becomes an incredible tool when used with the Splitter control, which enables certain objects to be resized on their own.

The Dock property allows you to place controls that fill a segment of the form or the entire form. When you dock a control to the left side of the form, the control maintains its width, but its height changes to fill the form's height. Likewise, the control's width will change if you dock it to the top or the bottom of the form. Finally, you can have a control (most likely a Text-Box or a PictureBox control) that fills the entire form. When you fill a form with a control, you can't have other controls on this form (except for a menu, of course).

On its own, the Docking property can't do much for your design. You can place a single TextBox control on a form and set its Dock property to Fill to fill the form with the text box. A form like this can't have buttons or other controls, short of menus, which don't interfere with the text box.

The settings of the Dock property are the members of the DockStyle enumeration: `Bottom`, `Fill`, `Left`, `None`, `Right`, and `Top`. When you open the Dock property of a control in the Properties window, you will see a small window with six buttons, which correspond to the available settings (see Figure 8.3).

**FIGURE 8.3:**

Setting a control's Anchor property in the Properties window

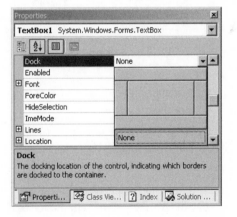

## Using the Splitter Control

In addition to anchoring and docking controls on the form, you can use the Splitter control to separate adjacent controls. The splitters are invisible vertical or horizontal separators between forms that make their presence known when the pointer hovers over them. When the pointer hovers over a horizontal splitter, its shape becomes a double vertical arrow, indicating that you can drag it up or down. As you drag the splitter, one of the two controls shrinks and the extra space is taken automatically by the other control. This is a powerful feature that will allow you to build truly elaborate interfaces, as you will see in the following section.

To demonstrate the use of the Splitter control in designing interfaces, we'll build the form shown in Figure 8.4. This is the form of the ExplorerStyle project, which you will find at www.sybex.com. The form contains three panes. The left pane is a TreeView control and the other two panes are two ListBox controls. This interface is very similar to the interface of Outlook. If you open the project you'll see that you can change the relative sizes of the various panes with the mouse. As you will see, all this functionality can be achieved with the Splitter control, without a single line of code. In the following chapter, we'll add code to populate the controls with data, but in this section we'll present the design of the form.

**FIGURE 8.4:**

This form contains three panes, and you can change the size of any pane at runtime with the mouse.

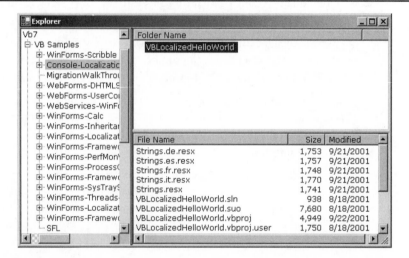

To build the form in Figure 8.4, start a new project, name it ExplorerStyle, and open its form in design mode. Follow these steps:

1. Place a TreeView control on your form (double-click the TreeView control's icon in the toolbox to create an instance of the control on the form), and don't worry about its placement yet.

2. Switch to the control's Properties window and set the new control's Dock property to Left. The control will be attached to the left edge of the form. Its width will remain the same, but its height will cover the height of the form. Change the width of the control so that it covers approximately one third of the form.

3. Now, place a Splitter control on the form. Double-click the control's icon in the toolbox and an instance of the Splitter control will be placed right next to the TreeView control. To see what you've done so far, run the application and place the cursor at the right edge of the TreeView control. The mouse pointer will assume the shape of a double horizontal arrow, and you can change the width of the TreeView control. Terminate the application and switch back to the Designer.

4. Place a Panel control on the form, and set its Dock property to Fill. The panel will fill the area of the form to the right of the Splitter control. The left section of the form is covered by the TreeView control, and the rest is covered by the Panel control. Everything you'll place on the Panel control will belong to the panel. If you dock a control on a panel, for example, the control will be docked to the panel's edges as if the panel were a form. The two ListView controls will be placed on the Panel control.

5. Place a ListView control on the panel and set its Dock property to Top. This control will fill the upper section of the panel.

6. Place a Splitter control on the panel and set its Dock property to Top. Because the panel's top section is taken by the top ListView control, the new Splitter will be docked to the bottom of the ListView control, in effect splitting it from the lower half of the panel.

7. Finally, place another ListView control on the form and set its Dock property to Fill. This control will fill all available area of the Panel control below the Splitter.

You have just designed an Explorer-style interface. Run the application now and check out the functionality of the interface. You can resize all three controls on the form in any way you like. The TreeView control will remain docked to the left edge of the form, and the two ListView controls will remain docked to the top and bottom of the form, respectively. The Splitter controls on the form are practically invisible, and their function is to allow you to resize the controls on either side of them. If you examine the properties of the Splitter control in the Properties window, you'll see that it provides a BorderStyle property and a Cursor property. Set the BorderStyle property to change the appearance of the control (don't expect any dramatic changes; after all, it's a narrow strip). The Cursor property determines the shape of the cursor when it hovers over the control.

You must place some data on the controls, but this is something we'll do in the following chapter. You can place data on the various controls at design time, but in most occasions we fill the controls at runtime from within our code. To put some sample data on the controls, locate the Nodes property of the TreeView control and the Items property of the ListView controls and add some data. You'll use this form as a navigational interface for folders and files in the following chapter. The same form can be used with many other applications. You can display customers, orders and order details, or accounts, transactions and transaction details. We've actually used similar interfaces in Chapter 5 and populated them with data from the Northwind database.

## Typical Windows Interfaces

Typical Windows applications deploy one of the following three styles of user interface:

**Single Document Interface**   Applications are made up of a main form, which is displayed at startup, and a number of auxiliary forms. Each form is independent of the others, although they can exchange information with one another and they can be positioned independently on the monitor. This type of interface is suitable for applications that are made up of different forms and need not open multiple documents at once. This is the most common type of interface, and you'll see later how to build applications with multiple forms and how to exchange information between the forms.

**Multiple Document Interface**   An MDI application consists of a single form, which acts as the host for other forms; the other forms are usually identical and host different documents of the same type. Most word processors and image processing applications, for example, use an MDI interface and they can open multiple documents or images. The application's form is the parent for all the forms it can host and the individual forms with the documents are the child forms. We use the MDI interface to build applications that can manipulate multiple documents through a common menu and/or toolboxes. We'll discuss briefly the MDI interface later in this chapter.

**Explorer Style Interface**   This interface consists of two panes arranged horizontally on the form. The left pane displays summary information, and the other pane displays details about the selected item in the left pane. Sometimes, the right pane is split in two panes and you can have two levels of detailed information. The interface of Outlook is a typical example. You can use this interface to display customers, orders and order details, or accounts, transactions and transaction details. This type of interface allows the user to start at the highest level of information and drill down to the details. The Explorer project is discussed in more detail in the next chapter.

Later in the chapter, we'll discuss interfaces with multiple forms, as well as the MDI interface, but let's continue with the new features of the Windows Form Designer, starting with the properties for sizing and positioning forms.

## Form Size and Position

You can use several properties to manipulate the size and position of your forms on the desktop, and they're discussed in this section. Your goal should be the design of a form that can be safely resized at runtime with the Anchor and Dock properties. You will most likely have to impose a minimum size to the form or attach scroll bars to the form if it's resized below a certain size (this is another new feature of the Windows Forms Designer). In general, you should avoid the direct manipulation of the form's appearance from within your code whenever possible.

### The TopMost Property

The TopMost property determines whether a form will be visible at all times or not. The property's default value is False, which means that the form will be covered by another form when another form is activated. If you want to keep the form visible at all times, set its TopMost property to True. Do this when you design Find and Replace forms, which must remain visible even when the user switches to the main form of the application (the form that contains the document being searched). When a form is set to be the application's topmost form, it's not displayed modally. You can switch to any other form of the application, but it will remain visible, even though it doesn't have the focus.

### The Opacity Property

This is a rather obscure property that allows you to make semitransparent forms. This property is a numeric value from 0 (complete transparency) to 1 (complete opacity). You can also specify integer values from 0 to 100 (the designer will display the Opacity's property value as a percentage, regardless of how you specify it). We can't think of a good reason to make your forms transparent, especially with business applications, but this is the tool.

### The Size Property

Most forms can be rearranged and resized at runtime by the user, which means that you must design forms that remain functional at various sizes. In earlier versions of Visual Basic, designing resizable forms was a major undertaking, and developers had to write code to resize and rearrange the controls on the form so that they would remain visible at various form sizes. Of course, there's a minimum form size beyond which there's not much you can do. Programmers also had to impose a minimum size for the form. The simplest trick was to set the form to a fixed size, but this isn't the most convenient interface you can design.

The form's size is given by the Size property, which returns a Size object with the same dimensions, and you can use the Width and Height properties of the Size object to read the current dimensions of the form. The form's width can be read with the following expression:

```
Me.Size.Width
```

The following statement, however, won't change the form's width:

```
Me.Size.Width = 2 * Me.Size.Width
```

The Width member is a value, and you can't use it in the left part of an expression. To set the form's dimensions through the Size property, create a new Size object and assign it to the Size property:

```
Me.Size = New Size(Me.Size.Width * 2, Me.Size.Height / 2)
```

Sometimes you'll want to prevent users from resizing certain forms because the controls on them may not maintain their relative positions and sizes. To force a minimum size, set the form's MinimumSize property to a Size object with the desired dimensions. To specify that the form shouldn't be reduced below a size of 400 by 300, create a Size object with these dimensions and assign it to the MinimumSize property with the following statement:

```
Me.MinimiumSize = New Size(400, 300)
```

When the form is resized by the user at runtime, the Resize event is fired. You need not code this event because you can use the Anchor and Dock properties to design forms that resize nicely. Programmers used to place quite a bit of code in this event's handler to resize and reposition the controls on the form. Despite the new Windows Form Designer's features, you may still have to control the resizing process. Let's say you have a form that must always maintain a certain aspect ratio. To force the desired aspect ratio, you can extract the smaller dimension and adjust the other dimension accordingly. The following statements show you how this is done (the aspect ratio of the form's width to its height is 4:3):

```
Private Sub Form1_Resize(ByVal sender As Object, _
                   ByVal e As System.EventArgs) _
                   Handles MyBase.Resize
    If Me.Width < Me.Height Then
        Me.Height = Me.Width * 0.75
    Else
        Me.Width = Me.Height / 0.75
    End If
End Sub
```

The Resize event doesn't take place as you resize the form with the mouse. It's fired once, after you release the mouse button. As a result, the form may assume any aspect ratio as it's being resized. After the release of the mouse button, however, the statements in the Resize event handler will be executed and the form dimensions will change once again—this time to the proper aspect ratio. Actually, the Resize event will be fired once again in response to the changing of the form's size from within your code. This time, however, the code won't resize the form because the form has the correct size already and no more Resize events will be fired.

## The SystemInformation Object

As you write code to arrange controls on a form, you will find the SystemInformation object very useful. This object exposes a number of properties that provide information about the sizes of certain items that are determined by the operating system; they're described in Table 8.1.

**TABLE 8.1:** The Properties of the SystemInformation Object

| Property | Description |
| --- | --- |
| Border3Dsize | Returns the dimensions of the 3D border in pixels. |
| BorderSize | Returns the width and height of the window's border as a Size object expressed in pixels. |
| CaptionHeight | Returns the height of the window's title bar in pixels. |
| ComputerName | Returns the computer name. |
| CursorSize | Returns the dimensions of the cursor in pixels. |

*Continued on next page*

**TABLE 8.1 CONTINUED:** The Properties of the SystemInformation Object

| Property | Description |
|---|---|
| DoubleClickSize | Returns a Size object that determines the area in which the user must click for the operating system to consider the two clicks a double-click. |
| DoubleClickTime | Returns the number of milliseconds allowed between mouse clicks for the operating system to consider the two clicks a double-click. |
| FixedFrameBorderSize | Returns the thickness, in pixels, of the border for a window that has a caption and is not resizable. |
| FrameBorderSize | Returns the thickness (in pixels) of the border for a window that can be resized. |
| HighContrast | Returns a Boolean value indicating whether the user has selected to run in high-contrast mode. |
| HorizontalScrollBarArrowWidth | Returns the width of the arrow in the horizontal scroll bar in pixels. |
| HorizontalScrollBarHeight | Returns the height of the horizontal scroll bar in pixels. |
| HorizontalScrollBarThumbWidth | Returns the width of the button that scrolls the contents of a horizontal scroll bar in pixels. |
| IconSize | Returns a Size object with the default dimensions of an icon in pixels. |
| MaxWindowTrackSize | Returns a Size object with the default maximum dimensions (in pixels) of a window with a caption and sizing borders. |
| MenuFont | Returns a Font object the operating system uses for the menus. |
| MenuHeight | Returns the height of the menu bar. |
| MinimumWindowSize | Returns a Size object with the minimum allowable dimensions of a window in pixels. |
| MouseButtons | Returns the number of buttons on the mouse. |
| MouseButtonsSwapped | Returns a Boolean value indicating whether the functions of the left and right mouse buttons have been swapped. |
| MousePresent | Returns a Boolean value indicating whether a mouse is installed. |
| MouseWheelPresent | Returns a Boolean value indicating whether a mouse with wheel is installed. |
| Network | Returns True if the computer is connected to a network. |
| ToolWindowCaptionButtonSize | Returns a Size object with the dimensions of small caption buttons. |
| ToolWindowCaptionHeight | Returns the height of a small caption. |
| UserDomainName | Returns the name of the current user domain. |
| UserName | Returns the name of the user currently logged on. |
| VerticalScrollBarArrowHeight | Returns the height (in pixels) of the arrow on the vertical scroll bar. |
| VerticalScrollBarThumbHeight | Returns the height (in pixels) of the button that scrolls the contents of a horizontal scroll bar. |
| VerticalScrollBarWidth | Gets the width in pixels of the vertical scroll bar. |
| WorkingArea | Returns a Size object with the dimensions of the working area in pixels. |

The properties of the SystemInformation object will come in handy when you write code to resize controls from within your code—in situations where the Dock and Anchor properties won't do. Notice that all the SystemInformation properties are read-only and that you can't change any of these settings. These settings are determined by the operating system, and most of them can be modified through the utilities of Control Panel.

## Scrolling Forms

The new Windows Form Designer can design scrolling forms, a feature that was sorely missing from previous versions of the IDE. Even if you don't want to bother with the Anchor and Dock properties to design elaborate forms, you can set the AutoScroll property to True so that users can always scroll into view the section of the form that interests them. To assist the design of scrolling forms, the following properties are supported (they're properties of the Form object; none of the controls supports them, except for the Panel control, whose function is to act as a container for other controls, similar to the Form object).

### AutoScroll

The AutoScroll property is a True/False value that determines whether scroll bars will be automatically attached to the form if it's resized to a point that not all its controls are visible. The CLR will determine whether one or more of the form's control are invisible, or partially visible, and attach the scroll bars to the form (see Figure 8.5).

**FIGURE 8.5:**

A typical scrollable form

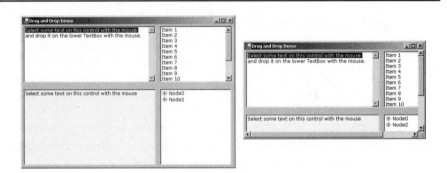

### AutoScrollMargin

This is a margin, expressed in pixels, that is added around all the controls on the form. If the form is smaller than the rectangle that encloses all the controls adjusted by this margin, the appropriate scroll bar(s) will be displayed automatically.

If you expand the AutoScrollMargin property in the Properties window, you will see that it's a Size object and its default value is (0,0). To set this property from within your code, use a statement like the following:

```
Me.AutoScrollMargin = New Size(40, 40)
```

Notice that you can't set the members of the Size object individually:

```
Me.AutoScrollMargin.Width = 40      ' WON'T WORK
Me.AutoScrollMargin.Height = 40     ' WON'T WORK
```

### AutoScrollMinSize

Use this property to specify the minimum size, in width and height, that the form can be resized to before the scrollbars automatically appear as part of the form. This does not control the form's minimum size; you should use the MinimumSize property for that purpose.

### MinimumSize, MaximumSize

These two properties determine the minimum and maximum size of a form. When users resize the form at runtime, the form won't become any smaller than the dimensions specified with the MinimumSize property nor any larger than the dimensions specified by Maximum-Size. They're both Size objects, and you can set them with a statement like the following:

```
Me.MinimumSize = New Size(400, 300)
```

The MinimumSize.Height property includes the height of the form's title bar; you should take that into consideration. If the minimum usable size of the form should be 400 by 300, use the following statement to set the MinimumSize property:

```
me.MinimumSize = new Size(400, _
                300 + SystemInformation.CaptionHeight)
```

### SizeGripStyle

This property gets or sets the style of the sizing handle to display in the lower-right corner of the form. Its value is a member of the SizeGripStyle enumeration, which is shown in Table 8.2. By default, forms are resizable, even if no special mark appears in their lower-right corner.

**TABLE 8.2:** The SizeGripStyle Enumeration

| Member | Description |
| --- | --- |
| Auto | The sizing handle is displayed as needed (default). |
| Show | The sizing handle is displayed at all times. |
| Hide | The sizing handle is not displayed, but the form can still be resized with the mouse (Windows 95/98 style). |

## The Controls Collection

The controls you place on a form can be accessed through the form's Controls property, which is a collection. Each item of the collection corresponds to a different control on the form. If a control acts as a container for other controls, like the Panel control does, it has its own Controls collection, which contains the controls sited on this container control.

The items of the Controls collection are of the same type as the controls they represent. When you place an instance of a control on the form, a new item is automatically added to the Controls collection. You can also add a new control to the form by adding an instance of the corresponding type to the Controls collection. The following statements declare a variable that references a new TextBox control, set its properties, and then add it to the Controls collection:

```
Dim txt As New System.WinForms.TextBox
txt.MultiLine = True
txt.Text = "This control was generated in code"
txt.Left = 100
txt.Top = 60
txt.Width = 400
txt.Height = 200
txt.Visible = True
Me.Controls.Add(bttn)
```

By default, controls added to the form's Controls collection are invisible and you must set their Visible property to True explicitly in your code. You can also remove a control with the Remove method, which accepts as argument either the index of a control in the Controls collection or a reference to the control to be removed. If the variable *txt* of the previous sample were declared outside any procedure in its form, you would be able to remove the control from the Controls collection with the following statement:

```
Me.Controls.Remove(txt)
```

You can also iterate through the Controls collection and retrieve the names and properties of all the controls on a form. This is what the following loop does:

```
Dim i As Integer
For i = 0 To Me.Controls.Count - 1
  Console.WriteLine(Me.Controls(i).Text)
  Console.WriteLine(Me.Controls(i).Width)
  Console.WriteLine(Me.Controls(i).Height)
Next
```

This code segment assumes that all the controls expose a Text property and that they have a width and a height. Because you can't be sure that a control provides a specific property, you can find out the type of each control in the collection with a statement like the following:

```
If Me.Controls(i).GetType Is _
            GetType(System.Windows.Forms.Panel) Then
' process an instance of the Panel control
End If
```

Once you know the control's type, you can manipulate it from within your code and request the values of properties that are unique to this control or call methods that apply to the specific control.

The Controls collection is used in building dynamic forms. A dynamic form contains a variable number of controls, which can be increased or decreased during the course of the application. It's not a very common situation, but it's fairly easy to create forms in your code. You can even write code to generate forms by populating the Controls collection.

The dynamically generated controls wouldn't be nearly as useful if you didn't have a method to connect them to events. What good would it do to add a dozen buttons to a form if you couldn't write event handlers to respond to their events?

To create an event handler at runtime, create a subroutine that accepts two arguments—the usual sender and e arguments—and enter the code you want to execute when a specific control receives a specific event. Let's say you want to add one or more buttons at runtime on your form and these buttons should react to the Click event. Create the ButtonClick() subroutine and enter the appropriate code in it.

Once the subroutine is in place, you must connect it to an event of a specific control. The ButtonClick() subroutine, for example, must be connected to the Click event of a Button control. The statement that connects a control's event to a specific event handler is the AddHandler statement, whose syntax is as follows:

```
AddHandler(control.event, New System.EventHandler(AddressOf subName))
```

For example, to connect the ProcessNow() subroutine to the Click event of a button called "Calculate," use the following statement:

```
AddHandler(Calculate.Click, _
            New System.EventHandler(AddressOf ProcessNow))
```

The ProcessNow() subroutine is a delegate for the control's Click event handler. In your delegate, you can use the sender argument to find out which control fired the event. The expression sender.Text, for example, returns the value of the Text property of the control that fired the event. Or, you can cast the sender argument to the proper control type. If the Process-Now() delegate handles the Click event of the controls Button1 and Button2, the sender.Text property's value will be the name of the button that was clicked.

## Multiple Form Applications

A typical Windows application consists of multiple forms and/or dialog boxes. In this section, you'll learn how to display one form from within another form's code and how to access the contents of a form from within another. The process isn't as simple as it used to be with VB6 because you can no longer access the controls on a form by prefixing their names with the name of the form to which they belong. Instead, you must create an instance of the control(s) you want to expose to other forms and make it available to the code of the other forms in the application.

To display a form from within another form's code, you must create an instance of the form to be invoked and then call its Show or ShowDialog method. The Show method displays the form modeless (you can switch to any other form of the application), and the ShowDialog method displays the form modally (you can't switch to any other form while this one has the focus). To return to the application after displaying a modal form, you must close the modal form. Let's say your application has two forms, named MainForm and AuxForm. As you can guess, the MainForm form is the application's startup object. To display the auxiliary form from within the main form, you can use the following statements:

```
Dim aForm As New AuxForm()
aForm.Show()
```

The declaration appears in the same procedure as the following statement—most likely the Click event handler of the button that invokes the form. When this event handler exits, the *aForm* variable ceases to exist.

This approach works well with modal forms, but not as well with modeless forms and here's why: Let's say you display an instance of the auxiliary form, switch to the main form, and click the same button again. Another instance of AuxForm will be created and it will be displayed. You will have two instances of the auxiliary forms on your screen. Then you can open a third instance, and so on. This is an unusual situation and most users will end up with dozens of auxiliary forms floating around. The *aForm* variable must be declared outside any procedure and be set in the form's Load event handler. This way, your code will be invoking the same instance of the auxiliary form rather than creating a new instance every time the user requests that form.

Figure 8.6 shows the MultipleForms application, which demonstrates how to invoke a form from within another and how to manipulate the controls on a form from within any other form's code. The main form of the application contains a TextBox control and a Find & Replace button. When this button is clicked, a very primitive Find & Replace dialog box appears, in which you can specify the string to be replaced and the replacement string. When the Replace button is clicked, all instances of the first string on the main form will be replaced by the second string. It's not the most functional text editing tool, but it demonstrates how to manipulate the controls on one form from within another form's code.

**FIGURE 8.6:**

The MultipleForms
application

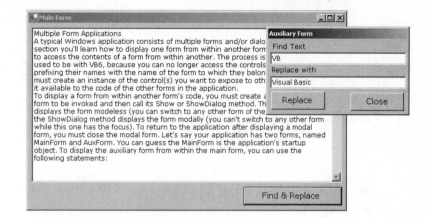

The project's startup object is the main form. To display the Find & Replace form (it's called *AuxForm* in the project), you must create a reference to this form and then call its Show method.

The auxiliary form needs to access the text on the TextBox control of the main form and perform the necessary replacements. In VB .NET, you can't simply prefix the name of the control by the name of the form it belongs to and access it. The main form must expose a reference of the control, and the auxiliary form will use this reference to access the control.

The following declaration must appear outside any procedure in the main form's file:

```
Public Shared txt As TextBox
```

In the form's Load event handler, you must set the *txt* variable to the instance of the TextBox control on the main form:

```
Private Sub MainForm_Load(ByVal sender As System.Object, _
                          ByVal e As System.EventArgs) _
                          Handles MyBase.Load
    txt = TextBox1
End Sub
```

The *txt* variable references the TextBox1 control on the main form, and you will see shortly how the auxiliary form uses this variable. When the Find & Replace button is clicked, the following code is executed. This event handler creates a new instance of the auxiliary form, copies the selected text on the main form's TextBox control to the FindBox TextBox control on the auxiliary form, and finally invokes the auxiliary form by calling the Show method:

```
Private Sub Button1_Click(ByVal sender As System.Object, _
                          ByVal e As System.EventArgs) _
                          Handles bttnFind.Click
```

```
    Dim aForm As New AuxForm()
    aForm.FindBox.Text = TextBox1.SelectedText
    aForm.Show()
End Sub
```

The code in the auxiliary form is located in the event handlers of the two buttons. When the Replace button is clicked, the following statements are executed; they replace all instances of the Find string with the Replace string:

```
Private Sub Button1_Click(ByVal sender As System.Object, _
                          ByVal e As System.EventArgs) _
                          Handles Button1.Click
    MainForm.txt.Text = MainForm.txt.Text.Replace( _
                          FindBox.Text, ReplaceBox.Text)
End Sub
```

When the Close button is clicked, the auxiliary form is closed with a call to the Close method:

```
Private Sub Button2_Click(ByVal sender As System.Object, _
                          ByVal e As System.EventArgs) _
                          Handles Button2.Click
    Me.Close()
End Sub
```

The best method to exchange data between forms is to create properties for each form and set the values of these properties from within the other forms' code. Let's say a form needs to expose a string variable. Create a public property and every other form will be able to access it. Properties are discussed in detail in Chapter 12, but here's the implementation of a simple form property:

```
Public Property MainText()
    Get
        Return TextBox1.Text
    End Get
    Set(ByVal Value)
        TextBox1.Text = Value
    End Set
End Property
```

This procedure exposes the text on the TextBox1 control as a property, the MainText property. To access this string from within another form's code, create an instance of the form and access the custom property as if it were a built-in property:

```
Dim MForm As MainForm
MForm.MainText = "new string"
```

You can also expose methods as public functions. Let's say that one of the forms contains the `Calculate()` function, which accepts two numeric values as arguments and returns another numeric value. You can implement the `Calculate()` function as a public function in one of the forms:

```
Public Function Calculate(ByVal a As Double, _
                          ByVal b As Double) As Double
    Return (a / b)
End Function
```

This function can be accessed from within another form of the same project as follows:

```
Dim MForm As MainForm
Dim a, b As Double
a = 1.001
b = 0.999
Console.WriteLine(MForm.Calculate(a, b))
```

## Dialog Boxes

Dialog boxes are special types of forms with rather limited functionality, which we use to prompt the user for data. Windows comes with several built-in dialog boxes for common operations, like the Open File and Save File dialog boxes. These dialog boxes are so common in user interface design that they're known as common dialog boxes. Technically, a dialog box is a form with its BorderStyle property set to FixedDialog and the ControlBox, MinimizeBox, and MaximizeBox properties set to False. You then add the necessary controls on the form and code the appropriate events, as you would do with a regular Windows form. Like forms, dialog boxes may contain a few simple controls, such as Labels, TextBoxes, and Buttons.

Another difference between forms and dialog boxes is that forms usually interact with each other. If you need to keep two windows open and allow the user to switch from one to the other, you need to implement them as regular forms. If one of them is modal, then you should implement it as a dialog box. A characteristic of dialog boxes is that they provide an OK and a Cancel button (sometimes a Yes and a No button or a Cancel and a Retry button). The OK button tells the application that the user is done using the dialog box and the application can process the information on it. The Cancel button signals to the application the user's intention to abort the current operation, and the application must act accordingly.

How do you initiate the dialog box from within another form's code? The process of displaying a dialog box is no different than the process for displaying another form. To do so, enter the following code in the event handler from which you want to initiate the dialog box (this is the Click event handler of the main form's button):

```
Private Sub Button1_Click(ByVal sender As System.Object, _
              ByVal e As System.EventArgs) _
              Handles Button1.Click
```

```
      Dim DLG as new DBoxForm()
      DLG.ShowDialog
   End Sub
```

Here, `DBoxForm` is the name of the dialog box. The ShowDialog method displays a dialog box as modal. When you display a modal dialog box, the statement following the one that called the ShowDialog method is not executed. The statements from this point to the end of the event handler will be executed when the user closes the dialog box. Statements following the Show method, however, are executed immediately when the dialog box is displayed.

You already know how to read the values entered on the controls of the dialog box. You also need to know which button was clicked to close the dialog box. To convey this information from the dialog box back to the calling application, you can use the DialogResult property provided by the Form object. This property can be set to one of the values shown in Table 8.3, which are the members of the DialogResult enumeration. The `DialogResult.OK` value indicates that the user has clicked the OK button on the form. There's no need to actually place an OK button on the form; just set the form's DialogResult property to `DialogResult.OK`.

**TABLE 8.3:** The DialogResult Enumeration

| Member | Description |
| --- | --- |
| Abort | The dialog box was closed with the Abort button. |
| Cancel | The dialog box was closed with the Cancel button. |
| Ignore | The dialog box was closed with the Ignore button. |
| No | The dialog box was closed with the No button. |
| None | The dialog box hasn't been closed yet. Use this option to find out whether a modeless dialog box is still open. |
| OK | The dialog box was closed with the OK button. |
| Retry | The dialog box was closed with the Retry button. |
| Yes | The dialog box was closed with the Yes button. |

The dialog box need not contain any of the buttons mentioned here as long as you set the form's DialogResult property to the appropriate value. This value can be retrieved by the calling application, which will take the appropriate action.

Let's say your dialog box contains a button named Done, which signifies that the user is done entering values on the dialog box, and a Cancel button, which aborts the current operation. The Click event handler of the Done button contains a single line:

```
Me.DialogResult = DialogResult.OK
```

Likewise, the Click event handler of the Cancel button contains the following line:

```
Me.DialogResult = DialogResult.Cancel
```

The event handler of the button that displays this dialog box should contain these lines:

```
Dim DLG as Form = new PasswordForm
If DLG.ShowDialog = DialogResult.OK Then
    { process the user selection }
End If
```

The value of the DialogResult property is usually set from within two buttons—one that accepts the data and one that rejects them. Depending on your application, you may allow the user to close the dialog box by clicking more than two buttons. Some of them must set the DialogResult property to `DialogResult.OK`, others to `DialogResult.Abort`.

If the dialog box contains a default Accept button (property AcceptButton), this button will automatically set the form's DialogResult property to `DialogResult.OK`. Likewise, the default Cancel button (property CancelButton) will automatically set the form's DialogResult property to `DialogResult.Cancel`.

## Menus

If there's a feature common to just about any application, it is the menu. The menu is the single element of the visual interface that is as popular with Windows applications as it was with DOS applications. Menus are designed with visual tools at design time. Unlike with previous versions of Visual Basic, they're designed right on the form and not on a separate dialog box. To add a menu to a form, place an instance of the MainMenu control on the form. Then select the control's icon in the controls tray at the bottom of the Designer and start entering the menu's captions right on the form, at the same location where the menu will appear at runtime. You can design multiple menus for a form and switch them from within your code, but you should use this feature very cautiously. Displaying totally different menus in the course of an application will most likely confuse the users.

To design multiple menus, place additional instances of the MainMenu control on your form. They'll be named MainMenu1, MainMenu2, and so on. Every time you select a different MainMenu control in the controls tray at the bottom of the Designer, a different menu structure will appear on the form. Notice that every instance of the MainMenu control is specific to a form.

Designing a menu is quite trivial. You enter the caption and then press Enter to move to the next item on the same menu. If you want to spawn a submenu from a specific item, press the right arrow and a submenu will be created next to the current item. To insert items or delete existing items, right-click an item and select the appropriate command from the context menu. Experiment with the new menu designer for a few minutes and you'll soon realize that it's as convenient as it can get.

To assign names to the menu items, right-click the menu and select the Edit Names command. You'll be switched to the name-editing mode of the Designer, where you can enter the names of the items just as you entered the captions of the various items. When you're done, right-click the menu again and select Edit Names to return to the caption-editing mode. You can select a menu item at any time and set its properties in the Properties window.

Once the menu has been designed, you can attach it to the form by assigning its name to the Menu property of the form:

```
Me.Menu = MainMenu1
```

You can also set the form's menu from within the Properties window. The form's Menu property displays the names of all available MainMenu objects, and you can select the appropriate one. The first MainMenu object you place on the form becomes the default menu, so you need not set the form's Menu property. If you have two main menus, you must switch them from within your code. You should avoid displaying totally different menus and try to simply disable/enable commands at different stages of the application and manipulate the commands of the same menu from within your code rather than switching between totally different menus. These comments don't apply to MDI applications, of course, which are discussed later in this chapter.

In addition to the form's main menu, you can also design context menus. A context menu is identical to a main menu, and it's invoked with the right-click of the mouse on a control or the form. You must add to your form an instance of the ContextMenu control for every context menu you want to design. The context menu is the same whether it's the context menu of a form or a control. You can even use the same context menu with multiple controls if it makes sense for the application.

Context menus are designed like main menus, but they're not displayed by default. To attach a context menu to a control, set the control's ContextMenu property to the name of the appropriate context menu. Other than that, context menus are no different than main menus. They may even contain commands that lead to submenus, although this isn't as common.

You can also create menus in your code. The commands of the menu are called items, and they're objects of the MenuItem type. Each command's items are members of the MenuItems collection, and you can manipulate them as members of a collection. The Item property, which is the default property, retrieves a specific item from the collection. To retrieve the third item of the collection, use the following expression:

```
MainMenu1.MenuItems.Item(2)
```

Or you can use this expression:

```
MainMenu1.MenuItems(2)
```

To add a new item to the MenuItems collection, use the Add method, which accepts as arguments the item's caption and a delegate for the item's Click event handler:

```
MainMenu.MenuItems.Add(caption, _
                    New System.EventHandler( _
                    AddressOf handler_name))
```

The statements of Listing 8.1 create a menu with the following structure:

File

    New

    Open

    Exit

Edit

    Copy

    Cut

    Paste

Format

    Font

        Verdana

        Tahoma

        Georgia

    Color

    Style

This menu contains three commands, and each command leads to a submenu. The File command leads to a submenu with the commands New, Open, and Exit. The statements that create the menu structure shown earlier must appear in the form's Load event handler:

---

**Listing 8.1**      **Creating a Menu in Code**

```
Private Sub Form1_Load(ByVal sender As System.Object, _
                    ByVal e As System.EventArgs) _
                    Handles MyBase.Load
Dim menu As New MainMenu()
Dim item As MenuItem
    item = New MenuItem("File")
```

```
        item.MenuItems.Add("New", _
            New System.EventHandler(AddressOf Me.MenuClick))
        item.MenuItems.Add("Open", _
            New System.EventHandler(AddressOf Me.MenuClick))
        item.MenuItems.Add("Exit", _
            New System.EventHandler(AddressOf Me.MenuClick))
        menu.MenuItems.Add(item)
        item = New MenuItem("Edit")
        item.MenuItems.Add("Copy", _
            New System.EventHandler(AddressOf Me.EditCopy))
        item.MenuItems.Add("Cut", _
            New System.EventHandler(AddressOf Me.EditCut))
        item.MenuItems.Add("Paste", _
            New System.EventHandler(AddressOf Me.EditPaste))
        menu.MenuItems.Add(item)
        item = New MenuItem("Format")
        item.MenuItems.Add("Font")
        item.MenuItems(0).MenuItems.Add("Verdana", _
            New System.EventHandler(AddressOf Me.FormatFont))
        item.MenuItems(0).MenuItems.Add("Tahoma", _
            New System.EventHandler(AddressOf Me.FormatFont))
        item.MenuItems(0).MenuItems.Add("Georgia", _
            New System.EventHandler(AddressOf Me.FormatFont))
        item.MenuItems.Add("Color", _
            New System.EventHandler(AddressOf Me.FormatColor))
        item.MenuItems.Add("Style", _
            New System.EventHandler(AddressOf Me.FormatStyle))
        menu.MenuItems.Add(item)
        Me.Menu = menu
    End Sub
```

All of the items of the File menu are serviced by the same event handler, the MenuClick subroutine. The same is true for the items of the Font menu of the Format command, which are handled by the FormatFont subroutine. The items of the Edit menu have their own event handlers; they're the EditCopy, EditCut, and EditPaste subroutines, which you must provide as well. The signature of a subroutine that will be used as a delegate for the Click event handler of the Click event of a menu item is as follows:

```
Sub MenuClick(ByVal sender As Object, _
            ByVal e As System.EventArgs)
    MsgBox("You selected the command " & _
            sender.text & " of the File menu")
End Sub
```

The event handler shown here is quite trivial. You must supply code to perform the necessary operations for each command. Notice how the common event handler figures out which menu item was clicked. The sender argument represents the item that was clicked. You can also cast the sender argument to the MenuItem type so that you can see the members of the MenuItem object in the Intellisense List Member: CType(sender, MenuItem).

To remove an item from the MenuItems collection, use the Remove and RemoveAt methods. The first method removes the item to which it applies, and the second removes an item by its index:

```
MainMenu1.MenuItems(3).Remove
MainMenu1.MenuItems.RemoveAt(3)
```

You can also remove all the items of a specific MenuItem object with the Clear method. If a MenuItem leads to a submenu, its IsParent property returns True. If a MenuItem has its own MenuItems collection, you can iterate through them with the following loop:

```
Dim item As MenuItem
For Each item In MainMenu.MenuItems
    ' process the current item
    ' the item variable exposes the
    ' properties of the MenuItem object
Next
```

## Owner-Drawn Menus

Menus are displayed in a font determined by the system. You can find out the menu font, or the height of the menu bar, through the corresponding properties of the SystemInformation object, which was discussed earlier in this chapter. However, you can't change this font from within your code. It is possible, though, to create custom menu items with some additional code. You can actually determine the appearance of each item by drawing the contents of its rectangle and give a custom appearance to your menus. These items are called *owner-drawn*, because their appearance is determined by the code in the form that owns them.

To customize the appearance of a menu item, you must set its OwnerDraw property to True (its default value is False). When the OwnerDraw property of a menu item is True, it raises two events: MeasureItem and DrawItem. These two events are raised in that order when the menu that contains them is opened. In the MeasureItem event, you must calculate the dimensions of the rectangle in which the item will be displayed, and in the DrawItem event, you must actually draw the menu item. The menu item is displayed in a rectangle, and you have absolute control over the appearance of this rectangle. You can call any of the drawing methods to customize the appearance of the item's rectangle, and each item may even have a different height. You can use a different background color (or bitmap), you can draw the item's caption in any font, or you can fill the rectangle with graphics.

The project OwnerDrawnMenu demonstrates the process of creating owner-drawn menus. It contains a main menu with two items, Color and Alignment, and each item leads to a submenu, as shown in Figure 8.7. The Color menu is made up of differently colored rectangles, and the Alignment menu contains three items with different alignment.

**FIGURE 8.7:**

An owner-drawn menu

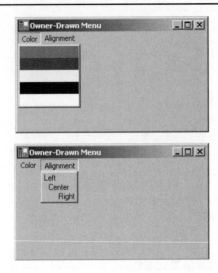

First, you must create a menu with the desired structure, as usual. You need not supply any captions for the items. Even if you do, these captions will be ignored. The Common Language Runtime will ignore them, and it will let the DrawItem event handler draw the item. Obviously, you must provide both a MeasureItem and a DrawItem event handler for each MenuItem object that has its OwnerDraw method set to True. The code that draws the Red and Green items of the Color menu is shown in Listing 8.2.

**Listing 8.2**    **The MeasureItem and DrawItem Event Handlers of the Color Items**

```
Private Sub Red_MeasureItem(ByVal sender As System.Object, _
    ByVal e As System.Windows.Forms.MeasureItemEventArgs) _
    Handles Red.MeasureItem

    Dim itemSize As SizeF
    itemSize = New SizeF(80, 18)
    e.ItemHeight = itemSize.Height
    e.ItemWidth = itemSize.Width
End Sub

Private Sub Red_DrawItem(ByVal sender As System.Object, _
    ByVal e As System.Windows.Forms.DrawItemEventArgs) _
    Handles Red.DrawItem

    Dim R As New RectangleF(e.Bounds.X, e.Bounds.Y, _
                            e.Bounds.Width, e.Bounds.Height)
    e.Graphics.FillRectangle(Brushes.Red, R)
End Sub
```

```
Private Sub Green_MeasureItem( _
    ByVal sender As System.Object, _
    ByVal e As System.Windows.Forms.MeasureItemEventArgs) _
    Handles Red.MeasureItem

    Dim itemSize As SizeF
    itemSize = New SizeF(80, 18)
    e.ItemHeight = itemSize.Height
    e.ItemWidth = itemSize.Width
End Sub

Private Sub Green_DrawItem(ByVal sender As System.Object, _
    ByVal e As System.Windows.Forms.DrawItemEventArgs) _
    Handles Green.DrawItem

    Dim R As New RectangleF(e.Bounds.X, e.Bounds.Y, _
                            e.Bounds.Width, e.Bounds.Height)
    e.Graphics.FillRectangle(Brushes.Green, R)
End Sub
```

The width of the item is more or less arbitrary. In many cases, the width of each item is determined by its contents. As a consequence, the MeasureItem and DrawItem event handlers contain similar code—just don't draw anything in the MeasureItem event handler. Calculate the proper dimensions and set the ItemHeight and ItemWidth properties of the event's DrawItemEventArgs argument. You can retrieve the same values from within the DrawItem event handler through the Bounds property of the second argument. The Bounds property is an object that represents the rectangle in which the drawing will take place. The DrawItem event's e argument also supports the State property, which determines the state of the menu, and its value is one of the members of the DrawItemState enumeration. The statement that determines the appearance of the menu item calls the FillRectangle method of the item's Graphics object and draws a rectangle filled with the corresponding color. The rectangle drawn has the exact same dimensions as the item's rectangle. If you make it smaller, then part of the item's box will be empty.

The code for drawing the items of the Alignment menu is similar. The width of each item is arbitrary, and the corresponding string is printed with a call to the DrawString method. This is a graphics method that has many overloaded forms. We use the overloaded DrawString method that lets us specify the string to be printed, its font, its color, the rectangle in which it must fit, and a special flag that determines the alignment of the string in the specified rectangle. Listing 8.3 contains the code that displays the item Right.

**Listing 8.3**    **The MeasureItem and DrawItem Event Handlers of the Alignment Items**

```
Private Sub AlignRight_MeasureItem( _
    ByVal sender As System.Object, _
    ByVal e As System.Windows.Forms.MeasureItemEventArgs) _
    Handles AlignRight.MeasureItem
```

```
    Dim itemSize As SizeF
    itemSize = New SizeF(40, 14)
    e.ItemHeight = itemSize.Height
    e.ItemWidth = itemSize.Width
End Sub

Private Sub AlignRight_DrawItem( _
    ByVal sender As System.Object, _
    ByVal e As System.Windows.Forms.DrawItemEventArgs) _
    Handles AlignRight.DrawItem

    Dim R As New RectangleF(e.Bounds.X, e.Bounds.Y, _
                            e.Bounds.Width, e.Bounds.Height)
    Dim strfmt As New StringFormat()
    strfmt.Alignment = StringAlignment.Far
    e.Graphics.DrawString("Right", Me.Font, Brushes.Black, _
                          R, strfmt)
End Sub
```

We've used the form's font to draw the menus. If you want to use a different font, you can either change the form's Font property at design time (the code will work as is) or create a new Font object in the DrawItem event handler, set its properties, and then pass it to the DrawString method as argument.

The same techniques apply to the ListBox control. You can customize the appearance of a ListBox control by taking control of the process that draws the control's items. The ListBox control has a DrawMode property, and it exposes the MeasureItem and DrawItem methods. The second argument of these methods, the e argument, supports the Index property (the index of the item being drawn).

## Drag-and-Drop Operations

A unique characteristic of the Windows user interface is the ability of the user to grab a control and drop it on another. You don't actually drop the control; you move the contents of the source control to the destination control. This feature is called drag-and-drop, and it's used extensively on the Windows Desktop. Nearly every item on the Desktop can be dragged and dropped on various other items, such as the Recycle Bin, a printer, a folder, and so on. You can use the same techniques in Visual Basic to enhance your applications.

Implementing drag-and-drop operations with Visual Basic .NET is substantially different than it was with earlier versions of the language. The outline of the control is no longer dragged (a feature that many users found annoying anyway). The changes in the shape of the pointer are adequate to indicate that a drag operation is in progress.

To enable a control to accept data when it's dropped, you must set its AllowDrop property to True. You must also insert a statement in its DragEnter event to determine the type of drop operation you allow the control to perform. The following statement prepares the control to accept a copy of the data on the control being dragged:

```
e.Effect = DragDropEffects.Copy
```

The Effect property determines what type of drop operations the destination control can accept, and its value can be one of the members of the DragDropEffects enumeration, which are shown in Table 8.4.

**TABLE 8.4:** The DragDropEffects enumeration

| Member | Description |
| --- | --- |
| All | The data is copied, removed from the source control, and scrolled in the drop target. |
| Copy | The data is copied to the destination control. |
| Link | The data from the source control is linked to the destination control. |
| Move | The data from the source control is moved to the destination control. |
| None | The control doesn't accept data. |
| Scroll | Scrolling is about to start or is currently occurring in the destination control. |

To initiate the drag operation, you must call the DoDragDrop method of the source control. In other words, you must detect when the user has started a drag-and-drop operation and call the DoDragDrop method of the appropriate control. This takes place in the MouseDown event, because this is the most intuitive method of starting a drag-and-drop operation. You can use any event as long as you make sure that it doesn't interfere with other operations. The MouseDown event of a TextBox control, for example, doesn't necessarily indicate the start of a drag-and-drop operation. In most cases, it doesn't—and you'll see shortly what you can do about it. The statement in Listing 8.4 will initiate a drag-and-drop operation on a TextBox control (the SourceTextBox control) when the mouse button is clicked.

**Listing 8.4    Initiating a Drag-and-Drop Operation**

```
Private Sub SourceTextBox_MouseDown( _
        ByVal sender As System.Object, _
        ByVal e As System.Windows.Forms.MouseEventArgs) _
        Handles SourceTextBox.MouseDown

    SourceTextBox.DoDragDrop(SourceTextBox.SelectedText, _
            DragDropEffects.Copy Or DragDropEffects.Move)

End Sub
```

The DoDragDrop method accepts two arguments: the data being dragged and the type of the allowed drop operation. This operation allows data to be copied or moved from the source control into the destination control. Once the operation has been initiated, all controls on the form will raise a DragEnter event when the pointer enters them and a DragLeave event when the point leaves them. While the pointer is over a control, the DragOver event is fired at short intervals. If a control doesn't allow data to be dropped, the pointer assumes a Stop icon's shape to indicate that the data can't be dropped on the control.

Identify the control that can act as destinations for a drop operation and enter the statement listed in Listing 8.5 in the DragEnter event.

**Listing 8.5**          **Handling the DragEnter Event**

```
Private Sub Destination_DragEnter( _
    ByVal sender As System.Object, _
    ByVal e As System.Windows.Forms.DragEventArgs) _
    Handles DestinationTextBox.DragEnter

    e.Effect = DragDropEffects.Copy
End Sub
```

When a drop operation takes place, the destination control raises the DragDrop event. It's your responsibility to actually copy the data on the destination control. The data has already been stored to a Data object, which you can access through the Data property of the e argument of the event. The following event handler inserts the data being dropped on the control into the current selection. If no text is currently selected, the data is inserted into the location of the pointer in the text, as shown in Listing 8.6.

**Listing 8.6**          **Handling the DragDrop Event**

```
Private Sub Destination_DragDrop( _
    ByVal sender As System.Object, _
    ByVal e As System.Windows.Forms.DragEventArgs) _
    Handles DestinationTextBox.DragDrop

    DestinationTextBox.SelectedText = _
            e.Data.GetData(DataFormats.Text).ToString
End Sub
```

If you attempt to start a drag operation on a TextBox control when the left mouse button is clicked, you will give up the editing operations of the mouse. Every time you attempt to select some text with the mouse, a drag operation starts and the editing features of the mouse are taken over by the dragging operations. Clearly, this isn't what users expect and you must handle it carefully. Our suggestion is to initiate drag-and-drop operations only if the Alt key is pressed while the left button is clicked or initiate them with the right mouse button (as long as the control doesn't have its own context menu).

The following event handler initiates a drag-and-drop operation if the MouseDown event was fired with the right mouse button:

```
Private Sub SourceTextBox_MouseDown( _
    ByVal sender As System.Object, _
    ByVal e As System.Windows.Forms.MouseEventArgs) _
    Handles SourceTextBox.MouseDown

    If e.Button = MouseButtons.Right Then
        SourceTextBox.DoDragDrop( _
            SourceTextBox.SelectedText, _
            DragDropEffects.Copy Or DragDropEffects.Move)
    End If
End Sub
```

To demonstrate simple drag-and-drop operations, we've included the DragDrop project on the Sybex website at www.sybex.com. This project demonstrates how to drag text from a TextBox control and drop it onto another TextBox control, as well as how to drag one or more items from a ListBox control and a TreeView control and drop it onto the same TextBox control. The form of the DragDrop operation is shown in Figure 8.8. The destination for all drop operations is the lower text box, and the other three controls can initiate a drag-and-drop operation. The ListBox control allows the selection of multiple items, and you can drag all selected items with a single operation to the TextBox control.

**FIGURE 8.8:**

The DragDrop project's main form

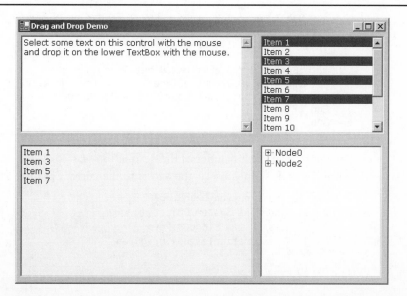

All drag-and-drop operations are initiated with the right mouse button. When we call the DoDragDrop method of the ListBox control, the event handler creates a string with all the selected items (each item on a separate line) and uses this string as the drag operation's data, as shown in Listing 8.7.

**Listing 8.7        Starting a Drag-and-Drop Operation in a ListBox Control**

```
Private Sub ListBox1_MouseDown(ByVal sender As Object, _
    ByVal e As System.Windows.Forms.MouseEventArgs) _
    Handles ListBox1.MouseDown

    If e.Button = MouseButtons.Right Then
        Dim i As Integer, selItems As String
        For i = 0 To ListBox1.SelectedItems.Count - 1
            selItems = selItems & _
                ListBox1.SelectedItems.Item(i) & vbCrLf
        Next
        SourceTextBox.DoDragDrop(selItems, _
            DragDropEffects.Copy Or DragDropEffects.Move)
    End If
End Sub
```

In the TreeView control's MouseDown event, we extract the selected node and use its caption as the operation's data, as shown in Listing 8.8.

**Listing 8.8        Starting a Drag-and-Drop Operation in a TreeView Control**

```
Private Sub TreeView1_MouseDown(ByVal sender As Object, _
    ByVal e As System.Windows.Forms.MouseEventArgs) _
    Handles TreeView1.MouseDown

    If e.Button = MouseButtons.Right Then
        TreeView1.DoDragDrop(TreeView1.SelectedNode.Text, _
            DragDropEffects.Copy Or DragDropEffects.Move)
    End If
End Sub
```

The DragDrop event handler of the destination text box is the same, no matter where the data originates. It simply inserts the data into the current pointer's location in the text:

```
Private Sub Destination_DragDrop( _
    ByVal sender As System.Object, _
    ByVal e As System.Windows.Forms.DragEventArgs) _
    Handles DestinationTextBox.DragDrop
```

```
        DestinationTextBox.Text = _
             e.Data.GetData(DataFormats.Text).ToString
    End Sub
```

## MDI Applications

To demonstrate the design of an MDI application, we'll build a simple project for viewing images. Each image will be loaded on a new child window, and you'll be able to have multiple images open at once. We'll also add a couple of primitive processing commands to the project. Figure 8.9 shows the MDIProject application's main form with several images open in their respective windows. Notice that the images can be scrolled on their forms. Images are displayed on PictureBox controls, and these controls have their SizeMode property set to AutoSize. They're resized according to the dimensions of the image you load onto them. The child forms have their AutoScroll property set to True, so that when the PictureBox doesn't fit in the window, the appropriate scroll bars appear automatically. In effect, the child windows look like scrolling PictureBox controls.

**FIGURE 8.9:**

The MDIProject application demonstrates the design of an MDI application.

Now let's build the application. Start a new project, and name it MDIProject. Select the project's form in the Solution window, and rename it from Form1.vb to MDIParent.vb.

To make this form the parent window that will host the child forms at runtime, set its IsMDI-Container property to True. The child form is a regular form. Add a new form to the project and name it MDIChild. This form will serve as a template for all child windows. By the way, not all child forms in an MDI application need be identical. It is possible for the parent form to host several types of child forms, but this is rather unusual.

When an MDI application starts, it displays an empty parent form with a minimal menu. This menu contains commands to load child forms and the usual Window menu, which we'll explore shortly. The File menu of the parent form contains a New or an Open item, which brings up a new child and, optionally, loads a document. In our case, we'll prompt the user with the FileOpen dialog box to select an image and we'll display it on a new child form. Let's start with the menu of the parent form. This menu contains two submenus with the following items:

File

   Open

   Exit

Window

   Tile Vertical

   Tile Horizontal

   Cascade

   Arrange Icons

Don't worry about the Window menu, we'll get to it shortly. Notice the lack of the Save and Save As items from the parent form's File menu? We haven't added these commands to the File menu because the corresponding operations are meaningless without a child form. All other operations that require a child window, like the Save command of the File menu and the Process menu, belong to the menu of the child form. Technically, it's possible to access any child form from within the parent form's code, but this will complicate the code. Operations that apply to child forms are best implemented in the child form's code.

But child forms don't have their own menus, or do they? Child forms have menus, but they're merged with the parent form's menu. As you already know, the menu of an MDI application is sketchy with no child documents open. Some MDI menus contain a full menu, but most of the items are disabled. As you will see in this section, it is possible to merge the menus of the parent and child forms (you'll actually specify how the two menus will be merged). When you design an MDI application, you build a child form with the full menu of the application.

This menu will appear as soon as the first child window is opened. Open the child form, and add the following menu to it:

File

    Close

    Save

    Save As

Process

    Rotate Left

    Rotate Right

    Flip Vertical

    Flip Horizontal

We have the two menus; now we must specify how they'll be merged. Both the parent and child forms have a File menu, but the application shouldn't have two File menus. The corresponding items will be merged under a single File menu.

First, let's see how they're merged by default. Switch to the parent form, place an instance of the FileOpenDialog control on the form, and insert the following statements in the Click event handler of the Open menu item. This event handler will create an instance of the child form and load an image on its PictureBox control, as shown in Listing 8.9.

**Listing 8.9**      **Displaying a Child Form in an MDI Application**

```
Private Sub FileOpen_Click(ByVal sender As System.Object, _
                        ByVal e As System.EventArgs) _
                        Handles FileOpen.Click
    OpenFileDialog1.Filter = "Images|*.jpg;*.tif"
    OpenFileDialog1.ShowDialog()
    If OpenFileDialog1.FileName = "" Then Exit Sub
    Dim child As New MDIChild()
    child.MdiParent = Me
    child.Text = System.IO.Path.GetFileName( _
                OpenFileDialog1.FileName)
    child.PictureBox1.Image = Image.FromFile( _
                OpenFileDialog1.FileName)
    child.ImageFileName.Text = OpenFileDialog1.FileName
    child.Show()
End Sub
```

To open a child window on the main form of the application, we create an instance of the child form, set its MDIParent property to the parent form, and then call its Show method. It's no different than displaying another form on the desktop, except for setting its parent form. There's another statement you may find odd in this listing. The ImageFileName control is a TextBox control that resides on the child form. It's a hidden control that stores the name of the file with the image that we loaded onto the PictureBox control of the child form. We need a simple method to access the paths of the images from within the Save command, and this is a very simple approach. You can't create a form variable with the name of the open document, as you would do with an SDI application, because there can be many open documents. You could create a collection with pathnames for each of the open documents, but this requires substantial overhead. The method suggested here is as simple as it gets. You can store any piece of information you may need later in your code to a hidden control and retrieve it at will.

If you run the application now, you will see the parent window with its minimal menu. Open a child form with the File ➢ Open command. As soon as the first child window opens, the menus of the parent and child forms will merge and the combined menu will appear on the parent form's menu bar (a characteristic of MDI applications). There will be two File menus on the form, the first one with the items of the parent form's File menu and the second one with the items of the child form's File menu. The two menus were merged, but not as you'd expect. We must set a few properties to specify how the menus will merge. These are the MergeType and MergeOrder properties.

The MergeType property determines how the items of two menus are merged, and its value can be one of the members of the MenuMerge enumeration, which are shown in Table 8.5.

**TABLE 8.5:** The MenuMerge Enumeration

| Member Name | Description |
|---|---|
| Add | The menu items of the child form are added to the menu items of the parent form (default). |
| MergeItems | The menu items of the child form are merged with the items of the parent form. The items are merged according to their order in the respective menus, not by their captions. |
| Remove | The menu item is ignored when two menus are merged. |
| Replace | The menu item replaces another item at the same position in the merged menu. The Replace option allows you to design the complete menu on the child form and have it replace the MDI form's menu as soon as the first child form is opened. |

When menu items are merged, the parent form's menu items appear first, followed by the child form's menu items. You can change the order in which the items are merged by setting their MergeOrder property, which is an integer value specifying the order in which the items will be merged. Items with a smaller MergeOrder value will appear in front of others with larger MergeOrder values. The Window item, for example, is always the last menu in an MDI application, with the exception of the Help menu. To make sure it is the last item in the merged menu structure, set its MergeType property to Add and its MergeOrder property to 100.

The File menu of the MDI form must be merged with the File menu of the child form, so you must set the MergeType property of both items to MergeItems. Their MergeOrder property must be 0. Menus are merged based on their MergeOrder value, not by their caption or their name.

Then you must set the MergeOrder property of the items in each menu. The settings for the File menu's item on the parent form are as follows:

| Menu Item | MergeType | MergeOrder |
|-----------|-----------|------------|
| File | Merge | 0 |
| Open | Add | 0 |
| Exit | Add | 4 |

The settings for the File menu's items on the child form are as follows:

| Menu Item | MergeType | MergeOrder |
|-----------|-----------|------------|
| File | Merge | 0 |
| Save | Add | 1 |
| Save As | Add | 2 |
| Close | Add | 3 |

The Process menu will be displayed next to the File menu, so its MergeType should be Add and its MergeOrder 1. If you run the project now, you'll see that the menus are displayed correctly when a child form is opened.

Let's switch back to the application's code. The Save and Save As commands call the Save method of the Image object to save the image of the current child form to a file. The Save command finds the filename in the hidden TextBox control we placed on the child form. The Save As command prompts the user for a new filename and saves the image to this file. It also stores the user-supplied filename to the hidden TextBox control so that the Save command will find it there. Listing 8.10 shows the code behind the Save and Save As commands.

---

**Listing 8.10**      **The Save and Save As Commands**

```
Private Sub FileSave_Click(ByVal sender As System.Object, _
                           ByVal e As System.EventArgs) _
                           Handles FileSave.Click
    PictureBox1.Image.Save(ImageFileName.Text)
End Sub

Private Sub FileSaveAs_Click( _
       ByVal sender As System.Object, _
       ByVal e As System.EventArgs) _
       Handles FileSaveAs.Click

    SaveFileDialog1.Filter = "Images|*.jpg;*.tif"
    SaveFileDialog1.ShowDialog()
    If SaveFileDialog1.FileName = "" Then Exit Sub
    PictureBox1.Image.Save(SaveFileDialog1.FileName)
    ImageFileName.Text
End Sub
```

---

The Close command calls the Close method of the child form. Normally, you should prompt the user to save any changes before closing the child window. You can add another hidden control to the child form, like a CheckBox control, and set it (or reset it) every time the user applies a transformation to the image (or saves the image to a file).

Now we can implement the processing commands. All the commands call the RotateFlip method of the Image object with the appropriate argument. The code behind the Flip Vertical command contains the following statements:

```
PictureBox1.Image.RotateFlip(RotateFlipType.Rotate180FlipX)
PictureBox1.Invalidate()
```

Run the MDIProject application and check it out. It doesn't perform any advanced tasks, but it works as expected. You can open any number of child forms and switch to any child form through the Window menu, or by clicking the desired child form, and apply transformations to any image. As you have noticed, we carefully divided the operations that must be performed from within the parent form and the operations that must be performed on the child forms, and we've added the appropriate code in different forms. Handling the document on a child form is no different than handling a document on a regular form from within its own code. There are situations, however, when you want to access a child form outside of its own form. Consider an MDI text editor, for example, with a Find & Replace dialog box. This form's code should be able to access the controls of the currently active child form and manipulate their contents.

### Accessing the Active Child Form

To access the active child form, use the ActiveMdiChild property of the parent form, which returns a reference to the active child form. To demonstrate how this works, we'll add a new form to our application. The new form will be invoked from within the parent form, and it will display the properties of the image on the active child form. Figure 8.10 shows this form in action.

Edit the File menu of the parent form and insert the command Properties below the Open command in its File menu. Then add a new form to the project and name it PropForm (this is where we'll display the properties of the active child form). The PropForm is not an MDI child form. There won't be multiple instances of this form. It's a regular form we're going to display modally. The user must close it to return to the application. This form should have a Close button, but the default Close icon at the top of the form will do for this example. The properties are displayed on a TextBox control that fills the form (Dock = Fill).

To invoke this form from within the parent form's code, we must create an instance of the PropForm and then call its ShowDialog method. Before showing the form, however, we must populate the TextBox control with the properties of the image on the currently active child form. To access the Image object with the properties of the image on the child form's PictureBox control, we access the active child form with the following expression:

```
Me.ActiveMdiChild
```

Then we cast this object to the MDIChild type:

```
CType(Me.ActiveChild, MDIChild)
```

This expression is a reference to the active child form. Then we obtain a reference to the image on the PictureBox1 control of the child form:

```
Dim img As Image
img = CType(Me.ActiveMdiChild, MDIChild).PictureBox1.Image()
```

Now, we can use the img object to retrieve the properties of the image and display them on the TextBox control of the PropForm. The code behind the Properties command in the parent form's File menu is shown in Listing 8.11.

---

**Listing 8.11        Displaying the Properties of the Active Image**

```
Private Sub FileProperties_Click( _
        ByVal sender As System.Object, _
        ByVal e As System.EventArgs) _
        Handles FileProperties.Click

    Dim img As Image
    img = CType( _
            Me.ActiveMdiChild, MDIChild).PictureBox1.Image()
    Dim props As New PropForm()
    props.TextBox1.Text = "WIDTH: " & vbTab & img.Width & _
            vbCrLf
    props.TextBox1.Text = props.TextBox1.Text & _
            "HEIGHT: " & vbTab & img.Height & vbCrLf
    props.TextBox1.Text = props.TextBox1.Text & "HRES: " & _
            vbTab & img.HorizontalResolution & vbCrLf
    props.TextBox1.Text = props.TextBox1.Text & "VRES: " & _
            vbTab & img.VerticalResolution & vbCrLf
    props.ShowDialog()
End Sub
```

---

When you code MDI applications, you should try to contain the operations in the child form to which they apply. You can manipulate the child forms through the parent form's code, but this will complicate your program. If you need to access the active child form from within the parent form's code, use the ActiveMdiChild property and cast this property to the appropriate type, as we did in the example. You can also activate a child form from within the parent form's code with the ActivateMdiChild method. This method requires as argument a reference to the child form to be activated.

### The Window Menu

A common feature among MDI applications is the Window menu, which contains two groups of commands. The first group of commands arranges the child windows on the MDI form, and the second group contains the captions of all open child windows. To create a Window menu, add a new item to the parent form's menu, name it Window, and insert the following items under it:

Tile Horizontally

Tile Vertically

Cascade

Arrange Icons

Then, locate the MDIList property of the Window menu in the Properties window and set it to True. This property causes the menu to keep track of all open child forms and display their names at the bottom of the Window submenu.

The other four items of the Window menu are implemented with a call to the LayoutMdi method of the parent form. This method can be called only if the IsMdiContainer property has already been set to True, and it accepts as argument one of the members of the MdiDILayout enumeration: TileHorizontal, TileVertical, Cascade, and ArrangeIcons. The following event handler will tile all child forms horizontally on the parent window:

```
Private Sub WindowTileH_Click( _
    ByVal sender As System.Object, _
    ByVal e As System.EventArgs) Handles WindowTileH.Click

    Me.LayoutMdi(MdiLayout.TileHorizontal)
End Sub
```

The MDILayoutMdi method of the parent form automatically rearranges the child forms; all you have to do is supply the proper argument.

At the bottom of the Window menu, you will see a list with all the child windows currently open on the parent form. This list is maintained automatically, and its purpose is to allow you to select one of the child windows.

## Summary

This chapter was a quick introduction to the new features of the .NET Windows Form Designer. There are several important new features, and many of the basic operations, like the design of a menu or the display of a form, are now done differently. We didn't describe minor new properties of the Form object or other trivial issues. Once you get started with the new Designer, you'll figure them out easily.

Among the most important new features of the Windows Form Designer are the tools for designing easily resizable forms. These tools are the Anchor and Fill properties, but mostly the Splitter and Panel controls. Use the Splitter control to divide your form into resizable sections. If a section contains more than a single control, place all the controls on a Panel and use the Panel's Anchor and Fill properties to make the controls adjust to the resizing of the Panel control.

Designing and programming menus has also been simplified in .NET. Even more important is the ability to create owner-drawn menus. Menus in .NET applications are not made up of captions, but they may contain graphics and colors. Drag-and-drop operations are a little different, and so is the process of designing MDI forms. Finally, you can implement dynamic forms in code and you no longer have to rely on control array. Experiment a little with the new features of the IDE and you'll find out for yourself that it's one of the most enhanced areas of Visual Studio .NET.

# CHAPTER 9

## Programming Windows Forms Controls

- Basic Windows controls

- Using the TreeView and ListView controls

- Printing in .NET

In this chapter, we'll review the major new features of some basic Windows controls. This isn't a summary of the new features of every enhanced control. Most of the Windows controls in the toolbox are similar to the controls of earlier versions of the language, and we will not discuss them in this book. Some of the controls you'll be using most often in your applications have undergone a major overhaul, and we'll look at these controls and how they're used in VB .NET. The controls we'll discuss here are the TextBox, the ListBox, the TreeView, and the ListView controls. Most programmers will attempt to use the new versions of these controls as they used the previous versions. For example, if you didn't know that the TextBox control provides a Lines property, which is an array of strings with the text lines of the control, you'd probably attempt to use string manipulation functions to extract individual text lines. Among the most profound changes in the new controls is the lack of the ItemData property of the ListBox control. The TreeView control doesn't support the Key and ParentKey properties—these were the basic properties in manipulating the hierarchy of the control's nodes. You won't miss the ItemData property because the new ListBox control can store objects, not just strings. However, you'll have to get used to using the ListBox control, or the TreeView control, in an entirely different way.

In the last part of the chapter, we'll explore the printing controls introduced with the new Framework. The process of printing with VB .NET is new, and several new controls are now available to facilitate the printing process. In addition to a discussion of these controls, you will find examples of code that generates printouts.

## The TextBox Control

The most important of the features of the new version of the TextBox control is that it can now hold up to 2 billion characters (2,147,483,647 characters, to be exact). Adding large amounts of text to the control will take a few seconds, and this is something you should keep in mind if you plan to work with large text files. By the way, if you plan to manipulate strings extensively, use the StringBuilder class and declare variables of this type. They're similar to String variables, but they're much faster to process.

---

**NOTE**   Notice that the default value of the MaxLength property is 32,767, which was the maximum length of text the old version of the control could store. Set this property to 0 (zero) to add large amounts of text to the control.

**NOTE**  This change in the maximum length of text you can place on a TextBox control brought about another important change in the behavior of the control. Earlier versions of the TextBox control generated a runtime error when the control's capacity was exceeded. The new TextBox control handles this situation silently. If you leave the MaxLength property set to its default value (32767) and then attempt to assign a longer string to the control's Text property, the string will be truncated and only its first 32,767 characters will be stored in the Text property. The rest of the string will be discarded silently. Practically, every instance of a multiline TextBox control should have its MaxLength property changed to 0.

The WordWrap property allows you to specify whether the control will wrap text lines. In the old version of the control, the ScrollBars property determined whether the text would wrap. Now, you can enter long lines of text even if no horizontal scroll bar is present. Finally, the properties that let you select or manipulate the selected text (or select text from within your code)—the SelStart, SelLength, and SelText properties—are now called Selection-Start, SelectionLength, and SelectedText. The AppendText method lets you add text to the control, and it's much faster than the equivalent statement:

```
TextBox1.Text = TextBox1.Text & textLine
```

If you want to prevent users from editing the text on a TextBox control, set the ReadOnly property to True. There's also a Locked property, but this one simply locks the control in its place at design time.

In addition to the Text property, you can access the text on the control with the Lines property. Unlike the Text property, however, the Lines property is read-only; you can't set the control's text by assigning strings to the Lines array. The Lines property is an array of strings, and each element of the array holds a line of text. The first line of the text is stored in the element Lines(0), the second line of text is stored in the element Lines(1), and so on. Because the Lines property is an array, you can retrieve the number of text lines on the control with the expression `Lines.Length`. You can iterate through the text lines with a loop like the following:

```
Dim iLine As Integer
For iLine = 0 To TextBox1.Lines.GetUpperBound(0)
    { process string TextBox1.Lines(iLine) }
Next
```

You must replace the line in brackets with the appropriate code, of course. Because the Lines property is an array, it supports the GetUpperBound method, which returns the index of the last element in the array. Each element of the Lines array is a string, and you can call any of the String class's methods to manipulate it. You can search for a string within the current line with the IndexOf and LastIndexOf methods, retrieve the line's length with the Length property, and so on—just keep in mind that you can't alter the text on the control by editing the Lines array.

In addition to properties, the TextBox control exposes the Select and SelectAll methods for selecting text. The SelectAll method selects all the text on the control and accepts no arguments. The Select method's syntax is shown next:

```
TextBox1.Select(start, length)
```

To select the characters 100 through 105 on the control, call the Select method, passing the values 99 and 6 as arguments:

```
TextBox1.Select(99, 6)
```

If the range of characters you select contains hard line breaks, you must take them into consideration as well. Each hard line break counts for two characters (carriage return and line feed). If the TextBox control contains the string "Visual Basic .NET", then the following statement will select the range "ual B":

```
TextBox1.Select(3, 5)
```

If you insert line breaks between the words and the text becomes

```
Visual
Basic
.NET
```

then the same statement will select the characters "ual" only. The other two characters are the line feed and carriage return characters that separate the first two lines. The length of the selection is 5, three letters and two unprintable characters.

The selected text can be retrieved with the SelectedText property. The starting location of the selected text is given by the property SelectionStart, and the length of the selected text is SelectionLength. You can also select text by setting these properties from within your code.

## Undoing Edits

An interesting feature of the TextBox control is that it can automatically undo the most recent edit operation. To undo an operation from within your code, you must first examine the value of the CanUndo property. If it's True, it means that you can undo the operation by calling the Undo method. An edit operation is the insertion or deletion of one or more characters. If you're entering text without deleting any, it's considered a single operation and it will be undone in a single step. If you call the Undo method again, the most recent operation will be undone. Because the most recent operation is the deletion of a number of characters, these characters will be restored.

To implement an Undo/Redo feature in your application, you can add a command to the application's Edit menu and toggle its caption between Undo and Redo. This command's code calls the Undo method to either undo or redo an operation. But, how do you know that the text has been edited? The TextBox control fires the TextChanged event every time its contents change. We'll use this event to restore the caption of the command to Undo. After undoing an operation, you must set the caption of the command to Redo.

### Undoing Selected Operations

The Undo method of the TextBox control would be much more useful if you could mark the beginning of the operation to be undone. After a paste operation, the Undo method will replace the pasted text with the original text . If the paste operation hasn't replaced any text, then the pasted text will be removed. You can implement a custom Undo/Redo command by storing the text into the Clipboard before a major operation—like the conversion of the text into uppercase, for example:

```
Editor.SelectAll()
Clipboard.SetDataObject(newText.ToString())
Editor.Paste()
```

Let's say you convert all (or selected) lines of text to uppercase. The next undo operation will replace the text with the converted lines with the original text. You can insert the same three lines after each statement you want to use as a "bookmark" for an undo operation. Clearing the control and pasting back its text is equivalent to resetting the Undo buffer.

### Copying and Pasting Text

There are also methods for copying, cutting, and pasting text on the control, and they're the Copy, Cut, and Paste methods. To copy the selected text to the clipboard, make sure that some text is selected and then call the control's Copy method:

```
If TextBox1.SelectionLength > 0 Then
    TextBox1.Copy()
End If
```

Do the same to cut the selected text and paste it onto the clipboard:

```
If TextBox1.SelectedText <> "" Then
    TextBox1.Cut()
End If
```

To paste data on the TextBox control, you must first make sure that the clipboard contains text, which is the data format you can paste on the TextBox control. If so, call the control's Paste method, as shown here:

```
If Clipboard.GetDataObject().GetDataPresent(DataFormats.Text) Then
    TextBox1.Paste()
End If
```

You can also manually copy the selected text (property TextBox1.SelectedText) to the clipboard or replace the selected text with the contents of the clipboard, but there's no reason to do so. You may wish to code the paste operations manually so that you can convert the contents of the clipboard to straight text in your code (for example, you can convert HTML code to text by skipping the HTML tags).

The TextBox control has no support for printing its text. Actually, none of the Windows controls has built-in support for printing. Later in this chapter, you'll see how to use the printing controls to print straight text.

These are the basic properties and methods of the TextBox control, and it's fairly easy to include a TextBox control in your interfaces. Programming the TextBox control isn't complicated either. We usually extract the selected text (or all the text on the control) and process it with the methods of the System.String class or the usual string manipulation functions of Visual Basic.

## The ListBox Control

The ListBox control and its cousins the CheckedListBox and ComboBox controls are some of the most basic elements of the Windows interface. In this chapter, we'll discuss in detail the changes in the ListBox control, which is now substantially different from its predecessor. Most of the properties and methods discussed in this section apply to all three controls.

The ListBox, CheckedListBox, and ComboBox controls present lists of choices from which the user can select one or more. The ListBox control occupies a user-specified amount of space on the form and is populated with a list of items. If the list of items is longer than can fit on the control, a vertical scroll bar appears automatically. The most prominent characteristic of the new ListBox control is that it can store objects, not just strings. Most of the applications you'll write will store strings to this control, but now you can store much more information to the ListBox control than was possible with earlier versions. The earlier versions of the ListBox control allowed you to store additional information in the DataItem property. This property could hold an integer, which programmers used as index to arrays or other indexed data structures. Now that the item itself can be an object, the DataItem property serves no purpose and it's no longer supported. As a consequence, the way you use the ListBox control in your applications is no longer the same, and many of the techniques you've developed are no longer applicable. You will see shortly how to use the ListBox control to store data of any type and even bind it to a data structure like an array, or even an ArrayList.

The items can be inserted in the ListBox control through the code or via the Items property in the Property Browser. To add items at design time, locate the Items property in the control's Property Browser and click the button with the ellipsis points. The String Collection Editor window appears, and you can add the items you want to display on the list. Each item is a string and must appear on a separate text line. When you run the project, the items will appear on the control in the same order they were entered on the String Collection Editor window—unless the control's Sorted property is set to True, of course.

At design time, you can only add strings to the ListBox control. Object items can be added to the control only from within your code, and you'll see how this is done in the next section, "Storing Objects to a ListBox Control."

The new ListBox no longer supports the List property. To access individual items on the control, you must use the Items property, which is a Collection object. The first item on the control is Items(0), the second is Items(1), and so on. The Items collection has the usual properties of the Collection object: the Count property, which is the number of items on the control, and the Add, Remove, Insert, and Clear methods to add items to, insert items in, or remove items from the control. The ListCount property has also disappeared. The number of items on the control is given by the expression `Items.Count`, and the AddItem and RemoveItem methods of the old version of the control have been replaced by the Add and Remove methods of the Items collection.

You can configure the control to support the selection of a single or multiple items with the SelectionMode property. If the control allows a single selection, the SelectedIndex and SelectedItem properties return the index and the value of the selected item respectively. If the control allows multiple selections, you can use the SelectedIndices and SelectedItems properties (which are also collections) to access the indices and values of the selected items.

In terms of new functionality, the most important enhancement to the new ListBox control is the search feature. The FindString method locates the closest match to the search argument and the FindStringExact method finds an exact match, if there is one. The FindString method returns the index of the first item that starts with the specified string and the FindStringExact method returns the index of the item that's identical to the specified string. Both methods perform case-insensitive searches. If you're searching for "visual" and the list contains the item "Visual", both methods will locate it, even though the case of the two string isn't identical.

The syntax of both methods is the same (the `searchStr` argument is the string you're searching for):

```
itemIndex = ListBox1.FindString(searchStr As String)
```

An alternative form of both methods allows you to specify the order of the item at which the search will begin:

```
itemIndex = ListBox1.FindString(search As String, startIndex As Integer)
```

The `startIndex` argument allows you specify the beginning of the search, but you can't specify where the search will end. The FindString and FindStringExact methods work even if the ListBox control is not sorted. You need not set the Sorted property to True before you call one of the searching methods on the control. Sorting the list will probably help the search operation a little, but it takes the control less than 100 milliseconds to find an item in a list of 100,000 items, so time spent to sort the list isn't worth it. Of course, even a moderately sized unsorted list is of no practical use to a user.

## Storing Objects to a ListBox Control

The Items property of the ListBox control is a collection that holds all the items on the control. At design time, you can populate this list through the String Collection Editor window, which you can invoke by clicking the Items entry in the Property Browser. At runtime, you can access and manipulate the items through the methods and properties of the Items collection, which are described in the following section, "Selecting Items."

Each member of the Items collection is an object. In most cases, we use ListBox controls to store strings, but it's also possible to store objects. When you add an object to a ListBox control, a string will be displayed on the control's visible area. This is the string returned by the object's ToString method. You can display any other property of the object by setting the control's ValueMember property to the name of the property. The following statements add two Color objects to the ListBox1 control:

```
ListBox1.Items.Add(Color.Red)
ListBox1.Items.Add(Color.Green)
```

Alternatively, you can create the objects first and then add them to the control:

```
Dim aColor As New Color()
aColor = Color.Blue
ListBox1.Items.Add(aColor)
aColor = Color.Yellow
ListBox1.Items.Add(aColor)
```

No matter how you add the Color objects to the ListBox control, they will appear as strings like the following:

```
Color [Red]
Color [Green]
```

You can display any of the properties of the Color object on the ListBox control instead of the string returned by the ToString method. The Color object doesn't expose many interesting properties, but you can display the value of the color's red component (a numeric value from 0 to 255) by setting the control's DisplayMember property to the name of the R property of the Color object:

```
ListBox1.DisplayMember = "R"
```

(The Color object exposes the R, G, and B properties—among others—and they return the red, green, and blue components of a color value.) If you insert this statement before adding the Color objects to the control (or set the control's DisplayMember property to the string "R" at design time), then a value from 0 to 255 will appear on the control in place of each Color object. You will see this technique in action in the following section.

The proper way to read the objects stored in a ListBox control is to examine the type of the object first and attempt to retrieve a property (or call a method) of the object only if it's of the appropriate type. Here's how you would read the green component of a Color object stored in the first item of the ListBox control:

```
If ListBox1.Items.Item(0).GetType Is GetType(Color) Then
    Console.WriteLine( ListBox1.Items.Item(0).G)
End If
```

To add items to the list, use the `Items.Add` or `Items.Insert` method. The syntax of the Add method is as follows:

```
ListBox1.Items.Add(item)
```

The `item` parameter is the object to be added to the list. You can add any object to the ListBox control, but items are usually strings. The Add method appends new items to the end of the list, unless the Sorted property has been set to True. The following loop adds the elements of the array `words` to a ListBox control one at a time:

```
Dim words(1000) As String
{ statements to populate array }
Dim i As Integer
For i = 0 To 999
    ListBox1.Items.Add(words(i))
Next
```

Similarly, you can iterate through all the items on the control with a loop like the following:

```
Dim i As Integer
For i = 0 To ListBox1.Items.Count - 1
    { statements to process item ListBox1.Items(i) }
Next
```

You can also use the For Each...Next statement to iterate through the Items collection, as shown here:

```
Dim itm As Object
For Each itm In ListBox1.Items
    { process the current item, represented by the itm variable }
Next
```

The Items collection supports the GetEnumerator method, which returns an IEnumerator object. You can use this object to iterate through the collection and retrieve each object in the ListItemCollection. The IEnumerator object exposes a few members:

**Current property**    Gets the current item in the collection

**MoveNext method**    Moves to the next item in the collection

**Reset method**    Moves before the first item in the collection

To iterate through the items of a ListBox control with an IEnumerator object, use a loop like the following:

```
Dim IEnum As IEnumerator
IEnum = ListBox1.Items.GetEnumerator()
While IEnum.MoveNext
    Console.WriteLine(IEnum.Current)
End While
```

The Current property of the IEnumerator object represents the current object in the list. You can also cast this object to the appropriate type—provided you know the type of objects stored in the ListBox control—and then call its properties and methods:

```
CType(IEnum.Current, type).member
```

In the preceding line, `type` is the type of the objects stored in the ListBox control and `member` is the name of a method or property of the specific object type.

You can also copy the contents of the ListBox to an array with the CopyTo method, which accepts as arguments the name of the array that will accept the items and the index of an element in the array where the first item will be stored:

```
ListBox.Items.CopyTo(destination_array, index)
```

The array that will hold the items of the control must be declared explicitly and must be large enough to hold all the items.

## Selecting Items

The ListBox control allows the user to select either one or multiple items, depending on the setting of the SelectionMode property. In a single-selection ListBox control, you can retrieve the selected item with the SelectedItem property and its index with the SelectedIndex property. The SelectedItem returns the selected item, which is an object. The text that was clicked by the user to select the item is reported by the Text property.

If the control allows the selection of multiple items, they're reported with the SelectedItems property. This property is a collection of objects, and it exposes the same members the Items collection exposes. The `SelectedItems.Count` property, for example, reports the number of selected items.

To iterate through all the selected items in a multiselection ListBox control, use a loop like the following:

```
Dim itm As Object
For Each itm In ListBox1.SelectedItems
    Console.WriteLine(itm)
Next
```

The itm variable was declared as Object because the items in the ListBox control are objects. They happen to be strings in most cases, but they can be anything. If all items are of the same type, you can convert them to the specific type and then call their methods. If the ListBox1 control holds Color objects, you can use a loop like the following to print the three components of each color:

```
Dim itm As Object
For Each itm In ListBox1.SelectedItems
    Console.WriteLine(Ctype(itm, Color).Red.ToString & _
            Ctype(itm, Color).Green.ToString & _
            Ctype(itm, Color).Blue.ToString)
Next
```

Quite often, you only need to know whether an object belongs to the list and not its exact location. This is when you use the Contains method of the Items collection—not to be confused with the control's Contains method. This method accepts an object as argument and returns a True/False value indicating whether the collection contains this object or not. Use the Contains method to avoid the insertion of identical objects to the ListBox control. The following statements add a string to the Items collection, but only if the string isn't already part of the collection:

```
Dim itm As String = "Visual Basic"
If Not ListBox1.Items.Contains(itm) Then
    ListBox1.Items.Add(itm)
End If
```

## The ListBoxDemo Project

The ListBoxDemo project demonstrates how to populate a ListBox with objects of a custom type. The main form of the ListBoxDemo project is shown in Figure 9.1. The top button clears the list, and the other two populate the list. The Populate List button populates the list directly by adding items to the Items collection, and the Populate Collection button populates a collection and then binds the collection to the ListBox control. The last button on the form goes through the items on the control with an Enumerator.

**NOTE** You'll find all the code from this chapter on www.sybex.com. Search for the book by its ISBN, 2879, or its title, *Visual Basic .NET Developer's Handbook*. You can download the code from the download button.

**FIGURE 9.1:**

The ListBoxDemo
project demonstrates
two different techniques
to populate a ListBox
control.

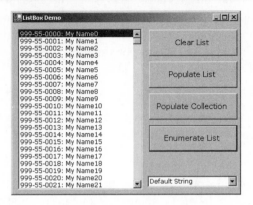

First, you must implement a class from which the objects will be created. Listing 9.1 shows
a simple class for storing persons (customers, contacts, and so on) that exposes a few properties and a custom ToString method. The value returned by the ToString method is the
string that represents the specific instance of the Person class (the string that will appear on
the control for each instance of the Person class you add to the Items collection).

**Listing 9.1    The Person Class**

```
Class Person
    Dim _name As String
    Dim _address As String
    Dim _SSN As String
    Dim _bdate As Date
    Public Property Name() As String
        Get
            Return _name
        End Get
        Set(ByVal Value As String)
            _name = Value
        End Set
    End Property
    Public Property Address() As String
        Get
            Return _address
        End Get
        Set(ByVal Value As String)
            _address = Value
        End Set
    End Property
    Public Property SSN() As String
        Get
            Return _SSN
```

```
        End Get
        Set(ByVal Value As String)
            _SSN = Value
        End Set
    End Property
    Public Property BDate() As Date
        Get
            Return _bdate
        End Get
        Set(ByVal Value As Date)
            _bdate = Value
        End Set
    End Property

    Public Overrides Function ToString() As String
        Return (SSN & ": " & Name)
    End Function
End Class
```

The method ToString returns a string made up of the current person's social security number and name. You can use any fields, or any combination of fields, as long as the value of the ToString property uniquely identifies an item. This isn't a restriction imposed by the control, but what good is it to display two or more items with the same description? The ToString method should return a string that identifies the current item, and it's used to display the list's items in a way that makes sense to a user.

The next step is to populate the control with objects of the Person type. We can do so by adding instances of the Person class, or we can create a collection of Person objects and then assign the name of the collection to the ListBox control's DataSource property. The Populate List button adds 100 Person objects to the list with the loop shown in Listing 9.2.

**Listing 9.2**     **Populating the ListBox Control with Person Objects**

```
Private Sub Button1_Click(ByVal sender As System.Object, _
                          ByVal e As System.EventArgs) _
                          Handles Button1.Click
    Dim P As Person
    Dim i As Integer
    For i = 0 To 99
        P = New Person()
        P.Name = "My Name" & i
        P.Address = "My Address" & i
        P.SSN = "999-55-00" & i.ToString("00")
        P.BDate = #5/14/1980#
        persons.Add(P)
        If ListBox1.FindStringExact(P.ToString) = -1 Then
            ListBox1.Items.Add(P)
```

```
        Else
            Console.WriteLine("Item " & P.ToString & " exists already")
        End If
    Next
End Sub
```

Notice that the code uses the ToString method to figure out whether each object exists in the list already. The method ToString returns the SSN of the person, along with the name. The SSN field makes each person unique, and the Name field will help the user locate a specific person. The FindStringExact method will work because it takes into consideration the SSN field, which is unique for each person. Any other field, or even combination of fields, wouldn't be unique.

To iterate through the list's items, you can use an enumerator, which you can retrieve automatically with the GetEnumerator method. Then, you can use the enumerator's MoveNext method to move to the next item in the collection and the Current property to retrieve the current person. Listing 9.3 includes the code behind the Enumerate List button.

**Listing 9.3    Enumerating the Items of the ListBox Control**

```
Private Sub Button2_Click(ByVal sender As System.Object, _
                          ByVal e As System.EventArgs) _
                          Handles Button2.Click
    Dim IEnum As IEnumerator
    IEnum = ListBox1.Items.GetEnumerator()
    While IEnum.MoveNext
        Console.WriteLine(IEnum.Current)
        Console.WriteLine(vbTab & CType(IEnum.Current, Person).Name)
        Console.WriteLine(vbTab & CType(IEnum.Current, Person).Address)
        Console.WriteLine(vbTab & CType(IEnum.Current, Person).SSN)
        Console.WriteLine(vbTab & CType(IEnum.Current, Person).BDate)
    End While
End Sub
```

The IEnumerator object exposes two methods, MoveNext and Reset (which resets the current location to the beginning of the list), and the Current property, which returns the current object in the list. This object is cast to the appropriate type with the CType() function and then we extract the properties of the current object.

If you double-click an item on the ListBox control, the values of its properties will be displayed on a message box with the statements shown in Listing 9.4.

**Listing 9.4**        **Retrieving the Properties of the Selected Object**

```
Private Sub ListBox1_DoubleClick(ByVal sender As System.Object, _
                              ByVal e As System.EventArgs) _
                              Handles ListBox1.DoubleClick
    Dim str As String
    str = CType(ListBox1.SelectedItem, Person).Name & vbCrLf
    str = str & CType(ListBox1.SelectedItem, Person).Address & vbCrLf
    str = str & CType(ListBox1.SelectedItem, Person).SSN & vbCrLf
    str = str & CType(ListBox1.SelectedItem, Person).BDate & vbCrLf
    MsgBox(str)
End Sub
```

As you can see, the ListBox control's Items collection contains objects, and you can retrieve all the properties of the selected item (or call its methods to manipulate the selected item). You can always set up a For...Next loop to iterate through the control's Items collection. If all the items are of the same object, you can create a variable of the same type and then set up a For Each...Next loop like the following:

```
Dim person As Person
For Each person In ListBox1.Items
    { process the current person }
Next
```

You can open the project and uncomment the statements as indicated by the comments to iterate through the items with a For Each...Next loop.

If you want to display a different property of each object on the control, set the control's Display Member property to the name of the property. The ComboBox at the bottom of the form contains the names of the properties of the Person object, and every time a new property is selected in the ComboBox control, the selected object property becomes the value of the control's DisplayMember property. The code behind the ComboBox control sets the ListBox control's DisplayMember property to the appropriate string, as shown in Listing 9.5.

**Listing 9.5**        **Setting the Display Member of the ListBox Control**

```
Private Sub ComboBox1_SelectedIndexChanged( _
            ByVal sender As System.Object, _
            ByVal e As System.EventArgs) _
            Handles ComboBox1.SelectedIndexChanged
    If ComboBox1.SelectedIndex <> 0 Then
        ListBox1.DisplayMember = ComboBox1.Text
    Else
        ListBox1.DisplayMember = ""
    End If
End Sub
```

A more flexible method to populate a ListBox control is to create a collection with the appropriate objects and then bind the collection to the ListBox control. When you bind a collection to a ListBox control, you can also specify which member will be displayed on the control. The Populate Collection button creates a collection with the same objects and then binds the collection to the control (see Listing 9.6).

---

**Listing 9.6**　　　**Binding the ListBox Control to a Collection**

```
Private Sub Button4_Click(ByVal sender As System.Object, _
                ByVal e As System.EventArgs) Handles Button4.Click
    Dim P As Person
    Dim i As Integer
    For i = 0 To 99
        P = New Person()
        P.Name = "My Name" & i
        P.Address = "My Address" & i
        P.SSN = "999-55-00" & i.ToString("00")
        P.BDate = #5/14/1980#
        persons.Add(P)
    Next
    ListBox1.DataSource = persons
End Sub
```

---

When you bind the control to a collection, you can't clear the items with the Clear method. Instead, you must remove all the elements from the collection. There's another interesting feature in binding a collection to a ListBox control. When you populate the control manually and then change the DisplayMember property through the ComboBox control at the bottom of the form, nothing will happen. You must populate the control again with the Populate List button for the new DisplayMember to take effect. When the control is bound to a collection, however, every time you change the DisplayMember property, the new setting takes effect and the list is repopulated. Again, no matter which property you display on the control, you can always access all the properties and methods of the object. The Enumerate List button will work as before and the double-click event on the ListBox control displays the properties of the selected object. The exact same code will work no matter how the control has been populated.

## The TreeView and ListView Controls

In this section, we'll review two of the more advanced Windows controls, the TreeView and ListView controls. These two controls are the ingredients of very functional interfaces, but they're not among the simplest controls to code. We'll use the information presented in this section to flesh out the ExplorerStyle application you developed in Chapter 8 to demonstrate the design of a form with an Explorer-style interface.

We'll start with an overview of the basic operations of the two controls—how they store items and how to populate them at design time and runtime—and then we'll look at the Explorer application's code, which demonstrates how to use the two controls in tandem.

## The TreeView Control

The simplest method of populating the TreeView control is to do so at design time, provided that the values of the nodes are known at design time. Locate the Nodes property in the Property Browser and click the button with the ellipsis points next to the property setting to open the TreeNode Editor window, shown in Figure 9.2. To add a root item, just click the Add Root button. The new item will be named Node0 by default. You can change its name by selecting the item in the list. When its name appears in the Label box, change it to anything you like.

**FIGURE 9.2:**

The TreeNode Editor window

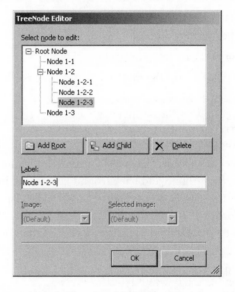

You can add items at the top level by clicking the Add Root button, or you can add items under the selected node by clicking the Add Child button.

In most cases, the nodes are added at runtime and you should be able to manipulate the control's Nodes collection from within your code. All the nodes belong to the control's Nodes collection, which is made up of TreeNode objects. The collection of all root nodes is given by the following expression:

```
TreeView1.Nodes
```

To access the first item of the Nodes collection, use the expression `TreeView.Nodes(0)`. The nodes under a root node form another collection, which you can access with this expression:

```
TreeView1.Nodes(0).Nodes
```

Each node in this collection is a child node of the first root node. The second root node's children are given by this expression:

```
TreeView1.Nodes(1).Nodes
```

If a child node has its own children, you can access them through the Nodes collection as well. The following expression returns the collection of nodes under the first child node of the root node:

```
TreeView1.Nodes(0).Nodes(0).Nodes
```

The Add method adds a new node to the Nodes collection and it accepts as argument a string or a TreeNode object and returns a reference to the newly added node. The simplest form of the Add method is as follows, where *nodeCaption* is a string that will be displayed on the control:

```
newNode = Nodes.Add(nodeCaption)
```

The other form of the Add method allows you to add a TreeNode object directly:

```
newNode = Nodes.Add(nodeObj)
```

To use this form of the method, you must first declare and initialize a TreeNode object:

```
Dim nodeObj As New TreeNode
nodeObj.Text = "Node Caption"
nodeObj.Tag = "Node Tag"
TreeView1.Nodes.Add(nodeObj)
```

The TreeNode object exposes a number of properties for setting its appearance. You can change its foreground and background colors, the image to be displayed in front of the node (property ImageIndex property), the image to be displayed in front of the node when the node is selected (property SelectedImageIndex property), and more, including the NodeFont property. You will see shortly how to assign images to the nodes of a TreeView control.

The last overloaded form of the Add method allows you to specify the index in the current Nodes collection, where the node will be added:

```
newNode = Nodes.Add(index, nodeObj)
```

The nodeObj Node object must be initialized as usual. If you call the Add method on the TreeView1.Nodes collection, as we've done in the last few examples, you'll add a root item. If you call it on a child's Nodes collection, you'll add another item to the existing collection of children items. If your control contains a root item already, then this item is given by the following expression:

```
TreeView1.Nodes(0)
```

To add a child node to the root node, use a statement like the following:

```
TreeView1.Nodes(0).Nodes.Add("Node 0")
```

The expression `TreeView1.Nodes(0)` is the first root node. Its Nodes property represents the nodes under the root node, and the Add method of the Nodes property adds a new node to this collection. To add another element on the same level as the previous one, just use the same statement with a different argument:

```
TreeView1.Nodes(0).Nodes.Add("Node 1")
```

### Adding Nodes at Runtime

To add nodes to a TreeView control at runtime, we start with the root nodes. The Add method returns a reference to the newly added node, and we use this reference to add child nodes under the root node. The following statement adds the first root node to the TreeView1 control, and then it adds two child nodes under it:

```
Dim Nd As TreeNode
Nd = TreeView1.Nodes.Add("Root Node")
Nd.Nodes.Add("Child Item 1")
Nd.Nodes.Add("Child Item 2")
```

Let's say we want to add child nodes under the "Child Item 2" node. We must store the reference to this node to a TreeNode variable and then use it to add the child nodes:

```
Dim Nd As TreeNode
Nd = TreeView1.Nodes.Add("Root Node")
Nd.Nodes.Add("Child Item 1")
Dim cNode As TreeNode
cNode = Nd.Nodes.Add("Child Item 2")
cNode.Nodes.Add("Child Item 2-1")
cNode.Nodes.Add("Child Item 2-2")
cNode.Nodes.Add("Child Item 2-3")
```

Notice that the new version of the TreeView control doesn't support the ParentKey property and any VB6 code you've written to populate a TreeView control can't be ported to VB .NET. To add a new node, you need a reference to its parent node (unless it's a root node). In the section "Mapping a Folder to a TreeView Control" later in this chapter, you'll see how to map the structure of an entire drive to a TreeView control. Each time we run into a directory, we add a new node under the node that represents the parent directory. Then we use the Node object returned by the Add method and we create a child node for each file in the directory. We'll overview the ListView control in the following section and then we'll look at the code that populates the TreeView control of the ExplorerStyle project.

## The ListView Control

The ListView control is similar to the ListBox control except that it can display its items in many forms, along with any number of subitems for each item. To use the ListView control in your project, place an instance of the control on a form and then sets its basic properties, which are described in the following sections.

There are two properties that determine how the various items will be displayed on the control: the View property, which determines how the items will appear, and the Alignment property, which determines how the items will be aligned on the control's surface. The View property's value can be one of the members of the View enumeration:

**LargeIcon**    Each item is represented by an icon and a caption below the icon.

**SmallIcon**    Each item is represented by a small icon and a caption that appears to the right of the icon.

**List**    Each item is represented by a caption.

**Detail**    Each item is displayed in a column with its subitems in adjacent columns.

The Alignment property determines how the items will be arranged on the control, and its possible settings are the members of the ListViewAlignment enumeration:

**Default**    When an item is moved on the control, it remains where it is dropped.

**Left**    Items are aligned to the left side of the control.

**Top**    Items are aligned to the top of the control.

**SnapToGrid**    Items are aligned to an invisible grid on the control; when the user moves an item, the item moves to the closest grid point on the control.

When the items are displayed in Detail view, you can use the HeaderStyle property to specify the style of the headers. The possible settings for the HeaderStyle property are the members of the ColumnHeaderStyle enumeration:

**Clickable**    The column headers react to clicking.

**Nonclickable**    The column headers don't react to clicking.

**None**    The column headers are invisible.

To display items and their subitems in Details view, you must first set up the appropriate columns. The first column corresponds to the items, and the following columns correspond to its subitems. If you don't set up at least one column, no items will be displayed in Details view. The items of the Columns collection are of the ColumnHeader type, and the properties of the headers are usually known at design time. The simplest method for setting up the column headers is to use the ColumnHeader Collection Editor, a visual tool you can invoke by clicking the button with the ellipsis points next to the Columns property in the Property Browser. In the ColumnHeader Collection Editor window, you can add and edit the appropriate columns and set properties like their captions and their widths, as shown in Figure 9.3.

**FIGURE 9.3:**

Setting up the headers
of the ListView control's
columns with the
ColumnHeader
Collection Editor

To add items to a ListView control at design time, click the button with the ellipsis points next to the Items property in the control's Properties window. The ListViewItem Collection Editor will appear, where you can type the caption of each item and set the item's basic properties. Notice in Figure 9.4 that each item can be displayed in a different font—you can use the Font property to make selected items stand out.

**FIGURE 9.4:**

Adding items to ListView
control with the List-
ViewItem Collection Editor

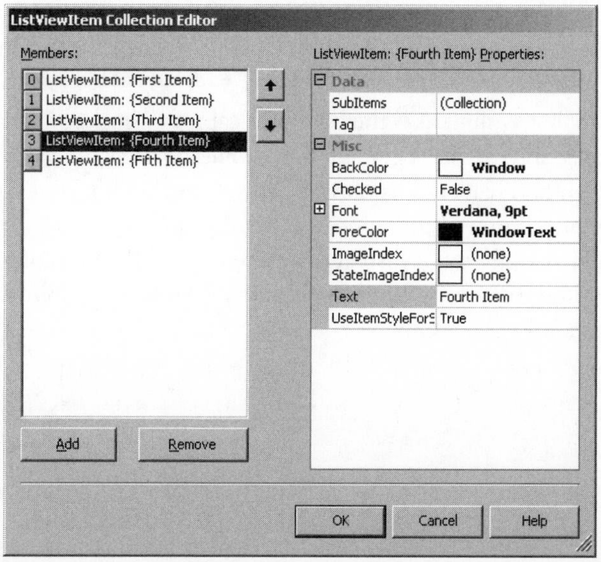

You can also set the control's columns at runtime by manipulating the properties of the Columns collection. The following statement adds a header. First, it creates a ColumnHeader object, then sets its properties, and then adds the new object to the control's Columns collection:

```
Dim cHeader As New ColumnHeader()
cHeader.Text = "Column Caption"
cHeader.Width = 75
cHeader.TextAlign = HorizontalAlignment.Center
ListView1.Columns.Add(cHeader)
```

You can also add new columns to the control by adding a ColumnHeader object for each new column to the Columns collection. The Columns collection provides the Insert method, which accepts as argument the index of the new column and a ColumnHeader object that represents the new column. The following statement inserts the column for the first subitem:

```
ListView1.Columns.Insert(1, cHeader)
```

Each item has a Tag property as well, where you can store additional information about the item. At design time, you can set the Tag property to a string or numeric value, but at runtime, you can assign any object to it.

Each item has a SubItems collection, as you can see in Figure 9.4. This collection contains the subitems of the current item. To add one or more subitems to the current item, click the button with the ellipsis points next to the SubItems property and you will see the ListView-SubItem Collection Editor, shown in Figure 9.5. On this dialog box, you can add the subitems of the current item, along with a couple of basic properties, like their font and background color.

Another overloaded form of the Add method accepts three arguments:

```
ListView.Columns.Add(caption, width, textAlign)
```

The first argument is the column's caption, the second argument is the column's width in pixels, and the last argument determines how the text will be aligned. The Add method returns a ColumnHeader object, which you can use later in your code to manipulate the corresponding column. You can add more subitems than there are columns in the control, but the excess subitems will not be displayed. To remove individual columns, use the Remove and RemoveAt methods of the Columns collection. The Clear method removes all the elements of the Columns collection.

**FIGURE 9.5:**

Adding subitems under an item of the ListView control

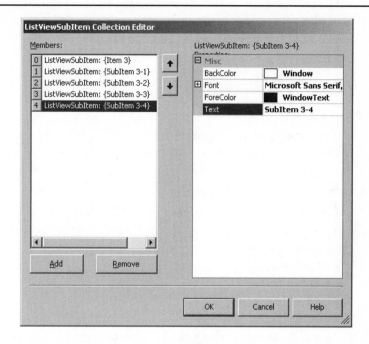

## The Items and SubItems Collections

The items on a ListView control are of the ListViewItem type and they form the Items collection. Likewise, the subitems are of the ListViewSubItem type and they form the SubItems collection. Both collections expose the usual members, like the Count property and the Add/ Remove methods that add and remove items to the collection. To set or read the caption of an item, use the Text property. To add an item to the ListView control, call the Add method of the Items collection. The following statements add two items to the ListView1 control:

```
Dim LItem As New ListViewItem()
LItem.Text = "Item 1"
ListView1.Items.Add(LItem)
LItem = New ListViewItem()
LItem.Text = "Item 2"
ListView1.Items.Add(LItem)
```

To add subitems to an item, use the Add method of the SubItems collection. To create a new item with three subitems, use the following statements:

```
Dim LItem As New ListViewItem()
LItem.Text = "New Item"
LItem.SubItems.Add("SubItem 0")
LItem.SubItems.Add("SubItem 1")
LItem.SubItems.Add("SubItem 2")
ListView1.Items.Add(LItem)
```

If you want to add a subitem at a specific location, use the Insert method. The Insert method of the SubItems collection accepts two arguments: the index of the subitem before which the new subitem will be inserted and the subitem to be inserted:

```
LitemLItem.SubItems.Insert(idx, subitem)
```

The subitem argument must be declared as a ListViewSubItem type. The following statements insert a new subitem between the second and third subitems of the item we added in the previous code segment:

```
Dim LSubItem As New ListViewItem.ListViewSubItem()
LSubItem.Text = "A new subitem"
LItem.SubItems.Insert(2, LSubItem)
```

To retrieve a specific subitem from the SubItems collection, you must specify both an item (to which the subitem belongs) and a subitem (the subitem to be removed):

```
sitem = ListView1.Items(itm1).SubItems(itm2)
```

Here, itm1 is the index of the item and itm2 the index of the desired subitem.

To remove subitems, use the Remove or RemoveAt method of the SubItems collection. The Remove method accepts as argument the SubItem object to be removed. The RemoveAt method accepts as argument the index of the subitem to be removed.

> **NOTE** The distinction between items and subitems is largely arbitrary. The first subitem of each item, SubItems(0), is the item itself. The expressions ListView1.Items(0).Text and ListView1.Items(0).SubItems(0).Text will return the same value, which is the caption of the first item in the control. However, the two expressions represent two different objects. If you call their GetHashCode method, it will return two different values.

The following loop iterates through the items of the ListView1 control and displays them on the Output window. Below each item, its subitems are displayed, indented by a few spaces:

```
Dim Item As ListViewItem
Dim itm As Integer
For Each Item In ListView1.Items
    Dim sItem As ListViewItem.ListViewSubItem
    itm = 0
```

```
        For Each sItem In Item.SubItems
            If itm = 0 Then
                Console.WriteLine(sItem.Text)
            Else
                Console.WriteLine(vbTab & sItem.Text)
            End If
            itm += 1
        Next
    Next
```

The first element in the SubItems collection is the item itself; that's why the code examines each subitem's order before printing it. Alternatively, you can write a loop that iterates through the SubItems collection but skips the first subitem:

```
For i = 1 To Item.SubItems.Count - 1
    Console.WriteLine Item.SubItems(i).Text
Next
```

---

**TIP**    The nodes of the TreeView control, as well as the items of a ListView control, are strings. To store additional information in each node or item, use the Tag property, which can store an object. The controls have their own Tag property, where you can also store an object; the TreeNode and ListViewItem/ListViewSubItem also have their own Tag property, and you can store a different object for each node and each item. You can use the Tag property to store anything from strings to DataSets (and everything in between).

## Mapping a Folder to a TreeView Control

The ExplorerStyle project, shown in Figure 9.6, loads the TreeView control with the structure of the folder C:\Program Files. The form was designed in the preceding chapter to demonstrate the use of the Dock property and the Splitter control in user interface design. The three panes of the form shown in Figure 9.6 can be resized in any way you wish. In this section, you'll add the proper code to populate the TreeView control with the names of the subfolders under the specified folder.

You can expand and collapse any folder on the TreeView control by clicking the plus sign in front of its name. When the user selects a folder by clicking its name, the selected folder's subfolders are displayed on the top ListView control. When the user selects one of these subfolders, the subfolder's files are displayed on the lower ListView control.

The Program Files folder contains a large number of subfolders with many files, and it will take a while to populate the control. You can change the name of the initial folder and even scan an entire volume. While the code is executing in the form's Load event handler, the application will appear to be frozen. In the next chapter, you'll learn how to execute this code in a background thread so that the form will continue to react to the various events.

**FIGURE 9.6:**

The ExplorerStyle project

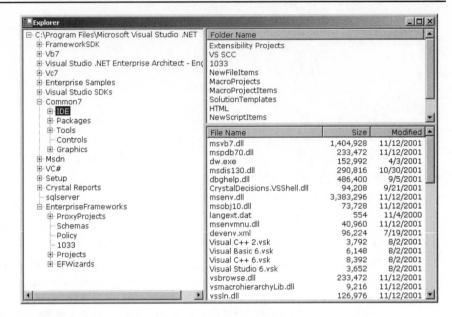

**FIGURE 9.6:**

The ExplorerStyle project

The root node is added to the control with the following statement:

```
Dim initFolder As String = _
            "C:\Program Files"
Nd = TreeView1.Nodes.Add(initFolder)
Nd.Tag = initFolder
```

The last statement sets the new node's Tag property to the path of the root folder. As you will see shortly, the nodes of the TreeView control will be named after each folder's name, and the Tag property will store the corresponding folder's pathname. The statements in Listing 9.7 are executed when the form is loaded.

**Listing 9.7     Mapping a Folder or Drive to a TreeView Control**

```
Private Sub Form1_Load(ByVal sender As Object, _
                ByVal e As System.EventArgs) Handles MyBase.Load
    Dim orgCaption As String
    Me.Show()
    orgCaption = Me.Text
    Me.Cursor = Cursors.WaitCursor
    Application.DoEvents()
    Dim Nd As New TreeNode()
    ' change the name of the folder to be scanned
    ' in the following statement
```

```
        Dim initFolder As String = _
                    "C:\Program Files\Microsoft Visual Studio .NET"
        Nd = TreeView1.Nodes.Add(initFolder)
        Nd.Tag = initFolder
        ScanFolder(initFolder, Nd)
        Me.Cursor = Cursors.Default
        Me.Text = orgCaption
    End Sub
```

The code adds a root node to the control and this node corresponds to the initial folder. All other nodes of the TreeView control are children of the root node (the folder we're mapping to the control). To map the remaining folders, we call the `ScanFolder()` subroutine and pass to it the name of the folder to be mapped and a reference to the root node. The `ScanFolder()` subroutine, which is the core of the application, is quite short (see Listing 9.8).

**Listing 9.8    The *ScanFolder()* Subroutine**

```
Sub ScanFolder(ByVal folderSpec As String, _
                ByRef currentNode As TreeNode)
    Dim thisFolder As String
    Dim allFolders() As String
    allFolders = Directory.GetDirectories(folderSpec)
    For Each thisFolder In allFolders
        Dim Nd As TreeNode
        Nd = New TreeNode(thisFolder)
        Nd = currentNode.Nodes.Add(Path.GetFileName(thisFolder))
        Nd.Tag = thisFolder
        folderSpec = thisFolder
        ScanFolder(folderSpec, Nd)
        Me.Text = "Scanning " & folderSpec
        Me.Refresh()
    Next
End Sub
```

The subroutine retrieves the subfolders under the folder passed to the subroutine as argument with the GetDirectories method of the Directory class. The folder names are stored in the `allFolders` array. The code iterates through all the folders in the `allFolders` array with a For Each…Next loop and adds a child node under the current node for each subfolder. At each node, the subroutine must scan the current folder. It does so by calling itself, passing as arguments the current folder and the newly added node. If the current folder has subfolders, they must be added to the TreeView control as child nodes under their parent folder's node. This process is repeated until all subfolders of the initial folder are added to the control.

Populating the TreeView control with a recursive subroutine is straightforward. When a folder is clicked on the TreeView control, we must extract the path of the selected folder and display its subfolders on the ListView control. This takes place from within the AfterSelect event of the TreeView control, as shown in Listing 9.9.

**Listing 9.9**          **Processing the Selected Node**

```
Private Sub TreeView1_AfterSelect(ByVal sender As System.Object, _
            ByVal e As System.Windows.Forms.TreeViewEventArgs) _
            Handles TreeView1.AfterSelect
    Dim Nd As TreeNode
    Dim pathName As String
    Nd = TreeView1.SelectedNode
    pathName = Nd.Tag.ToString
    ListView1.Items.Clear()
    If Directory.GetDirectories(pathName).Length > 0 Then
        ShowSubFolders(pathName)
    End If
    ShowFiles(pathName)
End Sub
```

The code retrieves the path of the selected folder through the node's Tag property (the node's text is the folder's name, not the entire path). The ShowSubFolder() subroutine, which retrieves the subfolders of the selected folder and displays them on the ListView control, is shown in Listing 9.10.

**Listing 9.10**          **The *ShowSubFolders()* Subroutine**

```
Sub ShowSubFolders(ByVal selFolder As String)
    ListView1.Items.Clear()
    ListView2.Items.Clear()
    Dim folders() As String
    Dim folder As String
    Dim LItem As New ListViewItem()
    folders = Directory.GetDirectories(selFolder)
    For Each folder In folders
        LItem = New ListViewItem()
        LItem.Text = System.IO.Path.GetFileName(folder)
        ListView1.Items.Add(LItem)
    Next
End Sub
```

Finally, when the user clicks a folder name in the ListBox control, we retrieve the files of the selected folder and display their names, along with some basic attributes, on the second ListView control (see Listing 9.11).

---

**Listing 9.11          Processing the Selected Subfolder**

```
Private Sub ListView1_SelectedIndexChanged(ByVal sender As Object, _
                            ByVal e As System.EventArgs) _
                            Handles ListView1.SelectedIndexChanged
    Dim folder As String
    If ListView1.SelectedItems.Count > 0 Then
        folder = TreeView1.SelectedNode.Tag.ToString & "\" & _
                      ListView1.SelectedItems(0).Text
        ShowFiles(folder)
    End If
End Sub
```

---

This subroutine extracts the name of the selected folder from the TreeView control, then it appends the name of the selected folder on the ListView control to create the folder's path, and finally, it uses the pathname to create a FileInfo object for this folder. The files of this folder are retrieved with the GetFiles method of the Directory object and displayed on the lower ListView control (see Listing 9.12).

---

**Listing 9.12          The *ShowFiles()* Subroutine**

```
Sub ShowFiles(ByVal folder As String)
    Dim LItem As New ListViewItem()
    Dim files() As String
    Dim file As String
    files = Directory.GetFiles(folder)
    ListView2.Items.Clear()
    For Each file In files
        LItem = New ListViewItem()
        LItem.Text = System.IO.Path.GetFileName(file)
        Dim FI As New FileInfo(file)
        LItem.SubItems.Add(FI.Length.ToString("#,###"))
        LItem.SubItems.Add(FormatDateTime( _
                Directory.GetCreationTime(file), DateFormat.ShortDate))
        LItem.SubItems.Add(FormatDateTime(_
                Directory.GetLastAccessTime(file), DateFormat.ShortDate))
        ListView2.Items.Add(LItem)
    Next
End Sub
```

---

Notice that this explorer is a bit unusual. It displays the subfolder of the selected folder both in the TreeView control (if you click the plus sign in front of a folder's name) and in the ListView control (if you click a folder's name). In other applications, you may have information structured in three levels (like customers, order, and details), in which case the information displayed on the three controls will be different.

Run the ExplorerStyle project and check out its operation. We've used files and folders to demonstrate the design of an Explorer-style interface, but you can use the same principles to build a navigational interface for other hierarchical data. In a database application, you can use this style of interface to display company names in the TreeView control, their orders in the upper ListView control, and the order details in the lower ListView control.

## Sorting the ListView Control

Another interesting feature of the ListView control is that you can sort its items (in effect, the rows of the grid) according to any column. Each column corresponds to a subitem and different subitems may represent different data types (numeric values, strings, dates, and so on). The control can't handle all data types you may choose to store in it, so you must supply some code. You need to implement a custom comparer, which knows how to compare two values of a specific data type. The custom comparer is a method that compares two values and returns an integer indicating the order of the two items. If the first item is larger than the second item, this value is 1. If the second item is larger, this value is –1. Finally, if the two items are equal, the value returned by the custom comparer is 0 (zero).

So, all you need to supply is a simple function that compares two items of the same type. Once the custom comparer is in place (and you'll see shortly how you connect this function to the control), the ListView control can sort its items. Sorting a list of items consists of multiple comparisons and swapping of items.

The custom comparer must be implemented in a separate class and it must implement the IComparer interface. For more information on the IComparer (and IComparable) interfaces, see Chapter 12. The custom comparer in Listing 9.13 compares two Long values (the sizes of two files). We'll use this comparer to sort the files displayed on the lower ListView control according to their sizes.

**Listing 9.13**    **A Customer Comparer**

```
Class FileSizeSorter
    Implements IComparer
    Public Function CompareTo(ByVal o1 As Object, _
                    ByVal o2 As Object) As Integer _
                    Implements System.Collections.IComparer.Compare
        Dim item1, item2 As ListViewItem
        item1 = CType(o1, ListViewItem)
        item2 = CType(o2, ListViewItem)
        If CLng(item1.SubItems(1).Text) > _
                            CLng(item2.SubItems(1).Text) Then
            Return 1
        Else
```

```
            If CLng(item1.SubItems(1).Text) < _
                            CLng(item2.SubItems(1).Text) Then
                Return -1
            Else
                Return 0
            End If
        End If
    End Function
End Class
```

To sort the rows of the ListView control, assign the name of the custom comparer to the ListViewItemSorter property of the control and then set the Sorting property to Ascending or Descending, depending on the desired sort order. You can provide several custom comparers and sort the items in many different ways. If you plan to display subitems in Details view, you should make the list sortable by any column. It's customary for a ListView control to sort its items according to the values in a specific column each time the header of this column is clicked. Let's add this functionality to the lower ListView control that displays the files in the selected folder. The items are filenames and should be sorted alphabetically. The first column of subitems contains file sizes, which must be sorted numerically, and the last column is a date and it must be sorted chronologically. Listing 9.14 shows all three custom comparers for our project.

---

**Listing 9.14      The Three Custom Comparers for the Explorer Project**

```
Class FileNameSorter
    Implements IComparer
    Public Function CompareTo(ByVal o1 As Object, _
                    ByVal o2 As Object) As Integer _
                    Implements System.Collections.IComparer.Compare
        Dim item1, item2 As ListViewItem
        item1 = CType(o1, ListViewItem)
        item2 = CType(o2, ListViewItem)
        If item1.SubItems(0).Text > item2.SubItems(0).Text Then
        Return 1
        Else
            If item1.SubItems(0).Text < item2.SubItems(0).Text Then
                Return -1
            Else
                Return 0
            End If
        End If
    End Function
End Class

Class FileSizeSorter
    Implements IComparer
```

```
    Public Function CompareTo(ByVal o1 As Object, _
                    ByVal o2 As Object) As Integer _
                    Implements System.Collections.IComparer.Compare
        Dim item1, item2 As ListViewItem
        item1 = CType(o1, ListViewItem)
        item2 = CType(o2, ListViewItem)
        If CLng(item1.SubItems(1).Text) > _
                            CLng(item2.SubItems(1).Text) Then
            Return 1
        Else
            If CLng(item1.SubItems(1).Text) < _
                            CLng(item2.SubItems(1).Text) Then
                Return -1
            Else
                Return 0
            End If
        End If
    End Function
End Class

Class FileDateSorter
    Implements IComparer
    Public Function CompareTo(ByVal o1 As Object, _
                    ByVal o2 As Object) As Integer _
                    Implements System.Collections.IComparer.Compare
        Dim item1, item2 As ListViewItem
        item1 = CType(o1, ListViewItem)
        item2 = CType(o2, ListViewItem)
        If CDate(item1.SubItems(2).Text) > _
                            CDate(item2.SubItems(2).Text) Then
            Return 1
        Else
            If CDate(item1.SubItems(2).Text) < _
                            CDate(item2.SubItems(2).Text) Then
                Return -1
            Else
                Return 0
            End If
        End If
    End Function
End Class
```

The code is straightforward. The three functions are identical, except that they cast their arguments to different types before comparing them. Notice that each comparer is implemented in its own class, named after the type of comparison it performs, and that these classes are outside the application's class.

To use the custom comparers, we must write some code that intercepts the clicks on the control's headers and calls the appropriate comparer. The ListView control fires the ColumnClick event each time a column header is clicked. This event handler reports the index of the column that was clicked through the e.Column argument, and we can use this argument in our code to sort the items accordingly. Listing 9.15 shows the event handler for the ColumnClick event.

**Listing 9.15**     **The ListView Control's ColumnClick Event Handler**

```
Private Sub ListView2_ColumnClick(ByVal sender As Object, _
          ByVal e As System.Windows.Forms.ColumnClickEventArgs) _
          Handles ListView2.ColumnClick
    Select Case e.Column
        Case 0
            ListView2.ListViewItemSorter = New FileNameSorter()
            ListView2.Sorting = SortOrder.Ascending
        Case 1
            ListView2.ListViewItemSorter = New FileSizeSorter()
            ListView2.Sorting = SortOrder.Ascending
        Case 2
            ListView2.ListViewItemSorter = New FileDateSorter()
            ListView2.Sorting = SortOrder.Ascending
    End Select
End Sub
```

As you can see, sorting the rows of a ListView control is fairly straightforward, and it's actually possible to sort the rows according to any criteria. In your custom comparers, you can use complicated logic that takes into consideration any number of items or functions of the items. For example, you can sort a ListView control chronologically based on a date (as we did in our example) but gather the files that are more than a year old to the beginning or the end of the list. If you're sorting products according to the number of items sold, you can take into consideration the date of the last sale to sort the products that have identical sales.

## Persisting Nodes

There are situations in which you may have to store the contents of a TreeView or ListView control to a disk file and read them back in a later session. If the control is populated by the user at runtime, you should be able to save the items to a file and populate the control from this file in a later session. The Framework provides a very powerful class, the Serializer class, which can save arbitrary objects to disk (and any stream, in general) and reconstruct these objects from the persisted data. An object that can be serialized must be marked as serializable, and not all objects are serializable. The Nodes and Items collections are not serializable, and they can't be persisted to disk directly. You can create an ArrayList with the nodes of the TreeView control (or the items of a ListView control) and serialize the ArrayList.

The Serializer class can persist objects in two formats: in binary format, which is more compact, and in text format, which is XML. The text format is more verbose (it contains all kinds of XML tags), but it's easy to understand and you can share it with other computers over the Web. In most cases, we don't exchange nodes and items with other computers, nor do we open the file to view a control's contents, so you're better off with the binary format.

To save an object to a stream, you must *serialize* the object with the Serialize method of a Formatter object. The Serialize method will generate a representation of the object, which can be stored to a file. If you use the XML format, you can view the representation of the object. To populate the control, you can read the file and deserialize it with Deserialize method of the appropriate Formatter object. The ListView and TreeView controls contain multiple items, which can't be serialized individually. We'll use an ArrayList to store all the items (or nodes) and then serialize the ArrayList.

### Serializing a ListView Control

To demonstrate the serialization of the Items collection of the ListView control, we've prepared the PersistListView project, which persists the items of a ListView control. The control is populated at design time, but the code will persist the current state of the control regardless of how the control was populated.

To save the control's contents, the program prompts the user for a file path with the File Save dialog box (it uses the `.bin` extension for the file it generates) and then calls the `SaveListView()` subroutine, passing the names of the file as argument. Listing 9.16 shows the `SaveListView()` subroutine.

**Listing 9.16**     **The *SaveListView()* Subroutine**

```
Sub SaveListView(ByVal fname As String)
    Dim formatter As New BinaryFormatter()
    Dim saveFile As FileStream
    saveFile = File.Create(fname)
    formatter = New BinaryFormatter()
    Dim ItemList As New ArrayList()
    Dim itm As Integer
    For itm = 0 To ListView1.Items.Count - 1
        ItemList.Add(ListView1.Items(itm))
    Next
    formatter.Serialize(saveFile, ItemList)
    saveFile.Close()
End Sub
```

To use the BinaryFormatter, you must import the following class:

```
Imports System.Runtime.Serialization.Formatters.Binary
```

The inverse operation is performed by the `LoadListView()` subroutine, which accepts as argument the name of a file selected by the user on a File Open dialog box. The `LoadListView()` subroutine clears the Items collection of the control and then prompts the user again with a message box. We've inserted this statement so that you can verify that the ListView control is emptied and then populated again. Listing 9.17 shows the `LoadListView()` subroutine.

**Listing 9.17    The *LoadListView()* Subroutine**

```
Sub LoadListView(ByVal fname As String)
    Dim formatter As New BinaryFormatter()
    Dim openFile As FileStream
    openFile = File.Open(fname, FileMode.Open)
    Dim ListViewItems As New ArrayList()
    ListViewItems = CType(formatter.Deserialize(openFile), ArrayList)
    openFile.Close()
    Dim itm As Integer
    ListView1.Items.Clear()
    MsgBox("Click OK to reload the ListView control")
    Dim lvItem As ListViewItem
    For itm = 0 To ListViewItems.Count - 1
        lvItem = New ListViewItem()
        lvItem = ListViewItems(itm)
        ListView1.Items.Add(lvItem)
    Next
End Sub
```

The `LoadListView()` subroutine persists the control's items and subitems as text and ignores the Tag properties. The ListView control can accommodate many fields for each item, and we usually don't store any information in the Tag property. Next, we're going to look at the code for persisting a TreeView control, which will also persist the Tag property of each node.

### Serializing a TreeView Control

The process of serializing a TreeView control is similar in principle to the process for serializing a ListView control: we'll create an ArrayList with the control's nodes and then serialize it. Where the items of a ListView control have a linear structure, the nodes of a TreeView control are hierarchically structured and we must maintain this structure. In other words, we can't simply add the nodes of the controls to an ArrayList. We must also store some information that will enable us to reconstruct the control's Nodes collection later.

The PersistTreeView project, whose main form is shown in Figure 9.7, uses the XML format for persisting the Nodes collection of the control. To persist an object in XML format, we use the SoapFormatter class. First, you must add a reference to the class System.Runtime .Serialization.Formatters.Soap (open the Project menu, select Add Reference, and in the Add Reference dialog box, select the specified .NET component).

---

**FIGURE 9.7:**

The PersistTreeView
project persists a
TreeView control's
nodes in XML format

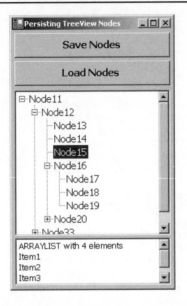

Like the items of a ListView control, the nodes of a TreeView control support the Tag property, where you can store additional information about each node. The code that demonstrates how to persist a TreeView control takes into consideration the Tag properties as well. Because the Node object itself isn't serializable, you must store the node's tag along with the node's text. In addition, you must also store information about the hierarchy of the nodes. This information is stored as an integer value that represents the indentation level of each node. When we run into a child node, we increase the indentation level by one. All the child nodes of a given node have the same indentation level, and when we return to the level of the parent node, we decrease the indentation level by one. This integer value is all the information you need to persist the structure of the control's Nodes collection.

Because the Node object isn't serializable, we must create a new class, or structure, with the <Serializable> attribute. The following structure stores the node's caption (Text property), the node's indentation level, and the node's Tag property:

```
<Serializable()> Structure sNode
        Dim node As String
        Dim level As Integer
        Dim tag As Object
    End Structure
```

Each node will be stored in an sNode variable, and all these variables will be added to an ArrayList, the AllNodes ArrayList, which is declared with the following statement:

```
Dim AllNodes As New ArrayList()
```

The code starts by calling the SaveTreeView() subroutine, passing the name of the file as argument. The SaveTreeView() subroutine sets up a SoapFormatter object, which will serialize the ArrayList. The ScanNode() subroutine scans the control's nodes and populates the AllNodes ArrayList. The code of the SaveTreeView() subroutine is shown in Listing 9.18.

**Listing 9.18    The *SaveTreeView()* Subroutine**

```
Sub SaveTreeView(ByVal fname As String)
    Dim formatter As New SoapFormatter()
    Dim saveFile As FileStream
    saveFile = File.Create(fname)
    formatter = New SoapFormatter()
    AllNodes.Clear()
    ScanNode(TreeView1.Nodes(0))
    formatter.Serialize(saveFile, AllNodes)
    saveFile.Close()
End Sub
```

The ScanNode() subroutine scans the Nodes collection of the TreeView control recursively. It starts with the root node and scans its child elements. Every time it runs into a node with child nodes, it calls itself, passing the parent node as argument. The ScanNode() subroutine will scan the child nodes one at a time and will add them to the ArrayList. Listing 9.19 shows the implementation of the ScanNodes() subroutine.

**Listing 9.19    The *ScanNode()* Subroutine**

```
Sub ScanNode(ByVal node As TreeNode)
    Static level As Integer
    Dim thisNode As TreeNode
    Dim myNode As sNode
    Application.DoEvents()
    myNode.level = level
    myNode.node = node.Text
    myNode.tag = node.Tag
    AllNodes.Add(myNode)
    If node.Nodes.Count > 0 Then
        level = level + 1
        For Each thisNode In node.Nodes
            ScanNode(thisNode)
        Next
        level = level - 1
    End If
End Sub
```

Every time it runs into a node with child nodes, the subroutine increases the level variable, which is the indentation level of the current node, by 1. After scanning the child nodes, the code decreases the level variable by 1. To load the TreeView control with the nodes persisted to an XML file, the code creates a SoapFormatter object and calls its Deserialize method to convert the XML file into an ArrayList. Then the items of the ArrayList, which are of the sNode type, are scanned in a serial mode. We use the information stored in each item to reconstruct the appropriate Node object and add it to the Nodes collection of the TreeView control. Listing 9.20 shows the code that populates the TreeView control by deserializing the XML file.

**Listing 9.20**    **Loading the TreeView Control**

```
Private Sub Button2_Click(ByVal sender As System.Object, _
                          ByVal e As System.EventArgs) _
                          Handles Button2.Click
    OpenFileDialog1.DefaultExt = "BIN"
    If OpenFileDialog1.ShowDialog = DialogResult.OK Then
        Dim fname As String
        fname = OpenFileDialog1.FileName
        TreeView1.Nodes.Clear()
        Dim formatter As SoapFormatter
        Dim openFile As FileStream
        openFile = File.Open(fname, FileMode.Open)
        formatter = New SoapFormatter()
        AllNodes.Clear()
        AllNodes = CType(formatter.Deserialize(openFile), ArrayList)
        openFile.Close()
        TreeView1.Nodes.Clear()
        MsgBox("Click OK to load the nodes")
        Dim o As Object
        Dim currNode As TreeNode
        Dim level As Integer = 0
        Dim fromLowerLevel As Integer
        Dim i As Integer
        For i = 0 To AllNodes.Count - 1
            o = AllNodes(i)
            Dim oNode As sNode = CType(o, sNode)
            If oNode.level = level Then
                If currNode Is Nothing Then
                    currNode = TreeView1.Nodes.Add(oNode.node.ToString)
                    currNode.Tag = oNode.tag
                Else
                    currNode = _
                        currNode.Parent.Nodes.Add(oNode.node.ToString)
                    currNode.Tag = oNode.tag
                End If
            Else
```

```
                   If oNode.level > level Then
                       currNode = currNode.Nodes.Add(oNode.node.ToString)
                       currNode.Tag = oNode.tag
                       level = oNode.level
                   Else
                       While oNode.level <= level
                           currNode = currNode.Parent
                           level = level - 1
                       End While
                       currNode = currNode.Nodes.Add(oNode.node.ToString)
                       currNode.Tag = oNode.tag
                   End If
               End If
               TreeView1.ExpandAll()
               Application.DoEvents()
           Next
       End If
End Sub
```

To demonstrate how the TreeView control stores the Tag property along with each node's caption, we've inserted the following code in the form's Load event handler. These statements set the Tag property of the Node12 node's child nodes to three different objects: a Rectangle object, a Bitmap object, and an ArrayList object. These objects are persisted along with the corresponding node, and they're loaded back when you read the control's contents from the file:

```
Private Sub Form1_Load(ByVal sender As System.Object, _
                       ByVal e As System.EventArgs) Handles MyBase.Load
    TreeView1.Nodes(0).Nodes(0).Nodes(0).Tag = _
            New Rectangle(0, 0, 30, 80)
    TreeView1.Nodes(0).Nodes(0).Nodes(1).Tag = _
            Image.FromFile("\My Documents\My Pictures\Iceberg.jpg")
    Dim AL As New ArrayList()
    AL.Add("Item1")
    AL.Add("Item2")
    AL.Add("Item3")
    AL.Add("Item4")
    TreeView1.Nodes(0).Nodes(0).Nodes(2).Tag = AL
End Sub
```

To verify that the objects of the Tag properties are loaded along with the control's nodes, you can click Node13, Node14, or Node15 and some description of the corresponding object will appear in the TextBox control at the bottom of the form. If you click the Node14 node, you will see the dimensions of the bitmap; if you click the Node15 node, you will see the count of the elements in the ArrayList as well as the elements themselves. Listing 9.21 shows the TreeView control's AfterSelect event handler.

---

**Listing 9.21**      **Retrieving the Object in the Selected Node's Tag Property**

```
Private Sub TreeView1_AfterSelect(ByVal sender As System.Object, _
            ByVal e As System.Windows.Forms.TreeViewEventArgs) _
            Handles TreeView1.AfterSelect
    If e.Node.Tag Is Nothing Then
        Exit Sub
    Else
        If e.Node.Tag.GetType() Is GetType(ArrayList) Then
            TextBox1.Text = "ARRAYLIST with " & _
                    CType(e.Node.Tag, ArrayList).Count.ToString & _
                    " elements"
            Dim AL As ArrayList
            AL = CType(e.Node.Tag, ArrayList)
            Dim i As Integer
            For i = 0 To AL.Count - 1
                TextBox1.AppendText(vbCrLf & AL.Item(i))
            Next
        Else
            If e.Node.Tag.GetType() Is _
                    GetType(System.Drawing.Bitmap) Then
                Dim img As Image = CType(e.Node.Tag, Image)
                TextBox1.Text = "BITMAP (" & _
                img.Width.ToString & " by " & _
                img.Height.ToString & ")"
            Else
                If e.Node.Tag.GetType() Is _
                        GetType(System.Drawing.Rectangle) Then
                    Dim rect As Rectangle = CType(e.Node.Tag, Rectangle)
                    TextBox1.Text = "RECTANGLE (" & _
                            rect.Width.ToString & " by " & _
                            rect.Height.ToString & ")"
                Else
                    TextBox1.Clear()
                End If
            End If
        End If
    End If
End Sub
```

---

The code is quite trivial, although a little lengthy. It reads the Tag property of the selected node, and if it's not Nothing, it examines the object's type. Then it casts the object to the appropriate type and displays some of its basic properties in the TextBox control.

**WARNING**   The Tag property of each node will be serialized along with the node's caption only if the object you've stored in this property is itself serializable. If not, an exception will be thrown. You can insert the appropriate handler or make sure that the objects you assign to the Tag property are serializable. In most cases, you'll use the Tag property to store integers or strings, so this isn't going to be a problem. The exception handler can't do much about nonserializable objects short of ignoring the corresponding Tag property and continuing with the following node. Practically speaking, you must make sure that all the Tag properties are serializable.

## Printing with VB .NET

A group of the new Windows controls that come with the Framework is related to printing. There's no longer a Printer object; to add printing capabilities to your VB applications, you must use these controls. We'll present the printing-related controls shortly, but let's start with an overview of the printing process. Printing on a page is equivalent to creating graphics on a form, or PictureBox control. VB .NET provides the Graphics object, which is exposed as a property of all controls that support graphics. This object in turn exposes a number of methods for drawing graphics primitives, such as simple shapes and text. Any output you can produce on the screen with the graphics methods can be directed to the printer to produce a printout.

The difference between a form (or the screen, in general) and the printer is that the size of the page is fixed. If the output doesn't fit on a single page, you must generate multiple pages. On the screen, you can create very long forms and attach scroll bars to allow users to view any part of the form. You will see shortly how to retrieve the dimensions of a page, send graphics commands to the printer, and detect the end of the page and start a new page. The graphics methods aren't discussed elsewhere in this book; we'll explain the basic graphics methods you'll need to generate text printouts as we go along.

### The Printing Objects

VB .NET introduced several controls for generating output for the printer, and we'll start with a quick overview of these objects. The main object for creating printouts is the PrintDocument object, which represents the printing surface and exposes a Graphics object. Everything you draw on the PrintDocument object with the usual graphics methods is sent to the printer. To print text, for example, you must call the DrawString method, which accepts as arguments the text to be printed, the font in which the text will be rendered, and the location of the first character in the text. There are many overloaded forms of the DrawString method, and we'll explore some of them here. You can also print frames around the text with the DrawLine or DrawRectangle method. In general, you can use all the methods of the Graphics object to prepare the printout.

## The PrintDocument Object

To send something to the printer, you must first add an instance of the PrintDocument control to the project. This control is invisible at runtime, and its icon will appear on the Components tray at design time. When you're ready to print, call the PrintDocument object's Print method. This method doesn't produce any output, but it raises the PrintPage event. This is where you must insert the code that generates output for the printer. The second argument of the PrintPage event exposes the Graphics property of the current printer, among other members, and you will use the methods of this object to create output for the printer.

The following statement initiates the printing; it's usually placed in a button's or a menu's Click event handler:

```
PrintDocument1.Print
```

To experiment with simple printouts, create a new project, place a button on the form, and add an instance of the PrintDocument object to the project. Enter the previous statement in the button's Click event handler. After you click this button, the `PrintDocument1_PrintPage` event handler takes over. This event is fired for each page of the output, so this is the handler where you insert the code to print the first page. If you need to print additional pages, you set the `e.HasMorePages` property to True just before you exit the event handler. This will fire another PrintPage event. The same process will repeat until all the pages have been printed. When you're finished, you set the `e.HasMorePages` property to False and no more PrintPage events will be fired. Listing 9.22 shows the structure of a typical PrintPage event handler. The PrintPage event handler prints three pages with the same text and a different page number on each page.

### Listing 9.22    A Simple PrintPage Event Handler

```vb
Private Sub PrintDocument1_PrintPage(ByVal sender As Object, _
                ByVal e As System.Drawing.Printing.PrintPageEventArgs) _
                Handles PrintDocument1.PrintPage
    Static pageNum As Integer
    Dim prFont As New Font("Verdana", 24, GraphicsUnit.Point)
    e.Graphics.DrawString("PAGE " & pageNum + 1, prFont, _
                    Brushes.Black, 700, 1050)
    e.Graphics.DrawRectangle(Pens.Blue, 0, 0, 300, 100)
    e.Graphics.DrawString("Printing with VB .NET", prFont, _
                    Brushes.Black, 10, 10)
    ' Should we print another page?
    pageNum = pageNum + 1
    If pageNum <= 3 Then
        e.HasMorePages = True
    Else
        e.HasMorePages = False
    End If
End Sub
```

The page number is printed at the bottom of the page with the first call to the DrawString method. The e argument exposes the printer's Graphics object, which in turn exposes all the graphics methods you'll need to generate any printout, including the DrawString method. The first argument of the DrawString method is the text to be printed. The text will be rendered with the font specified by the prFont object with a black brush, and the coordinates of the first character of the string are (700, 1050). In this example, we've hard-coded the coordinates of the various graphics elements. Later in this chapter, you'll learn how to take into consideration not only the dimensions of the physical page, but its orientation, too.

The sample code prints three pages, with the same text and different page numbers. While there are more pages to be printed, the program sets the e.HasMorePages property to True. After printing the last page, it sets the same argument to False to prevent further invocations of the PrintPage event. Note that the pageNum variable was declared as static so that it will retain its value between calls of the PrintPage event handler.

By default, the origin of the page's coordinate system is the upper-left corner of the page, and the coordinates extend to the right and the bottom of the page. The default units are 1/100 of an inch, so there are 850 by 1100 units on a letter-size page. You can draw anywhere you like on the page, but there's usually a margin around it. You can change the coordinate system by setting the PageUnit property of the Graphics object to one of the members of the Graphics-Unit enumeration, shown in Table 9.1.

**TABLE 9.1:** The GraphicsUnit Enumeration

| Member | Description |
| --- | --- |
| Display | Specifies 1/75 inch as the unit of measure. |
| Document | Specifies the document unit (1/300 inch) as the unit of measure. |
| Inch | Specifies the inch as the unit of measure. |
| Millimeter | Specifies the millimeter as the unit of measure. |
| Pixel | Specifies a device pixel as the unit of measure. |
| Point | Specifies a printer's point (1/72 inch) as the unit of measure. |
| World | Specifies the world unit as the unit of measure. |

## The Print Dialog Box

The PrintDialog control displays the standard Print dialog box (Figure 9.8), which allows users to select a printer and set its properties. If you don't display this dialog box, the output will be sent automatically to the default printer and the default settings of the printer will be used. Among other settings, the Print dialog box allows you to specify the range of pages to be printed. Before allowing users to select a range of pages, be sure that you have a way to skip any number of pages. If the user specifies pages 10 through 19, your code must calculate the section of the document that would normally be printed on the first 9 pages, skip it, and start printing after that. If the printout is a report with a fixed number of rows per page, skipping pages is trivial. If the printout contains formatted text, you must repeat all the calculations to generate the first 9 pages and ignore them (skip the statements that actually print the graphics). Starting a printout at a page other than the first one can be a challenge.

**FIGURE 9.8:**

The Print dialog box

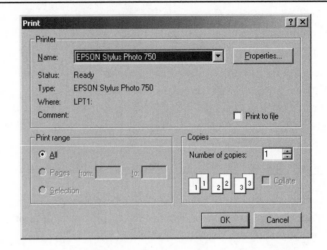

When you select a printer on this dialog box, it automatically becomes the active printer; you don't have to insert any code to switch between printers. It is also possible to set the printer from within your code with a statement like the following (where *printer* is the name of one of the installed printers):

```
PrintDocument1.PrinterSettings.PrinterName = printer
```

To retrieve the names of the installed printers, use the InstalledPrinters collection of the Printer-Settings object. This collection contains the names of the printers as strings, and you can access them with the following loop:

```
Dim i As Integer
With PrintDocument1.PrinterSettings.InstalledPrinters
    For i = 0 To .Count - 1
      Console.WriteLine(.Item(i))
    Next
End With
```

## The PageSetupDialog Control

The PageSetupDialog control displays the Page Setup dialog box, which allows users to set up the page (its orientation and margins). The dialog box returns the current page settings in a PageSettings object, which exposes the user-specified settings as properties. These settings don't take effect on their own; you simply examine their values and take them into consideration as you prepare the output for the printer from within your code. The Page Setup dialog box is shown in Figure 9.9. As you can see, there aren't many parameters to set on this dialog box, but you should display it and take into account the settings specified by the user.

**FIGURE 9.9:**

The Page Setup
dialog box

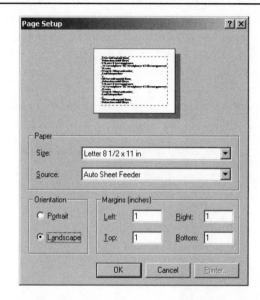

To display this dialog box in your application, you must drop the PageSetupDialog control on the form and then call its ShowDialog method. The one property of this control you'll be using exclusively in your projects is the PageSettings property. PageSettings is an object that exposes a number of properties reflecting the current settings of the page (margins and orientation). These settings apply to an entire document. The PrintDocument object has an analogous property, the DefaultPageSettings property. After the user closes the Page Setup dialog box, we assign its PageSettings object to the DefaultPageSettings object of the Print-Document object to make the user-specified settings available to our code. Here's how we usually display the dialog box from within our application and retrieve its PageSettings property:

```
PageSetupDialog1.PageSettings = PrintDocument1.DefaultPageSettings
If PageSetupDialog1.ShowDialog().DialogResult = OK Then _
    PrintDocument1.DefaultPageSettings = PageSetupDialog1.PageSettings
```

The statements that manipulate the printing objects can get fairly lengthy. It's common to use the With structure to make the statements shorter. The last example can also be coded as follows:

```
With PageSetupDialog1
    .PageSettings = PrintDocument1.DefaultPageSettings
```

```
        If .ShowDialog().DialogResult = OK Then _
                PrintDocument1.DefaultPageSettings = .PageSettings
    End With
```

### The PrintPreviewDialog Control

The Print Preview dialog box displays a preview of the printed document. It exposes a lot of functionality and allows users to examine the output, and when they're happy with it, they can send it to the printer. This dialog box, shown in Figure 9.10, is made up of a preview pane, in which you can display one or more pages and a toolbar. The buttons on the toolbar allow you to select the magnification, set the number of pages that will be displayed on the preview pane, move to any page of a multipage printout, and send the preview document to the printer.

**FIGURE 9.10:**

The Print Preview dialog box displaying a simple printout

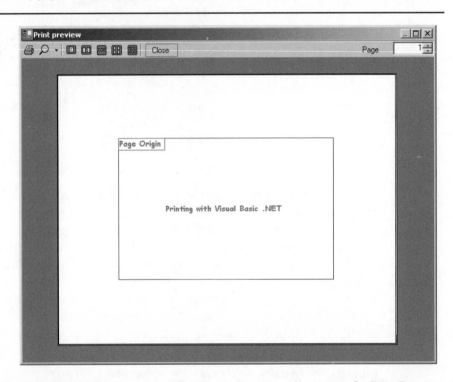

Once you've written the code to generate the printout, you can direct it to the PrintPreview control. You don't have to write any additional code; just place an instance of the control on the form and set its Document property to the PrintDocument control on the form. Then show the control instead of calling the Print method of the PrintDocument object:

```
PrintPreviewDialog1.Document = PrintDocument1
PrintPreviewDialog1.ShowDialog
```

After the execution of these two lines, the PrintDocument object takes over. It fires the PrintPage event as usual, but it sends its output to the preview dialog box and not to the printer. The dialog box contains a Print button, which the user can click to send the document being previewed to the printer. The exact same code that generated the preview document will also print the same document on the printer. The PrintPreview control will save you a lot of paper and toner while you're testing your printing code because you don't have to actually print every page to see what it looks like. Because the same code generates both the preview and the actual printed document, and because the Print Preview option adds a professional touch to your application, there's no reason why you shouldn't add this feature to your projects. In the examples in this section, we'll use this control to display the printouts on the screen.

The first example of printing code, shown in Listing 9.22, prints three simple pages to the printer. To redirect the output of the program to the PrintPreview control, replace the statement that calls the `PrintDocument1.Print` method in the button's Click event handler with the following statements:

```
PrintPreviewDialog1.Document = PrintDocument1
PrintPreviewDialog1.ShowDialog
```

If you run the project, this time you'll be able to preview the document on your monitor. If you're satisfied with its appearance, you can click the Print button to send the document to the printer. To avoid runtime errors as a result of a printer malfunction, you can use the following exception handler:

```
Try
    PrintPreviewDialog1.Document = PrintDocument1
    PrintPreviewDialog1.ShowDialog
Catch exc As Exception
    MsgBox "The printing operation failed" & vbCrLf & exc.Message
End Try
```

### The PrintPreview Control

The PrintPreview control is the preview pane of the Print Preview dialog box. The control has no buttons, and you must provide your own interface to allow users to navigate through the document's pages or change the current magnification. There are no compelling reasons to use this control, but it's an alternative to the PrintPreviewDialog control. Once you've understood how the PrintPreviewDialog control works, you will find it easy to program the control and preview the documents on a form of your own.

## Printer and Page Properties

A basic operation in any printing application is the retrieval of the settings of the current printer and the settings of the page as specified by the user on the Page Setup dialog box. The properties of these two items are reported to your application through the PrinterSettings and the PageSettings objects respectively. The PageSettings object is a property of the PrintPage-EventArgs class, and you can access it through the e argument of the PrintPage event handler. The DefaultPageSettings property of the PrintDocument object is a PageSettings object, which exposes the current page's settings. The PrinterSettings object is a property of the Print-Document object, as well as a property of the PageSetupDialog and PrintDialog controls. Finally, one of the properties exposed by the PageSettings object is the PrinterSettings object. The PrinterSettings and PageSettings objects provide all the information you may need about the selected printer and the current page through the properties listed in Tables 9.2 and 9.3.

**TABLE 9.2:** The Properties of the PageSettings Object

| Property | Description |
| --- | --- |
| Bounds | Returns the bounds of the page (`Bounds.Width` and `Bounds.Height`). If the current orientation is landscape, the width is larger than the height. |
| Color | Returns (or sets) a True/False value indicating whether the current page should be printed in color. On a monochrome printer, this property is always False. |
| Landscape | Indicates whether the page is printed in landscape or portrait orientation (this property is a Boolean value). |
| Margins | Returns (or sets) the margins for the current page (`Margins.Left`, `Margins.Right`, `Margins.Bottom`, and `Margins.Top`). |
| PaperSize | Returns (or sets) the size of the current page (`PaperSize.Width` and `PaperSize.Height`). |
| PaperSource | Returns (or sets) the page's paper tray. |
| PrinterResolution | Returns the printer's resolution for the current page. |
| PrinterSettings | Returns (or sets) the printer settings associated with the page. |

**TABLE 9.3:** The Members of the PrinterSettings Object

| Property | Description |
| --- | --- |
| InstalledPrinters | Retrieves the names of all printers installed on the computer. The same printer names also appear in the Print dialog box, where the user can select any one of them. |
| CanDuplex | Returns a True/False value indicating whether the printer supports double-sided printing. A read-only property. |
| Collate | Returns a True/False value indicating whether the printout should be collated or not. A read-only property. |
| Copies | Returns the requested number of copies of the printout. |
| DefaultPageSettings | The PageSettings object that returns, or sets, the default page settings for the current printer. |

*Continued on next page*

**TABLE 9.3 CONTINUED:** The Members of the PrinterSettings Object

| Property | Description |
|---|---|
| Duplex | Returns, or sets, the current setting for double-sided printing. |
| FromPage, ToPage | Returns the printout's starting and ending pages, as specified by the user on the Print dialog box. |
| IsDefaultPrinter | Returns a True/False value indicating whether the selected printer (the one identified by the PrinterName property) is the default printer. Note that selecting a printer other than the default one on the Print dialog box doesn't change the default printer. |
| IsPlotter | Returns a True/False value indicating whether the printer is a plotter. |
| IsValid | Returns a True/False value indicating whether the PrinterName corresponds to a valid printer. |
| LandscapeAngle | Returns an angle, in degrees, by which the portrait orientation must be rotated to produce the landscape orientation. |
| MaximumCopies | Returns the maximum number of copies that the printer allows you to print at a time. |
| MaximumPage | Returns, or sets, the largest value that the FromPage and ToPage properties can have. |
| MinimumPage | Returns, or sets, the smallest value that the FromPage and ToPage properties can have. |
| PaperSizes | Returns all the paper sizes that are supported by this printer. |
| PaperSources | Returns all the paper source trays on the selected printer. |
| PrinterName | Returns, or sets, the name of the printer to use. |
| PrinterResolutions | Returns all the resolutions that are supported by this printer. |
| PrintToFile | Indicates whether the printout will be sent to a file instead of a printer. |
| PrintRange | Returns, or sets, the numbers of the pages to be printed, as specified by the user. When you set this property, the value becomes the default setting when the Print dialog box is opened. |
| SupportsColor | Returns a True/False value indicating whether this printer supports color printing. |

You can also change the current printer by setting the PrinterName property of the PrinterSettings property with either of the following statements:

```
PrintDocument1.PrinterSettings.PrinterName = "HPLaser"
PrintDocument1.PrinterSettings.PrinterName = _
        PrintDocument1.PrinterSettings.InstalledPrinters(1)
```

Another property that needs some additional explanation is the PrinterResolution object. The PrinterResolution object provides the Kind property, which returns, or sets, the current resolution of the printer. Its value is one of the PrinterResolutionKind enumeration's members: Custom, Draft, High, Low, and Medium. To find out the exact horizontal and vertical resolutions, read the X and Y properties of the PrinterResolution object. When you set the PrinterResolution.Kind property to Custom, you must specify the X and Y properties.

Note that the PrinterResolution object is a property of the PageSettings object. The Printer-Settings object exposes a similarly named object, the PrinterResolutions property. This property is a collection that returns all resolution kinds, which are the members of the Printer-ResolutionKind enumeration.

The PrinterSettings object exposes a method, too: the CreateMeasurementGraphics method, which returns information about the printer. You can use this method to retrieve information about the printer in the `PrintDocument.Print` event handler.

### Page Geometry

Printing on a page is similar to generating graphics on your screen. Like the drawing surface on the monitor (the client area), the page on which you're printing has a fixed size and resolution. The most challenging aspect of printing is the calculation of the coordinates where each graphic element will appear. In business applications, the most common elements are strings (rendered in various fonts, styles, and sizes), lines, and rectangles (used as borders for tabular data). We print one element at a time, calculate the space it takes on the page, and then print the element next to or below it.

The printable area is determined by the size of the paper you're using and the margins specified by the user through the PageSetup dialog box. You can access the current page's margins through the Margins property of the `PrintDocument1.DefaultPageSettings` object. This object exposes the Left, Right, Top, and Bottom properties, which are expressed in the current coordinate system. The default coordinate system's unit is 1/100th of an inch and we believe that this coordinate system is quite adequate for most applications, especially for printing text and simple shapes. Because there are 100 units in an inch, all the variables that represent coordinates and sizes can be declared as Integer. You can also declare them as Single, but a fraction of a hundredth of an inch isn't going to make any difference in your printouts.

Another property exposed by the DefaultSettings object is the PageSize property, which in turn exposes the Width and Height properties. The width and height of the page are given by the following expressions:

```
PrintDocument1.DefaultPageSettings.PaperSize.Width
PrintDocument1.DefaultPageSettings.PaperSize.Height
```

The top of the page is at coordinates (0, 0), which corresponds to the top-left corner of the page. We never actually print at this corner; many printers can't print near the edges of the paper, and they assume that a reasonable margin is in effect. The coordinates of the top-left corner of the printable area of the page are given by the following expressions:

```
PrintDocument1.DefaultPageSettings.Margins.Top
PrintDocument1.DefaultPageSettings.Margins.Left
```

The dimensions of the printable area of the page are as follows:

```
PrintDocument1.DefaultPageSettings.PaperSize.Width - _
    PrintDocument1.DefaultPageSettings.Margins.Left - _
    PrintDocument1.DefaultPageSettings.Margins.Right

PrintDocument1.DefaultPageSettings.PaperSize.Height - _
    PrintDocument1.DefaultPageSettings.Margins.Top - _
    PrintDocument1.DefaultPageSettings.Margins.Bottom
```

This information is all you need to start printing on the page. In the following section, we'll build a project that demonstrates the basic printing operations.

## The Printing Project

To demonstrate the topics discussed in the previous sections, we'll build the Printing project, whose main form is shown in Figure 9.11. The Printing Demo button prints a rectangle that encloses the printable area of the page and a string, which is centered on the page. This printout is shown in preview mode in Figure 9.10. The code takes into consideration the orientation of the page as well as the margins, and you can copy parts of the code and reuse them in your applications. The Print Text button prints the text on the TextBox control, taking into consideration the current page settings. Both buttons use the PrintPreview control to display a preview of the printout. You can send the output to the printer by clicking the Print button on the Preview control. To completely bypass the PrintPreview dialog box and send the output directly to the printer, comment out the statement that calls the control's ShowDialog method and call the Print method of the PrintDocument object.

**FIGURE 9.11:**

The Printing project's main form

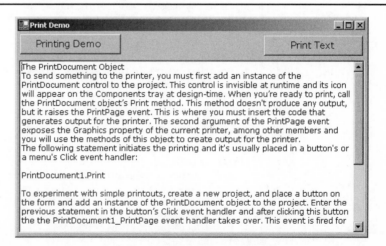

To generate the printout shown in Figure 9.10, the statements in Listing 9.23 are executed from within the Printing Demo button's Click event handler.

---

**Listing 9.23**     **The Printing Demo Button's Code**

```
Private Sub Button1_Click(ByVal sender As System.Object, _
                         ByVal e As System.EventArgs) _
                         Handles Button1.Click
    PrintPreviewDialog1.Document = PrintDocument1
    PageSetupDialog1.PageSettings = PrintDocument1.DefaultPageSettings
    If PageSetupDialog1.ShowDialog() = DialogResult.OK Then
        PrintDocument1.DefaultPageSettings = _
                        PageSetupDialog1.PageSettings
        PrintPreviewDialog1.ShowDialog()
    End If
End Sub
```

---

The code sets the PrintPreview control's Document property to the PrintDocument1 control so that any output you generate from within the PrintPage event handler will be directed to the preview window and not to the printer. Then it calls the Page Setup dialog box, where the user can select a paper size and set the orientation and the margins of the printed page. The new settings are stored in the DefaultPageSettings property of the PrintDocument1 object, from where they can be later retrieved and used by the code that creates the printout. The last statement displays the Print Preview dialog box. As soon as this dialog box is invoked, the PrintPage event of the PrintDocument1 control is fired. The code behind this event is shown in Listing 9.24.

---

**Listing 9.24**     **The PrintDemo Button's Code**

```
Private Sub PrintDocument1_PrintPage(ByVal sender As Object, _
            ByVal e As System.Drawing.Printing.PrintPageEventArgs) _
            Handles PrintDocument1.PrintPage
    Dim PageWidth As Integer = _
                PrintDocument1.DefaultPageSettings.PaperSize.Width
    Dim PageHeight As Integer = _
                PrintDocument1.DefaultPageSettings.PaperSize.Height
    If PrintDocument1.DefaultPageSettings.Landscape Then
        Dim tmp As Integer
        tmp = PageWidth
        PageWidth = PageHeight
        PageHeight = tmp
    End If
    Dim LeftMargin As Integer = _
                PrintDocument1.DefaultPageSettings.Margins.Left
    Dim RightMargin As Integer = _
                PrintDocument1.DefaultPageSettings.Margins.Right
    Dim TopMargin As Integer = _
                PrintDocument1.DefaultPageSettings.Margins.Top
    Dim BottomMargin As Integer = _
                PrintDocument1.DefaultPageSettings.Margins.Bottom
    Dim PrintPageWidth As Integer = _
                PageWidth - LeftMargin - RightMargin
    Dim PrintPageHeight As Integer = _
                PageHeight - TopMargin - BottomMargin
```

```
        Dim R As New Rectangle( _
                    LeftMargin, TopMargin, PrintPageWidth, PrintPageHeight)
        Dim PrintPen As New Pen(Color.Blue, 2)
        e.Graphics.DrawRectangle(PrintPen, R)
        Dim PrintFont As New Font("Comic Sans MS", 18, FontStyle.Bold)
        Dim PrintBrush As New SolidBrush(Color.Red)
        e.Graphics.DrawString("Page Origin", PrintFont, PrintBrush, _
                            LeftMargin, TopMargin)
        Dim StrSizeF As SizeF = _
                    e.Graphics.MeasureString("Page Origin", PrintFont)
        e.Graphics.DrawRectangle(Pens.Green, _
                    New Rectangle(LeftMargin, TopMargin, _
                                StrSizeF.Width, StrSizeF.Height))
        Dim pString As String = "Printing with Visual Basic .NET"
        Dim cstrSizeF As SizeF = e.Graphics.MeasureString(pString, _
                                PrintFont)
        Dim cX As Integer = LeftMargin + _
                        CInt((PrintPageWidth - cstrSizeF.Width) / 2)
        Dim cY As Integer = TopMargin + _
                        CInt((PrintPageHeight - cstrSizeF.Height) / 2)
        e.Graphics.DrawString(pString, PrintFont, PrintBrush, cX, cY)
    End Sub
```

This event handler starts by retrieving the width and height of the printable area of the page and stores them in the PageWidth and PageHeight variables. If the user selected the landscape orientation on the Page Setup dialog box, these two variables' values are swapped.

In Listing 9.24, we've used the PaperSize property to determine the dimensions of the printable area. The paper's size doesn't change when it's rotated, so we had to swap the width and height in our code. You can also use the Bounds property of the PageSettings object, which returns the correct width and height of the printable area, taking into consideration the current page orientation.

The code continues by extracting the page's margins from the properties of the DefaultPage-Settings object. Then it calculates the printed page's width and height by subtracting the corresponding margins from the page's total width and height.

The four margins are stored in the variables LeftMargin, RightMargin, TopMargin, and BottomMargin. The dimensions of the printable area of the page are stored in the variables PageWidth and PageHeight. All subsequent calculations for positioning the elements of the printout are based on these variables.

The first printing statement draws a rectangle with a pen that leaves a blue trace, 2 units thick. The rectangle encloses the entire printable area of the page. To print the string "Page Origin", the code sets up a Font and a Brush object. The pen draws in red and the Font object represents a bold Comic Sans MS font at 18 points. These two objects are passed as parameters to the DrawString method, along with the string to be printed.

The last two arguments passed to the DrawString method are the coordinates of the first character in the string, and they're set to the coordinates of the upper-left corner of the printable area of the page. The DrawString method prints the string so that the upper-left corner of the rectangle that encloses the string is at the specified coordinates. If you attempt to print a string at the lower-right corner of the page, the entire string will fall just outside the page and no visible output will be produced.

**NOTE**   It is possible to print outside the current margins of the page, even outside the page itself. The PrintDocument object isn't aware of the margins; it's your responsibility to limit the output within the user-specified margins. Even if you set the margins from within your code, you still have to make sure that your code doesn't produce any output outside the printable area of the page. To make sure your code doesn't print outside a specific area, set the Clip property of the Graphics object to the appropriate rectangle.

Then the code prints the string pString at the center of the page. To center the string on the page, the code calculates the width and height of the string, subtracts them from the width and height of the printable area of the page, and splits the difference to either side of the string. The MeasureString method returns the dimensions of a string when rendered on the Graphics object with a specific font. This method doesn't produce any output; it simply returns the dimensions of the rendered string. You can use these dimensions in your code to adjust the location of the string.

### Printing Text

The Print Text button prints the text on the TextBox control and a red rectangle indicating the area of the page within the specified margins, as shown in Figure 9.12. Listing 9.25 shows the code of the button's Click event handler. The code is identical to the code of the Printing Demo button, but it uses a different instance of the PrintDocument control. The PrintPage event, where all the printing code resides, is fired by the PrintDocument control. You can't use the same PrintDocument control for two different printouts. However, you can use the same PrintPreview control for all printouts.

**Listing 9.25**       **The Print Text Button's Code**

```
Private Sub Button2_Click(ByVal sender As System.Object, _
                          ByVal e As System.EventArgs) _
                          Handles Button2.Click
    txt = TextBox1.Text
    PrintPreviewDialog1.Document = PrintDocument2
    PageSetupDialog1.PageSettings = PrintDocument2.DefaultPageSettings
    If PageSetupDialog1.ShowDialog() = DialogResult.OK Then
        PrintDocument2.DefaultPageSettings = _
                                PageSetupDialog1.PageSettings
        PrintPreviewDialog1.ShowDialog()
    End If
End Sub
```

**FIGURE 9.12:**

Printing text in landscape mode with large left and bottom margins

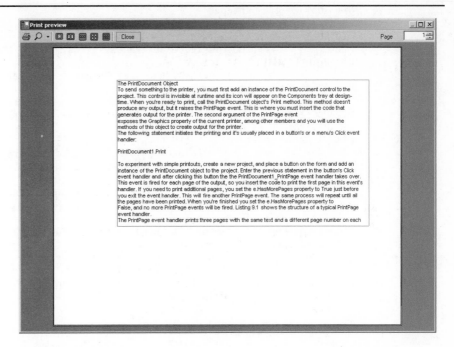

As soon as the PrintPreviewDialog control's ShowDialog method is called, the PrintPage event of the PrintDocument2 control is fired. This event handler's code is shown in Listing 9.26.

**Listing 9.26      Printing Text**

```
Private Sub PrintDocument2_PrintPage(ByVal sender As Object, _
            ByVal e As System.Drawing.Printing.PrintPageEventArgs) _
            Handles PrintDocument2.PrintPage
    Static Pos As Integer
    Dim PageWidth As Integer = _
            PrintDocument2.DefaultPageSettings.PaperSize.Width
    Dim PageHeight As Integer = _
            PrintDocument2.DefaultPageSettings.PaperSize.Height
    If PrintDocument2.DefaultPageSettings.Landscape Then
        Dim tmp As Integer
        tmp = PageWidth
        PageWidth = PageHeight
        PageHeight = tmp
    End If

    Dim LeftMargin As Integer = _
            PrintDocument2.DefaultPageSettings.Margins.Left
    Dim RightMargin As Integer = _
            PrintDocument2.DefaultPageSettings.Margins.Right
```

```
    Dim TopMargin As Integer = _
            PrintDocument2.DefaultPageSettings.Margins.Top
    Dim BottomMargin As Integer = _
            PrintDocument2.DefaultPageSettings.Margins.Bottom
    Dim PrintPageWidth As Integer = _
                    PageWidth - LeftMargin - RightMargin
    Dim PrintPageHeight As Integer = _
                    PageHeight - TopMargin - BottomMargin
    Dim PrintFont As New Font("Arial", 12, FontStyle.Regular)
    Dim PrintBrush As New SolidBrush(Color.Black)
    Dim pR As New RectangleF(LeftMargin, TopMargin, _
                    PrintPageWidth, PrintPageHeight)
    ' The following two statements print a red rectangle around the text
    Dim R As New Rectangle( _
            LeftMargin, TopMargin, PrintPageWidth, PrintPageHeight)
    e.Graphics.DrawRectangle(Pens.Red, R)
    Dim lines, chars As Integer
    Dim fmt As New StringFormat(StringFormatFlags.LineLimit)
    e.Graphics.MeasureString(Mid(txt, Pos + 1), PrintFont, _
                    New SizeF(PrintPageWidth, PrintPageHeight), _
                    fmt, chars, lines)
    e.Graphics.DrawString(Mid(txt, Pos + 1), PrintFont, _
                    PrintBrush, pR, fmt)
    Pos = Pos + chars
    If Pos < txt.Length Then
        e.HasMorePages = True
    Else
        e.HasMorePages = False
        Pos = 0
    End If
End Sub
```

The code starts by retrieving the margins of the page and then it calculates the dimensions of the rectangle where the text must appear. Then it creates a Rectangle object that delimits this area and prints it with a call to the DrawRectangle method. This is the R variable. Then it calls an overloaded form of the MeasureString method, which accepts the chars and lines arguments. The MeasureString method sets these variables to the number of characters and number of lines it can print in the specified rectangle. The code prints as many characters as can fit in the R rectangle and then sets the e.HasMorePages property. If there are more characters to be printed, the pos variable is set to the number of characters printed so far.

Notice that the pos variable is declared as Static so that it will retain its value between successive invocations of the PrintPage event. Every time the PrintPage event is invoked, a number of characters is printed. The exact number of characters is determined by the chars argument of the MeasureString method. After printing chars characters, we add the chars variable value to the pos variable. The next time this event is invoked, we start printing at location pos + 1 in the text.

The technique shown here is the simplest and fastest one for printing text. However, it works only with text that's formatted with a single font. To print formatted text, you should probably look into third-party controls, such as an enhanced TextBox with built-in printing capabilities. As far as the application presented in this section, you can easily add headers, page numbers, and related information near the margins or just outside the margins of the text to make a more functional text printing utility.

You can also use the other members of the Graphics object to generate graphics. The following statement will render the text on the page using an anti-alias technique (anti-aliased text looks much smoother than text rendered with the default method):

```
e.Graphics.TextRenderingHint = Drawing.Text.TextRenderingHint.AntiAlias
```

In Chapter 13, "Building Custom Windows Controls," you'll see how to add a Print command to the ListView control and print tabular.

## Summary

This chapter was an overview of some basic Windows controls and focused on the changes introduced by Visual Studio .NET. Some of the VB6 techniques you may be accustomed to no longer work with VB .NET and we hope the information in this, and the previous, chapter will help you learn the new ways of working with these controls. The printing controls are new to Visual Studio .NET and we explored them in more detail.

The next chapter is about a powerful programming technique that is totally new to VB6 programmers. You'll learn how to write multithreaded applications with Visual Basic .NET.

# CHAPTER 10

# Multithreading

- Creating and Starting Threads

- Building Responsive Interfaces

- Thread Communication

- Thread Synchronization

**T**his is the first time in the 10 years of Visual Basic's existence that you can use your favorite language to build multithreaded applications. It's easy to write a multithreaded application entirely in VB .NET, a feature many programmers were looking forward to. It's very likely that multithreading will also become one of the most abused features of the language, because writing multithreaded applications is inherently difficult and the process of debugging a multi-threaded application is quite a challenge. As simple as setting up and starting a thread may be, the potential for hard-to-fix bugs is enormous. Explore the topic of multithreading and familiarize yourself with the techniques, and once you feel comfortable with it, you may consider adding multiple threads to a real application.

As a developer, you have some idea of what multithreading is. A multithreaded application is capable of executing multiple code segments in parallel, by switching them in and out. No statements are executed in parallel, but the tasks appear to run in parallel because the CPU executes one task's code for a number of milliseconds, then switches to another task, and so on. Because the tasks appear to run in parallel, the application seems to run faster. This is the *perceived speed* of the application. Users see that something is happening and the interface is responsive, even though some computationally intensive tasks are executing at the same time.

This chapter is an introduction to multithreaded applications: the basic techniques and how to avoid the most common problems. With VB6, we had to insert calls the DoEvents function to make an application more responsive. The DoEvents function yields the control of the CPU and any pending events get a chance to be serviced. If your calculations take place in a loop, the application's interface will freeze until the loop is finished. To make sure the interface reacts to user actions, like the click of a Cancel button that aborts the execution of the loop, you can insert a call to the DoEvents method. All VB programmers are familiar with this technique. We're also familiar with the delay introduced by too many functions to this function. The solution was a satisfactory compromise between the responsiveness of the program and its speed.

This is known as cooperative multitasking. Multiple tasks can execute in parallel as long as each task is considerate of the others. One task that takes up all the CPU time can ruin the application. Windows NT (and all versions of Windows 2000 and Windows XP) deploy a different model, known as preemptive multithreading. The operating system no longer relies on the proper coding of the tasks, but it divides the CPU time between the threads. It inter-rupts each task to give another task a chance to execute. It also decides how much time to give to the threads based on their apparent need (how much CPU time they've used so far, how long it has been since they were switched, and so on). Threads that use the CPU more than others take more time. Of course, you can specify the priority at which a thread will be executed, but this is more like a vague request. There are only five possible settings, and the operating system isn't required to give two threads with the same priority the same time. If a thread is idle at any given time, its time-slice will be assigned to another thread and no CPU time will be wasted.

# When to Use Threads

So, the first question we must answer is what types of applications require multithread implementation. An application that goes out to the Internet and downloads files should be implemented as a multithreaded application. It may take several seconds to download a file from the Internet, but most of the time the CPU will be idle, waiting for the web server to respond. Mail applications are always multithreaded. You can read messages, or compose new ones, while the application is downloading or uploading mail. If the application can be broken into independent tasks that can be performed in parallel, you should consider implementing these tasks as separate threads.

Long-running tasks should also be coded as threads so that they will not lock the interface. This is the best reason for using a multithreaded application. As a VB programmer, you have probably not been exposed to multithreaded programming, so you should start with fairly simple multithreaded applications to understand how this technique can help your applications. A complicated application with threads will be a nightmare to debug. Until you understand the nature and implications of multithreaded programming, you shouldn't get carried away. Typical business applications won't benefit a lot from multiple threads.

Threads aren't all that common in business applications. A typical application doesn't execute tasks that take long to execute. Even when it does, users will most likely wait because of the way they use these applications. They're willing to wait for a long task to complete as long as they see an indication of its progress (never make users wonder whether the application is working or got stuck). Multithreaded applications can lead to peculiar bugs, which you can't reproduce and are very hard to fix. Ideally, you should design your multithreaded application very carefully and try to eliminate the sources of errors before you even begin coding. Every time you run a multithreaded application, different tasks may be executed in different order. There's no way to tell the operating system when to interrupt a task and switch in another task. As a result, a bug may surface once in a blue moon, and this is the worst kind of bugs you can run into. We'll have more to say about the common errors in multithreaded applications, but let's start with a review of the mechanics of setting up threads and executing them.

## Creating and Starting a Thread

To run a subroutine in its own thread, you must create a Thread object and then call its Start method. The Thread object's constructor accepts as argument a delegate for the subroutine you want to run as a thread. Let's say the subroutine that will run as a thread is called BusyThread. This is the thread's task subroutine, and it's an ordinary subroutine that performs a specific, well-defined task, just like any other subroutine. It can even call other subroutines or functions in the course of its execution. The difference is that it's running in parallel with the main application. By the way, the main application is also running in a thread, and it's called the main thread. The main thread is the code that handles the user interface and responds to user actions.

The following statements create a Thread object, the *Thrd* variable, which you can use to start the BusyThread subroutine:

```
Dim TStart As New ThreadStart(AddressOf BusyThread)
Dim Thrd As New Thread(TStart)
```

To start the execution of the subroutine, call the `Thrd` object's Start method with a statement like the following:

```
Thrd.Start()
```

You can also specify the delegate in the same line that declares the Thread object. The previous statements can also be written as follows:

```
Dim Thrd As New Thread(AddressOf BusyThread)
Thrd.Start()
```

The previous statements assume that you have imported the Threading namespace. If not, you have to fully qualify the class names. The Thread and ThreadStart classes are members of the `System.Threading` namespace, which you must import to your project to avoid having to fully qualify them (`Threading.Thread` and `Threading.ThreadStart`).

Note that the `BusyThread()` subroutine accepts no arguments. A thread's delegate can't be called with arguments. This seems like a serious drawback, but you will see later in the chapter how you can communicate with a thread. Moreover, the Start method doesn't start the thread instantly. Instead, it notifies the operating system that it must start the thread at its earliest convenience. It's quite likely that a few more statements in the main thread will be executed before the first statement in the thread.

As far as the thread itself is concerned, it's a VB subroutine, but there are a few things you shouldn't do in a thread's code. First, you shouldn't update the visible interface of the main thread. It's possible to update the application's interface, but it's not as simple as setting a control's property as you would do from within the main thread's code. Another trap when coding multithreaded applications is that you must be extra careful when multiple threads access a shared variable (a variable that's not local to the thread and can be accessed by multiple threads). A thread may read a variable's value and take some action based on this value, and before it gets a chance to update the variable, another thread may update the same variable. We'll get there soon, but let's look at the basic members of the Thread object.

### The Threaded MessageBox

This is the simplest multithreaded application you can build. It's as meaningless as the Hello World application, but we like it because it really exposes some interesting, unexpected behavior of multithreaded applications. Start a new project, place a button on its form, and enter the following statements in the button's Click event handler:

```
Private Sub Button1_Click(ByVal sender As System.Object, _
                          ByVal e As System.EventArgs) _
                          Handles Button1.Click
    Dim T As New Thread(AddressOf ShowMessageBox)
    T.Start()
End Sub
```

Then enter the declaration of the ShowMessageBox() subroutine:

```
Private Sub ShowMessageBox()
    MsgBox("I'm a threaded Message Box!")
End Sub
```

Don't forget to import the System.Threading namespace at the beginning of the file. Run the application and click the button. A message box will appear, as expected. This is an unusual message box, however, because it allows you to switch to the application's form. Not only that, you can pop up multiple messages boxes by clicking the button on the form several times. Each time, a new message box will appear, and all message boxes will remain on the screen until you click the OK button to close them.

You can also close the main application's form by clicking its Close button at the upper-right corner. The application won't terminate because some of the threads it spawned are still alive. The main application runs in its own thread, which you've terminated by closing the form. The other threads are still alive, so the application keeps running. Close the message boxes floating on your desktop and the application will terminate.

We think this is an interesting demonstration. First of all, it's really easy to set up and start a thread. The thread's task subroutine need not be any more complicated than a regular subroutine. Starting a thread is as simple as calling the Start method. Once started, the thread runs independently of the main thread, and you can start many threads from within your application. Finally, the application won't terminate until all the threads it initiated have been terminated.

If you interrupt the application by clicking the Break All button, you can see the running threads in the Threads tab of the Output window. Each thread has a unique ID and a name—we haven't assigned names to our threads, but you will soon learn how to name each thread. You may have also noticed that the message displayed on the message box is hard-coded in the line that calls the MsgBox() function. You can't pass an argument to the thread subroutine, but you will see later in this chapter how you can work around this limitation. In the following section we'll discuss the properties of the Thread class.

### Priority Property

This property determines how the operating system will prioritize the thread. You can set it to one of the members of the ThreadPriority enumeration: Lowest, BelowNormal, Normal, Above-Normal, and Highest. This is a general setting, and you don't know how much time the operating system will actually give to your thread or how frequently it will be switching it in and out because it may have to balance a number of threads at once. In general, you should avoid running threads with high priorities. Your main application will become almost unresponsive to user actions. You will be able to experiment with the settings of this property and see how it affects the main application in the sample application you'll build in the section "The Simple-Thread Project" later in this chapter.

### Name Property

Each thread can have a name, and you should always name your threads to ease your debugging efforts. To find out which thread is actually running, you can use the following statement:

```
Thread.CurrentThread.Name
```

### ThreadState Property

Each thread can be in one of several states, and this property returns the state of the specified thread at the time. The ThreadState property can have one of the values shown in Table 10.1.

**TABLE 10.1:** The Members of the ThreadState Enumeration

| Member | Description |
| --- | --- |
| Aborted | The thread has been aborted (terminated). |
| AbortRequested | The thread's abortion has been requested (with a call to the Abort method from within another thread), but the operating system hasn't aborted the thread yet. |
| Background | The thread is running in background mode (as opposed to a foreground thread). This member is a Boolean value. |
| Running | The thread is running. |
| Stopped | The thread has been stopped. |
| StopRequested | A request to stop the thread has been issued. |
| Suspended | The thread has been suspended. |
| SuspendRequested | A request to suspend the thread has been issued. |
| Unstarted | The thread hasn't been started yet. |
| WaitSleepJoin | The thread is blocked by a call to the Wait, Sleep, or Join method from within another thread. |

The ThreadState property is read-only; you can't put a thread into a specific state by setting this property. The operating system changes the state of a thread, and you can do so from within your code by calling the appropriate method, as discussed next.

A thread runs either in the background or in the foreground. The difference between the two is that background threads do not prevent the main application's thread from terminating. Once all foreground threads of the application have terminated, the Common Language Runtime ends the application by invoking the Abort on any background threads that are still alive.

### IsAlive Property

The IsAlive property returns True if the thread to which it's applied is active. The IsAlive property will return True even if the thread is currently inactive (it's sleeping or waiting to be switched in). It will return False if the thread's state is Unstarted, Stopped, or Aborted.

### IsBackground

The IsBackground property is a Boolean value that indicates whether a thread is a background thread. You can also set this property to make a thread run as a background thread. Background threads are like foreground threads, but they do not prevent a process from terminating. The CLR will not terminate an application if there are foreground threads. Normally, you call the Abort method on all running threads before you terminate the application.

### Start Method

Calling this method notifies the operating system that it should start the execution of the thread (allocate CPU time slices to the thread). The thread's execution doesn't start immediately when you call the Start method—just as the thread doesn't stop as soon as you call the Abort method. The Start method issues a request to start the thread, but there's no way to know for sure when exactly the thread will start.

### Abort Method

The Abort method begins the process of terminating the thread. Similar to calling the Start method, calling the Abort method doesn't immediately terminate the thread. Actually, according to the documentation, "calling this method usually terminates the thread." In nearly all cases, the Abort method will terminate the thread, except for rare occasions. One such occasion is when you call the MsgBox() function from within a thread. Calling this thread's Abort method won't terminate the thread.

If you want to be sure that the thread has terminated, examine the thread's ThreadState property or call the Join method to wait until the thread has actually terminated before you continue (for more information, see "The SimpleThread Project" later in this chapter).

### Join Method

This method blocks the current thread until the specified thread terminates or a specified time interval has elapsed. The Join method can be called without an argument, in which case it waits for the specified thread to terminate, or with an argument that determines how long to wait for the thread to terminate. The interval can be expressed as a number of milliseconds or a TimeSpan object. If you pass a time-out interval to the Join method, it will return True if the thread finishes in the specified time interval. Let's say the current thread needs the results of another thread, the *T1* thread. You can instruct the current thread to wait for the *T1* thread to complete its calculations before you use any of the results in the current thread. The following statements outline a subroutine that does that:

```
Sub CalcThread()
    ' perform other tasks
    T1.Join()
    '   use the results returned by the T1 thread
End Sub
```

The *T1* thread has been started elsewhere in the main application, but it's possible to start it from within the CalcThread() subroutine, then execute other statements, and finally, wait for the thread to return its results. As mentioned already, a thread can't be called with arguments and doesn't return a value, but you will see shortly how you can pass values from one thread to another.

If you call the Abort method and you want to be sure that the thread has terminated before you continue, call the Join method as shown here:

```
If T.ThreadState = ThreadState.Running Then
    T.Abort()
    T.Join()
End If
```

First make sure that the thread is running, because calling the Abort method on a thread that's not running will cause an exception to be thrown. After calling the Abort method, we call the Join method to block the current thread until the T thread has terminated. You can use more elaborate code to make sure that the program doesn't freeze should the thread not terminate.

### Sleep

The Sleep method blocks the thread for a specified interval. The interval for which the thread will be blocked is passed to the method as argument. You can specify the interval either as a number of milliseconds (an integer value) or as a TimeSpan. If you call the Sleep method with a zero argument, the thread will be suspended indefinitely and you must call the Interrupt method to wake up the task. If thread A needs some values that must be calculated by thread B, you can put thread A to sleep until thread B finishes its execution.

Because all applications in Visual Studio .NET are tasks, you can use the Sleep method to pause your application's main thread for a number of milliseconds. The thread in which the application runs is given by the expression `Threading.Thread`, and you can pause it for 3 seconds with the following statement:

```
Threading.Thread.Sleep(3000)
```

### Suspend

The Suspend method pauses the execution of a thread. You don't know when exactly the thread will be paused. Between the time you call the Suspend method on a thread and the time the thread is actually paused, the thread's state is SuspendRequested. To restart a suspended thread, call its Resume method.

### Resume

The Resume method resumes the execution of a thread that has been suspended. As with the Suspend method, the thread will not resume its execution as soon as you call the Resume method.

## The SimpleThread Project

Let's put together the information presented so far to demonstrate the basics of a multi-threaded application. The project uses a thread to perform calculations in the background while the main thread constantly updates a Label control by printing the current time. You can pause and restart the thread, request its state, and change its priority. Figure 10.1 shows the application's form. Click the Start Thread button to start the thread. The main thread will start the thread and then it will enter a loop, which updates the Label control with the current time. The code prints milliseconds, too, so that you can see that the main thread takes its share of the CPU time. You will also notice short breaks in the execution of the main thread (a second or two will pass and the Label won't be updated).

**FIGURE 10.1:**

The SimpleThread project's main form

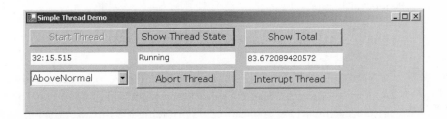

Enter the following declaration in the Code window, outside any procedure:

```
Dim Thrd As Thread
```

The *Thrd* variable will be accessed from within multiple event handlers, so it's declared at the form's level. In the "Start Thread" button's code, enter the following statements:

```
Private Sub bttnStart_Click(ByVal sender As System.Object, _
                            ByVal e As System.EventArgs) _
                            Handles bttnStart.Click
    Dim TStart As New ThreadStart(AddressOf BusyThread)
    Thrd = New Thread(TStart)
    Thrd.Priority = _
            CType(ComboBox1.SelectedItem, ThreadPriority)
    Thrd.Start()
    bttnStart.Enabled = False
    bttnInterrupt.Enabled = True
    bttnAbort.Enabled = True
    While True
        lblTime.Text = Now.TimeOfDay.ToString
        Me.Refresh()
    End While
End Sub
```

The first group of statements creates a new Thread object, in which the BusyThread() subroutine will execute. Then the thread's priority is set and the thread is started. The following loop displays constantly the current time on the *lblTime* Label control. The loop would normally lock up the interface; that's why we've inserted a call to the form's Refresh method. The thread will execute regardless of whether you refresh the form or not, but the interface will not be updated without it. You can also use the DoEvents method in the place of the Refresh method.

The thread's subroutine is quite trivial. It keeps generating random numbers and adding them to a variable, whose value you can display by clicking the Show Total button. Here's the BusyThread subroutine:

```
Sub BusyThread()
    Dim rnd As New System.Random()
    Dim rndValue As Double
    While True
        rndValue = rnd.NextDouble
        total = total + rndValue
    End While
End Sub
```

Notice that the loop in the subroutine would have locked your interface if it were executing in the main thread. Because it's executing in a thread, however, it doesn't seem to affect the responsiveness of the application. Try running the thread at the highest priority and you will see that is still doesn't block the interface. If you switch to the Task Manager, you will see that the application uses 97 percent of the CPU time, yet both processes are running nicely in parallel.

You can display the thread's state at any time by clicking the Show Thread State button. The code in this button's Click event handler displays a string, not a numeric value:

```
Private Sub bttnState_Click(ByVal sender As System.Object,_
                            ByVal e As System.EventArgs) _
                            Handles bttnState.Click
    lblState.Text = Thrd.ThreadState.ToString("G")
End Sub
```

You can also interrupt or abort the execution of the thread by clicking the appropriate button on the form. The code behind these two buttons is shown next:

```
Private Sub bttnInterrupt_Click(_
                ByVal sender As System.Object, _
                ByVal e As System.EventArgs) _
                Handles bttnInterrupt.Click
    If bttnInterrupt.Text = "Interrupt Thread" Then
        Thrd.Suspend()
        bttnInterrupt.Text = "Resume Thread"
    Else
        Thrd.Resume()
        bttnInterrupt.Text = "Interrupt Thread"
    End If
    lblState.Text = Thrd.ThreadState.ToString("G")
End Sub

Private Sub bttnAbort_Click( _
                ByVal sender As System.Object, _
                ByVal e As System.EventArgs) _
                Handles bttnAbort.Click
    If Thrd.IsAlive Then
        Thrd.Abort()
        Thrd.Join()
        bttnAbort.Enabled = False
        bttnInterrupt.Enabled = False
        bttnStart.Enabled = True
    End If
End Sub
```

# Building Responsive Interfaces

The main reason for writing multithreaded applications, at least nonspecialized applications, is to create applications that remain responsive even when they execute computationally intensive procedures—which is basically what we did in our last example. Let's say you've started a process that may take from several seconds to minutes to complete. You should make sure that while the task is executing, a Cancel button appears, which users can click to terminate the calculations. Implementing a responsive Cancel button in VB6 applications was quite a challenge. We had to insert calls to the DoEvents function in the code that performed the calculations to give the operating system a chance to process any pending events. And as you may recall, this was a trade-off between responsiveness and overall speed—too many calls to the DoEvents functions made the interface more responsive, but they also slowed down the application.

With VB .NET, you can code the calculations in a subroutine and start it as a thread. The main thread, which controls the application's visible interface, is running at the highest priority, and it always process its events timely. The thread may run at a lower priority. You can safely set the thread's priority below normal, because as long as users don't interact with the main thread, the spawned thread gets most of the CPU time.

To demonstrate the most basic, and simplest, use of multithreaded applications with VB .NET, we'll build an application that counts the files and folders on a drive. This process takes a while, and we'll implement it as a thread to keep the main thread responsive. The user can cancel the counting at any time by clicking the Cancel button. Figure 10.2 shows the application's main form.

**FIGURE 10.2:**
The ThreadDemo project

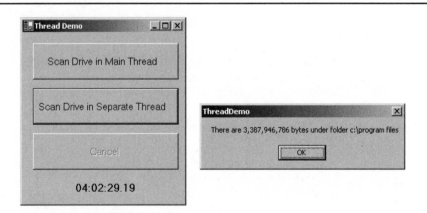

The project you'll build in this section is not included on the website. The ThreadDemo project on the website is an improved version of the project, which is discussed in detail in the following section.

Let's start with the nonthreaded version of the project. The Click event handler of the top button calls the ScanFiles() and then ScanFolder() functions to scan the files in the current folder and the files in the subfolders of the current folder. The ScanFolder() iterates through the subfolders of the parent folder recursively until it finds a folder without subfolders.

```
Private Sub bttnMain_Click(ByVal sender As System.Object,_
                        ByVal e As System.EventArgs) _
                        Handles bttnMain.Click
    Dim startingFolder As String = "c:\program files"
    Dim TSize As Long
    ScanFolder("")
    TSize = ScanFiles(startingFolder) + _
                ScanFolder(startingFolder)
    MsgBox("There are " & TSize.ToString("#,###") & _
            " bytes under folder " & startingFolder)
End Sub
```

The code calls the ScanFiles() function to retrieve the total size of the files in the initial path (*startingFolder*) and the ScanFolder() function to retrieve the total size of the files in the subfolders of the initial folder. As you can guess, the ScanFolder() function does all the work and is responsible for the delay.

The call to the ScanFolder() function with a zero length string simply resets the value of a static variable, as you will see shortly. The ScanFolder() function is recursive: after scanning the files in the folder passed as argument, it calls itself with the name of each subfolder under the current folder as argument. The process is repeated for each folder that has subfolders, at any depth. Listings 10.1 and 10.2 show the code of the ScanFolder() and ScanFiles() functions.

**Listing 10.1      The *ScanFolder()* Function**

```
Function ScanFolder(ByVal folderSpec As String) As Long
    Static TotalSize As Long
    If folderSpec = "" Then
        TotalSize = 0
        Return(0)
    End If
    Dim thisFolder As String
    Dim allFolders() As String
    allFolders = _
            System.IO.Directory.GetDirectories(folderSpec)
    For Each thisFolder In allFolders
        TotalSize += ScanFiles(thisFolder)
        folderSpec = thisFolder
        ScanFolder(folderSpec)
    Next
    Return (TotalSize)
End Function
```

---

**Listing 10.2**        **The *ScanFiles()* Function**

```
Function ScanFiles(ByVal folder As String) As Long
    Dim Total As Long
    Dim files() As String
    Dim file As String
    files = System.IO.Directory.GetFiles(folder)
    For Each file In files
        Dim FI As New System.IO.FileInfo(file)
        Total = Total + FI.Length
    Next
    Return (Total)
End Function
```

---

If you run the application, you'll see that it takes a substantial number of seconds to scan a large folder like C:\Program Files. While the code is executing, the Label control with the current time isn't updated. To display the time on a Label control, add a Timer control to the form, set its Interval property to 100 (milliseconds), and enter the following statement in its Tick event handler:

```
Private Sub Timer1_Tick(ByVal sender As System.Object, _
                        ByVal e As System.EventArgs) _
                        Handles Timer1.Tick
    Label1.Text = Format(Now(), "HH:MM:ss.ff")
End Sub
```

Let's make the application more responsive by executing the ScanFolder() function in a separate thread. First, create a subroutine to run as a separate thread. The StartCounting() subroutine is shown next:

```
Public Sub StartCounting()
    Dim startingFolder As String = "c:\program files"
    Dim TotSize As Long
    ScanFolder("")
    TotSize = ScanFiles(startingFolder) + _
              ScanFolder(startingFolder)
    MsgBox(TotSize)
End Sub
```

This subroutine calls the ScanFiles() and ScanFolders() functions as before. All you have to do now is create a new thread and run the StartCounting subroutine in this thread. Create a Thread variable at the form's level with the following statement:

```
Dim TSThread As Threading.Thread
```

Then insert the following statements in the Scan Drive in Separate Thread button's Click event handler to start the thread:

```
Private Sub bttnThread_Click(ByVal sender As System.Object,_
                             ByVal e As System.EventArgs) _
                             Handles bttnThread.Click
    TSThread = New Threading.Thread(AddressOf StartCounting)
    TSThread.Start()
End Sub
```

If you run the application, you will see a message box after a number of seconds (depending on how large the folder you're scanning is) with the total size of all files in the specified folder. The message box is initiated from within the StartCounting() subroutine, and this is a serious drawback of the application. Normally, we want to pass the results of the thread to the main thread of the application.

Another drawback of this project is that the main thread doesn't even know when the thread is done. The thread should be able to notify the main thread that it's done, at which point the main thread's code can read the values generated by the thread. In the following section, you'll see how to overcome these drawbacks: namely, how to exchange data with a thread and how threads can raise events to notify the thread that started them that they have finished their calculations.

## Passing Data between Threads

One of the shortcomings of the mechanism for starting threads is that the subroutine that implements the thread doesn't accept any arguments. More often than not, threads need to communicate with the main thread. To enable threads to communicate with one another, we create a class that exposes the values we want to exchange with the thread as properties and the task subroutines as methods. Let's say we want to pass a single argument, inArg, to the thread and accept two results back, outArg1 and outArg2. First create a class, let's call it TClass, and then implement these properties as public variables:

```
Class TClass
    Public inArg As String
    Public outArg1 As Long
    Public outArg2 As Long
```

The thread will be implemented as a subroutine in the same class, like this:

```
    Public Sub StartThread()
    '   insert the thread's code here
    '   read the value of inArg property
    '   set the values of the outArg1 and outArg2 properties
    End Sub
End Class
```

To start the thread, you must create an instance of the class, set the `inArg` property, and then create a Thread object passing the address of the `StartThread()` subroutine as argument. Then call the newly created thread's Start method:

```
Dim TS As New TClass
Dim TSThread As Threading.Thread
TS = New Threading.Thread(AddressOf TS.StartThread)
TS.inArg = "string value"
TS.Start()
```

So far you've managed to start the thread. You also need a way to read the results when they become available. To do so, you must raise an event from within the `StartThread()` subroutine, but not before you set the values of the return variables (`outArg1` and `outArg2`). The outline of the `StartThread()` subroutine is shown next (we're showing the entire TClass class):

```
Class TClass
    Public inArg As String
    Public outArg1 As Long
    Public outArg2 As Long

    Public Event Done()
    Public Sub StartThread()
        '  insert the thread's code here
        outArg1 = 9999999
        outArg2 = 1000000
        RaiseEvent Done()
    End Sub
End Class
```

In the Done event's handler, you can access the values of `outArg1` and `outArg2` as properties of the TS class:

```
Console.WriteLine(TS.outArg1.ToString)
Console.WriteLine(TS.outArg2.ToString)
```

Let's revise the project of the preceding section so that it notifies the main thread when it's done counting the files and the result is displayed on a control in the main thread.

## The Revised ThreadDemo Project

The TheadDemo project you will find on the website uses a class to allow the main thread to exchange information with the thread that counts the files. In this version of the application, we want to count the total number of files as well as the total number of folders under the initial path. The TotalSize class, shown in Listing 10.3, implements a thread with the task subroutine, auxiliary routines, the event to notify the main thread that the calculations have completed, and the variables we need to pass information to the thread (the path of the folder to be scanned) and retrieve the values returned by the thread (the number of the files under the specified folder and their total size).

The properties are declared as public variables and the task procedure is the `StartCounting()` subroutine. This subroutine is very short, because all the work is done by the `ScanFiles()` and `ScanFolder()` methods. `ScanFiles()` iterates through all the files in the folder specified by its argument, and `ScanFolder()` scans the subfolders of the folder specified by its argument recursively and calls the `ScanFiles()` method for each subfolder. Notice that these are not subroutines, like the ones we created in the previous section. They're quite similar, but this time they're implemented as methods of the class.

**Listing 10.3        The TotalSize Class**

```
Class TotalSize
    Public folderSpec As String
    Public Size As Long
    Public Count As Long
    Private TStart, TEnd As DateTime
    Public Event Done()

    Sub StartCounting()
        TStart = Now
        Size = 0
        Count = 0
        Size = ScanFiles(folderSpec) + _
                    ScanFolder(folderSpec)
        TEnd = Now
        Console.WriteLine(TEnd.Subtract(TStart))
        RaiseEvent Done()
    End Sub

    Function ScanFolder(ByVal folderSpec As String) As Long
        Static TotalSize As Long
        Dim thisFolder As String
        Dim allFolders() As String
        allFolders = _
              System.IO.Directory.GetDirectories(folderSpec)
        For Each thisFolder In allFolders
            TotalSize += ScanFiles(thisFolder)
            folderSpec = thisFolder
            ScanFolder(folderSpec)
        Next
        Size = TotalSize
        Return (TotalSize)
    End Function

    Function ScanFiles(ByVal folder As String) As Long
        Dim Total As Long
        Dim files() As String
        Dim file As String
        files = System.IO.Directory.GetFiles(folder)
```

```
        For Each file In files
            Dim FI As New System.IO.FileInfo(file)
            Total = Total + FI.Length
        Next
        Count = Count + files.Length
        Return (Total)
    End Function
End Class
```

To count the files in a folder by running the StartCounting() subroutine in a separate thread, insert the statements in Listing 10.4 in the Click event handler of the Scan Drive in Separate Thread button.

**Listing 10.4    Running the StartCounting Subroutine in a Thread**

```
Private Sub bttnThreaded_Click( _
                ByVal sender As System.Object, _
                ByVal e As System.EventArgs) _
                Handles bttnThreaded.Click
    TS = New TotalSize()
    TSThread = New Threading.Thread(AddressOf _
                    TS.StartCounting)
    TS.folderSpec = "c:\program files"
    TSThread.Start()
    bttnCancel.Enabled = True
End Sub
```

If you don't want to wait for the thread to complete the counting, you can interrupt it by clicking the Cancel button, which calls the Thread object's Abort method. The main thread calls the Abort method and then it's blocked by the call to the Join method, to make sure that the thread has terminated. Listing 10.5 shows the Cancel button's Click event handler.

**Listing 10.5    Terminating the Current Thread**

```
Private Sub bttnCancel_Click(ByVal sender As System.Object,_
                        ByVal e As System.EventArgs) _
                        Handles bttnCancel.Click
    TSThread.Abort()
    TSThread.Join()
    bttnCancel.Enabled = False
    MsgBox("Thread interrupted after counting " & _
                TS.Size.ToString & " bytes in " & _
                TS.Count.ToString & " files")
End Sub
```

The *TSThread* variable must be declared outside any procedure so that it can be accessed from within the Cancel button's event handler. The *TS* variable, which represents an instance of the TotalSize class, must also be able to handle the Done event, which is raised by the Start-Counting method. So, the following declarations must appear at the beginning of the form, outside any procedure:

```
Dim WithEvents TS As TotalSize
Dim TSThread As Threading.Thread
```

The last important piece of code in the project is the handler of the Done event. This event is raised by the TotalSize class when the counting ends and signals the main thread that it can read and display the results. Add the event handler in Listing 10.6 to the project's code.

**Listing 10.6      Handling the Done Event of the TotalSize Class**

```
Private Sub TS_Done() Handles TS.Done
    bttnCancel.Enabled = False
    MsgBox(TS.Size.ToString("#,###") & " bytes in " & _
          TS.Count.ToString("#,###") & " files")
End Sub
```

While the thread is running, the current time is displayed on a Label control from within a Timer control's Tick event handler. If you run the `ScanFolder()` subroutine in the main thread, the interface will freeze and the time won't be updated before the subroutine terminates. If you run the same subroutine in a separate thread, the interface will remain responsive.

## Updating the Interface from within a Thread

As mentioned already, one of the things you shouldn't do from within a thread is to update the visible interface of the main thread. In other words, you shouldn't manipulate the controls on the application's form from within a thread other than the main one. All Windows controls provide the Invoke method, which allows you to call a method safely from within a thread. You can also request the value of the InvokeRequired method, which returns True if the control's methods should be called through the Invoke method.

The Invoke method accepts as arguments a delegate to the method you want to call and an array of objects that contains the parameters you would normally pass to the method. Each argument of the control's method is stored in a separate element of the array—the first argument in the first element of the array, the second argument in the second element of the array, and so on.

The TreeView control is one of the controls whose methods must be called from within a thread with the Invoke method. To add a new node to the control, you must first declare a delegate with a statement like the following:

```
Public Delegate Function _
            Add_A_Node(ByVal aString As String) As TreeNode
```

This delegate has the same signature as the Add method of the control's Nodes collection—the method we want to call. It accepts as argument a string and returns a TreeNode object, which represents the node it added to the Nodes collection.

Then, from within the thread's code, you can call this method to add a new TreeNode object to the control with a statement like the following:

```
Nd = TreeView1.Invoke(New _
            Add_A_Node(AddressOf currentNode.Nodes.Add), _
            New Object() {"node's caption"})
```

The TreeView control requires that you call its methods from within another thread through the Invoke method, so you need not examine the InvokeRequired method. You could have also written the previous statement that calls the `Nodes.Add` method as follows:

```
If TreeView1.InvokeRequired Then
    Nd = TreeView1.Invoke(New _
            Add_A_Node(AddressOf currentNode.Nodes.Add), _
            New Object() {"node's caption"})
Else
    Nd = currentNode.Nodes.Add(Nd.Text)
End If
```

The expression `New Object() {item, item, item}` creates an array of objects and populates it with the items in the curly brackets. In the case of the Add method, you only need to specify a single argument, which is the caption of the node to be added.

In the following section, we'll build an application that is similar to Windows Explorer and that will map the structure of a drive to a TreeView control. The process isn't instant, so the code that populates the TreeView control will be executed on its own thread. The main thread remains responsive and the user can interact with the current contents of the control.

## The ThreadedExplorer Project

The ThreadedExplorer project demonstrates how to use the Invoke method to update a TreeView control from within a thread. The thread iterates through the folders of the C: drive and creates a tree structure that reflects the folder structure of the drive. The process of mapping the drive's folders on the TreeView control may take 30 seconds or more, depending on the number of folders on the drive. To avoid freezing the application's interface while the code in the form's Load event handler populates the TreeView control, you can execute the corresponding code from within a thread. This is exactly what the ThreadedExplorer does: it sets up a new thread in the form's Load event handler and starts it. The thread's code populates the TreeView control slowly and the user can expand the nodes added so far and examine their contents. Not all the information is readily available, but the user can interact with the nodes as they're being added to the control.

Figure 10.3 shows the application's form. It's a typical Explorer-style window that displays the names of the folders (along with their structure) on a TreeView control, the subfolders of the selected folder on the top ListView control, and the files of the selected folder (along with their basic attributes) on the lower ListView control.

**FIGURE 10.3:**

The ThreadedExplorer application

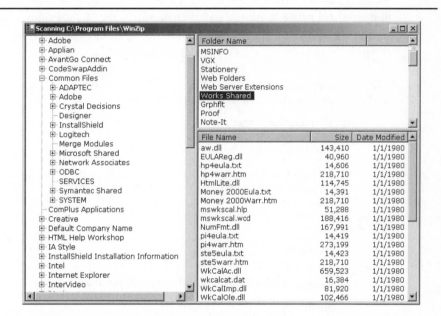

When the application starts, the statements in the Form's Load event handler create a new thread, in which the LoadTreeView subroutine will be executed (see Listing 10.7). This subroutine maps the structure of a folder to the TreeView control. The thread runs at a low priority, so that the main thread will remain as responsive as possible.

**Listing 10.7        Starting the LoadTreeView Thread**

```
Private Sub Form1_Load(ByVal sender As Object, _
                    ByVal e As System.EventArgs) _
                    Handles MyBase.Load
    bgThread = New Thread(AddressOf Me.LoadTreeView)
    bgThread.Priority = ThreadPriority.BelowNormal
```

```
        bgThread.Start()
        Dim Nd As New TreeNode()
        Me.Show()
    End Sub
```

The `bgThread` variable is declared at the form's level with the following statement:

```
Dim bgThread As Thread
```

The LoadTreeView thread's subroutine is shown in Listing 10.8. It creates an array with the arguments to be passed to the `Nodes.Add` method. The array contains a single element, which is the initial path. Then it calls the TreeView control's Invoke method to add the first node to the TreeView control. After that, it calls the `Show()` subroutine to iterate through the initial folder's subfolders (and their subfolders, to any depth) and map them to the TreeView control.

**Listing 10.8    The *LoadTreeView()* Subroutine**

```
Public Sub LoadTreeView()
    Dim Nd As New TreeNode()
    Dim initFolder As String = "C:\Program Files"

    Nd = TreeView1.Invoke(New Add_A_Node(AddressOf TreeView1.Nodes.Add), _
                New Object() {initFolder})
    Me.Show()
    ScanFolder(initFolder, Nd)
End Sub
```

The `Add_A_Node()` subroutine is a delegate for the Add method of the TreeView control's Nodes collection. This method accepts a single argument, which is the node's caption:

```
Public Delegate Function Add_A_Node( _
            ByVal aString As String) As TreeNode
```

This statement must be inserted in the code file outside any procedure. With this declaration in place, you can now code the ScanFolder subroutine, whose code is shown in Listing 10.9.

**Listing 10.9    The Revised *ScanFolder()* Subroutine**

```
Sub ScanFolder(ByVal folderSpec As String, _
            ByRef currentNode As TreeNode)
    Dim thisFolder As String
    Dim allFolders() As String
    allFolders = Directory.GetDirectories(folderSpec)
    System.Array.Sort(allFolders)
    For Each thisFolder In allFolders
```

```
            Dim Nd As TreeNode
            Nd = TreeView1.Invoke(New Add_A_Node( _
                    AddressOf currentNode.Nodes.Add), _
                    New Object() {Path.GetFileName(thisFolder)})
            folderSpec = thisFolder
            ScanFolder(folderSpec, Nd)
            Me.Text = "Scanning " & folderSpec
            Me.Refresh()
        Next
    End Sub
```

The program also monitors the keystrokes and aborts the thread's execution when the Escape button is clicked. Here's the form's KeyUp event, which captures all keystrokes before they're passed to the corresponding control (you must also set the form's KeyPreview property to True):

```
Private Sub Form1_KeyUp(ByVal sender As Object, _
        ByVal e As System.Windows.Forms.KeyEventArgs)_
        Handles MyBase.KeyUp
    If e.KeyCode = Keys.Escape Then
        bgThread.Abort()
    End If
End Sub
```

To complete the application, we've added the code to display the selected folder's subfolders in the upper ListView control every time the user clicks a folder name in the TreeView control. Likewise, when the user clicks a subfolder's name in the upper ListBox control, the corresponding files (along with their basic attributes) are displayed on the lower ListBox control.

The code in Listing 10.10 is executed when the user clicks an item on the TreeView control.

**Listing 10.10    Displaying the Subfolders of the Currently Selected Folder**

```
Private Sub TreeView1_AfterSelect( _
        ByVal sender As System.Object, _
        ByVal e As System.Windows.Forms.TreeViewEventArgs)_
        Handles TreeView1.AfterSelect
    Dim Nd As TreeNode
    Dim pathName As String
    Nd = TreeView1.SelectedNode
    pathName = Nd.FullPath
    ListView1.Items.Clear()
    ListView2.Items.Clear()
    If Directory.GetDirectories(pathName).Length > 0 Then
        ShowSubFolders(pathName)
    End If
    ShowFiles(pathName)
End Sub
```

This code clears the two ListBox controls and then calls the ShowSubFolders() subroutine to display the subfolders of the selected folder on the ListView1 control and the ShowFiles() subroutine to display the files of the selected folder on the ListView2 control. Listing 10.11 shows the ShowSubFolders() and ShowFiles() subroutines.

**Listing 10.11**    **The *ShowSubFolders()* and *ShowFiles()* Subroutines**

```
Sub ShowSubFolders(ByVal selFolder As String)
    ListView1.Items.Clear()
    ListView2.Items.Clear()
    Dim folders() As String
    Dim folder As String
    Dim LItem As New ListViewItem()
    folders = Directory.GetDirectories(selFolder)
    For Each folder In folders
        LItem = New ListViewItem()
        LItem.Text = System.IO.Path.GetFileName(folder)
        ListView1.Items.Add(LItem)
    Next
End Sub

Sub ShowFiles(ByVal folder As String)
    Dim LItem As New ListViewItem()
    Dim files() As String
    Dim file As String
    files = Directory.GetFiles(folder)
    System.Array.Sort(files)
    ListView2.Items.Clear()
    For Each file In files
        LItem = New ListViewItem()
        LItem.Text = System.IO.Path.GetFileName(file)
        Dim FI As New FileInfo(file)
        LItem.SubItems.Add(FI.Length.ToString("#,###"))
        LItem.SubItems.Add(FormatDateTime( _
                    Directory.GetCreationTime(file), _
                    DateFormat.ShortDate))
        LItem.SubItems.Add(FormatDateTime( _
                    Directory.GetLastAccessTime(file), _
                    DateFormat.ShortDate))
        ListView2.Items.Add(LItem)
    Next
End Sub
```

## The ThreadedImageProcessing Project

The example in this section demonstrates how to update the UI of the main thread from within a calculation-intensive thread. The ThreadedImageProcessing project lets you open one or more images and process them. The image processing techniques implemented in this project are quite basic, but they demonstrate how to process multiple images at once and update the main thread's interface from within each thread. Each processing thread processes a separate image, and all threads update their own images. As an image is being processed, you can scroll it up and down in its window or change the magnification factor (zoom in or out). The thread that processes the image will continue to work and update the image's window. Figure 10.4 shows the ThreadedImageProcessing project's form.

**FIGURE 10.4:**

The ThreadedImage-Processing project demonstrates how to process multiple images simultaneously.

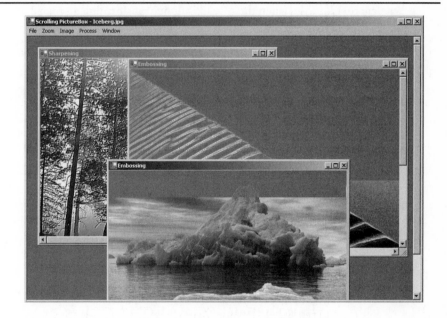

The ThreadedImageProcessing project is an MDI application. Each child form contains a PictureBox control, on which you can load an image and process it. You can load several images and process them simultaneously. You will be able to watch the progress as each image is processed. The effects of some image processing techniques are subtle and you must examine the images carefully to see them. The Emboss and Diffuse algorithms produce the most pronounced effect.

This project presents the following challenges: First, the transformation of the image takes place in a separate thread, which performs a very large number of calculations. The larger the image, the more calculations are required. The thread, however, can't wait until the entire image has been transformed before it updates the PictureBox control on the main thread's interface. This would offset any benefits from the multithreaded implementation of the application. We want to offer some visual feedback to the user and the progress of the processing is the best indication. On the other hand, if we update every pixel (or even every row of pixels) as we process them, the performance penalty will be substantial. We have decided to update the PictureBox with the transformed pixels every 10 rows.

To update the pixels, the thread must call the Invoke method, passing as argument the name of subroutine that will actually update the pixels, and an array with the pixels to be updated. The name of this subroutine is ImageDisplayCallback (it's a callback function). The thread can't pass the name of the subroutine directly, but a delegate to this subroutine, the _displayCallBack delegate. Likewise, when the thread is done transforming an image, it must notify the application by calling a delegate to the _doneCallback method.

Let's start with these two subroutines, whose code is shown in Listings 10.12 and 10.13.

**Listing 10.12       The *DoneProcessing()* Subroutine**

```
Public Sub DoneProcessing()
    Me.Text = "Done " & processCaption
    PictureBox1.Invalidate()
End Sub
```

**Listing 10.13       The *ShowPixels()* Subroutine**

```
Public Sub ShowPixels(ByVal Y As Integer, _
                      ByVal pixels() As Color, _
                      ByVal Refresh As Boolean)
    Dim i As Integer
    For i = 0 To _bitmap.Width - 1
        _bitmap.SetPixel(i, Y, pixels(i))
    Next
    Dim ratio As Single
    ratio = PictureBox1.Height / _bitmapheight
    If Refresh Then
        PictureBox1.Invalidate(New Region( _
                New Rectangle(0, 0, _
                PictureBox1.Width - 1, ratio * (Y + 10))))
    End If
End Sub
```

The DoneProcessing subroutine is straightforward. It updates the form's caption and invalidates the PictureBox control. The ShowPixels() subroutine is a bit more challenging. The first argument is the vertical coordinate of the first row of pixels to be updated. The second argument is an array of Color values, which are the values of the transformed pixels. This array contains a row of pixels, which will be displayed at the specified vertical co-ordinate. The last argument is a Boolean value that determines whether the PictureBox control should be invalidated or not. The ShowPixels() subroutine is called every time we process a row of pixels of the original image. The transformed pixels are copied onto the control, but the control isn't invalidated. Copying the transformed pixels on top of the original ones doesn't take too much time, but invalidating the control does. So we've decided to update the control (that is, show the pixels) after a certain a number of rows have been processed. We update the control every 10 rows of pixels, but you can change this value and find an optimal setting.

Next you must declare the delegates that the thread's code will pass as arguments to the invoke method:

```
Public Delegate Sub ImageDisplayCallback _
        (ByVal Y As Integer, ByVal pixels() As Color, _
        ByVal Refresh As Boolean)
Public Delegate Sub DoneProcessingCallback()
Private _displayCallBack As ImageDisplayCallback = _
        New ImageDisplayCallback(AddressOf ShowPixels)
Private _doneCallback As DoneProcessingCallback = _
        New DoneProcessingCallback(AddressOf DoneProcessing)
```

Now we're ready to use these definitions in the threads that transform the pixel values. We're not going to present all image processing techniques implemented in the project, but they all have the same structure. They scan the original pixels in two nested loops. The outer loop scans the rows of the bitmap and the inner loop scans the pixels of the current row. The smoothing algorithm takes the average of the surrounding pixels and replaces the current pixel with this average value. This technique smoothes out abrupt changes in the pixels and blurs the image.

The sharpening algorithm does the opposite: it subtracts the current pixel from the previous pixel on the same row or column and adds this difference (or a fraction of it) to the current pixel. This technique emphasizes the differences between pixels and, as a result, it sharpens the image.

The embossing algorithm is similar. It subtracts adjacent pixels and magnifies the difference. The diffusion algorithm swaps the values of pixels that are a few pixels away from each other and gives the image a "painterly" look.

You don't really have to understand how the image processing techniques work, unless you want to experiment with them. All the action takes place in the body of the inner loop. Listing 10.14 shows the BGSharpen() subroutine, which sharpens the current image.

**Listing 10.14    Sharpening an Image**

```
Sub BGSharpen()
    PictureBox1.Image = _bitmap
    Dim tempbmp As Bitmap
    tempbmp = _bitmap.Clone
    Dim pixels(tempbmp.Width) As Color
    Dim DX As Integer = 2, DY As Integer = 2
    Dim red, green, blue As Integer
    Dim args(2) As Object
    Dim i, j As Integer
    With tempbmp
        For i = DX To .Height - DX - 1
            For j = DY To .Width - DY - 1
                red = CInt(.GetPixel(j, i).R) + 0.5 * _
                        CInt((.GetPixel(j, i).R) - _
                        CInt(.GetPixel(j - DX, i - DY).R))
                green = CInt(.GetPixel(j, i).G) + 0.7 * _
                        CInt((.GetPixel(j, i).G) - _
                        CInt(.GetPixel(j - DX, i - DY).G))
                blue = CInt(.GetPixel(j, i).B) + 0.5 * _
                        CInt((.GetPixel(j, i).B - _
                        CInt(.GetPixel(j - DX, i - DY).B)))
                red = Math.Min(Math.Max(red, 0), 255)
                green = Math.Min(Math.Max(green, 0), 255)
                blue = Math.Min(Math.Max(blue, 0), 255)
                pixels(j) = Color.FromArgb(red, green, blue)
            Next
            args(0) = i
            args(1) = pixels
            If (i Mod 10) = 0 Then
                args(2) = True
            Else
                args(2) = False
            End If
            Me.Invoke(_displayCallBack, args)
        Next
    End With
    Me.Invoke(_doneCallback)
End Sub
```

Notice how the code sets up the args array with the arguments to the _displayCallBack function. The first element of the array is the order (coordinate) of the current row, the second argument is an array with the processed pixel values, and the last argument is set to True every 10 rows. The variable _tempbmp is created when the user selects an image-processing algorithm from the Process menu and it contains a copy of the image. Listing 10.15 shows the code in the Sharpen menu command's Click event handler.

**Listing 10.15    Starting the Sharpening Transformation on a Thread**

```
Private Sub ProcessSharpen_Click( _
                      ByVal sender As System.Object, _
                      ByVal e As System.EventArgs) _
                      Handles ProcessSharpen.Click
    If Not T Is Nothing Then
        If T.ThreadState = ThreadState.Running Then
            T.Abort()
            T.Join()
        End If
    End If
    processCaption = "Sharpening"
    Me.Text = processCaption
    _bitmapwidth = PictureBox1.Image.Width
    _bitmapheight = PictureBox1.Image.Height
    TStart = New ThreadStart(AddressOf BGSharpen)
    T = New Thread(TStart)
    T.Name = "Sharpen"
    T.Priority = ThreadPriority.BelowNormal
    ' Disable the Image and File menus while
    ' processing the image
    Me.ImageMenu.Enabled = False
    Me.FileMenu.Enabled = False
    T.Start()
End Sub
```

The $T$ variable is declared at the form's level and it's a Thread object. One algorithm can be applied to the current image at a time, so if the thread represented by this variable is active, we terminate it. Notice that this is an MDI application and the code resides in the child form. This allows you to process multiple images at once, but you can't start a transformation on an image before the currents one has ended. That's why the code examines the thread's state and terminates it if it's running. Then the code creates a new thread with the address of the BGSharpen() subroutine and starts it. Before starting the thread, however, the program disables the File and Image menus. You can't open a new image while the current one is being processed and you can't rotate, or flip, the image as it's being processed. However, you can use the commands of the Zoom menu and you can scroll the image as it's being processed.

The following variables are declared outside any procedure and are used throughout the application's code:

```
Dim T As Thread
Dim TStart As ThreadStart
Dim _bitmap As Bitmap
Dim _bitmapwidth As Integer, _bitmapheight As Integer
```

The _bitmap variable stores the pixels of the original and it's used by the thread's code to access the bitmap.

This section's sample application is fairly advanced, but it demonstrates how to put multiple threads to good use, and it's typical of an application that will benefit from a multithreaded implementation. The threads perform intensive computations and the update of the visible interface is quite demanding. Use the project on the website to experiment with its code and adjust it; we hope it will prove to be a useful tool in your exploration of multithreaded applications.

## Synchronization Issues

The threads we've implemented so far act on their own local variables, and they communicate with the main thread through a class's properties. Sometimes multiple threads must act on the same variable. Consider, for example, a program that performs several calculations in parallel through a number of threads. Every now and then the threads must exchange information with one another by setting and reading a number of shared variables. When multiple threads act on the same variable, all kinds of problems may surface. This is the source of the worst bugs in coding multithreaded applications. Let's see what happens when you attempt to update a shared variable from within multiple threads with a simple example.

### The ThreadedCalcs Project

In this section, we'll build a simple application with many threads, all of which act on a shared variable, the counter variable. This variable must be declared outside any procedure with the following statement:

```
Shared counter As Integer
```

The core of the thread's subroutine is shown here:

```
If counter > 0 Then
    Thread.Sleep(sleepTime)
    counter = counter - 1
Else
    Thread.Sleep(sleepTime)
    counter = counter + 1
End If
```

The counter variable is declared outside the subroutine so that all threads can access it. Its value should be between 0 and 1. A thread (any thread) reads its value and increases it by 1 if it's 0 or less or decreases it by 1 if it's larger than 0. The value of the counter variable should be either 0 or 1 at any given time. But is it?

The current thread may be interrupted at any point, even in midst of executing a simple statement like incrementing a variable by 1. This VB statement is translated into several machine language statements, and the thread may be interrupted between any two machine language statements. A thread may execute the If statement and determine that the variable must be increased. Before it gets a chance to increase the variable, however, another thread may be switched in. The new thread will read the same value and increase it, because the shared variable's value hasn't changed yet. When the previous thread (the one that was interrupted) is switched in again, it will modify the counter variable according to the result of the comparison it performed before it was switched out. As a result, it will increase the value of the counter variable once again and the new value will be 2. Even though the code we wrote would never allow the counter variable to reach this value when executed in a single thread, this is not true for the multithreaded implementation of the application.

To start the thread, insert the following statements in the Update Counter button's Click event handler:

```
Private Sub Button1_Click(ByVal sender As System.Object, _
                          ByVal e As System.EventArgs) _
                          Handles Button1.Click
    Dim aThread As Thread = New Thread(AddressOf Calculate)
    aThread.Start()
End Sub
```

The form of the ThreadedCalcs project on the website has one more button, the Run Many Threads button, which starts 100 threads, all with the same task subroutine. The code behind this button is shown next:

```
Private Sub Button3_Click(ByVal sender As System.Object, _
                          ByVal e As System.EventArgs) _
                          Handles Button3.Click
    Dim threads(99) As Thread
    Dim i As Integer
    For i = 0 To 99
        threads(i) = New Thread(AddressOf Calculate)
        threads(i).Start()
    Next
End Sub
```

You can start multiple threads by clicking the button repeatedly, before the current thread finishes. Run the application and click the Update Counter button several times. Even better, click the Run Many Threads button, which starts 100 different threads, all of which attempt to adjust the value of the same variable. You will see on the Output window something like this:

```
Thread 62 woke up. Counter=1
Thread 63 woke up. Counter=2
Thread 64 woke up. Counter=1
Thread 65 woke up. Counter=0
Thread 67 woke up. Counter=-1
```

```
Thread 66 woke up. Counter=-2
Thread 68 woke up. Counter=-3
Thread 66 woke up. Counter=-2
Thread 67 woke up. Counter=-1
Thread 69 woke up. Counter=0
Thread 70 woke up. Counter=1
Thread 71 woke up. Counter=2
Thread 72 woke up. Counter=3
Thread 73 woke up. Counter=4
```

Clearly, the output depends on the order in which the threads are being switched in and out. We've inserted the call to the Sleep method to make sure that virtually every thread will be interrupted after examining the values of the *counter* variable and before it has a chance to update it. Without the call to the Sleep statement, you'd have to run the program for hours until you witnessed this behavior.

If you don't take special care in coding threads that act on shared data, all kinds of bugs may surface. These bugs are very difficult to fix because they're not reproducible. They may surface or not, depending on when threads are interrupted. Because you have no control over the process that switches your threads in and out, you can't reproduce them. You can write a multi-threaded application that works as advertised during the test phase, even for days or weeks after you install it on a client's computer, and then fails. Your programmers may spend days testing the code and everything will appear to work fine. Even if it fails when the programmers are testing it, it's too difficult to find out what has happened with the traditional debugging tools.

Actually, there's only one method of dealing with bugs of this type: careful design of the application. If your application's threads act on shared data, you must follow the techniques described in the following section to avoid similar bugs. In the following section, you'll learn how to execute a section of code in a thread as a unit so that it won't be interrupted by another thread. We'll also revise the ThreadedCalcs project's code so that threads won't interfere with one another.

## The *SyncLock* Block

When two or more threads are accessing the same data, you must *synchronize* them. Synchronization in the context of multithreaded applications means that you must force certain segments of the thread's code to be executed without interruption. In other words, you mark a block of your code as non-interruptible. This tells the CLR that it can't switch out the current thread before the statements in this block are executing. When the block's statements have completed their execution, the thread can be swapped as usual. This critical block in the preceding example consists of the statements that examine the current value of the counter variable and then adjust it. The simplest way to synchronize multiple threads is to use the SyncLock statement. The critical segments of a thread can be placed in a pair of SyncLock ...End SyncLock statements so that they'll be executed as a single unit of code.

The SyncLock statement accepts as argument an object. While a thread is in a SyncLock block, it locks this object and no other thread can request a lock on the same object. After all the statements in the block have completed their execution, the lock on the object is released and the thread can be interrupted. Listing 10.16 shows how we've coded the segment of the thread's code that adjusts the shared variable.

**Listing 10.16**        **The Synchronized Version of the Calculate Task Subroutine**

```
Private Sub Calculate()
    Dim sleepTime As Integer
    Dim tmpCounter As Integer
    Dim rnd As New System.Random()
    sleepTime = rnd.Next(500, 2500)
    Console.WriteLine("Thread " & _
                Thread.CurrentThread.GetHashCode & _
                " will sleep for " & sleepTime & _
                " milliseconds")
    SyncLock locker
    If counter > 0 Then
        Thread.Sleep(sleepTime)
        counter = counter - 1
    Else
        Thread.Sleep(sleepTime)
        counter = counter + 1
    End If
    End SyncLock
    Console.WriteLine("Thread " & _
                Thread.CurrentThread.GetHashCode & _
                " woke up. Counter=" & counter)
End Sub
```

The locking object (the locker variable in this example) need not be an object used in any way by the thread. It's just a reference parameter, which the various threads can place a lock on. Since all threads should be able to access this object, you must declare it outside any procedure, with a statement like the following:

```
Shared locker As Object = New Object()
```

While the locker object is locked, no other thread can lock it; any other thread that needs to place a lock on the same object must wait for the thread that has the lock to release it.

**WARNING**   Another danger in multithreaded programming is the so-called *deadlock*. Let's say thread A has a lock on an object and it must wait for thread B to complete its calculations before it can release the lock. Thread B may also have to place a lock on the same object. The result is that thread B keeps waiting for thread A to release the lock but thread A waits for thread B to complete. This won't happen with two simple threads, but you may run into a deadlock situation if you have to manage multiple threads.

It's important to understand that you're not locking the code, but an object. While the object is locked, no other thread can interrupt the thread that placed the lock—so in effect you're locking a section of the code.

To test the ThreadCalcs application and see how synchronization affects the threads, you can comment out the statements SyncLock and End SyncLock. Without synchronization, the program runs faster, but it produces the wrong results. In synchronized mode, the program runs much slower, but the counter variable has always a valid value (a value between 0 and 1). The delay in this sample application is artificial—it was introduced with the Sleep statement— but it simply simulates the delay of code that performs some useful calculations.

As you can see, placing a lot of locks in your code has a serious impact in the application's performance. Lock only the segments of the code that adjust the shared variables and release the locks as early as possible. In our sample code, we've inserted calls to the thread's Sleep method to make sure that a thread will be interrupted in its critical code segment and another thread will be switched in. Remove the calls to the Sleep method and the code will appear to work just as well, even without the locks. This happens because the thread's code is so simple. If this were a real application, used on a daily basis, it would eventually fail and you would be hard-pressed to figure out what happened.

## Thread Pooling

Another method of writing multithreaded applications is by using the *thread pool*—as opposed to creating your own threads. The operating system provides and maintains a pool of threads, which you can use to run your tasks. Tasks are added to a queue and started as threads become available. This way, you can't overload the system with too many tasks. Actually, you should use the thread pool whenever possible, because it's easier to handle the threads.

The thread pool is ideal for executing multiple instances of the same task. If your application calls multiple identical tasks in separate threads, you should use the thread pool. Let's say your application needs to download a few dozen documents from one or more web servers. Some sites will respond faster than others, and you can't afford to wait for each document transfer to complete before you start downloading the next one. This type of application calls for a multithreaded implementation. Downloading multiple documents one at a time and waiting for each document to be downloaded before starting the download of the next one will result in a very slow-running application. Downloading multiple documents at once will improve not only the perceived speed, but the overall performance of the application as well. However, if you start all the tasks at once, too much time will be wasted in switching the tasks in and out. The best solution is to use the thread pool to queue the tasks and let the operating system itself handle them.

Each thread's subroutine will be the same—it will simply request a different URL. Instead of creating dozens of threads from within your code and managing them, you can queue all the threads and let the thread pool execute them as it sees fit. The thread pool will start each thread and share the CPU among them, and most important, it will not overload the CPU by running too many instances of the task subroutine.

To assign a task to a thread in the thread pool, you must call the QueueUserWorkItem method of the ThreadPool object, passing a delegate for the subroutine you want to run; the CLR will run the task in a thread. When all available threads are taken, tasks will remain in the queue and they'll be executed when one of the active tasks terminates. The following example shows how you could use thread pooling to start several tasks by queuing them with the ThreadPool object:

```
Dim TPool As System.Threading.ThreadPool
TPool.QueueUserWorkItem(New System.Threading.WaitCallback _
                        (AddressOf Task1))
TPool.QueueUserWorkItem(New System.Threading.WaitCallback _
                        (AddressOf Task2))
TPool.QueueUserWorkItem(New System.Threading.WaitCallback _
                        (AddressOf Task3))
```

This code shows how to queue three different tasks. You can also queue the same task multiple times, but this means that you must also pass some arguments to the tasks to differentiate them (each task will act on different arguments). One good reason for using the thread pool is that you can pass arguments to the task subroutine when you declare the delegate. In the following section, we will build an application to download multiple documents from the Web, using a separate thread for each document. The URL of each document will be passed to the appropriate thread as argument.

## The ThreadPool Project

The ThreadPool project, whose form in shown in Figure 10.5, demonstrates how to use the thread pool to request several documents on the Web. It creates a new task for each document, and all tasks are queued for execution by the thread pool. Each thread adds a line to the Text-Box control indicating that the download process has started and another line to indicate that the download process has ended.

Start by creating the objDocumentObj class, which contains the URL and the contents of the file. The Content property is empty until the file is actually downloaded. At that time, the Done property is also set to True so that the main thread knows that the file has been downloaded completely:

```
Public Class objDocument
    Friend URL As String
    Friend Done As Boolean = False
    Friend Content As String = ""
End Class
```

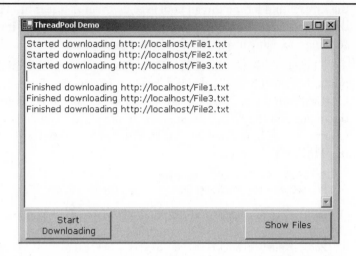

Then create an array of as many objDocument objects as you intend to download. Each thread will accept as argument an element of this array, download the file specified with the URL member, store the file's contents to the Content member, and set the Done member to True:

```
Dim Docs(99) As objDocument
```

To start the threads, enter the following code in the Click event handler of a button:

```
Private Sub Button1_Click(ByVal sender As System.Object, _
        ByVal e As System.EventArgs) Handles Button1.Click
    Dim TPool As System.Threading.ThreadPool
    Docs(0) = New objDocument()
    Docs(0).URL = "http://localhost/File1.txt"
    TPool.QueueUserWorkItem _
            (New System.Threading.WaitCallback _
            (AddressOf DownloadDocument), Docs(0))
    Docs(1) = New objDocument()
    Docs(1).URL = "http://localhost/File2.txt"
    TPool.QueueUserWorkItem _
            (New System.Threading.WaitCallback _
            (AddressOf DownloadDocument), Docs(1))
    Docs(2) = New objDocument()
    Docs(2).URL = "http://localhost/File3.txt"
    TPool.QueueUserWorkItem _
            (New System.Threading.WaitCallback _
            (AddressOf DownloadDocument), Docs(2))
End Sub
```

Listing 10.17 shows the DownloadDocument() subroutine's code.

**Listing 10.17    The DownloadDocument Task Subroutine**

```
Sub DownloadDocument(ByVal Doc As Object)
    TextBox1.AppendText("Started downloading " & _
            CType(Doc, objDocument).URL & vbCrLf)
    Dim myRequest As WebRequest = _
            WebRequest.Create(CType(Doc, DocumentObj).URL)
' This handler will catch runtime errors returned
' by the Web Server that prevent the successful download
' of the document (errors like "File not found")
    Dim Rsp As WebResponse
    Try
        Rsp = myRequest.GetResponse()
    Catch exc As Exception
        MsgBox(exc.Message)
    End Try
    Dim str As System.IO.Stream = Rsp.GetResponseStream
    Dim bytesread As Integer
    Dim length As Integer = 10240
    Dim Buffer(10240) As Byte
    Dim DocText As String
    Dim TextRead As String
    bytesread = str.Read(Buffer, 0, length)
    While bytesread > 0
        Dim i As Integer
        TextRead = ""
        For i = 0 To bytesread - 1
            TextRead = TextRead & Chr(Buffer(i))
        Next i
        DocText = DocText & TextRead
        bytesread = str.Read(Buffer, 0, length)
    End While
    CType(Doc, objDocument).Content = DocText.ToString
    CType(Doc, objDocument).Done = True
    str.Close()
    Rsp.Close()
    TextBox1.AppendText("Finished downloading " & _
            CType(Doc, objDocument).URL & vbCrLf)
End Sub
```

The code creates a WebRequest object to request the corresponding URL and then uses this object's GetResponse method to retrieve the stream returned by the remote server. You will find more information on Internet programming in Chapter 17 of this book.

The last issue is how to tell when all documents have been downloaded. A simple method is to deploy a Timer control and examine the value of the Done property of all instances of the objDocument objects. As far as the sample application is concerned, you can wait until all documents are downloaded and then click the Show Files button to display all three files in text format on the TextBox control.

You may have noticed that the thread updates the TextBox control from within its code. You can modify the code so that the thread updates the interface through the Invoke method (it's rather trivial), but in our experience, it's quite safe to update the TextBox and ListBox controls from within a thread's code.

## Summary

Multithreading is new to Visual Basic, and writing multithreaded applications is not trivial. Creating and starting new threads is deceptively simple. In this chapter we focused on some basic issues in multithreaded programming, namely exchanging information between threads and updating the interface of the main thread from within the background threads' code.

Another important issue in the communication between threads is synchronization. Multiple threads can access the same variable and update it. When this happens, you must make sure that while a thread accesses a variable, no other thread can access the same thread.

Before you start developing a multithreaded application, you must design the appropriate class carefully, minimize the number of variables shared among the threads, and pay special attention to synchronization among threads. Bugs caused by synchronization problems are difficult to fix. In general, most bugs in multithreaded applications are difficult to fix because they're almost impossible to reproduce.

# CHAPTER 11

# Debugging and Deploying .NET Applications

- Changes in debugging with VB .NET

- Creating debug and release versions

- Using basic debugging

- Setting conditional breakpoints

- Attaching to a running and/or remote program

- Debugging multiple processes

- Using the Debug and Trace classes

- The debugging windows

- Debugging from the command line

- Conditional compilation

- Distributing an application

- Other distribution types

**D**ebugging and deploying applications seem to be rather uncomfortably linked because it is usually when you are in the process of debugging that you come under pressure to deploy. Nevertheless, the two do run hand-in-hand because limited deployment is often part of the debugging process as you look to how your applications perform and behave "in the wild."

For many Visual Basic developers, the debugging tools in Visual Studio .NET offer a mix of the familiar and the decidedly different. If you have previously used the Visual Studio 6 debugger, though, you may find yourself on more familiar ground.

The big difference is that there is now just one debugger interface to handle all the .NET languages and application types. If you have built an application using a combination of VB and C#, you use a single set of debugging tools to look after the lot. This also applies to different application types, such as Windows- and web-based programs.

In this chapter, we will cover debugging tools and procedures in .NET. We will also be looking at the process of application deployment and how this is influenced by the .NET Framework. Deployment can be a not-quite-straightforward affair, particularly when working with web-based or distributed applications. To assist with this, .NET ships with a range of utilities for managing trusts and security in relation to .NET assemblies.

There are also various configuration files associated with .NET applications that can be altered to change aspects of the way an application executes without having to recompile the project.

We'll also consider the different methods of deployment, and what to use when, for the range of different application types that can be produced from Visual Studio .NET. For example, a web-based application may be simply transferred to IIS using the Copy Project command from the Project menu. This is not always appropriate, but it can be quite suitable for very basic projects and is simpler than creating a distribution.

Other possible methods include creating CAB projects (for Web download) and Merge Module projects (for updating components). Although not discussed here, third-party alternatives also exist for installation tools.

## Changes in Debugging with VB .NET

There have been a number of changes that have been introduced into the traditional VB debugging environment. Probably the main change is the creation of the single debugging environment for all .NET languages and application types, coupled with the ability to perform cross-language debugging. Web-based ASP.NET programs use the same debugger as other application types.

One potential surprise for VB programmers is that there is no longer the ability to drop into code while in Break mode and make changes on the fly. There is a work-around using the Command window (which replaces the old Immediate window in VB), but it is not quite the same thing.

Other changes include a number of different keyboard shortcuts and a range of additional features such as the ability to debug running programs outside the Visual Studio .NET environment and remotely debug a process running on another machine. It is also possible to debug multiple programs running either from within or outside the Visual Studio .NET IDE.

You can also monitor the execution of your programs by using the Trace and Debug classes to place appropriate statements at various points in your code. Debug statements are stripped out of code once the program is compiled in Release mode, but Trace statements remain by default. The process of using Trace (and Debug) statements to monitor and log performance and errors is referred to as *instrumenting* an application. This is a particularly useful technique for managing distributed applications. Apart from their different default behavior under Release mode compilation, the Trace and Debug classes are identical.

Visual Basic's `Debug.Print` method has been replaced with four new methods: `Debug.Write`, `Debug.WriteLine`, `Debug.WriteIf`, and `Debuf.WriteLineIf`. `Debug.Write` is very similar to `Debug.Print` and simply writes to the Output window via the trace listeners in the Listeners collection. Although the Write method overwrites information about the debug, the WriteLine method creates a new line. WriteIf and WriteLineIf provide conditional methods for the Debug class.

## Creating Debug and Release Versions

A Visual Studio .NET project created using the templates from the New Project menu has two different configurations: Debug and Release. The Debug configuration lacks optimization but has full debug capability. You use this configuration when you are building and testing the program. The release version is fully optimized and has most of its debug capability removed or disabled by default. (You can still set up tracing in a release version.) The release configuration is essentially for the distributable version of your application, although it may also be used for testing.

You can actively switch between the two configurations using the Solution Configurations drop-down box next to the Start arrow on the Standard toolbar. Alternatively, you can use Configuration Manager dialog box from the Build menu, as shown in Figure 11.1.

Settings for the two configurations can be changed using the Configuration Properties dialog box in the project's property pages (accessed by right-clicking the project's name in the Solution Explorer and selecting the Properties option). (See Figure 11.2.) Note that the Configuration Manager can also be accessed from the Configuration Properties dialog box.

FIGURE 11.1:

The Configuration
Manager

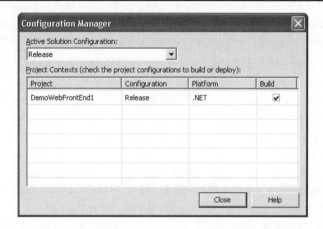

FIGURE 11.2:

The Configuration
Properties dialog box

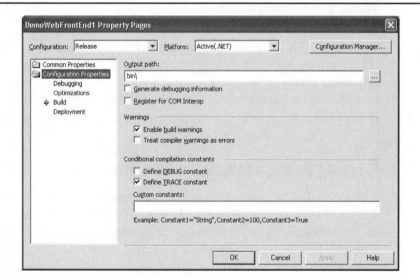

## Considerations for ASP.NET Applications

There are a few extra considerations that you need to take into account when setting up to debug or release ASP.NET applications.

First, you need to ensure that the `<compilation defaultLanguage="vb" debug="true" />` tag has been set in the Web.config page (accessed via Solution Explorer). This page is an XML document that contains a number of configuration settings for the ASP.NET application. The debug value of the compilation tag is set to true by default and needs to be changed to false when deploying your application to help maximize performance. Note that XML is case sensitive, so it is important to write these values correctly.

Additionally, to debug the individual ASPX pages, you can set their individual debug property to true. This property can be found in the properties window for DOCUMENT associated with each Web Form in your application. (Alternatively, the value can be set in the @Page directive in HTML view.)

## Using Basic Debugging

Basic debugging with .NET still consists of setting breakpoints, inspecting contents of variables, etc as in previous versions.

Breakpoints are set by inserting the cursor at the relevant point in the code and clicking in the left-hand margin of the code editor or by pressing F9. More sophisticated breakpoints can be determined and inserted by choosing the New Breakpoint option from the Debug menu (or by pressing Ctrl+B). Figure 11.3 shows the New Breakpoint dialog box. Conditional breakpoints can be set that halt execution according to the number of hits on the breakpoint or whether a predetermined condition has been met. We will look at using the New Breakpoint dialog box in the section on setting conditional breakpoints later in this chapter. To investigate the debugging features further we will set up a simple project and use it throughout the chapter.

**FIGURE 11.3:**

The New Breakpoint
dialog box

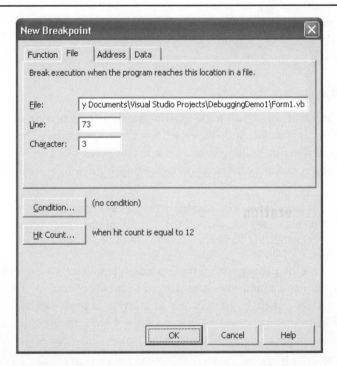

## The Debugging Project

We can set up a simple project to demonstrate the debugging tools. Open a new Windows application in Visual Basic .NET and name it DebuggingDemo1.

Set up Form1 with a ListBox control and Button control. Double-click the button to enter Code Behind and add the code in Listing 11.1.

**Listing 11.1**     **Code for the Button1_Click Event for DebuggingDemo1**

```
Private Sub Button1_Click(ByVal sender As _
 System.Object,  ByVal e As System.EventArgs) Handles Button1.Click

        Dim n As Integer
        Dim x As Integer
        Dim y As Integer = 1

        For n = 1 To 20
            x = 3 * n
            ListBox1.Items.Add(x)
            If n = 10 Then
                y = 2
            End If
        Next
    End Sub
```

Compile and run the project by selecting the Start command on the Standard toolbar. Clicking Button1 should populate the ListBox with the numbers 3 to 60.

## Simple Breakpoints

Run your cursor down the narrow gray left-hand margin of the code in the code editor window. If you click at the line x = 3 * n, a breakpoint (large brown dot) will be set at this point. Additionally, holding your cursor at this point will give additional information in ToolTip format on the point that you have chosen (including its line number).

**TIP**     You can display line numbers in the IDE by choosing Options from the Tools menu. In the Options dialog box, expand the Text Editor node and choose All Languages and General. Check the Line Numbers box in the Display section.

Run the program from the Start arrow. Click Button1 and drop into Break mode. The Command window replaces the old Immediate window and can be used to get the values of variables, change variables and properties, execute methods, and so on. For example, press F11 to step into the next line, type **x = 4 * n** into the Command window, and press the Enter key. Then type **?x** and press Enter. This should give the new value of x.

Placing the cursor over a variable in the main code window also gives the current value of that variable.

Figure 11.4 illustrates how this debugging session might look. The Command window is down in the right-hand corner of the IDE. Notice that the Autos window in the lower-left corner also lists the current variable values.

**FIGURE 11.4:**

Debugging session in Visual Studio .NET

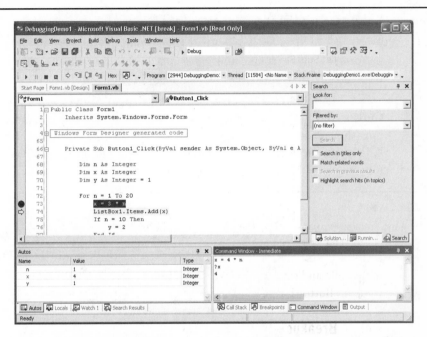

Unlike in previous versions of Visual Basic, you cannot make changes to the code from Debug mode. However, you can try something by typing code in the Command window, and if it works, copy the contents to the Clipboard and then insert it into your code properly when back in Design mode.

As with previous versions of Visual Basic, you can step through the code line by line using the Step Into option from the Debug menu (or pressing the F11 key). This will step you through every line of code, including any called procedures. The yellow highlight shows which line is being executed. You can step over procedures (running but not going through them line by line) using the Step Over command (F10) and step out of a procedure (and back to the calling procedure) using the Step Out command (Shift+F11) from the Debug menu.

You can move the next execution point away from the breakpoint by selecting the breakpoint in Break mode and dragging the yellow highlight to the point you choose. You can also delete a breakpoint in Break mode by simply clicking it or add a new breakpoint in similar fashion.

If you have set multiple debug points, they can also be globally deleted or disabled from the Debug menu. Pressing F5 (or the Start/Continue arrow) will run the program up to the next breakpoint.

In the next section, we will use the DebuggingDemo1 project to illustrate how to set conditional breakpoints.

## Setting Conditional Breakpoints

It is very easy to set breakpoints that trigger only after a certain number of loop iterations are performed or if a certain condition is met. In this example, we will create a breakpoint that triggers only after the loop in the DebuggingDemo1 project has cycled 12 times.

In Code Behind for the project, set your cursor to the x = 3 * n line (line number 73). Choose New Breakpoint from the Debug menu (Ctrl+B). This opens the New Breakpoint dialog box (shown previously in Figure 11.3). Select the File tab and click the Hit Count button. This opens the Breakpoint Hit Count dialog box. Set the drop-down box to "break when the hit count is greater than or equal to" and the value to 12, as illustrated in Figure 11.5.

**FIGURE 11.5:**

Setting the breakpoint hit count

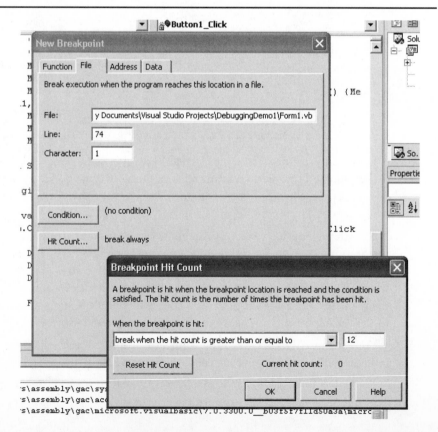

Click OK to exit out of the dialog boxes and run the program in Debug mode. This should open Form1. Click Button1 to begin executing the loop and drop into the breakpoint. If you take a look in the Autos window, you will see that execution broke when the value of *n* equaled 12.

You can also use the New Breakpoint dialog box to set a conditional breakpoint. Set your cursor at the x = 3 * n line in the code (line 73) and delete any existing breakpoints. Select New Breakpoint from the Debug menu. Select the File tab in the New Breakpoint dialog box and click the Condition button. This opens the Breakpoint Condition dialog. Make sure that the Condition check box is checked and set the condition to y=2. Leave the Is True radio button selected. Click OK to exit the dialog box. Leave the Hit Count setting at Break Always and click OK.

Run the program again in Debug mode. It should break at n = 11 when y = 2.

## Attaching to a Running and/or Remote Program

It's easy to attach the debugger to a program running outside the Visual Studio .NET IDE. The program may be on the same machine as the debugger or on a remote machine and accessed via some form of network connection. This technique is particularly useful for debugging XML Web services, SQL Server 2000 stored procedures, and web-based applications, all of which may typically be stored on machines other than the development machines once they have achieved some level of production status. They also represent programs and services that may have been developed independently but are required to support a new application being developed.

To access a running application, fire up Visual Studio .NET and from the Tools menu, choose Debug Processes (Ctrl+Alt+P). This will open the Processes dialog box. The processes running on the local machine are displayed by default. Clicking the small button with the ellipsis points next to the Name drop-down box will allow you to browse the network for a remote machine. (Make sure that you have administrative or debugging rights to the machine that you are attempting to debug.)

Identify the process that you wish to debug, select it, and click the Attach button. This opens the Attach to Process dialog box, shown in Figure 11.6.

In the Attach to Process dialog box, choose the type of process that you are attaching to and click OK. Back at the Processes dialog box, you will now be given the choice of whether to terminate the application or simply detach the debugger from it once debugging has finished. Being able to detach from the process is particularly useful when debugging server-side ASP.NET applications that are running in a production environment. Click the Close button to close the dialog box and carry out the debugging. You can use the Break command in the Processes dialog box or the Break All command from the Debug menu in the VS .NET IDE to break to the program being debugged. If there is no source code available to debug, you have the choice of using the Disassembly window to view the assembly code generated by the compiler.

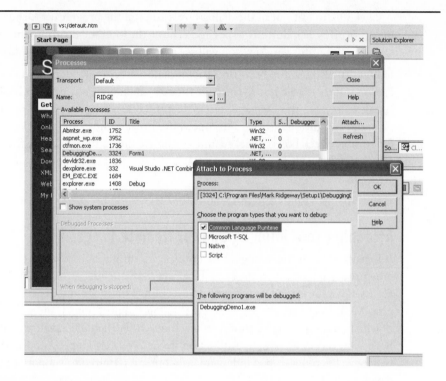

## Debugging Multiple Processes

You can also use the Processes dialog box to attach to and debug multiple processes at the same time. Simply select and attach each process that you wish to debug, as shown in Figure 11.7.

**FIGURE 11.7:**

Attaching and debugging
multiple processes from
the Process dialog box

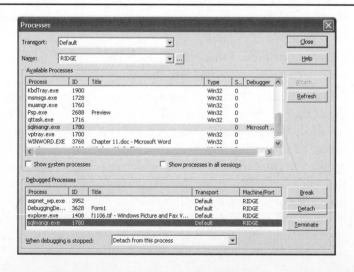

You can also debug multiple projects within the VS .NET IDE by using the Add Project ➢ Existing Project option to add other projects to the current solution. You can then debug the additional projects from the Solution Explorer by right-clicking the project name and choosing Debug ➢ Start New Instance from the context menu.

Figure 11.8 shows two separate projects being simultaneously debugged within the Visual Studio .NET IDE.

**FIGURE 11.8:**

Debugging multiple projects within the Visual Studio .NET IDE

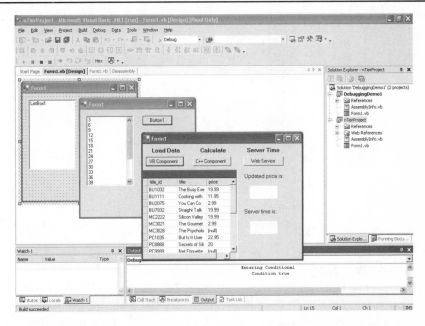

Using these methods, you can also simultaneously debug multiple projects written in different languages, such as VB .NET and C#.

## Using the Debug and Trace Classes

You can also use the Debug and Trace classes to provide information about your application's execution. You can use the Write, WriteLine, WriteIf, and WriteLineIf methods mentioned earlier in this chapter to report information to the Output window in a fashion similar to the way you used the old `Debug.Print` method in VB. There is also a range of additional methods and properties available to help track bugs and errors. In particular, there is the Assert method, which can be used to report messages in a modal dialog box if a given condition evaluates to False.

The Debug and Trace classes are very similar in their methods and properties. The main difference is that Debug statements are automatically stripped from the code when it is compiled in Release mode whereas Trace code remains and can be used for error and performance reporting in the deployed application.

Listing 11.2 demonstrates how you might add Debug statements to the code for the DebuggingDemo1 project.

**Listing 11.2        Debug Statements Added to the DebuggingDemo1 Project**

```
Private Sub Button1_Click(ByVal sender As _
  System.Object, ByVal e As System.EventArgs) _
  Handles Button1.Click

        Dim n As Integer
        Dim x As Integer
        Dim y As Integer = 1

        For n = 1 To 20
            x = 3 * n
            ListBox1.Items.Add(x)
            Debug.WriteLine("The value of x is " & x)
            Debug.Indent()
            Debug.WriteLineIf(n = 10, "Entering the _
  If/Then condition")
            If n = 10 Then
                Debug.WriteLine("Condition true")
                y = 2
            End If
            Debug.Unindent()
        Next
    End Sub
```

The key players here are the Debug.WriteLine statements. These write to the Output window in the lower-right corner of the Visual Studio .NET IDE. Figure 11.9 illustrates the expected output from these statements in the Output window.

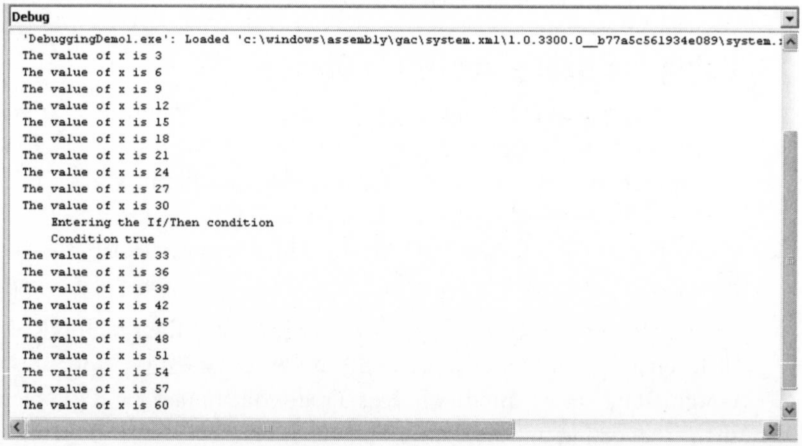

**FIGURE 11.9:**

Output window for Debug statements in the DebuggingDemo1 project

```
Debug
'DebuggingDemo1.exe': Loaded 'c:\windows\assembly\gac\system.xml\1.0.3300.0__b77a5c561934e089\system.:
The value of x is 3
The value of x is 6
The value of x is 9
The value of x is 12
The value of x is 15
The value of x is 18
The value of x is 21
The value of x is 24
The value of x is 27
The value of x is 30
    Entering the If/Then condition
    Condition true
The value of x is 33
The value of x is 36
The value of x is 39
The value of x is 42
The value of x is 45
The value of x is 48
The value of x is 51
The value of x is 54
The value of x is 57
The value of x is 60
```

The `Debug.WriteLine("The value of x is " & x)` statement writes the current value of *x* to the Output window. By using the WriteLine method, you get an intelligible output with each value on a separate line. If you just used the Write method, the output would be across one line.

The `Debug.Indent()` statement is used to control (in a fairly basic fashion) the formatting of content in the Output window. It indents the reports on the status of the If/Then statement. A conditional WriteLineIf example is then used to report when the If/Then statement should be active: `Debug.WriteLineIf(n = 10, "Entering the If/Then condition")`. A further `Debug.Writeline` is used inside the conditional statement, and then the `Debug.Unindent()` statement is used to prevent us from looping the Indent method to the point of extinction.

If you wished, you could replace all the Debug statements with their equivalent Trace statements—for example, `Trace.WriteLine`, `Trace.Indent`, and so on.

## Using the *Debug.Assert* Method

As an example of using the Assert method, we could replace the `Debug.WriteLineIf(n = 10, "Entering the If/Then condition")` statement with `Debug.Assert` statement: `Debug.Assert (n <> 10, "Entering the If/Then block")`. This is not really the purpose for which this method was intended—it is ideally more suited to capturing and reporting nasty exceptions—but it does illustrate the basic process involved.

Running the code now will throw the dialog box shown in Figure 11.10. The user is given the options Abort (to kill the application), Retry (to enter Debug mode), or Ignore (continue the application).

**FIGURE 11.10:**

Modal dialog box thrown by the `Debug.Assert` method

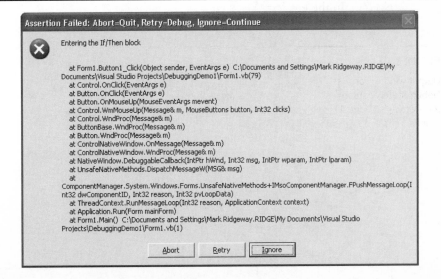

Output from the Trace and Debug statements is collected in objects called *listeners* that derive from the TraceListener class. So far, we have made use of the DefaultTraceListener that is created automatically to handle the Write and WriteLine messages. You can add extra listeners to a project if you wish to direct output to log or text files. Apart from the DefaultTraceListener, there are two other predefined listeners:

**EventLogTraceListener**　Redirects the output to an event log

**TextWriterTraceListener**　Redirects output to an instance of the TextWriter class or to a derivative of the Stream class

To add a listener, you simply reference the `Trace.Listeners` collection and call the Add method as follows: `Trace.Listeners.Add(NewTrace1)` or `Debug.Listeners.Add(NewDebug1)`. Listing 11.3 illustrates how you can add a new listener to the DebuggingDemo1 project to write debugging information to a text file.

**Listing 11.3**　　**Adding an Extra Listener to the DebuggingDemo1 Project**

```
Private Sub Button1_Click(ByVal sender As _
  System.Object, ByVal e As System.EventArgs) _
  Handles Button1.Click

        Dim n As Integer
        Dim x As Integer
        Dim y As Integer = 1

        Dim NewDebugListener As New _
  TextWriterTraceListener(System.IO.File.CreateText _
  ("C:\DebugTest.txt"))
        Debug.Listeners.Add(NewDebugListener)

        For n = 1 To 20
            x = 3 * n
            ListBox1.Items.Add(x)
            Debug.WriteLine("The value of x is " & x)
            Debug.Indent()
            Debug.WriteLineIf(n = 10, "Entering the _
  If/Then condition")
            If n = 10 Then
                Debug.WriteLine("Condition true")
                y = 2
            End If
            Debug.Unindent()
        Next

        Debug.Flush()

    End Sub
```

In this example, we create a new listener, NewDebugListener, that writes to a text file DebugTest.txt, stored in the root directory. The Debug.Flush statement at the end of the routine is required to flush the buffers of the listeners to ensure that all Listener objects receive their output. Naturally, we would use Trace statements (as opposed to the Debug statements) if we wished to generate output from a release version of our application.

## The Debugging Windows

There are a number of windows that you can use when debugging your applications. You have already seen and used a few of these in the shape of the Output, Command, Autos, and Disassembly windows. Some of the windows can be accessed from the tabs along the bottom of the Visual Studio .NET IDE while in Debug mode. The remaining windows can be accessed from the Windows option under the Debug menu. Choosing a window from the Debug ➤ Windows option will open the window and add it as a tab to the bottom of the IDE. The following list briefly describes the role of each window:

**Output**  Displays output from the debugger, including messages generated by the Debug and Trace methods.

**Breakpoints**  Shows the status of any breakpoints set in the program.

**Running Documents**  Lists any additional documents attached to the program.

**Watch**  Similar to Autos except that you determine which variables to view. It is possible to set up to four Watch windows.

**Autos**  Displays the state of variables used in the current and previous statements.

**Locals**  Gives the state of local variables.

**This**  Allow you to view the object associated with current method.

**Command (or Immediate)**  Lets you view, manipulate, and test variables, properties, and code.

**Call Stack**  Shows the calling path to the current function, including parameter types and values.

**Threads**  Allows you to gather information on and switch between various threads running in the program.

**Modules**  Displays the DLLs and EXEs used by the program.

**Memory**  Displays contents of memory. You can set up to four Memory windows.

**Disassembly**   Shows assembly code generated by the compiler (useful if you know assembly).

**Registers**   Lets you view the contents of the registers.

**NOTE**   Note that apart from the Output, Breakpoints and Immediate (Command) windows, the windows in the list are available only in Debug mode.

From the Debug menu itself, you can access two other potentially useful windows. The first, the Processes window, is essentially the same dialog box that we looked at earlier for connecting to and debugging remote and multiple processes (it was accessed via the Debug Processes option from the Tools menu). The second useful window accessed directly from the Debug menu is the Exceptions dialog box. This window shows the exceptions from the .NET Framework and is particularly useful for identifying the exceptions that are available. It is also used to control response to individual exceptions that are not handled specifically in the code.

In the next section, we will complete our discussion of debugging with a brief look at debugging from the command line.

## Debugging from the Command Line

As mentioned in Chapter 1, you can compile and debug .NET programs from the command line. In most cases, this is fairly unnecessary, but there are some instances in which it can be useful. For example, you might want only certain sections of code to compile depending on which flavor of Windows the code is to run on. This is called a *conditional compilation*.

The Visual Basic .NET compiler normally resides at `C:\Windows\Microsoft.NET\Framework\v1.0.3705\vbc.exe`. Note that the name of the `v1.0.3705` directory may vary depending on which release of .NET you are using.

You can run the compiler either from a batch file or from the command line (it's simplest from a Command window). Open a Command window and `CD` to the directory holding the compiler. You can invoke the compiler by typing **vbc**. If you type **vbc /?**, you will be rewarded with the list of options available for use with the compiler, as shown in Figure 11.11.

**FIGURE 11.11:**

Compiler options for the vbc compiler displayed in a Command window

To set up a simple example of using the compiler, open Notepad and enter the code in Listing 11.4.

**Listing 11.4**    **Simple VB Application for Use with vbc Compiler**

```
Imports System
Module Simpleapp
    Sub Main()
        Console.WriteLine("This is a simple app")
    End Sub
End Module
```

Save the file as Simpleapp.vb (make sure that you set the Save as Type option to All Files in the Save As dialog box in Notepad) in a C:\SimpleApp directory.

Compile the program with the following line from the Command window (having CD'd to the directory holding the vbc compiler).

**vbc C:\SimpleApp\Simpleapp.vb**

This should create a small executable in the directory holding vbc. You can run the executable by calling Simpleapp.exe from the Command window. It displays "This is a simple app" in the Command window. You can also run the application by double-clicking the EXE file in the directory, but you need to be quick to catch it! Adding the line Console.Readline() after the WriteLine statement and then recompiling will effectively cause the application to pause and be viewable when running it from the EXE file.

---

**NOTE**    You can also write console applications within the Visual Studio .NET IDE by choosing the Console Application option from the New Project dialog box.

To compile an application in Debug mode (as opposed to Release mode) from the command line, add the flag /debug:

**vbc /debug C:\SimpleApp\Simpleapp.vb**

If you wish to employ a number of compiler options in your compile, you need to use a *response file*. This is a text file that specifies the options to be carried out. Each command for the compiler is placed on a separate line. The # sign is used to denote any comments in the response file.

For example, type the code from Listing 11.5 into Notepad and save it into the C:\SimpleApp directory as response.txt.

**Listing 11.5        Response File for SimpleApp Example**

```
#Response file to compile Simpleapp.vb into Simple.exe
/out:C:\SimpleApp\Simple.exe
c:\SimpleApp\Simpleapp.vb
```

This response file compiles the Simpleapp.vb code into the Simple.exe application and outputs it to the same directory that you are using for the source code.

The first line comments out the purpose of the file. The second line directs the output of the compiler, and the third line identifies the location of the source file.

You call the response file using the following command line from the directory containing the vbc compiler:

**vbc @C:\SimpleApp\response.txt**

Command-line compiling is useful for setting up conditional compiles that allow you to compile particular portions of your code. You will see how to do this in the next section.

## Conditional Compilation

Code can be compiled conditionally using the #Const directive to declare conditional compiler constants and the #If...Then...#Else directives to determine which blocks of code are compiled. Conditional compilation is useful for compiling code for different platforms or creating different language versions of a particular application.

The value of a compiler constant can be entered in the code (using the #Const) or from the command line (or response file) at compile time. Listing 11.6 illustrates how our SampleApp application can be set up for a conditional compile based on an entry we will make in the response file.

**Listing 11.6**   **Conditional Compilation Example Using SampleApp**

```
Imports System

Module Simpleapp
    Sub Main()
        #If testOK then
        Console.WriteLine("This is a simple app")
        Console.ReadLine()
        #Else
        Console.WriteLine("This is not a simple app")
        Console.ReadLine()
        #End If

    End Sub
End Module
```

In this example, we test for a conditional compiler constant (*testOK*). To set the value of this at the command line, we use the /d switch as follows:

**/d:testOK=0**   Flags the *testOK* as False and returns the line "This is not a simple app."

**/d:testOK=-1**   Flags the *testOK* as True and returns the line "This is a simple app."

Listing 11.7 illustrates how we might add this to the response file.

**Listing 11.7**   **Setting the *testOK* Variable in the Response File**

```
#Response file to compile SimpleApp.vb into Simple.exe
/out:C:\SimpleApp\Simple3.exe
/d:testOK=0
c:\SimpleApp\Simpleapp.vb
```

Listing 11.8 illustrates how the conditional compile constant can be directly included in the code of Simpleapp.vb. Note that you need to remove the *testOK* line from the response file.

**Listing 11.8**        **Using #Const in the Simpleapp Application**

```
Imports System

Module Simpleapp
    Sub Main()
        #Const testOK = 0
        #If testOK then
        Console.WriteLine("This is a simple app")
        Console.ReadLine()
        #Else
        Console.WriteLine("This is not a simple app")
        Console.ReadLine()
        #End If

    End Sub
End Module
```

Here, we have set *testOK* to False and should expect the line "This is not a simple app" printed to the console when we run the program.

## Distributing an Application

When you set up an application for distribution in .NET, you must make sure that the target machine has all the files required to support your application.

To do so, you need to create a Windows installer program that contains all the necessary bits and pieces required to run and support your program. This is done by adding a separate setup project to your solution. For basic applications, the .NET version of the process involves more work than what you may have been used to with earlier versions of VB, but it's ideal for creating flexible and powerful solutions.

When adding a setup project, you are given the choice of a number of different options. By far the easiest is the Setup Wizard, and we will use it do a quick walk-through here.

We will create a distributable version of the DebuggingDemo1 application that we built earlier in the chapter. Begin by opening the DebuggingDemo1 project in Visual Studio .NET, and from the File menu, choose Add Project ➤ New Project.

Choose Setup and Deployment Projects from the Project Types menu in the Add New Project dialog box. Then choose the Setup Wizard option from the Templates window and set the name to SetupDebuggingDemo1. Click OK.

This opens the Setup Wizard. The wizard is fairly self-explanatory, enabling you to choose the appropriate distribution package for your application and to choose whatever contents (including external files) belong to the project.

For this example, choose the Create a Setup for a Windows Application option on the second screen of the wizard. (The first screen is a simple splash screen.) The third screen allows you to choose the project outputs to include in the setup. Typically, this will include the primary output (DLLs and EXE files). Other options exist that may be selected depending on the nature of your project and what you have included with it. The fourth screen enables you to add external files to your project, and the fifth screen (shown in Figure 11.12) provides a confirmation dialog on the settings of your project.

**FIGURE 11.12:**

Using the Setup Wizard to create a Windows installer for the DebuggingDemo1 project

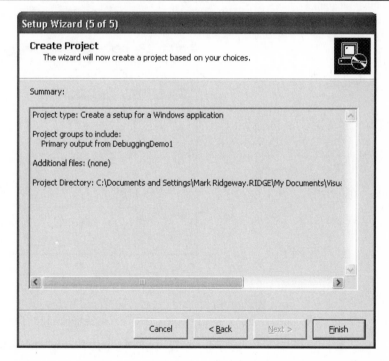

Once you've completed the wizard, you can set the various properties for your installer from the Properties window in Visual Studio. These include the title of the program, whether setup will detect a newer version of the application, the add/remove program icon, manufacturer and support details, and so on.

For this example, we will leave the default property settings. The main design window presents you with a number of folders representing the end user's desktop, application folder, and start menu/programs group. You can determine what shortcuts you wish to appear in these locations by selecting the relevant folder, right-clicking the workspace, and making the necessary selections from the context menu. By default, the application folder contains the primary output (i.e., the DebuggingDemo1 application).

For example, to add a desktop shortcut for the user, select the User's Desktop folder and right-click in the right pane of the split designer window. Choose the Create New Shortcut option. This opens the Select Item in Project dialog box. Choose Application Folder from the drop-down menu. This exposes the Primary Output from DebuggingDemo1 item, as shown in Figure 11.13. Click OK.

**FIGURE 11.13:**

Setting a Desktop shortcut for the user in the installer program.

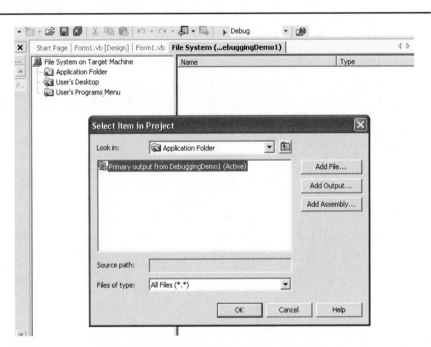

To test the installer, compile the program. You might want to set the Debug/Release mode to Release. The installation package(s) can be found in (assuming that you have followed the defaults) My Documents\Visual Studio Projects\SetupDebuggingDemo1\Debug.

The installer will walk you through a typical setup wizard that will install the DebuggingDemo1 program on your computer.

## Other Distribution Types

When you first choose the type of setup project to create, you are given the option of (as well as using the Wizard) Setup, Web Setup, Merge Module, or a CAB file. In the previous section, we showed you how to use the wizard to create a basic Setup project. You can also use the wizard to create any of the other distribution types.

At their basic level, each setup type is quite straightforward to create. The principal decision is which type you are going to use to begin with. The following list briefly describes each distribution type:

**Setup**    Traditional application that is installed to the file system of the client computer via distributable media such as CD-ROM or floppy disk. Setup files are produced as a Windows installer (.msi) file, which can be copied to the relevant media.

**Web Setup**    For applications that are to be deployed on a web server or made available on a web server for later download to client machines. This has an advantage over the Copy Project option (discussed in the introduction to this chapter) in that much of the configuration and deployment issues on the web server are automatically taken care of.

**CAB file**    For packaging ActiveX controls in a single CAB file for download from a web server to a web browser.

**Merge Module**    For installing shared components. Merge Module packages (.msm) are used in conjunction with a Windows installer (.msi) package when installing an application plus any shared components that it may use. Use a Merge Module where you expect your component to be used by multiple applications. Generally use one Merge Module per component.

Although we added the Setup project to our DebuggingDemo1 project in the previous example, we could also have created it quite separately. In this instance, the project we wish to create a setup for is added as external files. As a simple example, create a new Setup project and start the wizard. Make sure that you have previously, compiled DebuggingDemo1 and located the EXE file (in the Debug folder in the project directory). Add the DebuggingDemo1.exe file in screen 4 of the wizard and complete and build the Setup project as before.

It is also worth experimenting with the other types of distribution packages to get a feel for how they are put together.

## Summary

We have only scratched the surface of the debugging and deployment topics with this chapter. However, it is clear that Microsoft has come a long way with its debugging and deployment tools in .NET. As the use of these tools is very much uniquely driven by the particular situation for each application that you build, it is worth spending some time getting to know the tools as well as you can. Particularly with debugging, it is often easy to fall into the trap of constantly only using one or two tools and virtually forgetting that the others exist.

However, it is always worthwhile to take some time to reacquaint yourself with the full range of tools available, even the Disassembly window, whether you plan to learn assembly and make use it or not.

This completes this section of the book on Windows forms projects. In the next section, we will be covering custom components. Chapter 12 starts off by looking at the process of authoring custom components.

# PART III

# Custom Components

# CHAPTER 12

## Authoring Custom Components

- Classes vs. objects

- Building custom classes

- Abstraction and encapsulation

- Inheritance

- Interfaces

- The IComparable interface

- The IEnumerable interface

To make the most out of Visual Basic .NET, you must understand the role of classes and objects in programming. Classes are not new to Visual Basic .NET, but in this version of the language, they've assumed a new role. Everything in VB.NET is an object; even the humble integer is now implemented by a class. This chapter seems like a book within a book, but it's really an overview of objects and how to create your own objects. We anticipate that most of you are more or less familiar with the material in this chapter, but we're also confident that you'll find some interesting new information that will help you understand the role of classes and objects in VB programming a little better. Before you skip this chapter, please take a look at the last section, where we discuss callbacks and delegates—a topic that's new to most VB programmers.

The largest section of this chapter deals with implementation inheritance, the new type of inheritance you can implement with Visual Basic .NET. Inheritance means that you can create new classes (or Windows controls, as you will see in the following chapter) based on existing classes. The simplest application of implementation inheritance is to extend existing classes by adding features that are specific to your applications.

We'll also discuss interface inheritance, which isn't new to VB.NET, but it's a powerful aspect of object-oriented programming. Interface inheritance allows you to specify the signature of certain members and skip their implementation. These members will be implemented in the derived classes. A signature is the name and type of a property, or the name and arguments of a method. You will also learn how to build classes that implement some of the Framework's interfaces, like the IEnumerable and IComparable interfaces. The first topic, however, is an overview of classes and objects in VB.NET programming.

## Classes and Objects

Classes are not objects; they're the factories that produce objects. A class is a code module, whereas an object is just a variable that represents a class. Quite frequently the two terms are used interchangeably, but a class isn't something you can access directly. After creating a variable to represent a specific class, you create an instance of the class in memory and then you access the methods of the class through the variable that represents the instance of the class. To demonstrate the relationship between classes and objects, we'll explore a very useful class of the Framework, the `System.ArrayList` class. The following statement declares the `List` variable of the ArrayList type:

```
Dim List As ArrayList
```

At this point, the `List` variable is just a name. You can't add an item to the `List` collection with the Add method and you can't request the number of items in the list. Both statements will throw an exception if executed before the `List` variable is instantiated. If you attempt to call any of the List object's methods, you'll get the following exception:

```
Object reference not set to an instance of an object.
```

The compiler knows that it can store an ArrayList to this variable, but it will not do so until it runs into a statement like the following:

```
List = New ArrayList
```

This statement creates an instance of the ArrayList class. You can also say that this statement *instantiates* the ArrayList class. What this really means is that the System.ArrayList class's code is loaded into memory, the class's local variables are initialized, and you can add items to the List variable. The List variable exposes the Items property, which is another object, a Collection object. Each item in this collection represents a different item of the ArrayList. To add a new item, call the Items collection's Add method. To find out the number of items in the collection, call the Count method of the Items property. The following statements create a new ArrayList variable, populate it with a few items, and then print all the items in the Output window:

```
Dim List As New ArrayList()
List.Add("First Item")
List.Add("Second Item")
List.Add(999)
List.Add("Last Item")
Dim LEnum As IEnumerator
LEnum = List.GetEnumerator
While LEnum.MoveNext
    Console.WriteLine(LEnum.Current.ToString)
    End While
End Sub
```

When an object variable is instantiated, the class's code is loaded into memory, local variables are properly initialized, and a pointer to the block of memory allocated to this instance of the class is assigned to the object variable. You can create additional instances of the class. The class's code isn't loaded more than once; all instances share the same code. However, each instance has a separate copy of local variables and you can store different data to each variable.

You can also assign a variable of the ArrayList type to another variable of the same type:

```
Dim List1 As New ArrayList
Dim List2 As ArrayList
List2 = List1
```

Both List1 and List2 variables see the same block of memory, and therefore they see the same object. The items you add to the List1 variable can be also accessed through the List2 variable. Consider what happens if you reverse the order of the two variables in the assignment statement as shown next:

```
List1 = List2
```

List2 doesn't represent an object—it's value is Nothing. The same will happen to the List1 variable after the assignment; it will no longer point to an instance of the ArrayList class. This brings us to a very important keyword, the Nothing keyword.

## What an Object Is (and Isn't)

A variable that hasn't been properly initialized, or a variable that's been initialized and then assigned an uninitialized variable, has a value of Nothing. To find out whether a variable has been initialized, use the Is operator to compare it to the value Nothing. The following statements make sure the *Obj* variable represents an object before they use it:

```
If Not Obj Is Nothing Then
    ' Do something with Obj
End If
```

Many methods will return an object that's Nothing to indicate the absence of a result.

You can also find out the type of an object variable with the GetType method, and all classes expose a GetType method. The GetType method returns the type of the object to which it's applied. To find out whether a variable is of a specific type, use an expression like the following:

```
Dim dbl As Double = Math.PI
If dbl.GetType Is GetType(System.Double) Then
    Console.WriteLine("Variable is a double")
End If
```

To find out the name of the type, use the TypeName() function, which returns a string. The following statement will return the string "Double":

```
Console.WriteLine(TypeName(Dbl))
```

The GetType method is commonly used in applications that create dynamic forms. For example, the following statements iterate through all the controls on the form and change the background color of all PictureBox controls. We usually access each control by its name, but the control names may be known at design time; if the controls have been added to the form's Controls collection from within your code at runtime, as explained in Chapter 8, you should use a loop like the following:

```
Dim ctrl As Control
For Each ctrl In Me.Controls
    If ctrl.GetType Is System.Windows.Forms.PictureBox Then
        ctrl.BackColor = Color.Black
    End If
Next
```

By the way, there's a simpler method for iterating through the PictureBox controls on a form. If you use a variable of the PictureBox type in the For Each loop, you will iterate through the PictureBox controls on the form, and not through all controls on the form, as shown in the following loop:

```
Dim PB As PictureBox
For Each PB In Me.Controls
    PB.BackColor = Color.Black
Next
```

## Initializing Objects with Constructors

When you instantiate an object variable, the variable is also initialized. The ArrayList is initialized to an empty list, for example. Arrays are initialized according to their type when they're declared. If the array is numeric, its elements are zero; if its elements are of the String type, they're all set to zero-length strings. It's possible, however, to initialize an array by passing the values of the elements you want to store in it as arguments to its constructor. The following declaration creates an array of decimals and initializes it:

```
Dim numbers As Decimal() = {1, 2, 4, 8, 16, 32, 64, 256}
```

Notice that you don't have to specify the dimensions of the array; they're determined by the number of values in the brackets with the array's elements.

Object variables must be instantiated by calling their *constructor*. To generate random numbers, you can create the System.Random class with a statement like the following:

```
Dim rnd As New System.Random
```

If you declare the *rnd* variable without the New keyword, an exception will be thrown when you attempt to generate a random number later in your code.

To create a variable of the TimeSpan type, which represents a time interval, you can call the TimeSpan class's constructor with a statement like the following:

```
Dim TS As New TimeSpan(0, 0, 1, 59, 999)
```

The TS variable is an object of the TimeSpan type and represents an interval of 0 days, 0 hours, 1 minute, 59 seconds, and 999 milliseconds. However, you can create a zero-length TimeSpan object by omitting the New keyword in the declaration of the variable:

```
Dim TS As TimeSpan
MsgBox(TS)
```

This time you won't get an exception, but the variable TS will be initialized to a time interval of 0 milliseconds. You can set the duration of the TS variable in your code with the members of the TimeSpan class or initialize it by calling one of its overloaded constructors:

```
TS = New TimeSpan(1, 23, 59, 59)
```

All objects have a constructor, but sometimes this constructor is not visible—you can't access it through your code. Most classes provide an overloaded constructor. The ArrayList class's constructor for example, has three overloaded forms: one that accepts no arguments (it creates the default ArrayList object), one that accepts an integer argument (the ArrayList's capacity, which is the number of elements you intend to store in it), and another one that accepts a Collection object as argument. The last form of the constructor adds the items of the Collection object to the ArrayList.

The constructor usually accepts a few arguments, which are the basic properties of the object, and uses the values of the arguments to initialize the new instance of the object. The following constructor creates a Rectangle object and initializes it to the location and dimensions specified by the four arguments:

```
Dim Rect As New Rectangle(0, 0, 100, 20)
```

This statement is equivalent to the following statements, which set the rectangle's properties explicitly:

```
Dim R As Rectangle
R.X = 0
R.Y = 0
R.Width = 100
R.Height = 20
```

## Basic Data Types as Objects

The basic data types, such as integers, strings, and dates, don't behave quite like objects. You can declare an Integer variable and use it in your code without having to initialize it (actually, an integer is initialized to zero when it's declared). A purely object-oriented approach requires that even the basic data types are implemented and treated as objects. The Integer data type is implemented by the System.Integer class, but Visual Basic allows us to use it like an old-fashioned variable (a non-object variable). The same is true for all the basic data types. Even date variables are initialized to "1/1/0001 12:00:00 AM," and you need not call the New constructor. Actually, the basic data types have no constructors, and if you attempt to initialize an Integer variable with the New constructor, you'll get an error message.

You have certainly noticed that all the basic data types of the Framework are implemented as objects, which (conceptually) is something of a shock to "traditional" programmers. The Integer class exposes a few basic properties, like the MinValue and MaxValue properties that return the minimum and maximum numeric values one can represent with the Integer data type. It also exposes the ToString method, which in effect replaces the Format() function of previous versions of the language.

Other data types, like the String and Date types, expose many properties and methods. All the traditional string manipulation functions of Visual Basic have been replaced with methods. To find out the length of a string stored in a String variable, you can call the variable's Length method:

```
Dim Name As String = "My name"
Console.WriteLine Name.Length
```

The following statement shows how the members of the basic types are commonly used:

```
Dim Name As String = "Some name"
Console.WriteLine("There are " & Name.Length.ToString & _
                  " characters in " & Name)
```

The Length property returns an integer, and then we apply the ToString method to this integer value to convert it to a string. You can skip the conversion of the numeric value to a string value if you're using the default setting of the Option Strict statement (which is Off) and let the compiler convert it to a string. It is suggested, however, that you turn on the strict option.

**NOTE**    You can still use the Len() function of Visual Basic, but you should get into the habit of using the new members of the various data types. In future versions of the language, new features that are specific to a data type will be added as members of the specific data type and not as separate functions. All string manipulation functions will be members of the System.String class and they will no longer inflate the core language. By the way, the Framework includes a very powerful class for manipulating strings, the System.Text .StringBuilder class. The StringBuilder class exposes functionality similar to the functionality of the String class, but it's much faster.

## Building a New Class

In this section, we're going to look at the process of creating new classes and how to use them in our code. A class is a program that communicates with other programs through properties, methods, and events. These items, collectively known as members, constitute the object's interface. Objects expose a programmatic interface, not a visible interface. Just as the users of your application manipulate it through the application's visible interface, developers can manipulate your class programmatically, through its members.

Properties determine the object's state and methods perform actions on the object. Methods usually change the state of the object—they act on the object. Methods change the state of an object in ways that would be inconvenient, or impossible, through properties. The Clear method of many objects, for example, resets the values of their properties to their initial values. Without the Clear method, you'd have to reset each property individually. The Sort method of the objects that represent collections is another typical example. Without a Sort method, you'd have to retrieve all the items in the collection, sort them, and then clear the collection and add them back to it. The names of the properties are usually nouns and the names of the methods are verbs, to indicate that they perform an action.

A class starts with the Class keyword followed by the name of the class and ends with the End Class statement:

```
Class myCustomClass

End Class
```

At the beginning of the class, we declare the local variables: variables that will be used in the class's code but are invisible by any code outside the class. Then we write the procedures to implement the class's properties and methods, as discussed in the following sections. In effect, classes combine data and the code to manipulate the data in a single unit.

The Public access modifier appears usually in front of the Class keyword, because we want to be able to access the custom class from within other projects. The custom class may contain its own internal classes, too, which may be either private or public. If some classes contain code that's specific to your custom class and you don't want users of your class to access these additional classes, declare them as Private or Friend.

## Implementing Properties

Properties are implemented with Property procedures, which have two segments: a Get segment, which is invoked when the property is read, and a Set segment, which is invoked when the property is set. Read-only properties have a Get segment only. The code segment in Listing 12.1 shows a simple class that exposes two properties: the Name and Age properties.

**NOTE**     You'll find all the code from this chapter on www.sybex.com.

**Listing 12.1**     **A Simple Class for Representing Persons**

```
Public Class person
    Private _PersonName As String
    Private _PersonAge As Integer = 0
    Public Property Name() As String
        Get
            Return _PersonName
        End Get
        Set(ByVal Value As String)
            _PersonName = Value
        End Set
    End Property
    Public Property Age() As Integer
        Get
            Return _PersonAge
        End Get
        Set(ByVal Value As Integer)
            If Value > 0 And Value < 100 Then
                _PersonAge = Value
            End If
        End Set
    End Property
End Class
```

The properties are stored in private variables, which can't be accessed by code outside the class. The code in the Property procedure's Set section validates the value passed to the property and either sets the corresponding private variable or rejects the value. The sample code rejects invalid values (ages outside the range from 1 to 100) silently. You can also throw an exception when the user attempts to set a property to an invalid value (we'll discuss exceptions shortly). The code shown here simply rejects incorrect values silently.

To exercise the Person class, use a few statements like the following in a button's Click event handler:

```
Dim P As New person()
P.Name = "My Name"
P.Age = 300
Console.WriteLine(P.Name & ", " & P.Age)
P = New person()
P.Name = "Another Name"
P.Age = 30
Console.WriteLine(P.Name & ", " & P.Age)
```

We're assuming that both the test form's code and the class reside in the same module. If you implement the class in its own file, you should add to the test project a reference to the class.

To add a reference to a custom class in another project, open the Project menu and select Add Reference. When the Add Reference dialog box appears (Figure 12.1), select the Projects tab and locate the corresponding project with the Browse button. Select the desired class and then click OK to close the Add Reference dialog box.

**FIGURE 12.1:**

Adding a reference to a custom class in your project

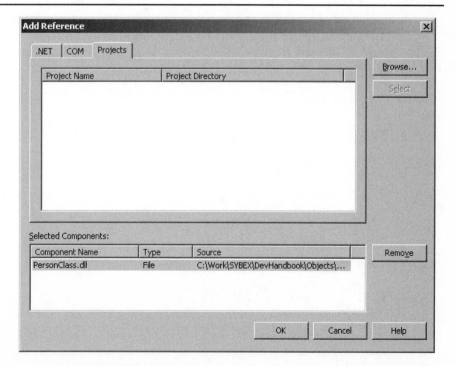

The sample projects shown in this chapter can be found on sybex.com. You can create a Windows application and insert the class's code after the form's code. If you want to separate the class from the test code, you should create a Class Library solution and enter the class's code in the Class module of the project. Then add a Windows Application project to the solution and set it as the Startup Object (right-click the test project in the Solution Explorer and select the command Set as Startup Project). Don't forget to add a reference to the class in the test project—if you don't, you won't be able to create instances of the class.

When the P variable is declared, class's code is loaded and the private (local) variables are initialized. If you declare another variable of the same type, the P1 variable, another set of private variables will be created. Each object will act on its own local variables and the two instances of the Person class don't interfere with one another. As you can see, a class embodies code and data into a single unit and the variables of each instance of the same class are totally independent.

The first group of statements attempt to assign the value 300 to the Age property, but the value is rejected and the property retains its default value, 0. The second group of statements successfully set the Age property to 30.

You can implement read-only properties by supplying the Get section of the Property procedure and prefixing the Property's name with the ReadOnly attribute. The Age property of the Person object is of no use because it's valid only for a few months after setting it for the first time. The Person class should store the date of birth (a constant value that doesn't change from year to year) and calculate the person's age as needed. Revise the Person class's code by adding the BirthDate property (read/write) and editing the Age property (read only) as shown in Listing 12.2.

**Listing 12.2     A Better Implementation of the Age Property**

```
Private _PersonBDate As Date
Public Property DateOfBirth() As Date
    Get
        Return _PersonBDate
    End Get
    Set(ByVal Value As Date)
        _PersonBDate = Value
    End Set
End Property

Public ReadOnly Property Age() As Integer
    Get
        Return DateDiff(DateInterval.Year, _PersonBDate, Now())
    End Get
End Property
```

## Objects vs. Structures

A common question is, why implement properties with Property procedures rather than declare structures with the equivalent fields? In other words, what's the difference between the Person class and the following structure?

```
Structure Person
    Dim name As String
    Dim bDate As Date
End Structure
```

As far as the data types of the fields are concerned, and the information you can store in them, there's no difference between a class and a structure. But a structure can't validate its data. If you assign a future date to the bDate property, it will gladly accept it as long as the value is within the range that can be represented by the Integer data type. Validation is a perfectly good reason for implementing an object's attributes as properties. You can even declare a few variables as Public (these variables are called fields) and they'll become properties of the object. Don't be tempted to do so, because you'll have to revise your code sooner or later. Let's say that changing the value of a property necessitates changes to another variable. That's something you can't do with fields. Or you may wish to raise an event when a property assumes a specific value—when the quantity in stock becomes 0, for example. It's trivial to raise an event from within a property's Set code, but it's impossible to raise an event when a field's value is set.

The best reason to use classes is that you can contain the code that applies to a specific class along with the data in a single module. If you're using structures, you must also provide code that acts on the data. Classes are modules that combine data and code, and users of your classes need not see the code. This feature, known as encapsulation, is discussed in more detail later in this chapter.

## Implementing Methods

Methods are nothing more than Public functions. They usually accept arguments, act on them, and may return a value. The return value can be anything; it can even be an object of the same type as the class itself. You can overload methods just as you would overload regular functions.

Let's say you have a method that accepts a time interval as argument. There are many ways to specify the interval, but the method's functionality doesn't change whether you specify the interval in milliseconds, in seconds and milliseconds, or even as a TimeSpan object. Let's say the method's name is Wait() and it waits for something to happen for a specified time interval, which is passed to the method as argument. The method may wait to read data from a stream or a web server. We won't discuss its implementation here. The important thing is that you shouldn't have to provide multiple methods with names like WaitInputMilliseconds,

WaitInputMinutes, and so on. What you need is a single method that accepts arguments of different types:

```
WaitInput(ByVal ms As Integer)
WaitInput(ByVal seconds As Integer, ms As Integer)
WaitInput(ByVal TS As TimeSpan)
```

Let's return to the Person class and add a method, the CalculateRate method. We're assuming that the Person class stores adequate information about the person it represents (income, profession, medical status, and so on) to calculate insurance rates. The CalculateRate method performs some calculations and returns a Decimal value, which is the suggested insurance rate for a person. Because it's applied to an instance of the Person class, all the information it needs is available to the method:

```
Public Function CalculateRate() As Decimal
    ' function's code
End Function
```

This is a very simple method. You can also pass arguments to a method. If you want the insurance rate for a specific plan, you can pass the name of the plan (or the desired insurance amount) to the method, as shown in the following implementation of the method:

```
Public Function CalculateRate(ByVal plan As Integer) As Decimal
    ' function's code
End Function
```

The function's code can use its argument(s) as well as the local variables in its calculations. It can even call the other methods of the object, because they're local functions. The two methods can coexist in the class: they're overloaded forms of the same function. As long as the arguments differentiate the various forms of the functions, you can overload your methods.

Not all methods return a value. A ChangeStatus method, which changes the current insurance status of a person, need not return a result. It simply sets another local variable to indicate the current status. However, you can return a value that may, or may not, be used by the code that calls the method. A Boolean value that indicates whether the method completed successfully is fairly common. The ChangeStatus method, for example, could also return the new status: attempt to set a field in a database table, then retrieve the same field's value and return it. The main application can easily determine whether the value was changed.

## Implementing Constructors

Nearly all of the Framework's classes have a constructor, which is basically a function that initializes a new instance of the class. The function's name is always New() and it's usually overloaded. There's always a New() function that accepts no arguments—it simply creates a new instance of the class and initializes all properties to their default values. Other overloaded forms of the constructor allow you to pass values to the basic properties of the class. For the Person class, you can create a constructor that accepts a name and a date of birth and initializes a new instance of the Person class to these values. Here are two overloaded forms of the Person class's constructor:

```
Public Sub New()

End Sub

Public Sub New(ByVal name As String, ByVal DOB As Date)
    Me.Name = name
    Me.DateOfBirth = DOB
End Sub
```

The Me keyword represents the class and the second form of the New constructor actually sets the class's properties, not the local variables. We avoid assigning the arguments directly to the private variables to make sure that the values passed to the constructor are properly validated (and there's no need to repeat the validation code in the constructor's code).

Notice that you can always call a class's default constructor (without arguments), even if the class doesn't contain a New() subroutine. If you decide to overload the constructor, however, you must also supply the implementation of the default constructor.

Even though Age is a read-only property, it can be still used with a parameterized constructor. We'll add a third form of the constructor that accepts a name and an age value and calculates the date of birth:

```
Public Sub New(ByVal name As String, ByVal Age As Integer)
    Me.Name = name
    Me.DateOfBirth = Now.Subtract(New TimeSpan(Age * 365))
End Sub
```

The value of the DateOfBirth property isn't the actual birth date, but it serves the purpose of calculating the person's age in calendar years.

## Implementing Events

Classes can also raise events, although this isn't very common. Controls raise a lot of events, but classes don't. An event is usually triggered by an external action, and classes don't interact with users. However, you can implement classes that raise events to indicate an unusual condition, the elapse of a time interval, the completion of an asynchronous operation, and so on.

To raise an event, use the RaiseEvent statement followed by the name of the event and possibly an argument. The name of the event must be declared as Public with a statement like the following:

```
Public Event customEvent()
```

This declaration must appear on the form's level. Then, you can raise the customEvent event from within any method with a statement like the following:

```
RaiseEvent customEvent
```

Most events, by means of their arguments, convey some information to the application that uses the class. Events pass two arguments, the sender argument, which identifies the object that raised the event, and an argument of the EventArgs type that contains information about the event itself.

To create your own EventArgs type, create a new class that inherits from the EventArgs class and add the appropriate members to the class. The EventArgs class provides a few basic members and the custom members will be added to them. Let's say you want to detect books with "peculiar" ISBN values. If you detect a valid ISBN that begins with three zeros ("000"), it's a fake ISBN. You can still use it in your application because it identifies a specific book, but you don't want to display this ISBN as if it were a real ISBN. Many programmers use the ISBN as key, and when they run into a book without ISBN, they make up a fake ISBN.

Every time the application detects such an ISBN, it can raise an event, the FakeISBN event. This event should report to its handler the fake ISBN through the EventArgs argument. Here's the definition of a class that derives from the EventArgs class and adds a new member, the ISBN member:

```
Public Class BookEvent
    Inherits EventArgs
    Public Shared ISBN As String
End Class
```

Then you must declare the event and its arguments with a statement like the following:

```
Public Event FakeISBN(ByVal sender As Object, ByVal e As BookEvent)
```

In your code, you must first set the ISBN property of the BookEvent class and then raise the FakeISBN event with a few statements like the following:

```
Dim oddISBN As New BookEvent()
oddISBN.ISBN = ISBN
RaiseEvent FakeISBN(Me, oddISBN)
```

These statements may appear in any member's code in the class. To intercept this event in the application that uses the custom class, you must create an instance of the class with the WithEvents keyword:

```
Dim WithEvents myObject As New myClass()
```

In the application that uses this class, you must program the myObject object's FakeISBN event handler. If you drop down the list of objects in the editor's window, select the myObject object, and then drop the list with the events, you will see the name of the custom event there. Select it and then enter the following lines in its handler:

```
Private Sub myObject_FakeISBN(ByVal sender As Object, _
                        ByVal e As CustomClass.BookEvent) _
                        Handles CustomClass.FakeISBN
    MsgBox("You've added a title with fake ISBN " & e.ISBN)
End Sub
```

Classes rarely trigger events, and when they do they usually notify the application about an external condition or the progress of an operation. Events are much more common with controls, as you will see in the following chapter.

## Handling Errors

When an application runs into an error (whether it was caused by a user action or any other source), we usually display a message to the user. Classes don't have a visible interface and can't interact with the user directly. Besides, error handling is the responsibility of the application that uses the class. When errors occur in a class, you must raise an exception and let the application handle it. This is how errors in all of the Framework's classes are handled, and your custom classes shouldn't be any different.

To raise an exception in a class, use the Throw method followed by an exception. The simplest method of passing an exception to the component that uses your custom class is to call the Throw function followed by a description of the error. The following statement will cause an exception when executed:

```
Throw New Exception("Age can't be negative")
```

The description of the error should be as specific as possible, and different conditions should produce different errors. This example initializes an Exception object and then throws the corresponding exception in a single statement.

We're going to add some validation code to the DateOfBirth property of our Person class. To validate the value passed to the DateOfBirth property, we will subtract it from the current date, and if the difference exceeds 100 years, we'll throw an exception (see Listing 12.3).

---

**Listing 12.3        Throwing an Exception from within a Property Procedure**

```
Public Property DateOfBirth() As Date
    Get
        Return _PersonBDate
    End Get
    Set(ByVal Value As Date)
        If DateDiff(DateInterval.Year, value, Now) > 0 And _
            DateDiff(DateInterval.Year, value, Now) < 100 Then
            _PersonBDate = Value
        Else
            Throw New Exception("Invalid date of birth")
        End If
    End Set
End Property
```

---

You can also define your own exceptions with a class that inherits from the ApplicationException class. Your class should contain three constructors, one without arguments, another constructor with a description, and a third constructor with a message and another exception object. Listing 12.4 shows a custom AgeException class.

**Listing 12.4**    **Defining a Custom Exception**

```
Public Class AgeException
    Inherits ApplicationException

    Public Sub New()
    End Sub

    Public Sub New(ByVal message As String)
        MyBase.New(message)
    End Sub

    Public Sub New(ByVal message As String, ByVal inner As Exception)
        MyBase.New(message, inner)
    End Sub
End Class
```

In the class's code, you will most likely create an instance of the exception with the second form of the constructor:

```
Throw New AgeException("Invalid value for the Age property!")
```

It's also likely that some other conditions, beyond your control, will cause an exception in your code. In this case, you may wish to pass the exception you detected in the class's code to the application. Here's the outline of a property procedure that passes an inner exception to the application:

```
Public Property PropName() As String
Get
    Try
        ' statements
        Return _propName
        Catch Exc As Exception
            Throw New customException("Error in XXX class", Exc)
    End Try
End Get

Set(ByVal Value As String)
    Try
        ' statements
        _propName= Value
    Catch
        Throw New customException("Error in XXX class", Exc)
    End Try
End Set
```

The application that uses the custom class should provide a structured exception handler to catch the custom exception, to avoid a runtime error, like the one shown in Figure 12.2. When you throw a custom exception from within your code, you provide the exception's description (the exception's Message property) and the inner exception (the exception's Inner-Exception property).

## Instance and Shared Members

The methods discussed so far are called *instance methods* because they can only be applied to an object that represents an instance of the class. The Name property applies to an instance of the Person class (an instance that represents a specific person with a name and a date of birth).

Sometimes we want to be able to call a method without having to create an instance of the class. The members of the Math class are typical examples. To calculate the absolute value of a number, you can't apply the Abs method to a numeric variable. You must call the `Math.Abs()` function, passing the numeric variable as argument. The methods of the DateTime class's members work the same way: you call them and pass the value on which they act as argument. These methods are called *shared*, because they do not act on private variables, and therefore, they do not require an instance of the class before they can be called. To create a shared method, simply prefix it with the Shared keyword.

Let's say you want to be able to write a simple application that allows the user to quote insurance rates over the phone. Since no sale has been made, we need not create an instance of the Person object just to get a rate and then discard it. We'll create a shared GetSampleRate method that accepts as arguments the person's age and returns the rate. This is an oversimplified approach, but you get the idea: we provide all the information needed to calculate the insurance rate in the form of arguments and we get back a result. (By the way, this is where the Age property may come in handy, because a customer is willing to reveal his age to get a quote, but not his actual birth date.) The data need not be stored anywhere, because most persons asking for our rates won't become our customers. The following is the implementation of a method that accepts as argument a person's age (in a real application you'd have to provide more information) and returns the insurance rate for the specific person (a pretty meaningless method of calculating insurance rates, but it takes into consideration the argument and returns a numeric value):

```
Public Shared Function GetSampleRate(ByVal age As Integer) As Decimal
    ' calculate insurance rate
    Return age / 2 + 104.55
End Function
```

To use this method, you can add statements like the following in a button's Click event handler on the test form:

```
Dim P As Person
Dim Age As Integer = _
            InputBox("Customer's age:")
Console.WriteLine(P.GetSampleRate(Age))
```

As you can see, there's no need to create an instance of the class; you simply call its shared methods and pass the appropriate arguments.

You can also implement shared properties. A shared property is common among all instances of the same class—in other words, all instances of the class "see" the same instance of the shared variable. If you want to keep track of the number of applications that use your class at any given time, you should implement a shared property:

```
Shared _Sessions As Integer
ReadOnly Property Sessions() As Integer
    Get
        Sessions = _Sessions
    End Get
End Property
```

The *_Sessions* local variable is increased and decreased elsewhere in your code (when a user instantiates and terminates the class).

At this point, you should have a fairly good idea of what a class does and we can discuss two major buzzwords in object-oriented programming: *abstraction* and *encapsulation*. These terms don't correspond to programming techniques; they're the two advantages of object-oriented programming.

## Abstraction

*Abstraction* means moving away from the details into a more conceptual treatment of a problem. In the past, programmers were thinking in terms of the problem they were trying to solve and wrote code to deal with the problem directly. Today, we try to express the problem with basic entities and then implement the objects that represent these entities. Let's consider an application for maintaining a database like Northwind. Instead of writing code to deal with specific operations on the tables of the database, we can come up with classes that represent the entities we deal with in our code. A Product object, which represents the products we sell, would be one of them. Other objects could be the Invoice object, which represents the sales, and the Order object, which represents purchases. Each object provides properties that describe the entity it represents: the product's name and price, the customer's name, address, and so on.

The next step is understanding the operations we need to perform on these objects and implementing them as methods. You'll need a method to add a product or a customer to the database, another method to delete a product, and a method to edit a product's fields. Once the objects are in place, you can write code that manipulates these objects rather than the tables of the database. You can request a Product object by calling a method like GetProductByID and passing the ID of the product as parameter or by calling a method like GetProductsByName and passing the name (or part of) of the product as argument. The GetProductByID method will return a single product, and the GetProductsByName will return a set of products.

You'll probably question the amount of work involved: If I can work directly with tables, why build another layer of objects between my application and the database? The benefits of using classes are not obvious in small projects. In very large projects, however, they become a necessity. You can't afford to have members of a team duplicating code, and you can't rely on many programmers implementing business logic. You incorporate basic database operations and business logic in one or more classes, and all programmers in the team use these objects. In effect, the classes help programmers produce consistent code, just as the basic controls allow you to create consistent Windows interfaces.

A database management system like SQL Server abstracts a very complicated structure for storing data. What you see is a collection of tables, which are made up of rows, their indices, relations, and so on. No one really cares how the data is actually stored on disk or how indexing works. SQL Server abstracts the complexity of the data storage and offers you a relational view of the data that makes sense programmatically.

### Encapsulation

*Encapsulation* is the ability to hide implementation details. Adding an invoice to the database is a complicated operation: we must make sure that all the detail lines refer to existing product IDs, the quantities ordered are available in the warehouse, and that all actions take place as in a transaction (i.e., if one line of the invoice fails, then the entire invoice must be rejected). Using classes, you can easily encapsulate the complexity of this operation into a method that accepts a few arguments, like the ID of the customer and an array of product IDs, quantities, and prices. Once this method is in place, any number of programmers can use it from different parts of the application.

Database constraints and T-SQL triggers are typical examples of encapsulation. Constraints allow you to impose rules on the values of each field (prices shouldn't be negative, for example) and embed these rules into the database. No programmer will be able to insert a row that violates these rules, intentionally or by mistake. Triggers allow you to update selected field values when other field values change. For example, you can create a trigger that adds a new line to a table every time the stock drops below a certain threshold. You can retrieve the rows of this table every morning and create purchase orders. Once a trigger is in place, you no longer have to worry about flagging products for reorder. Another benefit is that you don't have to rely on multiple programmers to understand business rules and implement them in multiple modules.

The Security.Cryptography class of the .NET Framework provides objects that securely encrypt documents. The encryption algorithms are quite complicated (the DES and RSA encryption algorithms), but you can encrypt a file with a few statements. You must supply the data to be encrypted and a password, and the encryption method will do the rest. All you really care about is that you have a securely encrypted document—you needn't (or shouldn't) even care about the actual encryption algorithm.

### Building the BookStore Class

In this section, you'll build a simple class for maintaining a collection of books. It's a simple class and certainly doesn't address many of the practical issues of a real-world application, but it demonstrates many interesting techniques. When we design a new class, it's important to keep in mind that the class should do the following:

- Abstract the actual objects we're modeling
- Encapsulate mundane or complicated operations

Our class will abstract a collection of books. No matter how books are stored in a data store (which could be a database or an XML file), the users of the class shouldn't have to understand the structure of the underlying data source. They should be able to create new book objects and add them to the data store, edit or delete existing books, and retrieve a collection of objects that represent books based on various criteria. The programmers using the class should be able to manipulate the collection of books with simple methods like GetBookByISBN, GetBook-Authors, and so on. These methods could be implemented as Web methods on a remote web server. Actually, if you create a class that exposes the necessary functionality for manipulating books, you can easily convert its members to Web methods, so that other developers can access them remotely.

Let's consider how we could simplify our code if we were developing an application to maintain a collection of books. First, we need a class that represents a collection of books; we'll call it BookStore. BookStore is a class that represents a collection of books—a few hundred or a few million. In our sample application, we'll store the books into an ArrayList, which can be persisted to an XML file between sessions. In a real application, you should use a database—you'll just have to implement the same methods differently. The BookStore class should also expose methods for retrieving books by ISBN, title, and so on, as well as methods for adding, editing, and removing Book objects from the collection. The users of the class need not be concerned with the implementation of the class's methods. You can implement a class that stores the books to an ArrayList and later change the code to use a database. The front-end application will work with the new implementation of the class without any changes in its code.

The BookStore class should expose a Book object to represent books. The Book class exposes properties that model the physical object they represent (the book's ISBN and title, its page count, price, and so on). In addition to these properties, each book can have one or more authors. The Authors property of the Book object, therefore, is a collection, and we'll implement it with another class, the Authors class. The Authors class will expose the standard members of a collection: the Count property and the Item, Add, and Clear methods.

Let's start with an outline of the BookStore class. Listing 12.5 shows the methods of the BookStore and Book classes. In essence, the definitions determine how the users of the two classes will manipulate the collection of books.

**Listing 12.5        The Outline of the BookStore, Book, and Authors Classes**

```
Public Class BookStore
    Public Function GetBookByISBN(ByVal ISBN As String) As Book
    End Function

    Public Function GetAuthorBooks(ByVal AuthorName As String) As Book()
    End Function

    Public Function AddBook(ByVal thisBook As Book) As Boolean
    End Function

    Public Function RemoveBook(ByVal thisBook As Book) As Boolean
    End Function

    Public Class Book
        Public BookAuthors As New Authors()

        Public Property Title() As String
        End Property

        Public Property SubTitle() As String
        End Property

        Public Overridable Property ISBN() As String
        End Property
```

```
        Public Property Price() As Decimal
        End Property

        Public Property Pages() As Integer
        End Property

        Public Class Authors
            Public Function Add(ByVal authorName As String)
            End Function

            Public Function Clear()
            End Function

            Public Function Count() As Integer
            End Function

            Public Function Item(ByVal idx As Integer) As String
            End Function
        End Class
    End Class
```

Notice that the Book class is defined in the BookStore class and the Authors class is defined in the Book class. This hierarchy indicates how classes will be used. The BookStore class is a container for Book objects. It simply provides methods for adding and removing Book objects to a collection. A real-world class would contain code to interact with a database. Actually, you can modify the BookStore class so that it gets its data from the Pubs database. The applications that use the BookStore and Book classes will not be affected by the changes. They will see the same members and they'll continue to handle a collection of books. The Book, Authors, and BookStore classes *abstract* the physical model we're emulating. They allow applications to access entities like books and authors and not have to worry about how these entities are stored or the relations between them. The application programmer can write an application for manipulating books without even knowing where, or how, the data is stored.

We'll start with the innermost class, the Authors class, which is a typical collection.

### Collection Properties

One of the noteworthy features of the Book class is that one of its properties is a collection. The Authors property is a collection—in other words, one of the properties exposed by a Book object is also an object. For each book, we'll maintain an ArrayList object with the names of the authors because we don't know how many authors each book may have. Some books may have no author; others may have a dozen authors. We'll provide a property to return the number of authors and three methods: The Add method to add an author, the Clear method to clear the collection, and the Item method, which accepts an index value as argument and returns the

author at the specified location in the collection. Listing 12.6 shows the implementation of the
Authors class.

**Listing 12.6     The Authors Property Is Implemented by Another Class**

```
Public Class Authors
    Private authorNames As New ArrayList()

    Public Function Add(ByVal authorName As String)
        authorNames.Add(authorName)
    End Function

    Public Function Clear()
        authorNames.Clear()
    End Function

    Public Function Count() As Integer
        Return (authorNames.Count)
    End Function

    Public Function Item(ByVal idx As Integer) As String
        If idx < authorNames.Count Then
            Return authorNames(idx)
        Else
            Throw New Exception("The book has only " & _
                        authorNames.Count.ToString & " authors")
        End If
    End Function
End Class
```

The code is straightforward and provides the few members that are necessary to access the
items of the Authors collection. Later in the chapter, you'll see how to implement the Authors
class with a single statement that takes advantage of inheritance. The class shown in Listing 12.6
is not a futile exercise. It demonstrates how to create object properties with their own interface.
Authors is a collection, so why not implement it by inheriting from a collection class? Its implementation can be as simple as this:

```
Public Class Authors
    Inherits ArrayList
End Class
```

Actually, you can switch between the two implementations of the Authors class and the rest
of the application will work without any changes. We'll discuss inheritance in detail shortly; all
you need to understand at this point is that the Inherits keyword brings all the functionality of
an existing class into our custom class.

So far, we've implemented the Authors class, which will become a property of the Book class. The implementation of the Book class is shown in Listing 12.7.

**Listing 12.7**    **The Book Class**

```
Public Class Book
    Private _Title As String
    Private _ISBN As String
    Private _Subtitle As String
    Private _Pages As Integer
    Private _Price As Decimal
    Public BookAuthors As New Authors()

    Public Property Title() As String
        Get
            Title = _Title
        End Get
        Set(ByVal Value As String)
            _Title = Value
        End Set
    End Property

    Public Property SubTitle() As String
        Get
            SubTitle = _Subtitle
        End Get
        Set(ByVal Value As String)
            _Subtitle = Value
        End Set
    End Property

    Public Overridable Property ISBN() As String
        Get
            ISBN = _ISBN
        End Get
        Set(ByVal Value As String)
            _ISBN = Value
        End Set
    End Property

    Public Property Price() As Decimal
        Get
            Price = _Price
        End Get
        Set(ByVal Value As Decimal)
            _Price = Value
        End Set
    End Property

    Public Property Pages() As Integer
        Get
            Pages = _Pages
```

```
            End Get
            Set(ByVal Value As Integer)
                _Pages = Value
            End Set
        End Property

        Public Class Authors
            Inherits ArrayList
        End Class
    End Class
End Class
```

The implementation of the various properties is quite trivial; we haven't even included any validation code for the ISBN. We'll return to this class and add more features later. But first, let's complete the example with the implementation of the BookStore class. The BookStore class is basically a collection of Book objects, but it's more than a simple collection. It exposes methods to retrieve books based on their title or ISBN, methods to retrieve the books of a specific author, or the authors of a book, and so on. Listing 12.8 shows a simple implementation of the BookStore class.

**Listing 12.8        The BookStore Class**

```
Public Class Bookstore
    Private allBooks As New ArrayList()

    Public Function GetBookByISBN(ByVal ISBN As String) As Book
        Dim i As Integer
        For i = 0 To allBooks.Count - 1
            If CType(allBooks(i), Book).ISBN = ISBN Then
                Return allBooks(i)
            End If
        Next
        Return Nothing
    End Function

    Public Function GetAuthorBooks(ByVal AuthorName As String) As Book()

    End Function

    Public Function AddBook(ByVal thisBook As Book) As Boolean
        allBooks.Add(thisBook)
    End Function

    Public Function RemoveBook(ByVal thisBook As Book) As Boolean
        allBooks.Remove(thisBook)
    End Function
```

Now that the BookStore class is in place, we can test-drive it. Add a new project to the solution and set it as the solution's Startup Object. A class can't be executed on its own; it must be instantiated from within another application, and this is what we're going to do. The test form of the BookStore project is shown in Figure 12.3. The grid is a ListView control that displays the basic properties of the Book objects stored in an instance of the BookStore class.

**FIGURE 12.3:**

Testing the Book-
Store class

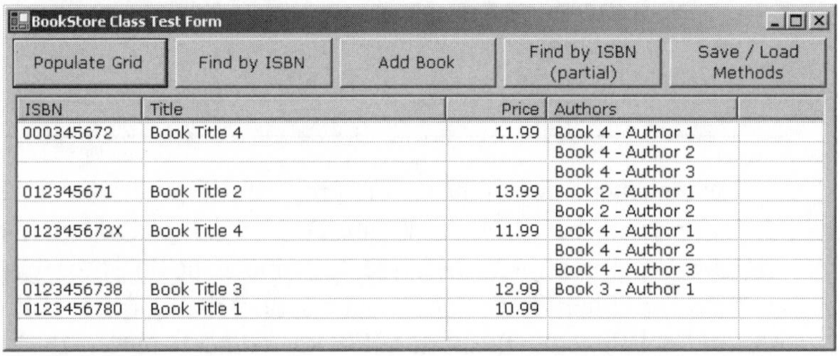

The following code adds books to the collection in the form's Load event handler:

```
Dim aBook As New Book()
aBook.ISBN = "0123456780"
aBook.Title = "Book Title 1"
aBook.Price = 10.99
Books.AddBook(aBook)

aBook = New Book()
aBook.ISBN = "012345671"
aBook.Title = "Book Title 2"
aBook.Price = 13.99
aBook.BookAuthors.Add("Book 2 - Author 1")
aBook.BookAuthors.Add("Book 2 - Author 2")
Books.AddBook(aBook)
```

The ShowAllTitles() subroutine populates the ListView control with the titles. Listing 12.9 demonstrates how to display each book's title and ISBN, and each author on a separate row under the corresponding book's row. Call this subroutine to display the members of the Books collection on the grid.

**Listing 12.9**      **The *ShowAllTitles()* Subroutine Populates the ListView Control**

```
Sub ShowAllTitles()
    Dim aBook As New Bookstore.Book()
    Dim LItem As ListViewItem
    Dim au As Integer
    ListView1.Items.Clear()
    For Each aBook In Books
        LItem = New ListViewItem()
        LItem.Text = aBook.ISBN
```

```
            ListView1.Items.Add(LItem)
            LItem.SubItems.Add(aBook.Title)
            LItem.SubItems.Add(aBook.Price.ToString)
            For au = 0 To Math.Min(0, aBook.BookAuthors.Count - 1)
                LItem.SubItems.Add(aBook.BookAuthors.Item(0))
            Next
            For au = 1 To aBook.BookAuthors.Count - 1
                LItem = New ListViewItem()
                LItem.SubItems.Add("")
                LItem.SubItems.Add("")
                LItem.SubItems.Add(aBook.BookAuthors.Item(au))
                ListView1.Items.Add(LItem)
            Next
        Next
    End Sub
```

## Persisting the BookStore Class

We need to add two more methods to our class to persist the collection of Book objects to a disk file and load the collection with the data stored in a file. The Save method accepts as argument a file's path and stores the ArrayList with the books to the specified file. The Load method accepts the same argument and loads the ArrayList with the data already persisted to the file.

To persist the ArrayList collection, we'll use the Serialization class. To use this class in a project, you must import the following namespace to your project: `System.RunTime`
`.Serialization.Formatters`. In Listing 12.10, we use the fully qualified name of the class. The Save and Load methods, shown in the listing, accept a single argument, which is the path of the file they're going to open (to either read from or write to). To serialize an object, we create an instance of the BinaryFormatter class and call its Serialize method, passing as arguments a FileStream object and the object to be serialized. To read the serialized data back, we call the same object's Deserialize method, passing as argument a FileStream object pointing to the file where the data has been stored.

**Listing 12.10    Implementing the Add and Save Methods of the BookStore Class**

```
    Public Function Save(ByVal path As String)
        Dim FS As New System.IO.FileStream(path, IO.FileMode.OpenOrCreate)
        Dim BS As New _
            System.Runtime.Serialization.Formatters.Binary.BinaryFormatter()
        BS.Serialize(FS, allBooks)
        FS.Close()
    End Function

    Public Function Load(ByVal path As String)
        Dim FS As New System.IO.FileStream(path, IO.FileMode.Open)
        Dim BS As New _
            System.Runtime.Serialization.Formatters.Binary.BinaryFormatter()
        allBooks.Clear()
```

```
        allBooks = CType(BS.Deserialize(FS), ArrayList)
        FS.Close()
    End Function
```

Notice that the Serialization class persists the entire ArrayList with a single statement, even though each element of the ArrayList contains a smaller ArrayList with the Author names. A real application would use a database to store the information, and it would also store books and authors in two different tables, but the user of the class need not be aware of the specifics. The Load and Save methods encapsulate complicated operations and programmers using your class need not worry about the structure of the database.

**NOTE**     Any class you plan to serialize must be prefixed by the Serializable attribute. Since it doesn't cost anything to mark a class as serializable, you might as well prefix all of your classes with this attribute. The declaration of the BookStore class must be changed to `<Serializable()>` Public Class Bookstore.

To test the Save and Load methods, insert the following statements in a button's Click event handler. The code exercises both methods at once (it saves and then reloads the data), but it demonstrates the use of the two methods:

```
Books.Save("c:\allbooks.bin")
Dim bk As Bookstore.Book
For Each bk In Books
    Books.RemoveBook(bk)
Next
Books.Load("c:\allbooks.bin")
```

The BookStore class handles many of the mundane, low-level operations. Of course, implementing a real class isn't trivial. In most cases, the class itself involves quite a bit of code. The benefits of using classes to encapsulate complicated operations become obvious in very large projects, where the same class will be reused by a large number of programmers. The BookStore class isn't the best example of abstraction, but it demonstrates the basic idea of abstraction. Programmers use objects that represent the physical entities they manipulate. Working with the properties of the Book class and the methods of the BookStore class is much simpler than manipulating tables with ADO .NET.

### Overriding Default Members

In addition to the class members you implement, the class exposes a few standard members. To see them, enter the name of a variable of this type and the following period. In the IntelliSense box, you will see the following standard members:

**Equals**   Determines whether the current instance is equal to the object passed as argument

**GetHashCode**   Returns the class's hash code (a unique integer value)

**GetType**   Returns the variable's type

**ReferenceEquals**   Returns True if the current instance of the class is the same as the object passed as argument

**ToString**   Returns a string that describes the variable

You can override the default implementation of these methods, and you will most likely have to override two of them: the Equals and ToString methods. The default implementation of the Equals method behaves like the ReferenceEquals method, and the ToString method returns a string like "ProjectName.ClassName". This string doesn't convey much information about the object.

The Equals method compares two objects and returns True if the two objects are equal. When you compare built-in objects, the compiler knows how to compare two of their instances. The following statements, for example, will print the value True in the Output window:

```
Dim rect1, rect2 As Rectangle
rect1 = New Rectangle(New Point(0, 0), New Size(100, 20))
rect2 = New Rectangle(New Point(0, 0), New Size(100, 20))
Console.WriteLine(rect1.Equals(rect2))    ' will print True
```

If you use Person objects as shown in the following example, however, the same statement will print False:

```
Dim P1 As New person("My Name", 30)
Dim P2 As New person("My Name", 30)
Console.WriteLine(P1.Equals(P2))             ' will print False
```

The two objects, P1 and P2, are equal, but the compiler doesn't know how to compare two arbitrary objects. The compiler doesn't assume that two objects are equal when all their properties are identical. Two shapes may be equal if they have the same area, but their coordinates may be different. How two custom objects will be compared is entirely up to you and you must provide some additional information to enable the compiler to compare two instances of your custom class. For the Person class, you can implement a custom Equals method with the code shown in Listing 12.11.

**Listing 12.11**     **Overriding the Equals Method of the Person Class**

```
Public Overloads Function Equals(ByVal obj As Object) As Boolean
    Dim P As person = CType(obj, person)
    If P.Name = _PersonName And P.Age = _PersonAge Then
        Equals = True
    Else
        Equals = False
    End If
End Function
```

Of course, you can use any combination of properties to determine whether two instances of the class are equal. You can transform the values of the properties and make the comparison as complicated as required. A real class for representing persons would compare social security numbers, which uniquely identify each person. No other combination of properties will be unique.

Overriding the default implementation of the ToString method is just as simple, and you can include any combination of properties you wish. The custom ToString method shown in Listing 12.12 returns a string with the person's name and age.

**Listing 12.12    Overriding the ToString Method of the Person Class**

```
Public Overloads Function ToString() As String
    Return _PersonName & ", " & _
           DateDiff(DateInterval.Year, Now, _PersonBDate)
End Function
```

The default ToString method would return a string that identifies the object's type:

```
PersonClass.Person
```

The custom ToString method returns this:

```
My Name, 33
```

## Inheritance

*Inheritance* is a powerful technique that gives you the ability to create a new class based on an existing one. You can create a new class by simply specifying that it inherit another class. The new class contains all the functionality of the inherited (or parent) class, and it's called the derived class. You can add new members to the derived class or override some members of the parent class. A typical example is the Person base class, from which you can inherit classes like Employee, Customer, Contact, and so on. All the derived classes expose the same basic characteristics, and they can be based on a common class.

Inheritance is not new to Visual Basic .NET, but for the first time Visual Basic supports implementation inheritance (true inheritance, as many developers like to call it). The other type of inheritance is interface inheritance. In our view, both types of inheritance are equally important, and each has its own applications. The emphasis in this chapter is on implementation inheritance, because it's new to VB programmers—it's also more flexible than interface inheritance. With interface inheritance, you write a class and specify that certain members are implemented as placeholders in the base class and that their code is supplied in the derived class.

When should you use inheritance? Use inheritance when you expect to implement classes, which can be based on a primary class. The Person class contains a few basic properties like a person's name, date of birth, and so on. Employees have all these properties, as well as a salary or wage, a position, and more. Customers share the same properties with the Person class, but they have an address, credit, and so on. The Employees and Customers classes may inherit the Person class.

Inheritance promotes encapsulation—another buzzword in OO programming. You write a class, test it, and debug it, and you make it available to a team of programmers. If you allow individual programmers to edit the class's code, they'll end up with their own, "customized" versions of your class. This isn't what we mean by code reuse, and sharing source code is out of the question. Programmers can use the class as is, but what if they need some extra features? Do they request an updated version of your code? Actually, consider how you would handle the update of your own code. In the past, you had to edit the code, make sure you didn't break the interface, and distribute the new class. If you were very careful, the old applications would work with the new class and new applications could also take advantage of the new members.

What do we mean by "breaking the interface"? All existing members should work as they did in the old version of the class. The methods should accept the same arguments and return the same types. Properties should also have the same type. If you decide to change the return type of a function from Single to Double, then some of the existing applications may not work with the new version of the class. This can be fixed easily, but what good is it to promote code reuse in terms of classes if you have to edit the applications that use them? You can't change the arguments of a method, either, not even their order. If you do, some of the applications that use this class will break.

You can change the implementation of a method or a property procedure at will. If you come up with a more efficient technique of implementing the same task, you can edit your class and distribute it to others. As long as the "signature" of the method remains the same (in other words, as long as you don't touch the function's declaration and you return the same type), all existing applications will not only work, but they will take advantage of the new algorithm you've implemented.

Yet what piece of code will remain unchanged for the lifetime of the applications that use it? What if other developers want to add features to your class to better integrate it with their applications? Here's where inheritance comes in. Developers can add to the functionality of your class without touching the code. This guarantees that any application using the original class will still work. In effect, developers won't replace the original class with another one. On the contrary, they will create another class that provides all the functionality of the original class (that's what inheritance is all about) and then some extra functionality. The extra functionality consists of new, or overloaded, members.

We'll start our discussion of inheritance with a simple example that demonstrates the best of inheritance. We'll move to more advanced topics later in the chapter, but our first example demonstrates the most important aspects of inheritance.

### Inheriting an Existing Class

Many of the Framework's classes can be inherited and you can take advantage of the functionality already built into the original class. In addition, you can add functionality that's unique to your application. For example, you can create an ArrayList class that processes its items, or you can add a Save and a Load method. To inherit from an existing class, use the Inherits keyword followed by the name of the class you want to inherit from. The class being inherited is the base class and the class that inherits is the derived class. The Inherits keyword must appear immediately after the Class keyword, as in the following example:

```
Class MyList
    Inherits System.ArrayList
End Class
```

These lines create a new class, the MyList class, which is identical to the ArrayList class: it exposes the exact same interface. Of course, we don't inherit from a class to create an identical one. The new class should add more members to the original class (properties and methods) or override some of the existing ones.

The custom Load and Save methods will make use of the Serialization class to persist the contents of the ArrayList to a file. Let's look at the implementation of these two methods. Both methods must establish a Stream object to the file in which the data will be stored. This object will be passed as argument to the Serialize (or Deserialize) method of the appropriate Formatter object. Start a new project of the Class Library type, name it MyClasses, and then rename default class to PersistableAList. The name of the project will become the default namespace and the class's full name will be MyClasses.PersistableAList. The name of the project is usually a company name or a product name. Enter the code shown in Listing 12.13 in the class's code window.

**Listing 12.13**    **Adding a Save and Load Method to the ArrayList Class**

```
Imports System.IO
Imports System.Runtime.Serialization.Formatters.Binary

<Serializable()> Public Class PersistableAList
    Inherits ArrayList
```

```
        Public Sub Save(ByVal fileName As String)
            Dim saveFile As FileStream
            saveFile = File.OpenWrite(fileName)
            Dim Formatter As BinaryFormatter = New BinaryFormatter()
            Formatter.Serialize(saveFile, Me)
            saveFile.Close()
            Formatter = Nothing
        End Sub

        Public Sub Load(ByVal fileName As String)
            Dim readFile As FileStream
            readFile = File.OpenRead(fileName)
            Dim BFormatter As BinaryFormatter
            BFormatter = New BinaryFormatter()
            Dim ATable As New ArrayList()
            ATable = CType(BFormatter.Deserialize(readFile), ArrayList)
            Dim ALEnum As IEnumerator = ATable.GetEnumerator
            While ALEnum.MoveNext
                Me.Add(ALEnum.Current)
            End While
        End Sub
    End Class
```

The code uses the Binary Formatter class to serialize the ArrayList, and the methods are no different than the subroutines you'd write to serialize an ArrayList in your code. The most interesting part of this code is the Inherits statement, which tells the compiler to create a new class based on the ArrayList class. The very first word in the class's declaration is an attribute, which tells the compiler that any object of this type is *serializable* (a long term describing that the object can be converted to a series of bytes that can be stored to a stream). In the case of our code, the stream is a FileStream object.

To test the new custom class, add another project to the solution, the TestProject project. Then set the TestProject as the Startup Project by selecting the Set as Startup Project command in the project's context menu. Add a reference to the class with the Project ➤ Add Reference command. Create a small custom ArrayList, persist it to a disk file with the Save method, and then reset the list and load it with the Load method:

```
Dim cTable As New MyControls.PersistableAList()
cTable.Add("First Item")
cTable.Add(2222)
cTable.Add(Now())
cTable.Save("c:\table.bin")
```

As you saw, adding custom features to an existing class is fairly straightforward. You will find it convenient to add features specific to your application to many of the Framework's classes. In the following chapter, you will see how to inherit Windows controls (in other words, add custom functionality to existing controls).

There are classes, however, that can't be inherited. The Array class, for example, is not inheritable. The simplest method of finding out whether you can inherit from an existing class is to attempt to inherit from it. If the class can't be inherited, an exception will be thrown and the name of the class following the Inherits keyword will be marked as being in error by the editor.

The Authors class in the BookStore example you've built earlier in this chapter stores the names of the authors in an ArrayList object and implements the members of a collection. Now that you've read about inheritance, you know a better way of implementing the Authors property. Derive it from the ArrayList class and you needn't implement a single member. The revised implementation of the Authors class is shown next:

```
Public Class Authors
    Inherits ArrayList
End Class
```

It still exposes the same members as the implementation shown in Listing 12.5 and the test project works just as well.

### Inheriting the Book and BookStore Classes

The BookStore and Book classes are not typical examples of inheritable classes, but you can create new classes by deriving from these two classes. Any class can be inherited as long as it's not marked with the NonInheritable attribute. The derived class contains the functionality of the original class, and it may add new members to the original class or override certain members.

The BookStore class treats the ISBN like a product ID, but the last digit of an ISBN is a check digit for the first 9 digits. Our class will accept any check digit, and this isn't what we want in a production environment. To minimize typing errors, we must validate the check digit and either reject ISBNs with the wrong check digit or fix the check digit in our code. We'll create a new class that derives from the BookStore class and validates the ISBNs of the books. The new class will override the ISBN property and it will add a new property, the OnOffer property. This is a Boolean value indicating whether the book is on offer.

Because the ISBN is a property of the Book class, we must inherit both the Book and the BookStore classes. The new classes are called newBook and newBookStore, and they inherit from the Book and BookStore classes respectively. The newBook class overrides the ISBN property with a better implementation of the same property and adds a Boolean property, the OnOffer property, which specifies whether the book is discounted or not. The outline of the newBook class is shown next:

```
Public Class newBook
    Inherits Bookstore.Book
```

```
      Public Overrides Property ISBN() As String
      Public Property OnOffer() As Boolean
   End Class
```

The newBookStore class inherits from the BookStore class and overrides the GetBookBy-ISBN method. The new implementation of the GetBookByISBN takes into consideration the check digits (if a check digit is missing, the function appends the proper one to the ISBN). The outline of the newBookStore class is shown here:

```
Public Class newBookStore
   Inherits Bookstore
   Public Overrides Function GetBookByISBN(ByVal ISBN As String) _
                           As book
```

The first line indicates the class from which the new class inherits. The newBook class inherits the Book class and the newBookStore class inherits the BookStore class. Notice that the overridden GetBookByISBN class returns a value of the Book type. Shouldn't it return a new-Book type? Overridden members must have the same signature as the matching members in the parent class, so the GetBookByISBN() method can't return a newBook type. However, the Book object can be used anywhere you would use a newBook object.

**NOTE** An important point to remember is that a class can inherit from another class only if you can use an object of the parent class in the place of an object of the child class. Let's say the parent class is Person and Employee is a derived class. The Employee class exposes more members than the Person class, and every object of the Person class can be used in the place of an object of the Employee class. The inverse is not true, though, because an Employee object has members that may not exist in its parent class. In our example, we should be able to use the Book object instead of the newBook object. If not, then we should design the newBook class from scratch rather than derive from the Book class.

The core of the newBook class is a private function, the CheckDigit() function, which calculates the check digit. The ISBN property calls this function to make sure all books have valid ISBNs. If not, an exception is thrown. Listing 12.14 shows the complete implementation of the newBook class.

**Listing 12.14      Inheriting from the newBook Class**

```
Public Class newBook
   Inherits Bookstore.Book
   Dim bookISBN As String
   Public Overrides Property ISBN() As String
      Get
         ISBN = bookISBN
```

```
        End Get
        Set(ByVal Value As String)
            If Value.Length = 10 Then
                bookISBN = Value.Substring(0, 9) & CheckDigit(Value)
            ElseIf Value.Length = 9 Then
                bookISBN = Value & CheckDigit(Value)
            Else
                Throw New Exception("Invalid ISBN!")
            End If
        End Set
    End Property

    Dim _onOffer As Boolean
    Public Property OnOffer() As Boolean
        Get
            Return _onOffer
        End Get
        Set(ByVal Value As Boolean)
            _onOffer = Value
        End Set
    End Property

    Private Function CheckDigit(ByVal ISBN As String) As String
        Dim i As Integer, chksum, chkDigit As Integer
        For i = 0 To 8
            chksum = chksum + (10 - i) * ISBN.Substring(i, 1)
        Next
        chkDigit = 11 - (chksum Mod 11)
        If chkDigit = 10 Then
            Return ("X")
        ElseIf chkDigit = 11 Then
            Return ("0")
        Else
            Return (chkDigit.ToString)
        End If
    End Function
End Class
```

The overridden newBook class examines the value of the ISBN property and throws an exception if it's not a valid ISBN value. If the length of the supplied value is 9 digits, the property's code sets the check digit to the appropriate value. If the supplied ISBN value is 10 digits long, the code doesn't correct the check digit because the error is not necessarily in the check digit. The OnOffer property's code is trivial.

Now we can switch our attention to the newBookStore class. This class, shown in Listing 12.15, inherits from the newBookStore class and overrides the GetBookByISBN method. The new method's code calls the GetBookByISBN method of the parent class (the MyBase keyword), passes the user-supplied ISBN as argument and returns the result returned by this method.

Notice that the new GetBookByISBN method doesn't pass the ISBN as it was entered by the user. Instead, it validates the ISBN first. If it's passed a 9-digit ISBN, it calculates the proper check digit and then uses the new, complete ISBN to search.

**Listing 12.15    Inheriting from the newBookStore Class**

```
Public Class newBookStore
    Inherits Bookstore

    Public Class BookEvent
        Inherits EventArgs
        Public Shared ISBN As String
    End Class
    Public Event FakeISBN(ByVal sender As Object, ByVal e As BookEvent)

    ' CAN'T OVERRIDE A BASE METHOD AND RETURN A DIFFERENT TYPE
    Public Overrides Function _
                    GetBookByISBN(ByVal ISBN As String) As Book
        Dim book As New newBook()
        If ISBN.Length = 9 Then ISBN = ISBN & book.CheckDigit(ISBN)
        book = MyBase.GetBookByISBN(ISBN)
        If ISBN.Substring(0, 3) = "000" Then
            Dim oddISBN As BookEvent
            oddISBN.ISBN = ISBN
            RaiseEvent FakeISBN(Me, oddISBN)
        End If
        Return book
    End Function
End Class
```

The following statements demonstrate how the derived GetBookByISBN method works:

```
Dim abook As New newBook()
abook.Title = "new Title"
abook.ISBN = "012345679"
abook.BookAuthors.Add("new Author 1")
abook.BookAuthors.Add("new Author 2")
abook.Pages = 350
abook.Price = 21.95
Books.AddBook(abook)

Console.WriteLine(abook.ISBN)
abook = Books.GetBookByISBN("0123456797")
If Not abook Is Nothing Then
    Console.WriteLine(abook.ISBN & vbTab & abook.Title)
```

```
Else
    Console.WriteLine("ISBN 0123456797 was not found")
End If
abook = Books.GetBookByISBN("012345679")
If Not abook Is Nothing Then
    Console.WriteLine(abook.ISBN & vbTab & abook.Title)
Else
    Console.WriteLine("ISBN 012345679 was not found")
End If
```

First, we add a book with a valid ISBN (012345679) to the collection. Then the code calls the GetBookByISBN method, passing the complete ISBN as argument (in the first call) and the same ISBN without the check digit as argument (in the second call). The method returns the same book regardless of which argument was passed to it. Notice that the derived GetBook-ByISBN method relies on the GetBookByISBN method of its parent class to perform the search. It simply appends the proper check digit to the ISBN (if it's missing) to make sure that the original GetBookByISBN method is called with a proper argument. It's worth mentioning that you don't need access to the source code of the parent class. Even though the parent class's code resides in the same module, we didn't touch it. We could have created the newBookStore class by inheriting the executable file of the BookStore class (the DLL that's created in the project's bin folder).

### Raising Custom Events

At the beginning of this chapter we briefly described how to raise custom events from within a class. To demonstrate the use of custom event arguments, we've added an event to the new method. The code in the GetBookByISBN method examines the ISBN passed as argument, and if it starts with 000, it fires an event, the FakeISBN event. Some publications don't have an ISBN, and many applications generate fake ISBNs. Because no valid ISBN starts with three zeros, our code treats this prefix as a fake ISBN and raises the FakeISBN event. This event is declared with the following statement:

```
Public Event FakeISBN(ByVal sender As Object, ByVal e As BookEvent)
```

The first argument, sender, is the current instance of the class and it's set to Me. The second argument is a custom type. You'll have to create custom event arguments when you want to pass information from the class that raised the event to the application that consumes the event. To create a custom event argument, declare a new class that inherits from the EventArgs class:

```
Public Class BookEvent
    Inherits EventArgs
    Public Shared ISBN As String
End Class
```

In the body of the class, declare the public members—properties that can be set by the class prior to triggering the event. In our example, we'll use a simple member, the ISBN property. This property is set to the value of the ISBN passed as argument to the GetBook-ByISBN method. To use the custom event argument, declare a variable of the custom event type, set its properties, and pass it as argument to the FakeISBN event when you raise the event:

```
If ISBN.Substring(0, 3) = "000" Then
    Dim oddISBN As BookEvent
    oddISBN.ISBN = ISBN
    RaiseEvent FakeISBN(Me, oddISBN)
End If
```

To test the custom event argument, switch to the test project and add the following declaration in the form's code:

```
Dim WithEvents Books As New newBookStore()
```

If you drop down the list of objects in the editor's window and select the Books object, the FakeISBN event will appear in the drop-down list of events. Select it and enter the following code to handle the FakeISBN event:

```
Private Sub Books_FakeISBN(ByVal sender As Object, _
                    ByVal e As Objects.newBookStore.BookEvent) _
                    Handles Books.FakeISBN
    MsgBox("You've added a title with fake ISBN " & e.ISBN)
End Sub
```

The code is quite trivial, but it demonstrates how you can retrieve custom values from the event's argument.

## Inheritance Modifiers

In this section, we're going to look at the class-related modifiers, which are keywords, like the Public and Private keywords you can use in variable declarations. These keywords apply to classes that can be inherited as well as the derived classes, and they appear in front of the Class keyword or in front of their members. By default, all classes can be inherited, but their members can't be overridden. You can change this default behavior with the following modifiers:

**NotInheritable**    The NotInheritable modifier prevents the class from being inherited (no other class can be derived from this class). The base data types of the Framework, for example, are not inheritable. You can inherit from the ArrayList class and build a custom ArrayList class, as we did earlier, but you can't inherit from the Array class.

**MustInherit**    A class marked with the MustInherit attribute can't be used directly in an application. It must be inherited by another class, which can then be used in an application. A derived class can access the members of the base class through the keyword MyBase.

**Overridable**    Every member with this modifier may be overwritten. Members declared as Public can't be overridden. You should allow developers to override as many of the members of your class as possible, as long as you don't think there's a chance that they may break the code in the process. Members declared with the Overridable keyword don't necessarily need to be overridden, so they should provide a basic functionality.

**NotOverridable**    Members declared with this modifier can't be overridden in the inheriting class. If the member contains functionality that affects the state of the object, mark the corresponding member as NotOverridable.

**MustOverride**    Members declared with this modifier must be overridden. You may skip the overriding of a member declared with the MustOverride modifier in the derived class as long as the derived class is declared with the MustInherit modifier. This means that the derived class must be inherited by some other class, which then receives the obligation to override the original member declared as MustOverride. It seems complicated, but it's really common sense. If you can't provide the implementation of a member that must be overridden, then the class must be inherited by another class, which will provide the implementation.

**Public**    This modifier tells the compiler that the specific member can be accessed from any application that uses the class. Most members of a custom class are declared as Public. Even a variable declared with the Public modifier will become a property of the class.

**Private**    This modifier tells the compiler that the specific member can be accessed only in the module in which it was declared. All the local variables must be declared as Private, and no other class (including derived classes), or application, will see them.

**Protected**    Protected members have scope between public and private, and they can be accessed in the derived class, but they're not exposed to applications using either the parent class or the derived classes. In the derived class, they have a private scope. Use the Protected keyword to mark the members that are of interest to developers who will use your class as a base class but not to developers who will use it in their applications.

**Friend**    Friend members have a project scope and can't be accessed from outside the project. Friend members are invisible from within the derived class's code, unless the base and derived classes reside in the same project.

**Protected Friend**    This modifier tells the compiler that the member is available to the class that inherits the class, as well as to any other component of the same project.

**Inherits**   The Inherits statement tells the compiler which class it derives from, and it must be the first executable statement in the derived class's code. A class that doesn't include the Inherits keyword is by definition a base class.

**Overrides**   Use this keyword to specify the member of the parent class you're overriding. If a member has the same name in the derived class that it has in the parent class, this member must be overridden. You can't use the Overrides keyword with members that were declared with the NotOverridable or Protected keywords in the base class.

**Shadows**   This is a rather obscure modifier that totally hides the equivalent member of the parent class. A method or property of the derived class marked with this modifier hides any members of the parent class by the same name. In effect, it's like removing a member from the parent class and adding a new member with the same name to the derived class.

## Interfaces

Interfaces are another major component of object-oriented programming with VB .NET. Sometimes, we know that our class must expose certain members, usually methods, but we can't code them because their implementation depends on how the class will be used. It's the responsibility of the programmer that will use our class to supply the implementation of the specific member(s). When you write the class's code, you can create placeholders for code that will be supplied later. A typical example is the comparison of objects. The collection classes of .NET (ArrayLists, HashTables, and even arrays) expose Compare and CompareTo methods, but these two methods can only compare simple data types like numbers and strings. If the collection holds objects, the Compare method will fail because it doesn't know how to compare objects. The class that uses the collection class must provide a function to compare the objects stored in the collection. This information was not available at the time the collection classes were written, so the designers inserted a placeholder for the Compare method. The class contains a method signature but no code.

If you want to supply your own Compare method, you must create a class that implements the IComparable interface. This interface has already been defined in the parent class and you must write the code of a function with a known signature. An interface is like a contract between your class and any other class that uses it. Any component that uses your class must provide a function with the same signature as the one listed in the interface. In the following paragraphs we'll add a couple of interfaces to our Person class and you'll see through the examples the type of functionality you can bring to your classes through interfaces.

We created the Person class earlier in the chapter. This class is of very little use as is. The idea is to provide a class from which other, related classes can inherit. We'll use the Person class as the base class for two new classes, the Manager and Programmer classes. Each class will add specific members to the base class (the Person class) to better describe managers and programmers. The focus in this section isn't the additional members, but members that perform similar tasks in both classes.

Let's say you want to add members to handle payroll functions (calculating the wages of programmers and managers every month, figuring out withholding taxes, and so on). Obviously, we don't want the programmers that use our class to make up names and add similar methods with different names. On the other hand, we can't implement these members in the parent class. The solution is to create an interface. You'll provide the signatures of the various members and others will have to provide the actual implementation.

For demonstration purposes, we'll create two interfaces, the Pay and TaxPayer interfaces. The Pay interface provides the following methods:

```
Public Interface Pay
    Property Wage() As Decimal
    ReadOnly Property NetPay() As Decimal
End Interface
```

The Wage() property returns the total amount earned by a specific manager or programmer at the end of the month (or week or any other period). This amount includes a basic salary, overtime, various bonuses, and so on. The NetPay property returns the net amount payable to the person. To add a little twist to the sample, we'll assume that no withholdings are applied to managers. Programmer salaries, on the other hand, are subject to withholdings. The Pay interface applies to both the Programmer and Manager classes.

We need additional information for calculating the withholdings. To manage this information, we'll create another interface, the TaxPayer interface, which is shown next:

```
Public Interface TaxPayer
    Property WithHoldingsPercent() As Single
    ReadOnly Property WithHoldings() As Decimal
End Interface
```

The TaxPayer interface contains the members for calculating programmer withholdings and it applies to the Programmer class. The developers responsible for the Manager and Programmer classes must specify that their classes implement the appropriate interfaces, which means that they must implement the members listed in the definitions of the interfaces.

The definitions of the interfaces appear in the Person class, but there's no way to specify from within the Person class which of the derived classes will implement them. The developer that will code a class will determine if the class will implement any of the parent class's interfaces. However, once you decide to implement an interface, you must supply code for all the members listed in the interface.

Let's build the Manager class. This class will inherit the Person class and it will implement the Pay interface. By that, we mean that the class must implement the methods specified in the

Pay interface. Listing 12.16 shows the Manager class. Notice the first two statements that reference the inherited class and the interface class.

---

**Listing 12.16**      **Deriving the Manager Class from the Person Class**

```
Public Class Manager
    Inherits PersonClass.Person
    Implements PersonClass.Pay

    Private _SSN As String
    Public Property SSN() As String
        Get
            Return _SSN
        End Get
        Set(ByVal Value As String)
            _SSN = Value
        End Set
    End Property

    Private _Wage, _Bonus As Decimal

    Public Property Wage() As Decimal _
            Implements PersonClass.Pay.Wage
        Get
            Return _Wage
        End Get
        Set(ByVal Value As Decimal)
            If Value > 0 Then _Wage = Value
        End Set
    End Property

    Public ReadOnly Property NetPay() As Decimal _
            Implements PersonClass.Pay.NetPay
        Get
            Return Wage + Bonus
        End Get
    End Property

    Public Property Bonus() As Decimal
        Get
            Return _Bonus
        End Get
        Set(ByVal Value As Decimal)
            If Value > 0 Then _Bonus = Value
        End Set
    End Property

End Class
```

Do something similar for the Programmer class. This class inherits the Person class, and it also implements the Pay interface. Because the Programmer class's Pay method calculates tax withholdings, it must also implement the TaxPayer interface. Once the proper Inherits and Implements keywords have been specified at the top of the class, the rest is straightforward. Listing 12.17 shows the Programmer class.

**Listing 12.17     Deriving the Programmer Class from the Person Class**

```
Public Class Programmer
    Inherits PersonClass.Person
    Implements PersonClass.Pay
    Implements PersonClass.TaxPayer

    Dim BaseSalary As Decimal
    Dim HoldPercent As Single

    Private _SSN As String
    Public Property SSN() As String
        Get
            Return _SSN
        End Get
        Set(ByVal Value As String)
            _SSN = Value
        End Set
    End Property

    Public Enum Evaluation
        Fire
        Boost
        Promote
    End Enum

    Dim _ReportsTo As Manager
    Public Property ReportsTo() As Manager
        Get
            Return _ReportsTo
        End Get
        Set(ByVal Value As Manager)
            _ReportsTo = Value
        End Set
    End Property

    Public Property Wage() As Decimal _
                Implements PersonClass.Pay.Wage
        Get
            Return BaseSalary
        End Get
        Set(ByVal Value As Decimal)
```

```
                If Value > 0 Then BaseSalary = Value
            End Set
        End Property

        Public Property WithHoldingsPercent() As Single _
                    Implements PersonClass.TaxPayer.WithHoldingsPercent
            Get
                Return HoldPercent
            End Get
            Set(ByVal Value As Single)
                If Value > 0 And Value < 1 Then HoldPercent = Value
            End Set
        End Property

        Public ReadOnly Property WithHoldings() As Decimal _
                    Implements PersonClass.TaxPayer.WithHoldings
            Get
                Return BaseSalary * HoldPercent
            End Get
        End Property

        Public ReadOnly Property NetPay() As Decimal _
                    Implements PersonClass.Pay.NetPay
            Get
                Return BaseSalary * (1 - HoldPercent)
            End Get
        End Property
    End Class
```

Notice that the Programmer class implements both interfaces. Although a class can inherit only from one class, it can implement any number of interfaces.

Let's exercise the members that implement the interfaces. The statements in Listing 12.18 create a Manager and a Programmer object and set their properties. Then they call the NetPay method on both objects. The NetPay method is implemented differently in each class, but it does the same for both classes: it returns the amount payable to the person represented by the current instance of the class.

---

**Listing 12.18     Testing the NetPay Method**

```
Private Sub Button4_Click(ByVal sender As System.Object, _
                          ByVal e As System.EventArgs) _
                          Handles Button4.Click
    Dim Manager1 As New Employee.Manager()
    Manager1.Name = "Tom Hearthill"
    Manager1.Wage = 130000
    Manager1.Bonus = 17500
```

```
Console.WriteLine("Manager " & Manager1.Name & _
                  " will be paid " & Manager1.NetPay & _
                  " this month.")
Dim Programmer1 As New Employee.Programmer()
Programmer1.Name = "Richard Applebaum"
Programmer1.DateOfBirth = "3/6/1965"
Programmer1.Wage = 45000
Programmer1.WithHoldingsPercent = 0.225
Console.WriteLine(Programmer1.Name & " will be paid " & _
                  Programmer1.NetPay & " this month.")
End Sub
```

The manager will make the sum of his wage and bonuses (147500), and the programmer will be paid his wage after subtracting the tax withholding (34875). The previous statements will produce the following output:

```
Manager Tom Hearthill will be paid 147500 this month.
Richard Applebaum will be paid 34875 this month.
```

As you can see, both implementation and interface inheritance have their role in designing classes for large projects. In a way, designing base classes and specifying interfaces is very similar to top-down design. We start with the "broad" classes, which represent the most basic entities of the application. Interface inheritance allows a designer to specify the desired functionality of a class and delegate its implementation to the developers. The benefits of inheritance may not be obvious in small-scale projects, but it becomes necessary in large-scale projects that involve a team of developers.

## When Do We Use Inheritance?

Is inheritance the bread and butter of application programmers? No, it's not. Most VB programmers don't even use custom objects in their projects, but this is going to change soon. You can't go far with VB .NET without objects (not elegantly, or in style, at least). Inheritance, especially interface inheritance, requires extreme planning and design of an application, and only lead programmers in very large projects will design object hierarchies that depend on inheritance. If implemented by inexperienced designers, inheritance can lead to more trouble than it's worth.

However, you can use implementation inheritance to customize general classes, like the ones that come with the Framework, for specific applications. For example, you can create Array-Lists that store items of a specific type only (usually instances of a custom class) by overriding the Add method. The following class inherits the functionality of the ArrayList class but stores only instances of the Person class:

```
Class PersonList
    Inherits ArrayList
```

```
Public Overrides Function Add(ByVal Obj As Object) As Integer
    If Obj.GetType Is GetType(Person) Then
        Return MyBase.Add(Obj)
    Else
        Return -1
    End If
End Function
End Class
```

First, it examines the type of the object passed as argument, and if it's a Person type, it adds it to the ArrayList by calling the Add method of the base class. If not, it returns the value –1 to indicate that the Add method failed. If the object was added successfully to the ArrayList, the Add method returns the index returned by the Add method of the base class. You can test the PersonList class with a few statements like the following:

```
Dim persons As New PersonList()
Dim P As New Person("name", 40)
Console.WriteLine(persons.Add(P))
Dim C As Color = Color.Aquamarine
Console.WriteLine(persons.Add(C))
P = New Person("another name", 25)
Console.WriteLine(persons.Add(P))
```

After these statements are executed, the persons list will contain two items, not three. You can easily add code to this class to throw an exception every time an application attempts to add an object of another type, add methods to return specific properties of each object (like GetNames, GetAges, and so on), and create a class to simplify many programming tasks for an application that handles persons. The PersonList class is probably useless to any other developer, but it can save you (and other team programmers) tedious coding and testing. The most important aspect of adding simple customized features to existing classes is that you don't need to rely on a number of programmers to fully understand the specifications of a large application. Programmers that use the PersonList class can't use it to store objects other than Person objects. In the following chapter, you'll see how, using the Inherits keyword, you can create new controls by inheriting from existing controls.

The examples we presented in this section are very simple and not typical of programming tasks that call for inheritance. Inheritance pays off in very large projects, parts of which will be developed by different programming teams. Hopefully, we've helped you to understand what inheritance is and the mechanics of interface and implementation inheritance. In the following section, we'll look at a few very important interfaces of the .NET framework so that you can make the most out of it.

## The IComparable and IComparer Interfaces

In addition to your own interfaces, there are many interfaces in .NET and you can add a lot of functionality to your custom classes by implementing one or more of the existing interfaces.

Most of the objects that implement collections, like the Array and ArrayList objects, provide a Sort method, which sorts the data in the collection. They also provide an enumerator, which allows you to iterate through the collection with a For Each...Next loop. You can add sorting and enumeration features to a custom class by implementing the IComparable and IEnumerator interfaces, which are discussed in detail in this section.

The Sort method can handle simple data types, like integers and strings. If the collection contains objects, like books, calling the Sort method won't help because it doesn't know how to sort the elements—basically, it doesn't know how to compare two elements and therefore can't sort the collection. If the objects in the collection represent books, the Sort method doesn't know how you want them sorted (by ISBN, by price, and so on). One of the overloaded methods of the Sort method accepts as argument a Comparer object, which is an instance of a class that exposes a CompareTo method. This method compares the current instance of the object to another object of the same type passed as argument and returns one of the following values, depending on the outcome of the comparison:

- A negative value if the current instance is less than the object
- Zero if the object is equal to the current value
- A positive value if the current instance is greater than the object

Once you provide the CompareTo method, the Sort method will use it to sort the items of the collection. All sorting algorithms compare values and swap the corresponding items if they're out of place, so all the information that the Sort method needs is a function that knows how to compare two items.

Before you can add a CompareTo method to a class, you must inform the compiler that the class knows how to compare two objects of that type. This is done by implementing a special interface, the IComparable interface. To implement the IComparable interface, you must insert the following line right after the class declaration:

```
Implements IComparable
```

Then you must provide the CompareTo method, which compares the current instance of the class to another object of the same type. The outline of the CompareTo method is shown next:

```
Public Function CompareTo(ByVal obj As Object) As Integer _
     Implements IComparable.CompareTo
If obj.property < Me.property Then
    Return -1
ElseIf obj.property = Me.property Then
    Return 0
Else
    Return 1
End If
```

To make your code more robust, you must cast the object passed to the CompareTo function to the same type as the class and catch any exceptions. You'll see a complete example shortly.

Objects can be sorted in many different ways, and you may not wish to sort the collection always in the same order. The IComparer interface allows you to specify multiple comparison methods and pass the appropriate one to the Sort method. The IComparer interface requires that your class provide the Compare method, which compares two objects passed as arguments (note that the CompareTo method compares the current instance of the class to the object you pass as argument). You can provide as many classes that implement the IComparer interface as you need, each one exposing its own Compare method, and use any one of them at will. Listing 12.19 shows the outline of a class that implements the IComparer interface.

**Listing 12.19**　　**Implementing the IComparer Interface**

```
Public Class CustomComparer
    Implements IComparer
    Public Function Compare(ByVal obj1 As Object, _
                            ByVal obj2 As Object) As Integer _
                            Implements IComparer.Compare
        If obj1.property < obj2.property Then
            Return -1
        ElseIf obj1.property = obj2.property Then
            Return 0
        Else
            Return 1
        End If
    End Function
End Class
```

Let's return to our BookStore class and add sorting capabilities. No built-in method could possibly sort our collection of books because we don't even know how we want them sorted, so we must first decide how we want to sort our list. In most cases, including our collection of Book objects, we want to be able to sort objects in several ways. When you display data on a ListView control, for example, you should allow users to sort the rows according to any column. We would like to be able to sort our books by ISBN, title, price, and so on. For this example, we'll implement three different sorting methods: by ISBN, by price, and by cost. The cost is the ratio of the book's price divided by its number of pages—in effect, the cost per page. To sort the elements of the collection, we'll call the ArrayList object's Sort method, passing as argument a callback function to a procedure that we'll implement as a separate class. We'll build three classes that implement the IComparer interface, and each class will expose a Compare method, which compares two items of the collection. Each class will compare the two items with different criteria. The Compare method of the ByISBN class will compare two Book objects based on their ISBNs. The Compare method of the ByPrice class will compare two Book objects based on their prices. The Compare method of the ByCost class will compare two Book object based on their cost per page. Listing 12.20 shows the implementation of these classes.

**Listing 12.20    Three Different Compare Methods for the BookStore Class**

```
Public Class ByISBN
    Implements IComparer
    Public Function Compare(ByVal obj1 As Object, _
                            ByVal obj2 As Object) As Integer _
                            Implements IComparer.Compare
        Dim Book1, Book2 As Book
        Book1 = CType(obj1, Book)
        Book2 = CType(obj2, Book)
        Return String.Compare(Book1.ISBN, Book2.ISBN)
    End Function
End Class

Public Class ByPrice
    Implements IComparer
    Public Function Compare(ByVal obj1 As Object, _
                            ByVal obj2 As Object) As Integer _
                            Implements IComparer.Compare
        Dim Book1, Book2 As Book
        Book1 = CType(obj1, Book)
        Book2 = CType(obj2, Book)
        If Book1.Price < Book2.Price Then
            Return -1
        ElseIf Book1.Price = Book2.Price Then
            Return 0
        Else
            Return 1
        End If
    End Function
End Class

Public Class ByCost
    Implements IComparer
    Public Function Compare(ByVal obj1 As Object, _
                            ByVal obj2 As Object) As Integer _
                            Implements IComparer.Compare
        Dim Book1, Book2 As Book
        Book1 = CType(obj1, Book)
        Book2 = CType(obj2, Book)
        If Book1.Pages / Book1.Price < Book2.Pages / Book2.Price Then
            Return -1
        ElseIf Book1.Pages / Book1.Price = _
                    Book2.Pages / Book2.Price Then
```

```
            Return 0
        Else
            Return 1
        End If
    End Function
End Class
```

Listing 12.20 shows three classes, each one exposing a Compare method. The three methods, however, have different implementations and you can use any one of the available comparison procedures by passing an instance of the corresponding class to the Sort method.

We've implemented three classes that implement the IComparer interface and, therefore, we can add three different sorting methods to the BookStore class, all of them using the base class's Sort method. Here are the three sorting methods of the BookStore class:

```
Public Function SortByISBN()
    allBooks.Sort(New ByISBN())
End Function

Public Function SortByCost()
    allBooks.Sort(New ByCost())
End Function

Public Function SortByPrice()
    allBooks.Sort(New ByPrice())
End Function
```

As you can see, we didn't have to supply the implementation of the Sort method, because the ArrayList class knows how to sort items; sorting consists of comparing items and swapping them if they're out of order. The implementation of an efficient Sort method is highly non-trivial, as opposed to the implementation of a function that compares two elements of the same custom type. The code of the Sort method contains all the necessary logic for scanning the items and swapping the items that are out of order. Once the logic for comparing two elements is in place, it will sort the collection's items.

You will see shortly how to build your own classes that expose methods that accept pointers to functions as arguments (*delegates* is the proper term). But first, let's take a closer look at another equally important interface, the IEnumerable interface.

## The IEnumerable Interface

Another standard feature of collections is that they can be enumerated: you can request an IEnumerator object (with the built-in GetEnumerator method), which returns a snapshot of the collection's items and allows you to iterate through the items with a For Each...Next loop. You can provide an enumerator for your own classes by implementing the IEnumerable and IEnumerator interfaces, and you'll do so for the BookStore class shortly.

To implement the IEnumerable and IEnumerator interfaces, you must insert the following line right after the class declaration:

```
Implements IEnumerable, IEnumerator
```

Then, you must provide the code for the following members:

- GetEnumerator
- Current
- MoveNext
- Reset

The actual implementation of these methods is quite trivial. The GetEnumerator method returns an instance of the current class. The Current method returns the current item in the list, and the MoveNext method advances to the next item. This means that you must maintain an internal counter to keep track of the current item's location. Notice that there's no Move-Previous (or any other navigational) method. A collection's enumerator can only scan the collection forward and in a read-only fashion: you can read the Current object, but you can't edit it.

The Reset method resets the internal counter to –1. The first time the MoveNext method is called, the internal counter is increased by one and it points to the first item in the collection.

To add the IEnumerator and IEnumerable interfaces to the BookStore class, you must insert the Implements statement shown earlier at the beginning of the class. Then declare a local variable that holds the current position in the list. The MoveNext method will increase this variable by one and the Reset method will set it to –1. Insert the following declaration in the class's code:

```
Private index As Integer = -1
```

Then implement the methods of the IEnumerator interface as shown in Listing 12.21.

**Listing 12.21**     **Implementing the IEnumerator Interface**

```
Public Function GetEnumerator() As IEnumerator _
              Implements IEnumerable.GetEnumerator
    Return Me
End Function

Public ReadOnly Property Current() As Object _
          Implements IEnumerator.Current
    Get
        Return allBooks(index)
    End Get
End Property
```

```
Public Function MoveNext() As Boolean Implements IEnumerator.MoveNext
    index = index + 1
    If index < allBooks.Count Then
        Return True
    Else
        Return False
    End If
End Function

Public Sub Reset() Implements IEnumerator.Reset
    index = -1
End Sub
```

The implementation of the IEnumerable and IEnumerator classes is straightforward, and it's practically the same for all classes. After adding support for the IEnumerator interface to the BookStore class, you can iterate through all the books in the collection with a loop like the following:

```
Dim bookEnumerator As IEnumerator
bookEnumerator = Books.GetEnumerator
bookEnumerator.Reset()
While bookEnumerator.MoveNext
    Console.Write(bookEnumerator.Current.ISBN & "     ")
    Console.Write(bookEnumerator.Current.Title & "     ")
    Console.Write(bookEnumerator.Current.Price.ToString & "     " )
    Console.WriteLine
    For au = 1 To bookEnumerator.Current.BookAuthors.Count - 1
        Console.WriteLine("     " & _
                          bookEnumerator.Current.BookAuthors.item(au))
    Next
End While
```

In the project's code on the website, you will find the EnumerateAllTitles() subroutine, which is similar to the ShowAllTitles() subroutine in that it populates the grid on the form. The difference is that the EnumerateAllTitles() uses the BookStore class's enumerator, whereas the ShowAllTiles() iterates through the collection with a For...Each loop.

## Delegates

Delegates are at the heart of object-oriented programming with VB .NET, but they're totally new to VB programmers. To understand what delegates are, you must first understand callback functions. An application is basically a collection of interacting objects. Objects set the properties of other objects, call their methods, and notify one another when an event takes place. Picture your application as a world of objects that communicate with one another by sending and receiving messages. However, an object need not inform all other objects that an event has taken place. If this were the case, there would be no time left for anything else.

What's needed is a mechanism to not only raise events, but also to register the objects that will be listening for a specific event. This is what delegates do: they associate events (in the source object) with objects (the listeners).

In most cases, VB hides delegates from you, the application programmer, by taking care of the necessary plumbing. An example is the WithEvents keyword. When you declare a variable with the WithEvents keyword, the Common Language Runtime knows that it should listen for events raised by the corresponding class. The class that implements the object will fire events, but if the object hasn't been declared with the WithEvents keyword, it will not listen to them.

When you code an application, you can program any event of any control on the form. At runtime, however, VB registers the objects that should listen for events. If you open the segment marked as #Region "Windows Form Designer generated code," you'll see that the controls are declared with the WithEvents keyword.

There are occasions when you have to explicitly declare delegates. A typical example is when you want to call a method indirectly, as we did in Chapter 10. When you update the user interface of an application from within a thread other than the main thread, you must call the methods of the controls through the Invoke method. This method accepts as argument a delegate to the actual method you want to call. Let's review the process in detail here.

In the main thread of the application, we create a Thread object with a statement like the following:

```
Dim bgThread As Thread
```

Then we assign a process to this thread and start the process. The process is the LoadTree-View() subroutine, which maps a drive's structure to a TreeView control. Because this process takes a while to complete, we execute it as a separate thread. The subroutine is running in the background, while at the same time the user can interact with the form—in other words, the application's interface will not freeze while the TreeView is being populated. Here's how we start the background process:

```
bgThread = New Thread(AddressOf Me.LoadTreeView)
bgThread.Start()
```

All the action takes place in the LoadTreeView() subroutine, which scans the current drive and creates a tree with the same hierarchy as the folders on the drive. The LoadTreeView() subroutine keeps adding nodes to the TreeView control on the main form. However, the same control may also be accessed by the main thread's code. The user may expand or collapse a branch of the tree, resize the control, and so on. A thread should never attempt to update a control on the main form on its own. This situation is so common in multithreaded programming that all Windows controls provide the Invoke method. Instead of calling one of the TreeView control's methods directly, you issue a request through the Invoke method. The main thread will receive the request and execute the method when it knows it's safe to do so.

The Invoke method accepts as argument a delegate to the method to be called and its arguments. To use the Invoke method, you must first create a delegate to the method of the control you plan to call. In the case of our example, we want to be able to add a new node to the TreeView control, so our delegate is for the Add method of the control's Nodes collection:

```
Public Delegate Function Add_A_Node(ByVal aString As String) As TreeNode
```

The delegate has the same signature as the actual method we want to call. The `Nodes.Add` method accepts as argument a string (the new node's label) and returns a TreeNode object that represents the newly added node. The `Nodes.Add` method is overloaded, but we're interested in this form of the method.

Finally, in the `LoadTreeView()` subroutine's code, we can call the Invoke method passing as argument the `Add_A_Node` delegate:

```
Nd = TreeView1.Invoke(New _
        Add_A_Node(AddressOf currentNode.Nodes.Add), _
        New Object() {Path.GetFileName(thisFolder)})
```

We create a new instance of the delegate by specifying the actual method it should call. Notice that the delegate contains the signature of the method, not the name of the method to be called. When we create an instance of the delegate with its constructor, we pass the address of the method to be called (the Add method of the Nodes collection of the current node) and an array of the Object type with the arguments. The Add method requires a string as argument, and it's passed as the first element of an Object array. All arguments must be placed to an array, in the same order as expected by the method.

You saw this technique in action in Chapter 10. If you attempt to call the control's `Nodes.Add` method directly from within the thread, you'll crash the application sooner or later, when the thread will attempt to update the TreeView control while the main thread is doing the same.

## A Custom Class with Delegates

To demonstrate another interesting use of delegates, we'll build a class that exposes two methods to act on arrays. The project we present in this section is called Delegates, and you will find it in this chapter's file on sybex.com. It's a Windows application that contains a test form and two classes: the MyObjects and ObjectMethods classes. The class MyObjects exposes a Sort method, which sorts the array passed to it as argument, and a Transform method, which transforms the elements of the array passed to it and stores the transformed values back to the same array. If you know that all instances of the class will store elements of the same type and the transformation will always be the same, go ahead and implement the methods in the class's code. But the class would be far more useful if you could let the user supply the functions for these two operations. You could store objects of any type to your class and manipulate them, even though the class knows nothing about the types of these objects.

Sorting an array is no problem; there are more sorting algorithms than you care to read about. The only problem is how to compare two elements. An instance of the class may be populated with integers, another one with custom objects, and a third with objects of many different types. Therefore, we can't make any assumptions as to the type of the data stored in each instance of the class. The bottom line is that we can't sort the array because we don't know how to compare two elements of the array. However, we can provide a Sort method and leave a "gap" in our code, where the user of our class can "insert" a function that compares two elements. The program that populates the array knows how to compare its elements, and once this function becomes available, our sorting method will work. This is what collections do, and you know how to provide a custom Compare method to sort a collection. In this section, you'll see how to write a class that accepts a user-supplied function.

The Transform method is quite trivial. It must iterate through all the elements of the array and call a function, passing the current element as argument. The user-supplied function will transform the object and pass the result back to our method as its return value.

Start a new project and add a class to it, the MyObjects class. Then enter the statements of Listing 12.22 in the class.

---

**Listing 12.22**    **The MyObjects Class**

```
Public Class MyObjects
    Public Delegate Function _
                TransformCallback(ByVal obj As Object) As Double
    Public Shared Sub Transform(ByVal objects() As Object, _
                ByVal TransformMethod As TransformCallback)
        Dim i As Integer
        For i = 0 To objects.GetUpperBound(0)
            objects(i) = TransformMethod(objects(i))
        Next
    End Sub

    Public Delegate Function _
                CompareCallBack(ByVal obj1 As Object, _
                                ByVal obj2 As Object) As Integer
    Public Shared Sub Sort(ByVal objects() As Object, _
                ByVal CompareMethod As CompareCallBack)
        Dim i, j As Integer
        Dim tmp As Object
        For i = 0 To objects.GetUpperBound(0)
```

```
            For j = i + 1 To objects.GetUpperBound(0)
                If CompareMethod(objects(j), objects(i)) = 1 Then
                    tmp = objects(i)
                    objects(i) = objects(j)
                    objects(j) = tmp
                End If
            Next
        Next
    End Sub
End Class
```

This class contains two methods (public functions). Because the functions call an external component—a function that will be provided by another class—we create two delegates with the signatures of the corresponding functions and then use the callback functions in our code. Both functions accept the address of the corresponding delegate as argument.

The class's Sort method is implemented with the most trivial (and least efficient) algorithm, the BubbleSort algorithm. This algorithm is very simple and can be implemented with a few lines of code, so we used it to keep the example as simple as possible. The Sort method can perform all the operations for sorting the array except for comparing two elements. To compare two elements, the Sort method calls the CompareMethod method, which is passed to it as a callback argument.

The CompareCallBack delegate declaration tells the compiler that an external application will supply the actual implementation of the function, but the compiler knows how it should be called. The Sort method accepts two arguments: an array with the elements to be compared and a delegate to the CompareMethod:

```
Public Shared Sub Sort(ByVal objects() As Object, _
                ByVal CompareMethod As CompareCallBack)
```

In the actual implementation of the Sort method, you can call the CompareCallBack function as if it were part of the class.

The Transform method is simpler because it contains hardly any code at all. This method iterates through the elements of an array, and for each element, it calls another callback function that actually transforms the element. The code of the MyObjects class contains two methods (the Sort and Transform methods) and two delegate declarations. Each method uses a callback function to call a function that will be supplied by an external component—the class, or application, that will use the class MyObjects.

To use this class, you must supply the TransformCallBack and CompareCallBack functions. Let's design an application that uses the MyObjects class and exercises its members. First, you must create a new class with the definitions of the two callback methods. Add a new class to the solution, name it ObjectMethods, and enter the statements in Listing 12.23 in its code window.

**Listing 12.23    The ObjectMethods Class**

```
Public Class ObjectMethods
    Public Shared Function CompareMethod(ByVal obj1 As Object, _
                    ByVal obj2 As Object) As Integer
        If obj1.ToString < obj2.ToString Then
            Return 1
        Else
            Return -1
        End If
    End Function

    Public Shared Function TransformMethod(ByVal obj As Object) _
                    As Double
        Dim i As Integer
        If IsNumeric(obj) Then
            Return Math.Exp(Math.Abs(1 / CType(obj, Double)))
        Else
            Return -999
        End If
    End Function
End Class
```

The CompareMethod function converts its two arguments to string values and compares them. Notice that the code doesn't treat the equals case differently, but this isn't really relevant when you sort items, only when you compare items. The TransformMethod performs a math transformation on its numeric arguments. If the argument is not numeric, it returns the value –999.

Finally, you can write an application that creates instances of the MyObjects class and calls its methods. Add a form to the solution, set it as the project's Startup Object, and place a Text-Box and two Button controls on it (or open the Delegates project, shown in Figure 12.4). The statements in Listing 12.24 create an array that contains a few numeric and a few string elements, the objs array. The elements of the array are printed by the PrintArray() subroutine in the order in which they were supplied. Then the array is sorted and its elements are printed again.

**Listing 12.24    Testing the Sort Method of the MyObjects Class**

```
Private Sub Button1_Click(ByVal sender As System.Object, _
                    ByVal e As System.EventArgs) _
                    Handles Button1.Click
    Dim objs() As Object = {23.4, "Visual", 56.2, "Basic", 62.3, 19.3}
    Dim Obj As Interfaces.MyObjects
    Dim CompareMethodCallback As MyObjects.CompareCallBack
    Dim i As Integer
    Console.WriteLine("Before sorting")
```

```
        PrintArray(objs)
        CompareMethodCallback = AddressOf ObjectMethods.CompareMethod
        Obj.Sort(objs, CompareMethodCallback)
        Console.WriteLine("After sorting")
        PrintArray(objs)
    End Sub
```

The second button's code, shown in Listing 12.25, exercises the Transform method. The code is nearly identical to the code for sorting the elements, only instead of sorting the array, it transforms it. The following transformed elements will appear on the TextBox control:

```
1.04366133256142
-999
1.01795284344116
-999
1.01618087955221
1.05317927624275
```

The value –999 that appears twice in the output is the transformed value of the strings. All numeric values were mapped onto other numeric values, slightly larger than 1.

**FIGURE 12.4:**

Testing the
Delegates class

**Listing 12.25      Testing the Transform Method of the MyObjects Class**

```
Private Sub Button2_Click(ByVal sender As System.Object, _
                      ByVal e As System.EventArgs) _
                      Handles Button2.Click
    Dim objs() As Object = {23.4, "Visual", 56.2, "Basic", 62.3, 19.3}
    Dim Obj As Interfaces.MyObjects
    Dim TransformMethodCallback As MyObjects.TransformCallback
    Dim i As Integer
    TextBox1.Clear()
    TextBox1.AppendText("Before transformation" & vbCrLf)
    PrintArray(objs)
```

```
        TransformMethodCallback = AddressOf ObjectMethods.TransformMethod
        Obj.Transform(objs, TransformMethodCallback)
        TextBox1.AppendText("After transformation" & vbCrLf)
        PrintArray(objs)
    End Sub
```

The variables *CompareMethodCallback* and *TransformMethodCallback* are delegates. They're telling the compiler, "When you run into a call to the CompareMethod function in the MyObjects class, call the function specified by the *CompareMethodCallback* variable."

In the last section of the chapter, we'll discuss a class for manipulating matrices. This is a real-world project, although it's of interest to mathematically inclined readers. Even if math isn't your strongest point, you'll be able to follow the example and ignore the implementation of the methods. The Matrix project demonstrates many of the techniques discussed in this chapter, and we hope some readers will use it as a starting point for building a class that manipulates matrices.

## A Class for Handling Matrices

The example of this section is a bit involved, but it demonstrates some of the most important topics discussed in this chapter. We are going to build a class for manipulating matrices (two-dimensional arrays). The Matrix class contains only two matrix manipulation methods (for adding and multiplying matrices), but it's easy to add your own methods. The starting point is the specification of the matrix: how we specify the matrix's dimensions and how to populate the matrix with data. The matrix is a two-dimensional array, which we'll store in a local variable declared as follows:

```
Private _table(0, 0) As Double
```

The dimensions of the array are stored in the *_rows* and *_cols* private variables, which are declared with the following statement:

```
Private _rows, _cols As Integer
```

Now we must decide how the application that uses the Matrix class will create a new matrix. Obviously, we must give programmers the ability to specify the dimensions of the matrix and its elements. The Rows and Cols properties will map the supplied values to the *_rows* and *_cols* variables:

```
Public Property Rows() As Integer
    Get
        Rows = _rows
    End Get
    Set(ByVal Value As Integer)
        _rows = Value
    End Set
End Property
```

```
Public Property Cols() As Integer
    Get
        Cols = _cols
    End Get
    Set(ByVal Value As Integer)
        _cols = Value
    End Set
End Property
```

We must also provide a method for setting (or reading) individual cells. This is the Cell method, which accepts as arguments the indices of an array element:

```
Public Property Cell(ByVal row As Integer, _
                     ByVal col As Integer) As Double
    Get
        If row > _rows Or col > _cols Then
            Throw New Exception("Row or column number outside range")
            Exit Property
        End If
        Cell = _table(row, col)
    End Get
    Set(ByVal Value As Double)
        If row > _rows Or col > _cols Then
            Throw New Exception("Row or column number outside range")
            Exit Property
        End If
        _table(row, col) = Value
    End Set
End Property
```

To create a new matrix and populate it with doubles, we must use a few statements like the following:

```
Dim a As Matrix = New Matrix()
a.Rows = 3
a.Cols = 4
' You can also use the following
' constructor to initialize the matrix
'     Dim mrtx As Matrix = New Matrix(3, 4)
Dim i, j As Integer
Dim rnd As System.Random = New System.Random()
For i = 0 To a.Rows
    For j = 0 To a.Cols
        a.Cell(i, j) = rnd.Next(100)
    Next
Next
```

We should also provide a convenient constructor for our class. Clearly, the Book class must have a default constructor that doesn't require any arguments and simply initializes the private array:

```
Sub New()
    MyBase.new()
    _rows = 0
    _cols = 0
    ReDim _table(_rows, _cols)
End Sub
```

Another form of the constructor should allow programmers to create a matrix by specifying its dimensions:

```
Sub New(ByVal R As Integer, ByVal C As Integer)
    MyBase.new()
    _rows = R
    _cols = C
    ReDim _table(_rows, _cols)
End Sub
```

Finally, a third form of the constructor will allow programmers to initiate a matrix in a single statement by passing a two-dimensional array of doubles:

```
Sub New(ByVal values(,) As Double)
    MyBase.new()
    _rows = values.GetUpperBound(0)
    _cols = values.GetUpperBound(1)
    ReDim _table(_rows, _cols)
    Dim i, j As Integer
    For i = 0 To _rows
        For j = 0 To _cols
            _table(i, j) = values(i, j)
        Next
    Next
End Sub
```

To use the last form of the constructor from within our code, we must first create an array of doubles and then pass it to the New constructor with a set of statements like the following:

```
Dim numbers(3, 3) As Double
Dim i, j As Integer
For i = 0 To 3
    For j = 0 To 3
        numbers(i, j) = i * 10 + j
    Next
Next
Dim mtrx As New Matrix(numbers)
```

If all elements are known, this is the most convenient method of declaring the matrix. If not, one of the other two forms of the constructor should be used.

The matrix manipulation methods are quite simple. They operate on the elements of two matrices and write the result to the elements of a third matrix. To add two matrices, for example, you add the elements with the same indices (coordinates) and assign the result to the element with the same indexes in the third table, which holds the result of the addition. The matrix manipulation methods will also be overloaded: we'll provide a shared method, which will act on the two matrices passed as arguments and return a third matrix with the results, and an instance method, which will act on the matrix represented by the current instance of the Matrix object and a matrix passed as argument. The implementation of the overloaded forms of the Add method is shown next:

```
' Shared Add Method
Public Overloads Function Add(ByVal A As Matrix, _
                              ByVal B As Matrix) As Matrix
    Dim Row, Col As Integer
    If Not (A.Rows = B.Rows And A.Cols = B.Cols) Then
        Add = New Matrix()
        Exit Function
    End If
    Dim newMatrix As New Matrix(A.Rows, A.Cols)
    For Row = 0 To A.Rows
        For Col = 0 To A.Cols
            newMatrix.Cell(Row, Col) = _
                        A.Cell(Row, Col) + B.Cell(Row, Col)
        Next
    Next
    Return(newMatrix)
End Function

' Instance Add Method
Public Overloads Function Add(ByVal A As Matrix) As Matrix
    Dim Row, Col As Integer
    If Not (A.Rows = MyClass.Rows And A.Cols = MyClass.Cols) Then
        Add = New Matrix()
        Exit Function
    End If
    Dim newMatrix As New Matrix(MyClass.Rows, MyClass.Cols)
    For Row = 0 To MyClass.Rows
        For Col = 0 To MyClass.Cols
            newMatrix.Cell(Row, Col) = _
                        A.Cell(Row, Col) + MyClass.Cell(Row, Col)
        Next
    Next
    Return(newMatrix)
End Function
```

Let's say you've set up two matrices, Matrix1 and Matrix2. You can add them using the instance method with the following statements:

```
Dim Matrix1 As New Matrix(4, 5)
Dim Matrix2 As New Matrix(5, 4)
' populate the matrices
Dim Matrix3 As New Matrix(4, 4)
Matrix3 = Matrix1.Add(Matrix2)
```

To call the shared method, use the following statements:

```
Dim MTRX As Matrix
Dim Matrix1 As New Matrix(4, 5)
Dim Matrix2 As New Matrix(5, 4)
' populate the matrices
Dim Matrix3 As New Matrix(4, 4)
Matrix3 = MTRX.Add(Matrix1, Matrix2)
```

The Multiply method is a little more interesting, because the matrices passed to the method may not be compatible. To multiply two matrices, you must make sure the number of columns in the first matrix is the same as the number of rows in the second matrix. Let's say you have declared two matrices with the following dimensions:

```
Dim Matrix1 As New Matrix(4, 5)
Dim Matrix2 As New Matrix(3, 4)
```

If you call the Multiply method with these two matrices in the order shown, the result is undefined (the two matrices can't be multiplied). However, you can multiply the two matrices in reverse order:

```
Dim Matrix3 As Matrix()
Matrix3 = MRTX.Multiply(Matrix2, Matrix1)
```

The result, Matrix3, will be a matrix with dimensions (3, 5). The Multiply method could throw an exception when the two matrices to be multiplied have incompatible dimensions, but we've chosen to return an empty matrix instead. Instead of an exception handler, your code must examine the matrix returned by the Multiply method and act accordingly. Here are the two overloaded forms of the Multiply method:

```
' Shared Multiply method
Public Function Multiply(ByVal A As Matrix, ByVal B As Matrix) As Matrix
    Dim Row, Col As Integer
    Dim i As Integer
    If Not (A.Cols = B.Rows) Then
        Multiply = New Matrix()
        Exit Function
    End If
    Dim newMatrix As Matrix = New Matrix(A.Rows, B.Cols)
```

```
        Dim pSum As Double
        For Row = 0 To A.Rows
            For Col = 0 To B.Cols
                pSum = 0
                For i = 0 To A.Cols
                    pSum = pSum + A.Cell(Row, i) * B.Cell(i, Col)
                Next
                newMatrix.Cell(Row, Col) = pSum
            Next
        Next
        Multiply = newMatrix
    End Function


    ' Instance Multiply method
    Public Function Multiply(ByVal A As Matrix) As Matrix
        Dim Row, Col As Integer
        Dim i As Integer
        If Not (A.Cols = MyClass.Rows) Then
            Multiply = New Matrix()
            Exit Function
        End If
        Dim newMatrix As Matrix = New Matrix(A.Rows, MyClass.Cols)
        Dim pSum As Double
        For Row = 0 To A.Rows
            For Col = 0 To MyClass.Cols
                pSum = 0
                For i = 0 To A.Cols
                    pSum = pSum + A.Cell(Row, i) * MyClass.Cell(i, Col)
                Next
                newMatrix.Cell(Row, Col) = pSum
            Next
        Next
        Multiply = newMatrix
    End Function
```

The following statements demonstrate how to call the Multiply method. They set up two matrices, pass them to the Multiply method, and upon return, examine the matrix returned by the method. If it's empty, the multiplication failed because the arguments passed to it were incompatible:

```
' Statements to set up matrices a and b
Dim c As New Matrix()
c = MTR.Multiply(a, b)
If c.Rows = 0 Or c.Cols = 0 Then
    MsgBox("Invalid martices")
    Exit Sub
End If
```

This operation is quite common (testing for empty matrices), so we added the IsEmpty method to the class. Its implementation is shown next:

```
Public Function IsEmpty() As Boolean
    If _rows = 0 Or _cols = 0 Then
        IsEmpty = True
    Else
        IsEmpty = False
    End If
End Function
```

The Matrix class demonstrates many aspects of class design and object-oriented programming, and you can experiment with the Matrix project you'll find in this chapter's file on sybex.com. The test form of the application, shown in Figure 12.5, allows you to perform a few simple operations with matrices. You can add more methods (if you have a practical use for the Matrix class, you'll have to implement a method for calculating the inverse of a matrix). The Matrix class is inserted in the same file as the project's form for convenience, but you can copy all the statements of the class and put them into a separate project—it must be a Class Library project.

**FIGURE 12.5:**

Testing the Matrix class

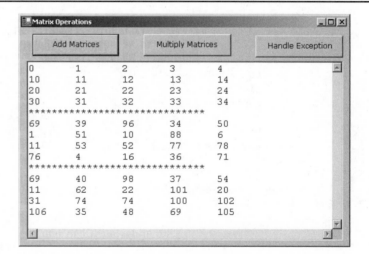

## Summary

Even if you've never built your custom classes in VB6, you can no longer afford to program without custom classes. They're central in VB .NET and you must get into the habit of implementing any part of the application you expect to reuse later as a class.

The main advantage of breaking up an application into classes is that you can combine data and their related code into single, reusable components. This not only promotes code reuse, it also helps you design more robust applications, because the classes should represent the entities you manipulate with your code. It's important for you to understand these entities, their functionality, and how entities communicate with one another (if they do).

Besides building custom classes, you can inherit existing ones and add functionality that's specific to your applications. Implementation inheritance is one of the most requested features of VB .NET and we're sure that most developers will create new classes by inheriting existing ones. In the following chapter you'll learn how to build custom Windows controls—a process that's not much different from building custom classes.

# CHAPTER 13

# Building Custom Windows Controls

- User-drawn custom controls

- Inherited custom controls

- Design-time features

- Custom data-bound controls

V isual Studio .NET is rapid application development (RAD) environment. The host of built-in controls and the visual tools make it easy to develop prototypes with point-and-click operations. Once the visual interface of the application is in place, you can write the classes for your data types and start coding the application. A good deal of the code deals with the manipulation of property values and calling the methods of the various controls. The controls that come with Visual Studio, however, are not adequate for every programming task. Most developers will eventually purchase third-party controls for specific tasks (a market that Microsoft wants to make sure will continue to exist and expand), while others will develop custom controls for in-house use. The custom controls will be specific to an application and will shorten the development time because they'll be used by many developers in the course of developing an application.

In this chapter, we'll look at the basics of building custom controls, as well as how to integrate them nicely in the Property Browser. An important aspect of building custom controls is how to make them easy to use, and this includes the ability to edit their properties in the Property Browser with visual tools. We'll start our discussion of custom controls with an overview of a control's function in the development environment, a quick comparison of controls and classes, and an explanation of the types of controls you can develop with Visual Studio .NET.

## What Is a Windows Control?

A control is basically a class with a visible (user) interface. It does everything a class can do, but it also provides an interface through which the control interacts with the user: it can display data, accept user-supplied data, react to events, and raise its own events. You can think of a control as a Windows form that can be placed on an actual Windows form and interact with the user at runtime. Of course, controls exhibit a design-time behavior as well. When another developer is using your control, they should be able to set the control's properties in the Property Browser and program the control's events. So, a control is a component that will be used by another developer and will eventually become part of an application. It goes without saying that building a control makes sense if you're going to use it in multiple applications or many forms.

From a designer's point of view, a control abstracts a complicated aspect of the visual interface. Let's say you need a TextBox control that changes color when it loses the focus and it's empty (a TextBox control that's mapped to a mandatory field). All it takes is a few lines of code in the control's Leave event handler. However, on a form with a dozen mandatory fields, you will have to repeat these statements for each TextBox. Some programmers will write a single event handler for all TextBox controls on the form. Even so, you will have to repeat the code in multiple forms. Clearly, the best approach is to create a custom control that provides all the functionality of the original TextBox control and the extra statements that implement the custom functionality (the conditional changing of the control's background color).

There are three types of controls you can develop, and the steps in implementing a custom control depend on the type. The most common type is the so-called *inherited control*. This type of control is based on existing controls and adds custom functionality as new properties, new methods, and new events. As mentioned earlier, you can create a new control by inheriting the TextBox control. The new control will expose all the functionality of the TextBox control as well as some custom functionality, which you must implement yourself. Such functionality may include a Print command, automatic number formatting, and so on.

The second type of control is a *composite control*. A composite control is similar to a form: it contains built-in controls (or other custom controls) and interacts with the user like a form. Developing this type of control is very similar to developing Windows forms. Composite controls are most appropriate in applications that perform similar or identical operations from within multiple forms. For example, a segment of a form that accepts search criteria and displays the results on a gridlike control is suitable for implementing as a composite control. This segment of the form can be packaged as a custom control and be used by multiple developers on multiple forms.

A typical composite control contains a number of Label and TextBox controls that display information about an entity like a person or a product. The various controls correspond to the fields of a table's row (the person's name, address, e-mail address, and so on). The same control can be used to display the information on many different forms, and users can edit its fields. It can even be used on a search form, where users supply search criteria. The control is designed once and can be used on many forms by many developers on the same team. Your knowledge of Windows forms and the information presented in the Chapter 12 is adequate for building composite controls.

The last type of control is the *user-drawn control*. This is the most demanding type of control from a developer's point of view because you're responsible for drawing the control's interface as well as providing the code for its properties and methods.

## Building Custom Controls

We'll start our presentation of custom Windows controls by building a composite custom control. The control we'll build in this section is quite simple and it will help you understand the process of designing and testing a custom control. For the sake of VB6 programmers moving into .NET, we'll start with a composite control (VB6 programmers are mostly familiar with this control). By the way, if you're a VB6 programmer accustomed to the ActiveX Migration Wizard, you should know that there are no control-related wizards in Visual Studio .NET.

To build a custom control, you must create a project of the Windows Control Library type. This type of project doesn't contain a Form, but a UserControl object. This object is the control's client area. You can place any control you wish on the UserControl object to create its visible interface. This is what users will see when they will create an instance of the custom control on their forms.

A project of this type can't be tested as is. The control must reside on a form, so you must add a Windows project to your application and place an instance of the custom control on it. As soon as you compile the control's code, a new item will be automatically added to the Toolbox and you can double-click it to create a new instance of the control on your test form. Then you can examine the custom control's design and runtime behavior. The test project is used in designing and debugging the application, but the control is compiled separately and can be referenced by any other project, independently of the test project you use to develop the control.

## Building the Contact Control

In this section, you'll build a control for displaying and editing a Person record, as shown in Figure 13.1. The form contains an instance of the Contact control with a thin border around it and no other controls. The Contact control is made up of Label and TextBox controls as well as two buttons. They're called *constituent controls* and they're hosted on a UserControl object. The code behind the constituent controls is identical to the code you'd use to build a Windows application for presenting and editing a Person structure. The e-mail and SSN (Social Security number) fields can be validated. If one of these fields loses the focus and it contains an invalid entry, the corresponding control's background color is changed to a light cyan shade. We use two different colors to indicate valid/invalid entries, and these two colors are exposed as properties of the control: the ValidEntryColor and InvalidEntryColor properties.

**FIGURE 13.1:**

The Contact custom control used on a test form

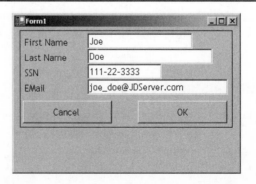

The data is stored in an instance of the Person class, which is declared as public. Any application that uses this control can create an instance of this class and populate it to pass a record to the control. When the user clicks the OK button, the data of the various fields is returned to the application in a Person variable. Both buttons raise an event to indicate the action that took place: the AcceptEdit event for the OK button and the AbortEdit event for the Cancel button. Finally, the Contact custom control exposes three methods: the Clear method, which clears the field values, the EnableEdit method, which enables the editing of the fields, and the Disable-Edit method, which disables the editing of the fields and hides the OK/Cancel buttons.

Start a new Windows Control Library project and name it DataEntry (this is the project's name at the book's pages at www.sybex.com). The Solution Explorer will contain an object called UserControl1, which is an instance of the UserControl object. Change its name to Contact. The control's full name is DataEntry.Contact. Then double-click the UserControl object in the Solution Explorer to open it in Design mode. The UserControl object is very similar to a form, but it doesn't have a visible frame and title bar.

Create the control's interface by dropping the corresponding controls on the UserControl object's surface. All of the tools you'd use to create an interface on a Form object can be used with the UserControl object as well. Use the Anchor and Dock properties to create an interface that resizes itself and the Format menu's tools to align the controls on the design surface. Figure 13.2 shows the UserControl object of the Contact custom control at design time.

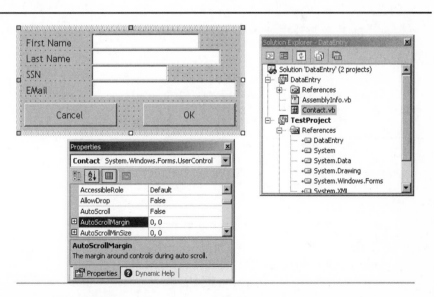

Once you're done with the visible part of the control, you can start coding it. Writing code for a composite control is very similar to coding a Windows application. In addition to the code that handles the appearance and the function of the constituent controls, you must also write some code to expose properties, methods, and fire events. You already know how to create properties for classes (with the Property procedure), how to expose methods (they're public functions), and how to fire events with the RaiseEvent method. Practically, you can start coding.

Let's start with the validation routines, which are the IsValidEMail() and IsValidSSN() functions. These functions, shown in Listing 13.1, validate the corresponding field's value and return a True/False value.

**Listing 13.1**     The *IsValidSSN()* and *IsValidEMail()* Functions

```
Private Function IsValidSSN() As Boolean
    If txtSSN.Text.Trim = "" Then
        txtSSN.BackColor = _InvalidEntryColor
        Return False
    Else
        Dim i As Integer
        For i = 0 To txtSSN.Text.Length - 1
            If Not (Char.IsDigit(txtSSN.Text.Substring(i, 1)) Or _
                txtSSN.Text.Substring(i, 1) = "-" Or _
                    txtSSN.Text.Substring(i, 1) = " ") Then
                txtSSN.BackColor = _InvalidEntryColor
                Return False
            End If
        Next
        txtSSN.BackColor = _ValidEntryColor
        Return True
    End If
End Function

Private Function IsValidEMail() As Boolean
    If txtEMail.Text.IndexOf("@") = -1 _
                And txtEMail.Text.IndexOf(".") = -1 Then
        txtEMail.BackColor = _InvalidEntryColor
        Return False
    Else
        txtEMail.BackColor = _ValidEntryColor
        Return True
    End If
End Function
```

These functions are called from within the corresponding control's Leave event handler as well as from within the OK button's Click event handler. The _*ValidEntryColor* and _*Invalid-EntryColor* private variables hold the values of the ValidEntryColor and InvalidEntryColor properties. The two properties are implemented with the statements in Listing 13.2.

---

**Listing 13.2    The Implementation of the ValidEntryColor and InvalidEntryColor Properties**

```
Private _InvalidEntryColor As Color = Color.LightCyan
<Description("The background color of fields with invalid data")> _
Public Property InvalidEntryColor() As Color
    Get
        Return _InvalidEntryColor
    End Get
    Set(ByVal Value As Color)
        _InvalidEntryColor = Value
    End Set
End Property

Private _ValidEntryColor As Color = Color.White
<Description("The background color of fields with valid data")> _
Public Property ValidEntryColor() As Color
    Get
        Return _ValidEntryColor
    End Get
    Set(ByVal Value As Color)
        _ValidEntryColor = Value
    End Set
End Property
```

---

You see an odd construct in front of the definitions of the two properties. This is an attribute that tells the compiler to include additional information about the control in the executable. The Description attribute adds a description to the property; this is the description that appears in the Property Browser when the property is selected. There are many more attributes you can add to a member of a custom control and we'll come back to discuss them shortly.

Let's see now how the validation routines will be used. Controls are usually validated when they lose focus, so enter the following statements in the Leave event's handler of the txtEMail and txtSSN controls:

```
Private Sub txtSSN_Leave(ByVal sender As Object, _
            ByVal e As System.EventArgs) Handles txtSSN.Leave
    IsValidSSN()
End Sub

Private Sub txtEMail_Leave(ByVal sender As Object, _
            ByVal e As System.EventArgs) Handles txtEMail.Leave
    IsValidEMail()
End Sub
```

So far, we've taken care of the unique aspects of our custom control: the validation routines and the changing of the color of fields that are in error. Now we must think about the data that will be displayed on this control. Instead of individual fields, we can create a custom type, the Person class. Because the Person class must be visible from within any application that uses the Contact control, enter the following class declaration outside the control's Class section:

```
Public Class Person
    Public LastName As String
    Public FirstName As String
    Public SSN As String
    Public EMail As String
End Class
```

Now we have a structure for storing our data and we can write the code for the OK and Cancel buttons. First, declare the two events that the two buttons will fire:

```
Public Event AcceptEdit(ByVal P As Person)
Public Event AbortEdit()
```

Then enter the code for the OK button's Click event handler (Listing 13.3).

**Listing 13.3    Handling the OK Button**

```
Private Sub bttnOK_Click(ByVal sender As System.Object, _
                        ByVal e As System.EventArgs) Handles bttnOK.Click
    If IsValidEMail() And IsValidSSN() Then
        Dim p As New Person()
        p.LastName = txtLast.Text
        p.FirstName = txtFirst.Text
        p.SSN = txtSSN.Text
        p.EMail = txtEMail.Text
        RaiseEvent AcceptEdit(p)
    End If
End Sub
```

The OK button's code creates an instance of the Person class, stores the field values in it, and passes it to the host application through the argument of the AcceptEdit event. The Cancel button, whose Click event handler is shown in Listing 13.4, simply raises the AbortEdit event.

**Listing 13.4    Handling the Cancel Button**

```
Private Sub bttnCancel_Click(ByVal sender As System.Object, _
                        ByVal e As System.EventArgs) _
                        Handles bttnCancel.Click
    RaiseEvent AbortEdit()
End Sub
```

Last, we can implement the methods of the Contact control as public functions. The Show-Person method accepts an instance of the Person class as argument and displays the object's fields on the TextBox controls of the control. The Clear method clears all TextBox controls and the EnableEdit/DisableEdit methods enable and disable the editing operations on the control, respectively. Their code manipulates the ReadOnly property of the TextBox controls and the Visible property of the two buttons. Listing 13.5 shows the implementation of all four custom methods.

**Listing 13.5      The Methods of the Contact Custom Control**

```
Public Sub ShowPerson(ByVal p As Person)
    txtLast.Text = p.LastName
    txtFirst.Text = p.FirstName
    txtSSN.Text = p.SSN
    txtEMail.Text = p.EMail
End Sub

Public Sub Clear()
    txtLast.Text = ""
    txtFirst.Text = ""
    txtSSN.Text = ""
    txtEMail.Text = ""
End Sub

Public Sub EnableEdit()
    txtLast.ReadOnly = False
    txtFirst.ReadOnly = False
    txtSSN.ReadOnly = False
    txtEMail.ReadOnly = False
    bttnOK.Visible = True
    bttnCancel.Visible = True
End Sub

Public Sub DisableEdit()
    txtLast.ReadOnly = True
    txtFirst.ReadOnly = True
    txtSSN.ReadOnly = True
    txtEMail.ReadOnly = True
    bttnOK.Visible = False
    bttnCancel.Visible = False
End Sub
```

Now we can test our custom control. Designing a control with constituent controls is very similar to creating a Windows form. Controls usually have many properties, support methods, and fire events. Implementing these members is similar to adding members to a Class.

The custom control can't be tested on its own. We must create a Windows project, place the control on its form, and test it. Add a new project to the solution and name it TestProject. The test project's folder must be under the solution's folder. If you don't specify a new folder for the project, a `TestProject` folder will be created at the same level as the control's folder.

To test the custom control, compile it with the Build Contact command of the Build menu. The custom control's project must be selected in the Solution Explorer window or the Build Contact command will not appear in the Build menu. After you have built the custom control, you must add to the test project a reference to the new control. Right-click the test project's name in the Solution Explorer, and from the context menu, select the Add Reference command. When the Add Reference dialog box appears, switch to the Projects tab and select the Contact component. Then click OK to add a reference to this control and close the dialog box.

When you switch to the form of the test project and open the Toolbox, you'll see that the last item on the Toolbox is your new custom control. Place an instance of the new control on the test form and then enter the following statements in the form's Load event handler:

```
Private Sub Form1_Load(ByVal sender As System.Object, _
                       ByVal e As System.EventArgs) Handles MyBase.Load
    Dim person As New DataEntry.Person()
    person.LastName = "Doe"
    person.FirstName = "Joe"
    person.EMail = "joe_doe@JDServer.com"
    person.SSN = "111-22-3333"
    Contact1.ShowPerson(person)
End Sub
```

If you run the application now, you will see the fields of the Person object passed to the control with the ShowPerson method. You can also edit the fields on the control and click the OK button when you're done. The control will raise the AcceptEdit event, which you can intercept in the application's code. The sample application contains the following statements in the control's AcceptEdit and AbortEdit event handlers:

```
Private Sub Contact1_AbortEdit() Handles Contact1.Abort
    Console.WriteLine("Edit Aborted")
End Sub

Private Sub Contact1_AcceptEdit(ByVal P As DataEntry.Person) _
                              Handles Contact1.AcceptEdit
    Console.WriteLine(P.LastName & " , " & _
            P.FirstName & vbCrLf & P.SSN & vbCrLf & P.EMail)
End Sub
```

Stop the application, select the Contact1 control on the form, and examine its properties. Our control doesn't expose many properties, but you can see how the two Color properties can be set with the Color dialog box and the Font property can be set with the Font dialog box. The appropriate editor will appear automatically in the Property Browser depending on the type of the property. You can set the properties of the new control at design time and check it out. It behaves just like the built-in controls.

As you work with the control on the test form, you will discover a problem as you resize the control. The control isn't being redrawn as you resize it. To add the finishing touches to the control, switch to the UserControl object and enter the following statement in the control's New subroutine:

```
SetStyle(ControlStyles.ResizeRedraw, True)
```

This statement causes the control to be redrawn as it is resized. Notice also that the User-Control object doesn't have a visible border and its default background color is the same as that of the form. You can add a simple border around the control by drawing a rectangle from within the control's OnPaint method. Locate this method in the code window and enter the following statement in its event handler:

```
Protected Overrides Sub OnPaint(ByVal e As System.Windows.Forms.PaintEventArgs)
    e.Graphics.DrawRectangle(Pens.Black, 1, 1, Me.Width - 2, Me.Height - 2)
End Sub
```

You have completed the design of your first custom control. A composite control is fairly straightforward to build. You can actually write a Windows application that exhibits the same behavior as your control and then transfer the logic from the Windows application to the control. Just keep in mind that the control doesn't usually interact with the other controls on the form on which it will be placed. You can access the control's parent form with the Parent property and then use the properties of the Parent object to access the properties of the form as well as any other controls that happen to be on the form at the time.

## Building a User-Drawn Control

In this section, we'll build a user-drawn control. This time you're responsible for drawing the control's surface, because the control doesn't contain any constituent controls. The FancyLabel project, which you will find at the book's pages at www.sybex.com, is a custom control similar to the Label control. It displays a string centered horizontally and vertically on the control and it has a double frame. Among other members, it exposes two methods that allow you to set the control in a flashing mode (the text alternates between white and any other color a few times per second). The border is drawn with two thin, adjacent lines, a dark one and a light one. Depending on which line is dark (the inside or the outside) and which one is light, we achieve two types of effects: an inset (carved) frame and a raised frame. The colors of the two lines are exposed as properties and you can change them to achieve the desired effect. The FancyLabel control is shown in Figure 13.3.

Let's start with a description of the custom control's basic properties:

**BorderStyle property**    This property determines the style of the control's border, and its value is a member of the BorderStyle enumeration: None, SingleBorder, and DoubleBorder.

**Caption property**    This property is the string that will be displayed on the control (it's usually called Text, but we think the "caption" term is more suitable). The control doesn't wrap the text, so its caption should be fairly sort.

**CaptionColor property**    This is the color in which the caption will be rendered.

**LightBorderColor, DarkBorderColor properties**    These two properties determine the two colors used to create the border. The default values of these properties result in a raised frame. Swap their settings for an inset (carved) effect.

You will notice that there's no Font property. The UserControl object itself exposes a Font property, and we'll use it to draw the control's caption.

In addition to the properties, the custom control will expose a few methods, which are the following:

**Clear method**    This method accepts as argument a Color value, and it clears the control by setting its caption to an empty string and its background to the specified color.

**StartFlashing method**    Call this method to put the control in flashing mode. The caption's color alternates between the color specified by the CaptionColor property and white.

**StopFlashing Method**    Call this method to terminate flashing mode. The text will be displayed in the color specified by the CaptionColor property.

Finally, the custom control will fire a few events:

**FlashingBright event**    This event is fired when the control's caption switches to white.

**FlashingNormal event**    This event is fired when the control's caption switches to its normal color. The two events are practically meaningless because there's not much you can do as the control's caption changes color, but they demonstrate how to raise events from within a custom control.

**CaptionChanged, CaptionColorChanged events**    These events take place when the Caption or CaptionColor properties change value, and they may be needed by developers to adjust the appearance of another control when the appearance of the SimpleControl changes.

## Building the FancyLabel Control

Start a new project, and on the Templates section of the New Project dialog box, select the Windows Control Library project type. In the Name field, enter the name of the project, Simple-Control. This is the project's name, not the control's name. In the new project's Solution Explorer, there will be an item called UserControl1. This is the surface of the custom control. The UserControl object is very similar to a Form object in the sense that it exposes a Graphics object that you can use to draw on and it can act as a host for other controls. In this example, we're not going to use any constituent controls; we're going to write code that controls the appearance of the custom control when it's placed on a form.

Change the name of the UserControl1 object to a meaningful name for your custom control. Let's change it to FancyLabel. Changing the name of the object in the Solution Explorer will only change the name of the VB file in which the control's code will be saved. To change the object's name, you must open the Property Browser of the UserControl object, locate its Name property, and change it.

---

**NOTE**    To change the name of a control during its design phase, you must change the User-Control object's Name property. Then, you must switch to the code window and change all instances of *UserControl1* to the new name. Actually, as soon as you change the UserControl object's Name property, a list of errors will appear in the Task List window. Double-click each error to see the corresponding line in your code that refers to the old name and change it manually.

The control is an object that must be hosted on a form; you can't run the project you just created. To test the control, you need a test project as well. Open the File menu and select the command Add Project ➢ New Project. In the New Project dialog box that will appear, you must change the suggested project type from Windows Control Library to Windows Application.

Name the new project TestProject and change the name of its main Form to TestForm. Now you're ready to build a control, place it on a form, and test it both at design time and runtime. You must also change the solution's Startup Project to the TestProject project so that when you press F5, the IDE will run the test project and display its main form (which, presumably, contains an instance of the custom control).

The UserControl object exposes quite a bit of the custom control's functionality. In effect, it's a generic custom control. To find out the functionality of the UserControl object, let's use it on our test form. Double-click the UserControl object in the Solution Explorer to open it in Design mode. Then open the Build menu and select Build SimpleControl. This action will create an executable for the custom control in the project's bin folder. Switch to the test project and add a reference to the custom control as explained already.

Now switch to the test form and open the Toolbox and you'll see that a new item was placed at the bottom of the Toolbox. It's the custom control's icon and it's called FancyLabel. Double-click its icon to place an instance of the control on the test form. The control has no special appearance; it's a square with the same background color as the form. Take a look at its properties in the Property Browser. It has the AutoScroll properties like all controls, the Anchor and Dock properties, and a BackColor and a BackgroundImage property. You can experiment with this generic control and explore the functionality already built into the control. You can set its BackgroundImage property to a large image and its AutoScrollMinSize property to the dimensions of the image.

If you expand the BackgroundImage property, as shown in Figure 13.4, you will see the dimensions of the image. Enter the same dimensions in the AutoScrollMinSize box and two scroll bars will be automatically attached to the control. Do you see what kind of control you've created? It's a scrolling PictureBox control. All you need in order to turn the generic control into a functional scrolling PictureBox is a statement that sets the control's AutoScrollMinSize property every time you load a different image. This action is signaled with the OnBackground-ImageChanged event, so creating a scrolling PictureBox custom control is almost trivial. The PictureBox control doesn't expose a Scrollbars property, nor does it expose an AutoScroll property. This means that a scrolling PictureBox is trivial to build, by setting its AutoScrollMinSize property to the dimensions of the current image from within the OnBackgroundImageChanged event's handler. The UserControl object is closer to a Form object than it is to any other control, and thanks to its support for automatic scrolling, it can be easily turned into a more flexible PictureBox control.

So, a generic user-drawn custom control is not as generic as you might have thought. It exposes much of the functionality you'd expect from any custom control—just consider what it would take to write code for the Dock and Anchor properties if you had to implement these properties yourself. The generic control is ready to be used in designing new Windows forms. All you have to do is add a few members that will make your control unique.

**FIGURE 13.4:**

A generic custom control can be easily turned into a scrolling PictureBox control.

Let's start by implementing the members of the FancyLabel control. The first property we'll look at is the Border property. It must be implemented as a Property procedure and its type is a custom enumeration, the BorderStyle enumeration. Listing 13.6 shows the members of the BorderStyle enumeration and the implementation of the Border property.

**Listing 13.6**    **Implementing the BorderStyle Enumeration and the Border Property**

```
Public Enum BorderStyle
    None
    SingleBorder
    DoubleBorder
End Enum

Private _BorderStyle As BorderStyle = BorderStyle.SingleBorder

Public Property Border() As BorderStyle
    Get
        Return _BorderStyle
    End Get
    Set(ByVal Value As BorderStyle)
        _BorderStyle = Value
        Invalidate()
    End Set
End Property
```

Compile the control again and switch to the test form. You'll see that the Border property is displayed as a drop-down list that contains all the members of the BorderStyle enumeration (see Figure 13.5). Users can't set this property to an unacceptable value.

**FIGURE 13.5:**

Setting the Border property in the Property Browser

The Caption property is quite trivial. It's a string value, which is stored to the _caption private variable. The statements in Listing 13.7 implement the Caption property.

**Listing 13.7        Implementing the Caption Property**

```
Private _caption As String = "Simple Label"
Public Property Caption() As String
    Get
        Return _caption
    End Get
    Set(ByVal Value As String)
        _caption = Value
        Invalidate()
    End Set
End Property
```

The CaptionColor property is just as easy. We implement a Color property and the compiler is intelligent enough to supply a color editor for setting its value in the Property Browser. The implementation of the CaptionColor property is shown in Listing 13.8.

**Listing 13.8        Implementing the CaptionColor Property**

```
Private _captionColor As Color = Color.Blue
Public Property CaptionColor() As Color
    Get
        Return _captionColor
    End Get
    Set(ByVal Value As Color)
        _captionColor = Value
        Invalidate()
    End Set
End Property
```

The last two custom properties of the control are also of the Color type, and they're implemented as shown in Listing 13.9.

**Listing 13.9        Implementing the LightColor and DarkColor Properties**

```
Private _LightColor As Color = Color.White
Private _DarkColor As Color = Color.DarkGray
Public Property LightBorderColor() As Color
    Get
        Return _LightColor
    End Get
    Set(ByVal Value As Color)
        _LightColor = Value
        Invalidate()
    End Set
End Property

Public Property DarkBorderColor() As Color
    Get
        Return _DarkColor
    End Get
    Set(ByVal Value As Color)
        _DarkColor = Value
        Invalidate()
    End Set
End Property
```

Adding custom properties to a UserControl object is identical to adding properties to a Class. You create a local variable in which you store the property's value and then write a Property procedure. Note that the Invalidate method is called after setting each property. We didn't have to do that with the composite control in the first example in this chapter because the constituent controls contain their own redraw logic. When you're responsible for drawing the control's surface, however, keep in mind that every time the value of a property that affects the control's appearance is changed, you must redraw the control. This is exactly what the Invalidate method does: it causes the control to redraw itself. But how is the control redrawn? This is what really makes our control tick, and it takes place from within the control's OnPaint event handler. We need to override the default OnPaint event handler and insert the code that will draw our custom control's surface. Before we examine the OnPaint event handler, let's test the custom properties we've added so far.

Compile the control again and switch to the test form. Select the control on the form, or place a new instance of the FancyLabel control on the form if you haven't done so already, and set its various properties. Nothing will happen on the control's surface because we haven't provided the code to redraw the control's surface. Let's return to the control and add the statements to redraw its surface. These statements are no different than the statements you'd use to redraw the surface of a Form object. Many developers find it simpler to write a form that exhibits the same functionality as their custom control and then copy the code and reuse it with their controls.

To program the control's OnPaint event handler, switch to the control's code window and select the overridable events in the drop-down list with the object names (select the Overrides item), and in the events drop-down list, locate and select the OnPaint event. Then enter the statements in Listing 13.10 in this event's handler.

### Listing 13.10    Drawing the FancyLabel Control's Border(s)

```
Protected Overrides Sub OnPaint(ByVal e As System.Windows.Forms.PaintEventArgs)
    Dim CaptionSize As SizeF
    ' Draw the control's caption, centered in both directions
    CaptionSize = e.Graphics.MeasureString(_caption, Me.Font)
    Dim X, Y As Integer
    X = Fix((Me.Width - CaptionSize.Width) / 2)
    Y = Fix((Me.Height - CaptionSize.Height) / 2)
    e.Graphics.DrawString(_caption, Me.Font, _
                New SolidBrush(captionColor), X, Y)
    ' If the control has no border, we're done.
    ' Or else, draw the outer border.
    If _BorderStyle = BorderStyle.none Then Exit Sub
    e.Graphics.DrawLine(New Pen(_LightColor, 2), _
                1, 1, 1, Me.Height - 1)
    e.Graphics.DrawLine(New Pen(_LightColor, 2), _
                1, Me.Height - 1, Me.Width - 1, Me.Height - 1)
    e.Graphics.DrawLine(New Pen(_LightColor, 2), _
                Me.Width - 1, Me.Height - 1, Me.Width - 1, 1)
    e.Graphics.DrawLine(New Pen(_LightColor, 2), _
                Me.Width - 1, 1, 1, 1)
```

```
                e.Graphics.DrawLine(New Pen(_DarkColor, 1), _
                                Me.Width - 1, Me.Height - 2, Me.Width - 1, 2)
                e.Graphics.DrawLine(New Pen(_DarkColor, 1), _
                                Me.Width - 1, 1, 1, 1)
                e.Graphics.DrawLine(New Pen(_DarkColor, 1), _
                                1, 2, 1, Me.Height - 2)
                e.Graphics.DrawLine(New Pen(_DarkColor, 1), _
                                2, Me.Height - 1, Me.Width - 2, Me.Height - 1)
                ' If the control has a double border, draw the inner border
                If _BorderStyle = BorderStyle.SingleBorder Then Exit Sub
                e.Graphics.DrawLine(New Pen(_LightColor, 2), _
                                3, 3, 3, Me.Height - 3)
                e.Graphics.DrawLine(New Pen(_LightColor, 2), _
                                3, Me.Height - 3, Me.Width - 3, Me.Height - 3)
                e.Graphics.DrawLine(New Pen(_LightColor, 2), _
                                Me.Width - 3, Me.Height - 3, Me.Width - 3, 3)
                e.Graphics.DrawLine(New Pen(_LightColor, 2), _
                                Me.Width - 3, 3, 3, 3)
                e.Graphics.DrawLine(New Pen(_DarkColor, 1), _
                                Me.Width - 3, Me.Height - 4, Me.Width - 3, 4)
                e.Graphics.DrawLine(New Pen(_DarkColor, 1), Me.Width - 3, 3, 3, 3)
                e.Graphics.DrawLine(New Pen(_DarkColor, 1), 3, 4, 3, Me.Height - 4)
                e.Graphics.DrawLine(New Pen(_DarkColor, 1), 4, Me.Height - 3, _
                                Me.Width - 4, Me.Height - 3)
End Sub
```

The code is quite trivial, even though a little lengthy. First it prints the control's caption, centered in both directions. To do so, it first calculates the dimensions of the rendered string by calling the MeasureString method. This method returns the dimensions of the string passed as argument when rendered in the specified font, but it doesn't actually render the string. The code then subtracts these dimensions from the dimensions of the control and splits the difference on either side of the string, vertically and horizontally.

After it prints the text, the code draws the border by drawing two adjacent lines near the control's perimeter. The colors of the two lines are the two colors specified with the DarkColor and LightColor properties.

You will notice a very disturbing problem as you test this control. As you resize it, it's not being always redrawn. It's automatically redrawn when you reduce its size, but not when you enlarge the control. Windows doesn't fire the OnPaint event when the control is expanded, so we must do something about it. The solution is to force the control to be redrawn every time it's resized by setting the ResizeRedraw style to True. To do so, enter the following statement in the control's New subroutine (you will find this subroutine in the Windows Form Designer Generated Code segment, at the top of the code editor's window):

```
Me.SetStyle(ControlStyles.ResizeRedraw, True)
```

The new control works as intended both at design time and runtime. Let's look at the control's methods now. The Clear method is quite straightforward:

```
Public Sub Clear(ByVal bgColor As Color)
    _caption = ""
    Me.CreateGraphics.Clear(bgColor)
    Invalidate()
End Sub
```

This method accepts as argument a Color value and fills the control with the specified color.

Now we can look at the two methods for placing the control in flashing mode. We want to change the color of the text every so often, so we must introduce a Timer control. We'll set the Timer's Interval property to 300 milliseconds so that the control's caption will change color nearly three times per second. The StartFlashing method enables the Timer control and the StopFlashing method disables it. The code behind these two methods is quite simple, as you can see in Listing 13.11.

**Listing 13.11    Programming the FancyLabel Control's Methods**

```
Private WithEvents T As New Timer()

Public Sub StartFlashing()
    T.Interval = 300
    T.Enabled = True
End Sub

Public Sub StopFlashing()
    FlashNow = True
    T.Enabled = False
     Flash(Me, New System.EventArgs())
End Sub
```

The *FlashNow* variable is declared outside the two procedures, because it's also used in the Tick event's handler, as you will see next.

```
Private FlashNow As Boolean
```

The Timer control's Tick event is handled by the Flash subroutine, which is shown in Listing 13.12. This subroutine prints the control's caption in an alternating color. The code doesn't change the *_captionColor* variable's value. It maintains a Boolean variable, the *FlashNow* variable, which alternates between True and False. When *FlashNow* is True, it draws the caption in white; when *FlashNow* is False, the code draws the same string in the color of the *_captionColor* variable. Each time, the *FlashNow* variable changes value with the statement FlashNow=Not FlashNow. The rest of the listing is straightforward.

**Listing 13.12    Alternating the Caption's Color**

```
Sub Flash(ByVal sender As System.Object, _
          ByVal e As System.EventArgs) Handles T.Tick
    FlashNow = Not FlashNow
    Dim CaptionSize As SizeF
    CaptionSize = Me.CreateGraphics.MeasureString(_caption, Me.Font)
    Dim X, Y As Integer
    X = Fix((Me.Width - CaptionSize.Width) / 2)
    Y = Fix((Me.Height - CaptionSize.Height) / 2)
    If FlashNow Then
        Me.CreateGraphics.DrawString(_caption, _
                        Me.Font, New SolidBrush(Color.White), X, Y)
    Else
        Me.CreateGraphics.DrawString(_caption, _
                        Me.Font, New SolidBrush(_captionColor), X, Y)
    End If
End Sub
```

Switch to the test form and test the methods added to the control. Place a Button on the form, set its Text property to Start Flashing and enter the statements in Listing 13.13 in its Click event handler.

**Listing 13.13    Testing the StartFlashing and StopFlashing Methods**

```
Private Sub Button1_Click(ByVal sender As System.Object, _
                          ByVal e As System.EventArgs) Handles Button1.Click
    If Button1.Text = "Start Flashing" Then
        UserControl11.StartFlashing()
        Button1.Text = "Stop Flashing"
    Else
        UserControl11.StopFlashing()
        Button1.Text = "Start Flashing"
    End If
End Sub
```

Every time the button is clicked, its caption is toggled between "Start Flashing" and "Stop Flashing." Run the application and check it out. It works as intended, and you have a functional Label control with a custom border that can flash a message.

Finally, we can add a few events to our custom control. First, we must add the events that indicate that a property has changed value. When the property Caption changes value (either through the Property Browser or from within the application's code), the OnCaptionChanged method is invoked automatically. In this event's handler, we must fire another event, which will be passed to the host application (the CaptionChanged event is consumed by the control's code and the host application will never receive it). Let's call the event that will signify changes in the Caption property's value CaptionChanged. CaptionChanged is the name of an event, which must be fired from within the control's OnCaptionChanged event handler. Our custom control contains two such events, the CaptionChanged and CaptionColorChanged events, and their implementation is shown next:

```
Public Event CaptionChanged As EventHandler
Protected Sub OnCaptionChanged(ByVal e As EventArgs)
    RaiseEvent CaptionChanged(Me, e)
End Sub

Public Event CaptionColorChanged As EventHandler
Protected Sub OnCaptionColorChanged(ByVal e As EventArgs)
    RaiseEvent CaptionColorChanged(Me, e)
End Sub
```

Now we'll add the two events that are unique to our custom control, the FlashingBright and FlashingNormal events. Both events are raised from within the Flash subroutine, depending on the caption's current color. When the color is switched to bright, the FlashingBright event is fired, and when the color is switched to the normal color, the FlashingNormal event is fired. The two events are raised from within the control's revised Flash subroutine, which is shown in Listing 13.14.

---

**Listing 13.14    The Revised *Flash()* Subroutine**

```
Public Event FlashingBright()
Public Event FlashingNormal()
Sub Flash(ByVal sender As System.Object, _
        ByVal e As System.EventArgs) Handles T.Tick
    FlashNow = Not FlashNow
    Dim CaptionSize As SizeF
    CaptionSize = Me.CreateGraphics.MeasureString(_caption, Me.Font)
    Dim X, Y As Integer
    X = Fix((Me.Width - CaptionSize.Width) / 2)
    Y = Fix((Me.Height - CaptionSize.Height) / 2)
    If FlashNow Then
        Me.CreateGraphics.DrawString(_caption, _
                    Me.Font, New SolidBrush(Color.White), X, Y)
        RaiseEvent FlashingBright()
    Else
        Me.CreateGraphics.DrawString(_caption, Me.Font, _
                    New SolidBrush(_captionColor), X, Y)
        RaiseEvent FlashingNormal()
    End If
End Sub
```

---

There's not much to do about testing the events, short of adding an indication about the current color. The test project for the FancyLabel control changes the caption of the test form to indicate the current color of the control's caption with the following event handlers:

```
Private Sub FancyLabel1_FlashingBright() Handles FancyLabel1.FlashingBright
    Me.Text = "White"
End Sub

Private Sub FancyLabel1_FlashingNormal() Handles FancyLabel1.FlashingNormal
    Me.Text = "FancyLabel Control Test Form"
End Sub
```

## Using Attributes

As with classes, many characteristics of the members of a custom control can be specified with attributes. Attributes are classes themselves, and they allow you to add specific properties, or behaviors, to a member. To add an attribute to a member, prefix its declaration with the name of the attribute in angle brackets. In a pair of parentheses following the name of the attribute, you can specify an argument. The following attribute assigns a description to the Character-Case property. The description will appear in the lower section of the Property Browser when the user selects the property, as well as in a ToolTip box when the user selects the same property in the IntelliSense box (presumably CharCase is an enumeration):

```
<Description("Determines the casing of the control's caption"> _
Public Property CharacterCase As CharCase
' your code here
End Property
```

There are many attributes, some quite trivial (like the Description attribute) and some others quite complicated to use. Following is a list with the most common attributes. They're all members of the System.ComponentModel.Design namespace, which you must import to your project with the Imports statement.

**AmbientValue**    This attribute specifies a value, which when passed to a property, causes the property to get its value from another source. If you have a control on a Form and the BackColor property of the control is set to a different color than the BackColor property of the Form, you can reset the BackColor property of the control to that of the Form by setting the BackColor property of the control to Color.Empty.

**Bindable**    This attribute specifies that the property can be bound to a data source. You'll see how to build data-bound controls later in this chapter:

```
<BindableAttribute(True)> Public Property DisplayColumn() As DataColumn
    ' Insert your code here
End Property
```

**Browsable**    This attribute specifies whether a property should be displayed in the Property Browser. The default value of this attribute is True, so you need not include it with every property (use this attribute only with properties you don't want to appear in the Property Browser and set it to False):

```
<Browsable(True)> Public Property customProperty() As String
    ' Insert your code here
End Property
```

**Category**    This attribute determines the category under which the property should appear in the Property Browser. To place a property under the category "Appearance", prefix it with the following attribute:

```
<Category("Appearance")> Public Property captionColor() As Color
```

If you specify a category that doesn't exist, a new category by that name will be added to the Property Browser. Create a new category if your custom control has multiple properties that belong to the same category.

**DefaultEvent**    This attribute specifies the default event of the control. This is the event that will appear in the code window when a developer double-clicks the control on the form. To make the EditComplete event the default event for your control, prefix it with the following attribute:

```
<DefaultEventAttribute> Public Event EditComplete
```

**DefaultProperty**    This attribute specifies the default property of the control. To make the Caption property the default property of your custom control, use the following statement:

```
<DefaultPropertyAttribute()> Public Property Caption
    ' your code here
End Property
```

**DefaultValue**    This attribute specifies the default value of a property. This value will appear next to the property's name in the Property Browser in regular font. When a developer changes the property's value, the new setting will appear in bold in the Property Browser. When the property's value is reset (with the Reset command of the context menu), the property is set to this value:

```
<DefaultValue(False)> Public Property customProperty() As Boolean
    ' your code here
End Property
```

**Description**    This attribute specifies a description for a property; the description will appear in the lower segment of the Property Browser when the property is selected:

```
<Description("The color in which the text will be rendered on the control"),
Category("Appearance")> _
```

```
Public Property Caption() As String
    ' you code here
End Property
```

**DesignOnly**   This attribute specifies that a property can only be set at design time. If you set it to True, the property won't be editable at run time.

**Editor**   This attribute specifies the custom editor to use to change a property. We'll look into custom designers in detail later in this chapter.

**Localizable**   This attribute specifies whether a property should be localized.

**MergeableProperty**   This attribute specifies that this property can be combined with identical properties of other controls in the Property Browser. If your control exposes a property like Font, when a developer selects the custom control along with other controls on the form, the Font property of your control will be merged with the Font property of the other controls. The new value set by the developer will apply to all selected controls, including your custom control.

**ReadOnly**   This attribute specifies whether a property is editable in the Property Browser. Notice that the property itself may be read-write. This attribute determines the behavior of the property in the Property Browser only.

**RefreshProperties**   This attribute determines how a designer refreshes when the associated property value changes. It can have one of the following values:

   **All**   All properties are requeried and refreshed if the property value is changed.

   **Default**   No other properties are requeried and refreshed if the property value is changed.

   **Repaint**   The control is repainted if the property value is changed.

**TypeConverter**   This attribute specifies the type of the converter that will be used to set the property's value. We'll look into type converters in detail later in this chapter.

As you can see, attaching attributes to the members of your custom control simplifies considerably the task of developing new Windows controls, and you should get into the habit of using the basic attributes like `Description`, `Category`, and `DefaultValue`. Some of the attributes are anything but trivial, but they address issues that were impossible to resolve earlier versions of VB.

## Inheriting Existing Controls

The majority of VB programmers will build custom controls that extend the functionality of existing ones by inheriting from them. Most of us would suggest some extra functionality for just about every one of the built-in controls. None of the built-in controls expose a Print method, yet how many applications deploy a TextBox control but don't provide a print command? Our sample control will be a fairly advanced one, but we hope many readers will find it useful in their day-to-day projects. You're going to build a custom ListView control that exposes all the functionality of the original control plus a Print method, a single method that will make the ListView control so much easier to include in your projects. Figure 13.6 shows the test form of the application and a Print Preview window with the control's data. The control's data will be printed as shown on the preview window. Notice that the long lines that don't fit in the control's cells are printed on multiple lines.

**FIGURE 13.6:**

The PrintListView control provides a custom Print method.

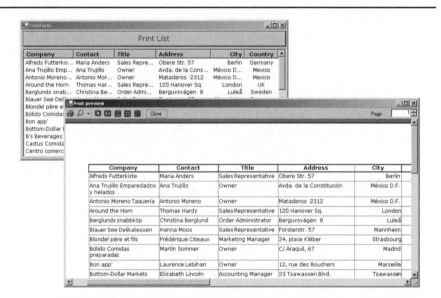

Before we look at the code, let's start with an overview of the control's operation and a few basic concepts of the Drawing class (printing in VB .NET is nothing more than drawing characters on the paper's surface). The control is populated programmatically—the ListView control can't be edited by the user at runtime.

To print from within an application, you normally add an instance of the PrintDocument component and, optionally, the PrintPreview and PageSetupDialog controls to the form. In our inherited control, we'll create these instances from within our code:

```
Private PPView As New PrintPreviewDialog()
Private PSetup As New PageSetupDialog()
Private vSpacing As Integer = 6
Private WithEvents PD As System.Drawing.Printing.PrintDocument
```

The PPView variable is an instance of the PrintPreview control. We'll use this control to preview the printout before sending it to the printer. The PSetup variable is an instance of the Page–SetupDialog control, which allows you to configure the printout (select the printer, the printout's orientation, and so on). The PD variable represents an instance of the PrintDocument class—all the printing takes place on this object. The last variable is the horizontal and vertical spacing of the cells on the printout.

The PListView control exposes a single method, the Print method, which is implemented with the statements shown in Listing 13.15.

**Listing 13.15     The Control's Print Method**

```
Public Sub Print()
    PD = New Printing.PrintDocument()
    PSetup.PageSettings = PD.DefaultPageSettings
    PSetup.ShowDialog()
    PPView.Document = PD
    PPView.ShowDialog()
End Sub
```

The first statement creates a new PrintDocument object, the PD variable, and you'll see how this object is used shortly. The next statement prepares the PageSetupDialog control and the following statement displays it. When the user closes the Page Setup dialog box, the code assigns the PrintDocument object to the PrintPreview control's Document object and shows the PrintPreview dialog box. The last statement, in effect, initiates the printing.

When you print in .NET, the PrintPage event of the PrintDocument object is fired. In this event's handler, you insert all the printing code. The event's PrintPageEventArgs argument exposes the surface of the page as a Graphics object, and you can call the drawing methods to generate the printout. When the bottom of the page is reached and there's more text to be printed, set HasMorePages property of the Graphics object to True and the PrintPage event will be fired again. When you're done, set the HasMorePages property to False to terminate the printing.

The PrintPage event handler is quite lengthy and we've inserted comments to explain how it works. The code reads the number of columns of the PListView control and divides the width of the page into as many segments as there are columns in the ListView control. The width of each column on the page is the same percentage of the page's width as the corresponding column is to the width of the control. To change the relative widths of the printed columns, resize the columns of the control with the mouse. The dimensions and margins of the page are retrieved with the properties of the DefaultPageSettings property of the PD variable. This object exposes the user-supplied margins and the total width and height of the page. The program takes into consideration the orientation of the page as well.

To print the data, the code goes through each row of the control, reads its items, and figures out the height of the cell required by each item. An item may take up one or more lines, so its text may have to be broken into multiple lines. The width of each column is fixed, so we need only to figure out the height of the cell. The MeasureString method returns this information. This method accepts as arguments the string to be printed, the font in which it will be rendered, and a SizeF object that represents the area in which the string should fit, and it returns the number of characters per line as well as the number of lines in which the string will be broken. Once you have this information, you can decide about the cell's height and then print the string. You must also keep track of the tallest cell on a line because its height will become the height of the entire line. Listing 13.16 shows the PrintPage event handler of the PrintDocument object, which is the heart of the custom control.

**Listing 13.16       The PrintPage Event's Handler**

```
Private Sub PD_PrintPage(ByVal sender As Object, _
         ByVal e As System.Drawing.Printing.PrintPageEventArgs) _
         Handles PD.PrintPage
    Static startItem As Integer
    Dim ColWidths(Me.Columns.Count - 1) As Integer
    ' calculate the width of each column and the total width of the grid
    Dim i As Integer, totWidth As Integer
    For i = 0 To Me.Columns.Count - 1
        ColWidths(i) = Me.Columns(i).Width
        totWidth = totWidth + ColWidths(i)
    Next
    ' X and Y are the coordinates of the current subitem
    ' and are updated after printing each subitem
    Dim X, Y As Integer
    ' cellWidth and cellHeight are the width and height
    ' of the current subitem's cell
    Dim cellWidth, cellHeight As Integer
    X = PD.DefaultPageSettings.Margins.Left
    Y = PD.DefaultPageSettings.Margins.Top
    Dim PWidth As Integer = PD.DefaultPageSettings.PaperSize.Width
    Dim PHeight As Integer = PD.DefaultPageSettings.PaperSize.Height
    If PD.DefaultPageSettings.Landscape Then
        Dim tmp As Integer
        tmp = PWidth
        PWidth = PHeight
        PHeight = tmp
    End If
    Dim PageWidth As Integer = PWidth - _
                            (PD.DefaultPageSettings.Margins.Left + _
                             PD.DefaultPageSettings.Margins.Right)
    Dim PageHeight As Integer = PHeight - _
                            (PD.DefaultPageSettings.Margins.Top + _
                             PD.DefaultPageSettings.Margins.Bottom)
```

```vbnet
Dim R As Rectangle, RF As RectangleF
Dim caption As String
Dim titleFont As Font = Me.Font
Dim itemFont As Font
Dim titleBrush As New SolidBrush(Color.Black)
Dim itemBrush As System.Drawing.Brush
itemBrush = Brushes.Black
Dim borderPen As New Pen(Color.Black, 2)
Dim txtWidth As Integer
Dim fmt As New StringFormat(StringFormatFlags.FitBlackBox)
Dim txtSize As SizeF
For i = 0 To Me.Columns.Count - 1
    caption = Me.Columns(i).Text
    cellWidth = ColWidths(i) * PageWidth / totWidth
    txtSize = e.Graphics.MeasureString(caption, titleFont)
    txtSize.Height = txtSize.Height
    cellHeight = txtSize.Height
    R = New Rectangle(X, Y, cellWidth, cellHeight)
    RF = New RectangleF(X, Y, cellWidth, cellHeight)
    e.Graphics.DrawRectangle(borderPen, R)
    RF = New RectangleF(X + (cellWidth - txtSize.Width) / 2, _
                        Y, cellWidth, cellHeight)
    e.Graphics.DrawString(caption, titleFont, titleBrush, RF, fmt)
    X = X + cellWidth
Next
Dim itm, sitm As Integer
Y = Y + cellHeight ' + vSpacing / 2
Dim SF As SizeF
' Now iterate through a number of items and print them.
' The exact number of items that will be printed varies,
' depending on the height of each cell. Some of the items/subitems
' may not fit on a single line
' The index of the last item printed is stored in the startItem static
' variable, so that printing will resume with the following item the
' next time the PrintPage event is fired
For itm = startItem To Me.Items.Count - 1
    X = PD.DefaultPageSettings.Margins.Left
    Dim tallestCell As Integer = 0
    For sitm = 0 To Me.Items(itm).SubItems.Count - 1
        caption = Me.Items(itm).SubItems(sitm).Text
        cellWidth = ColWidths(sitm) * PageWidth / totWidth
        ' itemFont is set to the font used to render
        ' the corresponding subitem on the control
        itemFont = Me.Items(itm).Font
        SF = New SizeF(cellWidth, 100)
        txtSize = e.Graphics.MeasureString(caption, itemFont, SF, fmt)
        ' keep track of the tallest cell in the current item
        txtSize.Height = txtSize.Height + vSpacing / 2
        If txtSize.Height > tallestCell Then tallestCell = txtSize.Height
        ' print the subitem with its original alignment
        Select Case Me.Columns(sitm).TextAlign
```

```
                Case HorizontalAlignment.Center _
                        : fmt.Alignment = StringAlignment.Center
                Case HorizontalAlignment.Left _
                        : fmt.Alignment = StringAlignment.Near
                Case HorizontalAlignment.Right _
                        : fmt.Alignment = StringAlignment.Far
            End Select
            e.Graphics.DrawString(caption, itemFont, itemBrush, RF, fmt)
            X = X + cellWidth
        Next
        Y = Y + tallestCell + vSpacing / 2
        e.Graphics.DrawLine(Pens.Gray, _
    PD.DefaultPageSettings.Margins.Left, _
                    Y, PD.DefaultPageSettings.Margins.Left + PageWidth + 1, Y)
        ' start a new page is the current row's cells exceed
        ' 95% of the page's printable area
        If Y > 0.95 * (PHeight - PD.DefaultPageSettings.Margins.Bottom) Then
            ' now print the vertical lines
            X = PD.DefaultPageSettings.Margins.Left
            For i = 0 To Me.Columns.Count - 1
                e.Graphics.DrawLine(Pens.Gray, X, _
                            PD.DefaultPageSettings.Margins.Top, X, Y)
                cellWidth = ColWidths(i) * PageWidth / totWidth
                X = X + cellWidth
            Next
            ' draw the last vertical line
            e.Graphics.DrawLine(Pens.Gray, X, _
                            PD.DefaultPageSettings.Margins.Top, X, Y)
            ' and the bottom horizontal line
            e.Graphics.DrawLine(Pens.Gray, _
                            PD.DefaultPageSettings.Margins.Left, Y, _
                            PD.DefaultPageSettings.Margins.Left + _
                            PageWidth + 1, Y)
            e.HasMorePages = True
            ' store the index of the last printed item in the startItem variable
            startItem = itm
            Exit Sub
        End If
    Next
    ' draw the grid of the last page, which is usually smaller than
    ' the other pages
    X = PD.DefaultPageSettings.Margins.Left
    For i = 0 To Me.Columns.Count - 1
        e.Graphics.DrawLine(Pens.Gray, X, _
                PD.DefaultPageSettings.Margins.Top, X, Y)
        cellWidth = ColWidths(i) * PageWidth / totWidth
        X = X + cellWidth
    Next
    e.Graphics.DrawLine(Pens.Gray, X, PD.DefaultPageSettings.Margins.Top, X, Y)
    e.Graphics.DrawLine(Pens.Gray, PD.DefaultPageSettings.Margins.Left, Y, _
                PD.DefaultPageSettings.Margins.Left + PageWidth, Y)
    e.HasMorePages = False
    ' Reset the startItem variable so that it's ready for the next printout
```

```
      ' This is a static variable and won't be reset automatically
      startItem = 0
End Sub
```

The PrintPage event handler shown here will work with any data and any number of columns. The only requirement is that all the information fits in the width of the page, even sideways. You can examine the code and edit it so that it splits the width of each logical page into multiple physical pages. For example, you can print the first five columns on the first page and the remaining columns on another page. The code won't be trivial, and if your applications call for advanced printing features, you should probably look into a third-party component, including Crystal Reports. The example of this section was meant to demonstrate how easily you can implement custom controls with functionality that's unique to your applications by inheriting the functionality of an existing control.

You can experiment with far less complicated inherited custom controls, which may be just as useful for your purposes. A few examples that come to mind are a multiline TextBox control with a Print method and a single-line TextBox control that accepts numeric data only (digits, a period, and one or more commas as thousand separators). The ability to inherit the functionality and visual elements of existing controls will help developers create the very controls they need. Those of you still skeptic about inheritance, consider how much you can achieve by inheriting existing classes and controls and using them to develop new tools.

## Custom Type Editors

The Property Browser allows you to set a control's properties with visual tools, depending on the property's type. Enumerated properties, for example, are set by selecting an item from a drop-down list with the enumeration's members. All properties declared as enumerations are set in this manner—you don't have to do anything in your code. Another interesting property editor is the Collection Editor, which applies to properties that are collections. There's also an Array Editor for array properties.

Being able to make the most of the Property Browser by incorporating custom visual editors is a must for your custom controls, especially if they're going to be used by other developers as well. Visual Studio promotes RAD, and there's no reason why your components shouldn't incorporate RAD features.

In the following sections, we'll look at some of the lesser known type editors for the Property Browser and how to design properties that take advantage of the built-in type editors. We need not show you the editors for selecting an image or setting the Font property of a control. Simply define a property as Image or Font type and the appropriate custom editor will appear in the Property Browser. Later in this section, you'll learn how to create your own custom editors.

## Array Properties

To implement a property as an array of strings, declare an array of strings and then write a Property procedure like the following:

```
Private _items() As String

Public Property Items() As String()
    Get
        Return _items
    End Get
    Set(ByVal Value As String())
        _items = Value
        ShowElements()
        OnItemsChanged(New EventArgs())
    End Set
End Property
```

When the Items property is displayed on the Property Browser, its value will be "String[] Array" and the button with the ellipsis points will appear next to the property's value. Click this button and you'll see the String Collection Editor's window, where you can edit the array's elements. The editor consists of a TextBox, where you can enter strings, as shown in Figure 13.7. Each text line on the control corresponds to an element of the array. You can also expand the property itself by clicking the plus button in front of its name and you will see a line for each item.

**FIGURE 13.7:**

Editing a String array property

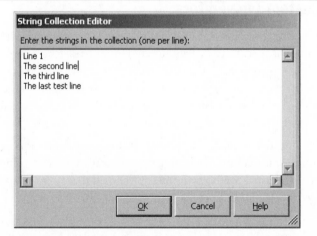

Creating an array of integers (or other numeric types) is just as easy. You declare a private variable in which the items will be stored and then create the usual Property procedures. The

Integer Collection Editor (shown in Figure 13.8) is a bit different. Each item of the collection is listed in the Members box, and you can edit an item's value by selecting it in this list. The following statements create a property that holds an array of integers:

```
Dim Data() As Integer
Public Property DataSet() As Integer()
    Get
        Return Data
    End Get
    Set(ByVal value As Integer())
        Data = value
        Me.Invalidate()
    End Set
End Property
```

**FIGURE 13.8:**

Editing an Integer array property

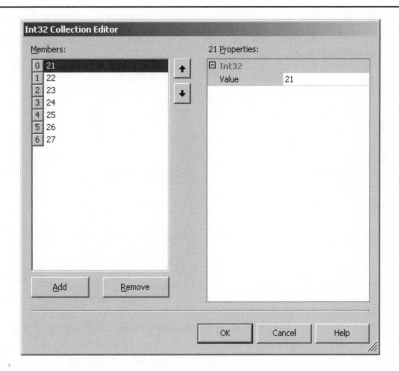

## Type Converters

Sometimes you'll have to create your own editors for the Property Browser, and there are many ways to create custom editors. The most common editor is a type converter. The fields of the

Property Browser accept string values. Everything you type is treated as a string (no validation takes place as you type a value), and then the string is validated and converted to the appropriate type. When entering a Point value, for example, you type two integer values separated by a comma. A Point property is also expandable: if you click the plus button in front of its name, you'll see a list of its members (the X and Y members), and each member is assigned the proper value.

You can implement your own drop-down editors for custom properties that have no single values. If your control exposes a property called Person, which is implemented as a class with various fields, you can provide individual control properties like FirstName, LastName, Age, and so on, or you can provide a property called Person or Employee. Users can then enter a value like "Doe, Joe, 35" or edit the individual fields of the property. Figure 13.9 shows a property with fields.

**FIGURE 13.9:**

Viewing a property with individual fields in the Property Browser

To create a property with fields (subitems in the Property Browser), you must implement a Type Converter. A Type Converter is a class that inherits the ExpandableObjectConverter class and knows how to combine the individual fields into a string (the value's property) as well as how to parse a string and extract the values of the individual fields. The string value combines the values of the fields in a predetermined format. A comma-separated list of values is very common, but you can use other delimiters, parentheses, and so on. You can make the converter as complicated as needed, but the general format of the string value should be intuitive. A default value is also useful, because it can act as a hint about the property value's format. The type converter is basically a pair of string parsing functions.

To create a property with fields, you must first decide the format of the string that combines the values of the fields. This format must ensure unambiguous parsing of the property's fields. Then you must create a class that derives from the ExpandableObjectConverter class. This class should override the following methods of the parent class:

**CanConvertFrom**   Accepts as argument a type and returns a Boolean value, indicating whether the string can be converted from the specified type to a string.

**CanConvertTo**   Accepts as argument a type and returns a Boolean value, indicating whether the string can be converted to the specified type.

**ConvertFrom**   Parses the string entered by the user and returns an instance of the class of the property. For the Person property example, it should convert a string like "Doe, Joe, 35" to an instance of the Person class with the following field values: `Person.Last = "Doe"`, `Person.First = "Joe"`, `Person.Age = 35`.

**ConvertTo**   Combines the fields of the property and returns a string.

The class in Listing 13.17 implements a Type Converter for a property with three fields: LastName, FirstName, and Age. The string value of the property has the form `LastName, FirstName, Age`.

**Listing 13.17**      **A Custom Type Converter for the Person Class**

```
Public Class PersonConverter
    Inherits ExpandableObjectConverter

    Public Overloads Overrides Function _
            CanConvertFrom(ByVal context As ITypeDescriptorContext, _
                        ByVal srcType As Type) As Boolean
        If srcType.Equals(GetType(String)) Then
            Return False
        Else
            Return MyBase.CanConvertFrom(context, srcType)
        End If
    End Function

    Public Overloads Overrides Function _
            CanConvertTo(ByVal context As ITypeDescriptorContext, _
                        ByVal destType As Type) As Boolean
```

```
            If destType.Equals(GetType(String)) Then
                Return True
            Else
                Return MyBase.CanConvertTo(context, destType)
            End If
    End Function

    Public Overloads Overrides Function _
            ConvertFrom(ByVal context As ITypeDescriptorContext, _
                        ByVal info As CultureInfo, _
                        ByVal value As Object) As Object
        Try
            Dim parts() As String
            parts = CType(value, String).Split(New Char() {","})
            Dim p As New Person(parts(0), parts(1), parts(2))
            Return p
        Catch
            MsgBox("Can't convert to Person")
            Return Nothing
        End Try
    End Function

    Public Overloads Overrides Function _
            ConvertTo(ByVal context As ITypeDescriptorContext, _
                        ByVal culture As CultureInfo, _
                        ByVal value As Object, _
                        ByVal destType As Type) As Object
        If (destType.Equals(GetType(String))) Then
            Dim p As Person = CType(value, Person)
            Return p.LastName & ", " & p.FirstName & _
                        ", " & p.Age.ToString()
        Else
            Return MyBase.ConvertTo(context, culture, value, destType)
        End If
    End Function

    Public Overloads Overrides Function _
            GetPropertiesSupported(ByVal context As _
                        ITypeDescriptorContext) As Boolean
        Return True
    End Function

    Public Overloads Overrides Function _
            GetProperties(ByVal context As ITypeDescriptorContext, _
                        ByVal value As Object, _
                        ByVal Attribute() As Attribute) _
                        As PropertyDescriptorCollection
        Return TypeDescriptor.GetProperties(value)
    End Function

End Class
```

The TypeConverter class is straightforward and you need only change the two functions:

**ConvertFrom()**   This is the function that parses the property value (a string) and extracts the individual fields.

**ConvertTo()**   This is the function that combines the property's individual fields to create a string value that will be displayed on the Property Browser, next to the property's name.

The rest of the code is always the same and you can use it as is. Once the Type Converter is in place, you can create the Person class and specify the PersonConverter class's type as the value of its TypeConverter attribute (see Listing 13.18).

---

**Listing 13.18        A Person Class with a Custom Type Converter**

```
<TypeConverter(GetType(PersonConverter)), Serializable()> _
Public Class Person
    Private _firstName As String = "unknown"
    Private _lastName As String = "unknown"
    Private _age As Integer = 0

Public Sub New(ByVal first As String, _
                ByVal last As String, ByVal age As Integer)
    _firstName = first.Trim
    _lastName = last.Trim
    _age = age
End Sub

Public Sub New()
    _firstName = ""
    _lastName = ""
    Age = 0
End Sub

Public Property Age() As Integer
    Get
        Return _age
    End Get
    Set(ByVal Value As Integer)
        Me._age = Value
    End Set
End Property

Public Property FirstName() As String
    Get
        Return _firstName
    End Get
    Set(ByVal Value As String)
        Me._firstName = Value.Trim
    End Set
End Property
```

```
Public Property LastName() As String
    Get
        Return _lastName
    End Get
    Set(ByVal Value As String)
        Me._lastName = Value.Trim
    End Set
End Property

End Class
```

With the two classes in place, you can now create a property of the Person type. Let's call this property Member and implement it with the statements in Listing 13.19.

**Listing 13.19    The Implementation of the Member Property**

```
Public Property Member() As Person
    Get
        Return p
    End Get
    Set(ByVal Value As Person)
        p = Value
    End Set
End Property
```

The property's implementation is quite trivial; all the information for handling it in the Property Browser exists in the definition of the class and its type converter. If you locate the Member property in the Property Browser, you'll see that it's value can be expanded as shown in Figure 13.9. You can edit the property either by editing its fields or as a string.

Now we'll combine the built-in Collection Editor with a multivalued property. We'll add a new property to our control, the Members property, which is an array of Person objects. To create the Members property, you must first declare a private array of Person objects. The Members property is an array, so a Collection Editor window will be automatically added to the property's value. Because the Person class has its own Type Converter, the Collection Editor knows about each member's fields and will display them automatically on the editor's window. Listing 13.20 shows the definition of the Members property.

**Listing 13.20    The Implementation of the Members Property**

```
Private _Members(0) As Person

Public Property Members() As Person()
    Get
```

```
            Return _Members
        End Get
        Set(ByVal Value As Person())
            ReDim _Members(Value.Length)
            _Members = Value
        End Set
    End Property
```

In the control's constructor (the New subroutine created by the Windows Form Designer for you), enter the following statement:

**_Members(0) = New Person()**

If you look up the Members property in the Property Browser, you will see the button with the ellipsis points next to the property name. The value of the property is the string "Person[] Array", indicating that the property is an array of Person objects. If you open the property's Collection Editor by clicking the button with the ellipsis points, you will see the Person Collection Editor, which is shown in Figure 13.10. Notice that Visual Studio knows about the structure of the Person objects and prompts you to enter each field separately. It will also perform some basic validation on the data you enter. For example, it won't let you enter a word or a date in the Age field's box.

**FIGURE 13.10:**

Using the Person Collection Editor to populate the Members property

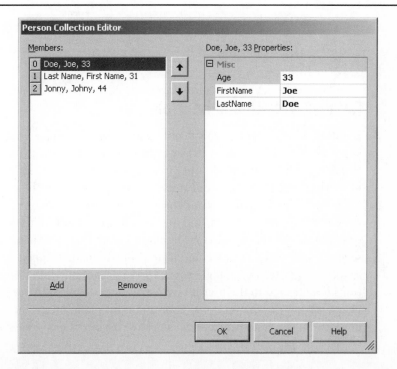

The Members property is also expandable, because its Type Converter inherits from the ExpandableObjectConverter. To view its items, click the plus button in front of the property name and you will see a list like the one shown in Figure 13.11. Each item's property can be specified as a string, or you can expand each element and edit its fields.

**FIGURE 13.11:**

Expanding an item of the Members property

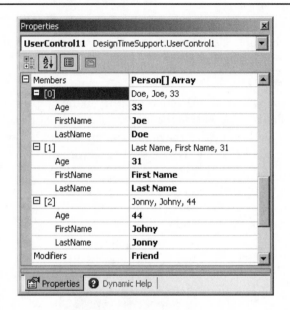

## Building Data-Bound Controls

Building data-bound controls is not complicated. To make your control data bound, just apply the Bindable attribute to one or more of its properties. To make the FancyLabel control data bound, you can add the Bindable attribute to its Caption property and change the property's type (it should be DataColumn). If you do so, the control will automatically detect any DataSets on the same form and display the appropriate drop-down editor in the Property Browser. If you expand the drop-down list next to the setting of the Caption property, you will be able to select a column of a DataTable and bind it to the property. In this section, we'll build a more complicated control, namely a control that can be bound to a set of rows, instead of a single row. A good deal of effort in designing data-driven applications is dedicated to the user interface: how do we allow the user to specify the data they need and how do we present it? A program for maintaining the Customers table shouldn't download all the customers to the client when the user wants to view a phone number. Likewise, we can't expect the user to select the desired customer by specifying an ID. We should provide enough criteria for the user to specify the rows they're interested in yet avoid downloading enormous amounts of information to the client. Not that we really care about the network's bandwidth, but what's a user supposed to do with a few hundred (let alone a few thousand) customers?

## The DBControl

One approach that works in many situations is to provide a control where users can type the first few characters of a customer name (or a product name) and then populate a list with the matching rows. The user can specify additional characters until they narrow down to the desired name or use the arrow keys to select the desired name from the list. Figure 13.12 shows a control that retrieves the product names matching a few characters entered in a TextBox and displays them on the ListBox control.

**FIGURE 13.12:**

Locating products by name

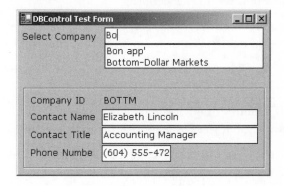

This is a useful control to have in designing data-driven applications. To make it really useful and reusable, we must design it so that it's not tied to a single database or table. We'll allow the developer to bind the control to any table and then specify the column to be displayed on the ListBox control as well as the column with the table's primary key. The user will select a row based on a meaningful key (like a product's or customer's name), and the control will retrieve the selected row with its primary key.

Once the DataSet is populated, the control knows how to search the table with the data. As the user types characters, the control's code retrieves the matching rows from the specified table and displays them on a ListBox control. The column displayed on the ListBox control is also exposed as a property of the control. To avoid a very long list of rows, the program limits the selected rows to 10 (you can change this value in the code, or even expose the maximum number of rows as a property). When the user has entered enough characters to narrow down the selection, they can press the Down arrow key to select an item in the ListBox control.

If they want to specify additional characters, they can press Escape to return to the editing area of the control.

The control is quite functional, but only if the entire table is downloaded to a DataSet at the client. Moreover, the search column must be indexed. In most applications, we can't afford to download very large tables to the client, but you can edit the control's code. Instead of searching the local DataSet every time a new character is entered, you can program the TextBox control's Enter key (or a function key) to populate the DataSet with the appropriate data from its data source. Another approach is to download only a few columns of the table with an SQL statement and pass to the application the ID of the selected row. Then the application will be responsible to retrieve the entire row.

We'll use this simple control to demonstrate how to develop advanced data-bound controls. In the context of this book, we'll ignore binding controls to data sources other than Data-Tables. Therefore, we can create the following properties:

**DataSource**   A DataSet object.

**DataMember**   A DataTable object. The DataMember property must be set to one of the tables of the DataSet represented by the DataSource property.

**DisplayColumn**   The column to be displayed on the ListBox control. This property must be set to one of the rows in the selected table.

**IDColumn**   Another column of the selected table. This property is usually the table's primary key, but you can set it to any column that uniquely identifies each row.

First, add these two statements at the beginning of the code to simplify the references to the members of these two classes:

```
Imports System.ComponentModel
Imports System.Globalization
```

Now we can implement the properties of our data-bound control. The DataSource and DataMember properties are quite simple. They're simply declared as DataSet and DataTable, respectively, and their values are stored in two local variables, the _DataSource and _DataMember variables, as shown in Listing 13.21.

---

**Listing 13.21**      **Implementing the DataSource and DataMember Properties**

```
Private _DataSource As DataSet
<Bindable(True)> Public Property DataSource() As DataSet
    Get
        Return _DataSource
    End Get
```

```
        Set(ByVal Value As DataSet)
            _DataSource = Value
        End Set
    End Property

    Private _DataMember As DataTable
    <Bindable(True)> Public Property Datamember() As DataTable
        Get
            Return _DataMember
        End Get
        Set(ByVal Value As DataTable)
            _DataMember = Value
        End Set
    End Property
```

The other two custom properties are of the DataColumn type and they're implemented with the statements shown in Listing 13.22. Their values are stored in two local variables as usual.

**Listing 13.22      The Implementation of the DisplayColumn and IDColumn Properties**

```
Private _DisplayColumn As New DataColumn()
<TypeConverter(GetType(ColConverter)), Bindable(True)> _
Public Property DisplayColumn() As DataColumn
    Get
        Return _DisplayColumn
    End Get
    Set(ByVal Value As DataColumn)
        _DisplayColumn = Value
    End Set
End Property

Private _IDColumn As DataColumn
<TypeConverter(GetType(ColConverter)), Bindable(True)> _
Public Property IDColumn() As DataColumn
    Get
        Return _IDColumn
    End Get
    Set(ByVal Value As DataColumn)
        _IDColumn = Value
    End Set
End Property
```

As you can see, all properties that represent DataColumns have their Bindable and Type-Converter attributes set. The Bindable attribute is set to True and the TypeConverter attribute is set to the type of a custom type converter, the ColConverter. As you can guess, you will have to implement this type converter's class yourself. The custom converter should inherit the ExpandableObjectConverter class, and its implementation is shown in Listing 13.23. The class that implements it always has the same structure as the PersonConverter class. It's actually simpler, because the ConvertFrom method returns the name of the table associated with the control's DataMember property.

**Listing 13.23**   **The ColConverter Custom Type Converter**

```
Public Class ColConverter
    Inherits ExpandableObjectConverter

    Public Overloads Overrides Function _
        CanConvertFrom(ByVal context As ITypeDescriptorContext, _
                        ByVal srcType As Type) As Boolean
        If srcType.Equals(GetType(String)) Then
            Return True
        Else
            Return MyBase.CanConvertFrom(context, srcType)
        End If
    End Function

    Public Overloads Overrides Function CanConvertTo( _
                ByVal context As ITypeDescriptorContext, _
                ByVal destType As Type) As Boolean
        If destType.Equals(GetType(String)) Then
            Return True
        Else
            Return MyBase.CanConvertTo(context, destType)
        End If
    End Function

    Public Overloads Overrides Function ConvertFrom( _
                ByVal context As ITypeDescriptorContext, _
                ByVal info As CultureInfo, _
                ByVal value As Object) As Object
        Return CType(value, DataColumn).ColumnName
    End Function

    Public Overloads Overrides Function ConvertTo( _
                ByVal context As ITypeDescriptorContext, _
                ByVal culture As CultureInfo,
                ByVal value As Object, _
                ByVal destType As Type) As Object
        If (destType.Equals(GetType(String))) Then
            Return CType(value, DataColumn).Caption
        Else
            Return MyBase.ConvertTo(context, culture, value, destType)
        End If
    End Function

    Public Overloads Overrides Function GetPropertiesSupported( _
                ByVal context As ITypeDescriptorContext) As Boolean
```

```
        Return True
    End Function

    Public Overloads Overrides Function GetProperties( _
                ByVal context As ITypeDescriptorContext, _
                ByVal value As Object, ByVal Attribute() _
                As Attribute) As PropertyDescriptorCollection
        Return TypeDescriptor.GetProperties(value)
    End Function
End Class
```

Now we can examine the code that actually makes the control work. Every time the user types a character in the TextBox control, we select a subset of a table's rows with the Select method. The string entered on the TextBox is passed to the Select method as argument. The rows selected by the Select method are stored in the rows local array. Then the code iterates through the elements of this array and populates the ListBox control.

To simplify the code that populates the ListBox control, we've created the displayItem class, which exposes two fields: the Text and ID fields. In the Text field, we store the value of the column specified with the DisplayColumn property (the text to be displayed on the ListBox control), and the ID field stores the value of the column specified with the IDColumn property (the row's ID):

```
Private rows() As DataRow
Class displayItem
    Public Text As String
    Public ID As String
    Public Overrides Function ToString() As String
        Return Text
    End Function
End Class
```

The TextBox control's TextChanged event is fired every time the user edits the control, and this is a good place to select the matching columns and display them on the ListBox control. The event's handler is shown in Listing 13.24.

**Listing 13.24     Selecting the Matching Rows and Displaying Them**

```
Private maxDisplayRows As Integer = 8
Private ListBoxHeight As Integer

Private Sub TextBox1_TextChanged(ByVal sender As System.Object, _
                        ByVal e As System.EventArgs) _
                        Handles TextBox1.TextChanged
    If Me.Height < TextBox1.Height + ListBoxHeight Then
        Me.Height = ListBox1.Top + ListBoxHeight
    End If
```

```
        Dim companyName As String = TextBox1.Text
        companyName = companyName.Replace("'", "''")
        rows = _DataSource.Tables(_DataMember.TableName).Select( _
                        "CompanyName LIKE '" & companyName & "%'")
        Dim i As Integer, totRows As Integer = rows.Length
        If rows.Length > maxDisplayRows Then totRows = maxDisplayRows
        ListBox1.Items.Clear()
        For i = 1 To totRows
            Dim itm As New displayItem()
            itm.Text = rows(i - 1).Item("CompanyName")
            itm.ID = rows(i - 1).Item("CustomerID")
            If i = totRows And rows.Length > totRows Then
                itm.Text = itm.Text & " ..."
            End If
            ListBox1.Items.Add(itm)
        Next
        ListBox1.DisplayMember = "DisplayItem.Text"
        ListBoxHeight = ListBox1.ItemHeight * totRows
        Me.Height = ListBox1.Top + ListBoxHeight + 4
    End Sub
```

When the user hits the Enter key, or the Down arrow key, in the TextBox control, the code switches the focus to the ListBox control and selects the top item. The user can then move down the list with the arrow keys:

```
    Private Sub TextBox1_KeyUp(ByVal sender As Object, _
                    ByVal e As System.Windows.Forms.KeyEventArgs) _
                    Handles TextBox1.KeyUp
        Select Case e.KeyCode
            Case Keys.Down, Keys.Enter
                If ListBox1.Items.Count > 0 Then
                    ListBox1.Focus()
                    ListBox1.SelectedIndex = 0
                End If
        End Select
    End Sub
```

When the user presses Enter or Escape while the ListBox control has the focus, we must detect the keystroke and respond accordingly. If the Enter key is pressed, the control will raise the RowSelected event and pass the selected row as argument. If the Escape key is pressed, the control will move the focus to the TextBox control. These actions take place in the ListBox control's KeyUp event handler, which is shown in Listing 13.25.

---

**Listing 13.25    Handling the Enter and Escape Keystrokes**

```
    Public Event RowSelected(ByVal row As DataRow)

    Private Sub ListBox1_KeyUp(ByVal sender As Object, _
```

```
                        ByVal e As System.Windows.Forms.KeyEventArgs) _
                        Handles ListBox1.KeyUp
        Select Case e.KeyCode
            Case Keys.Enter
                RaiseEvent RowSelected(rows(ListBox1.SelectedIndex))
                If ListBox1.Text.EndsWith("...") Then
                    Me.TextBox1.Text = _
                        ListBox1.Text.Substring(0, ListBox1.Text.Length - 4)
                Else
                    Me.TextBox1.Text = ListBox1.Text
                End If
                Me.Height = TextBox1.Top + TextBox1.Height
            Case Keys.Escape
                TextBox1.Focus()
        End Select
    End Sub
```

Compile the new control, switch to the test project and add a reference to the DBControl custom control. Then place an instance of the control on the test project's form. To configure the control, you must create a DataSet by dropping a table from the Server Explorer onto the form. Select the control on the form and set its properties in the Property Browser. Set the DataSource property to the DataSet's name, the DisplayMember property to the name of one of the tables in the DataSet, the DisplayMember to the name of one of the columns of the DataMember property, and the IDColumn property to the name of the key column of the DataMember property. Figure 13.13 shows the editor for the DisplayColumn property (the DataSet on the test form contains the Products table of the Northwind sample database).

**FIGURE 13.13:**

Setting the data-bound control's DisplayColumn property

As you can see, the DataSource and DataMember properties are not really necessary for this control. The other two data-bound properties can pick their values from any table in any DataSet on the form. We've included these two members in the sample application because some control may not require the specification of a DataColumn. Using the DataSource property, you can access any of the DataSets on the form, and using the DataMember, you can access all the columns in a specific table.

To test the custom data-bound control, switch to the test form and program the control's RowSelected event handler. The following sample shows how to retrieve the Person object returned by the UserControl1 control and display its fields on the Output window:

```
Private Sub UserControl11_RowSelected( _
                    ByVal row As System.Data.DataRow) _
                    Handles UserControl11.RowSelected
    lblID.Text = row.Item("CustomerID")
    txtContact.Text = row.Item("ContactName")
    txtTitle.Text = row.Item("ContactTitle")
    txtPhone.Text = row.Item("Phone")
End Sub
```

You should also include the statements to populate the DataSet from within your code (usually from within the form's Load event handler).

## Summary

In this chapter, you learned how to build custom Windows controls and you saw examples of all three types of custom controls you may run into: user-drawn controls, composite controls, and inherited controls. In our view, the most practical types of custom controls for application developers are the ones that inherit from existing controls. It's fairly easy to build custom controls that inherit the functionality of existing controls and add custom members suitable for a specific task.

One of the cool features of the language is the design time support you can add to your custom components through the members of the System.ComponentModel.Design namespace. We've shown you how to create custom editors for special properties and make your custom control look and feel very much like a Windows control.

# CHAPTER 14

# Building Windows Services

- Creating and installing Windows services

- Controlling Windows services programmatically

- Debugging a Windows service project

- Interacting with Windows services

One of the features of Windows is the ability to run a number of programs in the background. These programs are called services and they don't interfere with your applications. The operating system, however, relies on these services for numerous tasks. Internet Information Server (IIS) is such a service, and so is any antivirus software you may have installed on your computer. A service starts executing when you start the computer (some services must be started manually) and doesn't interfere with your work. Windows services are not new to the Framework (they were known as Windows NT services in earlier versions of Windows), but the .NET Framework makes it possible for the first time to write Windows services with Visual Basic. It's actually quite simple to write a basic Windows service. In this chapter, we'll discuss the process of building services in detail.

## Understanding Windows Services

A Windows service is a program that doesn't interact with the user. As a result, it should be a very robust application that handles errors and continues without user interaction. Most users are not even aware of the services running on their computer, so any message you display on their desktop will confuse them. Some services, like an antivirus service, may contact the user by displaying a window on the desktop and asking for information (whether to delete an infected file, prohibit an operation, and so on). In general, Windows services don't interact with the user, but you will see how you can bring up a window from within a service and get information from the user.

To view the services running on your computer, open the Control Panel (Start ➢ Settings ➢ Control Panel), open the Administrative Tools folder, and double-click the icon of the Services utility. On the Services window, you will see many services like the ones shown in Figure 14.1.

**FIGURE 14.1:**

The Services window

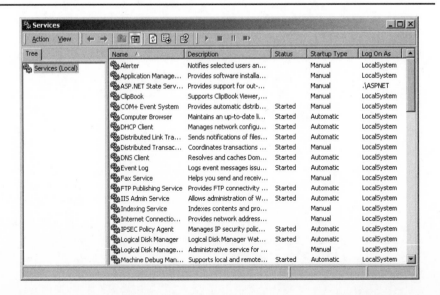

The Plug and Play service, for example, is always on and it's activated every time you add or remove a plug-and-play device. The Print Spooler service loads files into memory for later printing. When an application prints, it doesn't wait for a printer to become available and then print the entire document. Instead, it sends the printout to the spooler, which is then responsible for sending the data to the printer. There are many more services and you can view them all in the Services window (just don't change the settings of any service and don't start any services that aren't running). You're going to add a custom Windows service to this window.

Most Windows services don't interact directly with the user, but they log all types of messages. If a service can't perform its task, it must log a message to that effect. Sometimes services won't even start automatically when the computer powers on. The messages (information, warnings, and error messages) generated by the various services can be viewed in the Event Viewer, shown in Figure 14.2. The Event Viewer is one of the most valuable tools for administrators. In this chapter, we'll use it as a quick method to test our sample services. We'll add entries to the Event Viewer from within our service's code and we'll follow the progress of the service by monitoring the Event Viewer.

**FIGURE 14.2:**

The Event Viewer window

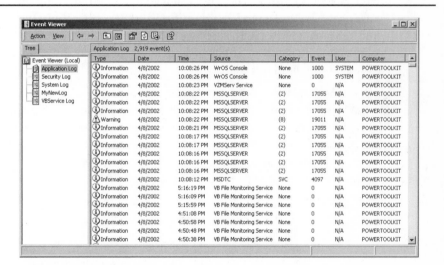

## Creating a Windows Service

The process of creating a Windows service isn't complicated. However, writing a practical service is quite a task because you have to write code to enable the service to interact with components like the file system, device drivers, remote computers, and so on. You can also contact any component that resides on the same computer and call its methods. We'll look at a simple

Windows service that monitors a selected folder and process any files in this folder. We'll assume that other applications (or users) place files in this folder and the service must act on these files. These files could represent orders, stock prices, even instructions for the service. Once you have the mechanism to detect the presence of a new file in a specific folder, you can process it in any way you see fit. The code that processes the file(s), which is the core of the Windows service, is identical to the code you'd use in a Windows application. It simply runs quietly in the background and users don't notice it, except that the hard disk may start reading or writing while the computer appears to be idle. You can write code to connect to a database and store information there about the file, the time it was created, it size, and so on. Later in this chapter, you'll see how you can create mail messages and send them to any recipient from within your service.

A service can be started and stopped, and you must program these two events. You enter the service's initialization code in its OnStart method and its termination and clean-up code in the OnStop method. Services can also be paused, an action that is signaled with the OnPause method. Paused services can be continued, and this action is signaled by the OnContinue method. Services are usually stopped, paused, and continued from within the Services window, but you can also control a service from within another application, and you'll see toward the end of this chapter how to control a service programmatically. Basically, you insert the appropriate code to handle a number of commands and you can invoke any of these commands from within a Windows application's code.

To create a new Windows service start a new project and select the Windows Service type in the New Project dialog box. The project's default name is WindowsService1, and for the first example, we're going to use the name VBService. Once the project is created, a single item will appear in the Solution Explorer (besides the usual references and the assembly file, of course). This item is a class and it's called Service1. Leave the default name so that you can spot it easily and remove it when you're done. Open the Service1 class and you'll see that Windows has created the following code:

```
#Region " Component Designer generated code "
    Public Sub New()
        MyBase.New()
        ' This call is required by the Component Designer.
        InitializeComponent()

        ' Add any initialization after the InitializeComponent() call

    End Sub

    'UserService overrides dispose to clean up the component list.
    Protected Overloads Overrides Sub _
                    Dispose(ByVal disposing As Boolean)
        If disposing Then
```

```
        If Not (components Is Nothing) Then
            components.Dispose()
        End If
    End If
    MyBase.Dispose(disposing)
End Sub

' The main entry point for the process
<MTAThread()> _
Shared Sub Main()
    Dim ServicesToRun() As System.ServiceProcess.ServiceBase

    ' More than one NT Service may run within the same process. To
    ' add another service to this process, change the following line
    ' to create a second service object. For example,
    '
    '    ServicesToRun = _
    '        New System.ServiceProcess.ServiceBase () _
    '            {New Service1, New MySecondUserService}
    '
    ServicesToRun = _
                New System.ServiceProcess.ServiceBase() _
                {New Service1()}
    System.ServiceProcess.ServiceBase.Run(ServicesToRun)
End Sub

'Required by the Component Designer
Private components As System.ComponentModel.IContainer

' NOTE:
' The following procedure is required by the Component Designer
' It can be modified using the Component Designer.
' Do not modify it using the code editor.
<System.Diagnostics.DebuggerStepThrough()> Private Sub _
                    InitializeComponent()
    '
    'Service1
    '
    Me.ServiceName = "Service1"

End Sub

#End Region
```

Notice that this class contains a Main() subroutine. Because the project has no visible interface, it must be started with a call to its Main subroutine. The name of the service (Service1) appears several times in the code. If you change the service's name in the Explorer window, you must also edit the class's code and change all instances of Service1 to the new service name.

First, select the Windows service and open the Property Browser. A Windows service exposes the following properties:

**AutoLog**   By default, all Windows services write information to the application event log. Set this property to automatically log actions like the starting and stopping of the service as well as critical errors.

**CanHandlePowerEvent**   This property is a Boolean value that determines whether the service can handle notifications of computer power status changes. If you set this property to True, you must also code the OnPowerEvent method.

**CanPauseAndContinue**   This property is a Boolean value that determines whether the service can be paused and resumed.

**CanShutDown**   This is another Boolean value that determines whether the service should be notified when the system is shut down. If you set this property to True, you must also code the OnShutdown method.

**CanStop**   This property is a Boolean value that determines whether the process can be stopped. Set this property to True for critical services that you don't want users to stop at any point.

Let's start by coding the OnStart method, which will be executed every time the service is started. Instead of using the FileSystemWatcher component, we'll create a Timer object that will fire events every so often. If it's critical that the changes are detected the moment they occur, you should use the FileSystemWatcher component. Our approach is simpler in terms of the required code, and it can be used in other similar scenarios, where there's no component to provide your code with the necessary notifications (like the arrival of a message from a specific account, for example).

Start by declaring a `Timer` variable at the beginning of the code:

```
Imports System.Timers
Dim WithEvents TMR As Timer
```

Then enter the statements in Listing 14.1 in the OnStart method. These statements initialize the `TMR` variable, connect the Timer object's Elapsed event (which takes place every 10 seconds) to the OnTick subroutine, and write the first entry to the Event Viewer.

**Listing 14.1**     **Starting the Service**

```
Protected Overrides Sub OnStart(ByVal args() As String)
    Me.AutoLog = False
    TMR = New Timer(10000)
    TMR.Enabled = True
```

```
    AddHandler TMR.Elapsed, AddressOf OnTick

    'set the source property
    Log.Source = mSource
    'log an initial entry
    Log.WriteEntry("Service Started", EventLogEntryType.Information)
End Sub
```

The *Log* variable is declared outside the procedure with the following statements:

```
Imports System.Diagnostics

Dim mSource As String = "VB File Monitoring Service"
Dim Log As New EventLog()
```

In the OnStop method, we'll insert the code to stop the timer and log the appropriate entry (Listing 14.2).

**Listing 14.2      Stopping the Service**

```
Protected Overrides Sub OnStop()
    TMR.Enabled = False
    Log.WriteEntry("Service Stopped", EventLogEntryType.Information)
End Sub
```

For now, let's add a trivial statement in the OnTick event handler. This is where all the action will take place, but we'll simply log a message to monitor the service's operation:

```
Private Sub OnTick(ByVal sender As Object, ByVal e As ElapsedEventArgs)
    Log.WriteEntry("Processed Files", EventLogEntryType.Information)
End Sub
```

## Installing the Service

The next step is to install the service on the target machine. Obviously, you can't test a Windows service by pressing F5 as you would do with a regular Windows application. Windows services run in the context of the Service Manager, so we must create the executable file and then install it with the `InstallUtil.exe` application.

The IDE hides the details of the installation of a Windows service with the help of the ServiceProcessInstaller and ServiceInstaller components. Right-click on the service's design surface, and from the context menu, select Add Installer. A new item will be added to the solution, the ProjectInstaller item. This item contains two components, the `ServiceProcessInstaller1` and the `ServiceInstaller1` components. The ServiceInstaller component, which will actually install the service, allows you to specify the name of the service (Service1) and how the service will be started. The StartType property can be set to one of the following values:

**Automatic**   The service starts when the computer powers on.

**Manual**   The service must be started manually in the Event Viewer's window. You can also start it programmatically from within another application.

**Disabled**   The service will be installed but can't be started until it's enabled.

Another property of the ServiceInstaller1 component is the ServiceName property. This is the name of the service as it will appear in the Services utility, and you should set it to a meaningful name, like VBService1. If you don't set this property, the service's name will be Service1 regardless of the project's name or the executable's filename.

Users can change the service's StartType property from within its Properties dialog box in the Services window.

The ServiceProcessInstaller component specifies an account (and optionally a username and password) under which the service will run. For a service to run at all times regardless of the current user, you must set the service's Account property to LocalSystem. If you specify a user account, then the service won't start when another user logs in and an error message will be logged. If you set the Account property to User, you must also specify the name and password of the user that can start the service.

Now we're ready to build and install the new service. Open the Build menu and select Build VBService. If the code compiles successfully, the VBService.exe file will be created in the project's bin directory. To install the newly created EXE file, you must process it with the InstallUtil.exe program, which is located in the Framework folder. The folder C:\WINNT\ Microsoft.NET\Framework\vXXX will be in the path. The exact name of the folder (vXXX) may vary, depending on the build and revision of the .NET Framework installed on your computer. To make sure this long folder name is part of the path, edit the environment variable Path in the Advanced tab of the System Properties window (Control Panel ➤ System). Once you've edited the Path environment variable, you can open a Command window, switch to the bin folder of the VBService1 project, and issue the following command:

```
InstallUtil VBService.exe
```

At this point, you may be prompted to set a username and a password for the service, depending on the setting of the Account property of the project's ServiceProcessInstaller component. Enter the administrator's username and password in the dialog box shown in Figure 14.3.

If you open the Services window (Control Panel ➤ Services), you will see the name of the new service, as shown in Figure 14.4. The service hasn't started yet. To start it, right-click its name and select Start. Don't forget to stop the service soon, because if left running, it will generate too many messages in the Event Viewer.

Services usually run
under the local system
account.

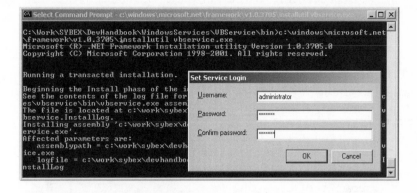

Starting the new service
in the Services event
dialog box

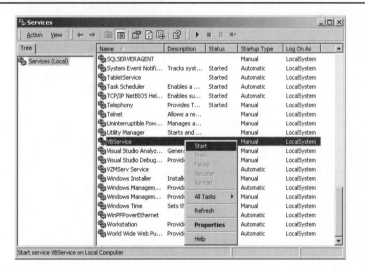

You can also view the service's properties by double-clicking its name in the Services window. The service's Properties dialog box contains four tabs:

**General**   Here you can change the name and description of the service. You can also set its Startup type, as well as start, stop, pause, and resume the service. The General tab is shown in Figure 14.5.

**Log On**   Here you can specify an account under which the service will run. You can also check the option Allow Service to Interact with Desktop if the service can bring up a dialog box and interact with the current user. You'll see later how this can be done. The Log On tab is shown in Figure 14.6.

**Recovery**   On the Recovery tab, you can specify how the service will recover from errors.

**Dependencies** On this tab, you can view other services that depend on Service1 as well as the names of the services VBService depends on. Our simple service doesn't depend on any other services and no other services depend on it.

The General tab of the service's Properties dialog box

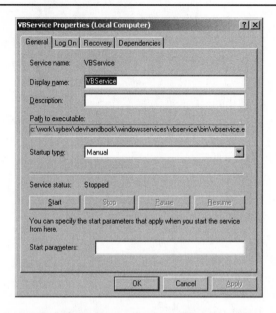

The Log On tab of the service's Properties dialog box

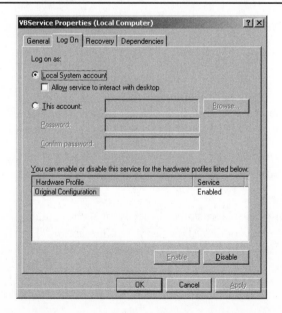

To test the new service, start it by selecting Start from its context menu and then open the Event Viewer window (Control Panel ➢ Administrative Tools ➢ Event Viewer). The first few entries generated by the new service are identified by the name of their source (VB File Monitoring Service) and will appear at the top of this window, and a new entry should be logged every 10 seconds, as shown in Figure 14.7. The window isn't refreshed automatically, so you must click the Refresh button on the window's toolbar to view the latest entries. As you can see, the service works: the Elapsed event takes place every 10 seconds and the OnTick() subroutine is executed. Now you can insert code that does something useful in this subroutine. You can iterate through the files in a specific folder and process them, move them to another folder, and so on. The code you'll add to the OnTick() subroutine is identical to the code you'd use in a Windows application. You may find it easier to start with a Windows application that does the required processing and then copy the code and paste it into the service's code window. Avoid using visual elements and use the Output window to test your code. Once it works, you can reuse it in a Windows service. Even better, build a class that exposes the required functionality and include it in the Windows service project.

**FIGURE 14.7:**

The entries made to the Application Event Viewer by the sample service

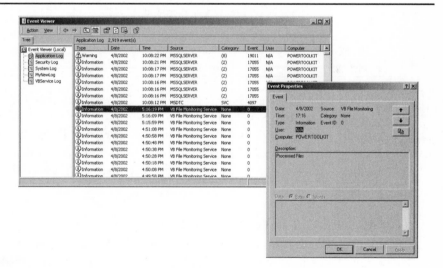

## Adding Custom Commands to the Service

Another event of the Windows service is the OnCustomCommand event. The service can recognize custom commands, and you can send commands to it from within another application's code. You'll see how you can invoke a service's custom commands shortly, but first let's see how the custom commands are implemented in the service's code (see Listing 14.3).

The service's command are just numbers, and you can't call them with arguments. A command number is a value from 129 to 255 (the first 128 values are reserved for use by the system). The Service Control Manager doesn't validate the command's number; it passes it directly to the service, and if the service does not recognize it, nothing happens. The various commands are handled in the OnCustomCommand event's handler with a long Select Case statement. Add the following statements to the service's OnCustomCommand event handler to handle the commands 129 and 130. The command 129 displays a message box and logs an entry to the viewer. The command 130 logs a different entry, but we'll return to this module and add the code to display a dialog box through which the user can interact with the service.

**Listing 14.3    Programming the Service's OnCustomCommand Event Handler**

```
Protected Overrides Sub OnCustomCommand(ByVal command As Integer)
    Select Case command
        Case 129 : Log.WriteEntry("Received Command 1")
            MsgBox("Executing command 129")
        Case 130 : Log.WriteEntry("Received Command 2")
            MsgBox("Executing command 130")
    End Select
End Sub
```

The two custom commands are quite trivial, but we'll return to this topic and you'll see how to implement a more complicated custom command. You'll actually see how to display a dialog box to the user from within a Windows service (a practice that doesn't always make sense, but some services may need to interact with the user). First, let's see how you can activate the custom commands of a Windows service. After that, we'll discuss the process of debugging Windows services.

## Controlling a Windows Service

As we mentioned already, it's possible to control a Windows service from within another application. You can retrieve a handle to a specific service and use it to start, stop, and pause the service and execute commands against it. To access the Windows services on your machine, you must use the System.ServiceProcess class. First, add a reference to the System.Service-Process component in your project, and then enter the appropriate Imports statement. In this section, you'll write a small application that retrieves the names of all services installed on your computer, starts and stops the service we developed earlier (VBService), and executes a command against VBService. The test project's interface is a form with three buttons; their captions are Show All Services, Start, and Execute Service Command. You will find the ServiceController project in the book's pages at www.sybex.com. Start a new project, this time a Windows application, and name it ServiceController. Place three buttons on the project's form and set their captions to Start (this button starts and stops the VBService service you developed earlier in this chapter), Execute Service Command (this buttons executes the command 130 of the VBService), and Show All Services (this button displays the names of all services in the Output window).

To access the services, you must create a ServiceController object and call its GetServices method, which returns an array of ServiceController objects. Each element of the array represents a different service. The code in Listing 14.4 retrieves the services installed on the local machine and displays their names on the Output window.

**Listing 14.4    Retrieving Information about the Installed Services**

```
Private Sub ShowServices_Click(ByVal sender As System.Object, _
                        ByVal e As System.EventArgs) _
                        Handles ShowServices.Click
    Dim sc As New System.ServiceProcess.ServiceController()

    Dim allServices() As ServiceController
    allServices = sc.GetServices()
    Dim i As Integer
    For i = 0 To allServices.GetUpperBound(0)
        Console.WriteLine(allServices(i).MachineName & _
                        "    " & allServices(i).ServiceName)
    Next
End Sub
```

The ServiceController object represents a Windows service and it can report information about the service, as well as control it, through the following members:

**CanPauseAndContinue, CanShutDown, CanStop**    These three properties return a Boolean value indicating whether the service can be paused and continued, shut down, and stopped.

**Pause, Start, Stop**    Use these methods to pause, start, and stop the service.

**ExecuteCommand**    Use this method to execute one of the service's commands.

The second button on the project's main form starts and stops the service. This button behaves like a toggle and changes its caption from Stop to Start (and back) to reflect the current status of the service. The statements in Listing 14.5 change the status of the Service1 service.

---

**Listing 14.5**    **Programmatically Starting and Stopping a Service**

```
Private Sub bttnStart_Click(ByVal sender As System.Object, _
                        ByVal e As System.EventArgs) _
                        Handles bttnStart.Click
    Dim sc As New System.ServiceProcess.ServiceController()
    sc.MachineName = "."
    sc.ServiceName = "Service1"

    If sc.Status = ServiceControllerStatus.Running Then
        sc.Stop()
        bttnStart.Text = "Start"
    ElseIf sc.Status = ServiceControllerStatus.Stopped Then
        sc.Start()
        bttnStart.Text = "Stop"
    End If
End Sub
```

---

To execute one of the service's commands, you simply pass the command number as argument to the ExecuteCommand method of the ServiceController variable that represents the Service1 service. Declare a variable of the ServiceController type and set its MachineName and ServiceName properties. Then call the ExecuteCommand, passing as argument one of the two command numbers (129 or 130) that the service recognizes. Here's the code of the Execute Service Command button:

```
Private Sub bttnCommand_Click(ByVal sender As System.Object, _
                        ByVal e As System.EventArgs) _
                        Handles bttnCommand.Click
    Dim sc As New System.ServiceProcess.ServiceController()
    sc.MachineName = "."
    sc.ServiceName = "Service1"
    sc.ExecuteCommand(129)
End Sub
```

All the command 129 does is tell the service to pop up a message box. In the following section we'll replace the message box with an actual window, which will allow you to interact with the user from within a Windows service.

## Adding User Interaction to the Service

As you saw, in the Properties dialog box of a Windows service you can allow the service to interact with the current user. This means that a Windows service can display a dialog box in which the user can enter data, as a means to pass parameters to the service. Going back to the file processing example of the previous section, you may wish to instruct the service to no longer process the files but simply move them to a different folder, or you may want the service to process the files and then delete them instead of moving them to another folder. The service can pop up a dialog box at any time (based on any internal criteria or an event) and interact with the user.

To demonstrate how Windows services can interact with users, we'll add to the service a new command that will display a dialog box to allow the user to select the folder to be monitored. The new command's number will be 130 and it will be processed in the OnCustomCommand event of the service. The dialog box that will pop up is an instance of a form; we'll look at the design of the form later. Add a form to the project and then add the code in Listing 14.6 to the OnCustomCommand event handler of the VBService service.

---

**Listing 14.6**    **The Revised OnCustomCommand Subroutine**

```
Protected Overrides Sub OnCustomCommand(ByVal command As Integer)
    Select Case command
        Case 129 : Log.WriteEntry("Received Command 1")
            MsgBox("Executing command")
        Case 130 : Log.WriteEntry("Received Command 2")
            TMR.Enabled = False
            Dim frm As New Form1()
            If frm.ShowDialog = Windows.Forms.DialogResult.OK Then
                Log.WriteEntry("Monitoring " & frm.selFolder, _
                                EventLogEntryType.Information)
                TMR.Enabled = True
            End If
    End Select
End Sub
```

---

The code creates a new instance of the Form1 object, the *frm* variable, and displays it modally. Then it retrieves the name of the selected folder, which is exposed as a property of the form. The code can use this information, as well as other data entered in the dialog box by the user, to alter its course of execution. Notice that the timer is disabled while the command is being processed to avoid a recursive behavior.

**TIP**    The ExecuteCommand method of the ServiceController object is synchronous. However, it will wait for a maximum of 30 seconds before it times out and an exception is thrown. The code that processes the command in the service must complete its execution in this time span or queue some work for later and return. If the command requires the processing of a very long file, for example, you should store the name of the file to be processed in a local variable (or a list structure) and exit the command before the actual processing of the file.

The dialog box used by the Service1 service to interact with the user is shown in Figure 14.8. It's a simple interface for selecting the folder to be monitored. To test the revised service, compile it and then switch to the Services window and start it.

Service1 interacts with the user with this dialog box.

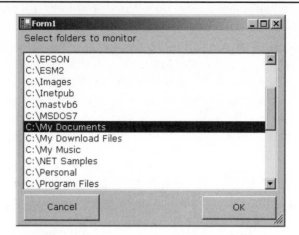

Open the ServiceController project in another instance of Visual Studio and change the number of the command passed to the ExecuteCommand method from 129 to 130. Then run the project and click the Execute Service Command button. The service's dialog box will pop up and you can select a folder name. Switch to the Event Viewer and you will find an entry indicating the folder you selected on the dialog box, similar to the one shown in Figure 14.9.

The result of the custom command 130

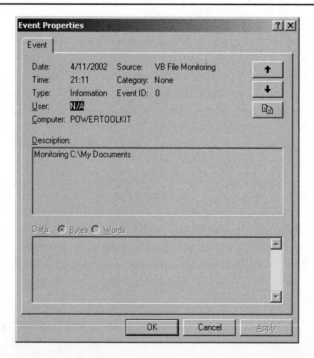

The dialog box of the Service1 Windows service is a simple form that allows the user to select a folder. The name of the selected folder is stored to the form's *selFolder* property, which is a public variable, and it's set from within the OK button's code. The code of the auxiliary form is fairly trivial. It populates a ListBox control with the names of the folders in the C: drive when it's loaded. The code is no different than the code you'd use in a similar form for a Windows application. This form interacts with the user and contains no statements specific to a Windows service. The form is being instantiated from within a Windows service, but it doesn't matter. To complete the example, Listing 14.7 shows the code of the auxiliary form.

**Listing 14.7        The Code behind the Form1 Auxiliary Form**

```
Public Shared selFolder As String

Private Sub ListBox1_SelectedIndexChanged( _
                   ByVal sender As System.Object, _
                   ByVal e As System.EventArgs) _
                   Handles ListBox1.SelectedIndexChanged
    selFolder = ListBox1.SelectedItem.ToString
End Sub

Private Sub Form1_Load(ByVal sender As System.Object, _
                   ByVal e As System.EventArgs) Handles MyBase.Load
    Dim Folders() As String
    Folders = Directory.GetDirectories("C:\")
    Dim folder As String
    ListBox1.Items.Clear()
    For Each folder In Folders
        ListBox1.Items.Add(folder)
    Next
End Sub

Private Sub bttnOK_Click(ByVal sender As System.Object, _
                   ByVal e As System.EventArgs) _
                   Handles bttnOK.Click
    Me.DialogResult = Windows.Forms.DialogResult.OK
End Sub

Private Sub bttnCancel_Click(ByVal sender As System.Object, _
                   ByVal e As System.EventArgs) _
                   Handles bttnCancel.Click
    Me.DialogResult = Windows.Forms.DialogResult.Cancel
End Sub
```

## Debugging a Windows Service

Another important issue in developing Windows services is testing and debugging them. Windows services run in the context of the Service Control Manager (SCM), not in the IDE. As a result, you can't start a Windows service by pressing F5, you can't insert breakpoints, and you can't even display messages in the Output window. However, you can pop up message boxes from within the service's code. We've all used message boxes in debugging, but messagesage boxes aren't debugging tools. For any serious debugging, we should be able to insert breakpoints, examine the values of the variables, and continue with the execution. It's quite possible to debug a Windows service with the traditional debugging tools of the IDE, but a few additional steps are required.

To debug a Windows service, you must first install it and start it with the Services utility as described earlier. Once the service has been installed, you can edit and recompile it as many times as you wish. The new EXE file will take effect automatically because the SCM loads the EXE file every time you start the service.

**NOTE**    If the service is running, you won't be able to compile its code. The EXE file in the project's `bin` folder is being used and it can't be overwritten. Stop the service and then compile the project. The changes will take effect the next time you start the service—you don't have to install the service again or take special action for the new EXE to take effect.

Once the service has been installed and is running, you can switch to the IDE and attach the service to the current instance of the IDE. To do so, open the Debug menu and select Processes. When the Processes dialog box appears, check the option Show System Processes as shown in Figure 14.10, select the name of the service, and click the Attach button on the dialog box.

**FIGURE 14.10:**

Attaching a process to be debugged to the current instance of the IDE

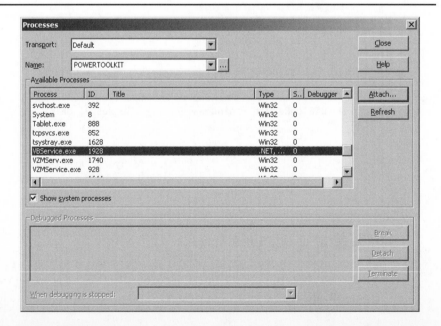

When you do so, the Attach to Process dialog box will appear (Figure 14.11). Here you must check the option Common Language Runtime and click OK to close the dialog box. You'll return to the Processes dialog box, where the ComboBox control at the bottom of the dialog box will be enabled. This control gives you the option to either terminate the process or terminate it after debugging. Select the first option (Detach from This Process) if you want the service to continue running after the debugging. In most debugging scenarios, we terminate the process after debugging (Terminate this Process) so that we can build a new EXE for the Windows service.

**FIGURE 14.11:**

The Attach to Process dialog box

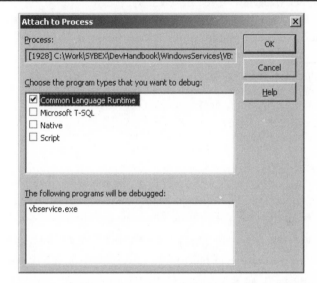

Close the Processes dialog box to return to the IDE. Now you can set breakpoints and single-step through the code. When you're done, select Stop Debugging from the Debug menu to terminate the service. At this point, you can further edit your code and build a new EXE.

The process of debugging a Windows service is simple, and once you attach the process to be debugged to the IDE, it's like debugging a Windows application. The development and debugging of Windows services is another example of the RAD capabilities built into Visual Studio.

## Sending Messages from within a Windows Service

Some services interact with users silently instead of interactively. Normally, you shouldn't expect a user to interact with your services. User interaction will happen in rather unusual situations, such as when a service detects the modification of an EXE from another file (a virus), critical Windows files are being deleted, and so on. Most services, however, work silently—the typical user isn't even aware of all the services running on their machine. A common technique for notifying the user about unusual conditions is to send messages to a specific account. If the files monitored by the sample Windows service you developed earlier in this chapter are orders, you can accumulate the orders and combine them into a single file every few hours. You can also write a service that queries SQL Server every few hours, prepares summary reports, and mails them to an account. By the way, you can also program SQL Server to mail the results of one or more queries, but you don't have as much flexibility in formatting the results. A Windows service can access all the resources on the system, just like a regular Windows application. It can automate Excel to prepare worksheets and embed them in a Word document and then send the document to one or more recipients.

Mailing from within a Windows service is not uncommon, so we'd like to end this section with a quick overview of the process. To create a message from within a VB .NET application with Simple Mail Transfer Protocol (SMTP), you must use the System.Web.Mail class. To send a message, you must first create one with the MailMessage object. Create an instance of the MailMessage class and then set its properties:

```
Dim message As MailMessage()
With message
    .From = "sender@localserver.net"
    .To = "recipient@yourserver.net"
    .Subject = "VBService Report"
    .Body = "the message's body"
End With
```

You can also add attachments to the message through the Attachments property, which is a collection. The following statement adds an attachment to the *message* variable, where *file_name* is the path of the file to be attached:

```
message.Attachments.Add(New MailAttachment(file_name))
```

Finally, create an instance of the SMPTMail class and call its Send method to send the message:

```
Dim Mail As New SmptMail()
mail.send(message)
```

## Summary

Windows services are not among the common types of applications, but when required, they'll come in very handy. In the past, VB developers had to rely on Timer controls to write applications that ran in the background, came alive every so often to perform certain tasks, and went back to sleep again. If you need a program to remain active at all times and perform certain tasks without interfering with the user, you should implement it as a Windows service. Now that it is possible to write (and debug) Windows services with Visual Basic, there's no reason not to take advantage of the new feature and use standard logging techniques.

Apart from installing them and a few minor complications in debugging them, Windows services are very similar to Windows applications. Actually, it's the IDE that makes it so simple to develop, install, and debug Windows services. As for the code of a Windows service, it's not any different than the code of a regular Windows application, with the exception of the OnStart and OnStop methods.

# PART IV

# Developing for the Web

# CHAPTER 15

# Developing Web Applications with ASP.NET

- The Web Forms controls

- The HTML controls

- Exploring the web controls

- Exploring the HTML controls

- Configuration settings

- Managing cache

- Optimizing performance

In Chapter 6, "Building Data-Driven Web Applications," we introduced some of the features associated with building web applications using the .NET technology. One of the great things about working with Visual Studio .NET is the way in which Microsoft has enabled the seamless integration of web-based components into your applications.

Superficially at least, building web applications with the Web Forms or HTML controls is not terribly different from building standard Windows applications. You drop some controls on a form, set the properties, write some VB code, compile, debug, and deploy. (If only it were all that easy!) However, to really take advantage of what .NET has to offer us and to build really compelling web applications that are fully optimized and give great performance, you need to be aware of the differences that do exist and how they can be accommodated and exploited.

For example, *fragment caching* can be used to cache portions of an ASPX page that are constantly reused. This helps create a performance boost over an equivalent page that is completely regenerated each time it is called. This is particularly useful in situations in which part of the page contains dynamic data but another part (such as a heading, a link, or a navigation bar) remains static.

In the first part of this chapter, we will examine the range of controls available for use with ASP.NET. Because many of these controls have an almost identical equivalent in the Windows Forms controls, we will focus only on those that are truly unique to the web arena or have significant variations from their Windows application cousins.

Later in the chapter, we will look at some of the more advanced features of working with web applications, such as configuration settings, caching, and performance factors.

## The Web Forms Controls

As you saw in Chapter 6, there are two main sources of controls available for the developer in the web application Toolbox: the server-side Web Forms controls and the client-side HTML controls. Table 15.1 contains a list of the web controls and a brief description of each.

**TABLE 15.1:** Web Controls

| Web Control | Description |
| --- | --- |
| AdRotator | Randomly inserts content (advertisements) within a specified area according to a weighted index. |
| Button | Creates a command-style button to enact code back on the server. |
| Calendar | Renders a calendar with calendar-style functionality on the target page. |
| CheckBox | Renders a single check box. |

*Continued on next page*

**TABLE 15.1 CONTINUED:** Web Controls

| Web Control | Description |
|---|---|
| CheckBoxList | Renders a list with check box functionality against each item. |
| CompareValidator | Validation control for comparing the contents of two fields; e.g., when constructing a password creation confirmation check. |
| CrystalReportViewer | For hosting a report in a web application. |
| CustomValidator | Validation control that enables customized validation requirements to be set. |
| DataGrid | Renders a data grid for displaying and interacting with data in a customizable table format. |
| DataList | Renders a control for displaying and interacting with data as a list. |
| DropDownList | Enables creation of a drop-down list of items from which user can make a selection. |
| HyperLink | Creates links for navigating within the site and externally. Link properties can be set dynamically at runtime. |
| Image | Control for placing an image on a page. |
| ImageButton | Enables a graphic to be specified as a button. |
| Label | Renders text on a page. Text content and properties can be determined at runtime. |
| LinkButton | Renders a button as a link. Effectively creates a link that posts back to the server and executes whatever code has been set for it. |
| ListBox | Displays a list of items that may be selected individually or in multiples by the user. |
| Literal | Renders text to a web page, but does so without adding any additional HTML tags. Similar to the Label control. |
| Panel | Container control that can be used to set global properties (style, color, etc.) for a group of controls at either design or runtime. |
| PlaceHolder | Is used as a container by controls that are added at runtime and that may vary in number. |
| RadioButton | Renders a single radio button control. |
| RadioButtonList | Renders a list with radio button functionality against each item. |
| RangeValidator | Validation control for checking that specified content or entries fall with a set range of values. |
| RegularExpressionValidator | Validation control for checking that a field entry follows a particular specified template (e.g., zip code). |
| Repeater | Creates customized lists out of any data available to a page. List format is specified by the developer. |
| RequiredFieldValidator | Validation control for checking that a user has made an entry into a specified field. |
| Table | Enables the establishment of dynamically rendered tables at runtime. |
| TableCell | Enables display of content in the Table control. |

*Continued on next page*

**TABLE 15.1 CONTINUED:** Web Controls

| Web Control | Description |
|---|---|
| TableRow | Enables display of content in the Table control. |
| TextBox | Provides a date entry field on a web page. Can be set as a password box with the contents obscured. |
| ValidationSummary | Validation control that reports validation status of other validation controls being used on the form. |
| XML | Writes an XML document into a web page. |

We will look at a number of these controls in more detail in the section "Exploring the Web Controls" later in this chapter. The next section lists the HTML controls and their individual roles.

## The HTML Controls

The HTML controls are client-side controls that essentially consist of the standard range of tools available for any web page that can be deployed using HTML code. They already have certain attributes specified. For example, the various input-based controls have the `type` attribute preset. Table 15.2 lists these controls and gives a basic description of each.

**TABLE 15.2:** HTML Controls

| HTML Control | Description | HTML Code Equivalent |
|---|---|---|
| Button | HTML input-style button | `<input type="button">` |
| CheckBox | HTML check box | `<input type="checkbox">` |
| DropDown | HTML drop-down combo box | `<select><option></option></select>` |
| File Field | HTML field for handling file upload | `<input type="file">` |
| Flow Layout Panel | Uses the Div element to arrange contents in "flow" style | `<div></div>` |
| Grid Layout Panel | Uses the Div element to arrange contents depending on placement | `<div></div>` |
| Hidden | Hidden field for displaying application-specific content | `<input type="hidden">` |
| Horizontal Rule | Horizontal line | `<hr>` |
| Image | HTML image control | `<img src="">` |
| Label | Uses the Div element to arrange text on a page | `<div></div>` |
| ListBox | Creates a list box (single- or multi-select) based on the Select tag | `<select size=" "><option></option></select>` |

*Continued on next page*

**TABLE 15.2 CONTINUED:** HTML Controls

| HTML Control | Description | HTML Code Equivalent |
|---|---|---|
| Password Field | HTML password field | `<input type="password">` |
| Radio Button | HTML radio button field | `<input type="radio">` |
| Reset Button | HTML reset button for clearing the content of all fields on a form | `<input type="reset">` |
| Submit Button | HTML submit button for submitting content entered in fields on a form | `<input type="submit">` |
| Table | HTML table | `<table><tr><td></td></tr></table>` |
| Text Area | HTML text area | `<textarea></textarea>` |
| Text Field | HTML text-style input field | `<input type="text">` |

It is important to note that, although some of the Web Forms and HTML controls share similar names and superficial functionality, they are in fact quite different controls. The Web Forms controls are server-side controls and the default behavior of the HTML controls is that of client-side controls. The following ASPX code snippets illustrate the differences between some of these controls.

Here is the code for an HTML Label control:

```
<DIV style="DISPLAY: inline; Z-INDEX: 104; LEFT: 62px; _
  WIDTH: 70px; POSITION: absolute; TOP: 367px; HEIGHT: _
  15px" ms_positioning="FlowLayout">Label</DIV>
```

Compare the HTML Label control with the code for the Web Forms label control:

```
<asp:Label id="Label1" style="Z-INDEX: 106; LEFT: 65px; _
  POSITION: absolute; TOP: 447px" _
  runat="server">Label</asp:Label>
```

Here is the code for an HTML Button control:

```
<INPUT style="Z-INDEX: 105; LEFT: 62px; POSITION: _
  absolute; TOP: 405px" type="button" value="Button">
```

Notice the difference in the code for the Web Forms Button control:

```
<asp:Button id="Button1" style="Z-INDEX: 107; LEFT: _
  65px; POSITION: absolute; TOP: 475px" runat="server" _
  Text="Button"></asp:Button>
```

It is possible to convert an HTML control to a server-side control by right-clicking the control and selecting the Run as Server Control option. This inserts a `runat = "server"` attribute into the HTML tag, as shown in the following code snippet for the HTML Label control:

```
<DIV style="DISPLAY: inline; Z-INDEX: 101; LEFT: 51px; _
  WIDTH: 70px; POSITION: absolute; TOP: 52px; HEIGHT: _
```

```
15px" ms_positioning="FlowLayout" id="DIV1" _
runat="server">Label</DIV>
```

However, the HTML Label control has a more limited range of configurable properties than the Web Form version, so in most cases, there are really not a great deal of good reasons for choosing the server-side HTML control over its Web Form equivalent.

## Exploring the Web Controls

In this section, we will take a look at a number of the Web Form controls available to the developer. Some of these controls are covered elsewhere in this book. In particular, the data-bound web controls (DataGrid, Repeater, and DataList) will be covered in Chapter 18. Chapter 18 will also cover the use of the CrystalReportViewer control. In Chapter 22, "Targeting Mobile Devices," we look at the AdRotator control (admittedly the mobile version, but it is very similar to the ASP.NET version). Previously, in Chapter 6, some of the validation controls have been demonstrated. Most of the simple controls have been covered in one form or another throughout this book.

We will begin by taking a look at the Calendar control.

### The Calendar Control

The Calendar control enables the developer to attach a rich calendar with broad functionality to web applications. Perform the following steps:

1. Create a new web-project in Visual Basic .NET and name it WebDemo1.

2. From the Web Forms Toolbox, drag a Calendar control to WebForm1.aspx. You can alter the appearance of the calendar using the Auto Format option below the Properties window. This opens the Calendar Auto Format dialog box (shown in Figure 15.1), which offers a range of predefined calendar layouts. We chose Professional 1. Click OK to confirm your selection.

**NOTE**  There may be some regional variation as to which day of the week is displayed as the default first day of the week. This can be altered with the FirstDayOfWeek property.

3. Within the Properties window, set the Selected Date and Visible Date properties to Today. When using these properties, you are presented with a little calendar from which you can pick dates. To choose Today, click the Today option at the bottom of this calendar. This will set the calendar to highlight the current date and will set the Selected Date property for the current date when the calendar is manipulated programmatically.

4. Click the Start arrow to run the calendar in Internet Explorer. (If you don't have IE as your default Browse option, you can change it using the Browse With option from the File menu of Visual Studio .NET.)

**FIGURE 15.1:**

The Calendar Auto Format dialog box

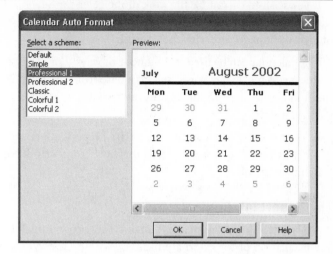

Figure 15.2 illustrates how the calendar should look running in Internet Explorer.

**FIGURE 15.2:**

The Calendar control running in Internet Explorer

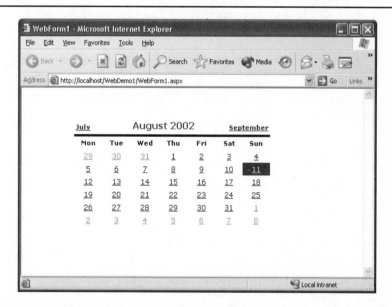

Clicking any of the dates will post back to the server and change the value of the Selected Date property, but it will have little other impact at this stage. You can browse forward and back through the months by clicking the next or previous month listed at the top of the calendar.

If you wish to customize the look of the calendar beyond the preset style that we used, you can use the Style options in the Properties window. The Calendar properties offer a wide range of style options for use with the control.

The calendar can be used in a number of ways. For example, it can be tied to a database that stores messages. When a user selects a date from the calendar, the value of the Selected Date method can be used to locate and retrieve any messages stored against the user on that particular date.

In the next section, we will look at the HyperLink control and extend the WebDemo1 project by building some functionality into a hyperlink based on the selected date in the Calendar control.

## The HyperLink Control

The HyperLink control enables you to create programmable links that can be used for internal site navigation or for external links. We will use the WebDemo1 project with its Calendar control as a simple example of how to use both these controls.

Drag a HyperLink (HyperLink1) control to WebForm1.aspx in WebDemo1. Double-click the Calendar control to enter Code Behind and add the code from Listing 15.1.

---

**Listing 15.1**          **Using the Calendar and Hyperlink Controls to Generate a Dynamic Hyperlink**

```
Private Sub Page_Load(ByVal sender As System.Object, _
ByVal e As System.EventArgs) Handles MyBase.Load

        ChooseDate()
    End Sub

    Private Sub Calendar1_SelectionChanged(ByVal sender _
As System.Object, ByVal e As System.EventArgs) Handles _
Calendar1.SelectionChanged
        ChooseDate()
    End Sub

    Private Function ChooseDate()
        Select Case Calendar1.SelectedDate.DayOfWeek()
            Case DayOfWeek.Monday
                HyperLink1.NavigateUrl = _
"http://www.sybex.com"
                HyperLink1.Text = "Sybex Books"
            Case DayOfWeek.Tuesday
                HyperLink1.NavigateUrl = _
"http://www.microsoft.com"
                HyperLink1.Text = "Microsoft"
            Case Else
                HyperLink1.NavigateUrl = _
```

```
            "http://www.gotdotnet.com"
                        HyperLink1.Text = "GotDotNet"
            End Select
      End Function
```

This is a straightforward piece of code that uses the SelectedDate property of the Calendar control to determine which value to assign to the NavigateURL method of the HyperLink control. We use a Case construct to apply different URLs for different dates and wrap it all up in a function that can be called separately from the PageLoad event (to assign the correct URL when the application first opens) and Calendar1's SelectionChanged event (to assign the URL when a date is chosen). We change the appearance of the HyperLink by changing its Text property.

Compile and run the application. Selecting different days of the week (Monday, Tuesday, rather than the other days for this example) should result in a corresponding change in the target URL of the HyperLink.

Next we will see how to use a Panel control to apply some global properties to portions of our application. We will also make use of the Literal control to add some text to the Panel control at runtime.

## The Panel Control (and the Literal Control)

Drag a Panel control (Panel1) to the WebForm1 in the WebDemo1 application and position it above the Calendar control.

You can add and edit text directly on the Panel control by clicking it once to select it and then clicking it once again. It enters Text Edit mode (indicated by thick gray edges around the Panel control), which can be used for adding and editing text and for positioning child controls within the panel.

Set the following Panel properties:

- Font Bold to True
- Font Italic to True
- Font Size to Medium
- ForeColor to #C00000

These properties become the default for any control or text added to the Panel control unless they changed explicitly within the property settings for the individual controls or programmatically at runtime. (We will do both.) Next, carry out the following steps:

1. Add a Label control (Label1) to the Panel1 and set the Text property to **Today is:**. You will notice that the Label control has adopted the properties from the Panel control, even at design time.

At this stage the Panel control may have the string "Panel" in it. This can only be removed from the designer by entering Text Edit mode on the Panel control and deleting it. Alternatively, you can switch to HTML view and delete the string from the ASPX code.

2. Add a second Label control and set its ID property to Day and delete the contents of its Text property.

3. Enter Text Edit mode on Panel1 and use the Enter key to move the insertion point to the next line. Type **The Date is:** directly on this line. Entering text directly in this way saves you from having to use a Label control. The only advantage in using a Label control would be that it would allow you to vary some of the formatting.

4. Add a third Label control after the text entry and set its ID property to TodaysDate. Delete any entry in the Text property for this control and set its ForeColor property to Black. This will override the ForeColor setting imposed by the Panel1 control.

5. Last, enter Text Edit mode again for the Panel1 control and move the insertion point down another line. Drag a Literal control (Literal1) to this point. The purpose of using a Literal control is so that you can add text directly to the Panel at runtime.

Figure 15.3 illustrates how the finished setup should look.

**FIGURE 15.3:**

Layout for WebDemo1 with the Panel control

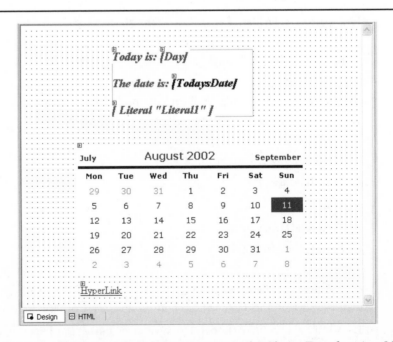

Switch to Code Behind and add the code from Listing 15.2 to the ChooseDate function. Note that we have also made some additions to the Case statement in the ChooseDate function.

**Listing 15.2        Expanded Code for WebDemo1 Sample to Cater for Panel Control**

```
Private Function ChooseDate()
        Select Case Calendar1.SelectedDate.DayOfWeek()
            Case DayOfWeek.Monday
                HyperLink1.NavigateUrl = _
    "http://www.sybex.com"
                HyperLink1.Text = "Sybex Books"
                Panel1.BackColor = Panel1.BackColor.Navy
                Panel1.ForeColor = Panel1.ForeColor.Yellow
            Case DayOfWeek.Tuesday
                HyperLink1.NavigateUrl = _
    "http://www.microsoft.com"
                HyperLink1.Text = "Microsoft"
                Panel1.BackColor = Panel1.BackColor.Coral
                Panel1.ForeColor = Panel1.ForeColor.Blue
            Case Else
                HyperLink1.NavigateUrl = _
    "http://www.gotdotnet.com"
                HyperLink1.Text = "GotDotNet"
                Panel1.BackColor = Panel1.BackColor.Wheat
                Panel1.ForeColor = Panel1.ForeColor.Red
        End Select
        Day.Text = Calendar1.SelectedDate.DayOfWeek.ToString
        TodaysDate.Text = Calendar1.SelectedDate.Date

        If Calendar1.SelectedDate.DayOfWeek = _
    DayOfWeek.Friday Then
            Literal1.Text = "Happy Birthday!!"
        Else
            Literal1.Text = ""
        End If
    End Function
```

The purpose of this code is to illustrate the effect of dynamically changing the properties of the Panel control at runtime on its child controls. For each of the selected dates, we have altered the BackColor and ForeColor properties, which should be reflected in the various child controls (with the exception of the ForeColor property of the TodaysDate Label, which has been set specifically for that control).

You can test this by compiling and running the program in IE. Selecting various days should produce a selection of fairly horrible color combinations of text and background.

Additionally, selecting Friday from the calendar should trigger the "Happy Birthday" string, which will appear in the Panel control via the Literal control that we added.

Figure 15.4 illustrates the program running in Internet Explorer after a "Friday" has been selected.

**FIGURE 15.4:**

WebDemo1 with Panel and child controls running in Internet Explorer

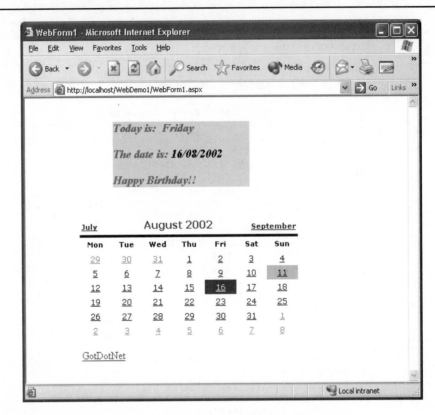

In the next section, we will demonstrate how to use a PlaceHolder control.

## The PlaceHolder Control

The PlaceHolder control is used to set an empty container control on a page to which additional controls can be added at runtime. This is particularly useful when you may not be sure as to the exact number of controls that are likely to be added.

The following example illustrates how to use the PlaceHolder control to programmatically add a set of Label controls to a Web page:

1. Create a new ASP.NET web application in Visual Basic .NET and name it WebDemo2. Create a second Web Form by using the Add Web Form option from the Project menu. We will use the first Web Form to enter some parameters specifying how many Label controls to generate and the text they will hold. The second Web Form will hold the PlaceHolder control and the dynamically generated Labels.

2. Switch to WebForm1 and drag two TextBox controls and two Label controls to the Web Form. We will use TextBox1 as a field to enter the text that will be reproduced in the

programmatically generated set of Label controls. Place one of the two Label controls next to TextBox1 and set the Label's Text property to **Type some text**. Place the second Label control next to the second TextBox and set the Label's Text property to **Number of Labels**.

3. Add a Button control to WebForm1 and double-click it to enter Code Behind. Enter the code from Listing 15.3 into the button's Click event.

**Listing 15.3**    **Code for Button1_Click Event for WebDemo2**

```
Private Sub Button1_Click(ByVal sender As System.Object,_
 ByVal e As System.EventArgs) Handles Button1.Click
        Session("labelContent") = TextBox1.Text
        Session("numLabels") = TextBox2.Text
        Response.Redirect("WebForm2.aspx")
      End Sub
```

The purpose of this code is to load the entries from the two TextBoxes into a pair of session variables and then open WebForm2 using the Response.Redirect method. At this stage, we haven't bothered with any validation processes, but we will come back to this later in the chapter when we look at the validation controls. Figure 15.5 illustrates how this WebForm1 should look at this stage.

**FIGURE 15.5:**

Control layout for WebForm1 in the WebDemo2 project

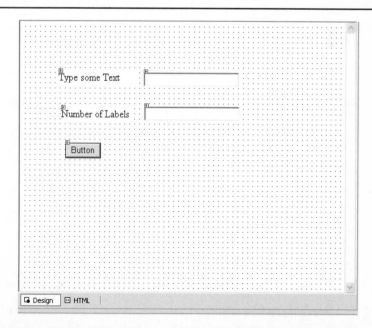

Switch to Web Form2 and add a PlaceHolder control to it. Double-click the form to switch to Code Behind and add the code from Listing 15.4 to the PageLoad event.

**Listing 15.4**  **Code for PageLoad Event for WebDemo2**

```
Private Sub Page_Load(ByVal sender As System.Object, _
ByVal e As System.EventArgs) Handles MyBase.Load
        Dim myLabel As Label = New Label()
        Dim n As Integer
        For n = 1 To Session("numLabels")
            myLabel = New Label()
            myLabel.Text = Session("labelContent") _
& n & ", "
            PlaceHolder1.Controls.Add(myLabel)
        Next n
    End Sub
```

In the code from Listing 15.4, we set up a loop based on the value of the session variable *numLabels*. We declare a new Label object and then use the loop to create multiple instances of the Label with the Text property set to the contents of the *labelContent* session variable. Running the sample application with a *numlabels* value of 100 and a *labelContent* string of "Hello there!!" produces the output illustrated in Figure 15.6.

**FIGURE 15.6:**

Running the WebDemo2 project

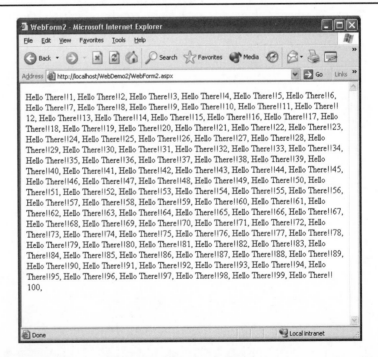

Note that the PlaceHolder control itself doesn't have any HTML representation on the form. Thus, it doesn't support the Style attribute, which would allow you to give it a specific location on the Web Form. However, you can precisely locate dynamically generated controls on the Web Form by setting their individual `Style` attributes at runtime. The following code snippet demonstrates how we might do this for a Button control.

```
Dim myButton As Button = New Button()

myButton.Style.Add("POSITION", "absolute")
myButton.Style.Add("LEFT", "153px")
myButton.Style.Add("TOP", "225px")
myButton.Text = "Test Button"

PlaceHolder1.Controls.Add(myButton)
```

In this code snippet, we use `myButton.Style.Add` to add text attributes to the `Style` attribute of the HTML tag for the myButton control when it is rendered at runtime. This will locate the button precisely where we want it on the web page.

We can use a similar approach to dynamically add controls to container controls other than the PlaceHolder control. For example, we could set up a Panel control in the WebDemo1 project and programmatically add Button controls to it each time a calendar date is clicked. The number of Buttons added depends on the day of the week, and one appropriately labeled button is added for each day of the current week.

Figure 15.7 illustrates how this might work when a Thursday is selected in the calendar.

**FIGURE 15.7:**

Programmatically adding Button controls in response to a calendar selection in WebDemo1

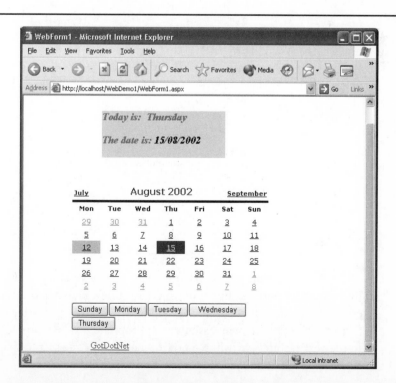

This can be achieved by dragging a Panel control (Panel2) to WebForm1 in the WebDemo1 project. Locate the Panel control directly under the existing Calendar control and above the HyperLink. Switch to Code Behind and add the code from Listing 15.5 to the Selection-Changed event of Calendar1.

**Listing 15.5     SelectionChanged Event Code for WebDemo1 Project**

```
Private Sub Calendar1_SelectionChanged(ByVal sender As _
System.Object, ByVal e As System.EventArgs) Handles _
Calendar1.SelectionChanged

        ChooseDate()

        Dim myButton As Button = New Button()
        Dim n As Integer = _
Calendar1.SelectedDate.DayOfWeek
        Dim x As Integer
        Dim day As String

        For x = 0 To n
            myButton = New Button()
            Select Case x
                Case 0
                    day = "Sunday"
                Case 1
                    day = "Monday"
                Case 2
                    day = "Tuesday"
                Case 3
                    day = "Wednesday"
                Case 4
                    day = "Thursday"
                Case 5
                    day = "Friday"
                Case 6
                    day = "Saturday"
            End Select
            myButton.Text = day
            Panel2.Controls.Add(myButton)
        Next x

    End Sub
```

We employ a similar approach to this in the previous example of using the PlaceHolder control, by using the Controls collection to create a new instance of myButton in the Panel2 control. The button generator is looped depending on the day of week selected and the SELECT CASE statement assigns an appropriate text label to each button as it is generated. In the next example, we will see how to make use of the server-side Table control.

## The Table Control

The Table control and its associated TableRow and TableCell controls are used to dynamically generate and manipulate tables at runtime.

Create a new web project in VB and name it WebDemo3. Drag a Table control (Table1) to WebForm1.

You can stretch out and resize the Table as much as you like. It also helps to set the Grid-Lines property to Both while working in Design mode. It is best to use this control if you plan on adding and manipulating cells and rows at runtime. If the table is likely to be fairly static, then it is easier to use the HTML Table control.

Adding cells and rows to the table is simply a matter of selecting the button with the ellipsis points in the Rows property at the bottom of the Table Properties window. This opens the TableRow Collection Editor dialog box (Figure 15.8). Rows can be easily added in this dialog box by simply clicking the Add button. Properties can be set for individual rows in the associated TableRow Properties window.

**FIGURE 15.8:**

The TableRow Collection Editor dialog box

To add and manage cells, click the button with the ellipsis points in the Cells property row at the bottom of the TableRow Properties window in the TableRow Collection Dialog box. This, in turn, opens the TableCell Collection Editor dialog box (shown in Figure 15.9), which can be used to add cells and edit cell properties. Note that you need to open this dialog box for each row that you have created.

**FIGURE 15.9:**

The TableCell Collection Editor dialog box

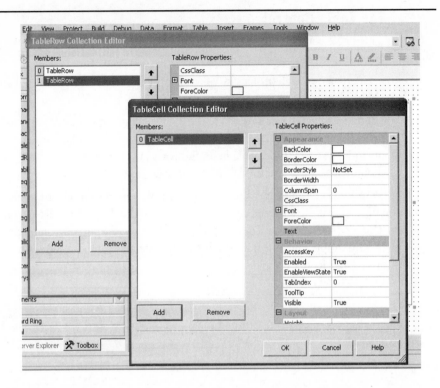

The main advantage, however, of using this control is that it can be manipulated programmatically. The code in Listing 15.6 illustrates how you can dynamically add rows and columns to a Table control at run-time.

Drag the Table1 control out to fill WebForm1 in the WebDemo3 project. Double-click somewhere in the form to enter the Page_Load event in Code Behind. Enter the code from Listing 15.6. This should create a simple two-column and two-row table with the cell in the bottom row spanning both columns.

**Listing 15.6      Programmatically Generating a Table in WebDemo3**

```
Private Sub Page_Load(ByVal sender As System.Object, _
   ByVal e As System.EventArgs) Handles MyBase.Load

        Dim myRow As New TableRow()
        Table1.Rows.Add(myRow)

        Dim myCell As New TableCell()
        myCell.Text = "Hello"
```

```
myRow.Cells.Add(myCell)
Dim myNextCell As New TableCell()
myNextCell.Text = "Hello"
myRow.Cells.Add(myNextCell)

Dim myNextRow As New TableRow()
Table1.Rows.Add(myNextRow)

Dim anotherCell As New TableCell()
anotherCell.Text = "Hello again"
anotherCell.ColumnSpan = 2
myNextRow.Cells.Add(anotherCell)

End Sub
```

As can be seen from Listing 15.6, you build the table row by row and cell by cell. You can also set various other properties, such as ColumnSpanning. The full range of table attributes is available. Figure 15.10 illustrates how the table appears when run in Internet Explorer.

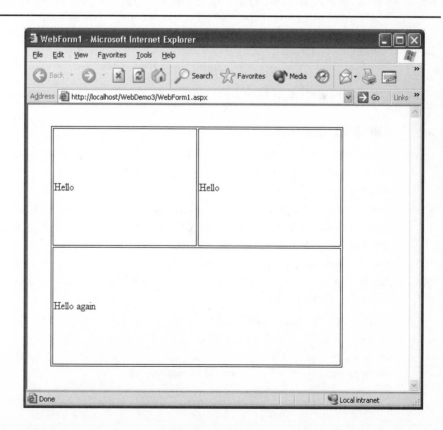

Typically, it is far more efficient to use a loop to generate the table. For example, the following code snippet illustrates a nested loop that will create a 6 × 4 table with each cell numbered:

```
Dim n As Integer
Dim x As Integer

For n = 1 To 6
    Dim newRow As New TableRow()
    For x = 1 To 4
        Dim newCell As New TableCell()
        newCell.Text = "Cell " & x
        newRow.Cells.Add(newCell)
    Next x
    Table1.Rows.Add(newRow)
Next n
```

**TIP**    It is often a good idea to set the EnableViewState property of the Table control to False when dynamically rendering tables because content changes can be lost when the page is refreshed at the server. Setting EnableViewState to False prevents earlier data values from being preserved and inadvertently overwriting newer values. This can also apply to other dynamically generated controls and their respective containers.

Next, we will take a look at using the XML control.

## The XML Control

The XML control can be used to write an XML document or the outcome of an XSLT transformation into a web page. The XML data can be sourced externally or written into the control itself.

Using the control to access an XML document is quite straightforward; simply use the Document Source property to locate the XML document to be loaded; alternatively, drag the XML control to the Web Form Designer, switch to HTML view, and write the XML code between the opening and closing tags of the XML control. A third strategy consists of using the Load method in the Page_Load event to load the XML document and then assign it to the Document property of the XML control.

To transform some XML data using an XSLT style sheet, set the TransformSource property of the XML control to the location of the XSLT page. Alternatively, you can create an instance of the XslTransform class (that points to your XSLT style sheet) and attach the Transform property of the XML control to that object.

In the following example, we will create a simple XML data file, an XSLT file to knock the data into some form of presentable format, and a Web Form running the XML control to view the output of the XSLT style sheet. Open a new ASP.NET project (Visual Basic) and name it WebDemo4.

We begin by creating the XML data file. In this case, we will build a simple address book (two entries only).

Listing 15.7 contains the code for the XML file. You can create the file by selecting the Add New Item option from the Project menu and choosing XML File from the Templates window. Alternatively, you could write it in Notepad, save it to the application directory of WebDemo4, and then manually add it to the project by using the Add Existing Item option from the Project menu. Whichever approach you use, name the file myAddresses.xml.

**Listing 15.7**      *myAddresses.xml*

```xml
<?xml version="1.0" ?>
<addresses>
   <address id="1">
      <name>Fred</name>
      <surname>Smith</surname>
      <phone>555 555 555</phone>
   </address>
<address id="2">
      <name>Mary</name>
      <surname>Jones</surname>
      <phone>444 444 444</phone>
   </address>
</addresses>
```

The next step is to create the XSLT style sheet. Again, you can take your pick between your favorite text editor and the XSLT template available in Visual Studio .NET. Listing 15.8 gives the code for the style sheet. Save the file as myAddrStyle.xslt.

**Listing 15.8**      *myAddrStyle.xslt*

```xml
<?xml version="1.0" ?>
<xsl:stylesheet version="1.0" _
 xmlns:xsl="http://www.w3.org/1999/XSL/Transform">
<xsl:template match="/">
<html>
<body>
<table border="1">
```

```
<xsl:for-each select="addresses/address">
<tr>
<td>
Name: <b><xsl:value-of select="name" /> <xsl:value-of _
  select="surname" /></b><br></br>
Phone number: <b><xsl:value-of select="phone"/></b>
</td>
</tr>
</xsl:for-each>
</table>
</body>
</html>
</xsl:template>
</xsl:stylesheet>
```

The purpose of the code in Listing 15.8 is to extract the data from the myAddresses XML file and present it in a readable format in an HTML table.

If you have used the templates in Visual Studio .NET, it is a good idea to save the project at this point. Next, we set up the Web Form to process the data. Select the WebForm1.aspx tab and add an XML control (Xml1) to the form. Set the control's DocumentSource property to myAddresses.xml. This will directly present the raw data from the XML file on the Web Form.

Add another XML control (Xml2) to the Web Form. Set the DocumentSource property to myAddresses.xml and the TransformSource property to myAddrStyle.xslt. The purpose of this control is to display the output of the XSLT file that we created.

The final layout of the Web Form is shown in Figure 15.11. Figure 15.12 shows the project running in Internet Explorer.

**FIGURE 15.11:**

Layout of WebForm1 .aspx for WebDemo4 project

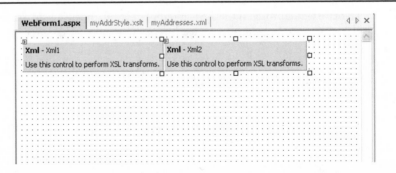

**FIGURE 15.12:**

The WebDemo4 project running in IE displaying "raw" output from an XML file and formatted output from an XSLT file

You can also load XML data directly into the XML control tags in HTML view of WebForm1. Drag a third XML control (Xml3) to WebForm1 in WebDemo4 and switch to HTML view. Locate the opening and closing tags for the Xml3 control and add the code from Listing 15.9.

**Listing 15.9    Adding XML Data Directly to the XML Control Tags**

```
<asp:Xml id="Xml3" runat="server">
    <addresses>
       <address id="1">
          <name>Fred</name>
          <surname>Smith</surname>
          <phone>555 555 555</phone>
       </address>
       <address id="2">
          <name>Mary</name>
          <surname>Jones</surname>
```

```
        <phone>444 444 444</phone>
      </address>
    </addresses>
  </asp:Xml>
```

Compile and run the project again and the XML data should be displayed as it was with the Xml1 control. To make use of the XSLT style sheet, simply insert the `TransformSource=` `"myAddrStyle.xslt"` attribute into the Xml3 tag as shown in the following code snippet:

```
<asp:Xml id="Xml3" runat="server" _
  TransformSource="myAddrStyle.xslt">
```

Running the project should now display the XML data in the same format used by the Xml2 control.

To load the XML document as an object and assign it to the XML control, drag another XML control (Xml4) to WebForm1. Double-click the designer to enter Code Behind and then add the code from Listing 15.10 to the Page_Load event.

---

**Listing 15.10      Working from an Instance of the XML Document**

```
Private Sub Page_Load(ByVal sender As System.Object, _
  ByVal e As System.EventArgs) Handles MyBase.Load

     Dim myXML As System.Xml.XmlDataDocument = New _
System.Xml.XmlDataDocument()
     myXML.Load(Server.MapPath("myAddresses.xml"))
     Xml4.Document = myXML

End Sub
```

---

This code example should load the unformatted data as previously demonstrated with the Xml1 control. You can take a similar approach employing `System.Xml.Xsl.XslTransform` to make use of the XSLT document.

In the next section, we will cover the use of the various Validation controls available with ASP.NET.

## The Validation Controls

A number of very useful validation controls that you can use to manage various aspects of data entry by your users are available to ASP.NET. We demonstrated the basic use of some of these controls in Chapter 6. In this section, we will look at all of them in a little more detail.

The following validation controls are available:

**CompareValidator**    Compares entries in two separate fields

**CustomValidator**   Creates custom validation expressions

**RangeValidator**   Ensures that entries fall within a certain range of values

**RegularExpressionValidator**   Checks data entry to make sure it follows a certain pattern or template

**RequiredFieldValidator**   Checks to see an entry has been made in a field

**ValidationSummary**   Lists the output of multiple validation controls in one place

To demonstrate the use of these controls, we will return to the WebDemo2 project. You will recall that we used this project to experiment with the use of the PlaceHolder control and set up a couple of fields that can result in a nasty exception (aren't all exceptions nasty?) if the fields are left empty. We could easily manage this with some structured exception handling, but in this particular case, we will use the validation controls.

Open the WebDemo2 project and set up WebForm1 with the controls and properties listed in Table 15.3.

**TABLE 15.3:** Controls and Properties for WebForm1 in WebDemo2

| Control | Control ID | Property | Value |
|---------|-----------|----------|-------|
| Label | Label1 | Text | "Type some text:" |
| Label | Label2 | Text | "Number of Labels" |
| Label | Label3 | Text | "Confirm Number of Labels:" |
| Label | Header | Text | "Label Mania" |
| | | Font | Comic |
| | | Bold | True |
| | | Size | X-Large |
| | | ForeColor | Red |
| TextBox | TextBox1 | Text | <empty> |
| TextBox | TextBox2 | Text | <empty> |
| TextBox | TextBox3 | Text | <empty> |
| Button | Button1 | Text | "Load Labels" |
| RequiredField-Validator | RequiredField-Validator1 | ErrorMessage | "Please enter some text in the Type some Text box" |
| | | Text | "Please enter some text" |
| | | ControlToValidate | TextBox1 |
| RequiredField-Validator | RequireFieldValidator2 | ErrorMessage | "Please enter a number in the Number of Labels box" |
| | | Text | "Please enter a number" |
| | | ControlToValidate | TextBox2 |

*Continued on next page*

**TABLE 15.3 CONTINUED:** Controls and Properties for WebForm1 in WebDemo2

| Control | Control ID | Property | Value |
|---|---|---|---|
| CompareValidator | CompareValidator1 | ErrorMessage | "Please confirm your number in the Confirm Number of Labels box" |
| | | Text | "Please confirm your number" |
| | | ControlToCompare | TextBox3 |
| | | ControlToValidate | TextBox2 |
| RangeValidator | RangeValidator1 | ErrorMessage | "Please enter a valid number between 1 and 99" |
| | | Text | "Enter a valid number" |
| | | ControlToValidate | TextBox2 |
| | | MaximumValue | 99 |
| | | MinimumValue | 1 |
| ValidationSummary | ValidationSummary1 | ShowMessageBox | True |
| | | ShowSummary | False |

The completed form should appear as shown in Figure 15.13.

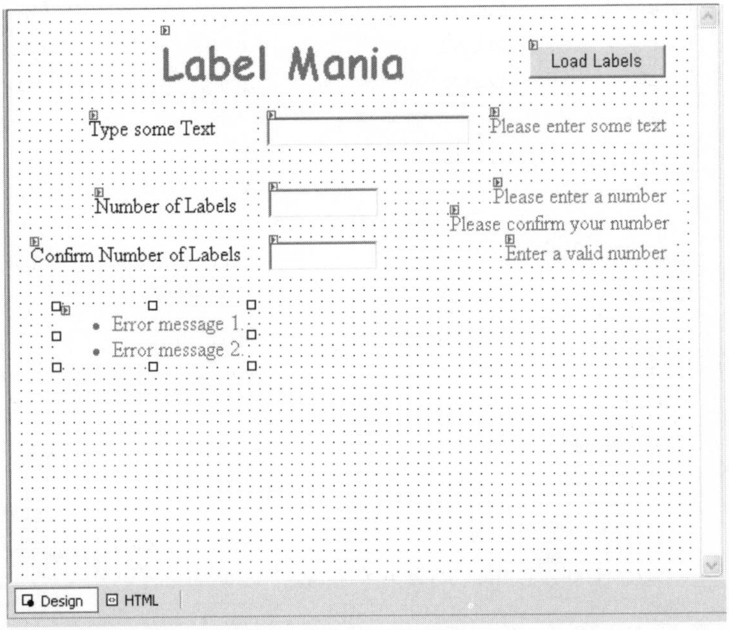

**FIGURE 15.13:**

The completed WebForm1 for the WebDemo2 project

The validation controls themselves are self-explanatory. If you leave their Display property at the default Static value, each control will display an individual error message after the initial post back from the Button control. You can disable the individual messages by setting the Display property for each validation control to None. You have the option of creating a shortened error message by using the Text property. In this example, the longer, more detailed ErrorMessage is displayed by the ValidationSummary control.

Additionally, we have chosen to display the validation summary using a message box. By setting the ShowSummary property to True, we could display the summarized error messages on the Web Form itself.

Figure 15.14 and Figure 15.15 demonstrate the validation process in action.

**FIGURE 15.14:**

Using the Validation controls (1)

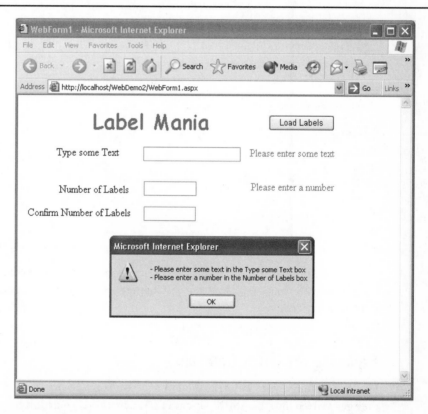

Two additional validation controls that we have not covered in this example are the Custom-Validator and the RegularExpressionValidator. Each of these controls works in a fashion similar to how the other validation controls work. The CustomValidator enables you to set up your own customized validation requirements, and the RegularExpressionValidator validates against a template that you can either specify or choose from a list.

**FIGURE 15.15:**

Using the Validation controls (2)

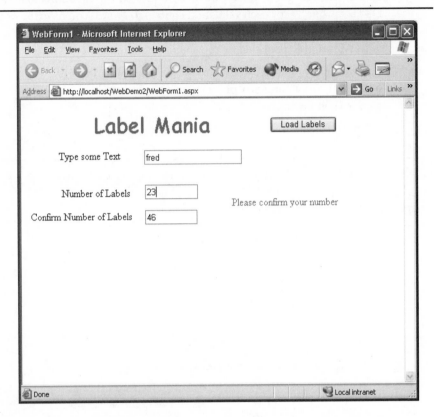

This completes our tour of the Web Form controls (with the exception of the data-bound controls that we will look at in Chapter 18. In the next section, we will explore the HTML controls.

## Exploring the HTML Controls

For those familiar with HTML, the HTML controls will present few surprises. Essentially, they get written into the ASPX page as HTML markup. Microsoft has created a set of controls based on HTML tags with a number of attributes already preset, and the controls have been given their own names. Thus, some of the names, such as Flow Layout Panel, might look a little unfamiliar to HTML programmers, but they are not particularly hard to use. The list of controls and their HTML equivalents is presented in Table 15.2 earlier in this chapter.

Because of their nature, the controls are not as flexible as their server-side equivalents, but because they are client-side controls, they remove processing load from your web servers. As a lot of the content on pages is often fairly static, not terribly complicated, and easily supported by the HTML controls, it pays to use the HTML controls wherever you can.

As you have seen, it is possible to convert the HTML controls to server-side processing, but in most cases, this is unnecessary. If you need to go server-side, you are far more likely to want to use the richer server-side equivalent controls from the Web Forms Toolbox. However, there are still occasions when you may need to convert an HTML control to server-side, and later in this section, we will show you how to do this with the HTML Listbox control.

In the following example, we will set up a simple static web page using the HTML controls and then examine the HTML generated for use at the client end. It is also worth noting that you can import an HTML page into Visual Studio .NET and then use the HTML controls to edit it.

## Building an HTML Page Using the HTML Controls

It will help to understand the HTML controls if you have an existing understanding of HTML. We won't launch into an HTML tutorial at this point, but there are plenty of Web- and book-based resources available to help you out. *Mastering Visual Basic .NET* by Evangelos Petroutsos (Sybex, 2002) contains an HTML primer sufficient to cover most of your needs with these controls.

To set up the project, complete the following steps.

1. Create a new ASP.NET project in Visual Basic .NET and name it WebDemo5. In the Toolbox, switch to the HTML controls. Drag a Label control to the form and set its Align property to Center.

2. Click again in the Label control to enter Text Edit mode (indicated by a broader gray serrated border). Change the text to read **HTML Controls Page**.

3. Right-click the Label control and select Build Style from the context menu. This opens the Style Builder dialog box, which gives you control over font, size, backgrounds, and so on. As you can see in Figure 15.16, it also enables you to create lists and apply various other effects.

   You might find the Style Builder dialog a little fiddly to work with at first, but it does offer quite a range of options to apply to the various controls. For the Label control that we are using, click Font in the list on the left and then set the color to blue, select the Absolute radio button under Size and choose XX-Large from the drop-down menu, and select the Absolute radio button under Bold and choose Bold from the drop-down menu. Click OK to exit the builder.

**FIGURE 15.16:**

The Style Builder dialog box for the HTML controls

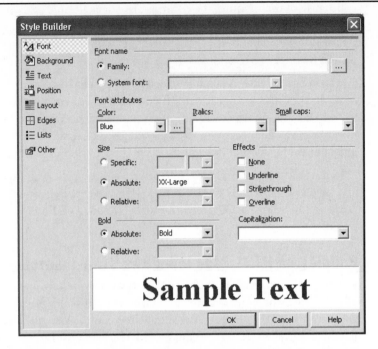

4. Resize the Label control using the handles to position the heading across the Web Form. If you switch to HTML view, you will see that the Label control is in fact a set of DIV tags and the settings that we made in the Style Builder are held in the `style` attribute, as shown in the following code snippet (this code may vary a bit depending on system defaults and the exact settings that you choose, such as position and size):

```
<DIV style="DISPLAY: inline; FONT-WEIGHT: bold; _
  FONT-SIZE: xx-large; Z-INDEX: 101; LEFT: 38px; _
  WIDTH: 459px; COLOR: blue; LETTER-SPACING: normal; _
  POSITION: absolute; TOP: 45px; HEIGHT: 69px" _
  align="center" ms_positioning="FlowLayout"> _
HTML Controls Page</DIV>
```

5. Drop a HorizontalRule control onto the form under the heading. From the Properties window, set the color to #ff0000 (red), noshade to True, and the size to 5.

6. Click somewhere on the page itself to select its properties. In the Properties window, set the title to myPage, vLink to Teal, and Link to Green. You will notice that the color names immediately convert to their hex format.

7. You can give the page a background image by setting the background property. In this case, we have pointed it to one of the background images in the Microsoft Office clip art directory at `file:///C:\Program Files\Microsoft Office\Clipart\Publisher\Backgrounds\ WB02218_.GIF`.

8. Drop a Table control onto the page under the horizontal line. You can adjust most of the properties of the Table using the Properties window. For example, set its bgcolor to#ffff99 (a pale yellow).

9. You can then drop content into your table either by typing directly into each cell or by adding other controls. In this example, we typed *Cell 1*, *Cell 2*, and *Cell 3* into the top row of cells and then dropped an Image control into the first cell of the second row. We adjusted the colspan property of this cell to 2 and deleted the third cell from this row by right-clicking it and selecting Delete.

10. Select the Image control that you just added and assign its src property to an appropriate image somewhere on your machine (we used a jelly bean image).

We could go on adding more controls and playing with their attributes, but you most likely get the idea. Figure 15.17 shows how the page looks at this point when it is run in Internet Explorer.

**FIGURE 15.17:**

WebDemo5 running in IE

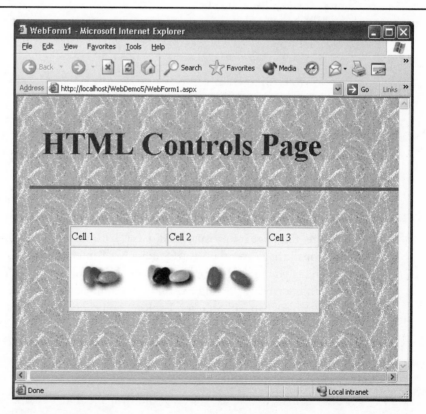

If you open the page in HTML view, you will see that what we have created is pretty much straight HTML. If you run the page in IE and check the source, you will see that the contents of the HTML view have been pretty much replicated exactly at the client end without much server intervention.

Next, we will show you how you can import and edit an existing web page.

## Editing an Existing HTML Page with Visual Studio .NET and the HTML Controls

Begin by creating a page to edit. Open Notepad (or your favorite text editor) and add the code from Listing 15.11.

---

**Listing 15.11**     **Simple Web Page**

```html
<html>
  <head>
    <title>My Page</title>
  </head>
  <body bgcolor="cornsilk">
    <center>
      <h1>My Page</h1>
      <br>
      <p>Hello there</p>
    </center>
  </body>
</html>
```

---

Save the page as index.html (remember to use the Save As and All Files options). Save it to somewhere accessible, such as the Desktop.

You can open the file in Internet Explorer to make sure everything is OK. Figure 15.18 shows how it should look.

You can get this page into Visual Studio .NET in two ways. The first method is to simply drag and drop the page over the Visual Studio .NET interface. This is quick and has the advantage of enabling you to edit the actual page in place. The other method is to add the page to an existing solution using the Add Existing Item command from the Project menu (or by right-clicking the project name in Solution Explorer and choosing Add Existing Item from the context menu). This fully incorporates the page into Visual Studio (and ultimately into the web application that it's now a part of), but the page you are editing is a copy of the original page and it now resides in the application folder for the current project. Any changes that we make will not appear in the original page.

For this example, we will use the drag-and-drop method. Make sure that you have the page open and running in Internet Explorer because you will be refreshing the page to show any changes that occur.

**FIGURE 15.18:**

The simple web
page in IE

Open up Visual Studio .NET and reduce the size of the window so that you can see your desktop. Drag and drop index.html onto the Start Page screen. This will open the page in the design environment with the HTML controls available from the Toolbox. You may have to open the Properties window separately. Click around the page with your mouse and look at the Properties window. You will notice that the window will reflect the various tags in the document, including the <p> and <center> tags. Figure 15.19 shows the web page open in the design environment.

The properties of the body section of the page itself can be a little hard to get to without dropping into HTML view. However, once in HTML view; you can quite happily edit the code from there.

In Design view, drag a HorizontalRule control to the web page. The range of properties available is a little more limited than when working inside a full Visual Studio .NET project. For example, you do not get the Build Style dialog box when right-clicking the control. You can, however, change its width, size, and noshade attributes.

Save the changes made and refresh the view of the page in Internet Explorer. It should now display the line that you added.

Alternatively, you could import the page into an existing project such as WebDemo5. Open WebDemo5 in Design mode, and from the Project menu, select Add Existing Item and then locate and add the `index.html` file. A copy of `index.html` is loaded into the application directory for WebDemo5 and any changes that you make are recorded there. The original page is left untouched.

**FIGURE 15.19:**

The simple web page open in the Visual Studio .NET design environment

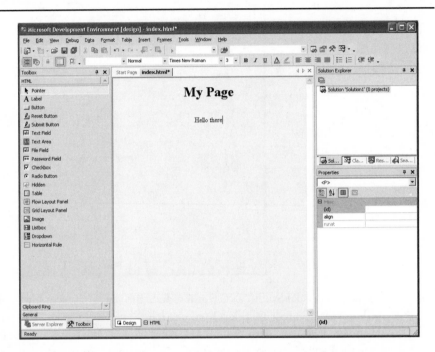

We will complete this section with a look at converting an HTML Listbox control to a server-side control and using the server-side functionality to populate the control at runtime.

## Converting an HTML Control to a Server-Side Control

We will begin looking at how to convert an HTML control to a server-side control by opening the WebDemo5 project and adding a Listbox control (Select1) from the HTML controls to WebForm1. Now perform the following steps:

1. Set the size property to 5.

2. Right-click the Listbox control and select the Run as Server Control option. This is as hard as it gets! The Select1 control is now available with a range of methods and properties in Code Behind.

3. Double-click the form to enter Code Behind and add the code to the Page_Load event from Listing 15.12.

4. Run the project. It should appear as in Figure 15.20 with a fully populated Listbox.

**Listing 15.12     Code to Populate HTML Listbox Control in WebDemo5**

```
Private Sub Page_Load(ByVal sender As System.Object, _
    ByVal e As System.EventArgs) Handles MyBase.Load
        Dim n As Integer
        For n = 1 To 10
            Select1.Items.Add("Fred " & n)
        Next n
    End Sub
```

**FIGURE 15.20:**

WebDemo5 with HTML
Listbox control

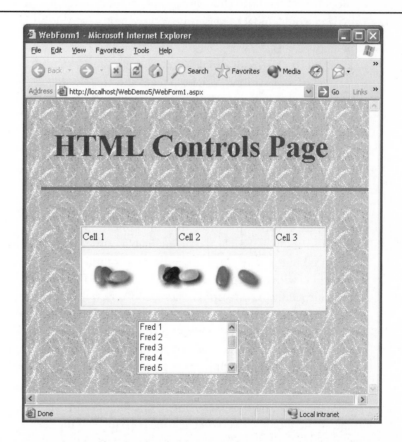

This completes our look at the HTML controls. In the rest of this chapter, we will be covering a range of more advanced topics associated with working with ASP.NET, such as caching and configuration settings.

## Configuration Settings

A number of the configuration settings for an ASP.NET application can be set, updated, or revised at any point during development, as well as during the deployment process and even once the application is "live" (and you can make changes to a live application without rebooting the server hosting the application). This is made possible by storing the configuration settings in XML files known as Web.config files.

Web.config files apply configuration settings for the contents of the directory in which they reside and any associated child directories. You can have multiple Web.config files resident on a single machine. In fact, every time you create a new ASP.NET project, a Web.config file is created for that project.

Thus, it is quite possible to develop a hierarchical structure of Web.config files that apply to a range of applications at the top level and steadily focus down to a single application as you move through the subdirectories. Additionally, there are other configuration files, such as the machine.config file that contains global settings that apply to the whole computer. Typically, this file is found in the C:\WINDOWS\Microsoft.NET\Framework\v1.0.3705\ CONFIG directory. Other configuration files can also be found in this directory, such as the security.config and enterprisesec.config files, which are mainly concerned with security settings.

The machine.config file is a good place to store settings that may be required by multiple applications. It is the first place that an application looks for configuration settings and provides an easily accessible and maintainable central repository for these types of values. Settings stored in this way are stored under the <appSettings> element. If you are developing applications with the Mobile Internet Toolkit (MIT), you will find that the MIT stores a lot of device-specific information in there, and as new devices appear on the market, it is a great place to update your system to be able to recognize them. One danger, however, of using machine.config is that it can grow to an unwieldy size very quickly. So it pays to be a little judicious about the precise content that goes in. Entries that are application specific and really only apply to one application should be saved for the application-specific configuration files.

The configuration files are plaintext documents and can be accessed and edited using any simple text editor such as Notepad (or Word for that matter). You can easily access and edit the Web.config file specific to your application from the Solution Explorer within the Visual Studio .NET IDE. Figure 15.21 illustrates the Web.config file open for the WebDemo5 project.

**FIGURE 15.21:**

Web.config open in
Visual Studio .NET for
the WebDemo3 project

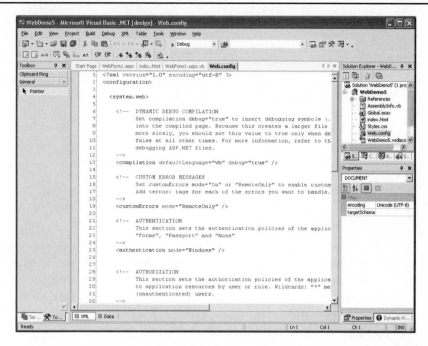

The Web.config file is very well documented internally, which makes it easy to modify to meet your needs. (In fact, the bulk of the file's contents are documentation.) Without the comments, the file looks a bit like Listing 15.13.

**Listing 15.13**    *Web.config* **File for WebDemo5**

```xml
<?xml version="1.0" encoding="utf-8" ?>
<configuration>

  <system.web>

    <compilation defaultLanguage="vb" debug="true" />
    <customErrors mode="RemoteOnly" />
    <authentication mode="Windows" />
    <authorization>
        <allow users="*" />
    </authorization>
    <trace enabled="false" requestLimit="10" _
pageOutput="false" traceMode="SortByTime" _
localOnly="true" />

    <sessionState
            mode="InProc"
```

```
            stateConnectionString="tcpip=127.0.0.1:42424"
            sqlConnectionString="data _
  source=127.0.0.1;user id=sa;password="
            cookieless="false"
            timeout="20"
    />
    <globalization requestEncoding="utf-8" _
  responseEncoding="utf-8" />

  </system.web>

</configuration>
```

We will run through each of the tags in the Web.config file. The initial tags are self explanatory. The <compilation> tag contains the debug attribute that should be set to false for performance reasons when you plan to deploy the project.

The <customErrors> tag enables you to create custom error pages that appear when something goes pear shaped rather than relying on the standard responses provided by .NET. The mode attribute of the tag can be set to On (it works), Off (it doesn't work), or RemoteOnly (works on remote clients only). You use a subtag <error> to identify the error code to then display the custom page. The <error> tag has the attributes statusCode and redirect.

The <authentication> and <authorization> tags relate to securing applications built with ASP.NET. We look at these tags in detail in Chapter 21.

The <trace> tag can be used to set application-level tracing that can be used to generate a trace log output for every page of the application. This can be enacted by setting the enabled attribute to true. If you set the pageOutput property to true, the results of the trace appear at the bottom of the web page; if set to false, the trace is output to a trace.axd file in the application directory.

The trace is a very informative document that tells you just about everything you need to know about how your application is behaving on the server that is hosting it. Figure 15.22 illustrates some of the trace output for the WebDemo5 project.

The principle setting in the <sessionState> tag that is of interest is the cookieless attribute. You use this in situations in which you need to maintain state but it is likely that the client machines will be unable to accept cookies. This is typical in mobile scenarios because many mobile devices are unable to accept cookies. When the attribute is set, the server maintains state by munging the session identifier into the URL.

When editing the Web.config file, it is very important to watch your use of case because XML is case sensitive. Any mistake in the Web.config file will floor your entire application.

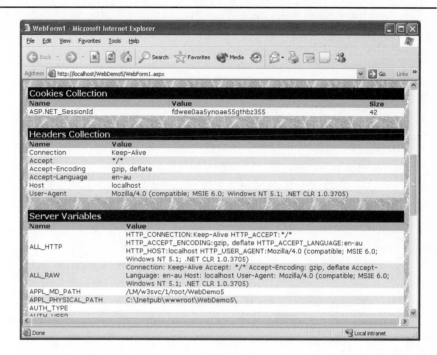

Other files that can be accessed via the Solution Explorer include the Global.asax and AssemblyInfo.vb files. The Global.asax file can be used to hold code for application-level events raised by ASP.NET, or by HttpModules. It supports visual design with Windows Forms controls and in Code view provides a framework of application-level events that you can apply code to.

The AssemblyInfo.vb file enables you to provide meta information about your project, such as the tile, product version, company name, copyright information, and so on.

## Managing Cache

There are a number of ways that developers can work with cache in ASP.NET. The first is using the Cache class to directly manipulate the cache of application data. Items can be retrieved or added directly to the cache using the Cache.add or Cache.insert methods. Expiry times can be manipulated and priority can be given to particular items using the CacheItem .priority enumeration value. Items can be deleted from cache using the Cache.remove method.

The second and third methods make use of the output cache to cache entire pages or, in the case of fragment caching, portions of pages.

Last, you can make use of ViewState to preserve properties and settings of various controls in your applications so that a user effectively sees the same page each time they request it from the server during a particular session.

## Caching Application Data

Working directly with the cache is an advantage when you have objects that consume a lot of server resources when they are set up. The following code snippet demonstrates how to store the contents of a TextBox control in cache:

```
Cache("myData") = Textbox1.text
```

You can test this quite simply by opening a new ASP.NET project (WebDemo6) and dragging two Button controls, a TextBox control, and a Label control to WebForm1. Double-click the first of the Button controls to enter Code Behind and enter the code from Listing 15.14.

**Listing 15.14     Simple Cache Management for Application Data**

```
Private Sub Button1_Click(ByVal sender As _
  System.Object, ByVal e As System.EventArgs) _
  Handles Button1.Click
        Cache("myData") = TextBox1.Text
    End Sub

    Private Sub Button2_Click(ByVal sender As _
System.Object, ByVal e As System.EventArgs) _
  Handles Button2.Click
        Label1.Text = Cache("myData")
    End Sub
```

Compile and run the application. Enter some text into the TextBox and click Button1. This should load the text into cache as myData. Click Button2. This should copy the value from cache into Label1.

## Output Caching

The second technique for cache management is to use the output cache to store the entire web page for a preset time period. You do this by adding the output cache directive to the ASPX page (in HTML view).

The directive takes the following format:

```
<%@ OutputCache Duration="120" VaryByParam="None" %>
```

The Duration parameter is used to set the cached duration of the page (in this case, 120 seconds). The VaryByParam attribute must be present in the directive (set to none if not used). It can be used along with two other attributes to enable the caching of multiple versions of a page. The other two attributes are VaryByHeader and VaryByCustom.

To use the VaryByParam attribute, you might have a page that provides a response to user input on the user's age (as either GET or POST). You can then specify VaryByParam="age". This would result in pages being cached separately based on different ages.

The VaryByHeader attribute can be used to cache pages based on specified header content, such as device. The VaryByCustom attribute can be used to write customized strings to cache multiple pages.

## Fragment Caching

The third technique involves caching portions of a page in the output cache in a technique known as *fragment caching*. This is achieved by bundling those portions of a page that are likely to remain static (headers, for example) into one or more user controls. You then apply output caching to the user controls and they are effectively cached separately to the rest of the main page when used.

Output caching can also be managed programmatically using the HttpCachePolicy class and the Page.Response property.

## ViewState

ViewState is used to store property values for controls as part of the particular session's state. It can be applied to a whole document or disabled for particular controls. Generally, the default setting for enableViewState for any control is true. Setting the enableViewState to false disables it for that particular control (or document).

Although it can be a very powerful tool for maintaining a user's session, it is not always necessary or desirable to activate ViewState. For example, if you expect high traffic on a particular page, having ViewState enabled could potentially result in a very large number of copies of that page on your server at any one time. If the page was fairly static, it would be better to disable ViewState, cache the page using output caching, and serve it up that way.

The ViewState is actually stored on the client's machine in a hidden field that is passed backward and forward between the client and server at each post back.

There is quite a bit more to ViewState (and to the whole caching arena) than we have covered here. If you want to get the most out of your ASP.NET applications, it is worth spending some time with the Microsoft documentation to familiarize yourself thoroughly with the various scenarios and possibilities available. One of the things with caching is that the requirements of each application are usually quite unique and you need to carefully structure your caching to take into account your user requirements, data structures, application design, and available equipment and network infrastructure.

In the final section of this chapter, we will look at a few issues associated with maximizing performance with web-based applications.

## Optimizing Performance

There are a number of general things that you can do to improve overall performance of your applications. These include a sensible approach to state management and cache management and some specific techniques such as not using autoeventwireup except where absolutely necessary and making use of the Page.IsPostback property to only process code once.

Naturally, there will be application-specific things you can do to improve performance, but the following list is a collection of approaches that we have found useful and that seem to be recommended by most commentators when looking at performance:

- Don't use a session if the application doesn't need it. Disable ViewState, avoid session variables, and set the enableSessionState property for your Web Form to False. (You can also knock ViewState on the head here as well.) If you need to use SessionState, but only to read session data (and not to write) then use the ReadOnly option.

- Even if you do need SessionState, you may not need ViewState. Disable it, either globally or for individual controls wherever practical. (However, remember that it is still very useful, and don't deprive yourself of functionality for the sake of a few microseconds!)

- When in doubt, cache! Cache everything that can be possibly cached. Make use of output and fragment caching wherever possible; they are easy to configure and work wonderfully well. In a dynamic setting, think ahead and make use of the VaryBy attributes in output caching to handle multiple pages.

- Remember to disable Debug mode (in Web.config) before you deploy. This includes disabling application tracing if you turned it on and making sure that you compile in Release mode.

- On the topic of errors and debugging, try to minimize the number of exceptions thrown by your code. Structured exception handling is easy to use, but it carries some overhead. Try to keep it focused on handling emergencies; it is easy to get sloppy with your code and rely on structured exception handling to pick up the pieces.

- Use SQL Server and the optimized SqlDataAdapter where possible for data connections. It is currently the fastest way to get rich data into .NET from a DBMS, and it is very reliable too. Additionally, use the DataReader where appropriate as opposed to using a DataSet.

- When accessing data, use stored procedures wherever possible. It is also worth writing your own data access and manipulation commands for use with a data adapter rather than using the auto-generated ones. It is much easier to optimize your own code.

- And finally, keep as much of your business code as possible in Code Behind rather than in HTML. Not only is it precompiled down a few steps, it also makes for a cleaner code structure, aiding post development additions, maintenance, and future upgrades.

## Summary

Visual Studio .NET introduces a powerful mechanism for creating rich, dynamic websites without moving too far from the comfort zones of the language that you are most familiar with. However, as you have seen from this chapter, it still helps a great deal to know HTML and, increasingly these days, XML. Although you can get away with little or no understanding of these languages, if you wish to really exploit the capabilities offered by ASP.NET, you need to have a good grip on more than just Visual Basic .NET.

Working with ASP.NET itself is a huge topic and very difficult to do justice to in just a couple of chapters. There are a number of areas that we have only just touched on (or left completely alone), and although our coverage here is sufficient to get you going and provide a measure of web support for most projects, it is worth spending some serious time with the Microsoft documentation if you plan on building prime-time, major league web-based applications with these tools.

There is an amazing depth to this technology. Just when you think you have exhausted a particular area, that there's nothing more that can be learned or exploited in it, you're likely to find a whole new set of methods or properties or different ways of doing things. In working with .NET, keep in mind that there is always another approach to a solution. So, if it doesn't want to work the first time, keep digging—the solution is always there, somewhere.

In the next chapter, we see how to combine what we have covered in this chapter into a full-blown web application.

# Chapter 16

# Programming Web Forms

- Planning the Gallaghers application

- Creating the XML data files

- The XML advertisement list and images for use with the AdRotator control

- Building the user controls

- Creating a template form

- Additional Page options in Visual Studio .NET

- Developing the Web Forms

- Running the application

- A further look at session management

I n this chapter, we will show you how to construct an e-commerce application using ASP.NET. We have based the application on the project that we constructed back in Chapter 6, "Building Data-Driven Web Applications" (the Gallaghers Gourmet website).

However, there will be a number of fundamental differences between the two projects. The purpose of the original project was to demonstrate a range of techniques, whereas with the version in this chapter, we are looking to create a far more polished and complete application (which just happens to demonstrate a number of different techniques).

In this version of the project, we will use XML documents as our data sources. In practice, these documents might normally be generated by other applications, such as SQL Server 2000 working through SQLXML 3 (as discussed in Chapter 2, "Working with SQL Server 2000 and Visual Studio .NET"). However, for this example, we will create the XML documents ourselves. Although writing straight XML is not everyone's cup of tea, in situations in which the data is fairly static and fairly limited (such as a small café's menu), it can be a practical alternative to creating and running a database. Later in this book (Chapter 19, "Using XML and Visual Basic .NET"), you will have the opportunity to explore XML and .NET technologies in more detail.

Additionally, orders will be passed onto Gallaghers from the application using e-mail rather than writing to a database. Using e-mail in this fashion is quite an effective method of managing an online order system for a small business in which volume is relatively low and turnaround is very quick. It also saves writing and managing a front end for a database.

## Planning the Gallaghers Application

The purpose of the Gallaghers application is to provide an online ordering vehicle for customers of the Gallaghers Gourmet catering store. The application is associated with the Gallaghers Gourmet website and the user has the opportunity to navigate between the site and the application when online. The structure of the application is shown in Figure 16.1.

Data is stored in two XML documents, one for the food items (menu.xml) and one for the drinks (drinks.xml). Additionally, two style sheets will be created to transform this data for presentation (menuStyle.xslt and drinkStyle.xslt).

Orders are placed on the Online Order page (WebForm1.aspx). Details are confirmed on the Order Details page (WebForm2.aspx), and code on this page handles the task of e-mailing the order to Gallaghers. Once the order is sent, the process is confirmed using the Order Confirmation page (WebForm3.aspx).

Each of these Web Forms carries a navigation bar pointing to the rest of the Gallaghers website. We will build one page of this site (the About page, WebForm4.aspx) to illustrate the practical use of the XML Web control and the XSLT style sheets.

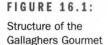

FIGURE 16.1:

Structure of the
Gallaghers Gourmet
application

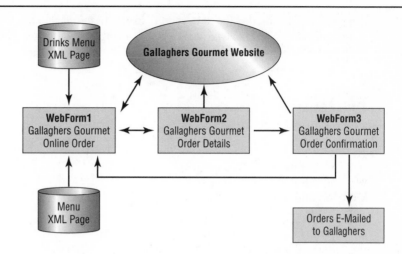

To help maximize performance, fragment and output caching will be used throughout where appropriate. Static areas such as the headings will be bundled into their own user controls (ASCX pages) to facilitate this. We will also disable ViewState and make use of the HTML controls as much as possible.

Layout on the Web Forms will be managed using a table structure provided by the relevant HTML control. WebForm1 will also feature the use of the AdRotator control to cycle a range of specials. An additional XML page will need to be built for use with this control (Ads.xml). We will use structured exception handling and the validation controls where appropriate.

Finally, information entered by the user will be stored in an array and managed as a single session variable.

## Creating the XML Data Files

The first step to building the Gallaghers application is to create the XML data and the XSLT transformation files. These files could be created using a text editor such as Notepad or using the Visual Studio .NET IDE. For this example, we will use Visual Studio.

Create a new web project (Visual Basic) in Visual Studio .NET and name it Gallaghers. From the Project menu, choose Add New Item and select the XML File template from the dialog box. Name it menu.xml and click OK.

In XML code view for the menu.xml page, delete the existing code skeleton and add the code from Listing 16.1.

---

**TIP**    A quick way of creating the XML code is to create the basic XML structure (without data) and then switch to the Data View window (using the tab at the bottom of the Designer window) and add the data from here. Figure 16.2 illustrates the Data View window.

---

**Listing 16.1**        *menu.xml*

```xml
<?xml version="1.0" ?>
<menu>
    <menuItem id="1">
        <food>Ploughman's Lunch</food>
        <price>5.20</price>
    </menuItem>
    <menuItem id="2">
        <food>Hot 'n Tasty</food>
        <price>5.50</price>
    </menuItem>
    <menuItem id="3">
        <food>Fruit Platter</food>
        <price>6.20</price>
    </menuItem>
    <menuItem id="4">
        <food>Gourmet Sandwiches</food>
        <price>5.50</price>
    </menuItem>
    <menuItem id="5">
        <food>Berry Pie</food>
        <price>4.50</price>
    </menuItem>
</menu>
```

---

Listing 16.1 is a simple XML-based database that includes details of the items on the Gallaghers food menu. We will create the drinks menu separately.

---

**FIGURE 16.2:**

The Data View window for XML files

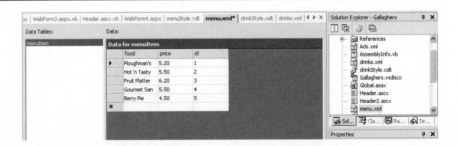

Save the file once you have completed it and create a new XML file in the project (using Project ➤ Add New Item) titled drinks.xml.

Delete the code skeleton from drinks.xml and add the code from Listing 16.2. Again you could use the Data View window to enter the data.

---

**Listing 16.2**    *drinks.xml*

```xml
<?xml version="1.0" encoding="utf-8" ?>
<drinks>
    <drinkItem id="1">
        <drink>Cola</drink>
        <drinkPrice>1</drinkPrice>
    </drinkItem>
    <drinkItem id="2">
        <drink>Orange</drink>
        <drinkPrice>1</drinkPrice>
    </drinkItem>
    <drinkItem id ="3">
        <drink>Fruit Juice</drink>
        <drinkPrice>1</drinkPrice>
    </drinkItem>
    <drinkItem id = "4">
        <drink>Soda</drink>
        <drinkPrice>1</drinkPrice>
    </drinkItem>
    <drinkItem id = "5">
        <drink>Mineral Water</drink>
        <drinkPrice>1</drinkPrice>
    </drinkItem>
</drinks>
```

---

This is a simple XML-based database containing the Drinks menu for Gallaghers. At this point, save the project.

Next, we will create the two style sheets to transform the XML data. Listing 16.3 provides the code for the style sheet to transform the menu.xml data. From the Project menu, select Add New Item and choose the XSLT File template. Name the page menuStyle.xslt. Delete the autogenerated code skeleton and add the code from Listing 16.3.

---

**Listing 16.3**    *menuStyle.xslt*

```xml
<?xml version="1.0" ?>
<xsl:stylesheet version="1.0" xmlns:xsl="http://www.w3.org/1999/XSL/Transform">
<xsl:template match="/">
<html>
<body>
<table border="0" cellpadding="5">
<tr>
```

```
<td colspan="2" align="center" bgcolor="khaki"><font _
 color="firebrick"><h2><i>Menu</i></h2></font></td>
</tr>
<xsl:for-each select="menu/menuItem">
<tr>
<td bgcolor="cornsilk">
<b><xsl:value-of select="food" /></b>
</td>
<td bgcolor="cornsilk"><b>$<xsl:value-of select="price" _
 /></b>
</td>
</tr>
</xsl:for-each>
</table>
</body>
</html>
</xsl:template>
</xsl:stylesheet>
```

The purpose of this code is to present the menu data in an HTML table formatted with an appropriate heading and back-colored cells. The table layout can be matched by the style sheet for the drinks.xml data and rendered side-by-side; they'll effectively make a single table.

Create another XSLT page from the Project menu and name it drinkStyle.xslt. Delete the existing code skeleton and add the code from Listing 16.4.

### Listing 16.4    *drinkStyle.xslt*

```
<?xml version="1.0" ?>
<xsl:stylesheet version="1.0" xmlns:xsl="http://www.w3.org/1999/XSL/Transform">
<xsl:template match="/">
<html>
<body>
<table border="0" cellpadding="5">
<tr>
<td colspan="2" align="center" bgcolor="khaki"><font _
 color="firebrick"><h2><i>Drinks</i></h2></font></td>
</tr>
<xsl:for-each select="drinks/drinkItem">
<tr>
<td bgcolor="cornsilk">
<b><xsl:value-of select="drink" /></b>
</td>
<td bgcolor="cornsilk"><b>$<xsl:value-of _
 select="drinkPrice" /></b></td>
</tr>
</xsl:for-each>
</table>
```

```
</body>
</html>
</xsl:template>
</xsl:stylesheet>
```

Again, this code presents the data from drinks.xml in a simple HTML table that is rendered with a heading and back-colored cells. Save the project. We have one more XML file to create, which we will look at in the next section.

# The AdRotator Control

Before we move onto creating the actual Web Forms for this project, there is one more XML page to create. We will use the AdRotator control to rotate a pair of images featuring current specials. The control works by randomly inserting an image from a predefined list into the Web Form each time it is called. The relative importance, or weight, of an image can be defined, ensuring that more heavily weighted images appear more often. You can also define group membership for various images and display only members of certain groups when required. The control is described in more detail in Chapter 22, "Targeting Mobile Devices." However, we will also illustrate its use in this example. The control is effectively configured using an XML file. This allows for runtime management of the control.

Listing 16.5 gives the code for an XML page to manage an AdRotator control. Add an XML file to the project by selecting Add New Item from the Project menu and choosing the XML File template. Name the file Ads.xml. Delete the existing code skeleton and add the code from Listing 16.5. Again, you can use the Data view from the Design surface to more easily (and quickly) add the data to the basic framework if you wish.

**Listing 16.5**    *Ads.xml*

```
<?xml version="1.0" ?>
<Advertisements>
    <Ad>
        <ImageUrl>http://localhost/Gallaghers/Images/_
image1.jpg</ImageUrl>
        <NavigateUrl></NavigateUrl>
        <AlternateText>Hot 'n Tasty</AlternateText>
        <KeywordFilter>Special</KeywordFilter>
        <Impressions>80</Impressions>
    </Ad>
    <Ad>
        <ImageUrl>http://localhost/Gallaghers/Images/_
image2.jpg</ImageUrl>
        <NavigateUrl></NavigateUrl>
```

```
        <AlternateText>Cherry pie</AlternateText>
        <KeywordFilter>Special</KeywordFilter>
        <Impressions>80</Impressions>
    </Ad>
 </Advertisements>
```

As you may have guessed from examining this code, we are going to have to create a couple of images for use as our advertisements. The framework itself is fairly straightforward. The <ImageUrl> tag is used to describe the location of the image to be used in the advertisement. The <NavigateUrl> tag can be used to provide an active link an appropriate page or site (which in the case of third-party advertising may be the third-party website). The <AlternativeText> tag provides a text substitute if the image cannot be displayed. The <KeywordFilter> tag provides a mechanism for sorting different advertisements, and the <Impressions> tag enables different weights to be applied to the advertisements to specify the "randomness" with which they appear. If the weights are the same (as they are in this case), each advertisement should have an equal chance of being displayed on any given server call.

Save the file. Next you will need to create the advertisement images for use by the control. Figures 16.3 and 16.4 show the images that we created for this project using clip art from the Microsoft Office folder.

**FIGURE 16.3:**

Advertisement1 for the Gallaghers application

**FIGURE 16.4:**

Advertisement2 for the Gallaghers application

Save the files as JPEG images (Image1.jpg and Image2.jpg). Save the two images to an Images folder in the application directory for Gallaghers (typically, C:\Inetpub\wwwroot\ Gallaghers). The dimensions of both images are 600px by 60px.

For the moment, we will simply create the Ads.xml file and its associated images. We will see in the section "Developing WebForm1" how to make use of the AdRotator control itself.

## Building the User Controls

We will employ two Web User controls in this application. Essentially, the user controls will be bundled heading components that can be fragment-cached and reused across forms. You will also see how to quickly confirm that fragment caching is in fact working for the application.

## Web User Control 1: *Header.ascx*

From the Project menu, select Add Web User Control and name the new control `Header.ascx`.

Switch to HTML view and add the following directive to the top of the page:

```
<%@ OutputCache Duration="60" VaryByParam="None" %>
```

This sets up fragment caching for when the control is used in a dynamic form that is not cached. The cache duration is 60 seconds. Switch back to Design view.

From the HTML controls, drag a Grid Layout Panel control onto the page. Set its Width attribute to 580px and Height to 135px. You can do this by dragging the handles in the visual designer or by editing the Style attribute in the Properties window or directly in HTML view.

Drag an HTML Label control to the Grid Layout Panel. Set the Label control's Style attribute and text content as indicated in the following code snippet:

```
<DIV style="DISPLAY: inline; FONT-WEIGHT: bold; _
  FONT-SIZE: xx-large; Z-INDEX: 103; LEFT: 23px; _
  WIDTH: 426px; COLOR: firebrick; _
  FONT-STYLE: italic; POSITION: absolute; TOP: 23px; _
  HEIGHT: 57px" ms_positioning="FlowLayout"> _
Gallaghers Gourmet</DIV>
```

Again you can do this by using the Build Style option from the right-click context menu on the control itself or by editing the Style attribute in the Properties window or directly in HTML view. You can add the text content (Gallaghers Gourmet) by editing the HTML or by clicking once in the control to enter Text Edit mode and typing the text directly.

Add an HTML Image control to the Grid Layout Panel. Position it to the right of the Gallaghers heading and attach it to the same image that you used back in the Chapter 6 example. (It may make some sense to copy the image and drop it into the `Images` folder in the root Gallaghers application directory. In this example, we have again gone with some clip art from Microsoft Office. Adjust the Style attribute appropriately. The final code in HTML view should look something like the following snippet:

```
<DIV style="WIDTH: 580px; POSITION: relative; _
  HEIGHT: 135px" ms_positioning="GridLayout"> _
<IMG style="Z-INDEX: 101; LEFT: 473px; _
  POSITION: absolute; TOP: 1px" height="83" _
  alt="" src="images/FD00306_.WMF" width="105"></DIV>
```

Directly under the Gallaghers heading, we will place the address and e-mail details. Unlike in earlier versions of this application, we will split this so that the e-mail address can be a mailto: link.

Although the address can be placed in an HTML Label control, we found that getting accurate placement on the page to align with the HyperLink control was best done using the

Label control from the Web Forms Toolbox. Drag a Label and a HyperLink control from the Web Forms Toolbox to the page, position them underneath the Gallaghers heading, and set their properties as indicated:

| Control | Property | Value |
| --- | --- | --- |
| Label | Font: Bold | True |
| | Font: Overline | True |
| | Font: Size | X-Small |
| | Text | 10 Rocky Rd, RockVille. Telephone: 555 555, Email: |
| | EnableViewState | False |
| | Width | 290px |
| | ID | LabelAddress |
| HyperLink | Font: Bold | True |
| | Font: Overline | True |
| | Font: Size | X-Small |
| | ForeColor | Black |
| | Text | gallaghers@gallaghers.gag |
| | EnableViewState | False |
| | ID | HyperLinkEmail |
| | NavigateUrl | mailto:gallaghers@gallaghers.gag |

The main thing to note with these controls is that we have turned off ViewState. This is purely for performance reasons. We don't need to use ViewState with this control and might as well remove whatever burden (no matter how nominal) it imposes.

The last control to add is the HTML Label containing the instructions for using the site. Switch back to the HTML controls and add an HTML Label control to the Grid Layout control directly under the previous controls. Using your preferred method (in the Properties window, directly in HTML view, or right-clicking and choosing Build Style), adjust the Style attribute and text content to match the following code snippet:

```
  <DIV style="DISPLAY: inline; Z-INDEX: 102; LEFT: 25px;_
 WIDTH: 514px; COLOR: firebrick; POSITION: absolute;_
 TOP: 107px; HEIGHT: 19px" ms_positioning="FlowLayout">_
For immediate delivery to your door, simply fill out your details and order from
our famous selection below. Then click the Submit button to
 check your order details.</DIV>
```

Figure 16.5 illustrates how the final setup of the user control should look. Listing 16.6 contains the complete code listing for the `Header.ascx` page.

**FIGURE 16.5:**

Layout for the Header `.ascx` Web User control

---

**Listing 16.6**      **Code for the *Header.ascx* Page**

```
<%@ Control Language="vb" AutoEventWireup="false" _
Codebehind="Header.ascx.vb" _
Inherits="Gallaghers.Header" TargetSchema= _
"http://schemas.microsoft.com/intellisense/ie5" _
enableViewState="False"%>
<%@ OutputCache Duration="60" VaryByParam="None" %>
<asp:hyperlink id="HyperLinkEmail" style="Z-INDEX: 107; _
LEFT: 314px; POSITION: absolute; TOP: 81px" _
ForeColor="Black" runat="server" Font-Size="X-Small" _
Font-Bold="True" Font-Overline="True" _
NavigateUrl="mailto:gallaghers@gallaghers.gag" _
EnableViewState="False">gallaghers@gallaghers.gag _
</asp:hyperlink><asp:label id="LabelAddress" _
style="Z-INDEX: 104; LEFT: 26px; POSITION: absolute; _
TOP: 81px" Width="290px" runat="server" _
Font-Size="X-Small" Font-Bold="True" _
Font-Overline="True" EnableViewState="False"> _
10 Rocky Rd, RockVille. Telephone: 555 555, _
Email:</asp:label>
<DIV style="WIDTH: 580px; POSITION: relative; _
HEIGHT: 135px" ms_positioning="GridLayout"> _
<IMG style="Z-INDEX: 101; LEFT: 473px; _
POSITION: absolute; TOP: 1px" height="83" _
alt="" src="images/FD00306_.WMF" width="105"> _
</DIV>
<DIV style="DISPLAY: inline; Z-INDEX: 102; LEFT: 25px; _
WIDTH: 514px; COLOR: firebrick; POSITION: absolute; _
TOP: 107px; HEIGHT: 19px" _
ms_positioning="FlowLayout"> _
For
    immediate delivery to your door, simply fill out your details and order from
    our famous selection below. Then click the Submit button to check your order
    details.</DIV>
```

```
<DIV style="DISPLAY: inline; FONT-WEIGHT: bold; _
  FONT-SIZE: xx-large; Z-INDEX: 103; LEFT: 23px; _
  WIDTH: 426px; COLOR: firebrick; FONT-STYLE: italic; _
  POSITION: absolute; TOP: 23px; HEIGHT: 57px" _
  ms_positioning="FlowLayout">Gallaghers _
    Gourmet</DIV>
```

Finally, disable enableViewState for the document (set it to False) in the Properties window for Document. Save the user control.

---

If you have been moving controls around a fair bit in the graphical designer window, it may be worth making a final check of the code in HTML view before moving on to something else. Visual Studio can create a lot of "orphan" <p> tags that have to be manually cleaned up (particularly when a lot of changes have been made).

For the next task, you will need to select the entire contents of the Header.ascx page, uncheck the Label control containing the instructions, and copy them to the Clipboard.

## Web User Control 2: *Header2.ascx*

From the Project menu, select Add Web User Control and name it Header2.ascx.

Paste the copied content of the Header.ascx control to the page. Tidy it up so that it appears as in Figure 16.6.

---

**FIGURE 16.6:**

Layout for the
Header2.ascx Web
User control

---

Add an Output Cache directive to the page as we did earlier for the Header.ascx Web User control. Set the enableViewState property for the page to False. Listing 16.7 gives the code for this page.

---

**Listing 16.7**    **Code for the *Header2.ascx* Page**

```
<%@ Control Language="vb" AutoEventWireup="false" _
  Codebehind="Header2.ascx.vb" _
  Inherits="Gallaghers.Header2" _
```

```
    TargetSchema="http://schemas.microsoft.com/_
    intellisense/ie5" enableViewState="False"%>
    <%@ OutputCache Duration="60" VaryByParam="None" %>
    <DIV style="WIDTH: 578px; POSITION: relative; _
     HEIGHT: 99px" ms_positioning="GridLayout"> _
    <IMG style="Z-INDEX: 101; LEFT: 473px; _
     POSITION: absolute; TOP: 1px" height="83" _
     alt="" src="images/FD00306_.WMF" width="105">
       <DIV style="DISPLAY: inline; FONT-WEIGHT: bold; _
    FONT-SIZE: xx-large; Z-INDEX: 102; LEFT: 31px; _
    WIDTH: 426px; COLOR: firebrick; _
    FONT-STYLE: italic; POSITION: absolute; _
    TOP: 14px; HEIGHT: 57px" ms_positioning="FlowLayout"> _
    Gallaghers Gourmet</DIV>
       <asp:Label id="LabelAddress" style="Z-INDEX: 103; _
    LEFT: 32px; POSITION: absolute; TOP: 75px" _
    EnableViewState="False" Font-Overline="True" _
    Font-Bold="True" Font-Size="X-Small" runat="server" _
    Width="290px">10 Rocky Rd, RockVille. _
    Telephone: 555 555, Email:</asp:Label>
       <asp:hyperlink id="HyperLinkEmail" style="Z-INDEX: 104; _
    LEFT: 319px; POSITION: absolute; TOP: 75px" _
    EnableViewState="False" _
    NavigateUrl="mailto:gallaghers@gallaghers.gag" _
    Font-Overline="True" Font-Bold="True" _
    Font-Size="X-Small" runat="server" _
    ForeColor="Black"> _
    gallaghers@gallaghers.gag</asp:hyperlink></DIV>
```

Save the page. In the next section, you will see how to quickly show that fragment caching is working as expected for your application.

## Demonstrating Fragment Caching

We can easily demonstrate fragment caching at work by adding some dynamic content to both of the Web User controls and then disabling output caching on one of the user controls. The controls can then be dropped onto a Web Form, which is then compiled and run and the respective outputs of the Web User controls compared.

To demonstrate this here, set the LabelAddress Text property on both controls to programmatically reflect the current time and then disable fragment caching for the Header2 control.

In both controls, double-click somewhere on the page to enter Code Behind. Add the following line to the Page_Load event handler for each control:

```
LabelAddress.Text = DateTime.Now.Second.ToString()
```

This will write the current number of seconds from the computer clock to the label's text property. Delete the output cache directive from the Header2 control (in HTML view).

Tab to the blank WebForm1 and drop a copy of both controls (from the Solution Explorer) onto the form. Compile and run the project.

The same number of seconds should be displayed for both controls. Wait a few seconds and refresh the page. The Header control (which is fragment-cached) shouldn't change, but the Header2 should be updated. This is illustrated in Figure 16.7. If you wait a minute or so for the cache to expire and hit refresh again, the times should be back in synch.

**FIGURE 16.7:**

Illustrating the use of fragment caching with the Web User controls

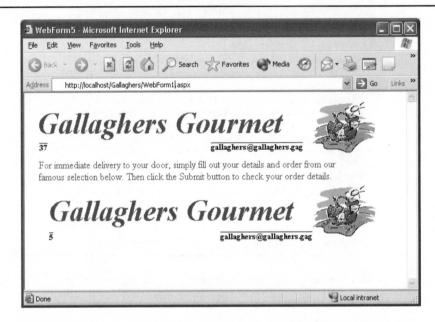

To continue building the project, delete the two user controls from WebForm1, add the output cache directive back into Header2, and delete the line of code you added to the Page_ Load events for the two controls.

## Creating a Template Form

The tried-and-true method of laying out web pages is to use a table. Although ASP.NET sites can be developed using the grid layout properties of the various container controls, using a table can give you the granular level of layout control you need when using a mix of HTML, Web User, and Web Form controls. It also enables the controls on the form to be dynamically relocated at runtime according to the size of controls such as CheckBoxLists and RadioButtonLists.

It is also useful to create a template form for use as a kind of scratch pad for creating and testing various layouts and for holding layouts that you may want to reuse across the project. You can, of course, use the Clipboard Ring for holding stuff that you wish to reuse, but you lose it when you quit out of the project.

**TIP**
You can quickly view any test layouts from the template form by right-clicking the form and choosing the View in Browser option. This will display the current form in your browser without compiling the whole project (although it may ask you whether you wish to save the current file before progressing, which we strongly recommend).

Once the project is complete, you can exclude the template from the project without actually deleting it by right-clicking the template file in Solution Explorer and choosing the Exclude from Project option. The file remains in the root application directory for the project and can be added in again later if necessary by choosing the Add Existing Item option.

To set up the template form, choose Add Web Form from the Project menu and name the new Web Form Template.aspx.

From the HTML controls, drag a Table control onto the form. In the Properties window for the Table, set the Style property to the following:

```
Z-INDEX: 101; LEFT: 34px; WIDTH: 608px; _
    POSITION: absolute; TOP: 8px; HEIGHT: 103px
```

Switch to HTML view and edit the <row> and <td> tags of the table as shown in Listing 16.8.

**Listing 16.8**    **Table Framework for *Template.aspx***

```
<TABLE id="Table1" style="Z-INDEX: 101; LEFT: 34px; _
WIDTH: 608px; POSITION: absolute; TOP: 8px; HEIGHT: 103px" _
cellSpacing="1" cellPadding="1" width="609" border="0">
    <TR>
        <TD style="HEIGHT: 22px" colSpan="2"></TD>
    </TR>
    <TR>
        <TD colSpan="2"></TD>
    </TR>
    <TR>
        <TD colSpan="2"></TD>
    </TR>
    <TR>
        <TD colSpan="2"></TD>
    </TR>
    <TR>
        <TD></TD>
        <TD></TD>
```

```
          </TR>
          <TR>
              <TD colSpan="2"></TD>
          </TR>
          <TR>
              <TD colSpan="2" align="middle"></TD>
          </TR>
          <TR>
              <TD colSpan="2"></TD>
          </TR>
          <TR>
              <TD align="middle" colSpan="2"></TD>
          </TR>
      </TABLE>
```

This creates a nine-row table in which the fifth row has two cells and the remaining rows all have a single cell.

**TIP**   If you copy HTML code in from an external source such as Word, use the Paste as HTML option under the Edit menu in the Visual Studio .NET IDE. This pastes the HTML without any extraneous formatting.

Switch back to Design view and drag a horizontal rule (from the HTML controls) to the second row of the table. Set the properties as shown:

| Property | Value |
| --- | --- |
| color | #b22222 (Firebrick) |
| noshade: | True |
| size | 3 |
| width | 600 |

In HTML view, the code for the <hr> tag should appear as follows:

```
<HR width="600" color="firebrick" noShade SIZE="3">
```

Copy and paste the horizontal rule into rows 4, 6, and 8. Drag a Label control (from the HTML controls) into the bottom row. Switch to HTML view and edit the <DIV> tag as follows:

```
<DIV style="DISPLAY: inline; WIDTH: 456px; _
 COLOR: firebrick; HEIGHT: 28px" align="center" _
 ms_positioning="FlowLayout">
      <address> Copyright 2002: Gallaghers Gourmet.
 Site last updated October 2002</address>
 </DIV>
```

Note that we have added an <address> tag to the listing.

Add five HyperLink controls from the Web Forms Toolbox to the seventh row of the table. Set their properties as outlined:

| Control | Property | Value |
| --- | --- | --- |
| HyperLink1 | ForeColor | Navy |
| | Text | Email Gallaghers |
| | EnableViewState | false |
| | Width | 113px |
| | ID | HyperlinkEmail |
| | NavigateUrl | mailto:gallaghers@gallaghers.gag |
| HyperLink2 | ForeColor | Navy |
| | Text | About Gallaghers |
| | EnableViewState | false |
| | Width | 125px |
| | ID | HyperlinkAbout |
| | NavigateUrl | WebForm4.aspx |
| HyperLink3 | ForeColor | Navy |
| | Text | Our Friendly Staff |
| | EnableViewState | false |
| | Width | 125px |
| | ID | HyperlinkStaff |
| | NavigateUrl | Staff.htm |
| HyperLink4 | ForeColor | Navy |
| | Text | Virtual Coffee |
| | EnableViewState | false |
| | Width | 113px |
| | ID | HyperlinkCoffee |
| | NavigateUrl | Coffee.htm |

| Control | Property | Value |
|---|---|---|
| HyperLink5 | ForeColor | Navy |
|  | Text | Order a Meal |
|  | EnableViewState | false |
|  | Width | 113px |
|  | ID | HyperlinkOrder |
|  | NavigateUrl | WebForm1.aspx |

In the actual application, we will build only the components accessed by HyperLink2 and HyperLink5 (Web Form 4 and Web Form 1, respectively). The purpose of the links is to provide wider access to the main Gallaghers site. If we were to develop the site further, the Staff link is fairly self-explanatory, and the Virtual Coffee link might be used to access a chat application or something similar. Figure 16.8 shows how the completed table will appear in the designer.

**FIGURE 16.8:**

Completed table in
`Template.aspx`

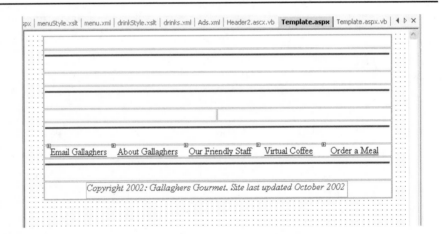

## Additional Page Options in Visual Studio .NET

Although we don't directly use any in the Gallaghers example, there are a number of other file types and page options that are available for use in web applications built using .NET. Code skeletons, tools, and templates for all of these options can be found through the Add New Item dialog box accessed from the Project menu.

The alternatives include Cascading Style Sheets (CSS), HTML pages, Framesets, and text files, among others. In the following sections, we will briefly look at a few of these additional options.

## Cascading Style Sheets

When you first create a Web Application project, a default style sheet is created. This can be found in the Solution Explorer as `Styles.css`. Selecting the `Styles.css` file in Solution Explorer opens the file in the style sheet editor format, as shown in Figure 16.9.

**FIGURE 16.9:**

The CSS Editor in Visual Studio .NET

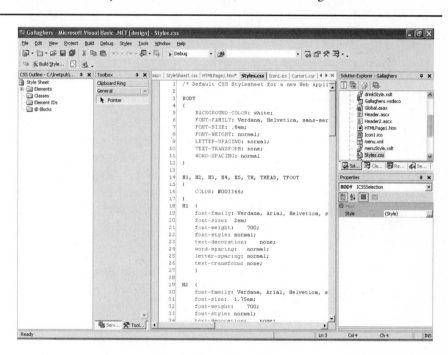

You can make global changes to your application by applying this style sheet (`Styles.css`) to each of your pages and editing it once. Simply drag the style sheet reference from Solution Explorer to any of your application's pages to apply it. This creates the following line of code inside the <head> tags of your page:

```
<LINK href="Styles.css" type="text/css" rel="stylesheet">
```

You can delete the reference to the style sheet by opening the page in HTML view and removing the line of code.

Additionally, you can create your own style sheets by selecting the Style Sheet template from the Add New Item dialog box accessed via the Project menu. You can use these style sheets on their own or together with the Style.css sheet to override particular default properties for a given page.

For example, create a new style sheet and name it StyleSheet1.css (the default). This opens the style sheet editor with a simple skeleton for the <body> tag. Add the code from Listing 16.9 to the editor and save the style sheet. We will experiment with this style sheet in the next section.

---

**Listing 16.9**    **Code for *StyleSheet1.css***

```
body
{BACKGROUND-COLOR: blue;}

h1
{ text-align:center; color:red; }
```

---

## HTML Pages

If you wish to work with plain vanilla HTML, you can add an HTML page (or three or four) to your project. This option can be selected directly from the Project menu or via the Add New Item option. You can use the HTML controls with such pages, but if you want to do more (such as use server-side controls), you'll be better off starting with a Web Form. You can add all the necessary code to the HTML page to extend it, but this effectively gives you what would have been autogenerated by the Web Form template.

We'll use an HTML page here to demonstrate the style sheet created in the previous section.

Select Add HTML Page from the Project menu. This will create HTMLPage1.htm (the default name). Switch to HTML view and add the following code snippet to the <body> tag.

```
<body MS_POSITIONING="GridLayout">
    <h1>Hello</h1>
</body>
```

Switch back to the Design view. You should see a large, black "Hello" displayed in the upper-left corner of the page.

Drag the Styles.css reference from the Solution Explorer onto the page. This changes the color and font of the text.

Drag the StyleSheet1.css that we created earlier to the page. This centers the text, changes its color, and changes the color of the page. If you switch back to HTML view, you will see that the reference to StyleSheet1.css appears after the reference to Styles.css, effectively applying its style attributes over the top of Styles.css. Listing 16.10 contains the full ASPX code for this example and illustrates the juxtaposition of the style sheet reference tags.

**Listing 16.10**    **Full ASPX Code for CSS Style Sheet Example**

```
<!DOCTYPE HTML PUBLIC "-//W3C//DTD HTML 4.0 _
 Transitional//EN">
<html>
   <head>
      <title>HTMLPage1</title>
      <meta name="vs_defaultClientScript" _
content="JavaScript">
      <meta name="vs_targetSchema" _
content="http://schemas.microsoft.com/intellisense/ie5">
      <meta name="GENERATOR" content="Microsoft Visual _
Studio.NET 7.0">
      <meta name="ProgId" content="VisualStudio.HTML">
      <meta name="Originator" content="Microsoft Visual _
Studio.NET 7.0">
      <LINK href="Styles.css" type="text/css" _
rel="stylesheet">
      <LINK href="StyleSheet1.css" type="text/css" _
rel="stylesheet">
   </head>
   <body MS_POSITIONING="GridLayout">
      <h1>Hello</h1>
   </body>
</html>
```

## Framesets

You can use the Frameset template to create a frameset for laying out a web page or website. When you choose this as an option, you are also given a choice as to the structure and layout of the frameset, as shown in Figure 16.10.

**FIGURE 16.10:**

The Select a Frameset Template dialog box

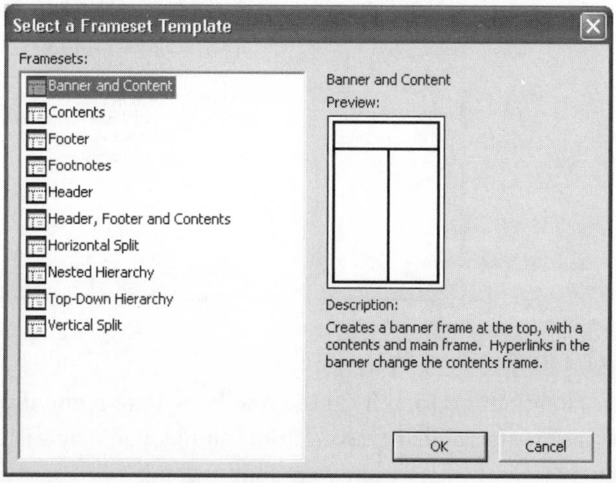

Once you have chosen your template, you need to go into HTML view and add references to the pages that you wish to use in the various frames in your set. These are simply added directly into the code skeleton that is provided and can be added as ASPX or HTML pages. The following code snippet illustrates how the <frameset> tag may end up looking after references have been added to Banner.aspx (a banner page), WebForm1.aspx (used as the main page), and Contents.html (the contents page):

```
<frameset rows="83,80%">
        <frame name="banner" src="Banner.aspx" _
  scrolling="no" noresize>
      <frameset cols="150,*">
          <frame name="contents" src="Contents.html">
          <frame name="main" src="WebForm1.aspx">
      </frameset>
```

Additionally, in this example, you would need to add the following tag to the <head> area of the Contents.html page:

```
<base target="main">
```

Figure 16.11 illustrates how a frameset may look using some of the elements of the yet to be completed Gallaghers Gourmet website.

**FIGURE 16.11:**

Example frameset

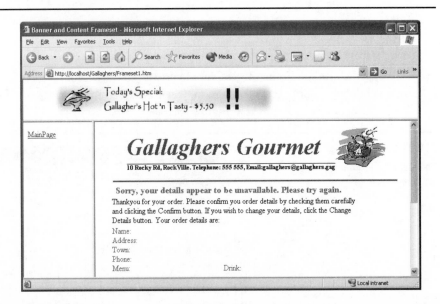

## Text Files

You can use this option from the Add New Item menu if you need to include a text file in the project for a particular reason. For example, you may wish to use it to hold a log of certain events as they occur within your application.

In the next section, we will return to the Gallaghers application and see how to create the various Web Forms used in the project. You may wish to close any of the additional pages that you created in this section because we will not be using them again in the project.

## Developing WebForm1

WebForm1 will be the main data entry dialog for customers wishing to place an order with Gallaghers. We will begin by specifying some of the global properties of the form and then setting up the AdRotator control.

Tab to WebForm1, click on the form, and in the Properties window for DOCUMENT, set the link and vlink properties to #000080 (Navy). Set the title property to Gallaghers Gourmet—Online Order.

Drag an AdRotator control onto WebForm1 from the Web Forms Toolbox. Although the rest of the page will be built into the table that we created earlier, we have kept the AdRotator separate to achieve a minor layout effect, which you will see later. The main property to set for this control is the AdvertisementFile property, which locates the XML file that lists the advertisements we want featured (created earlier). Set the properties for the control as outlined here:

| Property | Value |
|---|---|
| BorderColor | Red |
| BorderStyle | Outset |
| BorderWidth | 4px |
| AdvertisementFile | Ads.xml |
| EnableViewState | False |
| Height | 60px |
| Width | 600px |
| ID | AdRotator1 |

To precisely position the control on the Web Form, switch to HTML view and locate the tag for AdRotator1. Edit its Style attribute to appear as follows:

```
style="Z-INDEX: 104; LEFT: 34px; POSITION: absolute; TOP: 9px"
```

If you run the project at this point and refresh the page a couple of times in your web browser, you should see a cycling of the two advertisements. (It is a random posting, so you will see the same ad several times in a row.)

The next step is to add the table that we created earlier in the `Template.aspx` form. Tab to the `Template.aspx` form and copy the table along with its contents. Return to `WebForm1.aspx` and paste the table below the AdRotator control.

Locate the table precisely by editing the LEFT and TOP attributes of its style property as follows:

```
LEFT: 34px; TOP: 63px;
```

You will also need to add a number of additional rows to the table and edit some of the existing ones. Switch to HTML view and locate the third set of <tr> tags. Edit the tags by removing the `colspan` attribute of the existing <td> tag and add an additional set of <td> tags. The edited cells will each contain a CheckBoxList control that you can either add from the designer or type in as code at this point. The advantage of using the CheckBoxList over the RadioButton-List used in the previous version of Gallaghers is that users will now be able to make multiple selections from the menus. The code for establishing this row is demonstrated in the following snippet:

```
<TR>
    <TD style="WIDTH: 282px" align="middle"> _
  <asp:checkboxlist id="CheckBoxListDrinks" _
runat="server"></asp:checkboxlist></TD>
    <TD align="middle"><asp:checkboxlist _
id="CheckBoxListMenu" runat="server"> _
</asp:checkboxlist></TD>
</TR>
```

Add the code from the following snippet after the second set of <tr> tags in the table (to create a new third row). Note that any tags that we have added are in lowercase, whereas Visual Studio .NET usually (but not always) writes its HTML using uppercase:

```
<tr>
    <td style="WIDTH: 282px">
        <DIV style="DISPLAY: inline; FONT-WEIGHT: bold; _
WIDTH: 70px; HEIGHT: 15px" ms_positioning="FlowLayout">_
Drinks:</DIV>
    </td>
    <td>
        <DIV style="DISPLAY: inline; FONT-WEIGHT: bold; _
WIDTH: 70px; HEIGHT: 15px" ms_positioning="FlowLayout"> Meals:</DIV>
    </td>
</tr>
```

This effectively places an HTML Label control into each of the cells in the new third row.

In HTML view, locate what is now the fifth row (it contains the second horizontal rule). Add another row after this that contains a single cell according to the following code snippet:

```
<tr>
   <td style="HEIGHT: 107px" colSpan="2"></td>
</tr>
```

In the next row (now row 7), identify the first set of <td> tags and edit them as follows:

```
<td style="WIDTH: 282px">
   <DIV style="DISPLAY: inline; WIDTH: 280px; _
HEIGHT: 44px" ms_positioning="FlowLayout"> _
Click the Submit button to check your order _
details:</DIV>
</td>
```

This will effectively place an HTML Label control in this cell. The table should now have 11 rows.

Switch back to Design view. Figure 16.12 illustrates how the Web Form should look at this stage. Note that we have set the table to deliberately overlap the AdRotator control. There will probably be some minor differences between your page layout and the page layout in the figure.

**FIGURE 16.12:**

Progressive view of setting up WebForm1.aspx

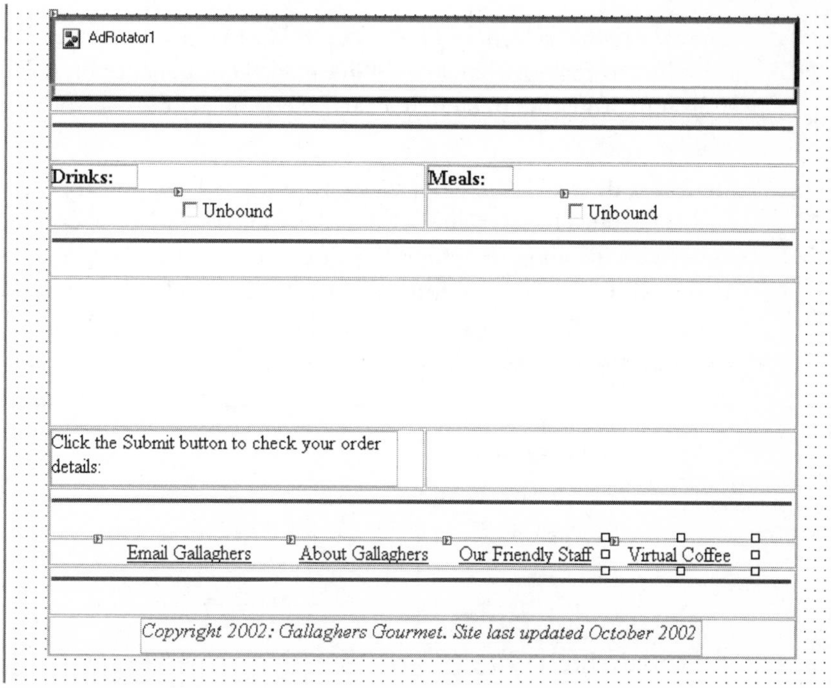

The purpose of overlapping the AdRotator control with the table is so part of the image used in the `Header.ascx` Web User control overlaps the AdRotator to help visually bring the two together on the page. You can determine the layer order of the elements by selecting the table, choosing Order from the Format menu, and clicking the Bring to Front option. Figure 16.13 illustrates the effect we were aiming to achieve.

**FIGURE 16.13:**

The Header Web User control and AdRotator control in WebForm1

You add the Web User control by selecting the `Header.ascx` reference in Solution Explorer and dragging it to the first row of the table. This will set an instance of the user control (Header1) on the form. In the Properties window, set the EnableViewState property to False.

In row 2 of the table, drag a Label control from the Web Forms Toolbox and place it underneath the existing horizontal rule. Give it an ID of LabelError, delete its Text property, and set its Font properties to Bold, Red, and Medium. Set the control's EnableViewState property to False.

In row 6, drag a Grid Layout Panel from the HTML controls into the cell and resize the panel to fill the cell. Place five HTML Label controls, each on a separate row in the cell. From the Web Forms Toolbox, drag four TextBox controls to the cell. Align the TextBoxes against the first, third, fourth, and fifth label controls. Also bring in four RequiredFieldValidator controls. Line these up against the TextBoxes. Drag over a RegularExpressionValidator and place it next to the second label. Figure 16.14 illustrates the layout for the cell.

**FIGURE 16.14:**

Control layout for row 6 of the table in WebForm1

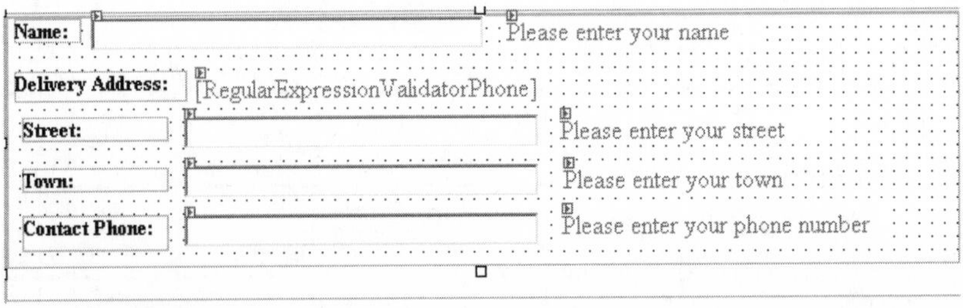

| Name: | | Please enter your name |
|-------|---|---|
| Delivery Address: | [RegularExpressionValidatorPhone] | |
| Street: | | Please enter your street |
| Town: | | Please enter your town |
| Contact Phone: | | Please enter your phone number |

The Property settings for the controls in row 6 are as follows:

| Control | Property | Value |
|---------|----------|-------|
| HTML Label | ID | lblName |
| | Style Attributes | bold; x-small |
| | Text content | "Name:" |
| HTML Label | ID | lblAddress |
| | Style Attributes | bold; x-small |
| | Text content | "Delivery Address:" |
| HTML Label | ID | lblStreet |
| | Style Attributes | bold; x-small |
| | Text content | "Street:" |
| HTML Label | ID | lblTown |
| | Style Attributes | bold; x-small |
| | Text content | "Town:" |
| HTML Label | ID | lblPhone |
| | Style Attributes | bold; x-small |
| | Text content | "Contact Phone:" |
| TextBox | Font: Size | X-Small |
| | Text | <empty> |
| | ID | TextBoxName |
| TextBox | Font: Size | X-Small |
| | Text | <empty> |
| | ID | TextBoxStreet |
| TextBox | Font: Size | X-Small |
| | Text | <empty> |
| | ID | TextBoxTown |
| TextBox | Font: Size | X-Small |
| | Text | <empty> |
| | ID | TextBoxPhone |

| Control | Property | Value |
| --- | --- | --- |
| RequiredFieldValidator | ErrorMessage | "Please enter your name" |
|  | ControlToValidate | TextBoxName |
|  | ID | RequiredFieldvalidatorName |
| RequiredFieldValidator | ErrorMessage | "Please enter your street" |
|  | ControlToValidate | TextBoxStreet |
|  | ID | RequiredFieldValidatorStreet |
| RequiredFieldValidator | ErrorMessage | "Please enter your town" |
|  | ControlToValidate | TextBoxTown |
|  | ID | RequiredFieldvalidatorTown |
| RequiredFieldValidator | ErrorMessage | "Please enter your phone number" |
|  | ControlToValidate | TextBoxPhone |
|  | ID | RequiredFieldvalidatorPhone |
| RegularExpressionValidator | Display | None |
|  | ErrorMessage | "Please enter a valid phone number" |
|  | ControlToValidate | TextBoxPhone |
|  | ValidationExpression | U.S. Phone Number |
|  | ID | RegularExpressionValidator-Phone |

Note that when building this project, we found it a little easier when testing to disable the RegularExpressionValidator control so that we didn't have to keep entering a full phone number!

Next we need to add a Button control (for a command button) and a ValidationSummary control to the second cell in row 7. Drop a Button control in this cell and set its ID to ButtonSubmit and its Text property to Submit. Insert a ValidationSummary control next to the Button. Set the ShowMessageBox property to True and the ShowSummary property to False.

The last step in setting up this form is to delete the Order a Meal link from row 9 because it is obviously not required for WebForm1. Figure 16.15 shows how the completed form appears in Design view.

Save the form and open it in your browser by right-clicking somewhere on the form itself and choosing the View in Browser option. The form is shown in Figure 16.16.

**FIGURE 16.15:**

The complete
WebForm1 in
Design view

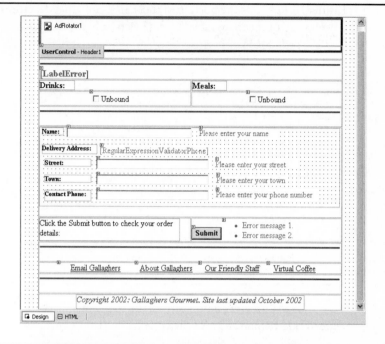

**FIGURE 16.16:**

The complete
WebForm1 open in
Internet Explorer

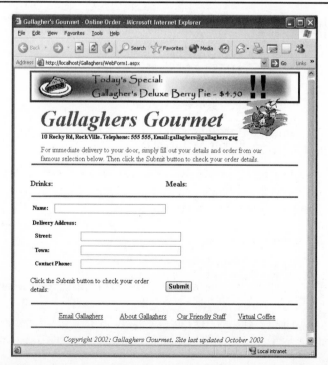

Listing 16.11 shows the portion of the ASPX code that describes the AdRotator control and the beginning of the main table. On the web page for this book, Listing 16.11 contains the full ASPX code for WebForm1. The listing is too large to be practically printed here.

**Listing 16.11      Sample ASPX code for WebForm1**

```
<FORM id="Form1" method="post" runat="server">
  <asp:adrotator id="AdRotator1" style="Z-INDEX: 104; _
  LEFT: 34px; POSITION: absolute; TOP: 9px" runat="server" _
  AdvertisementFile="Ads.xml" BorderColor="Red" _
  BorderStyle="Outset" BorderWidth="4px" Height="60px" _
  Width="600px" EnableViewState="False"></asp:adrotator>
  <TABLE id="Table1" style="Z-INDEX: 105; LEFT: 34px; WIDTH: _
  608px; POSITION: absolute; TOP: 63px; HEIGHT: 384px" _
  cellSpacing="1" cellPadding="1" width="608" border="0">
    <tr> .
      <td colSpan="2"><uc1:header id="Header1" runat="server" _
      EnableViewState="False"></uc1:header></td>
        </tr>
```

Next we need to start adding some code to make it all work. Double-click on WebForm1 to enter Code Behind and add the code from Listing 16.12 to the Page_Load code skeleton.

**Listing 16.12      Code for Page_Load event in WebForm1**

```
Private Sub Page_Load(ByVal sender As System.Object, _
ByVal e As System.EventArgs) Handles MyBase.Load


        If Not IsPostBack Then

            LabelError.Text = ""
            Dim n As Integer
            Dim x As Integer

            Try
                Dim menuXML As System.Xml.XmlDataDocument _
= New System.Xml.XmlDataDocument()
                menuXML.Load(Server.MapPath("menu.xml"))

                Dim drinksXML As _
System.Xml.XmlDataDocument = New _
System.Xml.XmlDataDocument()
                drinksXML.Load(Server.MapPath("drinks.xml"))

                For n = 0 To _
menuXML("menu").ChildNodes.Count - 1
                    CheckBoxListMenu.Items.Add _
```

```
(menuXML("menu").ChildNodes(n).Item("food").InnerText() _
 & " $" & menuXML("menu").ChildNodes(n). _
Item("price").InnerText())
                CheckBoxListMenu.Items(n).Value = _
 menuXML("menu").ChildNodes(n).Item("price"). _
InnerText()
            Next n

            For x = 0 To _
 drinksXML("drinks").ChildNodes.Count - 1
                CheckBoxListDrinks.Items.Add _
(drinksXML("drinks").ChildNodes(x).Item("drink"). _
InnerText() & " $" & drinksXML("drinks").ChildNodes(x). _
Item("drinkPrice").InnerText())
                CheckBoxListDrinks.Items(x).Value = _
 drinksXML("drinks").ChildNodes(x). _
Item("drinkPrice").InnerText()
            Next x

        Catch
            LabelError.Text = "Sorry, our
menu appears to be temporarily unavailable
at the moment.
Please try again."
            End Try
        End If

    End Sub
```

The purpose of this code is to load the contents of the two XML data files (menu.xml and drinks.xml) into the two CheckBoxList controls on WebForm1. The code is managed by a structured exception handler, which catches any problems and posts an appropriate message to the LabelError control.

Taking it from the top, we declare menuXML as an XML Data document and load it with the content from the menu.xml file. This is handled by the following code:

```
Dim menuXML As System.Xml.XmlDataDocument _
 = New System.Xml.XmlDataDocument()
menuXML.Load(Server.MapPath("menu.xml"))
```

We then do the same for drinksXML and the drinks.xml file.

The next step is to loop through the child nodes in menuXML and load the menu data into CheckBoxListMenu. Additionally, the prices are loaded as Values in the CheckBoxListMenu and are displayed as part of the text string for each item:

```
For n = 0 To menuXML("menu").ChildNodes.Count - 1

  CheckBoxListMenu.Items.Add _
(menuXML("menu").ChildNodes(n).Item("food").InnerText() _
```

```
    & " $" & menuXML("menu").ChildNodes(n). _
  Item("price").InnerText())

    CheckBoxListMenu.Items(n).Value = _
  menuXML("menu").ChildNodes(n).Item("price"). _
  InnerText()

  Next n
```

The data for drinks is then managed in a similar fashion. We complete the subroutine with the Catch statement for the SEH.

Next we need to add the code for the SubmitButton_click event. Add the code from Listing 16.13 underneath the Page_Load subroutine.

**Listing 16.13**    **SubmitButton_Click for WebForm1**

```
Private Sub ButtonSubmit_Click(ByVal sender As _
  System.Object, ByVal e As System.EventArgs) Handles _
  ButtonSubmit.Click

        Dim menuChoices As String
        Dim menuTotal As Double
        Dim menuItem As ListItem

        menuChoices = ""
        menuTotal = 0

        For Each menuItem In CheckBoxListMenu.Items
            If menuItem.Selected = True Then
                menuChoices = menuChoices & _
  "<BR>" & menuItem.Text
                menuTotal = menuTotal + menuItem.Value
            End If
        Next

        Dim drinkChoices As String
        Dim drinkTotal As Double
        Dim drinkItem As ListItem

        drinkChoices = ""
        drinkTotal = 0
        For Each drinkItem In CheckBoxListDrinks.Items
            If drinkItem.Selected = True Then
                drinkChoices = drinkChoices & "<BR>" & _
  drinkItem.Text
                drinkTotal = drinkTotal + drinkItem.Value
            End If
        Next

        Dim myArray As New ArrayList()
        myArray.Add(TextBoxName.Text)
```

```
        myArray.Add(TextBoxStreet.Text)
        myArray.Add(TextBoxTown.Text)
        myArray.Add(TextBoxPhone.Text)
        myArray.Add(menuChoices)
        myArray.Add(menuTotal)
        myArray.Add(drinkChoices)
        myArray.Add(drinkTotal)

        Session("detailsArray") = myArray

        Response.Redirect("WebForm2.aspx")

    End Sub
```

The purpose of this code is to read through the two CheckBoxLists and build a string for each consisting of the checked items in each list (menuChoices and drinkChoices). We also total up the value of each list into the *menuTotal* and *drinkTotal* variables. This is handled by the following snippet for the menu selections:

```
Dim menuChoices As String
Dim menuTotal As Double
Dim menuItem As ListItem

menuChoices = ""
menuTotal = 0

For Each menuItem In CheckBoxListMenu.Items
   If menuItem.Selected = True Then
      menuChoices = menuChoices &  "<BR>" & menuItem.Text
      menuTotal = menuTotal + menuItem.Value
   End If
Next
```

A similar code block looks after the drink selections.

This information, along with the customer details entered into the TextBox controls, is bundled into an array that is then assigned to a session variable. The application then redirects to the yet-to-be-built WebForm2.aspx. This is handled by the following:

```
Dim myArray As New ArrayList()

myArray.Add(TextBoxName.Text)
myArray.Add(TextBoxStreet.Text)
myArray.Add(TextBoxTown.Text)
myArray.Add(TextBoxPhone.Text)
myArray.Add(menuChoices)
myArray.Add(menuTotal)
myArray.Add(drinkChoices)
myArray.Add(drinkTotal)
```

```
Session("detailsArray") = myArray

Response.Redirect("WebForm2.aspx")
```

Compile and run the page. It should load with the CheckBoxLists filled out. The validation process should work, although the Submit button will generate an error because we have not yet created the WebForm2. Figure 16.17 shows how the running application should look at this stage. In the next section, we will create WebForm2.

**FIGURE 16.17:**

The completed WebForm1 in Internet Explorer

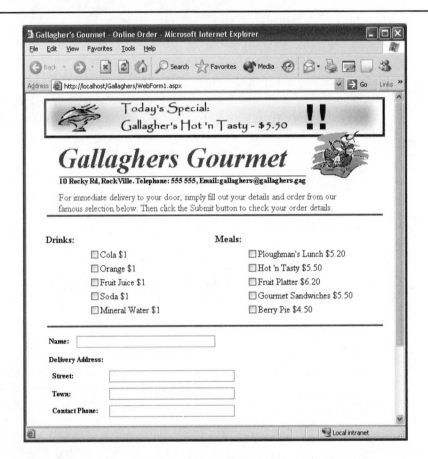

## Developing WebForm2

The purpose of WebForm2 is to provide a confirmation screen for customers to confirm their details and order before finally posting it to Gallaghers. Details of the orders will be automatically e-mailed through to Gallaghers from the application.

From the Project menu, select Add Web Form and leave the new form's name as the default WebForm2.aspx. In the Properties window for DOCUMENT, set the values of the vlink and link attributes to #000080 (navy) and the title to Gallaghers Gourmet—Order Details.

Open the Template.aspx form and copy the table and its contents. Paste the table into WebForm2. In the Properties window for the table, set the following attributes of style:

```
Z-INDEX: 111; LEFT: 34px; WIDTH: 609px; _
  POSITION: absolute; TOP: 9px; HEIGHT: 103px
```

Delete the Order a Meal link from row 7. Drag the Header2.ascx control reference from the Solution Explorer to row 1 of the table. Select the control (Header21) and set its Enable-ViewState property to False.

In row 2, drag a Label control from the Web Forms Toolbox and place it below the horizontal rule. Give it an ID of LabelError, delete its Text property, and set its Font properties to Bold, Red, and Medium. Set the control's EnableViewState property to False.

Into row 3, drag an HTML label and resize the control to fill the cell. Click on the label to enter Text Edit mode and add the following text: **Thank you for your order. Please confirm your order details by checking them carefully and clicking the Confirm button. If you wish to change your details, click the Change Details button. Your order details are:**.

After row 3, you will need to add a new row 4. Switch to HTML view, identify the <tr> tags for row 3, and add the code from Listing 16.14.

---

**Listing 16.14    Code Listing for Row 4 of Table in WebForm2**

```
<tr>
  <td>
    <DIV style="DISPLAY: inline; FONT-WEIGHT: normal; _
WIDTH: 70px; COLOR: firebrick; HEIGHT: 15px" _
ms_positioning="FlowLayout">Name:</DIV>

    <asp:Label id="LabelName" runat="server" _
Width="204px"></asp:Label>

    <br>

    <DIV style="DISPLAY: inline; FONT-WEIGHT: normal; _
WIDTH: 70px; COLOR: firebrick; HEIGHT: 15px" _
ms_positioning="FlowLayout">Address:</DIV>

    <asp:label id="LabelStreet" runat="server" _
Height="9px" Width="127px"></asp:label>

    <br>
```

```
        <DIV style="DISPLAY: inline; FONT-WEIGHT: normal; _
    WIDTH: 70px; COLOR: firebrick; HEIGHT: 15px" _
    ms_positioning="FlowLayout">Town:</DIV>

        <asp:label id="LabelTown" runat="server" _
    Height="9px" Width="127px"></asp:label>

        <br>

        <DIV style="DISPLAY: inline; FONT-WEIGHT: normal; _
    WIDTH: 70px; COLOR: firebrick; HEIGHT: 15px" _
    ms_positioning="FlowLayout">Phone:</DIV>

        <asp:label id="LabelPhone" runat="server" _
    Height="9px" Width="140px"></asp:label>

        <br>

        <DIV style="DISPLAY: inline; FONT-WEIGHT: normal; _
    WIDTH: 71px; COLOR: firebrick; HEIGHT: 19px" _
    ms_positioning="FlowLayout">Menu:</DIV>

        <asp:Label id="LabelMenu" runat="server" _
    Width="164px"></asp:Label>

        <DIV style="DISPLAY: inline; FONT-WEIGHT: normal; _
    WIDTH: 70px; COLOR: firebrick; HEIGHT: 15px" _
    ms_positioning="FlowLayout">Drink:</DIV>

        <asp:Label id="LabelDrink" runat="server" _
    Width="160px"></asp:Label>

    </td>
  </tr>
```

You may find it easier to simply create an extra <tr><td></td></tr> skeleton in HTML view, return to Design view, and add six HTML Label controls and six Label controls from the Web Forms Toolbox. Set the appropriate control properties and then return to HTML view to finalize layout, insert <br> tags, and generally tidy up the HTML. When you're inserting a mix of controls in this fashion, they tend to have a bit of a mind of their own as far as placement and you need to go in manually to sort this out at the end. The final layout of this row is shown in Figure 16.18.

**FIGURE 16.18:**

Layout of controls in row 4 of WebForm2.aspx

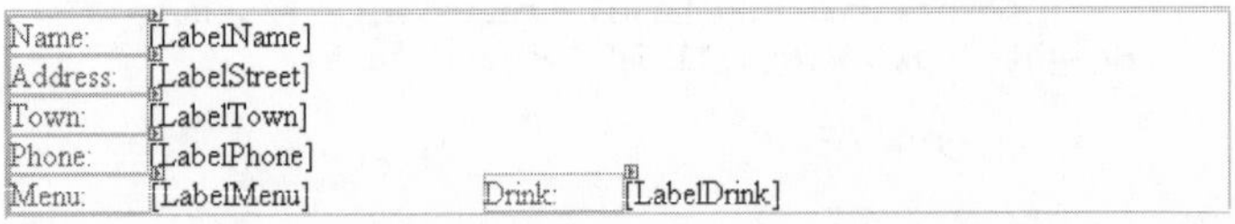

| Name: | [LabelName] | | |
| Address: | [LabelStreet] | | |
| Town: | [LabelTown] | | |
| Phone: | [LabelPhone] | | |
| Menu: | [LabelMenu] | Drink: | [LabelDrink] |

The HTML labels all have their font color set to Firebrick and have been given the relevant text content. The Web Forms Labels all have their ID set to the relevant value and their Text property cleared of content.

In what is now row 6, you will need to delete the second set of <td> tags in HTML view and insert a `colspan=2` attribute in the first set of <td> tags.

Return to Design view and add an HTML Label control. Enter the following text in the Label and set its font color to Firebrick: **The total cost of your order is:**. Immediately next to this control, place a Label from the Web Forms collection. Set its Bold property to True and its ID to LabelPrice. Delete the content from its Text property. The following code snippet illustrates how this should look in HTML view:

```
<TR>
    <TD style="HEIGHT: 13px">
        <DIV style="DISPLAY: inline; WIDTH: 187px; _
  COLOR: firebrick; HEIGHT: 19px" ms_positioning _
="FlowLayout">The total cost of your order is:</DIV>

        <asp:Label id="LabelPrice" runat="server" _
  Width="88px" Font-Bold="True"></asp:Label>
    </TD>
</TR>
```

After row 6, you need to insert another two rows. Do this in HTML view and include the horizontal rule in the first one. In the second row, place an HTML Label. Insert the following text into the Label: **Please check your details. Click Confirm to confirm or Change Details to start again.**

Place the insertion point after the Label and press the Enter key to move down a line. Place a Grid Layout Panel from the HTML controls in the cell. Position two Button controls from the Web Forms collection on the Grid Layout Panel. Set the Bold property of the first button to True, its Text property to Confirm, and its ID to ButtonConfirm. For the second button, set its Text property to Change details and its ID to ButtonChange. Set the EnableViewState property of both buttons to False.

The following code snippet illustrates how the code for these two new rows should appear in HTML view:

```
<TR>
    <TD style="HEIGHT: 34px">
        <HR width="600" color="firebrick" noShade SIZE="3">
    </TD>
</TR>

<tr>
    <td>
        <DIV style="DISPLAY: inline; WIDTH: 525px; _
  HEIGHT: 19px" ms_positioning="FlowLayout"> _
```

```
Please check your details. Click Confirm to _
confirm or Change Details to start again.</DIV>

    <br>
    <br>

    <DIV style="WIDTH: 528px; POSITION: relative; _
HEIGHT: 31px" ms_positioning="GridLayout">

    <asp:button id="ButtonChange" style="Z-INDEX: _
101;  LEFT: 291px; POSITION: absolute; TOP: 0px" _
runat="server" Width="108px" Text="Change Details" _
EnableViewState="False"></asp:button>

    <asp:Button id="ButtonConfirm" style="Z-INDEX: _
102; LEFT: 124px; POSITION: absolute; TOP: 0px" _
runat="server" Width="108px" Font-Bold="True" _
Text="Confirm"></asp:Button></DIV>
    </td>
</tr>
```

Figure 16.19 shows how the completed form should look in Design view. Figure 16.20 shown how the completed form should appear when run in Internet Explorer. Note that Figure 16.20 contains an error message that we still need to build the functionality for.

**FIGURE 16.19:**

The completed WebForm2 in Design view

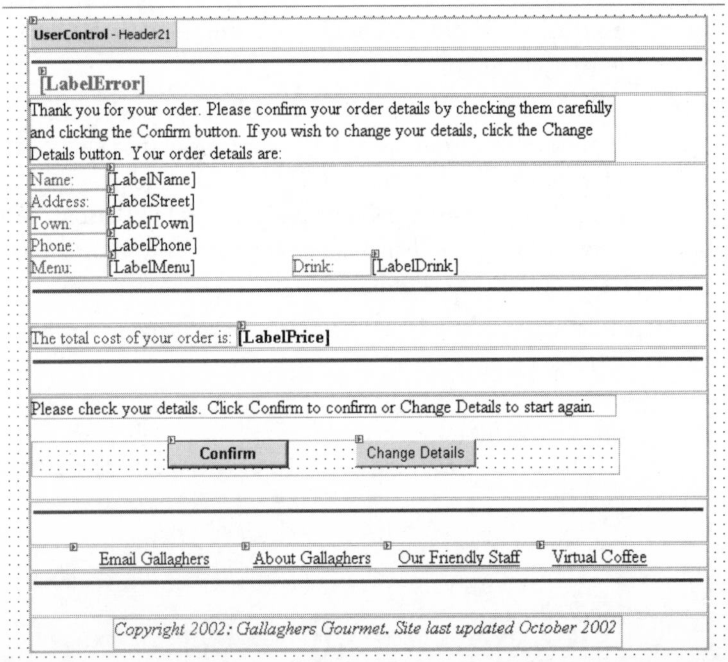

**FIGURE 16.20:**

The completed
WebForm2 in Internet
Explorer

*Gallaghers Gourmet*

10 Rocky Rd, RockVille. Telephone: 555 555, Email:gallaghers@gallaghers.gag

**Sorry, your details appear to be unavailable. Please try again.**

Thank you for your order. Please confirm your order details by checking them carefully
and clicking the Confirm button. If you wish to change your details, click the Change
Details button. Your order details are:

Name:
Address:
Town:
Phone:
Menu:                                                            Drink:

The total cost of your order is:

Please check your details. Click Confirm to confirm or Change Details to start again.

[ **Confirm** ]          [ Change Details ]

Email Gallaghers      About Gallaghers      Our Friendly Staff      Virtual Coffee

*Copyright 2002: Gallaghers Gourmet. Site last updated October 2002*

Double click the somewhere on WebForm2 to enter Code Behind. Add the code from
Listing 16.15 to the Page_Load code skeleton.

**Listing 16.15     Page_Load for WebForm2**

```
Private Sub Page_Load(ByVal sender As _
  System.Object, ByVal e As System.EventArgs) _
  Handles MyBase.Load

Try
          LabelError.Text = ""

          Dim detailsArray As New ArrayList()
          detailsArray = Session("detailsArray")

          LabelName.Text = detailsArray(0)
          LabelStreet.Text = detailsArray(1)
          LabelTown.Text = detailsArray(2)
          LabelPhone.Text = detailsArray(3)
          LabelMenu.Text = detailsArray(4)
```

```
        LabelDrink.Text = detailsArray(6)
        LabelPrice.Text = "$ " & detailsArray(5) _
           + detailsArray(7)

     Catch
        LabelError.Text = "Sorry, your details _
appear to be unavailable. Please try again."
     End Try

  End Sub
```

The purpose of this code is to create a new array and read into it the contents of the session variable (*detailsArray*). Once this is done, the various items from the array are assigned to the text properties of their respective Label controls. A Try...Catch statement looks after situations where the array may be empty.

The next step is to allow the customer to confirm their order and to mail the details of the order to Gallaghers. From Design view, double-click the Confirm button to enter Code Behind. Add the code from Listing 16.16 to the ButtonConfirm_Click skeleton.

**Listing 16.16    ButtonConfirm_Click for WebForm2**

```
Private Sub ButtonConfirm_Click(ByVal sender As _
  System.Object, ByVal e As System.EventArgs) Handles _
  ButtonConfirm.Click

     Dim n As Integer
     Dim messageStr As String

     Dim detailsArray As New ArrayList()

     Try
        detailsArray = Session("detailsArray")

        Dim mailMsg As New Mail.MailMessage()
        mailMsg.From = "orders@gallaghers.gag"
        mailMsg.To = "orders@gallaghers.gag"
        mailMsg.Subject = "Gallaghers Gourmet Order"

        messageStr = ""
        For n = 0 To 7
           messageStr = messageStr & _
detailsArray(n) & ", "
        Next
        mailMsg.Body = messageStr

        Mail.SmtpMail.SmtpServer = _
  "mail.mySMTPServer.com"
```

```
        Mail.SmtpMail.Send(mailMsg)

        Response.Redirect("WebForm3.aspx")
    Catch
        LabelError.Text = "Sorry, we were unable to _
confirm your order. Please try again."
    End Try
End Sub
```

This code reads the content of the *detailsArray* into a mail message (mailMsg) using the For…Next loop to cycle through the contents of the array and create a message string. The mail message is directed to the orders@gallaghers.gag address that our mythical company uses for collecting its orders. If the machine that hosts the application is also an SMTP server, we can ignore the Mail.SmtpMail.SmtpServer = _ "mail.mySMTPServer.com" line. Otherwise, we insert the name of our preferred SMTP server here. The mail is then sent and the application redirects to WebForm3. We have ensconced the whole thing with SEH to capture any problems that may occur with the mailing process. We will look at mail from Visual Studio .NET in more detail in Chapter 17, "Internet Programming."

The final step is to give the customer the opportunity to change their details or order if necessary. Double-click the Change Details button and enter the code from Listing 16.17 into its code skeleton. This code simply redirects the application back to WebForm1.

---

**Listing 16.17     ButtonChange_Click for WebForm2**

```
Private Sub ButtonChange_Click(ByVal sender As _
  System.Object, ByVal e As System.EventArgs) Handles _
  ButtonChange.Click
        Response.Redirect("WebForm1.aspx")
End Sub
```

---

Listing 16.18 contains the first portion of the ASPX code for WebForm2. The full listing of the ASPX code for this form can be found in Listing 16.18 on the web page for this book.

---

**Listing 16.18     Sample ASPX Code for *WebForm2.aspx***

```
<%@ Register TagPrefix="uc1" TagName="Header2" _
  Src="Header2.ascx" %>
<%@ Page Language="vb" AutoEventWireup="false" _
  Codebehind="WebForm2.aspx.vb" Inherits="Gallaghers.WebForm2"%>
<!DOCTYPE HTML PUBLIC "-//W3C//DTD HTML 4.0 Transitional//EN">
<HTML>
  <HEAD>
```

```
    <title>Gallagher's Gourmet - Order Details</title>
    <meta name="GENERATOR" content="Microsoft Visual _
Studio.NET 7.0">
    <meta name="CODE_LANGUAGE" content="Visual Basic 7.0">
    <meta name="vs_defaultClientScript" content="JavaScript">
    <meta name="vs_targetSchema" _
content="http://schemas.microsoft.com/intellisense/ie5">
  </HEAD>
  <body MS_POSITIONING="GridLayout" vLink="navy" _
link="navy">
```

This completes the setup for WebForm2. In the next section, we will create WebForm3.aspx.

## Developing WebForm3

The purpose of WebForm3 is to give the customer notification that their order has been successfully sent and will be processed. It also provides a jumping-off point for the rest of the website. Create a new Web Form from the Project menu and leave its name at the default WebForm3.aspx.

Because this page contains no dynamic content, we can output-cache the whole page. Switch to HTML view and add the following directive to the top of the page:

```
<%@ OutputCache Duration="60" VaryByParam="None" %>
```

Return to Design view, click somewhere on the form, and in the Properties window for DOCUMENT, set the values of the vlink and link attributes to #000080 (navy) and the title to Gallaghers Gourmet—Order Confirmation. Set the EnableViewState property for the DOCUMENT to False.

Open the Template.aspx form and copy the table and its contents. Paste the table into WebForm3. In the Properties window for the table, set the following attributes of style:

```
Z-INDEX: 111; LEFT: 34px; WIDTH: 609px; _
  POSITION: absolute; TOP: 9px; HEIGHT: 103px
```

Delete the Order a Meal link from row 7. Drag the Header2.ascx control reference from the Solution Explorer to row 1 of the table. Select the control (Header21) and set its EnableViewState property to False.

In row 3 of the table, place an HTML Label control. Resize the control to fit the row. Click inside the Label to enter Text Edit mode and add the following text: **Thank you for your custom. Your order is now being prepared by our chef and will be delivered soon.** Press Enter to move to the next line and then add the following text: **Click OK to return to our main page.**

Finally, in row 5 of the table, delete the second cell and add a `colspan=2` attribute to the first cell. Set its align attribute to center. Add a Button control from the Web Forms Toolkit to the cell. Set its Bold property to True, the Text property to OK, the EnableViewState to False, and the ID to ButtonOK.

Figure 16.21 shows how WebForm3 should appear in Design view, and Figure 16.22 shows it running in Internet Explorer.

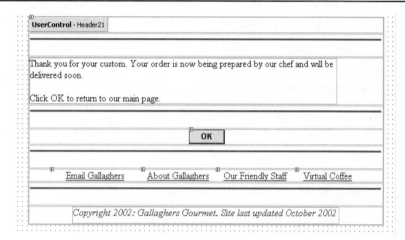

Gallaghers Gourmet

10 Rocky Rd, Rock Ville. Telephone: 555 555, Email:gallaghers@gallaghers.gag

Thank you for your custom. Your order is now being prepared by our chef and will be delivered soon.

Click OK to return to our main page.

OK

Email Gallaghers      About Gallaghers      Our Friendly Staff      Virtual Coffee

Copyright 2002: Gallaghers Gourmet. Site last updated October 2002

There is very little code to add to this page. Double-click the OK button to enter Code Behind and add the code from Listing 16.19 to the code skeleton for ButtonOK_Click. This is simply designed to redirect the user back to WebForm1, although if we actually had a Gallaghers website, it would be better to take the user into the main page of the actual site.

**Listing 16.19     ButtonOK_Click for WebForm3**

```
Private Sub ButtonOK_Click(ByVal sender As _
 System.Object, ByVal e As System.EventArgs) _
 Handles ButtonOK.Click
        Response.Redirect("WebForm1.aspx")
End Sub
```

This completes the construction of WebPage3. Listing 16.20 contains the first part of the ASPX code for Webpage3.aspx. The full listing can be found on the web page for this book.

**Listing 16.20     Sample ASPX Code for *WebPage3.aspx***

```
<%@ Register TagPrefix="uc1" TagName="Header2" _
 Src="Header2.ascx" %>
<%@ Page Language="vb" AutoEventWireup="false" _
 Codebehind="WebForm3.aspx.vb" Inherits="Gallaghers.WebForm3" _
 enableViewState="False"%>
<%@ OutputCache Duration="60" VaryByParam="None" %>
<!DOCTYPE HTML PUBLIC "-//W3C//DTD HTML 4.0 Transitional//EN">
<HTML>
    <HEAD>
        <title>Gallaghers Gourmet - Order Confirmation</title>
        <meta content="Microsoft Visual Studio.NET 7.0" _
name="GENERATOR">
        <meta content="Visual Basic 7.0" name="CODE_LANGUAGE">
        <meta content="JavaScript" name="vs_defaultClientScript">
        <meta _
content="http://schemas.microsoft.com/intellisense/ie5" _
name="vs_targetSchema">
    </HEAD>
    <body vLink="navy" link="navy"
```

Although we are not creating the main Gallaghers website in this example, we have included a sample About Gallaghers page to illustrate the use of the XML control. We will set this up in the next section.

## Developing WebForm4

WebForm4 would actually be part of the Gallaghers main site. It could be used to give visitors details about the company, such as it history, full menus, and information about its facilities. In this example, we will use XSLT style sheets in conjunction with the XML control to display the Gallaghers menu.

Create a new Web Form from the Project menu and leave the name at the default `WebForm4.aspx`.

Because the Gallaghers menu doesn't change that much over time, we can afford to output-cache this entire page. Switch to HTML view and add the following directive to the top of the page:

```
<%@ OutputCache Duration="60" VaryByParam="None" %>
```

Return to Design view, click somewhere on the form, and in the Properties window for DOCUMENT, set the values of the vlink and link attributes to #000080 (navy) and the title to Gallaghers Gourmet—About Gallaghers.

Open the `Template.aspx` form and copy the table and its contents. Paste the table into WebForm4. In the Properties window for the table, set the following attributes of style:

```
Z-INDEX: 111; LEFT: 34px; WIDTH: 609px; _
  POSITION: absolute; TOP: 9px; HEIGHT: 103px
```

Drag the `Header2.ascx` control reference from the Solution Explorer to row 1 of the table. Select the control (Header21) and set its EnableViewState property to False.

Drag an HTML Label control into row 3 of the table. Resize it to fit the row. Click within the control to enter Text Edit mode. Add the following text: **Welcome to the Gallaghers Gourmet website. Below you'll find our tasty menu, from which you can order in the store and over the Internet for personal delivery.**

In row 5, set the align attribute of the left-hand cell to right and that of the right hand cell to left. Drop an XML control into each of the two cells. For the first XML control in the left-hand cell, set the DocumentSource property to menu.xml, the TransformSource to menuStyle.xslt, and the ID to XmlMenu.

For the other XML control, set the DocumentSource property to drinks.xml, the Transform-Source to drinkStyle.xslt, and the ID to XmlDrinks.

This completes the layout for WebForm4. There is nothing to enter in Code Behind for this form. Figure 16.23 shows the completed page in Design view. Figure 16.24 shows the same page opened in Internet Explorer.

**FIGURE 16.23:**

WebForm4.aspx in
Design view

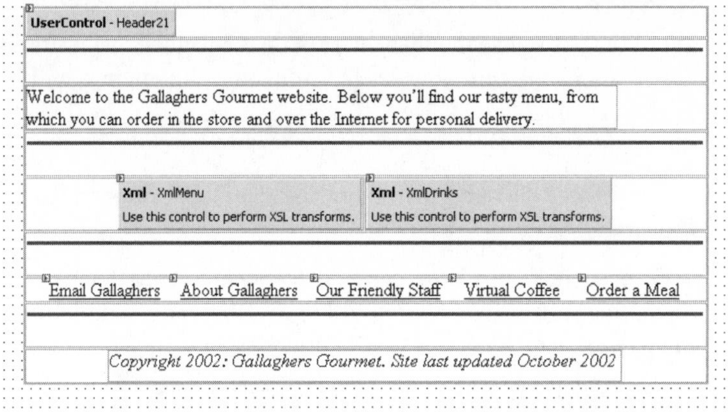

| UserControl - Header21 | | |
| --- | --- | --- |
| Welcome to the Gallaghers Gourmet website. Below you'll find our tasty menu, from which you can order in the store and over the Internet for personal delivery. | | |
| **Xml** - XmlMenu<br>Use this control to perform XSL transforms. | **Xml** - XmlDrinks<br>Use this control to perform XSL transforms. | |
| Email Gallaghers   About Gallaghers   Our Friendly Staff   Virtual Coffee   Order a Meal | | |
| Copyright 2002: Gallaghers Gourmet. Site last updated October 2002 | | |

**FIGURE 16.24:**

WebForm4.aspx in
Internet Explorer

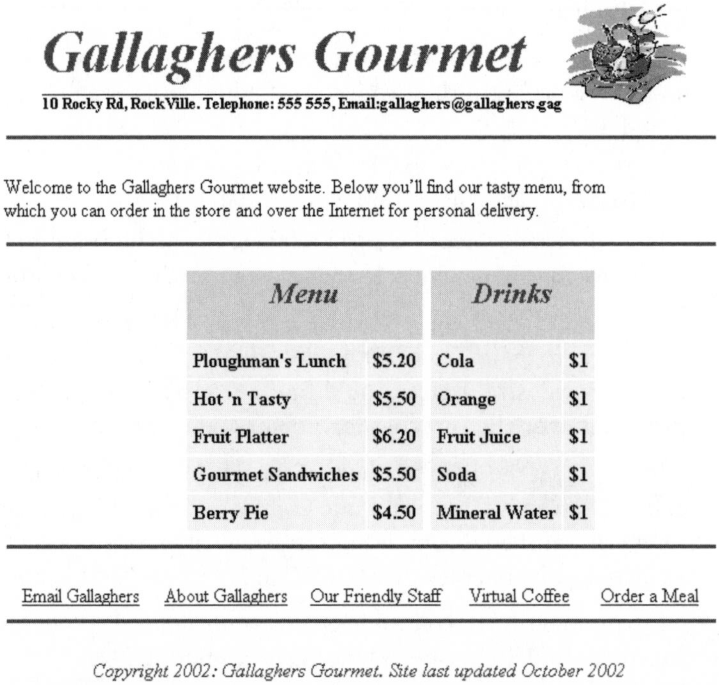

*Gallaghers Gourmet*

**10 Rocky Rd, Rock Ville. Telephone: 555 555, Email:gallaghers@gallaghers.gag**

Welcome to the Gallaghers Gourmet website. Below you'll find our tasty menu, from which you can order in the store and over the Internet for personal delivery.

| *Menu* | | *Drinks* | |
| --- | --- | --- | --- |
| Ploughman's Lunch | $5.20 | Cola | $1 |
| Hot 'n Tasty | $5.50 | Orange | $1 |
| Fruit Platter | $6.20 | Fruit Juice | $1 |
| Gourmet Sandwiches | $5.50 | Soda | $1 |
| Berry Pie | $4.50 | Mineral Water | $1 |

Email Gallaghers   About Gallaghers   Our Friendly Staff   Virtual Coffee   Order a Meal

*Copyright 2002: Gallaghers Gourmet. Site last updated October 2002*

Listing 16.21 contains the first part of the ASPX code for WebForm4. The full listing can be found on the web page for this book.

**Listing 16.21       Sample ASPX code for *WebForm4.aspx***

```
<%@ OutputCache Duration="60" VaryByParam="None" %>
<%@ Register TagPrefix="uc1" TagName="Header2" _
 Src="Header2.ascx" %>
<%@ Page Language="vb" AutoEventWireup="false" _
 Codebehind="WebForm4.aspx.vb" Inherits="Gallaghers.WebForm4"%>
<!DOCTYPE HTML PUBLIC "-//W3C//DTD HTML 4.0 Transitional//EN">
<HTML>
    <HEAD>
        <title>Gallaghers Gourmet - About Gallaghers</title>
        <meta name="GENERATOR" content="Microsoft Visual _
Studio.NET 7.0">
        <meta name="CODE_LANGUAGE" content="Visual Basic 7.0">
        <meta name="vs_defaultClientScript" content="JavaScript">
        <meta name="vs_targetSchema" _
content="http://schemas.microsoft.com/intellisense/ie5">
    </HEAD>
    <body MS_POSITIONING="GridLayout" vLink="navy" _
link="navy">
```

This completes the development of the Gallaghers application, at least as far as we are going to go here. In the next section, we will look briefly at running the application.

## Running the Application

As with any web application, before you do your final compile and deploy, make sure that you have disabled debug in the web.config file and that you compile in Release mode. In our example, you also need to check that you have excluded the Template.aspx form from the project. Also ensure that you have set the WeForm1.aspx as your start page.

When you run the application, it will open to WebForm1, where the customer can make their selection(s) and fill out their details. Note that the customer can make multiple selections. This is shown in Figure 16.25.

Once they get past the validation process, customers can click the Submit button and be presented with the confirmation form. This is shown in Figure 16.26.

Assuming that everything is in order, the customer can click the Confirm button and then be presented with the final order confirmation screen. Meanwhile, an e-mail message is sent to Gallaghers with the details of the order. Figure 16.27 shows the e-mail message for the order in this example as it appears in Outlook Express. (The formatting isn't pretty, but it's only for demonstration purposes.)

**FIGURE 16.25:**

Making selections
from the Gallaghers
application

**FIGURE 16.26:**

Confirming selections
on the Gallaghers
Application

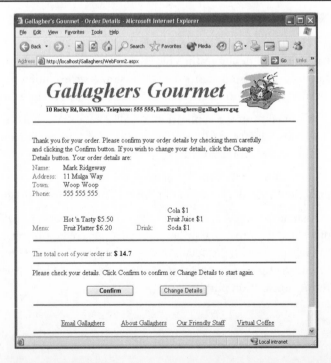

FIGURE 16.27:

E-mail message from
Gallaghers application

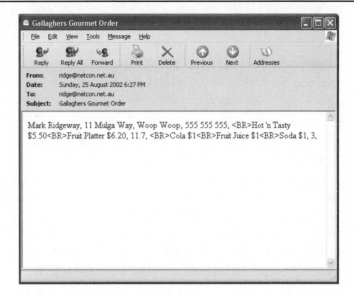

## A Further Look at Session Management

Session management is always a hot topic when it comes to developing applications for the Web. So far, we have used simple session variables to maintain state, but Visual Studio .NET enables you to maintain and control sessions using a range of techniques. We will briefly explore some of these techniques in this section.

An ASP.NET application generates a new session for a user when their request does not contain a valid SessionID. A unique SessionID is generated for each session and can be stored on the client in a cookie or munged into the URL for cookieless sessions. An application can be converted to cookieless by setting the `cookieless="false"` attribute to `true` in the session-State tag in the `web.config` file.

We need to distinguish at this point between session state and application state. Application state is a global condition that applies to the entire application and all users of it. Thus, an application variable has the same value for all users, and if one user changes it, then all users see the change. For this reason, application state has fairly limited usefulness when trying to set up unique connections for individuals. You can use the `Gloabal.asax` file to set a lot of the application-level events. Session state, on the other hand, applies to what the individual user actually experiences and can be very different from the experience of another user using the application at the same time.

In the rest of this section, we will experiment a little bit with session management. Open a new ASP.NET project and name it WebSessions. You can identify the current SessionID using `Session.SessionID`. For example, drag a Label control to the Web Form. Double-click the form, enter Code Behind, and insert the following snippet into the Page_Load skeleton:

```
Label1.Text = Session.SessionID
```

Compile and run the form. The SessionID should be available in Label1. Note that the particular SessionID that you have been issued will continue to be reused by your browser even if you abandon the session that initiated the ID and then start another one. You will be issued another SessionID only if you restart the browser or if the server is reset.

You can finish a session using `Session.Abandon` and alter the session time-out figure from the default 20 minutes using `Session.Timeout`.

SessionState itself can be set using the enableSessionState property for a Web Form. This can be set to True (yes, we have a session), False (no session), and ReadOnly (you need a session but don't need to write anything to it). Sessions consume resources, so to maximize performance, it is worth using the False or ReadOnly options wherever possible. (We could have applied these in some cases in the Gallaghers application.)

Drag three Button controls to the form and set their Text properties to Abandon, Set Variable, and Show Variable, respectively. Add a second Label control to the form and position it next to the Show Variable button. Enter Code Behind and copy in the code from Listing 16.22.

**Listing 16.22    Code for WebSessions Project**

```
Private Sub Page_Load(ByVal sender As System.Object, _
  ByVal e As System.EventArgs) Handles MyBase.Load
        Label1.Text = Session.SessionID
        Session.Timeout() = 1
    End Sub

    Private Sub Button1_Click(ByVal sender As _
  System.Object, ByVal e As System.EventArgs) Handles _
  Button1.Click
        Session.Abandon()
    End Sub

    Private Sub Button2_Click(ByVal sender As _
  System.Object, ByVal e As System.EventArgs) Handles _
  Button2.Click
        Session("variable1") = "fred"
    End Sub

    Private Sub Button3_Click(ByVal sender As _
  System.Object, ByVal e As System.EventArgs) Handles _
  Button3.Click
        Label2.Text = Session("variable1")
    End Sub
```

In the Page_Load event we expose the SessionID and set the session time-out to 1 minute. The Abandon button (Button1) ends the session. As discussed earlier, clicking this button and refreshing the page will not, however, result in a different SessionID being posted.

The Set Variable button (Button2) creates a session variable. The Show Variable button (Button3) displays the value of this variable. Thus, clicking Buttons 2 and 3 will display "fred" in Label2. However, if you set the variable by clicking Button2 and then kill the session by clicking Button1, "fred" will not be displayed when next you click Button3. You can use session variables to hold anything you like, but be aware that they do consume memory on the server. One way around this is to set the session time-out to much lower than the default 20 minutes. This is possible when you may have a small application and pages are not likely to be viewed for more than a couple of minutes at a time. In this example, we have set the time-out period to 1 minute. You can test this by clicking Button2 to set the session variable, wait about a minute, and then try to display the value of the variable by clicking Button3.

You can obviously do a lot more with sessions and session management than discussed here. The tools are essentially easy to use—it is just the execution that can get confusing!

Another method of storing session information is by using cookies on the client's computer. This is not always an ideal solution because many people are suspicious of cookies and disable them on their machines. However, they are easy to manipulate programmatically, and we will demonstrate a simple example here.

Add another Button (Button4) to the Web Form. Set its Text property to Set Cookie. Double-click the button and add the following code to its Click event:

```
Private Sub Button4_Click(ByVal sender As _
  System.Object, ByVal e As System.EventArgs) Handles _
  Button4.Click
        Response.Cookies("Cookie1").Value = "mary"
        Response.Cookies("Cookie1").Expires() = _
  "September 1, 2002"
End Sub
```

The first line sets the actual cookie as an in-memory cookie that evaporates when the browser is closed down. If you want the cookie to persist over a period of time and be stored on the client's machine as a text file (assuming that the client allows it), add the second line with your choice of date. Figure 16.28 shows how this cookie looks on a machine.

**FIGURE 16.28:**

The "mary" cookie as stored in Internet Explorer

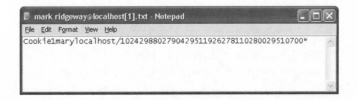

To display the cookie on the form, you need to add another Button (Button5) and a Label control (Label3—place it next to Button5) to the form. Set the Button's Text property to Read Cookie. Double-click the Button and add the following code to its Click event:

```
Label3.Text = Request.Cookies("Cookie1").Value
```

Again, we can do a lot more with cookies, but this illustrates the basics.

We looked earlier at ViewState as it applies to individual controls. It is possible to manipulate ViewState to store and manage information relevant to individual controls.

To illustrate this, add two more Button controls (Button6 and Button7) to the Web Form. Set Button6's Text property to Set ViewState and Button7's Text property to Restore Text-Box. Add a TextBox to the form and position it near these two buttons. Double-click Button6 and add the following code snippet to its Click event:

```
ViewState("TextBox1.text") = TextBox1.Text
```

Double-click Button7 and add the following code to its Click event:

```
TextBox1.Text = ViewState("TextBox1.text")
```

Compile and run the project. Experiment with the two buttons. If you type some text into the TextBox (say, **Wilma**) and refresh the form, you will lose the text. Retype **Wilma** and click Button6 (Set ViewState). Refreshing the page now results in the text remaining. If you change *Wilma* to *Betty* and click Button7 (Restore TextBox), *Wilma* will be restored.

We could have used these techniques in the Gallaghers application to keep a customer's details in WebForm1 so that they would be there if for any reason a customer needed to return to the form to make some minor changes. The way we left it, the customer has to type everything again.

The final method we'll look at for managing session information is the use of hidden fields. This is an HTML technique for embedding information into the actual page that the user is displaying. Whenever a user posts back to the server, the content of these hidden fields can be read and updated if necessary. ViewState itself relies on the use of hidden fields, but you can add additional fields to a form and exploit them. Remember, for every field that you add, you are adding weight to the application and potentially slowing its download time, so be careful what you actually put in these fields. The controls are available from the HTML controls in the Toolbox.

As an example, drag a Hidden Field control to the form. Right-click it and select the Run as Server Control option. The control's ID should now be Hidden1. Enter Code Behind and add the following line to the Page_Load event:

```
Hidden1.Value = "Barney"
```

Return to Design view, and from the Web Forms controls, add another Button control (Button8). Set its Text property to Hidden. Place a Label control (Label4) beside the Button. Double-click Button8 and add the following code snippet to its Click event:

```
Label4.Text = Hidden1.Value
```

Compile and run the project. Click the Hidden button. This should populate Label4 with the contents of the Hidden1 field (which you should not be able to see when the project is run in a web browser—hence, a hidden field).

## Summary

As you can see just from the Gallaghers example, Visual Studio .NET exposes you to a wide range of technologies and techniques for developing your web-based applications. This puts the focus back on planning and design when building these applications. To build a fully optimized application that fully leverages the available tools, you need to spend time carefully thinking through the design of the application, where and how it is likely to be used, available hardware, available support, user loads, and possibility of future development.

Spending time in planning enables the developer to make the most out of the broad toolset available with .NET. With the Gallaghers application, you have seen how to make use of an XML data source, exploit fragment and output caching, and mail from within the application. We also looked at the range of session management tools available.

In the next chapter, we will be looking at some more specific elements of Internet programming with .NET, including a close look at the `System.Net` class and sending and receiving mail with .NET.

# CHAPTER 17

# Internet Programming

- IP addresses and computer names

- The WebClient class

- The WebRequest and WebResponse classes

- The TcpClient and TcpListener classes

- The UdpClient class

- Sending and receiving mail

In this chapter, we'll discuss the members of the System.Net class, which allow you to connect to various resources on the Web and interact with other computers on the Internet. The most prominent type of Internet application is an ASP Web application, and Visual Studio has greatly simplified the process of developing web applications. However, in addition to applications that interact with web servers, there's a need for applications that communicate with one another over the Internet. For example, a computer might contact a remote server every so often and execute a command against it. Two users might initiate a chat session if an instance of the appropriate application is running on both computers.

Even web applications are not always limited to a browser connected to a web server. You can write a Windows application that contacts a web server, downloads one or more files, and processes them locally. It's also possible to upload files to the web server, as long as you specify the name of an application that runs on the server and knows what to do with the uploaded files.

Modern applications need access to information stored on remote servers, and this need has increased in recent years and will certainly continue to do so. The information we need resides on multiple computers and we can no longer afford to download it to a single computer and process it there. We want to access the information wherever it exists, retrieve the most up-to-date information, and process it as needed. Even the processing need not be local. Web services (also introduced with .NET) are programs that run on web servers and can be called from within any application. They're executed on the remote server, which returns the results of the processing to the client. In this chapter, we'll introduce the System.Net class and discuss some typical examples, like interacting with a web server and building a chat application.

## IP Addresses and Computer Names

Before we start our discussion of the System.Net class, let's go through some basic definitions. You're probably familiar with the topics of this section, but we'll repeat a few basic terms for the sake of VB programmers who are new to Internet programming.

Every computer on the Internet is identified by a unique address known as the *IP address*. The IP address is a long number that is written as a group of four numbers, each one in the range from 0 to 255, like 192.140.39.101. This is known as dotted-quad notation. When you connect to the Internet through an Internet service provider (ISP), your computer is assigned an IP address automatically by the ISP. This address remains the same for the duration of the session, and the next time you connect to the Internet, you get a new IP address. It is possible to request a fixed IP address from your ISP, and more and more people have a fixed IP address on the Internet.

To find out your computer's IP address, connect to the Internet as usual and then run the IPConfig utility, which is shown in Figure 17.1. Open the Start menu, select Run, and then enter CMD in the dialog box that will pop up. When the Command Prompt window appears, enter **ipconfig /all** and press Enter.

**FIGURE 17.1:**

The IPConfig utility

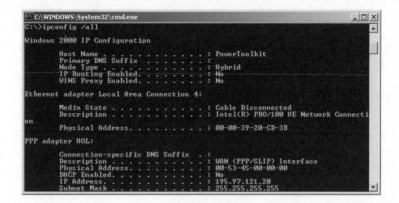

In addition to their IP address, computers on the Internet have a friendly name too, their *hostname*. You can find your computer's name in the Network Identification tab of your computer's Properties dialog box. If you're on a network with a registered domain name, your computer's friendly name is something like *name.domain.com*, where *name* is your computer's name and *domain.com* is the company's domain name.

In addition to the IP address you're assigned by your ISP when you connect to the Internet, your computer has another IP address on the local network (if you're on a local area network). The local network IP address was assigned to each computer on the local network by the administrator or by a special program that runs on a server and assigns an IP address to each computer as it's turned on. This is what the Dynamic Host Configuration Protocol (DHCP) utility does; it assigns a unique IP address to each workstation of the network as it connects.

If you're on a corporate network, you probably get on the Internet via a proxy server. The proxy server is an intermediary computer between the computers on the local network and the Internet. All the computers on the local network access the Internet through the proxy server. In addition, the proxy server can protect the local network from outside attacks, but we won't discuss this topic any further. It's also possible to share a fast Internet connection among multiple computers on the network by sharing one computer's Internet connection (the computer that's connected to the Internet through a DSL or even faster line). No matter how you connect to the Internet from a local network, your computer has an IP address for the Internet and another one for the local network. You can connect to other clients on the same local network with either IP address or simply with the client's hostname. Users on the Internet can connect to your computer only if they know the IP address assigned to your computer when you connected to the Internet. Of course, knowing a computer's address on the Internet doesn't mean that you can do anything more than request a connection to it. Whether you will actually connect and see its resources depends on the remote computer's security settings. The classes we'll discuss in this chapter enable two computers to communicate with one another on a specific port. The computer that accepts the request will decide whether to honor it or reject it. An application should be running on both machines and monitor the specific port. If you have shared one or more drives or folders for the Web (Web Sharing tab of the drive's property pages), then any user can access your drive. It's imperative to specify a password for all the drives you decide to share on the Web so that only trusted users can access them.

Finally, there's a special IP address that identifies the local computer: 127.0.0.1. This address refers to the local computer (the computer on which the program is running) regardless of whether the computer is on the Internet, a local area network, or both. You will use this address to test all applications presented in this chapter if you're using a stand-alone computer.

## The *System.Net.Dns* Class

To simplify the processing of IP addresses, the .NET Framework provides the System.Net.Dns class, which exposes several methods. All methods of this class make use of the IPAddress and IPHostEntry classes. The two classes are similar, and they allow you to discover IP addresses from hostnames or hostnames from IP addresses.

The IPHostEntry class exposes the following properties:

**AddressList property**    This property returns (or sets) a list of IP addresses associated with a hostname, which is passed to the method as a string. The list of addresses is returned as an array of addresses should the host have multiple addresses. You can't set the address of the local client, but you can create an IPHostEntry that represents a remote computer and set its AddressList property. You can use this object in your code to identify the specific computer.

**Aliases property**    This property returns (or sets) a list of aliases associated with a host.

**HostName property**    This property returns (or sets) the friendly name of the host.

The IPAddress class exposes the Address property, which is an IP address. The System .Net.Dns class exposes several methods to manipulate computer addresses:

**GetHostByAddress(IPAddress) method**    This method accepts an IP address as argument and returns an IPHostEntry object. On our computer, the following statement returned the string "PowerToolkit":

```
Console.WriteLine(GetHostByAddress("127.0.0.1").HostName)
```

The GetHostByAddress method will return a hostname if the client with the specified address is on the same local network or if it belongs to a network with a registered name.

**GetHostByName(hostname) method**   This method accepts a hostname as argument and returns the host's IP address. The following statement will return your computer's IP address if you change the hostname to your computer's hostname:

```
Console.WriteLine(System.Net.Dns.GetHostByName( _
                "myHost").AddressList(0))
```

If you're on a local area network and the Internet at the same time, the IPAddressList array will have multiple elements (multiple IP addresses).

**Resolve(hostname) method**   This method accepts as argument an IP address or a hostname and returns an IPHostEntry object that represents the host. The argument can be either a friendly name (like "PowerToolkit" or "www.domain.com"), or an IP address.

Now we can switch our attention to classes for programming Internet applications, starting with the simplest one, which is the WebClient class.

## The WebClient Class

The simplest class for requesting, downloading, and uploading documents over the Web is the WebClient class. This class provides methods for exchanging information with a web server through streams, similar to accessing local files. It's not the most flexible method of accessing a web server, but if all you need is to download a file (or upload a file) to a web server, this class is all you need.

The WebClient class is part of the System.Net namespace, which you must import to your application with the following statement:

```
Imports System.Net
```

Then, you can create instances of the WebClient class and call its methods. Let's start with a quick overview of the available methods for downloading and uploading data.

### Methods for Downloading Data

To download data from a web server, you can use the following methods of the WebClient class:

**OpenRead method**   This method creates a Stream object that acts as a channel between your application and the web server. Once the Stream object is in place, you can use its Read methods to retrieve the data. The syntax of the OpenRead method is as follows:

```
WebClient.OpenRead(documentURL)
```

The return value of the OpenRead method must be assigned to a Stream object:

```
Dim wClient As New WebClient
Dim webStream As Stream = wClient.OpenRead("142.18.191.10/File.html)
```

**DownloadData method**    This method downloads data from a web server and returns them in an array of bytes. The syntax of the method is as follows (where *documentURL* is the URI of the document to download):

```
WebClient.DownloadData(documentURL)
```

This argument can be the URI of a file, or the URI of an ASP application that generates its output on-the-fly and transmits it to the client.

**DownloadFile method**    This method downloads data from a web server directly to a local file. Use the following syntax for the DownloadFile method:

```
WebClient.DownloadData(documentURL, localFileName)
```

The first argument is the document's URL and the second argument is the path of a local file, where the downloaded data will be stored.

## Methods for Uploading Data

To upload a file to a web server, you can use the following methods of the WebClient class:

**OpenWrite method**    This method creates a Stream object that acts like a channel between your application and the web server. Once the Stream object is in place, you can use its Write methods to upload data. The simplest form of the OpenWrite method accepts a single argument, which is the URI of the resource that will accept the uploaded file:

```
WebClient.OpenWrite(URI)
```

A second overloaded form of the method allows you to specify the method to be used for sending the data to the server, and its value can be the "POST" or "GET" string:

```
WebClient.OpenWrite(URI, method)
```

The following statements create a Stream object for a specific document on a web server:

```
Dim wclient As New WebClient()
Dim outStream As Stream = wclient.OpenWrite(uri, "POST")
```

**UploadData method**    This method sends an array of bytes to the web server and returns another array of bytes with the server's response (if any):

```
WebClient.UploadData(URI, data)
WebClient.UploadData(URI, method, data)
```

The first argument is the URI of the resource that will accept the data, method is a string specifying the method to be used for uploading the data ("GET" or "POST"), and the last argument is an array of bytes with the information to be uploaded.

**UploadFile method**    This method uploads a file to the web server and returns an array of bytes with the server's response (if any). Here is the syntax of the UploadFile method:

```
WebClient.Upload(URI, path)
```

The first argument is the URI of the resource that will receive the file (most likely the name of an ASP application that runs on the server), and the second argument is the path of the local file that will be uploaded. An overloaded form of the method accepts another argument that specifies the method that will be used to transmit the file to the server:

```
WebClient(URI, method, path)
```

**UploadValues method**    This method uploads a collection of name/value pairs to the web server and returns an array of bytes with the server's response (if any). To call this method, you must first create a NamedValueCollection of the name and value pairs you want to upload and pass it along with the URI of the resource that will receive the data to the server. This is similar to submitting a form with several fields to the server (each field's name is the corresponding control name and its value is the data entered by the user). The syntax of the method is as follows:

```
WebClient.UploadValues(URI, data)
```

To upload a collection of three named values, use the following statements:

```
Dim data As New NameValueCollection()
data.Add("First Name", Joe)
data.Add("Last Name", "Doe")
data.Add("EMail", "user@domain.com")

Dim wClient As New WebClient()
WebClient.UploadValues("192.210.27.119", data)
```

All three methods for uploading data (except for the OpenWrite method) return an array of bytes with the server's response. This response can be used as a confirmation of the successful completion of the operation.

As you have noticed, the data is transmitted as arrays of bytes (unless you're uploading a local file or downloading directly to a local file, of course). What this means to developers is that you need some methods to convert strings to arrays of bytes and vice versa. The .NET Framework provides the System.Text.Encoding.ASCII class, which does exactly that. The System.Text.Encoding class contains a number of useful classes, like the Unicode, UTF7, and UTF8 class, which handle Unicode, UTF7, and UTF8 characters, respectively. All of these classes expose the same methods, so we'll present the methods of the System.Text.Encoding.ASCII class.

To convert a string to an array of bytes, call the GetBytes method, which accepts as argument a string and returns an array of bytes. The following statements convert a string variable (the cmdString variable) to a series of bytes and store them in the buffer array:

```
Dim cmdString As String = "Uploaded Filename"
```

```
Dim buffer() As Byte
System.Text.Encoding.ASCII.GetBytes(cmdString)
```

Likewise, the GetString method converts an array of bytes to a string. This method accepts as arguments an array of bytes and returns a string:

```
System.Text.Encoding.ASCII.GetString(buffer)
```

We'll use these two methods a lot in this chapter, so make a note of their syntax. We're showing here the simplest form of both methods. The GetBytes and GetString methods are overloaded, and you can look up the other forms of the methods in the documentation.

## Downloading Documents with WebClient

To download a document from a web server, create an instance of the WebClient class and call its Download method, passing as argument the URI of the resource you want to download. The resource can be a filename or the name of an executable (an ASP application) that generates data on-the-fly. The following statements request the main page of a website and display it on a TextBox control. What you will see on the control is the page's HTML code. The file need not be an HTML page; you can specify any document's URI with the argument of the DownloadData method.

```
Imports System.Net
Imports System.Text
Dim WClient As New WebClient()
Dim remoteUrl As String = "http://www.sybex.com"
Dim buffer As Byte() = WClient.DownloadData(remoteUrl)
TextBox1.Text = Encoding.ASCII.GetString(myDataBuffer)
```

The DownloadData method is synchronous: the application's interface will freeze until the entire document has been downloaded to the client. Of course, you can execute this method on a thread so that the interface will remain responsive. Even so, the data doesn't become available before the last byte has been downloaded to the client.

If you would rather download one line at a time and process the lines as they arrive, you can use create a Stream object with the OpenRead method and use the ReadLine method, as shown in the following code segment:

```
Dim WClient As New WebClient()
Dim WStream As Stream = WClient.OpenRead("http://www.sybex.com")
Dim SR As New StreamReader(WStream)
Dim txtLine As String
txtLine = SR.ReadLine
While Not txtLine Is Nothing
    TextBox1.AppendText(txtLine & vbCrLf)
    txtLine = SR.ReadLine
End While
WStream.Close
```

Finally, you can download the data directly to a file with the DownloadFile method. This method accepts two arguments, the URI of the document to be downloaded and the path of a file where the data will be stored. The following statements will download the HTML code of the Sybex main page and store it to the C:\SYBEX.HTML file:

```
Dim fileName As String = "C:\SYBEX.HTML"
Dim WClient As New WebClient()
WClient.DownloadFile("http://www.sybex.com", fileName)
```

## Uploading Documents with WebClient

Uploading a file doesn't mean that it will also be saved somewhere on the server's file system. Quite the opposite. When you upload a file, you also need a web application running on the server to intercept the file and process it.

If the data you want to upload resides in a file, you can upload the entire file with the UploadFile method, which accepts three arguments: the destination URI, the method to be used for upload, and the path of the file to be uploaded. The method that will be used for uploading the data is a string argument and its value can be either "POST" or "GET". The POST method allows you to upload a larger amount of data, but they're both limited when it comes to really long files.

To experiment with file uploading, you must create a client application that will upload some information to the server as well as a web application that will accept the data on the server. Create a new web application, the GetFile project. Then enter the following statements in the Web Form's Load event handler:

```
Private Sub Page_Load(ByVal sender As System.Object, _
                    ByVal e As System.EventArgs) Handles MyBase.Load
    Dim str As IO.Stream
    str = Request.InputStream
    Dim strLen As Integer = CInt(str.Length)
    Dim buffer(strLen) As Byte
    str.Read(buffer, 0, strLen)
    Response.Write("You submitted " & buffer.Length.ToString & _
                " bytes of data")
End Sub
```

This web application retrieves the data submitted by the client, stores them to an array of bytes, and returns a string with the length of the array. This is the server's response, and we'll use it in our client application to verify that the operation has completed successfully.

Then switch to the Web Form's HTML tab and delete everything except for the header of the page:

```
<%@ Page Language="vb" AutoEventWireup="false"
        Codebehind="WebForm1.aspx.vb" Inherits="GetFile.WebForm1"%>
```

Our application shouldn't have a visible interface because we want to contact it remotely from within our client and upload the file.

Now you can compile the project and contact it from a client. Create the appropriate EXE file with the Build GetFile command of the Build menu. Then start a new instance of VB and place the statements in Listing 17.1 behind a button's Click event handler.

---

**Listing 17.1**     **Uploading a File to a Web Server**

```
Private Sub Button1_Click(ByVal sender As System.Object, _
                          ByVal e As System.EventArgs) _
                          Handles Button1.Click
    Dim URI As String = "http://127.0.0.1/GetFile/WebForm1.aspx"
    Dim myWebClient As New WebClient()
    Dim fileName As String = "c:\products.xml"
    Dim buffer As Byte() = myWebClient.UploadFile(URI, "POST", fileName)
    MsgBox(System.Text.Encoding.ASCII.GetString(Buffer))
End Sub
```

---

If you run the Windows project and click the button on the form, the specified file will be submitted to the GetFile.aspx application and a few moments later you will see the server's response on a message box. The application running on the server doesn't process the data, but you can edit the code to perform any type of processing or store the buffer array to a file on the server. It's a matter of writing simple VB code, as you would for a Windows application.

The WebClient class is fairly straightforward to work with and should be used with simple applications that don't require extensive interaction between the client and the server. For more demanding applications, you can use the WebRequest and WebResponse classes, which are discussed next.

## The WebRequest and WebResponse Classes

Using the WebClient to exchange files with a web server is almost trivial, but the operation is synchronous: once you start reading the incoming stream (or sending the outgoing stream), your application will freeze until the entire document has been moved. The .NET Framework provides the WebRequest and WebResponse objects, which are more flexible and allow asynchronous transfers.

Behind the scenes, the WebClient class uses the WebRequest and WebResponse classes to connect to the remote server and retrieve its response. The WebClient class is used for very simple applications and textbook examples. Any real application that needs to access resources on the Internet should use these two classes and their descendants. One very good reason for using the WebRequest and WebResponse classes is that the WebClient class's methods are synchronous—you can't use them to download, or upload, a resource asynchronously. You can always use the WebClient class from within a separate thread, but as you will soon see, the WebRequest and WebResponse classes have built-in asynchronous capabilities.

The WebRequest and WebResponse classes are abstract classes and can't be used directly in your code. They abstract the operations of connecting to a server and requesting resources. The four descendant classes that are implemented in the .NET Framework are the HttpWebRequest/HttpWebResponse classes, which we use to access resources with the `http://` URI scheme, and the FileWebRequest/FileWebResponse classes, which we use to access resources with the `file://` URI scheme. In the section, we'll discuss in detail the HttpWebRequest and HttpWebResponse classes.

To access a Web page (or any document that can be returned by a web server), create an instance of the WebRequest class by calling its Create method, whose syntax is as follows (where the *URI* argument is a string representing the document's URL):

```
HttpWebRequest.Create(URI)
```

This method returns a WebRequest object, which you can use to set the properties of the connection, establish a connection, and then call the WebRequest object's GetResponse methods, which returns an object that represents the server's response, the WebResponse object. Another method of the WebRequest object, the GetResponseStream method, returns a Stream object, which you can use to read the data sent by the server. The following statements establish a connection to a remote server and read the specified document (the main page of this book's publisher's site):

```
Dim URI As Uri = New Uri("http://www.sybex.com")
Dim wReq as HttpWebRequest = HttpWebRequest.Create(URI)
Dim wResp As HttpWebResponse = wReq.GetResponse()
Dim InStream As Stream = wResp.GetResponseStream()
Dim reader As StreamReader = New StreamReader(InStream, Encoding.ASCII)
Dim HTMLdoc As String = reader.ReadToEnd()
Console.WriteLine(respHTML)
wResp.Close()
```

Notice that the HttpWebResponse object created by the GetResponse method must be closed or else you won't be able to use it to make additional requests later in your code.

To upload data to a server, call the GetRequestStream object and then use the Stream class's methods to write data onto the stream. The data will be uploaded to the remote server, where it must be processed by a web application or a plain old ASP page. The following statements upload a local file to a remote web server:

```
Dim Data() As Byte
' statements to populate Byte array
```

```
Dim wReq As HttpWebRequest = _
        HttpWebRequest.Create("http://127.0.0.1/GetFile.aspx")
wReq.Method = "POST"
wReq.ContentLength = Data.Length
Dim OutStream As Stream = wReq.GetRequestStream()
OutStream.Write(Data, 0, Data.Length)
OutStream.Close()
```

The two classes are straightforward to use, and we'll look at an example in a moment. To complete this introduction to the basic members of the two classes, we should discuss the methods that provide asynchronous support. They're the BeginGetResponse and EndGet-Response methods. The BeginGetResponse accepts two arguments: a callback delegate and an object containing information about the request. Here's the syntax of the BeginGetResponse method:

```
HttpWebResponse.BeginGetResponse(callback, state)
```

In this statement, `callback` is a delegate to the subroutine to be called when the HttpWeb-Response object is available and `state` is an object variable (you can store in it information you want to pass to the delegate). The BeginGetResponse method returns an IAsyncResult object, which is a reference to the asynchronous request. You'll see how it's used in the code momentarily.

In the callback delegate, you must call the EndGetResponse method explicitly. Once the HttpWebResponse object that represents the server's response becomes available, you can call its GetResponseStream method to retrieve the Stream object with the server's data. The delegate is the address of a subroutine that accepts a single argument, which is the object returned by the BeginGetResponse method.

Reading the data from the remote server is also a potentially slow process (the server may take a while to respond, or the client's connection to the server may be slow). You can perform the download operation asynchronously with the BeginGetRequestStream and EndGetRequest-Stream objects.

## The WebRequest Project

To demonstrate the members of the WebRequest and WebResponse objects, we've designed a simple application that downloads a document from a web server using these two classes. It's the WebRequest applications, whose main form is shown in Figure 17.2. As you know, downloading a file from a remote server is a slow process, and we can't allow the interface of our application to stop responding while the client computer waits for the server to start submitting data. This example demonstrates how to contact a web server and request a document both synchronously and asynchronously.

**FIGURE 17.2:**

The WebRequest application demonstrates how to contact a web server synchronously and asynchronously.

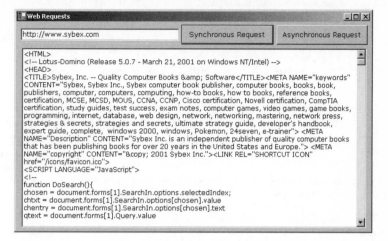

The Synchronous Request button makes a request for a specific URI and then waits for the request to be acknowledged. The request is made with the `HttpWebRequest.Create` method, which returns an HttpWebRequest object as soon as the server responds. You can then call the GetResponseStream method of this object to retrieve the requested URI. Once you retrieve the Stream object, you can assign it to a StreamReader and use the StreamReader class's methods to read the document. You can use the ReadToEnd method, which will wait until the entire document arrives, or the ReadLine method, which will read one line of the document at a time. In either case, the application will remain busy downloading the document until it's done. Listing 17.2 shows the code behind the Synchronous Request button.

**Listing 17.2**    **Downloading a File Synchronously with HttpWebRequest**

```
Private Sub SynchronousDownload(ByVal sender As System.Object, _
                                ByVal e As System.EventArgs) _
                                Handles bttnSynch.Click
    Dim WReq As HttpWebRequest = HttpWebRequest.Create(txtURL.Text.Trim)
    Dim WResp As HttpWebResponse = WReq.GetResponse()
    Dim RStream As Stream = WResp.GetResponseStream()
    Dim SR As StreamReader = _
        New StreamReader(RStream, Encoding.ASCII)
    Dim data As String = SR.ReadLine
    While Not data Is Nothing
        txtResponse.AppendText(data & vbCrLf)
        data = SR.ReadLine
    End While
    WResp.Close()
End Sub
```

The Asynchronous Request button calls the `HttpWebRequest.BeginGetResponse` method, which initiates the asynchronous download of the document specified with the Create method. This method accepts as argument a delegate, which is the address of the subroutine that must be invoked as soon as the server starts transmitting the document. The code behind the Asynchronous Request button is quite simple, as shown in Listing 17.3.

**Listing 17.3       Downloading a File Asynchronously with HttpWebRequest**

```
Private Sub AsynchronousDownload(ByVal sender As System.Object, _
                            ByVal e As System.EventArgs) _
                            Handles bttnAsynch.Click
    Dim WReq As HttpWebRequest = HttpWebRequest.Create(txtURL.Text.Trim)
    Dim ReqCallback As New AsyncCallback(AddressOf RequestComplete)
    WReq.BeginGetResponse(ReqCallback, WReq)
End Sub
```

The `RequestComplete()` subroutine is an asynchronous callback and it accepts a single argument, which is of the IAsyncResult type. This argument basically identifies the asynchronous operation that completed its execution. In the RequestComplete subroutine's code, you must call the EndGetResponse method, passing the argument passed to the RequestComplete subroutine by the system. The EndGetResponse method returns an HttpWebResponse object, similar to the GetResponse method. Once the instance of the HttpWebResponse object has been created, you can use it to read the document, either in its entirety or one line at a time (as we do in Listing 17.4, which shows the code of the RequestComplete delegate).

**Listing 17.4       The RequestComplete Delegate**

```
Private Sub RequestComplete(ByVal ar As System.IAsyncResult)
Dim webGet As HttpWebRequest = CType(ar.AsyncState, HttpWebRequest)
Dim wResp As HttpWebResponse
Dim RStream As IO.StreamReader
    wResp = CType(webGet.EndGetResponse(ar), HttpWebResponse)
    RStream = New IO.StreamReader(wResp.GetResponseStream)
    Dim data As String = RStream.ReadLine
    While Not data Is Nothing
        txtResponse.AppendText(data & vbCrLf)
        data = RStream.ReadLine
    End While
    wResp.Close()
End Sub
```

Reading lines off the incoming stream synchronously is not a very efficient process either. The Stream object exposes the BeginRead/BeginWrite and EndRead/EndWrite methods, which are very similar to the asynchronous methods of the WebResponse object: they accept a delegate and they invoke it when the read/write operation has completed. You can edit the code of the application and make the read operations asynchronous as well.

## The OnlineImages Project

The project in the preceding section demonstrates how to retrieve a text document, but you're not limited to text documents. You can download all types of files as long as you know what to do with the incoming data. In this section, we'll build a new application, the OnLineImages application, that downloads images and displays them on a Windows form as shown in Figure 17.3. The application connects to a web server and downloads a text document with the names of the available images. This document need not exist on the server. You can create it on-the-fly from within an ASPX application on the server. To keep the project simple, we'll create a text file with the image names and send it to the client. Once the file with names of the image files arrives at the client, the application displays them on a ListBox control and the user can download and view any of the images by clicking its name.

**FIGURE 17.3:**

The OnlineImages project downloads images from a web server with the WebRequest/ WebResponse classes.

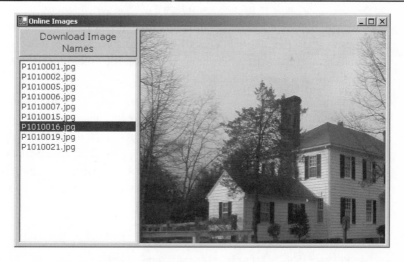

The Download Image Names button contacts a server (in this example, we're using the web server on the local machine) and downloads a file with the names of the images. This is a text file, but most likely it will be another application that returns the names of all image files in a specific folder or drive. Each image name is transmitted on a separate line, and the client reads them with the ReadLine method and places them on a ListBox control. Listing 17.5 shows the code behind this button.

---

**Listing 17.5**    **Downloading the List of Images**

```
Private Sub Button1_Click(ByVal sender As System.Object, _
                          ByVal e As System.EventArgs) _
                          Handles Button1.Click
    Dim WReq As HttpWebRequest = _
        HttpWebRequest.Create("http://127.0.0.1/OnLine/Images.txt")
    Dim WResp As HttpWebResponse = WReq.GetResponse()
    Dim RStream As Stream = WResp.GetResponseStream()
    Dim SR As StreamReader = _
            New StreamReader(RStream, Encoding.ASCII)
    ListBox1.Items.Clear()
    Dim data As String = SR.ReadLine
    While Not data Is Nothing
        ListBox1.Items.Add(data.Trim)
        data = SR.ReadLine
    End While
    WResp.Close()
End Sub
```

---

The image can be downloaded synchronously or asynchronously using any of the methods we discussed earlier. In this example, we use the synchronous method because we want to demonstrate how to use the incoming stream's binary data to reconstruct an image. The code doesn't store the image's bytes anywhere. Instead, it uses the FromStream method of the Image object to create a new image based on the incoming stream with the image's data and display it on a PictureBox control.

Listing 17.6 shows how the program handles the selection of an image file in the ListBox control. After the HttpWebResponse object has been created by a call to the GetResponse method of the appropriate HttpWebRequest object, it's fed to the FromStream method of the Image object. The *img* variable represents an image, whose bitmap is populated as the bytes arrive from the server. Once all the bytes making up the image have been downloaded, the code assigns the *img* variable to the Image property of a PictureBox control.

---

**Listing 17.6**    **Downloading the Image Selected by the User**

```
Private Sub ListBox1_SelectedIndexChanged(_
                        ByVal sender As System.Object,_
                        ByVal e As System.EventArgs) _
                        Handles ListBox1.SelectedIndexChanged
    Dim WReq As HttpWebRequest = _
            HttpWebRequest.Create("http://127.0.0.1/OnLine/" & _
            ListBox1.SelectedItem.ToString)
    Dim WResp As HttpWebResponse
    Try
        WResp = WReq.GetResponse()
```

```
        Catch exc As Exception
            PictureBox1.CreateGraphics.Clear(PictureBox1.BackColor)
            Dim msgFont As New Font("Verdana", 14, FontStyle.Bold)
            PictureBox1.CreateGraphics.DrawString(exc.Message, _
                    msgFont, Brushes.Red, _
                    New RectangleF(0, 0, PictureBox1.Width, _
                                    PictureBox1.Height))
            Exit Sub
        End Try
        Dim RStream As Stream = WResp.GetResponseStream()
        Dim img As Image
        img = Image.FromStream(RStream)
        PictureBox1.Image = img
        WResp.Close()
    End Sub
```

# The TcpClient and TcpListener Classes

These classes use the Transfer Control Protocol (TCP) to make requests over the Internet. The main characteristic of TCP is that it requires that a network connection be established before you can use it to actually send (or receive) data. Unlike with the User Datagram Protocol (UDP), which is discussed later in this chapter, the packets arrive in the same order as they were sent. This isn't exactly true, but TCP itself will rearrange the packets as they arrive.

To exchange information between two machines with TCP, you must use the TcpClient and TcpListener classes. The machines will exchange information with the methods of the TcpClient class, but the TcpListener class is necessary to establish a connection between them. The program running on one of the two machines will instantiate the TcpListener class and wait for the other machine to request a connection. Once a connection between the two machines is established, the two programs can exchange information with the help of the TcpClient class's methods.

## The TcpClient Class's Members

Let's start with an overview of the basic members of the TcpClient class:

**Connect method**    This method connects the client to a remote TCP host using a hostname and a port number. You can also combine the hostname (or IP address of the host) and the port number to create a network endpoint object. The following two lines show the syntax of the Connect method. To use the second form, you must first create an instance of the IPEndPoint class and initialize it to the desired host and port number:

```
TcpClient.Connect(host, Integer)
TcpClient.Connect(IPEndPoint)
```

The host argument can be either the host's name or its IP address. Assuming that a connection to a client has been established, you can use the properties of the IPEndPoint class to retrieve information about the network interface and port number of the client. The basic properties of the IPEndPoint class are the AddressFamily, Address, and Port properties. The IPEntryPoint class is similar to the IPHostEntry class, which was discussed earlier in this chapter.

You can also create an IPEndPoint object and pass it to the Connect method. The following statements prepare an IPEndPoint object that identifies a remote host:

```
Dim remoteTcp as IPEndPoint
remoteTCP.AddressFamily = AddressFamily.InterNetwork
remoteTcp.Address ="194.80.101.32"
remoteTcp.Port = 11000
```

**Close method**     This method closes the TCP connection to the remote server. To close the connection, call the Close method without any arguments:

```
TcpClient.Close()
```

**GetStream method**     Once you have established a TCP connection to a server, you call the GetStream method to obtain a NetworkStream object, which can send and receive data to and from a remote server. The NetworkStream object supports the usual Read and Write methods, which move information between the two computers as arrays of bytes. To use the Write method, you must convert the data you want to send to a byte array and pass it as argument to the Write method. The Read method stores the data received in an array of bytes, which you must convert to a string. These operations are easy to perform with the System .Text.Encoding class.

The following statements attempt to connect to a TCP server, send a command, and display the server's response. The outBuffer array holds the bytes that make up the string you want to send to the client, and the inBuffer array holds the bytes returned by the remote client:

```
Dim client As New TcpClient()
client.Connect("194.80.101.32", 11000)
Dim Strm As NetworkStream = client.GetStream()
Dim outBuffer() As Byte = _
        System.Text.Encoding.ASCII.GetBytes("TCP Connection request")
Strm.Write(outBuffer, 0, outBuffer.Length)
Dim inBuffer(client.ReceiveBufferSize) As Byte
Strm.Read(inBuffer, 0, CInt(client.ReceiveBufferSize))
Dim inData As String = System.Text.Encoding.ASCII.GetString(bytes)
MsgBox("The server's response was " & vbCrLf & inData)
client.Close()
```

## The TcpListener Class's Members

To test-drive the TcpClient class, you need another application that will act as a TCP server. The TCP server application is basically the same as the client and it uses the TcpClient object to send and receive data. However, the TCP server is distinguished from the TCP client by the fact that it must be set up to wait for a connection request from a client and either accept it or cancel it. To accept a TCP connection request, you must use the TcpListener class's members, which are the following:

**LocalEndPoint property**    This property returns the EndPoint of the current TcpListener. It's an instance of the IPEndPoint class.

**Start method**    Call this method to start listening to network requests on the port specified. To start listening for requests on a port, create an instance of the TcpListener class by passing the number of the port to listen to as argument to the class's constructor and then call the Start method:

```
localListener = New TcpListener(5000)
localListener.Start()
```

**Stop method**    This method closes the TcpListener object and stops listening to the port.

**AcceptTcpClient method**    This method, which is called without arguments, accepts a connection request. It's a blocking method and will return only after a client has been connected. As a result, it must be called from within its own thread so that you can end it.

The following statements accept a request from a client and send a string to the client as soon as the connection is established. The AcceptTcpClient method will not return unless a client requests a connection:

```
Dim client As TcpClient = tcpListener.AcceptTcpClient()
Dim str As String = "Connection request accepted"
Dim outBuffer As Byte() = System.Text.Encoding.ASCII.GetBytes(outBuffer)
client.Send(outBuffer)
```

## The TCPChat Project

To demonstrate the use of the TcpClient class, we've developed a chat application. The TCPChat application is running on two different machines and allows users to exchange text messages, one line at a time. The interface of the application is shown in Figure 17.4. The figures show the TCPChat application accepting an incoming request. Once the request is accepted, the two computers can engage in a conversation using the keyboard.

The machine that initiates the chat attempts to establish a connection to another machine, either on a local area network or on the Internet. Once it establishes connection, it sends the following string to the client to indicate that it desires to engage in a conversation:

```
CHAT_REQUEST
```

The remote machine must acknowledge the chat request by sending back the following string:

```
WHORU
```

**FIGURE 17.4:**

The TCPChat application allows two users to chat over the Internet with the help of the TcpClient class.

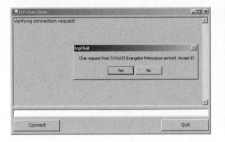

To this command, the computer that initiated the chat must reply by sending the machine name and username. The user of the remote client will see something like this:

```
Chat request from 194.19.230.18 : UserName arrived. Accept it?
```

If the client that receives this request accepts it, the two computers engage in a conversation. Every text line entered on the single-line TextBox at the bottom of the form is sent to the other client. When it arrives there, it's displayed as a separate line on the multiline TextBox at the top of the form. Either end can terminate the connection at any time by clicking the Quit button. You can use two instances of this application to chat with a friend over the Internet or automate the exchange of data between two machines. On a local network, you can request a connection with the machine name. On the Internet, you have to know the IP address of the other end. If one of the parties has a fixed IP address, it's easy to establish a connection at any time as long as an instance of the application is running on the machine with the fixed IP address. Otherwise, the two parties must exchange an IP address either by e-mail or by calling one another. If one of the machines is on a network with a registered IP address, you can use the name of the network and the name of the machine to request a connection.

Let's look at the various parts of the application. The TCPChat project's code is a bit involved because the same application acts as both client and server. The same application can either initiate a connection or accept a connection request from a remote computer. When the application starts, it must enter a "wait" mode, in which it waits for a connection request from the remote client. Both ends are using the same application and we don't know which one will initiate the chat, so the application must listen to the other end for a chat request.

To listen to a request from a remote client, you must call the AcceptTcpClient method of the TcpListener object. Because this method is synchronous, you must call it from within a thread. This thread should also raise an event when a client request arrives. We'll start with a class, the ListenClass, which contains both a subroutine to be executed on its own thread and the declaration of the event. The code of the ListenClass class is shown in Listing 17.7. The multithreading techniques we'll use in this chapter have been discussed in detail in Chapter 10.

**Listing 17.7        The ListenClass Class**

```
Class ListenClass
    Public client As TcpClient
    Public Event Connected()
    Public localListener As TcpListener

    Public Sub StartThread()
        If localListener Is Nothing Then
            localListener = New TcpListener(5000)
        End If
        localListener.Start()
        client = localListener.AcceptTcpClient
        RaiseEvent Connected()
    End Sub

    Public Sub StopListening()
        localListener.Stop()
    End Sub
End Class
```

When the application starts, it's placed in "wait" mode: the StartThread subroutine is executed on a background thread. The subroutine calls the AcceptTcpClient method and waits until a request arrives from a remote computer. When a client running the same application requests a connection, the AcceptTcpClient method returns and the Connected event is fired. The thread is instantiated in the Form's Load event handler with the statements in Listing 17.8.

**Listing 17.8        Starting a Thread to Listen for Incoming Connections**

```
Private Sub Form1_Load(ByVal sender As Object, _
                       ByVal e As System.EventArgs) Handles MyBase.Load
    TSThread = New Threading.Thread(AddressOf TS.StartThread)
    TSThread.Priority = Threading.ThreadPriority.BelowNormal
    TSThread.Start()
End Sub
```

Let's look now at the code that requests a connection. When the Connect button is clicked, the statements shown in Listing 17.9 are executed. The program prompts the user for the IP address of the remote computer and attempts to establish a TCP connection to port 5000 (any free port will do). If the connection attempt is successful, the code creates two Stream objects: a StreamWriter, which will be used to send commands to the remote computer, and a StreamReader, which will be used to read the commands sent by the remote client.

The commands exchanged between the two computers have the form "$$$[*XXX*]$$$," where *XXX* is the command. We've chosen this format to minimize the chances of interpreting a message sent from one computer to the other during the chat as a command. The first command sent by the computer that made the request is the CHAT_REQUEST command. The remote client must respond to this command with another command, the WHORU command. Then the local client must send the computer's name followed by a colon and the user's name. The remote computer will either accept the connection or respond with the QUIT command, which terminates the connection. The code behind the Connect button is shown in Listing 17.9.

**Listing 17.9** **Accepting a Connection Request**

```
Private Sub bttnConnect_Click(ByVal sender As System.Object, _
                              ByVal e As System.EventArgs) _
                              Handles bttnConnect.Click
    TS.localListener.Stop()
    TSThread.Abort()

    Dim remoteclient As TcpClient
    Dim remoteIP As String
    remoteIP = InputBox("Enter the IP of the remote computer")
    If remoteIP = "" Then Exit Sub
    Try
        remoteclient = New TcpClient(remoteIP, 5000)
    Catch exc As Exception
        MsgBox(exc.Message)
        Exit Sub
    End Try
    txtRemote.Focus()
    R = New IO.StreamReader(remoteclient.GetStream)
    W = New IO.StreamWriter(remoteclient.GetStream)
    W.WriteLine("$$$[CHAT_REQUEST]$$$")
    W.Flush()
    Dim resp As String = R.ReadLine
    If resp = "$$$[WHORU]$$$" Then
        W.WriteLine(Environment.MachineName & ":" & _
                    Environment.UserName)
        W.Flush()
    End If
    TSThread = New Threading.Thread(AddressOf CClass.StartThread)
    CClass.clientStream = R
    txtChat.AppendText("Connected to " & remoteIP & vbCrLf)
    TSThread.Start()
    bttnQuit.Enabled = True
    bttnConnect.Enabled = False
End Sub
```

The client that receives the request accepts it initially. Then the Connected event (whose handler is shown in Listing 17.10) is fired. This event is declared in the ListenClass class's code and can be raised by any part of the code that has access to the class. In this event handler, we create a StreamWriter and StreamReader, the *W* and *R* variables, to send data to the remote client and read the data sent by the remote computer respectively. These two objects are created with the GetStream method of the *localClient* variable. This variable is set in the ListenClass's Connected event handler when the computer initially accepts the request. The Connected event's handler is shown in Listing 17.10.

The two computers engage in a handshake, as explained already. During this process, either computer can terminate the connection by sending the QUIT command to the other end. If all ends well and the two ends agree to engage in a chat session, the StartChat subroutine is executed on a separate thread on both machines. The TCP protocol enables two computers to send and receive data simultaneously.

**Listing 17.10      Validating a Connection Request**

```
Private Sub TS_Connected() Handles TS.Connected
    localClient = TS.client
    txtChat.Text = "Verifying connection request" & vbCrLf
    W = New IO.StreamWriter(localClient.GetStream)
    R = New IO.StreamReader(localClient.GetStream)
    Dim resp As String
    resp = R.ReadLine
    If resp <> "$$$[CHAT_REQUEST]$$$" Then
        localClient.Close()
        Exit Sub
    End If
    W.WriteLine("$$$[WHORU]$$$")
    W.Flush()
    resp = R.ReadLine
    Dim reply As DialogResult
    reply = MsgBox("Chat request from " & resp & _
                " arrived. Accept it?", MsgBoxStyle.YesNo)
    If reply = DialogResult.No Then
        W.WriteLine("$$$[QUIT]$$$")
        W.Flush()
        localClient.Close()
        TSThread = New Threading.Thread(AddressOf TS.StartThread)
        TSThread.Start()
        txtChat.Text = "Awaiting connection request" & vbCrLf
        bttnQuit.Enabled = False
        bttnConnect.Enabled = True
        Exit Sub
    End If
    txtChat.AppendText("Request accepted, you're online" & vbCrLf)
```

```
        TSThread = New Threading.Thread(AddressOf CClass.StartChat)
        CClass.clientStream = R
        TSThread.Start()
        bttnQuit.Enabled = True
        bttnConnect.Enabled = False
    End Sub
```

To read the incoming lines, we must set up a loop that continuously monitors the client's stream. This loop, however, shouldn't freeze our interface, so we'll implement it as another thread. This thread should also exchange information with the main thread: it will monitor the incoming stream and send the characters entered by the user to the remote computer, and it will also raise two events:

**LineArrived event**    This event is raised every time a new line arrives from the remote client. This event passes to the main thread the string sent by the remote client.

**ConnnectionClosed event**    This event is raised when the remote client terminates the connection.

The actual chat takes place from within a procedure that runs in its own thread. We need another class, the ChatClass, with the subroutine that monitors the incoming stream. Listing 17.11 shows the ChatClass, which monitors the client stream. The StartChat subroutine enters a loop that keeps calling the ReadLine method of the StreamReader object created by the ListenClass. Every time the remote client sends a new line of text, the ReadLine method of the clientStream object returns and the LineArrived event is fired. The line of text is passed to the handler of this event as argument.

The connection can be terminated by the client with the QUIT command. When this command arrives, the ConnectionClosed event is fired. The connection may also be terminated unexpectedly, so we trap all errors and terminate the connection from within our code as well.

**Listing 17.11    The ChatClass Class**

```
Class ChatClass
    Public clientStream As IO.StreamReader
    Public Event LineArrived(ByVal txtLine As String)
    Public Event ConnectionClosed()

    Public Sub StartChat()
        Dim line As String
        While True
            Try
                line = clientStream.ReadLine
                If line = "$$$[QUIT]$$$" Then
                    RaiseEvent ConnectionClosed()
```

```
                    Exit Sub
                End If
            Catch exc As Exception
                RaiseEvent ConnectionClosed()
                clientStream.Close()
                Exit Sub
            End Try
            If Not line Is Nothing Then RaiseEvent LineArrived(line)
        End While
    End Sub
End Class
```

Once the two machines are connected, the program starts the TSThread (see Listing 17.10) thread on both clients. When you use the TCP protocol, the two machines can both talk and listen to one another at the same time. The characters entered by each user on the lower Text-Box control are sent to the other machine, where they're displayed on the upper (multiline) TextBox control.

You can add more commands to the TCPChat application. For example, you can add commands that initiate a process on the remote machine (commands to act on the local file system, start a console application, and so on). The remote computer can format the result of the process as text and send it to the computer that initiated the process.

## The UdpClient Class

The UdpClient class is similar to the TcpClient class, and it uses the User Datagram Protocol (UDP) to exchange information between clients. The difference between the two protocols is that UDP requires that the two clients exchange commands in a well-defined sequence. Where TCP allows the two ends to send and receive data at once, UDP requires that each client knows when it should transmit and when it should receive data.

The two computers that communicate through UDP use the UdpClient class. One instance of this class acts as a server, while the other one acts as a client. The server machine is the one that waits for a UDP client to make a request on a specific port and accepts it. The client is the machine that makes the request. The client machine knows the address of the server and uses it to request a connection. The server machine, on the other hand, is informed about the address of the machine that made a request when it accepts it.

To open a communication channel between two computers with UDP, you must create two different applications, one for each computer. The server computer must listen for an incoming request on a specific port. The server computer doesn't know where the request is coming from, but the address of the client computer is passed to the server as soon as the connection is established. The following statements create an instance of the UdpClient class and set it to listen to port 1011:

```
Dim localPort As Integer = 1011
client = New UdpClient(localPort)

Dim remoteEP As IPEndPoint
Dim data() As Byte = client.Receive(remoteEP)
```

The Receive method returns the data sent by the remote client. The argument of the Receive method is passed by reference, and it's set to an IPEndPoint variable that represents the remote client. The IP address of the remote client is given by the expression `remoteEP.Address`.

The client, on the other hand, will request a connection by calling the UdpClient class's Connect method and passing the remote server's address and port:

```
Dim udpClient As New UdpClient()
udpClient.Connect("193.29.79.102", 1011)
```

Alternatively, the client computer can connect to the server by creating a new instance of the UdpClient class and passing the address and port of the remote server:

```
Dim remoteClient As New UdpClient("193.29.79.102", 1011)
```

Once the connection between the two computers has been established, either computer can call the Send method to send data to the other computer and the Receive method to the retrieve data sent by the other computer. The Receive method is synchronous, and it will return only if the other has submitted an array of bytes.

The syntax of the Send method is as follows:

```
UdpClient.Send(buffer, length)
```

In this statement, `buffer` is an array with the data to be transferred and `length` is the number of bytes in the array. Here is another overloaded form of the function:

```
UdpClient.Send(buffer, length, endpoint)
```

This form of the method accepts a third argument, which is an IPEndPoint representing the remote server. A third form of the method is identical to the previous one, but it uses the remote server's hostname and port:

```
UdpClient.Send(buffer, length, hostname, port)
```

Here is the syntax of the Receive method:

```
UdpClient.Receive(remoteEP)
```

The `remoteEP` argument is set to an IPEndPoint that represents the computer that sent the data. Because the server is listening to a specific port but not a specific address, you must always examine the value of the Receive method's argument to make sure you're communicating with the desired client. The data sent by the remote computer is returned by the Receive method as an array of bytes.

## The UDPDemo Projects

To demonstrate how to use the UdpClient class, we've designed the UDPDemoClient and UDPDemoServer projects. The server project waits for a connection request from a remote client. When a request arrives, it validates the address of the remote client and accepts the request if the remote computer's name is PowerToolkit (or whatever name you specify). Then it sends the SEND_FILE string to the client and waits for the client to respond with the name of the file it's about to send and then the file's lines. The client and server projects of the UDP-Demo project group are shown in Figures 17.5 and 17.6.

**FIGURE 17.5:**

The UDPDemoClient project connects to the server and sends a file.

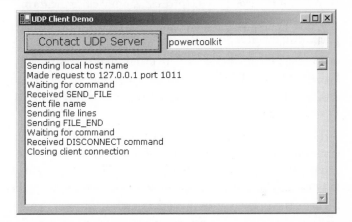

**FIGURE 17.6:**

The UDPDemoServer project accepts a client connection and requests a file upload.

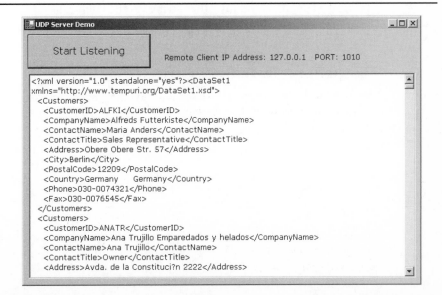

Let's start with the server program. When the Start Listening button is clicked, the program creates an instance of the UdpClient class and starts listening to port 1011:

```
Dim localPort As Integer = 1011
client = New UdpClient(localPort)
Dim remoteEP As IPEndPoint
Dim data() As Byte = client.Receive(remoteEP)
```

The Receive method is a blocking one, and it will not return unless it receives some data from a client. This call should take place from within a separate thread so you can terminate the process of listening. For the purpose of this example, we assume that a connection will arrive. If you want to terminate the process, simply close the form.

When a client sends some data to the server, the *remoteEP* variable is set to the address of the remote client. You can use this value to validate the client and initiate a session or to break the connection. The program displays the address of the remote client on a Label control and then examines the data sent by the client. We want the client to identify itself by sending a specific string (in our case, the name of the client machine, which is PowerToolkit).

If the data came from a known machine, the server sends a command, the SEND_FILE command. You decide the format of the commands and the set of commands both the server and the client should understand. The SEND_FILE command requests a file from the client. In our example, we'll let the client determine which file to send. You can also pass one or more filenames as argument to this command. If the two machines communicate to exchange specific files at certain times, the client knows which file it's supposed to transmit.

To send a command (or any other string) to the client, the server uses the SendString() subroutine, whose definition is shown in Listing 17.12.

**Listing 17.12**     **The SendString Subroutine**

```
Private Sub SendString(ByVal what As String, ByVal where As IPEndPoint)
Dim buffer(what.Length + 1) As Byte
Dim len As Integer = _
                    System.Text.Encoding.ASCII.GetBytes( _
                    what.ToCharArray(), 0, what.Length, buffer, 0)
    Try
        client.Send(buffer, len, where)
    Catch exc As Exception
        MsgBox(exc.Message)
    End Try
End Sub
```

The *client* variable represents the local instance of the UdpClient class. It's declared in the form's level and it's instantiated with the following statements:

```
Dim localPort As Integer = 1011
client = New UdpClient(localPort)
```

The first argument of the SendString() subroutine is the string to be transmitted and the second argument identifies the client to which the string will be sent. The IPEndPoint object includes the address and the port number of the client, which means that a client may be receiving data from multiple remote machines, each one on a different port. To send the command SEND_FILE to the remote client, the program creates a string with the command's name and passes it to the SendString() subroutine, along with the *remoteEP* variable:

```
cmdString = "SEND_FILE"
SendString(cmdString, remoteEP)
```

Then the server receives the name of the file to be transmitted from the client and responds by sending the "OK" string:

```
data = client.Receive(remoteEP)
Dim fileName As String = System.Text.Encoding.ASCII.GetString(data)
cmdString = "OK"
SendString(cmdString, remoteEP)
```

Then it enters a loop that's repeated for each line of the file. The remote client sends an XML file, one line at a time. When it's done, it sends the command FILE_END on a separate line. You should change the file delimiter to a string that's very unlikely to appear in the body of the information you transmit between the two machines.

When the UDP server sees this string, it responds by sending the DISCONNECT string, which closes the connection. The complete listing behind the Start Listening button is shown in Listing 17.13.

**Listing 17.13**      **Requesting and Receiving a File from a Remote Client**

```
Private Sub Button1_Click(ByVal sender As System.Object, _
                          ByVal e As System.EventArgs) _
                          Handles Button1.Click
    Dim localPort As Integer = 1011
    client = New UdpClient(localPort)

    Dim remoteEP As IPEndPoint
    Dim data() As Byte = client.Receive(remoteEP)
    Label1.Text = "Remote Client IP Address: " & _
                  remoteEP.Address.ToString & "   PORT: " & _
                  remoteEP.Port.ToString
```

```
    Application.DoEvents()
    Dim resp As String = System.Text.Encoding.ASCII.GetString(data)
    Dim cmdString As String, strLen As Integer
    If resp = "PowerToolkit" Then
        cmdString = "SEND_FILE"
        SendString(cmdString, remoteEP)
    Else
        MsgBox("Request from unrecognized client. " & _
               "Will close connection")
        Label1.Text = "Remote Client: None"
        client.Close()
        Exit Sub
    End If
    data = client.Receive(remoteEP)
    Dim fileName As String = System.Text.Encoding.ASCII.GetString(data)
    cmdString = "OK"
    SendString(cmdString, remoteEP)
    data = client.Receive(remoteEP)
    resp = System.Text.Encoding.ASCII.GetString(data)
    While resp <> "FILE_END"
        txtFile.AppendText(resp & vbCrLf)
        data = client.Receive(remoteEP)
        resp = System.Text.Encoding.ASCII.GetString(data)
        If resp = "FILE_END" Then
            cmdString = "DISCONNECT"
            SendString(cmdString, remoteEP)
            client.Close()
            MsgBox("Received File " & fileName & "(" & _
                   txtFile.Text.Length.ToString & " bytes)")
            Exit Sub
        Else
            SendString(cmdString, remoteEP)
        End If
    End While
    cmdString = "DISCONNECT"
    SendString(cmdString, remoteEP)
    MsgBox("Received file " & fileName & " (" & _
           txtFile.Text.Length.ToString & " bytes)")
    client.Close()
    Exit Sub
End Sub
```

Let's switch to the client's side. The client creates two instances of the UdpClient class. The *client* variable represents the local computer's UDP port and will be used to send data to the server. The *RemoteEP* variable is set to the remote server and will be used to receive data sent by the server program:

```
Dim remoteAddress As String = txtURL.Text
Dim remotePort As Integer = 1011
```

```
Dim localPort As Integer = 1010
client = New UdpClient(localPort)
Dim RemoteEP As IPEndPoint
```

The address of the remote server is picked from the TextBox control on the form. The client listens to port 1010 and talks to port 1011—the server uses the same ports, but their roles are reversed.

To send data, the client uses the same SendString() subroutine. To initiate a connection, it sends its name to the selected IP address and port:

```
RemoteEP = _
    New IPEndPoint(Dns.Resolve(txtURL.Text).AddressList(0), remotePort)
SendString(Dns.GetHostName, RemoteEP)
```

The Resolve method of the Dns class converts a computer name to an IP address. If the server is another computer on the same local network, you can specify its address by name. You can also specify the remote server by name if it's on a network with a registered name. If the server's name is Listener and it belongs to the domain MyCompanyInc.com, you can specify its address with the name Listener.MyCompanyInc.com.

Then the client enters a loop, which reads the commands sent by the server. Our sample application recognizes two commands, the SEND_FILE and DISCONNECT commands. You can modify the code to add more commands. When the user clicks the Contact UDP Server button, the code establishes a connection to the remote UDP server and reacts to the SEND_FILE command. The code behind this button is shown in Listing 17.14.

---

**Listing 17.14**    **Contacting a Remote UDP Server**

```
Private Sub Button1_Click(ByVal sender As System.Object, _
                          ByVal e As System.EventArgs) _
                          Handles Button1.Click
    Dim remoteAddress As String = txtURL.Text
    Dim remotePort As Integer = 1011
    Dim localPort As Integer = 1010
    client = New UdpClient(localPort)

    Dim RemoteEP As IPEndPoint
    RemoteEP = _
    New IPEndPoint(Dns.Resolve(txtURL.Text).AddressList(0), remotePort)
    TextBox1.AppendText("Sending local host name" & vbCrLf)
    SendString(Dns.GetHostName, RemoteEP)
    TextBox1.AppendText("Made request to " & _
                        RemoteEP.Address.ToString & " port " & _
                        RemoteEP.Port.ToString & vbCrLf)
    Dim resp As String = ""
    Dim endpoint As IPEndPoint
```

```
    Dim txtLine As String
    While Not resp = "DISCONNECT"
        TextBox1.AppendText("Waiting for command" & vbCrLf)
        Dim data() As Byte
        Try
            data = client.Receive(endpoint)
        Catch exc As Exception
            TextBox1.AppendText("Connection attempt failed " & _
                                "(UDP Server not running)")
            Exit Sub
        End Try
        resp = System.Text.Encoding.ASCII.GetString(data)
        If resp = "SEND_FILE" Then
            TextBox1.AppendText("Received SEND_FILE" & vbCrLf)
            TextBox1.AppendText("Sent file name" & vbCrLf)
            SendString("CUSTOMERS.XML", RemoteEP)
            TextBox1.AppendText("Sending file lines " & vbCrLf)
            Dim stream As New StreamReader("C:\Customers.xml")
            txtLine = stream.ReadLine
            Dim iLine As Integer = 1
            While Not txtLine Is Nothing
                SendString(txtLine, RemoteEP)
                data = client.Receive(endpoint)
                If System.Text.Encoding.ASCII.GetString _
                            (data) <> "OK" Then
                    MsgBox("File transfer failed")
                    client.Close()
                    Exit Sub
                End If
                txtLine = stream.ReadLine
            End While
            TextBox1.AppendText("Sending FILE_END" & vbCrLf)
            SendString("FILE_END", RemoteEP)
        End If
    End While
    TextBox1.AppendText("Received DISCONNECT command" & vbCrLf)
    TextBox1.AppendText("Closing client connection" & vbCrLf)
    client.Close()
    Exit Sub
End Sub
```

The client logs its actions on a TextBox control so that you can watch the progress of the operation.

## Sending and Receiving Mail

While we're on the topic of communicating with other machines over the Internet, a few words about exchanging e-mail messages through a message server are in order. We'll start by stating that the simplest method of accessing your messages (and creating new ones) is to automate Outlook. Outlook's object model is very rich, and it makes sending and receiving mail quite trivial. However, Outlook is not installed on all machines, and you may wish to exchange messages that need not appear in anyone's mailbox. You can use the tools discussed in this section to exchange messages between applications; these messages will not appear in the inbox or outbox of any e-mail application.

As you know, there are two protocols for exchanging mail messages: Post Office Protocol, version 3 (POP3) and Simple Mail Transfer Protocol (SMTP). POP3 interacts with a mail server and provides commands for reading messages and deleting them from a mail server. SMTP provides commands for creating new messages and sending them to a mail server. The .NET Framework's SmtpMail class exposes all the functionality you need to create new messages and upload them to a specific account on a mail server, which will then deliver the messages to their recipients. However, there's no equivalent class for the POP3 protocol. To access a POP3 account, you must use the TcpClient class to establish a connection to a POP3 mail server and execute any of the POP3 commands against it.

## The SmtpMail Class

To send a message with the SmtpMail class, you must create an instance of the `System.Web.Mail` class (which represents a mail message), create a message object, and then send it with the SmtpMail class's Send method. The message will be delivered through the SMTP mail service built into Windows 2000 (if it's addressed to another user on the same local network) or through an arbitrary SMTP server. To specify a mail server, use the SMTPServer property. If the SMTP Windows Service is running, you need not specify a mail server. The messages will be delivered through the default e-mail server.

The `System.Web.Mail` namespace exposes the MailMessage and MailAttachment classes, which you will need to create and send a message.

## The MailMessage Class

The MailMessage class provides properties and methods for creating a message. It exposes the following basic properties:

**Attachments**    A collection of attachments to be transmitted with the message.

**Bcc**    A list of e-mail addresses to receive a blind carbon copy (BCC) of the message. Mulitple BCC recipients are separated with semicolons.

**Body**    The message's body.

**BodyEncoding**    The encoding type of the message's body. This property's value is a member of the `System.Text.Encoding` enumeration: `ASCIIEncoding`, `UnicodeEncoding`, `UTF7Encoding`, and `UTF8Encoding`.

**BodyFormat**   The content type of the message's body. This property's value can be Html or Text.

**Cc**   A list of e-mail addresses to receive a carbon copy (CC) of the message. Mulitple CC recipients are separated with semicolons.

**From**   The address of the message's sender. You can specify any address, as the From property isn't validated.

**Headers**   The custom headers that are transmitted with the message.

**Priority**   The message's priority. Its value is a member of the MailPriority enumeration: High, Low, and Normal.

**Subject**   The message's subject.

**To**   The address of the message's recipient. It's your responsibility to specify a valid address, because you will not be notified about unsuccessful attempts to deliver a message.

**UrlContentBase**   The URL base for all relative URLs contained in the body of an HTML message.

**UrlContentLocation**   The Content-Location HTTP header for the message.

**NOTE**   The From property's setting isn't picked up automatically from the mail server. You can specify any sender name you wish with this property and the message will be delivered. If you've ever received annoying messages without a return address, this is how they were sent. You can even send a message using the recipient's address as the sender's address. Of course, this doesn't mean that you can send messages and remain totally anonymous, because the header of the message will contain information about your server. Also note that if you specify an address that doesn't exist, or if your message can't be delivered for any other reason, you will not receive any indication about the failure of the delivery.

## The MailAttachment Class

The MailAttachment class provides properties and methods for creating attachments:

**Encoding**   The encoding of the current attachment

**Filename**   The attached file's name

The SmtpMail class provides the Send method, which sends a message. You can call this method by passing a MailMessage object as argument or by passing four string arguments, which are the message's sender, recipient, subject, and body. The following statements create a short message and send it:

```
Dim from As String = "your_name"
Dim mailto As String = "recipients_name"
Dim subject As String = "SubjectLine"
Dim body As String = "Enter your message here"
SmtpMail.Send(from, mailto, subject, body)
```

Alternatively, you can create a MailMessage object and pass it to the Send method as argument:

```
Dim msg As New MailMessage()
msg.From = "your_name"
msg.To = "recipients_name"
msg.Subject = "SubjectLine"
```

To attach one or more files to the message, create a MailAttachment object and add it to the Attachments collection with the Add property:

```
Dim attch As New MailAttachment("C:\My Documents\Attached1.txt")
msg.Attachments.Add(attch)
attch = New MailAttachment("C:\My Documents\Attached2.txt")
msg.Attachments.Add(attch)
```

## Accessing a POP3 Mail Server

To access a POP3 mail server (all mail servers on the Internet support this protocol), you must create a TCPClient object, connect to the mail server, and log in. Once you're connected, you can issue any of the POP3 commands against the mail server. Let's start with a quick overview of the POP3 commands and then we'll look at the details of connecting to a mail server and accessing the messages for a specific account.

### The POP3 Commands

POP3 is a simple mail protocol, but it doesn't provide functionality equivalent to that of the SMTP protocol. The messages you retrieve from a POP3 mail server are returned as long strings. All the fields of the message are included in this string, with the appropriate headers and delimiters. Even the attachments are embedded in the message and it's the client's responsibility to extract them. Since the attachments can be binary files too, they're encoded as text and you must convert them to the appropriate format. In this section, we'll discuss how to retrieve simple messages and extract their fields. Extracting the attachments is fairly complicated, and you should leave this task to your mail program. However, you can look up the specifications of the POP3 protocol to learn how a message is encoded and how to extract the attachments from the message's body.

Most developers will write code to access a POP3 server and retrieve specific messages (messages from a specific account or messages with a specific string in their subject line) and process them silently. These are messages between applications that require no user interaction and should not end up in a user's mailbox.

POP3 recognizes the commands in Table 17.1. Each message on the server is identified by an integer value. The first (oldest) message on the server has an index of 1, the second oldest message has an index of 2, and so on. Most of the POP3 commands accept a message number as argument and act on the specified message.

**TABLE 17.1:**  POP3 Commands

| Command | Description |
|---------|-------------|
| USER | This command is followed by an account name and it passes it to the POP3 server for verification purposes. |
| PASS | This command is followed by a password and it passes it to the POP3 server for verification purposes. Once you have logged onto the server, you can issue any of the following commands. |
| STAT | This command displays the number of messages for a specific account in the mail server, as well as their total size. |
| LIST | This command accepts as argument a message number and displays the message's total size. |
| RETR | This command accepts as argument a message number and displays the message. The command retrieves the entire message (including its sender, subject, and attachments) as a single string. |
| DELE | This command accepts as argument a message number and deletes the message. Messages deleted with the DELE command are marked as deleted on the server and you can't access them, but they're not physically removed from the server's disk. To remove the deleted messages from the server, you must call the QUIT command. |
| QUIT | This command closes the connection to the server and removes all deleted messages. |
| TOP | This command accepts as arguments a message number and the number of lines to display. |

All commands are processed by the mail server, which responds with a string. The mail server's response starts either with the prefix +OK (if the command was executed successfully) or with the prefix –ERR (if the command failed). Following the prefix, there's usually an informative message, which may differ from server to server. The prefix is always one of the two strings shown earlier, and you can read them to find out whether the command was successful or not. Then you can extract the message and display it to the user. Here's how you can connect to a POP3 server and read your mail without a mail client like Outlook or Eudora Mail: Start Telnet from the Run menu (Select Start ➤ Run, enter **Telnet**, and press Enter). In the Command Prompt window that appears, you can issue the Open command to connect to your mail server. The Open command is a Telnet command; you use it only to connect to the server. Once you've established a connection, you can issue any of the POP3 commands discussed earlier.

Run Telnet and enter the following command to connect to your mail server:

```
OPEN mail.isp.com 110
```

Replace *mail.isp.com* with your mail server's name. 110 is the port; always use port 110 when connecting to a mail server. The server will respond with a string like this, but the server name will be different:

```
+OK POP3 wstation100.proto.biz server ready
```

Notice that the name of the server you use to connect is usually an alias and the server's response includes the actual server name.

Then enter the USER command followed by your username:

```
USER user_name
```

You will not see what you type from now on, just the server's responses. The server should respond with a string like the following:

```
+OK User name accepted, password please
```

Now you must enter this, where *password* is your password:

```
PASS password
```

The server will respond with a string like this:

```
+OK Mailbox open, 3 messages
```

Now enter the STAT command and you'll get back the number of messages waiting for you on the server followed by their total size:

```
+OK 3 124356
```

Obviously, this response indicates one or more messages with attachments. If you issue an invalid command, like SHOW, or you attempt to reissue the USER command, you'll get a different response:

```
-ERR Unknown TRANSACTION state command
```

This error message tells you that your command is not recognized in the TRANSACTION state (once you log in, you're automatically in TRANSACTION state). To view the first message, enter the following command:

```
RETR 1
```

To view the first line of the second message enter this command:

```
LIST 2 1
```

The first line is quite long, and it will be displayed on many lines in the window. This line contains the message's header (the sender's address, the date it arrived, the message's subject, and so on). Figure 17.7 shows how you interact with a POP3 mail server. You can only see the server's responses, but you can guess which command was issued and generated each response.

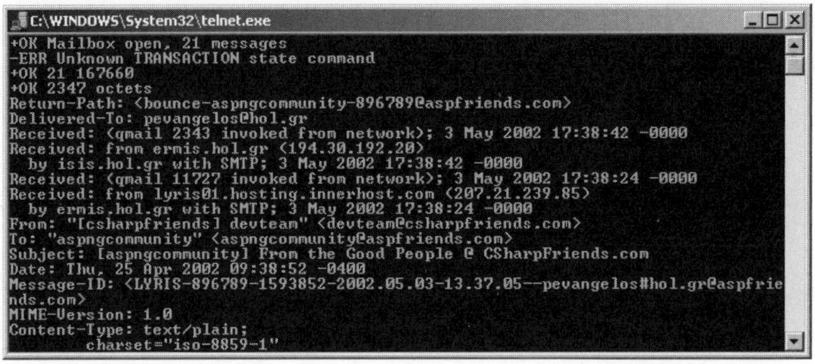

**FIGURE 17.7:**

Interacting with a POP3
mail server through
Telnet with POP3
commands

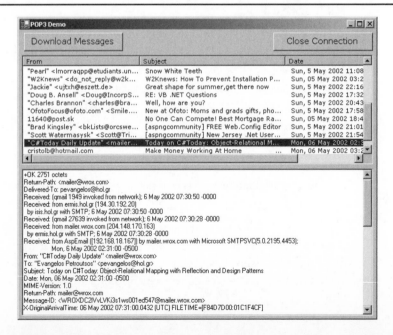

### The POP3Client Project

The POP3Client project, whose main form is shown in Figure 17.8, demonstrates the process
of connecting to a POP3 mail server and manipulating the messages on the server from within
a VB application. To connect, the program prompts the user for the name of the mail server
and the user's name and password. The mail server has the form `mail.server.com`. If your
username is `user@server.com`, the main server's name is probably `mail.server.com`. You can
find out the name of the mail server by looking at the properties of your mail application (it's
the setting of the POP3 property). Once the user is connected, the program downloads all the
messages on the server and displays their headers on a ListView control.

**FIGURE 17.8:**

The POP3Client
application downloads
the messages from a
POP3 mail server.

The selected message's body is displayed on a TextBox control at the bottom of the form. Users can select a message with the keyboard or the mouse and view its body. Pressing the Del key deletes the selected message. The message isn't removed from the server, so the code removes all the fields except for the message's subject on the ListView control. The deleted messages will be removed from the server when the Close Connection button is clicked, which closes the connection.

Because each message is returned as a long string, we must also write the appropriate functions to extract the parts of the message. These functions, along with some utility functions that connect to the server and execute commands against it, will be placed in a class, the POP3Message class, which is shown in Listing 17.15.

**Listing 17.15**     **The POP3Message Class**

```
Class POP3Message

    Dim Server As TcpClient
    Dim NetStrm As NetworkStream
    Dim RdStrm As StreamReader

    Public Function Connect() As Integer
        Dim POP3Account As String
        POP3Account = InputBox("Enter your POP3 account name " & _
                                "(e.g., mail.server.com)")
        If POP3Account.Trim = "" Then Exit Function
        Try
            Server = New TcpClient(POP3Account.Trim, 110)
            NetStrm = Server.GetStream()
            RdStrm = New StreamReader(Server.GetStream())
        Catch exc As Exception
            MsgBox(exc.Message)
            Exit Function
        End Try
        Dim user As String
        user = InputBox("Enter your user name")
        Dim data As String = "USER " + user.Trim + vbCrLf
        Dim szData() As Byte = _
            System.Text.Encoding.ASCII.GetBytes(data.ToCharArray())
        NetStrm.Write(szData, 0, szData.Length)
        Dim POPResponse As String
        POPResponse = RdStrm.ReadLine()
        If POPResponse.Substring(0, 4) = "-ERR" Then
            MsgBox("Invalid user name")
            Return -1
        End If

        Dim password As String
        password = InputBox("Enter your password")
        data = "PASS " & password & vbCrLf
```

```
            szData = System.Text.Encoding.ASCII.GetBytes(data.ToCharArray())
            NetStrm.Write(szData, 0, szData.Length)
            POPResponse = RdStrm.ReadLine()

            If POPResponse.Substring(0, 4) = "-ERR" Then
                MsgBox("Invalid password")
                Return -1
            End If
            data = "STAT" + vbCrLf
            szData = System.Text.Encoding.ASCII.GetBytes(data.ToCharArray())
            NetStrm.Write(szData, 0, szData.Length)
            POPResponse = RdStrm.ReadLine()
            If POPResponse.Substring(0, 4) = "-ERR" Then
                MsgBox("Could not log you in")
                Return -1
            End If
            Dim parts() As String
            parts = POPResponse.Split(" ")
            Dim messages, totSize As Integer
            messages = parts(3)
            Return messages
        End Function

        Public Function DeleteMessage(ByVal msgIndex As Integer)
            Dim data As String = "DELE " & msgIndex.ToString & vbCrLf
            Dim szData() As Byte = _
                    System.Text.Encoding.ASCII.GetBytes(data.ToCharArray())
            NetStrm.Write(szData, 0, szData.Length)
            Dim tmpString As String = RdStrm.ReadLine()
            If tmpString.Substring(0, 4) = -ERR" Then
                MsgBox("Could not delete message")
                Return -1
            Else
                Return 11
            End If
        End Function

        Public Function Quit()
            Dim data As String = "QUIT " & vbCrLf
            Dim szData() As Byte = _
                    System.Text.Encoding.ASCII.GetBytes(data.ToCharArray())
            NetStrm.Write(szData, 0, szData.Length)
            Dim tmpString As String = RdStrm.ReadLine()
        End Function

        Public Structure Message
            Dim _From As String
            Dim _To As String
            Dim _Date As String
            Dim _Subject As String
            Dim _CC As String
```

```
        Dim _BCC As String
        Dim _Received As String
        Dim _Body As String
    End Structure

    Public Function CreateFromText(ByVal strMessage As String) As Message
        Dim Mssg As New Message()
        Dim brkPos As Integer
        Dim Header As String
        Dim Headers() As String
        Dim Body As String
        Dim vField As Object
        Dim strHeader As String
        Dim HeaderName As String
        Dim HeaderValue As String

        brkPos = InStr(1, strMessage, vbCrLf & vbCrLf)
        If brkPos Then
            Header = strMessage.Substring(0, brkPos - 1)
            Body = strMessage.Substring(brkPos + 1, _
                        strMessage.Length - Header.Length - 3)
            Mssg._Body = Body
        Else
            Throw New Exception("Invalid message format")
            Exit Function
        End If

        Headers = Split(Header, vbCrLf)
        Dim _header As String
        For Each _header In Headers
            brkPos = _header.IndexOf(":")
            If brkPos >= 0 Then
                HeaderName = _header.Substring(0, brkPos)
            Else
                HeaderName = ""
            End If
            HeaderValue = _header.Substring(brkPos + 1)
            Select Case HeaderName.ToLower
                Case "received"
                    Mssg._Received = HeaderValue
                Case "from"
                    Mssg._From = HeaderValue
                Case "to"
                    Mssg._To = HeaderValue
                Case "cc"
                    Mssg._CC = HeaderValue
                Case "bcc"
                    Mssg._BCC = HeaderValue
                Case "subject"
                    Mssg._Subject = HeaderValue
```

```
                Case "date"
                    Mssg._Date = HeaderValue
            End Select
        Next
        Return Mssg
    End Function

    Function GetMessage(ByVal msgindex As Integer) As String
        Dim tmpString As String
        Dim Data As String
        Dim szData() As Byte
        Dim msg As String

        Try
            Data = "RETR " & msgindex.ToString & vbCrLf
            szData = _
                System.Text.Encoding.ASCII.GetBytes(Data.ToCharArray())
            NetStrm.Write(szData, 0, szData.Length)
            tmpString = RdStrm.ReadLine()
            If tmpString.Substring(0, 4) <> "-ERR" Then
                While (tmpString <> ".")
                    msg = msg & tmpString & vbCrLf
                    tmpString = RdStrm.ReadLine()
                End While
            End If
        Catch exc As InvalidOperationException
            MsgBox("Message retrieval failed: " & vbCrLf & _
                    Err.ToString())
        End Try
        Return msg
    End Function
End Class
```

This class contains some basic functions for connecting to and disconnecting from the mail server and retrieving specific messages, and it contains the CreateMessageFromText() function, which extracts the various fields of a message and creates a Message object. The Message object exposes the parts of a message as properties (From, To, Subject, and so on). The code is straightforward: it encodes the commands as arrays of bytes and sends them to the server with the Write method of the NetworkStream object. The various parts of the message are extracted from the string returned by the RETR command with the usual string manipulation functions of Visual Basic. Each field of the message is identified by a header followed by a colon on a separate line (see Figure 17.7).

When the Download Messages button is clicked, the program connects to the mail server, retrieves the headers of the unread messages, and displays them on the ListView control. Listing 17.16 shows the code behind the Download Messages button.

---

**Listing 17.16**    **Connecting to a POP3 Server and Downloading Messages**

```
Private Sub Button1_Click(ByVal sender As System.Object, _
                            ByVal e As System.EventArgs) _
                            Handles Button1.Click
    Dim i As Integer
    Dim msg As POP3Message.Message
    Dim msgString As String
    Dim messages As Integer
    Me.Cursor = Cursors.WaitCursor
    messages = objPOP3.Connect()
    If messages = -1 Then
        Me.Cursor = Cursors.Default
        Exit Sub
    End If
    Dim originalCaption As String = Me.Text
    For i = 1 To messages
        Me.Text = "Downloading message " & i.ToString & "/" & _
                    messages.ToString
        Dim msgItem As New ListViewItem()
        msgString = objPOP3.GetMessage(i)
        msg = objPOP3.CreateFromText(msgString)
        msgItem.Text = msg._From
        msgItem.SubItems.Add(msg._Subject)
        msgItem.SubItems.Add(msg._Date)
        ListView1.Items.Add(msgItem)
        TextBox1.AppendText(msg._Body & vbCrLf)
    Next
    Me.Text = originalCaption
    Me.Cursor = Cursors.Default
End Sub
```

---

When the user selects a message on the ListView control, the program requests the body of the selected message from the server and displays it on the TextBox at the bottom of the form. Listing 17.17 shows the code that displays the body of the selected message on the TextBox control. The selected message is retrieved from the client with the GetMessage method of the POP3Message class.

---

**Listing 17.17**    **Displaying the Selected Message**

```
Private Sub ListView1_Click(ByVal sender As Object, _
                            ByVal e As System.EventArgs) _
                            Handles ListView1.Click
    Dim messages As Integer
    TextBox1.Text = objPOP3.GetMessage(ListView1.SelectedIndices(0) + 1)
End Sub
```

---

To delete a message, the code calls the DeleteMessage method of the POP3Message class, passing the message's number as argument, as shown in Listing 17.18.

---

**Listing 17.18**      **Deleting a Message on the Mail Server**

```
Private Sub ListView1_KeyUp(ByVal sender As Object, _
                    ByVal e As System.Windows.Forms.KeyEventArgs) _
                    Handles ListView1.KeyUp
    If e.KeyCode = Keys.Delete Then
        If objPOP3.DeleteMessage( _
                ListView1.SelectedIndices(0) + 1) >= 0 Then
            ListView1.Items( _
                ListView1.SelectedIndices(0)).Text = "DELETED"
            ListView1.Items( _
                ListView1.SelectedIndices(0)).SubItems.Clear()
        End If
    End If
End Sub
```

---

Finally, when the Close Connection button is clicked, the program calls the Quit method of the POP3Message class, which in turn executes the QUIT command against the mail sever, as shown in Listing 17.19. This command removes the deleted messages and terminates the connection to the server.

---

**Listing 17.19**      **Terminating the Connection to a POP3 Server**

```
Private Sub Button2_Click(ByVal sender As System.Object, _
                    ByVal e As System.EventArgs) _
                    Handles Button2.Click
    objPOP3.Quit()
    ListView1.Items.Clear()
End Sub
```

---

## Summary

In this chapter, we explored the System.Net class, which provides the functionality you need to connect to various Internet resources from within a Windows application. The most basic applications will do little more than a browser does: they download a file from a web server or upload information to a web server. The downloaded document isn't usually an HTML file, but a text file, which will be parsed by the client. You can also download HTML documents and "scrape" them (remove the HTML tags and parse the text to locate the information you're interested in). Uploading data is similar to submitting a form with the browser. You can upload a text file or named values, which is what the browser does when you submit a form to the server.

The classes that support the TCP and UDP protocols allow you to build Windows applications that communicate with one another by listening to a specific port without the need of a web server. The two computers that communicate with these protocols should run the appropriate program and the two programs should use the same port to communicate with one another.

# CHAPTER 18

## The Data-Bound Web Controls

- Introducing the data-bound web controls

- The List controls

- The DataList control

- The DataGrid control

- The Repeater control

- The CrystalReportViewer

I n Chapter 6, "Building Data-Driven Web Applications," you saw how to data-bind Web Form controls such as the Label control. In this chapter, we will look at the range of controls that are designed specifically for data access from Web Forms.

These include the collection of List controls (ListBox, DropDownList, CheckBoxList, and RadioButtonList), the DataList control, the DataGrid control, and the Repeater control. Additionally, we will take a look at the CrystalReportViewer.

## Introducing the Data-Bound Web Controls

The List controls are the simple "display a column of data" type of controls. They enable single selections (and multiple selections in the case of the CheckBoxList and ListBox controls) and essentially all have similar properties and methods. The DataList control is like a List-Box on steroids. It is a templated control, enabling fine control over the way it is displayed and capable of displaying multiple fields. The DataGrid and Repeater controls can also display multiple fields. The DataGrid control presents data in a tabular format, whereas the Repeater control provides a container for building customized lists based on templates that you create.

You can bind the controls to a variety of sources, including databases, arrays, text files, XML data files, and so on. In this chapter, we will demonstrate the use of databases, arrays, and XML files as data sources.

The actual process of attaching data to these controls is very simple. It essentially involves setting the DataSource property of the control in question to the data source itself and then calling the DataBind method. DataBind is the method that enables ASP.NET data binding. It is used to invoke the relation between the target control and the source data fields.

You may also be required to identify which specific fields from the data source need to be used where in the target control. Then it's just a matter of compiling and running the program.

With controls such as the DataList, Repeater, and DataGrid controls, you can use the `DataBinder.Eval` method and templated columns approach to achieve a granular level of formatting control over the way they display data. The `DataBinder.Eval` method evaluates late-bound data-binding expressions. You can use it to grab the text that you require from the available fields and then employ the templating process to dress the resulting string(s) into something presentable. We will look at an example with the DataList control.

# The List Controls

For the purpose of working with the examples in this chapter, create a new ASP.NET project named WebDataDemo1.

There are a number of List controls, and they share most of the same features. We have previously used the RadioButtonList and the CheckBoxList controls in the two versions of the Gallaghers application in Chapters 6 and 16.

When you data-bind the List controls, you need to remember that one of their key limitations is that they are capable of displaying only one column of data at a time. (The exception occurs with the mobile versions of these controls in the Mobile Internet Toolkit. You can use `DataBinder.Eval` to stitch together the contents of multiple columns from the data source.)

However, the List controls are all capable of holding two values for each item of data. The DataTextField property stores the value to be displayed (such as an item's name) and the DataValueField property can be used to store some other value that might be useful to help manipulate the item programmatically (such as the item's catalog number).

We will begin by seeing how to data-bind a ListBox control to an XML Data document.

## Data-Binding a ListBox to an XML Document

In the WebDataDemo1 project, drag a ListBox control to `WebForm1.aspx`. From the Project menu, choose the Add Existing Item option and add the `menu.xml` file from Chapter 16. If you haven't yet worked from this chapter, choose Add New Item from the Project menu, select the XML File template and name the file `menu.xml`. Add the code from Listing 16.1 to the designer and save the file.

We cannot data-bind directly to the XML file. We need to dump its content into a DataSet and then pull the data from the DataSet. From the Data Toolbox, drag a DataSet to WebForm1. Check Untyped Dataset in the Add Dataset dialog box. Click OK. This creates an instance of DataSet1 at the bottom of the designer.

---

**NOTE**    Note that we will look at working with XML and VB .NET in more detail in Chapter 19.

Drag a Button control (Button1) to the designer and set the Button's Text property to Load ListBox. Double-click the button to enter Code Behind, and in the Button's Click event, add the code from Listing 18.1.

**Listing 18.1          Button1_Click for Load ListBox**

```
Private Sub Button1_Click(ByVal sender As _
  System.Object, ByVal e As System.EventArgs) _
  Handles Button1.Click

        DataSet1.ReadXml(Server.MapPath("menu.xml"))
        ListBox1.DataSource = DataSet1
        ListBox1.DataTextField = "food"
        ListBox1.DataBind()

End Sub
```

Begin by using the ReadXml method to load the data from the XML document into DataSet1. Then set the DataSource property for ListBox1. The next step is to tell ListBox1 which column out of the DataSet to load into its DataTextField for display. Then call the DataBind method and compile and run the program; you should end up with something that looks like Figure 18.1.

**FIGURE 18.1:**

Displaying the data from an XML data document in a data-bound ListBox

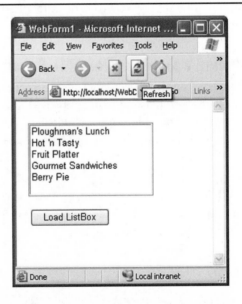

You could also have applied the contents of the price field for each menu item into the DataValueField of the ListBox. Additionally, you can use the ReadXmlSchema method to read XML schema into the DataSet.

## Data-Binding the DropDownList to an Array

In this example, you'll see how to data-bind a DropDownList control to an array. Drag a Drop-DownList control to WebForm1 in the WebDataDemo1 project. Double-click somewhere on the form to enter Code Behind and add the code from Listing 18.2.

**Listing 18.2     Data-Binding to an Array**

```
Private Class Menu
      Dim _menuItem As String

      Public Sub New(ByVal menuItem As String)
          _menuItem = menuItem
      End Sub

      Public ReadOnly Property menuItem() As String
          Get
              Return _menuItem
          End Get
      End Property
End Class


   Private Sub Page_Load(ByVal sender As _
System.Object, ByVal e As System.EventArgs) Handles _
MyBase.Load

      If (Not IsPostBack) Then
          Dim myArray As New ArrayList()

          myArray.Add(New Menu("Ploughman's Lunch"))
          myArray.Add(New Menu("Hot 'n Tasty"))
          myArray.Add(New Menu("Fruit Platter"))
          myArray.Add(New Menu("Gourmet Sandwiches"))
          myArray.Add(New Menu("Berry Pie"))

          DropDownList1.DataSource = myArray
          DropDownList1.DataTextField = "menuItem"
          DropDownList1.DataBind()
      End If
   End Sub
```

If you want to, you could have expanded the Menu class with the price data for the menu items and bound these to the DataValueField of the DropDownList control. As you can see, setting up the array occupies most of this code and the actual business end of attaching the data to the DropDownList control is taken care of in the last three lines of code. Figure 18.2 illustrates how the DropDownList should look when run in Internet Explorer.

**FIGURE 18.2:**

Running the WebData-
Demo1 project and the
DropDownList in
Internet Explorer

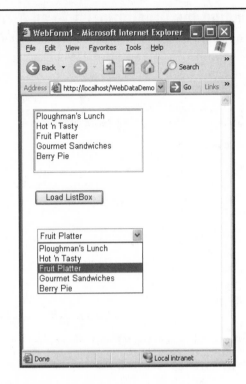

## Data-Binding a CheckBoxList to a Database

In most real-life data connection cases, connecting to a database is what it is all about. You have seen previously in this book how to work with ADO.NET and data connectivity in relation to Windows forms. There is little difference when working with Web Forms, and Chapter 6 included an example of data-binding a RadioButtonList control to an SQLServer database.

In this example, we'll show you how to connect a CheckBoxList to a database using a DataSet. We will also run through the Insert, Update, and Delete procedures. To begin, follow these steps:

1. Drag a CheckBoxList (CheckBoxList1) to WebForm1 in the WebDataDemo1 project. You might want to give it plenty of width on the page.

2. Drag a SqlDataAdapter to the form and establish a connection to the pubs database. Follow the Data Adapter Configuration Wizard through to the Query Builder and choose the titles table. Choose All Columns in the Titles table as shown in Figure 18.3.

3. Click OK and then click through and exit the wizard. You should have created a full deck of SQL statements in the wizard.

**FIGURE 18.3:**

Setting up the Query Builder

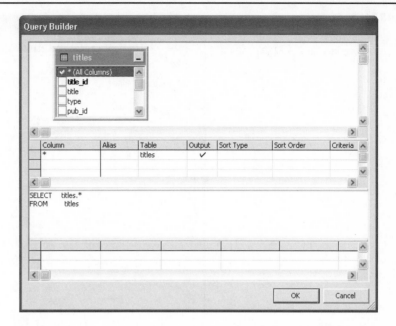

**4.** Right-click the SqlDataAdapter1 in the designer and choose Generate Dataset. Choose the New option as shown in Figure 18.4. This creates an instance of DataSet11 in the designer.

**5.** In the Property window for CheckBoxList1, set the following values:

DataSource: DataSet11

DataMember: titles

DataTextField: title

DataValueField: title_id

**6.** Switch to Code Behind and add the following two lines of code to the Page_Load event:

```
SqlDataAdapter1.Fill(DataSet11)
CheckBoxList1.DataBind()
```

**7.** Compile and run the project. It will resemble Figure 18.5.

You have the option with the CheckBoxList and RadioButtonList controls to play with their formatting to a limited extent. This option won't be that useful in this example because the sheer size of the entries prohibits the sort of formatting available. However, the options normally permit you to create multiple columns for presenting the data across the page in a more tabular form rather than just straight down the page. The relevant properties are accessed in the layout section of the Properties window for the respective controls.

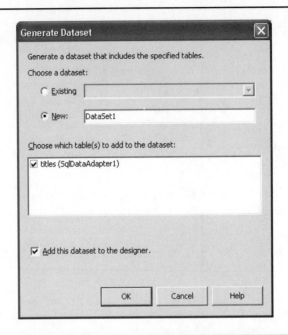

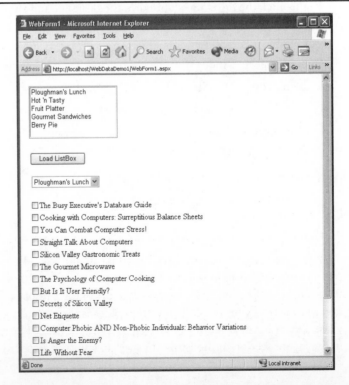

## Creating a New Record

Next we'll add a new record by adding a row to the table in the database. This is performed in two steps. First, we add a row to the DataSet and then we call the Update method of the DataAdapter to update the original database:

1. Drag four TextBox controls onto WebForm1. We dropped them toward the upper-right corner next to the ListBox.

2. Drag four Label controls and place one next to each of the TextBox controls. Set the Text properties of the Labels to Title, ID, Type, and Pub Date, respectively.

3. Place a Button control (Button2) underneath the TextBox controls and set its Text property to New Record.

4. Double-click the Button control to enter Code Behind and add the code from Listing 18.3 to the Button's Click event.

**Listing 18.3    Button2 (the New Record button)**

```
Private Sub Button2_Click(ByVal sender As _
  System.Object, ByVal e As System.EventArgs) Handles _
  Button2.Click

       Dim newTitle As DataRow

       newTitle = DataSet11.Tables(0).NewRow

       newTitle("title") = TextBox1.Text
       newTitle("title_id") = TextBox2.Text
       newTitle("type") = TextBox3.Text
       newTitle("pubdate") = TextBox4.Text

       DataSet11.Tables(0).Rows.Add(newTitle)
       SqlDataAdapter1.Update(DataSet11)

       CheckBoxList1.ClearSelection()
       SqlDataAdapter1.Fill(DataSet11)
       CheckBoxList1.DataBind()

   End Sub
```

This code is quite straightforward. We declare a new DataSet row (newTitle) and then define it as belonging to DataSet11. Next we read the contents of the various TextBoxes into the columns of the new row. We complete the process by inserting the completed row into DataSet11 and then update the original database with the contents of the DataSet. The last three lines of code refresh the CheckBoxList with the new entry. Compile and run the code. Figure 18.6 illustrates how it should appear.

**FIGURE 18.6:**

WebDataDemo1 with
the functionality to
create a new record

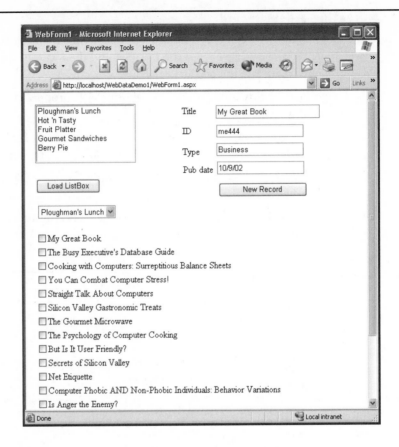

## Deleting a Record

Establishing code to delete a record is just as easy. In this example, we will add a Button control
that deletes any records that have been checked in the CheckBoxList:

1. Add another Button control (Button3) underneath the New Record button from the previous
   example. Set its Text property to Delete.

2. Double-click the Button to enter Code Behind and add the code from Listing 18.4 to the
   code skeleton for its Click event.

**Listing 18.4**    **Button3 (the Delete button)**

```
Private Sub Button3_Click(ByVal sender As _
  System.Object, ByVal e As System.EventArgs) Handles _
  Button3.Click
```

```
        Dim key As String
        key = CheckBoxList1.SelectedItem.Value
        SqlDataAdapter1.Fill(DataSet11)

        DataSet11.Tables(0).Rows.Find(key).Delete()
        CheckBoxList1.ClearSelection()
        CheckBoxList1.DataBind()

        'SqlDataAdapter1.Update(DataSet11)

    End Sub
```

In this example, we search the DataSet for the record containing the primary key matching the value in the selected item. The record is then deleted and the CheckBoxList is updated. We have commented out the last step that updates the original database. You can experiment with this to see how changes in the DataSet can be reflected in the client without having to write back to the original data source.

## Updating a Record

In the final example with the List controls, we'll create the functionality to make a change to a record. We will create an Update button that sets a title of a book selected in the CheckBox-List to a new value entered in TextBox1:

1. Drag a Button control (Button4) to WebForm1 and set its Text property to Update. Position the Update button below the Delete button.

2. Double-click the Update button to enter Code Behind and add the code from Listing 18.5 to the code skeleton for its Click event.

**Listing 18.5        Button4 (the Update button)**

```
Private Sub Button4_Click(ByVal sender As _
  System.Object, ByVal e As System.EventArgs) Handles _
  Button4.Click

        Dim key As String
        key = CheckBoxList1.SelectedItem.Value
        SqlDataAdapter1.Fill(DataSet11)

        DataSet11.titles.Rows.Find(key).Item("title") _
 = TextBox1.Text

        CheckBoxList1.ClearSelection()
        CheckBoxList1.DataBind()

        'SqlDataAdapter1.Update(DataSet11)

    End Sub
```

Again, in this code we have commented out the final update of the database. The rest of the code works in a fashion similar to how the code in Listing 18.4 for the Delete button works. We identify the value of the selected item, which happens to be the primary key. This value is then used to search the DataSet (notice that we have used `DataSet11.titles` as opposed to `DataSet11.Tables(0)` or `DataSet11.Tables("titles")`—all are legitimate), and the item in the title column is reassigned to the contents of the TextBox1.

Figure 18.7 illustrates the final layout of the controls for this project.

**FIGURE 18.7:**

Layout of controls for WebDataDemo1

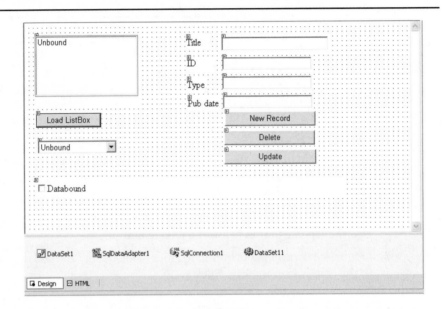

This completes our coverage of the List controls. In the next section, we will look at the DataList control.

## The DataList Control

The DataList control is the first of the controls that you can extensively manipulate using templates and styles. It is capable of presenting multiple fields of data from the data source.

A range of methods are available for editing the styles and templates associated with the control. You can right-click and choose either Auto Format or Property Builder to edit the styles. Alternatively, you can access the style settings in the Properties window and make your changes there. It's often easier to either use one of the Auto Format options or to go in and edit the HTML directly (or both).

You can edit the templates by right-clicking the control and choosing the Edit Template option. You can work with Header and Footer templates, Item templates (including Item, AlternatingItem, SelectedItem, and EditItem), and the Separator template.

You can also define the number of columns to use for the DataList, and you can set the associated properties such as CellPadding and CellSpacing. Essentially, as far as design goes, if you can do it in HTML, you can do it to the DataList control.

You can also add other controls to the DataList and give it additional functionality, such as allowing the user to select, edit, and delete items.

---

**TIP**   When working with the List controls, you often need to have an intimate understanding of your DataSets in case things go wrong. You can view the contents of your DataSets in the debugging windows, which is an excellent way of sorting out problems that can occur when setting up data driven applications. You can access the entire DataSet in the Autos window, although it may take some drilling down to locate specific data (or where it should be!). You can also use commands such as >? DataSet11.Tables(0).Rows.Item(0) .Item(0) in the Command window of the debugger to access specific information about the DataSet.

In the following demonstration project (WebDataDemo2), we will create a simple application that displays data from the titles table in the pubs database and then offer the user options such as detailed views of individual items and the opportunity to edit and delete items.

## Setting Up WebDataDemo2

To create the project to demonstrate the use of the DataList control, open a new ASP.NET project and name it WebDataDemo2. Perform the following steps:

1. From the Data Toolbox, drag a SqlDataAdapter to WebForm1 and connect it to the pubs database. Use the Data Adapter Configuration Wizard and the Query Builder (refer to Figure 18.8) to generate the following SQL statement:

   ```
   SELECT title_id, title, type, pub_id, price, advance,_
   royalty, ytd_sales, notes, pubdate FROM titles
   ```

2. Generate the full set of SELECT, UPDATE, and DELETE statements and exit the Wizard.

3. Right-click SqlDataAdapter1 on at the base of the WebForm1 Designer window and select Generate Dataset. This creates an instance of DataSet11 on the designer.

4. Drag a DataList control (DataList1) to WebForm1 and set its DataSource property to DataSet11 and its DataMember property to titles. Set the RepeatColumns property to 2 and CellPadding to 4. This will render the data presented by the control in two columns and ensure that there is a bit of visual space between adjacent records.

5. Right-click the DataList1control in the designer and choose the Auto Format option. As you can see in Figure 18.9, we chose the Colorful2 option from the dialog box, but we'll be editing this further in the project.

**FIGURE 18.8:**

Using the Query Builder for WebDataDemo2

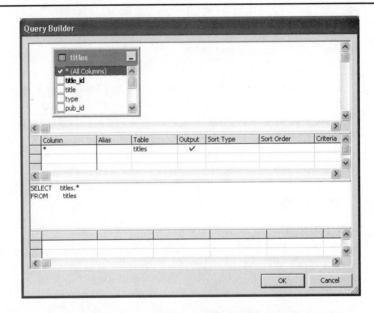

**FIGURE 18.9:**

The Auto Format dialog box for the DataList control

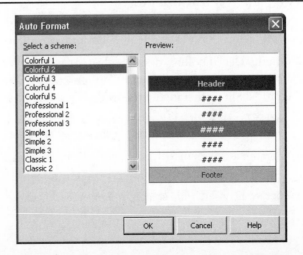

**6.** Select the WebForm1 itself and edit its link and vlink properties to navy (#000080). We will be adding LinkButton controls at a later point and the purpose of this setting is to regulate their appearance.

**7.** Right-click the DataList1control again and choose the Property Builder option. This opens the DataList1 Properties dialog box. Click the Format option and expand the Items node as shown in Figure 18.10.

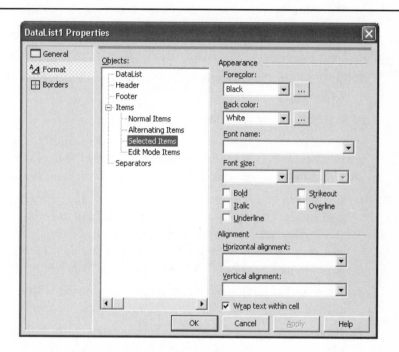

**8.** Set the ForeColor and BackColor properties as shown here and exit the dialog box.

| Item | ForeColor | BackColor |
|------|-----------|-----------|
| Normal Items | MediumBlue | CornSilk |
| Alternating Items | CornSilk | CornFlowerBlue |
| Selected Items | MediumBlue | White |
| Edit Mode Items | MediumBlue | White |

We will be setting up the Edit Mode template with an HTML table, and you will find that in an HTML table the Style settings from step 8 are ineffective. There are two main ways of getting around it: One is to go into the HTML and add `<FONT COLOR="MediumBlue">` tags to each cell in the table. Another method is to bulk-select the table in the Edit Template view (that we are about to use) and set the font color to MediumBlue. In practice, this adds the tags to each cell of the table, but Microsoft does the work for you.

1. Right-click the DataList1 control and choose Edit Template ➢ Header and Footer Templates from the context menu. In the Header template, type the heading **Titles List**.

2. Right-click the DataList1 control and choose the Edit Template ➢ Item Templates option. (To return to normal view, choose the End Template Editing option.)

3. In the ItemTemplate, type **Title:**, press the Enter key to move down a line, and type **Price:**.

4. Do the same in the AlternatingItemTemplate.

5. In the SelectedItemTemplate, type **Title:**, press Enter, type **Price:**, and then add **Type:**, **YTD Sales:**, and **Notes:**.

6. Repeat step 5 for the EditItemTemplate.

We will be adding LinkButton controls to all the templates and a number of TextBoxes to the Edit Item template, but first we need to edit the HTML to remove the <P> tags that Visual Studio seems to take great delight in scattering throughout the code.

1. Switch to HTML view and identify and remove the <P></P> tag combinations from the page. Where line breaks are required, replace them with <br> tags. The advantage of using <br> tags is that they don't generate anywhere near the same amount of white space between lines as do <P> tags. Leave the EditItemTemplate alone for the time being, because we will be performing a major HTML edit of this template later on.

2. While in HTML view, place <b></b> tag combinations around all the headings that were inserted.

3. The next step is to bind the relevant parts of the control to the related fields in the DataSet. This is handled using the `DataBinder.Eval` statement directly in HTML view. Listing 18.6 demonstrates how this code should look for the Item and AlternatingItem Template.

**Listing 18.6**     **ASPX Code for Item and Alternating Item Template**

```
<FooterStyle ForeColor="#003399" BackColor="#99CCCC"></FooterStyle>
    <HeaderStyle Font-Bold="True" ForeColor="#CCCCFF" _
 BackColor="#003399">
</HeaderStyle>
<AlternatingItemStyle ForeColor="Cornsilk" _
 BackColor="CornflowerBlue">
</AlternatingItemStyle>
<HeaderTemplate>
    Titles's List
</HeaderTemplate>
```

```
<ItemStyle ForeColor="MediumBlue" BackColor="Cornsilk"></ItemStyle>
<ItemTemplate>
     <B>Title: </B>
     <%# DataBinder.Eval(Container.DataItem, "title") %>
     <BR>
     <B>Price: </B>
     <%# DataBinder.Eval(Container.DataItem, "price", "{0:c}") %>
     <BR>
     <BR>
     <asp:LinkButton id="LinkbuttonItemDetails" runat="server" _
CommandName="select">Details</asp:LinkButton>  
     <asp:LinkButton id="LinkbuttonItemEdit" runat="server" _
CommandName="edit">Edit</asp:LinkButton>  
     <BR>
     </ItemTemplate>
     <AlternatingItemTemplate>
     <B>Title: </B>
     <%# DataBinder.Eval(Container.DataItem, "title") %>
     <BR>
     <B>Price: </B>
     <%# DataBinder.Eval(Container.DataItem, "price", "{0:c}") %>
     <BR>
     <BR>
     <asp:LinkButton id="LinkbuttonAltDetails" runat="server" _
CommandName="select">Details</asp:LinkButton>  
     <asp:LinkButton id="LinkbuttonAltEdit" runat="server" _
CommandName="edit">Edit</asp:LinkButton>  
     <BR>
     </AlternatingItemTemplate>
```

Listing 18.6 includes the code for the LinkButtons that need to added. You can either code them at this point or wait a bit and add them graphically in a few more steps.

1. The next step is to work on the ASPX code for the Selected Item template. Listing 18.7 contains the code for this template.

---

**Listing 18.7**      **ASPX Code for Selected Item Template**

```
<SelectedItemStyle ForeColor="MediumBlue" BackColor="White">
</SelectedItemStyle>
<EditItemStyle ForeColor="MediumBlue" BackColor="White">
</EditItemStyle>
<SelectedItemTemplate>
   <B>Title: </B>
   <%# DataBinder.Eval(Container.DataItem, "title") %>
   <BR>
   <B>Price: </B>
   <%# DataBinder.Eval(Container.DataItem, "price", "{0:c}") %>
   <BR>
```

```
    <B>Type: </B>
    <%# DataBinder.Eval(Container.DataItem, "type") %>
    <BR>
    <B>YTD Sales: </B>
    <%# DataBinder.Eval(Container.DataItem, "ytd_sales") %>
    <BR>
 <B>Notes:</B>
    <%# DataBinder.Eval(Container.DataItem, "notes") %>
    <BR>
    <BR>
    <asp:LinkButton id="LinkbuttonSelDeselect" runat="server"_
CommandName="deselect">DeSelect</asp:LinkButton>  
    <asp:LinkButton id="LinkbuttonSeEdit" runat="server" _
CommandName="edit">Edit</asp:LinkButton>  
    <asp:LinkButton id="LinkbuttonSelDelete" runat="server" _
CommandName="delete">Delete</asp:LinkButton><BR>
    </SelectedItemTemplate>
```

2. Switch back to the Design view and make sure that you are in the Template Edit mode. If you haven't already done so, add two LinkButton controls to the ItemTemplate. Set their Text properties to Details and Edit, respectively, and then set their CommandName properties to select and edit (*case is important*). Set their respective ID properties to Link-ButtonItemDetails and LinkButtonItemEdit.

3. Repeat step 2 for the AlternatingItem Template except set the ID properties to Link-ButtonAltDetails and LinkButtonAltEdit.

4. In the SelectedItem template, add three LinkButton controls. Set their Text properties to DeSelect, Edit, and Delete. Set their CommandName properties to deselect, edit, and delete. Set their respective ID properties to LinkButtonSelDeselect, LinkButtonSelEdit, and LinkButtonSelDelete.

5. In the EditItemTemplate, add a TextBox control next to each of the label items. Place a Table control from the HTML Toolbox below the existing items and three more Link-Button controls underneath the table. (All you are doing here is dumping a collection of controls on the form with the intention of editing them next from HTML view.) Switch to HTML view and edit the template according to Listing 18.8.

**Listing 18.8        ASPX Code for the Edit Item Template**

```
<EditItemTemplate>
    <TABLE id="Table8" cellSpacing="3" cellPadding="1" _width="300" border="0">
        <TR>
        <TD><B><FONT color="mediumblue">Title:</FONT></B></TD>
        <TD>
```

```
<asp:Label id=LabelTitle runat="server" _
 text='<%# DataBinder.Eval(Container.DataItem, "title") %>'>
      </asp:Label><FONT color="mediumblue"></FONT></TD>
      </TR>
      <TR>
         <TD><B><FONT color="mediumblue">Price:</FONT></B></TD>
      <TD>
      <asp:TextBox id=TextboxPrice runat="server" _
Text='<%# DataBinder.Eval(Container.DataItem, "price") %>' _
Width="63px">
      </asp:TextBox><FONT color="mediumblue"></FONT></TD>
      </TR>
      <TR>
      <TD><B><FONT color="mediumblue">Type:</FONT></B></TD>
      <TD>
      <asp:TextBox id=TextboxType runat="server" _
Text='<%# DataBinder.Eval(Container.DataItem, "type") %>' _
Width="122px">
      </asp:TextBox><FONT color="mediumblue"></FONT></TD>
      </TR>
      <TR>
      <TD><B><FONT color="mediumblue">YTD Sales: </FONT></B>
      </TD>
      <TD>
      <asp:TextBox id=TextboxYtd runat="server" _
Text='<%# DataBinder.Eval(Container.DataItem, "ytd_sales", _
"{0:N}") %>' Width="122px">
      </asp:TextBox><FONT color="mediumblue"></FONT></TD>
      </TR>
      <TR>
      <TD><B><FONT color="mediumblue">Notes:</FONT></B></TD>
      <TD>
      <asp:TextBox id=TextboxNotes runat="server" _
Text='<%# DataBinder.Eval(Container.DataItem, "notes") %>' _
Width="191px" TextMode="MultiLine" Height="50px">
      </asp:TextBox></TD>
      </TR>
   </TABLE>
   <BR>
      <asp:LinkButton id="LinkbuttonEditUpdate" runat="server" _
CommandName="update">Update</asp:LinkButton>  
      <asp:LinkButton id="LinkbuttonEditCancel" runat="server" _
CommandName="cancel">Cancel</asp:LinkButton>  
      <asp:LinkButton id="LinkbuttonEditDelete" runat="server" _
CommandName="delete">Delete</asp:LinkButton>
</EditItemTemplate>
```

This completes the basic setup of the DataList control. The next step is to code the functionality into Code Behind. Figure 18.11 shows how the control should now appear in the Designer window. Figure 18.12 shows as much of the control as will fit into a single screen shot in Edit Template mode.

**FIGURE 18.11:**

The completed
DataList1 control in
WebDataDemo2

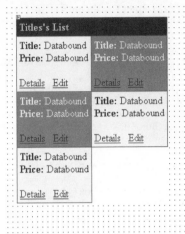

**FIGURE 18.12:**

The completed
DataList1 control in
Edit Template mode

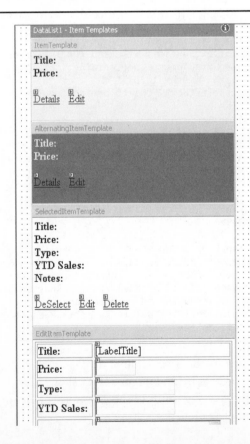

## Writing the Code Behind for WebDataDemo2

Although we have used LinkButton controls for this project, we could have also used the Button or ImageButton counterparts.

Clicking a Button control raises the DataList_ItemCommand event, and you can normally build functionality in by exploiting this event together with the CommandName property. However, there are some specific handlers that you can (and will) use that are keyed to common events. These include the Select, Edit, Update, and Delete events.

If you are using the templates (rather than just the styles), you must data-bind the DataList control again within any of the handlers that you create to ensure that data continues to be displayed when the control is rendered out again.

**WARNING**    One thing to watch when you are using DataSets and DataLists is that you must use the IsPostBack method at the Form_Load event, particularly if you are using Button controls and/or wish to create edit and delete functionality. You can get away without it if you are using LinkButton controls to simply select an item.

Listing 18.9 contains the first set of code that we will add to Code Behind. The purpose of this code is to populate the DataList1 control and provide us with selection/deselection functionality in our application.

**NOTE**    For simplicity's sake, we have avoided any exception handling in this example.

**Listing 18.9**        **Page_Load and Item Selection Code for WebDataDemo2**

```
Private Sub Page_Load(ByVal sender As System.Object, _
ByVal e As System.EventArgs) Handles MyBase.Load

        If Not IsPostBack Then
            SqlDataAdapter1.Fill(DataSet11)
            DataList1.DataBind()
        End If

    End Sub

    Private Sub DataList1_SelectedIndexChanged(ByVal _
sender As System.Object, ByVal e As System.EventArgs) _
Handles DataList1.SelectedIndexChanged
        SqlDataAdapter1.Fill(DataSet11)
        DataList1.DataBind()
    End Sub

    Private Sub DataList1_ItemCommand(ByVal source As _
Object, ByVal e As _
```

```
        System.Web.UI.WebControls.DataListCommandEventArgs) _
    Handles DataList1.ItemCommand

        If e.CommandName = "deselect" Then
            DataList1.SelectedIndex = -1
            SqlDataAdapter1.Fill(DataSet11)
            DataList1.DataBind()
        End If

    End Sub
```

The Page_Load subroutine simply loads up the DataSet and attaches it to DataList1. If you compile and run the project at this point, it should result in a nicely populated (and presented) page of data from the pubs database. We need to use the IsPostBack method here for more than just performance reasons as explained earlier. Without it, the DataBind call in Page_Load effectively prevents the Item_Command call from Button controls from happening. (It's not so much of a problem with LinkButton controls, but it does limit their potential functionality.) Figure 18.13 shows how it should look if you run it at this point.

**FIGURE 18.13:**

WebDataDemo2 in
Internet Explorer

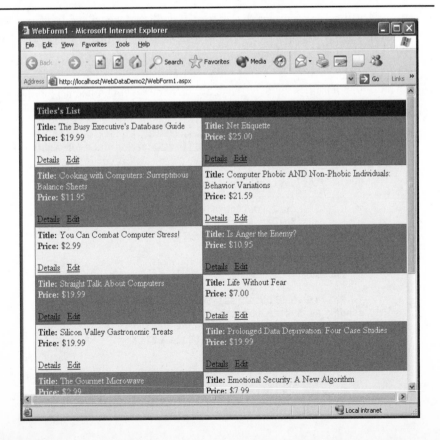

The SelectedIndexChanged event is raised in response to a different item being selected by a user clicking a button containing a `DataCommand = select` property. In this handler, we need to data-bind the DataList1 control again to update it against the additional information that we wish to display. If we hadn't added additional fields into the SelectedItem Template and had just used a style to change its color when it was selected, then we would not have needed to write this handler. We need to fill the DataSet again because it is not stored between visits to the server.

To deselect our item, we exploit the ItemCommand event, which is raised whenever a Button-type control is clicked in the DataList. In this instance, we have written a conditional statement to detect the content of the ItemCommand property, and if it is deselect, then we set the SelectedIndex back to −1 (nothing selected) and data-bind the DataList again to refresh it.

In Listing 18.10, we set up the edit functionality for our DataList.

**Listing 18.10**     **Edit Functionality for WebDataDemo2**

```
Private Sub DataList1_EditCommand(ByVal source As _
  Object, ByVal e As _
  System.Web.UI.WebControls.DataListCommandEventArgs) _
  Handles DataList1.EditCommand
        DataList1.EditItemIndex = e.Item.ItemIndex
        SqlDataAdapter1.Fill(DataSet11)
        DataList1.DataBind()
End Sub

Private Sub DataList1_CancelCommand(ByVal source As _
  Object, ByVal e As _
  System.Web.UI.WebControls.DataListCommandEventArgs) _
  Handles DataList1.CancelCommand
        DataList1.EditItemIndex = -1
        SqlDataAdapter1.Fill(DataSet11)
        DataList1.DataBind()
End Sub


Private Sub DataList1_UpdateCommand(ByVal source As _
  Object, ByVal e As _
  System.Web.UI.WebControls.DataListCommandEventArgs) _
  Handles DataList1.UpdateCommand

        SqlDataAdapter1.Fill(DataSet11)
        Dim Price As TextBox
        Dim Type As TextBox
        Dim Sales As TextBox
        Dim Notes As TextBox
```

```
        Price = e.Item.FindControl("TextboxPrice")
        Dim newPrice As Decimal = _
Convert.ToDecimal(Price.Text)

        Type = e.Item.FindControl("TextboxType")
        Dim newType As String = Type.Text

        Sales = e.Item.FindControl("TextboxYtd")
        Dim newSales As Decimal = _
Convert.ToDecimal(Sales.Text)

        Notes = e.Item.FindControl("TextboxNotes")
        Dim newNotes As String = Notes.Text

        Dim key As String
        key = DataSet11.titles.Rows.Item _
(e.Item.ItemIndex).Item("title_id")

        DataSet11.titles.Rows.Find(key).Item _
("price") = newPrice
        DataSet11.titles.Rows.Find(key).Item _
("type") = newType
        DataSet11.titles.Rows.Find(key).Item _
("ytd_sales") = newSales
        DataSet11.titles.Rows.Find(key).Item _
("notes") = newNotes

        SqlDataAdapter1.Update(DataSet11)

        DataList1.SelectedIndex = DataList1.EditItemIndex
        DataList1.EditItemIndex = -1
        DataList1.DataBind()

End Sub
```

In response to the EditCommand event, we assign `DataList1.EditItemIndex = e.Item.Item-Index`. This sets the EditItemIndex to the currently selected ItemIndex and opens the item in the EditItem Template (with a little help from a data-bind refresh).

Similarly, the handler for the CancelCommand sets the EditItemIndex back to −1 (nothing selected) and refreshes the DataList.

The third handler in this listing is designed to read the contents of the TextBox controls and use them to update the DataSet and ultimately the data source. Note that there is no exception handling used in this example, so mistakes such as leaving a field empty will cause the program to crash.

Contents of the controls in the DataList are read by using the `e.Item.FindControl` method to copy the control from the form into a locally declared version. We do this for each of the controls in question. Note that we fill the DataSet before we do anything else (it can be very frustrating and quite unproductive to try to read data from an empty DataSet!).

The next step is to identify the primary key of the current record from the DataSet. We then read the Text property of the local versions of the TextBox controls and use these values to update the relevant row in the DataSet. For example, `DataSet11.titles.Rows .Find(key).Item("price") = newPrice` updates the price field of the relevant record in the DataSet.

We then complete the process by updating the data source with `SqlDataAdapter1 .Update(DataSet11)` and drop back to selected mode by equating the SelectedItemIndex to the current EditItemIndex and setting the EditItemIndex to −1 (not selected). Figure 18.14 shows how the DataList1 control should appear in Edit mode when run in Internet Explorer.

**FIGURE 18.14:**

WebDataDemo2 in Edit mode

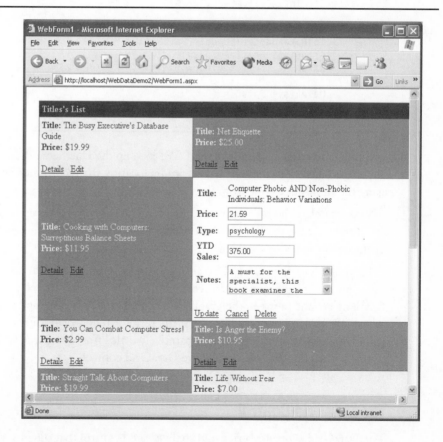

The final code listing for this project is Listing 18.11, where we add some delete functionality to the ListBox. Note that in this example, the functionality is very basic and doesn't give any warnings or confirmations.

---

**Listing 18.11**     **Delete Functionality for WebDataDemo2**

```
Private Sub DataList1_DeleteCommand(ByVal source As _
  Object, ByVal e As _
  System.Web.UI.WebControls.DataListCommandEventArgs) _
  Handles DataList1.DeleteCommand

      SqlDataAdapter1.Fill(DataSet11)

      Dim key As String
      key = DataSet11.titles.Rows.Item _
(e.Item.ItemIndex).Item("title_id")

      DataSet11.Tables(0).Rows.Find(key).Delete()
      SqlDataAdapter1.Update(DataSet11)
      DataList1.EditItemIndex = -1
      DataList1.SelectedIndex = -1

      DataList1.DataBind()

End Sub
```

---

This listing is quite straightforward. We load up the DataSet and then identify the value of the primary key from the selected record by locating the record index value in the DataSet using the ItemIndex value from the DataList (they should be the same).

Next we delete the relevant record from the DataSet and then update the data source. We finish off by setting the EditItemIndex and SelectedIndex values to −1 (not selected) and refresh the DataList by calling databind.

This completes the example. You can run the program and further experiment with layouts, styles, and templates. As you can see from this example, there can be a bit of work involved switching around between the graphical designer, HTML view, and Code Behind (as well as the various dialog boxes available), but the result can be worth it in creating a very rich and highly functional interface with comparatively little effort compared with other technologies. In the next section, we will look at the DataGrid control.

## The DataGrid Control

The DataGrid control is a rich and sophisticated control that offers a high level of data presentation and manipulation potential for the developer. In its default form, it is capable of quite a lot, but as you have seen from the DataList control, these types of controls are very extensible and the DataGrid is no exception.

You saw how to use the DataGrid control back in Chapter 2, "Working with SQL Server 2000 and Visual Studio .NET." In this section, we will revisit these techniques and put them into perspective with everything else we have covered so far in this chapter. To demonstrate the use of the DataGrid control, perform the following steps:

1. Open a new ASP.NET project in Visual Studio .NET and name it WebDataDemo3.

2. Drag and a DataGrid control (DataGrid1) onto WebForm1.

3. Drag a SqlDataAdapter to the Designer window and use the wizard to establish a connection that returns all the information from the authors table in the pubs database according to the following SQL statement:

   ```
   SELECT au_id, au_lname, au_fname, phone, address, city, _
   state, zip, contract FROM authors
   ```

4. Right-click the SqlDataAdapter1 and create a DataSet. This should place DataSet11 on the designer.

5. Select the DataGrid1 control and set its Width property to 100%. Set its DataSource property to DataSet11 and its DataMember property to authors.

6. Right-click the DataGrid1 control and choose Auto Format from the context menu. In the dialog box, choose an appropriate format; we chose Colorful 4 for this example.

7. Right-click the DataGrid1 control again and choose the Property Builder option. This dialog box for the DataGrid control is far more verbose than the one for the DataList control, and most of what you need to do can be performed directly from this dialog box. Figure 18.15 illustrates the DataGrid property builder box. Note that you can also access most of these settings from the normal Properties window, and of course much of it can also be set by coding directly into the HTML view or working in Code Behind.

8. In the Property Builder, click the Columns option and uncheck the Create Columns Automatically at Run Time option. Leaving this option checked is a quick way to display all columns in the data table, using their field names as column headings. In this case, we'll select some of the columns and customize the headings. Figure 18.16 shows the columns and their Header Text properties as they look in the designer.

9. You can click the Format option in the Property Builder and choose Columns and set their individual sizes if you feel it is necessary for layout purposes.

10. Exit the Property Builder and double-click the Web Form to enter Code Behind. Add the code from Listing 18.12 to the Page_Load code skeleton to populate the control.

**FIGURE 18.15:**

The property builder dialog box for the DataGrid control

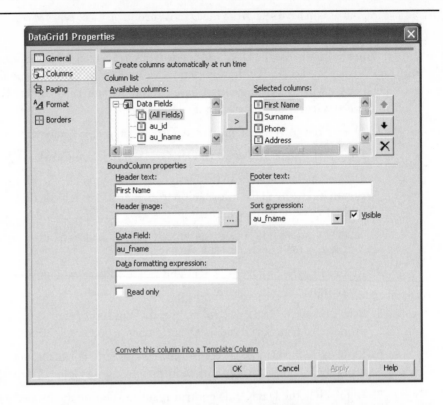

**FIGURE 18.16:**

Columns and Header Text properties for DataGrid1

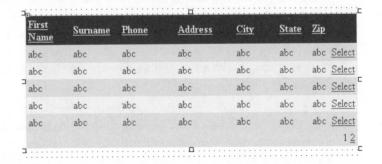

**Listing 18.12**   **Populating the DataGrid1 Control for WebDataDemo3**

```
Private Sub Page_Load(ByVal sender As System.Object, _
   ByVal e As System.EventArgs) Handles MyBase.Load
      If Not IsPostBack Then
```

```
            SqlDataAdapter1.Fill(DataSet11)
            DataGrid1.DataBind()
        End If
    End Sub
```

Compile and run the program. It should look similar to Figure 18.17 after an item has been selected.

**FIGURE 18.17:**

WebDataDemo3 running
in Internet Explorer

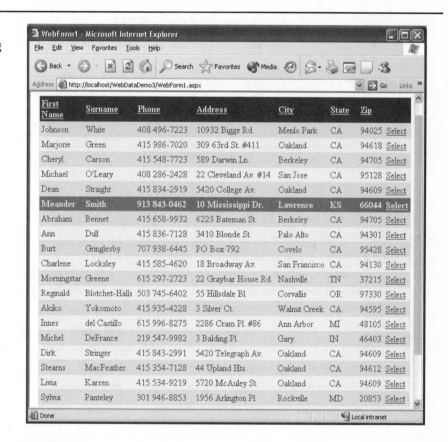

## Setting Pagination

If you are working with a large DataSet, it can be unwieldy for your users to load all the data onto a single page. ASP.NET offers a paging option that enables you to split the data across a number of pages. However, if you use this option, it is still a good idea to place a limit on the number of records returned by a query so that your users aren't fishing through several hundred pages!

To set paging for our WebDataDemo3 project, right-click the DataGrid1 control and choose the Property Builder option. Click the Paging option and check the Allow Paging box. For this example, set the Page Size property to 5 rows and set Mode to Page Numbers.

Click OK and enter Code Behind. Add the code from Listing 18.13. This handler responds to the PageIndexChanged event and displays the page chosen by the user.

**Listing 18.13    Paging Code for WebDataDemo3**

```
Private Sub DataGrid1_PageIndexChanged(ByVal source As _
  Object, ByVal e As _
  System.Web.UI.WebControls.DataGridPageChangedEventArgs)_
  Handles DataGrid1.PageIndexChanged
        DataGrid1.CurrentPageIndex = e.NewPageIndex
        SqlDataAdapter1.Fill(DataSet11)
        DataGrid1.DataBind()
End Sub
```

Compile and run the program. It should now display only five rows at a time and allow you to navigate between the different pages.

## A Master/Detail Form

One of the main uses of the DataGrid control is for creating a master/detail form setup in which two (or more) DataGrid controls are placed on a page. One of the controls acts as a master display of summary information. Clicking an item in the master control displays more details in the detail control. A typical use for this type of setup might be to retrieve details of all the transactions made by a particular client.

We set up a simple example of a master/detail form in Chapter 6. In this example, we will create a master/detail form that displays the books written by a particular author from the pubs database:

1. We begin by creating a new DataView for the pubs database. From the Server Explorer, expand the pubs node. Right-click the Views node and select the New View option. Add the authors, titleauthor, and titles tables.

2. In the authors table, check the au_lname and au_fname fields. In the titleauthor table, check the au_id field, and in the titles table, check all fields except the title_id field.

3. Save the DataView as AuthorsTitlesView. Figure 18.18 shows how it should look.

4. The next step is to create the master/detail form itself. The easiest way to approach this is to use the Data Form Wizard accessed by choosing the Add New Item option from the Project menu. In WebDataDemo3, select this template and use the default name, DataWebForm1.aspx.

**FIGURE 18.18:**

Creating the
AuthorsTitlesView

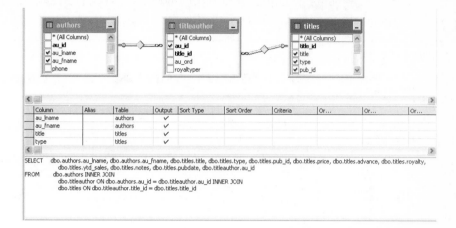

**5.** In the Data Form Wizard, create a new DataSet (DataSet2). Choose the pubs connection.

**6.** On the Choose Tables or Views screen, select the authors table and the AuthorsTitles-View view. Make sure that you move them over to the Selected Items window and click Next.

**7.** On the Create a Relationship between Tables screen, name the new relationship Authors-Titles. Select authors as the parent table and AuthorsTitlesView as the child table. Select au_id as the key field for both tables. Click the arrow to move the new relationship over to the Relations window. Click the Next button.

**8.** On the final screen, choose an appropriate range of fields that you wish to appear in the two DataGrids. We kept the authors' first and last name and address details for the master and the book details (without the authors' names) for the detail table. Click the Finish button.

This produces a fairly clunky-looking pair of tables in the DataWebForm1. We can now use the Auto Format and Property Builder options to clean them up. Most of the code we need to get started has been auto-generated and we can easily edit it to build any additional functionality. As a simple example, build the solution and then right-click somewhere in the form and choose the View in Browser option. The page loads with nothing on it except a Load button. Clicking the button displays the forms. This is a little unnecessary for normal usage, so we will look at getting rid of the button. Back in the designer, double-click the Load button to enter Code Behind and transfer its code to the Page_Load event handler. You can now delete the Load button and the form should open displaying the data.

To give the WebDataDemo3 project some form of completeness, return to WebForm1 and add a Hyperlink control to the page. Set its Text property to Book Details and its NavigateURL to DataWebForm1.aspx. Figure 18.19 illustrates how you can quickly begin to knock such a setup into some sort of shape without a great deal of effort.

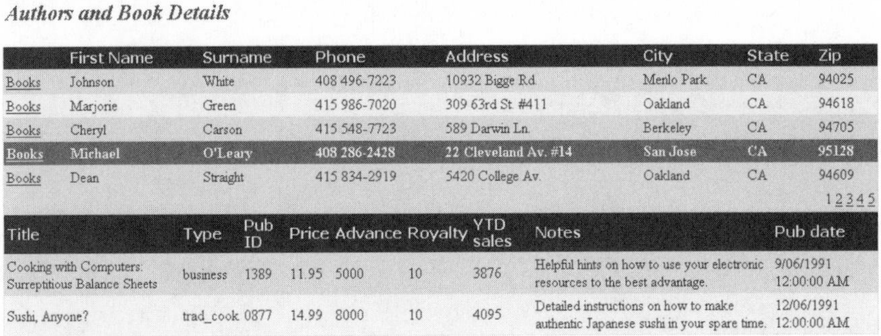

**FIGURE 18.19:**

WebDataDemo3 showing the master/detail form with basic formatting

*Authors and Book Details*

| | First Name | Surname | Phone | Address | City | State | Zip |
|---|---|---|---|---|---|---|---|
| Books | Johnson | White | 408 496-7223 | 10932 Bigge Rd | Menlo Park | CA | 94025 |
| Books | Marjorie | Green | 415 986-7020 | 309 63rd St. #411 | Oakland | CA | 94618 |
| Books | Cheryl | Carson | 415 548-7723 | 589 Darwin Ln. | Berkeley | CA | 94705 |
| Books | Michael | O'Leary | 408 286-2428 | 22 Cleveland Av. #14 | San Jose | CA | 95128 |
| Books | Dean | Straight | 415 834-2919 | 5420 College Av. | Oakland | CA | 94609 |

1 2 3 4 5

| Title | Type | Pub ID | Price | Advance | Royalty | YTD sales | Notes | Pub date |
|---|---|---|---|---|---|---|---|---|
| Cooking with Computers: Surreptitious Balance Sheets | business | 1389 | 11.95 | 5000 | 10 | 3876 | Helpful hints on how to use your electronic resources to the best advantage. | 9/06/1991 12:00:00 AM |
| Sushi, Anyone? | trad_cook | 0877 | 14.99 | 8000 | 10 | 4095 | Detailed instructions on how to make authentic Japanese sushi in your spare time. | 12/06/1991 12:00:00 AM |

In the next section, we will investigate the use of the Repeater control.

## The Repeater Control

The Repeater control provides a container that you can use to build your own custom data presentation/manipulation control using the range of web controls and tools available in Visual Studio .NET.

In this example, we will use the control to display a list of authors and some details from the pubs database:

1. Open a new ASP.NET project and name it WebDataDemo4. Drop a SqlDataAdapter onto WebForm1 and set it to pick up the contents of the authors table from the pubs database. Create a DataSet (DataSet11) to hold the details from the authors table.

2. Drop a Repeater control onto the Web Form. All the editing for the control is performed in HTML view. This is not a GUI affair! Switch to HTML view and locate the Repeater control. You will notice that its tags look very bare. You are entirely left to your own devices as to the range and type of templates that you might wish to add and the controls that you might want to include. Set the Repeater's DataSource property to DataSet11 and its Data-Member to authors.

**TIP**  You can also build functionality in at Code Behind because the Repeater control does raise the ItemCommand event. However, in this example, we will stick with a simple list.

3. Switch to HTML view and add the code from Listing 18.14 to the Repeater tags.

---

**Listing 18.14      ASPX Code for the Repeater Control in WebDataDemo4**

```
<asp:Repeater id="Repeater1" runat="server" _
 DataSource="<%# DataSet11 %>" DataMember="authors">
   <HeaderTemplate>
      <h1><font color="red">Authors' Names</font></h1>
      <hr>
   </HeaderTemplate>
   <ItemTemplate>
      <asp:Label id="Label1" runat="server" _
Text='<%# DataBinder.Eval(Container, "DataItem.au_fname")%>'>
      </asp:Label> 
      <asp:Label id="Label2" runat="server" _
Text='<%# DataBinder.Eval(Container, "DataItem.au_lname")%>'>
      </asp:Label>
      <br>
      <br>
   </ItemTemplate>
</asp:Repeater>
```

---

This is a nice simple little layout that provides a Header template with "Authors' Names" as the title with a horizontal rule underneath. The Item template provides two data-bound label controls that display the first and last name of each author.

---

**WARNING**  You can data-bind to other data sources within a Repeater control if you wish, but you won't be able to display all the rows as you would when data-binding to the Repeater's data source.

The last step is to add the necessary code to Code Behind to load up the DataSet and data-bind the Repeater control. Listing 18.15 contains the code for this.

---

**Listing 18.15      Code Behind for WebDataDemo4**

```
Private Sub Page_Load(ByVal sender As System.Object, _
 ByVal e As System.EventArgs) Handles MyBase.Load
       If Not IsPostBack Then
           SqlDataAdapter1.Fill(DataSet11)
           Repeater1.DataBind()
       End If
   End Sub
```

---

Compile and run the project. In Internet Explorer, it should appear as shown in Figure 18.20.

Next we will spend some time with the CrystalReportViewer control.

**FIGURE 18.20:**

WebDataDemo4 in
Internet Explorer

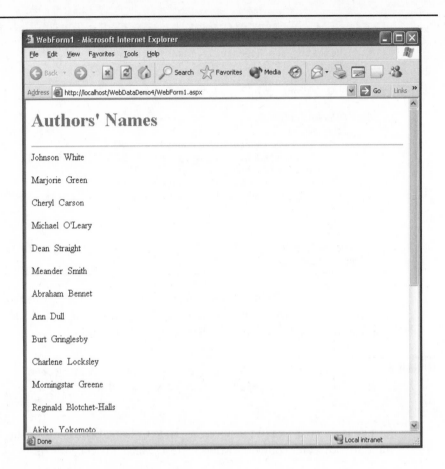

## The CrystalReportViewer Control

The CrystalReportViewer control provides a mechanism for retrieving and viewing reports from your web application. You have a number of options, from binding untyped external reports at runtime to viewing a strongly typed report that has been added to the project at design time. Additionally, you can cache strongly typed reports to improve efficiency.

Reports can be added to a project from an external location or created within Visual Studio .NET using the Crystal Report Wizard. This is accessed by choosing Add New Item from the Project menu and selecting the Crystal Report template in the dialog box that appears.

The copy of Crystal Reports that ships with Visual Studio .NET is capable of supporting five simultaneous users and can be distributed as part of a Windows or web application subject to a range of conditions specified in the Crystal Reports licensing details. If you wish to expand your application beyond the five-user limit, you will need to purchase additional licenses.

Once you first use Crystal Reports in Visual Studio .NET, you will be asked to register the product, which, although not essential, does provide access to some additional support. If you choose not to register, the product will work normally but you will get a reminder prompt every time you open a project containing reports.

Crystal Reports provide a rich and flexible feature set that goes beyond the scope of this chapter. For more information about application development with Crystal Reports, see *Mastering Crystal Reports 9* by Cate McCoy and Gord Maric (Sybex, 2003). In the following example, we will show you how to create a simple report based on the authors table from the pubs database and view it in an ASP.NET Web Form.

## Creating WebDataDemo5

To set up the CrystalReportViewer demonstration project, create a new ASP.NET project in Visual Studio .NET and name it WebDataDemo5. Then follow these steps:

1. We will begin by creating the report that we will be viewing in the project. From the Project menu, choose Add New Item and select the Crystal Report template. Name it `Crystal-Report1.rpt` (the default) and click Open. This will open the Crystal Report Gallery dialog box in the designer IDE for `CrystalReport1.rpt`.

2. Select the Using the Report Expert option and (be adventurous) choose the Standard template. See Figure 18.21.

**FIGURE 18.21:**

The Crystal Report Gallery dialog box

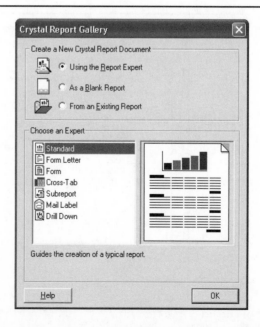

3. Click OK. This will open the Standard Report Expert. Setting up the report from here is simply a matter of making the appropriate selections and clicking the Next button. The first choice to make is the data source.

4. On the Data screen, click the OLE DB (ADO) option. This will open a wizard for setting up this connection. Choose the Microsoft OLE DB Provider for SQL Server provider and click the Next button.

5. The next screen asks you for connection information. You need to identify the server and the database. If you are not using integrated security on SQL Server, then add an appropriate account name and password; otherwise, click the Integrated Security check box. (Check the check box before trying to select the database!)

**WARNING**  If you are not using Integrated security, be aware that the SQL Server password is not persisted in Crystal Reports at runtime and you will need to hard-code the relevant details (username, password, server, and database) into your application.

6. At the Advanced Information screen, make any changes that you think are necessary (or as we did, leave well enough alone) and click Finish to exit the wizard.

7. This will return you to the Standard Report Expert where you can drill-down through the pubs connection to add the authors table to the Tables in Report box, as shown in Figure 18.22.

**FIGURE 18.22:**

Adding the authors table in the Standard Report Expert

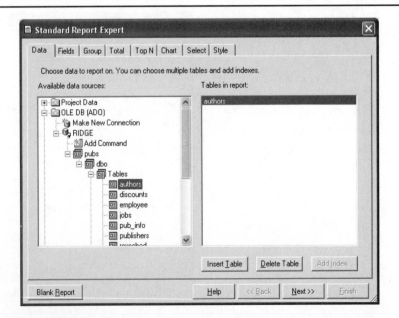

8. Clicking the Next button will take you to the screen to choose which fields to display. For the purposes of this exercise, we chose the authors' first and last names and the relevant address and contact details, as shown in Figure 18.23.

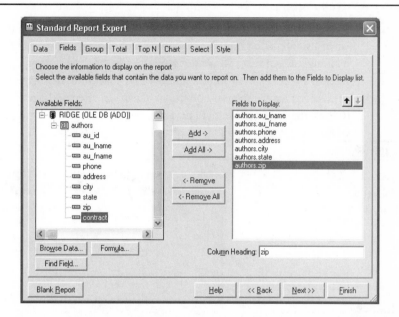

9. The remaining screens are optional, so just click through them. Have a look as you go and you will get some idea of the range of possibilities available, including the capacity to create graphs and charts very easily. At the last screen (the Style options), you can choose from a set of styles to give your report. You can edit the style you choose later, if needed. Type **Authors** into the Title field.

10. Exit the Standard Report Expert and take a look at the report that is created. You can edit most items on the report, although editing through the Properties window can be a bit of a hit-or-miss affair. You are better off right-clicking the object in question and choosing the Format option.

11. Save the report and return to WebForm1. We will now set up the CrystalReportViewer.

## Adding the CrystalReportViewer

To access the report through the CrystalReportViewer, we need to do three things:

- Place a CrystalReportViewer control on the Web Form.
- Set up a ReportDocument object linked to the source report file.
- Data-bind the CrystaReportViewer to the ReportDocument.

Let's step through this:

1. From the Web Forms Toolbox, drag a CrystalReportViewer control to WebForm1. At this point it won't look like much. Position the control in the upper-left corner of the Web Form.

2. From the Components Toolbox, drag a ReportDocument to the Web Form. This will open a small dialog box that enables you to choose your particular report (either directly as a strongly typed report from the project or as the default untyped report that you can attach later to a report stored somewhere on your machine). If you choose the typed report in your project (which we suggest you do), you can also elect to have the report cached, as you can see in Figure 18.24. This will place an instance of cachedCrystalReport11 down the bottom of the Designer window.

**FIGURE 18.24:**

The Choose a ReportDocument dialog box

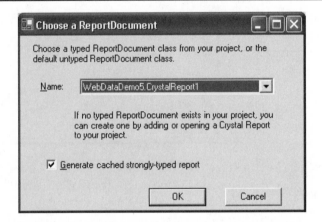

3. Click OK to exit the dialog box. Click the CrystalReportViewer1 control and select the DataBindings property from the Properties window. Click the button with the ellipsis points to pop up the dialog box.

4. In the dialog box, click ReportSource from the Bindable Properties window.

5. In the Simple Binding box, expand Page and click cachedCrystalReport11, as shown in Figure 18.25.

6. Click OK. If everything is still working properly, you should see a skeleton of your report appear in the Designer window, as shown in Figure 18.26.

7. To complete the process, double-click on the Web Form to enter Code Behind and add the code from Listing 18.16 to the Page_Load event handler.

**FIGURE 18.25:**

The CrystalReport-
Viewer1 DataBindings
dialog box

**FIGURE 18.26:**

CrystalReportViewer1
after partial data binding

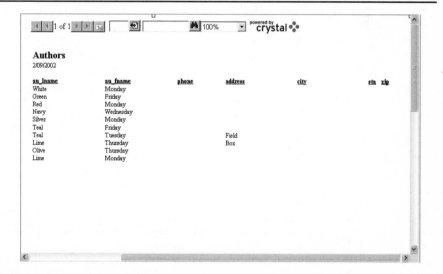

---

**Listing 18.16**    **Page_Load for WebDataDemo5**

```
Private Sub Page_Load(ByVal sender As System.Object, _
ByVal e As System.EventArgs) Handles MyBase.Load

        CrystalReportViewer1.DataBind()

End Sub
```

---

This code simply data-binds the CrystalReportViewer1 control. Compile and run the project. It should display the report as shown in Figure 18.27.

---

**FIGURE 18.27:**

WebDataDemo5 in Internet Explorer

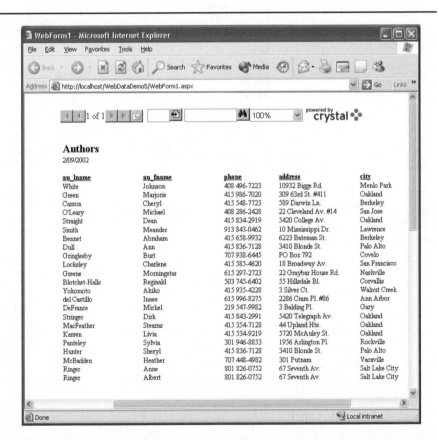

As you can see, this report is still fairly rough, but it can be easily formatted into something more presentable. Figure 18.28 shows the same report after only a few minutes of work laying out the fields and headings, retyping the column headings, positioning the report on the Web Form, adding some grid lines, and giving the main heading more prominence.

The completed
WebDataDemo5

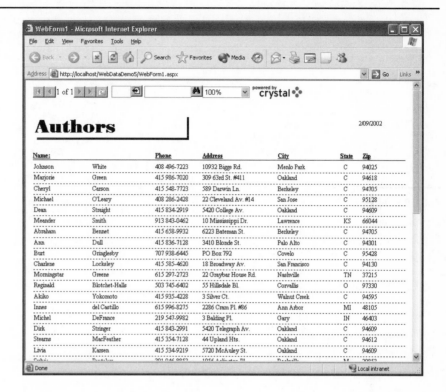

## Summary

In this chapter, we looked at the main data-bound controls for use with ASP.NET Web Forms. Although there are many similarities with their Windows applications counterparts, there are some key differences to be aware of such as the actual process of databinding the controls.

The controls are very flexible and you can combine them with other controls to greatly empower your applications, but there are a few traps for the unwary to watch out for. These include using the IsPostBack method in the Page_Load events where appropriate and the issue with Crystal Reports and SQL Server authentication in web applications where the SQL Server password is not persisted in Crystal Reports at runtime where integrated authentication isn't used.

You can easily data-bind the controls to a range of data sources, including databases, arrays, and XML files. This gives you the flexibility of choosing the appropriate data source for your application based on the needs of the application itself rather than the requirements of the design environment.

In the next chapter, you will see how VB .NET can be used to take advantage of the many recent developments in XML.

# CHAPTER 19

# Using XML and Visual Basic .NET

- XML in ADO.NET

- Creating an XML Schema

- Parsing XML Files

- SQL Server and XML

**Y**ou already know how to retrieve data from a database, how to update its tables using data adapters, and how to store structured, related data into DataSets. You also know that the information flows out of and into the DataSets and the database in XML format. XML is a standard that can represent all types of data as text. It's a simple standard and, because of this, it has the potential of becoming a universal standard.

XML is a very promising standard. People are using it with all types of applications, and it's permeating the computer industry. You shouldn't be surprised to see a programming language modeled after XML in the future. Actually, you can see how Microsoft uses XML to store the description of a form. Open a project, any project that happens to be on your hard disk. Click the Show All Files button on the Solution Explorer's toolbar, and you will see a few more files, which aren't displayed on the Solution Explorer by default. Among them are the RESX files of each form. These files describe the resources of each form. If you open any of the RESX files, you will see that the resources are described in XML format. Fortunately, you'll never have to create these files yourself, so it doesn't really matter whether you understand them or not. By the way, XML files are easy to understand, but they're not so easy to produce.

This is also how XML is used with ADO.NET. The data you move through the data adapters arrive to the DataSet in XML format, and this is how they're transmitted to the server. So far, you haven't had to look at the XML description of your data, and it would be nice if you could keep it that way. However, there are situations in which you may have to write code to parse XML files and extract the desired data (when you receive data in XLM format from a non-Windows database, for example). In this chapter, we'll look at how XML is used in database programming. Even if you don't plan to exchange data with other databases and/or systems, you should have an idea of what XML does and how it's used in ADO.NET. You'll also learn how to create DataSets in code by specifying their schema in XML, how to populate the table(s) of the DataSet, and how to persist them to local files.

We haven't attempted to condense an entire XML book into a single chapter. This chapter will help you develop a better understanding of XML and recognize when you might benefit from using XML in your projects. You can find out the details as you need them. To begin, it's important to understand how XML is used in ADO.NET and what it can do for you. To make the chapter practical, we've structured it around a few useful examples that implement common operations. We won't spend much time explaining the structure of XML documents, and we won't show you how to create valid and well-formed XML documents. Instead, we relied on Microsoft's tools to format the desired information in XML format.

## XML in ADO.NET

When you program with ADO.NET, the encoding of the data in XML format takes place behind the scenes and you need not even know that your data undergoes a transformation.

With ADO, there was a different, proprietary protocol that moved data from the database into Recordsets (it was of no use outside Windows). Each database uses its own format to store data, but a Windows application using ADO (or ADO.NET) expects to find its data in Recordsets (or DataSets in ADO.NET). XML is as useful outside Windows as it is inside Windows. A DataSet in XML format can be parsed and used on any other platform. You can actually read an XML document that represents a DataSet and figure out the information stored in it, and how the data is structured. If you need to exchange information with an IBM or a Linux database, you can package your data in XML format and send it to the other computer. You can also receive an XML document from the other computer, parse it, extract the information you need, possibly transform it, and finally save it in a SQL Server database.

Most of us have been doing this with some form of delimited files. As far as a mechanism for exchanging "dry" data, XML documents are quite similar to delimited files. In their simplest form, XML documents are simply another mechanism for exchanging data. Makes you wonder why no one thought of XML (or something similar) during the past decades, when "universal" formats appeared and disappeared like comets. However, XML is much more than a mechanism for moving data around. XML documents store more than just data; they store information about the structure of the data, which is called its *schema*. XML files have other benefits, as well. There are tools for parsing XML files, tools to transform XML files, and even tools to query XML files. It seems that the trick to a "universal" standard isn't the standard itself, but the tools to support it. And XML seems to have gained the support of the entire industry.

## XML Tags

Let's start with a few definitions. XML stands for eXtensible Markup Language, and it's a markup language, like HTML. HTML describes the appearance of a document (how the data will be rendered on a browser) with tags; XML describes the data itself, also with tags. Another difference is that HTML consists of a fixed number of tags that all browsers understand, whereas XML does not use predefined tags; you can create your tags to describe your information. Of course, you can't expect other applications to understand what your tags mean. The application that will process the XML document must know what each tag means. Even if you receive an XML document and you have no idea what it describes, you can easily extract the information and place it in one or more database tables. The structure of the information is there, and that's all that matters for the computer. You can get a good idea about the information stored in an XML file (after all, it's a text file). However, an XML document with names, ages, and other related data, could represent a list of customers, a baseball team, or the FBI's Most-Wanted List. The information will make sense to humans only if they're told what it represents. Only then can you write code to process the data.

To describe a list of books with XML, you could use a document like the following:

```
<books>
    <book>
        <title>All About Visual Basic .NET</title>
        <ISBN>972837559X</ISBN>
        <chapter>What's new in VB. NET</chapter>
        <chapter>The .NET Framework</chapter>
        <chapter>The new Windows Controls</chapter>
    </book>
</books>
```

The <books> tag describes the entire document: it's a document for storing information about books, and <books> is the *root element*. An XML document must contain a single root element. Its name could be anything, of course. XML doesn't understand English. We've chosen this name for the tag so that the file makes sense to humans.

Each "piece" of information is described by a special tag. The <title> tag describes the book's title, the <chapter> tag describes chapter titles, and so on. Someone else might have used different tags, like <BookTitle>, <ChapterTitle>, and so on. Notice that XML is case-sensitive.

When you parse an XML document, you can think of the elements making up the file as nodes. Each element is a node, and the nodes are nested. At any time, you can access a node's child nodes (which is a collection) or its parent node (this is a single node). If we included author information in our sample XML segment, it would look like this:

```
<books>
    <book>
        <title>All About Visual Basic .NET</title>
        <ISBN>972837559X</ISBN>
        <chapter>What's new in VB. NET</chapter>
        <chapter>The .NET Framework</chapter>
        <chapter>The new Windows Controls</chapter>
        <authors>
            <name>first author's name</name>
            <name>second author's name</name>
        </authors>
    </book>
</books>
```

The <authors> element is a child element of the <book> element, and it has its own child elements (the <name> elements). The outermost element is the root element of the document, and all other elements are child elements. The root element in this example is <books>. Each tag has a matching closing tag, which has the same name as the opening tag, but it's prefixed by a backslash. The example you saw contains information that authors would probably share between them.

A bookseller would use an XML document to store different data about the same book:

```
<books>
    <book>
        <title>All About Visual Basic .NET</title>
        <ISBN>972837559X</ISBN>
        <price>49.99</price>
        <discount>0.25</discount>
        <supplier>Books-a-Load</supplier>
        <publicationYear>2002</publicationYear>
    </book>
</books>
```

Because books are identified by their ISBNs, you can combine the two documents by matching their <ISBN> tags. If you load the last two XML sample documents into a DataSet as two tables, you can establish a relation based on the ISBN.

XML isn't limited to describing tabular data—the type of data that comes from a database or can be stored to a database table. The following is the XML description of a message:

```
<email>
    <from>evangelos@example.org</from>
    <to>Richard@example.org</to>
    <subject>Reminder</subject>
    <body>I'll be in town next week</body>
</email>
```

This document could be created by an e-mail application. We're not implying that this information couldn't be stored to a database, but its addresses and messages are stored in different data stores for this example. When a message is actually sent, a <sent> tag might be added to indicate the date and time the message was sent. When another application receives it, a <received> tag might be added, and so on. As long as the applications that deal with the XML-formatted messages understand what each tag means, they can use a text file to store the messages. Of course, searching through a large text file with many messages might be a problem, but as you will see later in this chapter, there are tools to automate the parsing of an XML document.

The two applications that exchange messages in this format need not be absolutely compatible. One of them might use the <from> tag to indicate the sender; the other one might use the <sender> tag. It is possible to apply a transformation that will automatically rename the tags to match the requirements of another application. One of the two systems may not even recognize all the tags. A tag like <priority> is not really required, and one of the applications may actually ignore it—or pass it around without processing it.

---

**NOTE**    There are few rules you should be aware of when you are creating tag names. The most important one is that tags may not start with the letters *xml*. Because XML tags are case-sensitive, no variation of these letters may be used (*XML*, *Xml*, and so on). Tag names may not start with a number or punctuation symbols, and they can't contain spaces.

Tags may also have attributes, which appear as name/value pairs following the name of the tag. The following tag represents a computer. Computers are classified into two categories, notebooks and desktops. Instead of creating two different tags, we can use the `<computer>` tag with a `type` attribute:

```
<computer type="notebook">
    { other tags }
</computer>
```

Attribute values always appear in double or single quotes, even if they're numeric. There are no hard rules regarding when you should use attributes. Most of the time we don't bother with attributes; we implement them as child tags. The preceding example is equivalent to the following:

```
<computer>
    <type="notebook">
    { other tags }
</computer>
```

Attributes shouldn't be used frequently with XML. If you go too far with attributes, you're actually misusing the new format.

## XML vs. DataSets

As you know, ADO.NET DataSets store their data in XML format. Because XML is a universal standard, we don't need to bother with proprietary formats when we can use a universal mechanism for storing data. Besides, when using XML-compatible applications, even different operating systems can exchange data with one another. DataSets contain a relational view of the data: they contain multiple tables with relations between them based on the values of one or more columns, the primary and foreign key columns. The underlying XML file contains the same data, but in a hierarchical view. The DataSet object maintains a synchronized XML description of its data, and you can view the data in either relational or hierarchical view at any time.

Why abandon the relational view of the data and the tools you've learned to use so far in the book? If you're developing database applications with ADO.NET, you'll never have to switch to the XML view. However, you may receive data from a different computer in XML format, or you may create XML files from your data and send them to a non-Windows system. You can send a price list in XML format to any other application or operating system. The recipient of the data can modify the data, possibly by adding a column with quantities, and return the revised XML file to your application, which should be able to extract the quantities and create a new order. You can also create a DataSet entirely in code and never use it to update a database table; you can bind DataSets to controls, populate them, and then persist the DataSet to a disk file, from which the DataSets can be read at later time.

### The XMLData Project

Let's start with a DataSet and explore the structure of the equivalent XML document. The project we'll develop in this section is called XMLData.

Start a new project, design a form like the one shown in Figure 19.1, and then drop the `publishers` and `titles` tables of the Pubs database on the design surface. A Connection and two DataAdapter objects will be created automatically, and you should configure the two data adapters, one for each table. You need not generate the SQL statements to update the database, just the `SELECT` statements to retrieve all the publishers and all the titles. After configuring the data adapters, create a new DataSet, the `PublishersTitles` DataSet, which contains both tables.

**FIGURE 19.1:**

The XMLData application demonstrates how DataSets are persisted in XML format.

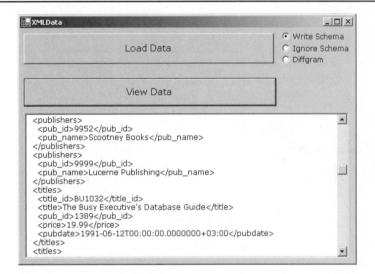

Insert the following statements into the Load Data button's Click event handler to populate the DataSet with two tables, the `publishers` and `titles` tables:

```
Private Sub Button1_Click(ByVal sender _
  As System.Object, ByVal e As System.EventArgs) _
  Handles Button1.Click
    PublisherTitles1.Clear
    DAPublishers.Fill(PublisherTitles1, "Publishers")
    DATitles.Fill(PublisherTitles1, "Titles")
End Sub
```

After populating the DataSet, you can view the XML representation of the data on the TextBox control. To extract the XML description of the data from a DataSet, use the DataSet's WriteXml method, which accepts two arguments: a Stream object to the file where the XML data will be stored and a constant that specifies the exact structure of the XML data:

```
Dataset.WriteXml(stream, mode)
```

The mode argument can have one of the values of the XmlWriteMode enumeration, as shown in Table 19.1.

**TABLE 19.1:** The XmlWriteMode Enumeration

| Member | Description |
| --- | --- |
| IgnoreSchema | Writes the data without schema information (default value). |
| WriteSchema | Writes the data with an inline schema. |
| DiffGram | Writes the data as a diffgram, which includes the original and current versions of each row. You will find more information on diffgrams later in this chapter. |

After saving the XML description of the data to a file, the code reads the same file and displays it on the TextBox control. Listing 19.1 shows the code behind the View Data button.

**Listing 19.1      Viewing a DataSet in XML Format**

```
Private Sub Button2_Click(ByVal sender As System.Object, _
 ByVal e As System.EventArgs) Handles Button2.Click
    Dim WStream As _
     New System.IO.StreamWriter("PublisherTitles.xml")
    Dim mode As XmlWriteMode
    If radioWriteSchema.Checked Then
        mode = XmlWriteMode.WriteSchema
    Else
        If radioDiffGram.Checked Then
            mode = XmlWriteMode.DiffGram
        Else
            mode = XmlWriteMode.IgnoreSchema
        End If
    End If
    PublisherTitles1.WriteXml(WStream, mode)
    WStream.Close()
    Dim RStream As _
     New System.IO.StreamReader("PublisherTitles.xml")
    TextBox1.Text = RStream.ReadToEnd()
    RStream.Close()
End Sub
```

The file in which we store the XML description of the DataSet is called PublishersTitles.xml, and it's created in the Bin folder under the project's folder. You can add a File Save dialog box to the project to make it a little more flexible. The code takes into consideration the settings of the radio buttons on the form to save the data in the format specified by the user. You can check out all three versions of the XML file and see how the *mode* argument affects the type of output generated by the WriteXml method.

Here are the first few publishers, followed by the first few titles. We've omitted many lines, but they all have the same structure:

```
<publishers>
  <pub_id>0736</pub_id>
  <pub_name>New Moon Books</pub_name>
</publishers>
<publishers>
  <pub_id>0877</pub_id>
  <pub_name>Binnet &amp; Hardley</pub_name>
{ more publisher entries }
  <titles>
    <title_id>BU1032</title_id>
    <title>The Busy Executive's Database Guide</title>
    <pub_id>1389</pub_id>
    <price>19.99</price>
    <pubdate>1991-06-12T00:00:00.0000000+03:00</pubdate>
  </titles>
  <titles>
    <title_id>BU1111</title_id>
    <title>Cooking with Computers: _
     Surreptitious Balance Sheets</title>
    <pub_id>1389</pub_id>
    <price>11.95</price>
    <pubdate>1991-06-09T00:00:00.0000000+03:00</pubdate>
  </titles>
{ more titles entries }
```

You can't experiment with the DiffGram option because the DataSet can't be modified, so the current version is the same as the original version. In the next example, we'll edit the DataSet's tables and you'll see how the XML file stores the changes in the data. But first, we must relate the two tables. If you examine the XML representation of the DataSet, you'll realize that it contains the rows of the two tables but no relation between them. Because the DataSet doesn't contain any relations, its XML representation couldn't be any different.

### Establishing Relations

Let's add a relation between the two tables. You can do so in your code, or you can edit the XSD file in the Designer. In this example, we've added the relation between the two tables in the code so that you can easily remove it (by commenting out the appropriate lines) or reinstate it (by uncommenting the same lines). The lines in Listing 19.2 add the relation between the two tables.

---

**Listing 19.2**     **Adding a Relation Between the Publishers and Titles Tables**

```
PublisherTitles1.Relations.Add(New _
        DataRelation("PubTitles", _
        PublisherTitles1.Tables("publishers").Columns("pub_id"), _
        PublisherTitles1.Tables("titles").Columns("pub_id")))
```

---

After we add the relation between the two tables, the resulting XML looks like the original, and only the following section was added. This section contains the description of the relation. The `<xs:unique>` tag makes the `pub_id` column of the Publishers table unique. The `<xs:keyref>` tag establishes a relation between the two tables based on the `pub_id` column.

```
<xs:unique name="Constraint1" msdata:PrimaryKey="true">
  <xs:selector xpath=".//mstns:publishers" />
  <xs:field xpath="mstns:pub_id" />
</xs:unique>
<xs:unique name="titles_Constraint1" msdata:
            ConstraintName="Constraint1"
            msdata:PrimaryKey="true">
  <xs:selector xpath=".//mstns:titles" />
  <xs:field xpath="mstns:title_id" />
</xs:unique>
<xs:keyref name="PubTitles" refer="Constraint1">
  <xs:selector xpath=".//mstns:titles" />
  <xs:field xpath="mstns:pub_id" />
</xs:keyref>
```

### Nesting Relations

The rest of the file contains the publishers and the titles. You may have noticed that typical XML files contain nested entries: each publisher section contains all the books of this publisher, then the next publisher with its books, and so on. To create a hierarchical XML file, you must declare that the relations between the tables are nested. To do so, set the Nested property of the relation to True (the default value of this property is False). Add the following statement to the Load Data button's Click event handler after the statement that adds the relation to the schema:

```
PublisherTitles1.Relations(0).Nested = True
```

This time the structure of the XML file reflects the hierarchy of the data. The `<title>` tags are nested within their matching `<publisher>` tags. The code in Listing 19.3 is a small section of the XML file generated by the WriteXml method when the relations between the tables of the DataSet are nested.

---

**Listing 19.3**     **The XML Description of a DataSet with Nested Relations**

```
<publishers>
  <pub_id>0736</pub_id>
  <pub_name>New Moon Books</pub_name>
  <titles>
    <title_id>BU2075</title_id>
    <title>You Can Combat Computer Stress!</title>
    <pub_id>0736</pub_id>
    <price>2.99</price>
    <pubdate>1991-06-30T00:00:00.0000000+03:00</pubdate>
  </titles>
  <titles>
    <title_id>PS2091</title_id>
    <title>Is Anger the Enemy?</title>
    <pub_id>0736</pub_id>
    <price>10.95</price>
    <pubdate>1991-06-15T00:00:00.0000000+03:00</pubdate>
  </titles>
</publishers>
<publishers>
  <pub_id>1389</pub_id>
  <pub_name>Algodata Infosystems</pub_name>
  <titles>
    <title_id>BU1032</title_id>
    <title>The Busy Executive's Database Guide</title>
    <pub_id>1389</pub_id>
    <price>19.99</price>
    <pubdate>1991-06-12T00:00:00.0000000+03:00</pubdate>
  </titles>
</publisher>
```

---

## Loading XML into DataSets

In this section, we'll load the `PublisherTitles.xml` file we created in the previous section into a DataSet. The XML file resides on the hard disk, and it could have originated anywhere. To fill a DataSet from an XML file, use the ReadXml method of the DataSet object, which reads its data from a file (or stream). The ReadXml method's arguments are the name of the file (or a Stream object) and an optional argument that determines which section of the file will be read:

```
Dataset.ReadXml(source, mode)
```

The first argument can be the name of a file, a Stream object, or a TextReader object. The value of the second argument can be one of the members of the XmlReadMode enumeration, which is shown in Table 19.2.

**TABLE 19.2:** The XmlReadMode Enumeration

| Member | Description |
|---|---|
| Auto | The ReadXml method examines the XML and chooses the most appropriate option. If the XML is a DiffGram, the entire DiffGram is loaded (the original and current versions of the rows). If the DataSet or the XML contains a schema, then the schema is read. If neither the DataSet nor the XML contains a schema, then the ReadXml method attempts to infer the schema from the data (see the InferSchema entry in this table). Auto is the default member. |
| ReadSchema | The DataSet loads the schema and the data from the XML. If the DataSet contains a schema, then the new tables are added to the existing schema. If there are common tables, an exception will be thrown. The DataSet understands XSD (XML Schema Definition language) and XDR (XML Data Reduced language) formats, but the preferred format is XSD. |
| IgnoreSchema | The ReadXml method ignores any schema information in the XML and loads the data into the DataSet. Any data that doesn't match the existing schema is ignored. |
| DiffGram | This member causes the ReadXml method to add data to the current schema. It merges the new rows with any existing rows if their primary keys match. |
| InferSchema | This member causes the ReadXml method to infer the schema from the XML data. If the DataSet contains a schema already, new tables may be created for the XML tables that don't match a table in the DataSet. If incompatible columns exist in the XML data and the DataSet, then an exception will be thrown. |
| Fragment | This member causes the ReadXml method to read XML fragments, which must match the DataSet schema. |

To load an XML file into a DataSet, call the simplest form of the ReadXml method as follows:

```
DS.ReadXml("c:\myContacts.xml")
```

DS is a properly declared DataSet object, and you need not create a schema for it. This DataSet isn't derived from a database; it's based on a stand-alone file. Once the data is in the DataSet, you can use any of the techniques discussed earlier in the book to process it. You can view its tables and edit them, navigate through its rows using the appropriate Relation objects, and so on. You can accept or reject changes, and you can do everything you can do with a table-based DataSet. You can bind the DataSet to a DataGrid control, allow users to edit the data, and then save the data to an XML file with the WriteXml method. This is what we'll do in the following section.

## The LoadXML Project

The LoadXML project demonstrates how to load a DataSet with an XML file, edit the data, and then save it back to an XML file. Create a new project and design a form with two buttons and a DataGrid control, as shown in Figure 19.2. This project's folder must reside under the same parent folder as the XMLData project because it uses the `PublisherTitles.xml` file created by the XMLData project. If you create the folder elsewhere, you must also change the reference to the XML file (the code uses a relative reference to the XML file generated by the preceding example).

**FIGURE 19.2:**

The LoadXML project demonstrates how to use an XML file as a data source.

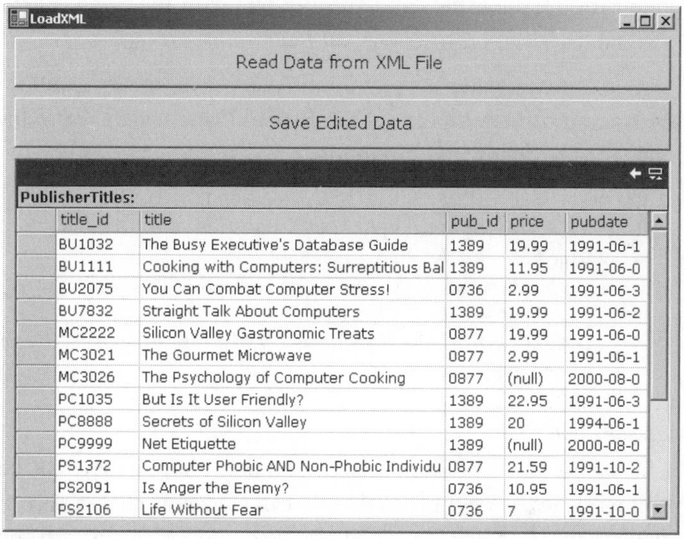

The Read Data From XML File button reads the `PublisherTitles.xml` file and loads it on a new DataSet with the statements shown in Listing 19.4. Then the code establishes a relation between titles and publishers and finally binds the DataSet to the DataGrid control by assigning it to the control's DataSource property.

**Listing 19.4    Loading XML Data on a DataGrid Control**

```
Private Sub Button1_Click(ByVal sender As System.Object, _
 ByVal e As System.EventArgs) Handles Button1.Click
    Dim RStream As New _
        System.IO.StreamReader("..\..\XMLData\Bin\" & _
        "PublisherTitles.xml")
    DataSet1.Clear()
    DataSet1.ReadXml(RStream)
    DataSet1.Relations.Clear()
    DataSet1.Relations.Add(New DataRelation("Pubs2Titles", _
            DataSet1.Tables(0).Columns("pub_id"), _
            DataSet1.Tables(1).Columns("pub_id")))
    DataGrid1.DataSource = DataSet1
    RStream.Close()
End Sub
```

The DataSet is cleared so that you can reload the DataSet by clicking the top button on the form. If you comment out this statement, you'll be able to load the XML file on the control the first time, but if you attempt to reload the control, you'll get an exception. The DataSet has a schema already, and the ReadXml method can't add a new table with the same name. The code reads the data into the DataSet with the ReadXml method, which will create two tables: one with the publishers and another one with the titles. Then it adds a relation between the two tables based on their pub_id field.

You can edit some rows of the titles table on the grid and then save the modified data. The second button on the form, Save Edited Data, saves the modified data back to the same XML file with the following statements:

```
Private Sub Button2_Click(ByVal sender As System.Object, _
 ByVal e As System.EventArgs) Handles Button2.Click
    Dim WStream As New _
        System.IO.StreamWriter("..\..\XMLData\Bin\" & _
        "PublisherTitles.xml")
    DataSet1.WriteXml(WStream, XmlWriteMode.DiffGram)
    WStream.Close()
    DataSet1.Clear()
End Sub
```

Why use the DiffGram mode? You don't have to save the changes, but we've chosen to use this mode in the example so that we can view how changes are stored in an XML file. Typically, you accept all the changes and create a new XML file with the most recent version of the data. If you're working with your notebook, however, you may create the DataSet when you're connected to the server, persist the data to a file, and update the database when you get back to the office. In this case, you should store the changes as well, so that your application won't change rows that have been updated already. The topic of performing multiple updates against the data source and handling update errors was discussed in detail in Chapter 5. All the techniques we presented in this chapter can be used with DataSets populated from an XML file. If the XML file and the database you want to update don't have the same structure, you'll have to design your own Command objects.

This project also demonstrates how to use the DataGrid control as a data-entry and editing tool. All you really need is an XML document that describes the schema of the data you want to display on the control—no data. You can load this schema, adjust the appearance of the DataGrid control, and allow users to enter data and edit it. You can then move the data back to the XML file and reload it at a later session. For more information on using the DataGrid control as a data entry tool, see the section "The MakeXMLFile Project" later in this chapter. But first, let's take a closer look at how changes in a DataSet are persisted in XML.

### The DiffGram of the Edited DataSet

In this section, we'll develop a project very similar to the LoadXML project, but we'll replace the TextBox control at the bottom of the form with a DataGrid control. You can edit the DataSet on the DataGrid and then persist it to an XML file. If you edit the XML file you loaded in the LoadXML example and then persist it, the changes won't be recorded to the file. The row versions are a trademark of DataSets; that's why we developed a different project to demonstrate how DataSets are persisted in XML.

You can copy the folder of the LoadXML project and rename the copied project to EditXML-Data. Replace the TextBox control with a DataGrid control and bind it to the project's DataSet, the *PublisherTitles1* DataSet. This DataSet contains two related tables, and you can edit them both on the DataGrid control. The code of the project didn't change substantially; we simply removed the statements that displayed text on the TextBox control.

Run the project, edit a few title rows, add a few rows, and delete one of the original rows. Then click the Persist DataSet button to persist the DataSet as a DiffGram, and open the `PublisherTitles.xml` file that the application has created in the project's `Bin` folder.

The following is the element corresponding to a title that has been edited:

```
<titles diffgr:id="titles3" msdata:rowOrder="2"
        diffgr:hasChanges="modified">
   <title_id>BU2075</title_id>
   <title>You Can Combat Computer Stress!</title>
   <pub_id>0736</pub_id>
   <price>33</price>
   <pubdate>1991-06-30T00:00:00.0000000+03:00</pubdate>
</titles>
```

This section is the XML representation of the current data. Notice the attribute `hasChanges`, whose value is `"modified"`. The most interesting segment of the file is at the end, and it's the `<diffgr:before>` segment. This segment contains the original version of the same title:

```
<diffgr:before>
    <titles diffgr:id="titles3" msdata:rowOrder="2"
       xmlns="http://www.tempuri.org/PublisherTitles.xsd">
      <title_id>BU2075</title_id>
      <title>You Can Combat Computer Stress!</title>
      <pub_id>0736</pub_id>
      <price>2.99</price>
      <pubdate>1991-06-30T00:00:00.0000000+03:00</pubdate>
    </titles>
</diffgr:before>
```

This section contains the original data. If you call the AcceptChanges method of the DataSet, the section with the original data will be removed from the XML representation of the DataSet. The values of the `<diffgr:before>` segment will be replaced by the current (edited) values. As you already know, the AcceptChanges and RejectChanges methods apply to individual rows as well. If you apply these two methods to individual rows, some of the titles in the `<diffgr:before>` section will be removed (the changed rows you accept) and some of the titles in the same section will replace the matching products in the `<diffgr:diffgram>` section.

If you delete a line, the corresponding entry in the `<diffgr:diffgram>` will be removed and the original line will be added to the `<diffgr:before>` section. This is how the DataSet knows about deleted lines, and you already know how it will handle a deleted row if you reject the changes.

If you add a row to the DataSet, a new item will be added to the section `<diffgr:diffgram>` and it will be marked as `"inserted"`, as shown here:

```
<titles diffgr:id="titles19" msdata:rowOrder="18"
        diffgr:hasChanges="inserted">
  <title_id>TC8888</title_id>
  <title>New Title</title>
  <pub_id>0736</pub_id>
  <price>3.99</price>
  <pubdate>2001-01-01T00:00:00.0000000+02:00</pubdate>
</titles>
```

As you can see, the XML description of the DataSet contains all the information needed to manipulate the data at the client and yet be able to update the underlying tables in the database. At any point you can accept and reject the changes (or selected changes) and the DataSet will be adjusted accordingly. This is also how the GetChanges method of the DataSet object works. To retrieve the edited rows, this method looks for rows marked as `"modified"`. Likewise, it retrieves the new rows by looking for rows marked as `"inserted"` and it retrieves the deleted rows by locating the rows that appear in the `<diffgr:before>` section and have no counterpart in the `<diffgr:diffgram>` segment. As you can see, using XML is a very convenient method of storing DataSets and the versions of their rows. This example showed you exactly how the DataSet works and why Microsoft has chosen this format for encoding the DataSet's contents.

The DataAdapter object uses the information stored in the DataSet to figure out whether it should update the underlying tables in the database. When using optimistic concurrency, the DataAdapter will not change a row if the current row's fields are not the same as the original versions of the row in the DataSet. If you look at the Update command of the DataAdapter, you will see that it compares the original versions of its modified rows to the current versions of the same rows in the table. If they're the same, it means that they haven't been modified since they were read, and it updates them. If they differ, then the row has been edited since it was read and the corresponding rows are not updated.

## Creating an XML Schema

In this section, we'll create a schema from scratch. Instead of retrieving the schema from one or more database tables, we'll add an XML Schema component to our project and we'll create its schema from scratch.

Create a new Windows application and name it MakeXMLFile. Right-click the project's name in the Solution Explorer and select Add ➢ Add New Item. In the Add New Item dialog box that appears, select XML Schema and click OK. The name of the XML schema that will be added is XMLSchema1.xsd by default. Double-click this file's name in the Solution Explorer to open it in the Designer. There are two ways to work with an XSD file: in the Schema mode you can create a schema with visual tools, and in the XML mode you can edit the XML description of the schema. You can switch between the two views by selecting the appropriate tab at the bottom of the Designer. We'll use the visual tools exclusively, but you can switch to the XML view at any time. You can edit the schema in either view and then see how the edits affected the other view.

Now we can create a simple schema for storing data about persons (customers, contacts, any collection of person your application may require). We'll create a table in which we'll store information like names, social security numbers, addresses, phone numbers, and the like. We'll also create a table with groups. Each group will have a name and a unique ID. It's quite useful to be able to classify the people into one or more groups, like customers, suppliers, press, and so on. The same person may belong to multiple groups, as well. To connect the two tables, we must introduce a third one, which will hold pairs of IDs that identify people and the groups to which they belong. If the same person belongs to two groups, then we simply add two lines to the middle table. The two rows will have the same person ID, but different group IDs.

Let's start by building the first table, the Person table. Right-click somewhere on the Designer's surface, and select Add ➢ New Element. A new box, which represents an element, will be added to the Designer. Start typing the name of the element (Person) and then click on the first empty line of the table. Enter the name of the first field (PersonID), and in the box next to it, select the data type of the column. Because this is an ID that identifies each person, make it an integer. While this row is selected, switch to the Property Browser and you will see that the Integer data type provides the AutoIncrement property. This element's value will be automatically set to the next integer every time you add a new row to the table (just like an Identity field in SQL Server).

Then move to the next row, enter the name of the next attribute, and select its type from the drop-down list in the next box. This attribute's name is LastName, and it's a string. The next attribute is FirstName and the last attribute's name is SSN (both are strings). To add a new element to the schema, right-click the Designer's surface and select Add ➢ Element.

Name the new element Group (it's the table that stores the names and IDs of the various groups to which a person belongs). This element has two attributes, the GroupID (an integer with AutoIncrement set to True) and the GroupName attributes (a string). To add the attributes, just type their names and select the appropriate type from the drop-down list next to the name.

The last step is to create a third element, the Members element. This element contains relations between persons and groups. Its attributes are named PersonID and GroupID, and they're both integers. Each time you want to add a person to a group, you can add a new row to the Members table and set its columns to the ID of the person and the ID of the group to which the person belongs.

To complete the schema, we must add the proper relations between the various elements. Add two relations to the schema (double-click the Relation icon on the toolbox) and then configure them as follows: The first relation should connect the Person table to the Members table by relating the PersonID columns in both tables. The second relation should connect the Members table to the Group table by relating the GroupID column in both tables, as shown in Figure 19.3.

**FIGURE 19.3:**

The Schema of the MakeXMLFile project

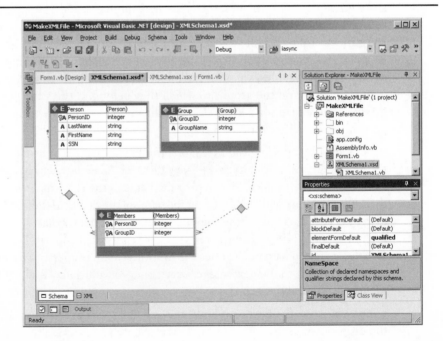

Once you've created the schema, you can create a DataSet object with the identical structure. Switch to the project's form and add a DataSet object from the toolbox (the icon of the DataSet object can be found in the Toolbox's Data tab). When the Add DataSet dialog box appears, check the option Typed DataSet, and in the Name box, select the name of the XSD file with the XML schema you just created. Then click the OK button to close the dialog box and add the appropriate DataSet to the project.

Now you can add a DataGrid control to the form and bind it to the DataSet just created. Set the DataGrid control's DataSource property to the name of the DataSet (XMLSchema11) and run the application. You will be able to enter and edit data on the grid and persist the data in an XML file (see Figure 19.4).

**FIGURE 19.4:**

Creating a DataSet based on the schema shown in Figure 19.3

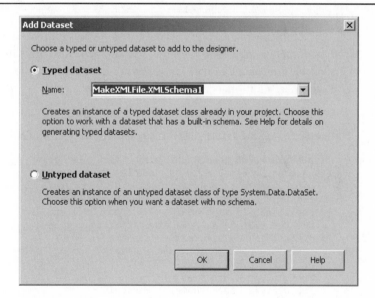

In the following section, we'll take a closer look at the code of the MakeXMLFile project.

## The MakeXMLFile Project

We have created a DataSet schema with three related tables, and we can bind a DataGrid control to it. Place a DataGrid control on the application's main form along with two buttons, as shown in Figure 19.5. Then bind the DataGrid control to the project's DataSet by setting its DataSource property to XmlSchema11 (or whatever you've named the DataSet generated by the wizard).

**FIGURE 19.5:**

The MakeXMLFile project demonstrates how to use the DataGrid control as a data entry tool.

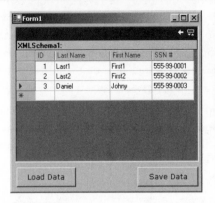

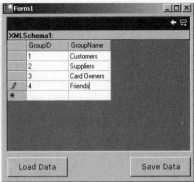

The default appearance of the DataGrid control is rather blunt, but you can customize it from within your code. The code that sets up the DataGrid control for the columns of the Person table is executed from within the form's Load event handler, and it's shown in Listing 19.5. You can insert additional code for the other tables.

**Listing 19.5**     **Customizing the Appearance of the DataGrid Control**

```
Private Sub Form1_Load(ByVal sender As System.Object, _
ByVal e As System.EventArgs) Handles MyBase.Load
    Dim PubTableStyle As New DataGridTableStyle()
    PubTableStyle.HeaderForeColor = Color.Blue
    PubTableStyle.MappingName = "Person"
    Dim PubColStyle As New DataGridTextBoxColumn()
    ' First column's format
    PubColStyle.Alignment = HorizontalAlignment.Center
    PubColStyle.HeaderText = "ID"
    PubColStyle.Width = 35
    PubColStyle.MappingName = "PersonID"
    PubTableStyle.GridColumnStyles.Add(PubColStyle)
    ' Second column's format
    PubColStyle = New DataGridTextBoxColumn()
    PubColStyle.Alignment = HorizontalAlignment.Left
    PubColStyle.HeaderText = "Last Name"
    PubColStyle.Width = 100
    PubColStyle.MappingName = "LastName"
    PubTableStyle.GridColumnStyles.Add(PubColStyle)
    ' Third column's format
    PubColStyle = New DataGridTextBoxColumn()
    PubColStyle.Alignment = HorizontalAlignment.Left
    PubColStyle.HeaderText = "First Name"
    PubColStyle.Width = 75
    PubColStyle.MappingName = "FirstName"
    PubTableStyle.GridColumnStyles.Add(PubColStyle)
```

```
' Fifth column's format
PubColStyle = New DataGridTextBoxColumn()
PubColStyle.Alignment = HorizontalAlignment.Left
PubColStyle.HeaderText = "SSN #"
PubColStyle.Width = 75
PubColStyle.MappingName = "SSN"
PubTableStyle.GridColumnStyles.Add(PubColStyle)
DataGrid1.TableStyles.Add(PubTableStyle)
End Sub
```

As a quick reminder, the DataGrid control provides a TableStyles collection, and there's one such collection for each table of the DataSet displayed on the control. Each member of the TableStyles collection is itself another collection, a GridColumnStyles collection. The GridColumnStyles collection contains a member for each column of the corresponding table, and each member is of the DataGridTextBoxColumn type (or the DataGridBoolColumn type for True/False columns). You can set the properties of this object to determine the appearance of the column. You shouldn't forget to set the MappingName property of each table and each column of the grid to the name of the table column you plan to map to each item. If not, the DataGrid will not be bound to the DataSet.

The code sets up a DataGridTextBoxColumn object for each element and then adds them to the GridColumnStyles collection of the DataGridTableStyle property of the control. Notice that you must create one DataGridTableStyle object for each table in the DataSet. If a table doesn't have its own member in the TableStyles collection, the corresponding table will have its default appearance. The code shown in Listing 19.5 sets up the columns of the Person table. You can insert similar statements for the remaining tables in the form's Load event handler.

The statements in the Save Data button's Click event handler persist the data to an XML file (see Listing 19.6). We've hard-coded the name of the file, but you can easily prompt the user with a File Open dialog box.

---

### Listing 19.6    Persisting the Data to an XML File

```
Private Sub SaveData(ByVal sender As System.Object, _
  ByVal e As System.EventArgs) Handles bttnSave.Click
    Dim fname As String
    fname = "c:\Persons.xml"
    Dim OutStream As New System.IO.StreamWriter(fname)
    XmlSchema11.WriteXml(OutStream, _
     System.Data.XmlWriteMode.IgnoreSchema)
    OutStream.Close()
End Sub
```

---

In a later session, you can load the DataSet with the data in the Persons.xml file. The Click event handler of the Load Data button is shown in Listing 19.7.

---

**Listing 19.7**      **Loading the DataSet with Data from an XML File**

```
Private Sub LoadData(ByVal sender As System.Object, _
  ByVal e As System.EventArgs) Handles bttnLoad.Click
    Dim fname As String
    fname = "c:\Persons.xml"
    Dim InStream As New System.IO.StreamReader(fname)
    XmlSchema11.ReadXml(InStream, _
      System.Data.XmlReadMode.Auto)
    InStream.Close()
End Sub
```

---

So far you've seen basic examples of using XML in database applications, as well as how to persist structured, related data to XML files. You can use XML files as data stores for many non-data bound applications that would otherwise be manipulating files. The advantage of XML is that you don't have to worry about the structure of the file, handle special characters, enforce relations between tables, and so on. XML is a text-based protocol, and it can store all types of information. Notice that you haven't had to deal directly with the structure of the XML files so far. This means that the DataSet does a fine job of abstracting the process of persisting data to XML files as well as loading a DataSet from an XML file. However, there's more you can do with XML, and we're going to look at a few more practical XML topics.

## Transforming XML Files

If you open an XML file in Internet Explorer, you will see the actual contents of the file. Internet Explorer understands XML, but it won't hide the tags when displaying XML files. However, you can apply a so-called XSL (eXtensible Style Sheet) transformation to the file and display it as you wish on the browser. We usually display XML files as tables, but you can also create a page with data-bound controls on it. To transform an XML document, you use XSL style sheets, which process an XML file and generate another text file. XSL style sheets are not executable; they contain instructions that will be processed by other programs, like the browser, or the XML server control.

Let's look at a style sheet for manipulating the `PublisherTitles.xml` file. This XML file contains publishers and titles. The style sheet will generate an HTML page with two tables, one for the publishers and another one for the titles. This is a very simple HTML page, but it's straight HTML and you can make it as complicated as you wish (or as you can). Listing 19.8 shows the contents of the `PublisherTitles.xsl` file. It starts with a standard header, and it contains mostly HTML tags. This style sheet transforms the XML document into an HTML page, so it's only natural that it's made up mostly of HTML tags. You can transform your XML data into a file of arbitrary structure. It's actually not uncommon to transform an XML file into another XML file, which has the identical structure, but different element tags that match the description of your database. You can even go as far as to create delimited text files from XML files, but this defeats the purpose of creating the XLM file in the first place.

**Listing 19.8**          **The *PublisherTitles.xsl* Stylesheet**

```
<xsl:stylesheet version = '1.0'
xmlns:xsl='http://www.w3.org/1999/XSL/Transform'>
<xsl:template match='/'>
<table cellspacing='3' border='2'>
<tr>
<th>PubID</th>
<th>Publisher</th>
</tr>
<xsl:for-each select='PublisherTitles/publishers'>
<tr>
<td>
<xsl:value-of select='pub_id'/>
</td>
<td>
<xsl:value-of select='pub_name'/>
</td>
</tr>
</xsl:for-each>
</table>
<br></br>
<table border='2'>
<tr>
<th>ID</th>
<th>Title</th>
<th>Price</th>
</tr>
<xsl:for-each select='PublisherTitles/titles'>
<tr>
<td>
<xsl:value-of select='title_id'/>
</td>
<td>
<xsl:value-of select='title'/>
</td>
<td>
<xsl:value-of select='price'/>
</td>
</tr>
</xsl:for-each>
</table>
</xsl:template>
</xsl:stylesheet>
```

All the HTML tags, or literals, that appear in the XSL file are copied to the output. The tags that are processed begin with the `xsl` prefix. The first such tag (after the header) is the following:

```
<xsl:for-each select='PublisherTitles/publishers'>
```

This tag starts a loop that iterates through the `<publishers>` tags of the XML file. These tags correspond to the rows of the Publishers table. All the statements from this tag to the matching closing tag are repeated for each `<publishers>` tag in the XML file. In this section, there are two columns one for the pub_id field and another one for the pub_name field. The `value-of-select` keyword is replaced by the appropriate field. The following line is replaced by the ID of the first publisher in the file during the first iteration, by the ID of the second publisher during the second iteration, and so on:

```
<xsl:value-of select='pub_id'/>
```

The loop ends with the tag `</xls:for-each>`. The style sheet of Listing 19.8 will translate the `PublisherTitles.xml` file into an HTML page with two tables, one with the publishers and another one with the titles, as shown in Figure 19.6.

**FIGURE 19.6:**

Translating an XML file into an HTML page with two tables

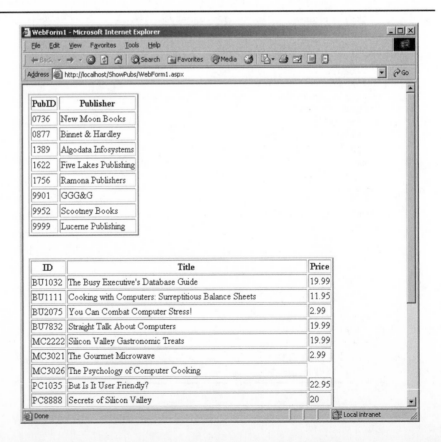

To use the XSL file, create a new Web application and place an instance of the XML control on the Web Form. This is a trivial control with two properties of interest: the Document-Source property, which is the URI of the XML file to be translated, and the TransformSource property, which is the URI of the XSL file with the description of the transformation to be applied to the XML file. Set these two properties to the `PublisherTitles.xml` and `Publisher-Titles.xsl` files and then run the application. Internet Explorer will come up displaying the two tables shown in Figure 19.6.

If you want to apply a transformation and save the result to a file, you must use the XslTransform object, load the style sheet, and then call the XslTransform object's Transform method to save the transformed file. The Transform method is overloaded, and its simplest form accepts as an argument the path of the XML file to be transformed and the path of the output file, as shown in the statements in Listing 19.9.

**Listing 19.9        Transforming an XML File with the XslTransform Object**

```
Dim objXSLT As New XslTransform()
objXSLT.Load("PublisherTitles.xsl")
objXSLT.Transform("PublisherTitles.xml", _
   "TransformedFile.html")
Dim InStream As _
   New System.IO.StreamReader("TransformedFile.html")
TextBox1.Text = InStream.ReadToEnd
InStream.Close()
```

The statements in Listing 19.9 transform an XML file and save the transformed data into another file. The new file is then displayed on a TextBox control. Place these statements in the Click event of a button and experiment with XSL transformations.

The XML control is a very simple but very powerful control. You can write components that extract the information you want to display on your site's pages (or create static XML files with data). By applying different transformations to your data, you can create widely different pages or change the XSL files at will to alter the appearance of your pages. Using XML to describe the data and XSL to describe how they'll be rendered allows you to decouple the contents from the look of your site. This is an enormous topic that is beyond the scope of this book.

## Parsing XML Files

In addition to storing data in XML format, you should also be able to parse XML files without storing them to DataSets. Most developers will use a DataSet to store XML data that originates outside a database (in other words, load the DataSet with an XML file generated by another application), but there will be occasions when you want to parse an XML file directly and extract the desired information.

The XML document is a hierarchical view of the data, and some web developers may find it simpler to work with the XML view of the data. Currently, there are no practical visual tools for working with XML files, but with the wide acceptance of the XML protocol, the situation may change in the very near future. You have seen how to create an XML file's schema in the IDE. In this section, you'll learn how to process XML files from within your code.

There are two classes for accessing XML data: the XmlDocument class and the XmlData-Document class. Both classes represent the XML file in memory, and they allow you to read or modify the XML document. For very large documents, you can use the XmlReader class, which provides forward-only, read-only access. This means that you can't edit the XML file with the XmlReader class. However, you can always create a new XML document based on an existing one and save it with the help of the XmlWriter class.

The XmlDocument and XmlDataDocument objects are very similar. The XmlData-Document class is new to .NET, and it provides a property called DataSet, which exposes the XML data as a DataSet. The XmlDocument represents an XML document and can't be used with DataSets. The DataSet property of the XmlDataDocument object provides a relational view of the XML data, and as a database programmer, you're more comfortable with this notation. In this chapter, we'll use the XmlDataDocument class to access XML files from within our code.

There are several methods to scan an XML file, but in this section we'll show you how to go through the elements, and their child elements, by treating them as nodes. You read a node and process its child nodes one at a time. If one of the child nodes has children of its own, you process them and continue.

To use the XmlDataDocument class, you must first create an instance of the class and load an XML file to it. The following statements create an instance of the XmlDataDocument class and load to it the data of the `PublisherTitles.xml` file:

```
Dim objXMLDoc As New XmlDataDocument()
objXMLDoc.Load("PublisherTitles.xml")
```

The XML document consists of nodes, and each node may have one or more child nodes. There are several ways to select groups of nodes. No matter which one you use, the selected nodes are returned as a collection of the XmlNodeList type. Each element of the collection is an XmlNode object, and you can use its properties to extract the node's name and value. The GetElementsByTagName method of the XmlDataDocument, for example, selects all the elements with a tag you specify and returns them as an XmlNodeList collection. The following statements will retrieve all the `<publishers>` tags in the file and store them in a collection, the oNodes collection:

```
Dim oNodes As XmlNodeList
oNodes = objXMLDoc.GetElementsByTagName("publishers")
```

How do we iterate through the oNodes collection? Because it's made up of XmlNode objects, we can use a For Each…Next loop like the following:

```
Dim oNode As XmlNode
For Each oNode In oNodes
    { statements to process the current node }
Next
```

The XmlNode object exposes a large number of properties, which we aren't going to discuss here. We'll look at only the properties you need to iterate through a collection of nodes and extract the desired information. Although it's possible to write code to iterate through the nodes of an arbitrary XML document, you should have a good idea about the structure of the document. Being able to iterate through the tables of an arbitrary DataSet and the rows of any of its tables is of questionable value. The idea is to extract useful information from the XML document and process it, not just print the values. Let's write a loop to iterate through the publishers of the `PublisherTitles.xml` file.

First, we set up a For Each…Next loop as shown earlier. At each iteration, the *oNode* variable represents another `<publishers>` node, which in turn has two child nodes, the `<pub_id>` and `<pub_name>` elements. To retrieve the values of these nodes, use the ChildNodes collection of the current node. Each element of this collection is another XmlNode object, and its two basic properties are the Name and InnerText properties. Name is the name of the node (its tag name), and the InnerText property represents the node's value (the string between the two tags). A related property is the InnerXml property, which returns the same string in XML encoding (the < character is represented as &lt;, for example).

```
Dim oNode As XmlNode
For Each oNode In oNodes
    If oNode.HasChildNodes Then
        Dim iNode, iNodes As Integer
        iNodes = oNode.ChildNodes.Count
        For iNode = 0 To iNodes - 1
            TextBox1.AppendText(oNode.ChildNodes(iNode).Name _
             & vbTab & oNode.ChildNodes(iNode).InnerText _
             & vbCrLf)
        Next
    End If
Next
```

The XmlNode object exposes a Value property, which returns the value of the node, but this value is not the same string as the InnerText property.

To demonstrate how to scan the nodes of an XML document, as well as how to query an XML document, we've prepared the XMLDataDoc project, whose main form is shown in Figure 19.7.

**FIGURE 19.7:**

The XMLDataDoc project demonstrates the members of the XmlDataDocument object.

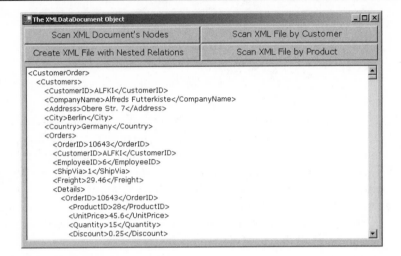

The "Scan XML Document's Nodes" button creates an XML document with the publishers and titles of the Pubs database and iterates through the publishers. The code shown in Listing 19.10 handles the Click event of the Scan XML Document's Nodes button. It will generate the following output (there are eight publishers in the file):

```
pub_id      0736
pub_name    New Moon Books
pub_id      0877
pub_name    Binnet & Hardley
pub_id      1389
pub_name    Algodata Infosystems
pub_id      1622
pub_name    Five Lakes Publishing
pub_id      1756
pub_name    Ramona Publishers
pub_id      9901
pub_name    GGG&G
pub_id      9952
pub_name    Scootney Books
pub_id      9999
pub_name    Lucerne Publishing
```

The `PublishersTitles.xml` file doesn't contain nested relations. It's made up of a section with the publishers followed by another section with the titles. The GetElementsByTagName method will work no matter how the elements are arranged in the XML file (whether they're nested or not).

---

**Listing 19.10**      **Scanning the <publishers> Nodes of the *PublisherTitles.xml* File**

```
Private Sub Button1_Click(ByVal sender As System.Object, _
 ByVal e As System.EventArgs) Handles Button1.Click
  TextBox1.Clear()
  Dim objXMLDoc As New XmlDataDocument()
  objXMLDoc.Load("PublisherTitles.xml")
  Dim oNodes As XmlNodeList
  oNodes = objXMLDoc.GetElementsByTagName("publishers")
  TextBox1.AppendText("There are " & _
   oNodes.Count.ToString & _
   " publishers in the file" & vbCrLf)

  Dim oNode As XmlNode
  For Each oNode In oNodes
    If oNode.HasChildNodes Then
      Dim iNode, iNodes As Integer
      iNodes = oNode.ChildNodes.Count
      For iNode = 0 To iNodes - 1
       TextBox1.AppendText(oNode.ChildNodes(iNode).Name & _
        vbTab & oNode.ChildNodes(iNode).InnerText & vbCrLf)
      Next
    End If
  Next
End Sub
```

---

The second button on the form, the "Create XML File with Nested Relations" button, creates an XML file with nested relations. This time we'll use data from the Northwind database; we'll read customers, their orders, and each order's details. In a real-world application, the resulting file would be enormous, but you can limit the number of selected rows through the SELECT statements. You can retrieve only customers in a particular state, or a single customer, and then only the orders that were placed within a week's or month's time span.

The statements in Listing 19.11 populate a DataSet with three tables—the Customers, Orders, and Details tables—and then they establish a nested relation between the customers and their orders and the orders and their details. The DataSet is then loaded into an XML document, which is saved in the `AllOrders.xml` file.

**Listing 19.11**     **Storing Customers, Orders, and Details in an XML File**

```
Private Sub Button2_Click(ByVal sender As System.Object, _
 ByVal e As System.EventArgs) Handles Button2.Click
  TextBox1.Clear()
  Dim CN As New SqlClient.SqlConnection("data source=.;" & _
              "initial catalog=northwind;user id=sa;" & _
              "workstation id=POWERTOOLKIT")
  Dim DS As New DataSet("CustomerOrder")
  CN.Open()
  Dim DACustomers As New SqlClient.SqlDataAdapter( _
      "SELECT * FROM Customers", CN)
  DACustomers.Fill(DS, "Customers")
  Dim DAOrders As New SqlClient.SqlDataAdapter( _
      "SELECT * FROM Orders", CN)
  DAOrders.Fill(DS, "Orders")
  Dim DADetails As New SqlClient.SqlDataAdapter( _
      "SELECT * FROM [Order Details]", CN)
  DADetails.Fill(DS, "Details")
  CN.Close()

  DS.Relations.Add(New DataRelation("CustomerOrders", _
     DS.Tables("Customers").Columns("CustomerID"), _
     DS.Tables("Orders").Columns("CustomerID")))
  DS.Relations.Add(New DataRelation("OrderDetails", _
     DS.Tables("Orders").Columns("OrderID"), _
     DS.Tables("Details").Columns("OrderID")))
  DS.Relations("CustomerOrders").Nested = True
  DS.Relations("OrderDetails").Nested = True

  Dim objXMLDoc As XmlDataDocument
  objXMLDoc = New XmlDataDocument(DS)
  TextBox1.Text = objXMLDoc.OuterXml
  objXMLDoc.Save("AllOrders.xml")
End Sub
```

The XML document is also displayed on the text box, and its first few elements are shown here:

```
<CustomerOrder>
  <Customers>
    <CustomerID>ALFKI</CustomerID>
    <CompanyName>Alfreds Futterkiste</CompanyName>
    <ContactName>Maria Anders</ContactName>
    <ContactTitle>Sales Representative</ContactTitle>
    <Address>Obere Str. 57</Address>
    <City>Berlin</City>
    <PostalCode>12209</PostalCode>
    <Country>Germany</Country>
    <Phone>030-0074321</Phone>
    <Fax>030-0076545</Fax>
    <Orders>
      <OrderID>10643</OrderID>
```

```
        <CustomerID>ALFKI</CustomerID>
        <EmployeeID>6</EmployeeID>
        <OrderDate>1997-08-25T00:00:00.00+03:00</OrderDate>
        <RequiredDate>1997-09-22T00:00:00+03:00</RequiredDate>
        <ShippedDate>1997-09-02T00:00:00.00+03:00</ShippedDate>
        <ShipVia>1</ShipVia>
        <Freight>29.46</Freight>
        <ShipName>Alfreds Futterkiste</ShipName>
        <ShipAddress>Obere Str. 57</ShipAddress>
        <ShipCity>Berlin</ShipCity>
        <ShipPostalCode>12209</ShipPostalCode>
        <ShipCountry>Germany</ShipCountry>
        <Details>
           <OrderID>10643</OrderID>
           <ProductID>28</ProductID>
           <UnitPrice>45.6</UnitPrice>
           <Quantity>15</Quantity>
           <Discount>0.25</Discount>
        </Details>
        <Details>
           <OrderID>10643</OrderID>
           <ProductID>39</ProductID>
           <UnitPrice>18</UnitPrice>
           <Quantity>21</Quantity>
           <Discount>0.25</Discount>
        </Details>
        <Details>
           <OrderID>10643</OrderID>
           <ProductID>46</ProductID>
           <UnitPrice>12</UnitPrice>
           <Quantity>2</Quantity>
           <Discount>0.25</Discount>
        </Details>
            ' more detail lines
      </Orders>
         ' more orders
    </Customers>
      more customers
 </CustomerOrder>
```

Let's say you have received this XML file and you want to process it in its native format—without converting it to a DataSet or storing it to a local database. First, you must load it into an XmlDataDocument object, and you already know how to do this:

```
Dim objXMLDoc As New XmlDataDocument()
objXMLDoc.Load("AllOrders.xml")
```

Next, you must retrieve the nodes that interest you. You can retrieve all the customer elements, or all the orders, with the GetElementsByTagName method, but this time we'll use a different approach. We'll retrieve all the orders of a specific customer, and then we'll scan all their child elements, which are the detail lines of the corresponding order.

Just as you can select rows from a database table with an SQL statement, you can select elements in an XML document using the XPath language. XPath is a language for performing queries against an XML document, but it's nothing like SQL. It has a rather odd syntax and it's not nearly as powerful. The current implementation of XPath allows you to specify simple criteria for selecting elements of the document. To select the elements that correspond to orders of the customer with ID of ALFKI, you must specify the element tag to which the selection applies by supplying the name of the table and the criteria in square brackets:

```
descendant::Orders[CustomerID="ALFKI"]
```

The first part of the expression indicates that we want all the child elements of the selected element that meet the selection criteria. In other words, we want the <Orders> elements (including their child elements) in which the CustomerID field is ALFKI. The code actually prompts the user for the ID of the desired customer, and it creates a string similar to the one shown in the preceding code statement. This expression must be passed to the SelectNodes method, which returns an XmlNodeList collection:

```
Dim ordNodes As XmlNodeList
ordNodes = _
  objXMLDoc.SelectNodes("descendant::Orders[CustomerID=""ALFKI""]")
```

Once you have retrieved the selected nodes, you can iterate through them with a For Each … Next loop. The <Order> elements have child nodes, some of which are <Detail> elements. Every time we run into a <Detail> element, we must set up another loop to iterate through its child nodes, which are the order's detail lines. The statements in Listing 19.12 iterate through the orders of the ALFKI customer and display all the related elements on the TextBox control.

**Listing 19.12    Scanning the Elements of a Specific Customer**

```
Private Sub Button3_Click(ByVal sender As System.Object, _
ByVal e As System.EventArgs) Handles Button3.Click

    Dim custID As String
    custID = InputBox("Please enter the desired " & _
      "customer's ID", "Search by Customer ID", "ALFKI")
    TextBox1.Clear()
    Me.Cursor = Cursors.WaitCursor
    Dim objXMLDoc As New XmlDataDocument()
    objXMLDoc.Load("AllOrders.xml")
    Dim ordNodes As XmlNodeList
    ordNodes = objXMLDoc.SelectNodes( _
      "descendant::Orders[CustomerID=""" & custID & """]")
    Dim ordNode As XmlNode
    Dim mRow As DataRow
```

```
For Each ordNode In ordNodes
    Dim i As Integer
    For i = 0 To ordNode.ChildNodes.Count - 1
        If ordNode.ChildNodes(i).Name <> "Details" Then
         TextBox1.AppendText(ordNode.ChildNodes(i).Name & _
          vbTab & ordNode.ChildNodes(i).InnerText & vbCrLf)
        End If
        If ordNode.HasChildNodes Then
            Dim detNodes As XmlNodeList
            detNodes = ordNode.ChildNodes(i).ChildNodes
            Dim detNode As XmlNode
            For Each detNode In detNodes
                Dim j As Integer
                For j = 0 To detNode.ChildNodes.Count - 1
                    TextBox1.AppendText(vbTab & detNode.Name & _
                     vbTab & detNode.InnerText & vbCrLf)
                Next
            Next
        End If
    Next
Next
Me.Cursor = Cursors.Default
End Sub
```

Another important property of the XmlNode object is the ParentNode property, which returns the parent element of the current element. Let's say you want a list of all customers who have ordered a specific product, along with their matching orders. The following XPath query will return all the detail rows that contain the product with an ID of 20:

```
descendant::Details[ProductID=20]
```

Once you have all the detail lines with the specified product, you can also retrieve the order to which they belong and the customer that placed the order. The order is the parent node of each selected element, and the customer is the parent node of the corresponding order. The statements in Listing 19.13 iterate through the detail lines that contain the product with the specified ID value (20). This is what the last button on the form does. It retrieves all the elements that correspond to orders that contain the user-supplied product ID. Then it displays the parent node of each detail line, which is the number of the order to which the detail line belongs. It also displays the order's parent node, which is the ID of the customer that placed the order.

**Listing 19.13       Scanning the Orders that Contain a Specific Product**

```
Private Sub Button4_Click(ByVal sender +
 As System.Object, ByVal e As System.EventArgs) _
 Handles Button4.Click
  Dim prodID As String
```

```
    prodID = InputBox("Please enter the desired " & _
        "product's ID", "Search by Product ID", "12")
    TextBox1.Clear()
    Me.Cursor = Cursors.WaitCursor
    Dim objXMLDoc As New XmlDataDocument()
    objXMLDoc.Load("AllOrders.xml")
    Dim detailNodes As XmlNodeList
    detailNodes = objXMLDoc.SelectNodes( _
     "descendant::Details[ProductID=" & prodID & "]")
    Dim detailNode As XmlNode
    Dim mRow As DataRow
    For Each detailNode In detailNodes
      Dim i As Integer
      Dim orderNode As XmlNode
      orderNode = detailNode.ParentNode
      TextBox1.AppendText("ORDER ID  " & vbTab & _
        orderNode.Item("OrderID").InnerText & vbCrLf)
      TextBox1.AppendText("PLACED ON " & vbTab & _
        orderNode.Item("OrderDate").InnerText & vbCrLf)
      TextBox1.AppendText("FREIGHT   " & vbTab & _
        orderNode.Item("Freight").InnerText & vbCrLf)
      Dim customerNode As XmlNode
      customerNode = orderNode.ParentNode
      TextBox1.AppendText(vbTab & "PLACED BY " & _
        customerNode.Item("CompanyName").InnerText & vbCrLf)
      For i = 0 To orderNode.ChildNodes.Count - 1
        If orderNode.ChildNodes(i).ChildNodes.Count = 1 Then
          TextBox1.AppendText(vbTab & _
            orderNode.ChildNodes(i).Name & vbTab & _
            orderNode.ChildNodes(i).InnerText & vbCrLf)
        Else
          If orderNode.HasChildNodes Then
            Dim orderDetailNodes As XmlNodeList
            orderDetailNodes = _
              OrderNode.ChildNodes(i).ChildNodes
            Dim orderDetailNode As XmlNode
            For Each orderDetailNode In orderDetailNodes
              Dim j As Integer
              TextBox1.AppendText(vbTab & vbTab & _
                orderDetailNode.Name & vbTab & _
                orderDetailNode.InnerText & vbCrLf)
            Next
          End If
        End If
      Next
    Next
    Me.Cursor = Cursors.Default
End Sub
```

The outer loop goes through the selected detail lines. With each iteration, the variable
*detailNode* represents another detail element. To extract the order element to which the

detail line belongs, we retrieve the ParentNode property of the current element, which is the detailNode element:

```
orderNode = detailNode.ParentNode
```

Then we print the fields of this order (who placed it, when, the ID of the employee who made the sale, and so on). To retrieve information about the customer who placed this order, we retrieve the ParentNode property of the orderNode element:

```
customerNode = orderNode.ParentNode
```

Once the headers of the order and the order's customer are printed, we can iterate through the child nodes of the orderNode element. These child nodes are the detail lines, and we print all the lines of the order:

```
For i = 0 To orderNode.ChildNodes.Count - 1
    { statements to print the current detail line }
Next
```

A segment of the output produced by the last button on the form is shown in Listing 19.14. Notice that all the selected orders contain the product with ID = 12.

**Listing 19.14    The Output of the SCAN XML File by Product Button of the XMLDataDoc Project**

```
ORDER ID    10633
PLACED ON    1997-08-15T00:00:00.0000000+03:00
FREIGHT    477.9
   PLACED BY Ernst Handel
   OrderID        10633
   CustomerID     ERNSH
   EmployeeID     7
   OrderDate      1997-08-15T00:00:00.0000000+03:00
   RequiredDate   1997-09-12T00:00:00.0000000+03:00
   ShippedDate    1997-08-18T00:00:00.0000000+03:00
   ShipVia        3
   Freight        477.9
   ShipName       Ernst Handel
   ShipAddress    Kirchgasse 6
   ShipCity       Graz
   ShipPostalCode 8010
   ShipCountry    Austria
      OrderID        10633
      ProductID      12
      UnitPrice      38
      Quantity       36
      Discount       0.15
      OrderID        10633
      ProductID      13
      UnitPrice      6
```

```
Quantity    13
Discount    0.15
OrderID     10633
ProductID   26
UnitPrice   31.23
Quantity    35
Discount    0.15
OrderID     10633
ProductID   62
UnitPrice   49.3
Quantity    80
Discount    0.15
```

This is the first order in the XML file that contains the specified product. The code displays all the relevant fields because it's a demo application. In a real application, you'd isolate the fields you need and use their values in your code.

As you experiment with XML, especially with scanning the nodes of an XML file, you will notice that the process is rather slow. XML is not a substitute for a database; it's a convenient method of storing limited amounts of information and sharing it with business partners. XML is a verbose, text-based format, and it can't be as efficient as a real database. However, it's the best method for exchanging data with other computers. It won't be long, however, before specialized tools that can process large XML documents very efficiently will become available.

This section was an overview of XML and the XmlDataDocument object, and it's not meant to be used as a reference. The XmlDataDocument object provides additional members to add new elements, edit elements, and even remove existing elements. The topics discussed in this chapter are the most useful ones, especially for a database programmer. If you want to manipulate XML data, you will find it much more convenient to create a DataSet with the same structure as the XML file and then use the members of the DataSet object, with which you're quite familiar. The last section of this chapter deals SQL Server's support for XML.

## SQL Server and XML

So far you've learned how to extract XML data from a DataSet and how to create your own XML files either form the DataSet's tables, or from scratch. SQL Server 2000 can return the results of a query directly in XML format. In other words, it's possible to execute a query against a SQL Server database and request that the result is returned in XML format. You can look at the results of a query in XML format right in the Query Analyzer's window by executing a query and appending the FOR XML clause. The following statement will return all the rows of the Customers table in XML format:

```
SELECT * FROM Customers FOR XML AUTO
```

The output of this query looks like this:

```
XML_F52E2B61-18A1-11d1-B105-00805F49916B
-----------------------------------------------------
<customers CustomerID="ALFKI" CompanyName=
 "Alfreds Futterkis ContactName="Maria Anders"
 ContactTitle="Sales

Representative" Address="Obere Str. 57" City="Berlin"
 PostalCode="12209" Country="Germany" Phone="030-0074321"

Fax="030-0076545"/><customers Cust
ce Lebihan" ContactTitle="Owner" Address=
 "12, rue des Bouche City="Marseille" PostalCode="13008"
 Country="France"

Phone="91.24.45.40" Fax="91.24.45.41"/><customers
 CustomerID CompanyName="Bottom-Dollar Markets"

ContactName="Elizabeth Lincoln"
```

The lines are too long to be displayed on the Results pane of Query Analyzer, and they're truncated. The problem is that each row displayed by the Query Analyzer has a size limitation. You can increase the length of each line, but not beyond 8,192 characters. As you will see, this limitation doesn't exist when the results are returned to the application as an XmlDataDocument.

The FOR XML clause allows you to retrieve the results of a query from SQL Server in XML format, and it accepts a single argument, the *mode* argument, which specifies how the XML document will be formatted. This argument can have one of the following values:

**RAW**   This mode transforms each row returned by the query into an XML element with a generic identifier <row /> as the element tag.

**AUTO**   This mode transforms the rows returned by the query into a nested XML tree. Each table in the FROM clause is mapped to an element and the table's columns are mapped to attributes of the corresponding element.

**EXPLICIT**   This mode requires that you specify explicitly the shape of the XML that will hold the query's results. To use this mode, you must write your queries in a particular way. Using the EXPLICIT mode is quite cumbersome, and we will not use it in our examples.

When you program against a local SQL Server database with ADO.NET, there's no reason to retrieve the results in XML format. The DataSet you'll populate with the result of the query will convert them to XML format anyway. However, SQL Server supports XML so that it can be accessed over the HTTP protocol. By appending the query to a URL that identifies the remote SQL Server, it is possible to execute a query against SQL Server from within Internet Explorer. A corporation may choose to expose some of its data to the Web, not through a web application or a web service, but by allowing applications to execute queries against their database over HTTP. The client applications don't have access to the entire database; the owner of the database can prepare a number of queries that the clients are allowed to execute against the database, either to retrieve data or even update some tables. For example, you may allow clients to add purchase orders to your database by submitting a query directly to SQL Server. In the next section, we'll explore selection queries. You'll learn how to contact SQL Server on a remote computer through a URL, execute specific queries, and retrieve the results in XML format.

You'll also learn how to create web pages with data by retrieving a result set from SQL Server in XML format and applying an XSL transformation on the result set. The next version of SQL Server will provide extensive support for XML. The following section is a brief introduction to the XML features of SQL Server 2000.

The SELECT statement of T-SQL supports the FOR XML clause, which specifies that the query's result be returned in the form of an XML document instead of a relational result set. Complex queries, or queries that you want to make secure, can be stored as templates in an IIS virtual directory and executed by referencing the template name. The template is basically an SQL query, or stored procedure, which resides in a special folder, a *virtual folder* as it's called. Clients have access to this folder rather than SQL Server itself, and they can execute only the templates stored in the virtual folder.

## Configuring a Virtual Directory for SQL Server

To enable SQL Server to interact with a client through XML, you must first create a virtual directory, as you would do for a web application. All the requests to be serviced by SQL Server must include the name of this virtual directory in their URL. To create a virtual directory, start the Configure SQL XML Support in IIS utility and you will see the IIS Virtual Directory Management for SQL Server window, as shown in Figure 19.8.

**FIGURE 19.8:**

Configuring a virtual directory

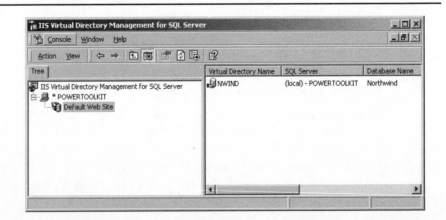

Open the Action menu and select New ➤ Virtual Directory. You will see the New Virtual Directory Properties dialog box, which is shown in Figure 19.9. The dialog box has six tabs on which you must specify the following:

**General**   Here you specify the name of the virtual directory and its path. The virtual directory is mapped to an existing path, which can be the path of any folder on the system. It's usually a subfolder under the web server's root folder.

**Security**   Here you specify how the requests made to the new virtual directory will be authenticated. You can use a SQL Server account, a Windows account, or basic authentication.

**Data Source**   On this tab, you can select the name of an instance of SQL Server that will be associated with the virtual directory and a database. Set the name of the virtual directory to NWIND (this is the name we'll use in the examples), and select the local server and the Northwind database.

**Settings**   Here you can specify the type of access you want to provide through the virtual directory. URL queries are SQL queries that can be submitted to SQL Server through a URL, as if clients were requesting a script on the server. You should disable this option and enable the Allow Template Queries option. A template is a file that contains a query and clients can call this query by specifying the server's URL, followed by the name of the template file. Templates don't allow users to execute queries directly against the database, just one of a number of predefined queries, which you have prepared ahead of time. The option Allow XPath Queries allows clients to execute XPath queries on SQL views.

**Virtual Names**   On this tab, you can specify additional virtual folders under the SQL Server's virtual folder. These folders will be used for storing specific types of items. The allowed types are database objects (like views and stored procedures), schemas, and templates. In this chapter, we'll use templates with specific queries. Add a new virtual name, the "Templates" virtual folder, and map it to the Templates folder under SQL Server's virtual folder. This is the folder in which we'll store the templates.

**Advanced**   This tab contains a couple of advanced settings, like the location of the SQLISAPI.dll file. It's unlikely that you will change the default settings on this tab.

Once the new virtual directory is added to the Web Server, its name will appear in the right pane of the IIS Virtual Directory Management for SQL Server utility, as shown in Figure 19.8. Close the window and you're ready to submit queries to the Northwind database over the HTTP protocol. You can think of the name of the virtual folder as the name of an ASP file that processes incoming requests. The actual query to be executed is passed as a parameter to this URL. To execute a query against the Northwind database, you must form a URL starting with the URL of the machine on which SQL Server is running and followed by the name of the virtual folder and the text of the SQL query.

**FIGURE 19.9:**

Specifying a new virtual
directory for SQL Server

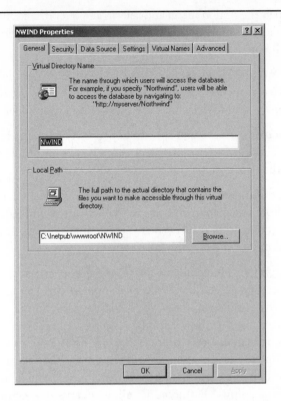

Of course, the query's text must be URL encoded. The following special characters must be replaced by the indicated strings:

| | |
|---|---|
| + (space) | %20 |
| / | %2F |
| ? | %3F |
| % | %25 |
| # | %23 |
| & | %26 |

To test the functionality of the new virtual folder we created, let's submit a query directly to the SQL Server running on the local machine. Start Internet Explorer and enter the following URL in the Address box:

```
http://localhost/nwind?sql=SELECT%20*%20FROM%20Customers%20FOR%20XML%20AUTO
```

To submit the query to another machine on the local network, or the Internet, replace the "localhost" address in the URL with the address of the remote server. On the local network you can also use the computer name.

You don't need to manually URL-encode the address as you type. Enter it as plain text and as soon as you press the Enter key, the URL will be encoded and submitted to the server. This query will return an error message to the effect that an XML document is allowed to have one top element only. If you examine the source code of the document, you'll see that it contains one <Customers> tag for each row of the table. To avoid this problem, specify a root element by appending the root=root parameter to the end of the URL:

```
http://localhost/nwind?sql=SELECT%20*%20FROM%20Customers
%20FOR%20XML%20AUTO&root=root
```

If you request this URL, the result will be an XML file with all the rows of the Customers table. Here are the first few lines of the document:

```
<root>
  <Customers CustomerID="ALFKI"
   CompanyName="Alfreds Futterkiste"
   ContactName="Maria Anders" ContactTitle="Sales
   Representative" Address="Obere Str. 57" City="Berlin" PostalCode="12209"
      Country="Germany" Phone="030-0074321"
   Fax="030-0076545" />
  <Customers CustomerID="ANATR"
   CompanyName="Ana Trujillo Emparedados y helados"
   ContactName="Ana Trujillo" ContactTitle="Owner"
   Address="Avda. de la Constitución 2222"
   City="México D.F." PostalCode="05021"
   Country="Mexico" Phone="(5) 555-4729"
   Fax="(5) 555-3745" />
```

As you can see, each customer is represented by a single element and its fields are attributes of the <Customers> tag. The entire document is contained within a <root> element (you can use any other name for the top element). You can create an XML document with separate elements for each field by specifying the ELEMENTS modifier to the FOR XML clause. If you request the following URL, you'll get back an XML document with a separate element for each field:

```
http://localhost/nwind?sql=SELECT%20*%20FROM%20Customers
%20FOR%20XML%20AUTO,%20ELEMENTS&root=root
```

Here is what the XML document would look like:

```
<Customers>
  <CustomerID>ALFKI</CustomerID>
  <CompanyName>Alfreds Futterkiste</CompanyName>
  <ContactName>Maria Anders</ContactName>
  <ContactTitle>Sales Representative</ContactTitle>
  <Address>Obere Str. 57</Address>
```

```
      <City>Berlin</City>
      <PostalCode>12209</PostalCode>
      <Country>Germany</Country>
      <Phone>030-0074321</Phone>
      <Fax>030-0076545</Fax>
   </Customers>
   <Customers>
      <CustomerID>ANATR</CustomerID>
      <CompanyName>Ana Trujillo Emparedados y helados
         </CompanyName>
      <ContactName>Ana Trujillo</ContactName>
      <ContactTitle>Owner</ContactTitle>
      <Address>Avda. de la Constitución 2222</Address>
      <City>México D.F.</City>
      <PostalCode>05021</PostalCode>
      <Country>Mexico</Country>
      <Phone>(5) 555-4729</Phone>
      <Fax>(5) 555-3745</Fax>
   </Customers>
```

The possible modifiers for the XML mode are the following:

**XMLDATA**  Specifies that the query must return an XML-Data schema, inserted at the top of the document.

**ELEMENTS**  Specifies that the columns are returned as subelements of an element. Otherwise, they are returned as attributes. This option is supported in AUTO mode only.

**BINARY BASE64**  Specifies that any binary data returned by the query is represented in base64-encoded format. You must specify this modifier if you plan to retrieve binary data using RAW and EXPLICIT mode.

## Using Templates

Appending your queries to the URL is awkward, at best. It's also dangerous, because users can also specify action queries to be executed against your database. You can create queries and store them as XML files in a virtual folder of your Web Server. As indicated earlier, the Template folder under SQL Server's virtual folder is where the templates are stored in the examples of this section.

A template is a text file that contains the text of the query to be executed against the database. However, the query must be XML formatted. This is done by embedding the text of the query in a pair of <sql:query> tags:

```
<sql:query>
   SELECT  Customers.CustomerID, CompanyName, ContactName, ContactTitle
   FROM    Customers
</sql:query>
```

To avoid the problem of multiple root elements, you can specify the root element of the document in the template file, with the statements shown here:

```
<ROOT xmlns:sql="urn:schemas-microsoft-com:xml-sql">
  <sql:query>
  SELECT  Customers.CustomerID, CompanyName, ContactName, ContactTitle
  FROM    Customers
  </sql:query>
</ROOT>
```

Store the statements of the last listing to the file `GetCustomers.xml` in the `Templates` virtual folder. Then request this file from within Internet Explorer by specifying the following URL in its Address box:

```
http://localhost/NWIND/Templates/GetCustomers.xml
```

This query will return information about all the customers in the database, which for a real database represents an enormous amount of information. A more practical query would return a subset of Customers table. Let's modify the query so that it selects customers from a specific country. Creating a parameterized query is straightforward, but we must specify that the template accept a parameter. The following is a template file with a query that retrieves the customers from a specific country (specified with a parameter). The parameter of the query is the *@country* variable, and it's declared with the `<sql:param>` tag. If this query is called without a value for the parameter, then the default value USA will be used:

```
<ROOT xmlns:sql="urn:schemas-microsoft-com:xml-sql">
  <sql:header>
    <sql:param name='Country'>USA</sql:param>
  </sql:header>
  <sql:query>
    SELECT  Customers.CustomerID, CompanyName, ContactName, _
     ContactTitle
    FROM    Customers
    WHERE   Country=@country
    ORDER BY Customers.CompanyName
    FOR XML AUTO, ELEMENTS
  </sql:query>
</ROOT>
```

If you enter the following URL in the browser's Address box, you will execute the Get-Customers query in the `Templates` folder, requesting all customers from Germany:

```
http://localhost/NWIND/Templates/GetCustomers.xml?
Country=Germany
```

Figure 19.10 shows a segment of the result of the query as displayed on the browser.

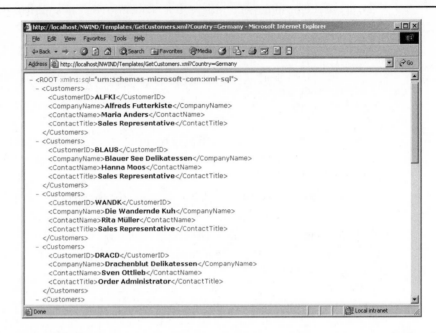

In the following section, we'll use a more interesting query, one that returns nested related tables. The revised query, Listing 19.15, returns all the customers from a specific country along with their orders, including the details of the orders.

**Listing 19.15    A Template for Retrieving Customer Orders**

```
<ROOT xmlns:sql="urn:schemas-microsoft-com:xml-sql">
  <sql:header>
    <sql:param name='Country'>USA</sql:param>
  </sql:header>
  <sql:query>
    SELECT  Customers.CustomerID, CompanyName,
            ContactName, ContactTitle, Orders.OrderID,
            OrderDate, Order Details].ProductID,
            [Order Details].UnitPrice, Quantity
    FROM    Customers
    JOIN Orders ON Orders.CustomerID=Customers.CustomerID
    JOIN [Order Details] ON Orders.OrderID =
         [Order Details].OrderID
    WHERE Country=@country
    ORDER BY Customers.CustomerID, Orders.OrderID
    FOR XML AUTO, ELEMENTS
  </sql:query>
</ROOT>
```

Create a text file with the statements of Listing 19.15, name it `GetCustomerOrders.xml`, and store it in the `Templates` virtual folder and then execute it from within your browser. As you can see, a template is basically a query embedded in a few XML tags.

Of course, XML queries aren't meant to be called from the browser's address box. Any program that can contact a web server and download a file can also execute queries against a remote server. Once the data arrives to the client, you can store it to a DataSet, process it locally, and present it to the user through a Windows application's interface. For more information on downloading information from a web server, see Chapter 17, "Internet Programming."

### The SQLServerXML Project

As you have guessed by now, it's fairly easy to connect to a remote SQL Server on the Web, extract data in XML format, and process it from within your application as usual. Let's build an application that retrieves data from a SQL Server database through a web server and uses it to create a DataSet and bind it to a DataGrid control. Figure 19.11 shows the SQLServer-XML project's main form. The Load XML Button contacts the local SQL Server through the Web server running on your machine. You can contact any computer running SQL Server on your network, but this is how you can test the application on a single machine. Make sure you have started IIS and you have configured SQL Server's support for XML as explained in the section "Configuring a Virtual Directory for SQL Server," earlier in this chapter. The XML data returned by SQL Server forms a long string, which is displayed on a TextBox control at the top of the form. The XML document you see in Figure 19.11 has been edited manually. If you run the project, you will see the same information in a very long string.

**FIGURE 19.11:**

The SQLServerXML project demonstrates how to request the result of a query from SQL Server in XML format.

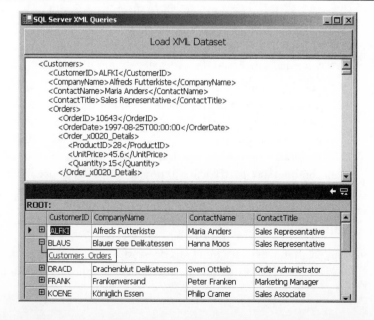

To execute the GetCustomerOrders query and retrieve the results in XML format, click the Load XML DataSet button, whose Click event handler is shown in Listing 19.16.

**Listing 19.16**     **Retrieving the Customers and Their Orders in XML Format**

```
Private Sub Button1_Click(ByVal sender As System.Object, _
  ByVal e As System.EventArgs) Handles Button1.Click
    Dim xmlDoc As New XmlDataDocument()
    xmlDoc.Load("http://localhost/NWIND/Templates/" & _
                "GetCustomerOrders.xml?Country=Germany")
    TextBox1.AppendText(xmlDoc.OuterXml)
    xmlDoc.Save("NWCustomerOrders.xml")
    SqlConnection1.Close()
    Dim DS As New DataSet()
    DS.ReadXml("NWCustomerOrders.xml")
    DataGrid1.DataSource = DS
End Sub
```

This event handler calls the Load method of the XMLDataDocument object passing a URL as an argument. The URL is the address of the GetCustomerOrders.xml template, followed by the name and value of the query's argument. If the query accepts multiple arguments, they should all appear after the address and be separated by ampersand (&) characters. The XML-DataDocument object's OuterXML property returns the entire document, which is displayed on a TextBox control. The same document is then saved to an XML file, which is read with the DataSet object's ReadXml method. Once the DataSet is populated with the customers and their orders, it's bound to the DataGrid control. The DataSet contains nested relations between its tables, and the data will be displayed hierarchically on the DataGrid control. You can view the customers, expand a customer to see their orders, and then expand an order to see its details. You can edit the SQL statement to display more or fewer fields for each table and display products names in the order detail lines instead of product IDs.

You can also submit action queries in XML format to SQL Server to update the database. The topic of SQL Server's support for XML is quite interesting, and it's worth exploring on your own. Note that you need not set up any objects to contact the computer running SQL Server. All you have to do is specify the computer's URL in the XMLDataDocument object's Load method. After reading the data into the XMLDataDocument object, you can use any of the techniques discussed earlier to process the data, or use them to populate a local DataSet.

## Summary

This chapter provided a quick overview of XML for database developers. XML is at the core of ADO.NET, but you need not fully understand the new format in order to write data-driven applications. We've presented the basics of XML and given several examples to demonstrate how the DataSet object uses XML and how you can switch between the relational (tables, columns, and relationships) and hierarchical (XML) views of the same data. XML is also the best method to pass data between remote computers. Actually, this is how information is passed between layers of an application. XML, as SOAP, is also used to pass data from a web service (an application running on a web server) to a client. ADO.NET is based on a "universal" protocol, and the best part of it is that you need not write any code to manipulate XML documents. Everything is done in the background by ADO.NET for you.

# CHAPTER 20

# Creating XML Web Services

- Introducing XML Web services

- The Simple Object Access Protocol (SOAP)

- Web Services Description Language (WSDL)

- Discovery

- Universal Description, Discovery and Integration (UDDI)

- Creating an XML Web service

- Consuming an XML Web service

- Securing XML Web services

**A**n XML Web service is essentially a program capable of communicating across a network (such as the Internet) using the open standard Simple Object Access Protocol (SOAP) and XML technologies. SOAP describes how data and commands should be represented using XML.

In this chapter, we will look at some of the technologies associated with SOAP and the process of creating and consuming a data-driven XML Web service. We will also examine some of the security considerations attached to working with XML Web services.

## Introducing XML Web Services

XML Web services may be either software components or resources such as data libraries (or a combination of both). They can be established as proprietary components only used by specified applications within a defined scope or they can be widely available to a variety of different users. They can be accessed only over the local computer, from within a local network, or over a wide area network or the Internet. They must be delivered by a web server. Owners of XML Web services may provide them free of charge to their users or they may charge for their use.

XML Web services can source other XML Web services for some of their functionality and/or data. Essentially, if you can write a program as a component, then you can write it as an XML Web service.

There are many advantages to writing components as XML Web services:

- Data and commands are communicated across Port 80, virtually guaranteeing easy passage around the Internet and into and out of networks.

- The use of common standards such as XML and SOAP enable wide support for components written as XML Web services.

- Web service directories (UDDI) and techniques for identifying Web services (Discovery) provide a mechanism for potential users to identify, locate, and access your Web services.

- Support for XML Web services by major players such as Microsoft and IBM suggests that the technology is likely to be around for a while, so it's worth your while to invest the time and effort to learn how to use it.

- Visual Studio .NET makes the creation and consumption of XML Web services very easy from a developer's perspective.

- The SOAP Toolkit enables existing components to be ported across to XML Web services by placing a SOAP wrapper around the components. You don't have to make any actual changes to the components themselves (well, not usually).

The main disadvantage of working with XML Web services is that at this stage they are subject to an evolving standard with a number of issues such as security still to be ironed out.

Websites such as www.salcentral.com and resources such as Universal Description, Discovery and Integration (UDDI) provide a huge range of examples (both free and commercial) that are available over the Internet, including the following:

- Games such as chess
- Statistical analysis services
- Map and directory services
- Credit card verifiers
- "Thought for the day" and "joke of the day" type services
- Weather reports

The search engine Google has made its services available as a set of XML Web services. These can be accessed from the Google website (www.google.com) and exploited with the assistance of an SDK download called the googleapi. It provides all of the information, documentation, WSDL files, and examples required to incorporate the Google services directly into your application. You will need to register with Google to obtain a free license key to use the Web services and this will entitle you to up to 1,000 queries per day from your application.

The major technologies of Web services are described in the following sections.

## The Simple Object Access Protocol (SOAP)

SOAP is a lightweight protocol for exchanging data in a distributed heterogeneous environment. It provides a set of rules about how data and commands (in XML) should be described.

You can download the SOAP Toolkit from Microsoft. It enables you to apply a SOAP wrapper to existing COM objects, thus giving them XML Web service functionality. The Toolkit can be obtained from the download site at http://msdn.microsoft.com/downloads. It includes these components:

- A high-level API for applying a SOAP wrapper to COM objects
- The SOAP Messaging Objects Framework
- A low-level API for direct control over the SOAP process
- Sample clients and services
- The Microsoft SOAP Trace Tool

The SOAP Toolkit Wizard (which is part of the high-level API) can be used to apply SOAP wrappers to most simple COM objects. However, if you have used custom data types in the object, or if it has some other form of complexity, then you can use the low-level API to manage all aspects of the process. (The latest versions of the SOAP Toolkit are beginning to identify and address these complexities, simplifying the process of applying the wrapper.)

There are other services related to SOAP that can be used to locate and access XML Web services. These include Web Services Description Language (WSDL), Discovery, and Universal Description, Discovery and Integration (UDDI).

## Web Services Description Language (WSDL)

WSDL is used to expose the capabilities of an XML Web service. It is an XML format that describes an XML document used to provide information about a particular XML Web service, including its functions, procedures, availability of services, message formats, and required communication protocols required.

You can author WSDL documents directly, but mostly they are auto-generated by Visual Studio .NET when you create an XML Web service. They are read and interpreted by VS .NET when the XML Web service is consumed.

## Discovery

SOAP Discovery is used to locate the WSDL documents that provide the descriptions for XML Web services. The process works by providing a file that gives information about the location of the WSDL and other XML Web service–related documents.

There are two types of files that can be created for this purpose: dynamic discovery files (with the extension `.vsdisco` and used for dynamic discovery) and static discovery files (with the extension `.disco` and used for static discovery). These are both XML-based file formats.

Dynamic discovery files are automatically generated by Visual Studio .NET when an XML Web service is created. They allow a potential user to search through the directory tree for XML Web services. The file can be edited to exclude specific subdirectories from the search. If a `default` `.vsdisco` file is placed in the root of the web server, it can be used to initiate discovery across an entire website. Microsoft recommends not using dynamic discovery on production servers (which is probably a very good idea!) and only using it in development scenarios. Dynamic discovery searches for files with the `.vsdisco`, `.disco`, and `.asmx` (XML Web service) extensions. If one of these files isn't found, then the search in that directory (and its sub-directories) is stopped.

For production servers, you are much safer using static discovery. You need to write these files yourself (you will see how later in this chapter). They provide specific access only to those resources that you choose to nominate.

Additionally, you cannot place dynamic and static discovery files in the same directory. When a directory search based on a dynamic file encounters a static file, it stops and will not search any further.

## Universal Description, Discovery and Integration (UDDI)

UDDI has been described as the "Yellow Pages" of Web services. It is basically a business services directory aimed at providing a searchable, categorized resource for XML Web services, among other things.

There is a lot more to UDDI than a simple directory. You can find out more about it at Microsoft's UDDI site at `http://uddi.microsoft.com` or the official UDDI.org site at `www.uddi.com`.

The Microsoft UDDI directory can be accessed directly from within the Visual Studio .NET IDE by selecting Add Web Reference from the Project menu. Figure 20.1 illustrates the Add Web Reference dialog box as it appears when accessing the Microsoft UDDI.

**FIGURE 20.1:**

The Microsoft UDDI directory

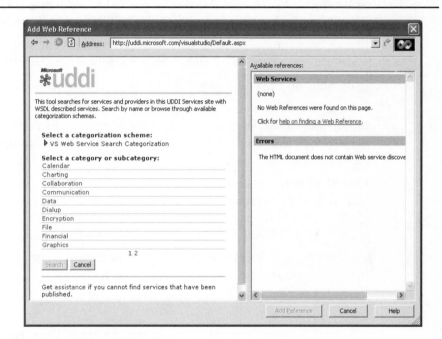

# Creating an XML Web Service

In Chapter 7, "The Business Tier," you saw how to create and consume a simple XML Web service. The important thing to realize from this was that the process itself is very straightforward. Any complexity that exists is what you choose to introduce into the business logic that you are packaging up as your XML Web service.

In the example for this section, we will return to the trusty old pubs database and consider how we might make use of the titles table from a commercial perspective.

For example, in a publishing company, we might consider making our list of titles available to retailers as an XML Web service. The advantage of this is that retailers can display the list of titles along with any additional information that we choose to provide. We can update this information centrally at our database, and those changes will be instantly reflected in the third-party sites making use of the XML Web service.

The advantage for retailers is that they have instant access to the latest information from us without any more work on their part, and the advantage to us is that retailers are always displaying the latest and most accurate information on our products.

We will begin by creating the XML Web service and setting up the data connections.

## Setting Up the XML Web Service

We will call the XML Web service WebServiceTitles. It will have one service, Titles, with a single method, GetTitles. To set up the XML Web service, complete the following steps:

1. Launch Visual Studio .NET and choose New Project. From the Visual Basic Projects folder, choose the ASP.NET Web Service template and name it WebServiceTitles.

2. In the Solution Explorer, right-click Service1.asmx and rename it Titles.asmx.

3. From the Data Toolbox, drag a SqlDataAdapter to the Designer and establish a connection to the pubs database. Work through the Data Adapter Configuration Wizard to the Choose a Query Type screen and select the Create New Stored Procedures option. We will use this approach to optimize performance for the connection.

4. Click Next, and at the Generate the Stored Procedures screen, click the Advanced Options button. Deselect everything in the advanced options dialog. The purpose of this connection is only to retrieve data; we will not need any of the additional SQL statements. Click OK to return to the Generate the Stored Procedures screen.

5. Click the Query Builder button to open the Query Builder and add the titles table. Create the following SQL statement in the Query Builder:

```
SELECT    title_id, title, type, notes, pubdate
FROM      titles
```

6. Click the OK button to return to the Generate the Stored Procedures screen and then click the Next button to enter the Create the Stored Procedures screen. Give the Select statement the name SelectAuthors. This should be the only one that is editable. Make sure that the Yes, Create Them in the Database for Me option is selected. Click the Next and Finish buttons to exit the wizard.

7. In the designer, right-click the SqlDataAdapter1 object and choose the Generate Dataset option. Don't change the default selections and do not select the Add This Dataset to the Designer option. This should generate a DataSet1 schema visible in the Solution Explorer.

8. Double-click the design surface to enter Code Behind. Adjust the second line of code (the class definition) to appear as in the following snippet:

```
<WebService(Namespace:="http://myWebServiceSite.com")> _
    Public Class Titles
```

This renames the class from Service1 to Titles. It also establishes the location of the XML Web service at the mythical site of http://myWebServiceSite.com. Normally, you would give the actual location of your XML Web service here. We could leave it as the default (`http://tempuri.org`), but changing the URL removes the warning that you receive concerning the `http://tempuri.org/` namespace when you call the XML Web service.

9. Delete the default sample XML Web service code that is provided, and add the code from Listing 20.1.

**Listing 20.1**    **The GetTitles Function for WebServiceTitles**

```
<WebMethod()> Public Function GetTitles() As DataSet1
        Dim TitlesData As New DataSet1()
        SqlDataAdapter1.Fill(TitlesData)
        Return TitlesData
End Function
```

This code simply declares an instance of the DataSet and fills it with the data from the titles table.

## Testing the XML Web Service

Test the XML Web service by clicking the Start button or pressing F5. This should open the Web service in Internet Explorer, as shown in Figure 20.2.

**FIGURE 20.2:**

WebServiceTitles in Internet Explorer

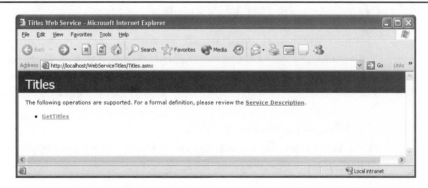

You can take a look at the service description for WebServiceTitles by clicking the relevant link. This will open the WSDL document that has been automatically generated for this XML Web service.

To call the GetTitles method, click the GetTitles link. This will open the page shown in Figure 20.3, which gives a range of information concerning this method.

To run the GetTitles method, click the Invoke button. This will open up the full XML (including the data) returned by the method and, in this instance, is a useful way to examine the XML structure of a DataSet.

The GetTitles method
for the Titles service

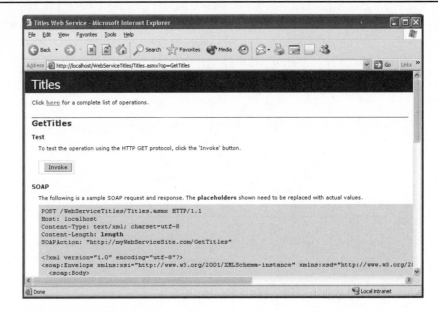

This completes setting up the XML Web service; our next step is look at how it can be consumed.

## Consuming an XML Web Service

The process of making use of an XML Web service is called *consuming* it. In this section, we will create a simple application to view the data returned by the Titles service in the WebService-Titles XML Web service. You will also see how to add to the root directory of your web server a discovery file that potential users can employ to locate the XML Web services that you provide.

## Creating the Discovery Files

Begin with the process of creating the discovery files by opening your favorite text editor and entering the code from Listing 20.2.

**Listing 20.2**      *MyDiscovery.disco*

```
<?xml version="1.0" encoding="utf-8" ?>
<discovery xmlns="http://schemas.xmlsoap.org/disco/">
<discoveryRef _
  ref="http://localhost/WebServiceTitles/Titles.asmx" />
</discovery>
```

Save the file as `MyDiscovery.disco` in your web server's root directory. The code is self-explanatory. It simply tells anyone who cares to look in it where they can find your XML Web service. This is a static discovery document and is safer and more reliable than the dynamic discovery file that is automatically generated with the creation of the XML Web service. (It is worth deleting any of these VSDISCO files on a production server.)

You can always include additional XML Web services simply by adding more <discoveryRef> tags.

Rather than have your users fishing around looking for your discovery documents, it is sensible to add a link to them from an appropriate place on your site. You can provide a direct link to them and/or write the link into your <HEAD> tag of the preferred page. This has the advantage of displaying the referenced services in the right-hand pane of the Add Web Reference dialog box used when adding XML Web services from within Visual Studio .NET.

Open your default web page for the root of `http://localhost` in your favorite text or web editor. Listing 20.3 illustrates a default web page with the link to the discovery document added into the header area as well as an additional direct link in the body of the document.

**Listing 20.3**     **A Default Web Page with Header and Body links to Discovery Files**

```
<HTML>
<HEAD>
<link type='text/xml' rel='alternate' _
 href='MyDiscovery.disco'/>

<TITLE>MySite - Web Service Discovery Links</TITLE>

</HEAD>
<BODY>
<H1>Web Service Discovery Links for MySite</H1>
<BR>
<a href="MyDiscovery.disco">XML Web Services available on this site</a>

</BODY>
</HTML>
```

You can try this example by saving it as something suitable (such as `default2.html`) and temporarily setting it as the default page for your site from the Default Web Site Properties dialog in IIS Manager.

**WARNING**  Be careful not to overwrite your existing default page!

**NOTE**  The default file extension in IIS is .htm. Some people use `.html`. Depending on your preference, you will need to sort this out in the IIS Manager.

Figure 20.4 shows this default web page when opened in the Add Web Reference dialog box, which is accessed from the Project menu in Visual Studio .NET.

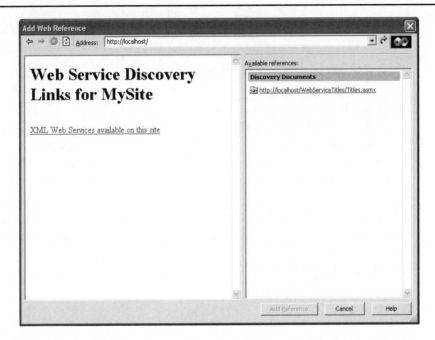

You can easily employ these links in an existing page by adding `<link type='text/xml' rel='alternate' href='MyDiscovery.disco'/>` to the header area of the page and/or `<a href="MyDiscovery.disco">XML Web Services available on this site</a>` somewhere to the body of the page.

The next step is to construct an application to consume the XML Web service.

## Building WebServiceConsumer1

To build the client for the XML Web service, complete the following steps:

1. Create a new ASP.NET Web application project in Visual Studio .NET (Visual Basic Projects) and name it WebServiceConsumer1. We will use this application to consume the WebServiceTitles Web service and to display the contents of the titles table.

2. From the Project menu, select the Add Web Reference option. If you followed the discovery process in the previous section, you should have a link into the XML Web service from your default page. If not, you will need to use the following URL:

   ```
   http://localhost/WebServiceTitles/Titles.asmx
   ```

   Once you have accessed this link/URL the Add Web Reference dialog box, shown in Figure 20.5, will appear.

**FIGURE 20.5:**

The Add Web Reference
dialog box open to the
Titles service

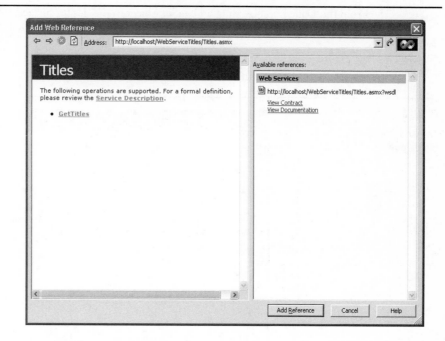

3. Click the Add Reference button to complete the process. This adds a reference to the XML
   Web service in the Solution Explorer, as shown in Figure 20.6.

**FIGURE 20.6:**

Web reference in the
Solution Explorer

4. From the Data Toolbox, drag a DataSet object to the design surface. This opens the Add DataSet dialog. Choose the Typed Dataset option and select the following (refer to Figure 20.7):

```
WebServiceConsumer1.localhost.DataSet1
```

Click OK to place an instance of DataSet11 on the designer.

**FIGURE 20.7:**

The Add DataSet
dialog box

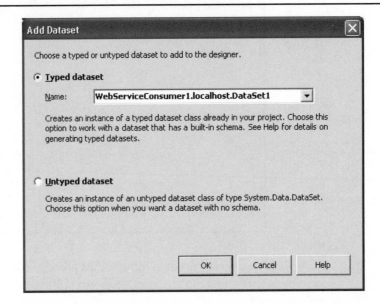

5. The next step is to add the relevant controls to the designer. Add six Label controls and a DropDownList control and set the properties as follows:

| Control | Property | Value |
| --- | --- | --- |
| Label | Font: Bold | True |
| | Font: Name | Comic Sans MS |
| | Font: Size | X-Large |
| | Text | Titles Available |
| Label | Text | Click a title for further details |
| DropDownList | AutoPostBack | True |
| | DataSource | DataSet11 |
| | DataMember | titles |
| | DataTextField | title |
| | DataValueField | title_id |

| Control | Property | Value |
| --- | --- | --- |
| Label | Text | <NULL> |
|  | ID | LabelID |
| Label | Text | <NULL> |
|  | ID | LabelType |
| Label | Text | <NULL> |
|  | ID | LabelPubdate |
| Label | Text | <NULL> |
|  | ID | LabelDetails |

Figure 20.8 illustrates the layout of these controls on the Web Form.

**FIGURE 20.8:**

Layout of controls for WebServiceConsumer1

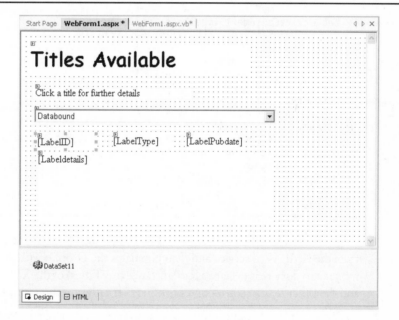

**WARNING** You must set the AutoPostBack property for the DropDownList control to True for this application to work properly.

Once the controls have been added to WebForm1, double-click the designer to switch to Code Behind and add the code from Listing 20.4.

**Listing 20.4        Code Behind for WebServiceConsumer1**

```
Private Sub Page_Load(ByVal sender As System.Object, _
ByVal e As System.EventArgs) Handles MyBase.Load

        If Not IsPostBack Then
            Dim myTitles As New _
WebServiceConsumer1.localhost.Titles()
            DataSet11.Merge(myTitles.GetTitles)
            DropDownList1.DataBind()
        End If

End Sub

Private Sub DropDownList1_SelectedIndexChanged(ByVal _
sender As System.Object, ByVal e As System.EventArgs) _
Handles DropDownList1.SelectedIndexChanged

        Dim myTitles As New _
WebServiceConsumer1.localhost.Titles()
        DataSet11.Merge(myTitles.GetTitles)

        Dim n As Integer
        n = DropDownList1.SelectedIndex
        LabelID.Text = "ID: " & _
DataSet11.titles.Rows(n).Item("title_id")
        LabelType.Text = "Type: " & _
DataSet11.titles.Rows(n).Item("type")
        LabelPubdate.Text = "Publication Date: " & _
DataSet11.titles.Rows(n).Item("pubdate")
        Labeldetails.Text = _
DataSet11.titles.Rows(n).Item("notes")

End Sub
```

We use two handlers in this code. The Page_Load handler merges the data into Dataset11 from the XML Web service and then populates the DropDownList control. As you can see, all we need to do here is declare a local instance (myTitles) of the XML Web service Titles service and then merge the return contents of its GetTitles method into DataSet11.

The second subroutine handles the SelectedIndexChanged event for the DropDownList control. It assigns the relevant contents out of DataSet11 into the various Label controls when an item has been selected from the DropDownList.

Note that at this stage, this code is not very robust and is easily knocked over by things such as empty database fields. You would need to at least add some exception management code such as structured exception handling for a production-level application.

Figure 20.9 shows how the application should appear when running and an item has been selected. In the next section, we will look at securing Web services.

**FIGURE 20.9:**

WebServiceConsumer1
in Internet Explorer

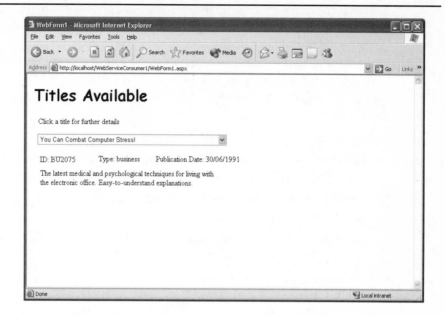

## Securing XML Web Services

As we were writing this book, native security for XML Web services (meaning the data and operations are encrypted in some way and only those that are entitled to use the Web service can get to it) was only trickling onto the scene.

It is important, however, to realize that the need for native security only applies to XML Web services from the perspective that they are entities that are independent of the various transport protocols. SOAP is a message format, and it is possible for a single SOAP message to be conveyed over several protocols. In this scenario, the security has to be inherent in the message format so that it is applied equally across all protocols.

The intention is that at some point the inclusion of native security will happen. However, at this stage security is still largely something that developers need to consider for themselves. To a large extent, you can rely on the technologies associated with the transport protocol and/or platform on which you are running the XML Web service (technologies such as HTTP security and the various security features of IIS).

One of the difficulties is that as soon as you start applying custom security solutions to your XML Web service, it is no longer part of an open standard and you begin to limit your potential range of users.

However, it is not too difficult to take some basic precautions to protect your server and code from attack. The other main worry is that you may have unsecured data flying around the Internet and it could potentially fall into the wrong hands. Of course, this is only a problem if the data itself is intrinsically sensitive or worth a lot of money. For a lot of XML Web service providers, this is not going to be a problem—the current time in Wellington, New Zealand, and the fishing conditions in the Coliban River, Malmsbury, are hardly going to be of interest to data hackers.

XML Web service security therefore has three main aspects:

- Protection of your Web server and system from attacks that may be launched via exploits of your XML Web service(s)

- Authentication and other processes to restrict access to only those that you wish to use your XML Web service

- Data and transmission encryption to protect the integrity of information that may get intercepted while in transit

In practice, because you are using ASP.NET to create and consume your XML Web services, you will be using Microsoft technologies such as IIS together with the HTTP protocol, and you can employ techniques specific to these technologies to create the necessary levels of protection for the aspects of security in the preceding list.

There are many different ways of approaching these different aspects of security, and largely they are the same technologies that you can use to protect any form of website or web transaction that you may set up. Many of the specific issues associated with security and ASP.NET are dealt with in Chapter 21, "Securing Applications in ASP.NET."

## Protecting Your Web Server

There are many possible approaches you can take to protecting your server, including hardware, software, and procedural. Individual requirements vary considerably depending on your individual circumstances and resources. However, there are a number of things that should be done as a matter of course, irrespective of what sort of system you are running.

If you are running a version of Microsoft's IIS, you need to keep it up-to-date with the latest patches. These are available through the Windows Update tools in Windows 2000 and Windows XP. It is also wise to subscribe to Microsoft's security bulletins, which are available through the security section of the company's website at `www.microsoft.com/security`.

In addition, there is a variety of tools that Microsoft has released to assist in strengthening security of potentially vulnerable software, such as the IIS Lockdown tool.

You should also be running an up-to-date virus scanner with current virus definitions and have some form of firewall.

Many other options exist, such as using a router, restricting access to your web server with IP filtering, and carefully designing your software so as to limit the amount of information that potential hackers can glean from your system via thrown exceptions or weaknesses that they may exploit. Even the structure of your website can be a factor in your security design.

## An Example of Enforcing Authentication

As an example of a sensible and achievable precaution, we can add a layer of authentication security to the WebServiceTitles service. This will restrict access to those who are capable of authenticating against the host network using integrated Windows authentication.

Begin by opening the MMC snap-in for IIS and configuring the directory security for the XML Web service.

Once you have opened the IIS Manager, expand the Web Sites node and then the Default Web Site node. Right-click WebServiceTitles and select the Properties option. From the Properties dialog box, select the Directory Security tab, and under Anonymous Access and Authentication Control, click the Edit button. This opens the Authentication Methods dialog box. Uncheck Anonymous Access and make sure that Integrated Windows Authentication is checked (see Figure 20.10).

**FIGURE 20.10:**

Setting directory access properties in IIS

This sets the directory access permissions and ensures that only authenticated domain members can access the service. Additionally, authentication details are encrypted.

**TIP**   Only use integrated Windows authentication when you are very sure of the nature of clients accessing your service. Some platforms do not work well with IWA, and in these cases it is better to go with basic authentication (passwords are passed in clear text) as long as having access takes precedence over any security precautions.

The next step is to enable the application to work with these security settings. Open WebServiceTitles in Visual Studio .NET and open the Web.config file by double-clicking it in the Solution Explorer. Add the following tag to a convenient location in the <system.web> section:

```
<identity impersonate="true"/>
```

Save your changes and open the WebServiceConsumer1 project. Add the following line of code to the two handlers in Code-Behind after the Dim MyTitles line:

```
myTitles.Credentials = _
  System.Net.CredentialCache.DefaultCredentials
```

The completed code should look like Listing 20.5.

**Listing 20.5**        **Code Behind for WebServiceConsumer1 with Authentication**

```
Private Sub Page_Load(ByVal sender As System.Object, _
ByVal e As System.EventArgs) Handles MyBase.Load

        If Not IsPostBack Then
            Dim myTitles As New _
WebServiceConsumer1.localhost.Titles()
            myTitles.Credentials = _
System.Net.CredentialCache.DefaultCredentials
            DataSet11.Merge(myTitles.GetTitles)
            DropDownList1.DataBind()
        End If

End Sub

Private Sub DropDownList1_SelectedIndexChanged(ByVal _
 sender As System.Object, ByVal e As System.EventArgs) _
 Handles DropDownList1.SelectedIndexChanged

        Dim myTitles As New _
WebServiceConsumer1.localhost.Titles()
        myTitles.Credentials = _
System.Net.Credential Cache.DefaultCredentials
        DataSet11.Merge(myTitles.GetTitles)

        Dim n As Integer
        n = DropDownList1.SelectedIndex
```

```
        LabelID.Text = "ID: " & _
DataSet11.titles.Rows(n).Item("title_id")
        LabelType.Text = "Type: " & _
DataSet11.titles.Rows(n).Item("type")
        LabelPubdate.Text = "Publication Date: " & _
DataSet11.titles.Rows(n).Item("pubdate")
        Labeldetails.Text = _
DataSet11.titles.Rows(n).Item("notes")

End Sub
```

If you log in from an unauthenticated client, you should now get the standard Windows login dialog, shown in Figure 20.11.

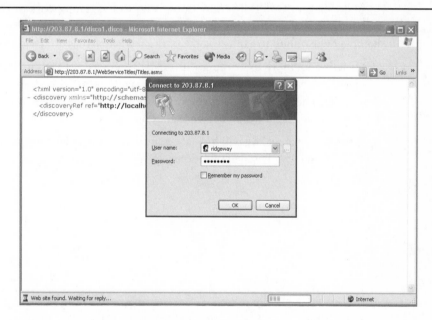

There are a number of other approaches that can also be taken as far as authentication is concerned. You can use either digest authentication or client certificates. You can set permissions for individual files to require authentication just as you can for directories. You can set permissions for individual users or groups by configuring the Web.config file of the XML Web service and employing URL authorization. Forms authentication, a popular method available with ASP.NET, is not available for use with XML Web services.

You can also create custom SOAP headers to pass the authentication details if you want to separate the process away from the transport protocol (HTTP). Microsoft's SOAP documentation contains instructions and examples on how to do this.

## Encryption

Over HTTP, encryption is easily available in the form of Secure Sockets Layer (SSL) technology. You can protect not only authentication details (in the case of basic authentication) but the integrity of the data stream itself. Alternatively, you can use client certificates in conjunction with SSL for your authentication. However, using SSL does introduce a performance hit, so there is some trade-off involved.

## Summary

Using XML Web services is an easy and reliable way to create middle-tier structures for both local use and for wider dissemination over a wide area network or over the Internet. You have seen in this chapter how to create and consume an XML Web service, and you have also had the opportunity to explore some of the security issues attached to working with them.

There is a lot more to working with XML Web services than we have covered here. For instance, you can build asynchronous functionality into XML Web services to overcome the issue of the client waiting for a response from a Web service (coming over the Internet, a response could take a while) before it goes on with something else.

In the next chapter, we will look at security in more detail and specifically as it relates to ASP.NET and web-based applications.

# CHAPTER 21

# Securing Applications in ASP.NET

- Security options

- Impersonation

- Using URL authorization

- Setting up SSL in IIS

- Building an example of forms-based security

S ecurity is an area that is becoming increasingly important as websites become more interactive and involved in the exchange and management of sensitive information. As developers, how you manage security should be a paramount consideration when you begin the design of virtually any site.

Unfortunately, many of the major security considerations—such as who has access to the host servers and what sort of firewalls and other forms of network protection to use—may well be out of your hands. This is particularly going to be the case when your role is simply to develop the site and others will take care of the network management and ongoing site maintenance.

However, you do have control over the security that is inherent to the site itself, and it is incumbent on you as the site creator to determine exactly what will be the security requirements for the site and to develop and implement an appropriate security model. Furthermore, ASP.NET and Visual Studio .NET—along with Windows and Internet Information Server (IIS)—offer a range of security models and techniques that you can choose from to use with your applications.

It is important to make these decisions early in the project to ensure that security is an inherent part of the application rather than an after-market bolt-on. We have probably all been guilty of taking the latter of these two approaches (and Microsoft's security technology lends itself to the approach), but taking the bolt-on path is more likely to leave holes and weaknesses that can be exploited by those of a nefarious nature.

## Security Options

Microsoft offers a wide range of options that can be utilized across the various technologies that contribute to a successful ASP.NET application. Some of these options can be used in conjunction with each other; others cannot.

Although in many instances, setting some form of security management at one level (such as IIS) and then setting similar restrictions at another level (such as NTFS permissions) may seem a little redundant; it is worth remembering that good security is often about how many layers you can put between yourself and a potential hacker. If you only have a single layer of defense, it doesn't matter how good it is; once it is breached, you are in trouble. Using multiple layers gives you an advantage in that, if a layer is accidentally or deliberately compromised, you still have other security layers in place.

In terms of security, you need to distinguish between the *authentication* process that identifies the user as the entity they claim to be (normally handled with some form of username and password combination) and *authorization*, which determines what resources the user has access to.

When you use ASP.NET, you normally determine the form of authentication both in IIS and within the application itself. Within the application, you use the `Web.config` file to set the authentication method. Open the `Web.config` file and identify the `<system.web>` section and then look for the following tag:

```
<authentication mode="Windows" />
```

This sets the authentication method to Windows, which is the default setting. You can also set the mode to Forms, Passport, or None. We will be discussing these authentication methods later in the chapter.

In the following sections, we will look at what options are available and some of their respective pros and cons.

## Directory and File Permissions

One of the first steps to consider when establishing your security regime is what NTFS permissions to apply to the actual files and directories you are making available through your application.

In order to set the NTFS access control list (ACL), you need to be using NTFS-formatted hard drives, typically with the Windows NT, 2000, or XP operating systems. You will also need to be running IIS 5 (or later) and your clients need to be on Windows platforms (and running recent versions of Internet Explorer).

In an environment in which you do not have network administrative privileges, your ability to set these permissions may be restricted. However, you can specify recommended permissions in the installation instructions. As a general rule in any sort of authenticated environment, it is worth making sure that the Everyone group is removed from the directories making up the application. (Although, be careful to give appropriate open access to a file or directory to which you may wish to redirect nonauthenticated users.) You can then take this to the next level by specifically granting access only to those users and groups entitled to use the various individual directories and files. This can be done on a directory-by-directory basis and even at the file-by-file level if necessary. (Normally, permissions are inherited down through the directory structure and a well-constructed application, in terms of its directory tree, will minimize the number of individual permission settings that you may have to make.

The approach is particularly useful in an intranet environment where you may need to manage access to various resources depending on an individual user's group membership. For example, members of an administrative group may be given access to resources not available to normal domain members.

Permissions are typically set by right-clicking the file or directory in question and choosing the Properties option. Select the Security tab and make the required settings. Figure 21.1 shows an example of setting file permissions. You can add or remove users, alter the permissions for each user (and explicitly deny users if necessary), and from the Advanced dialog box, you can exercise granular control over the precise aspects of the permissions you apply. You can also set ownership and group permissions from the Advanced dialog box.

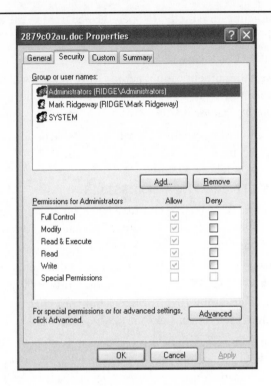

**TIP**   If you are setting permissions in Windows XP, you may need to expose the permissions dialog box by choosing Folder Options from the Tools menu in an open window and deselecting Use Simple File Sharing under the View tab.

To enable IIS to act as the authenticated client in accessing resources, you use a process called *ASP.NET impersonation*. This enables IIS to execute code under the identity of the authenticated user, with their associated privileges and rights. Previously with ASP, impersonation was set as the default (and in most cases, you never needed to think about it or even be aware that it was happening). With ASP.NET, you need to explicitly enable impersonation and set the level of impersonation that you wish to use.

## IIS Website Properties

Within IIS itself, you can set some general levels of protection for your website and the resources (the individual files, directories, and applications) that make it up. These include setting the Execute Permissions and Application Protection settings and various user rights, such as whether they can obtain a listing of the directory contents, write to the resource, access script source code, and so on. You can also determine whether visits should be logged.

These security decisions can be made hierarchically through the website, from a global level right down to individual files. You access them by opening the IIS Microsoft Management Console (MMC) snap-in and expanding the navigation tree nodes in the left-hand pane until you reach the resource you wish to work with. You then right-click the resource and choose Properties. Depending on the type of resource, the settings are available under the Home Directory, Directory, Virtual Directory, or the File tab. Figure 21.2 illustrates the settings for the QuickStart tutorials in a copy of IIS (version 5.1).

**FIGURE 21.2:**

Virtual Directory properties in IIS version 5.1

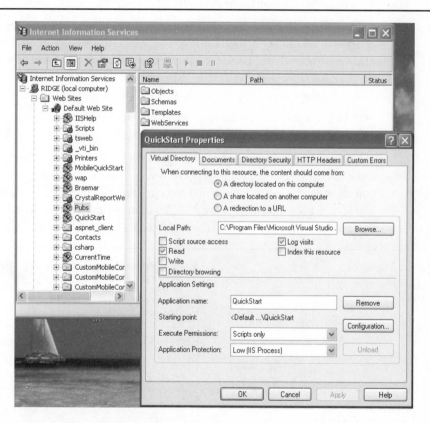

Execute Permissions determines the type of code that a user is able to run within a given directory. You may set it to Scripts Only, Scripts and Executables, or None. The Application Protection option determines how isolated your application's memory space will be. The Medium setting is appropriate for most applications and offers a reasonable balance between performance and security.

## IIS Authentication

There are a number of levels of IIS authentication available:

- Anonymous (default)

- Basic

- Digest

- Integrated Windows authentication (default)

- Client certificate mapping

- .NET Passport authentication (IIS 6)

From the ASP.NET applications perspective, you need to set the mode attribute of the <authentication> tag in Web.config. You would use the Windows default where you were planning to use Basic, Digest, or Integrated Windows Authentication and wished to run the ASP.NET application as the authenticated user. If you are running the Anonymous level, you would typically set the mode attribute to none.

You can employ SSL (Secure Sockets Layer) in conjunction with these forms of authentication, although it is typically used only with Basic Authentication or client certificates.

You can choose the method of authentication by right-clicking the desired resource and choosing Properties. You then select the Directory Security or File Security tab (depending on whether you are accessing a directory or file) and click the Edit button. This displays the Authentication Methods dialog, shown in Figure 21.3. You can set up authentication combinations by selecting more than one type of method. (Note that using Client Certificates is a separate process again.)

**FIGURE 21.3:**

The Authentication Methods dialog box

From within the Directory (or File) Security window, you can also restrict the IP and domain names able to access your resources.

## Anonymous

If Anonymous authentication is set, users are not prompted for a username and password unless you have enforced NTFS permissions on a particular resource (and provided an alternative authentication scheme).

Anonymous authentication authenticates the client using the IUSR_machinename account. By default, IIS controls the password for this account and it enables clients to access only public areas of the website. If you choose to manually control the password, you can enable the anonymous user to access network resources.

The main advantage of providing anonymous access is that your visitors do not need to have individual accounts to access the website and the scheme offers the best performance of any of the authentication methods.

## Basic

With Basic authentication, the user is prompted for a username and password. However, the user information is sent in plain text (encoded as Base64 strings), which potentially leaves it open to attack. Because the method is part of the HTTP 1.0 specification, it is widely supported across platforms and your users do not need to be strictly confined to a Microsoft Windows environment. It can be used with proxy servers and firewalls.

Combining Basic authentication with SSL allows for a secure exchange of details to be established. However, using SSL involves a performance hit.

Users authenticated with Basic authentication have access to the network resources to which they are entitled (assuming that the user has an account within your domain).

## Digest

Digest authentication provides a more secure form of authentication than Basic by providing an encryption scheme for the user's password. It can be used through proxy servers and firewalls but is only supported by Internet Explorer 5.0 or later.

It is also vulnerable to an attacker recording a communication and then replaying that communication for the purposes of getting themselves into the system. For this reason, it is still a good idea to combine it with SSL where a truly secure connection is required.

## Integrated Windows Authentication

Integrated Windows authentication requires Internet Explore 2.0 or later. You can use either NTLM or Kerberos authentication. However, to use Kerberos you need to be running IIS 5.0

(or later) and Windows 2000 Server (or later) as the server platform. Client machines under Kerberos must be running at least Windows 2000.

Integrated Windows authentication is the best option for an intranet environment, but it can be a bit problematic when used over the Internet. It cannot authenticate through a firewall via a proxy unless you use a Point-to-Point Tunneling Protocol (PPTP) connection.

### Client Certificates

Client Certificates provide for a very secure authentication environment because they require each client to obtain a certificate from a trusted certificate authority (CA) and then operate over an encrypted HTTP session. They are distinct from Server Certificates, which are used by the client to authenticate your website so that the client can securely send you sensitive information such as credit card details. Server certificates are used in a typical SSL scenario, and we will discuss them further later in this chapter in the section "Setting up SSL in IIS."

Once the client certificate has been established and set up on the client machine, the system administrator maps the certificate(s) to the user account. Client Certificates are used in conjunction with SSL to create an encrypted session between the client and server. Their purpose is for you to authenticate clients requesting information from your website.

Although secure, Client Certificates can be awkward to set up and do not work with all browsers.

## Secure Sockets Layer (SSL) Encryption

SSL is relatively easy to configure with IIS and provides a reliable and secure method for handling sensitive transactions across the Internet. It has the advantage of being widely supported and it works well in the various forms of authentication available within IIS.

## URL Authorization

URL authorization is set from the `Web.config` file. You can create subdirectories within your application that contain particular resources and control access to those resources by creating separate `Web.config` files for the subdirectories.

Using URL authorization, you can grant or deny access permission to individual users and groups. You can also specify the particular HTTP method (GET or POST) that the user is entitled to employ.

## Forms-Based Authentication

In Forms-based authentication, unauthenticated requests are sent to an ASP.NET Web Form using HTTP client-side redirection. Normally, the form is constructed as a login form, enabling the user to enter their details for authorization. You can attach the login form to any appropriate form of data store for your user's login credentials, such as a database or XML document.

However, it is worth remembering that passwords can be potentially stolen during communication, and without any form of encryption, they can be read. It is possible to apply SSL to encrypt the passwords and secure the communication. An additional issue is that forms-based security is normally based on cookies and it is possible for a cookie to be intercepted and deciphered. Applying SSL across the entire communication is one solution to this, but that may cause some problems with poor performance. One solution recommended by Microsoft is to regularly regenerate the cookies at appropriate intervals and expire the previous cookies.

The process of applying forms-based authentication is quite reliable and easy to set up. Later in this chapter, we will work through an example that uses an XML document to store user credentials for a web-based scenario. In Chapter 22, "Targeting Mobile Devices," we'll set up a forms-based authentication scenario for a cookieless environment and use a database as the credentials store.

## Passport

Passport is Microsoft's XML Web service–based central authentication mechanism. The advantage of using Passport in your application is that the authentication process is managed for you and your users are able to use an existing, common password. They do not have to develop a new password especially for your application, nor do they need to remember to change the password for your application when they alter their password elsewhere.

Microsoft stores all the user identities and details on its own Passport servers. Passport has become fairly ubiquitous these days because virtually anyone with a Hotmail account also has a Passport account. It is based on a cookie system (which restricts its use in environments that do not support cookies, such as some mobile computing environments) and can be a bit awkward from the developer's perspective if you need to make use of the usernames and passwords in your own code.

Users signing into your site have their request redirected to the .NET Passport sign-in page. Passport determines whether your site is authorized to use the Passport services (that you have registered and paid your money) and then processes the authentication request. If the authentication is successful, the necessary relationship is established between the host site and the client.

To set up Passport within an application, you will need to download the Passport SDK from the Microsoft download site. You may also need to consider running the connection under SSL to really lock down security because, although Passport uses heavily encrypted cookies, it is still (in a fashion similar to Digest authentication) vulnerable to replay attacks.

# Impersonation

As you saw earlier, impersonation is the process whereby IIS is able to act on behalf of the client using the client's own network credentials. Previously in ASP, impersonation was the default situation. However, in ASP.NET, you now need to explicitly enable impersonation and choose the level at which you wish it to function.

This is handled within the `Web.config` file. If you wish to use impersonation, add the following line to the `<system.web>` section of `Web.config`:

```
<identity impersonate="true" />
```

If you need to, you can disable impersonation with the following (remembering that impersonation is disabled is the default):

```
<identity impersonate="false" />
```

Additionally, you can set impersonation to impersonate a specific account with the following:

```
<identity impersonate="true" name="domain\username" password="password" />
```

There are a number of levels of impersonation available, but there are two that you should be aware of:

**Impersonate**   The service can impersonate the client but is restricted to accessing resources on the service's own computer. (Network services can be accessed if the client process and service are on the same machine.)

**Delegate**   Delegate is supported only in Windows 2000 and later. The service can impersonate the client across the network even if the client is remote to the service's own machine.

To set up delegation, you must enable both the actual user account (in Windows 2000 Server, Active Directory Users and Computers) and the specific service's account (also from Active Directory Users and Computers) for delegation. You may also need to set the computer that hosts the service so that it's trusted for delegation; you do so from the Computer object in Active Directory Users and Computers.

As an example of setting up impersonation, suppose you have a common shared directory called `Global_Shared` on your system. You can enable directory browsing under IIS so that authorized users of your intranet can see and access the files contained within it. It also contains a number of subdirectories that are used for various purposes. Members of the personnel team have a subdirectory called `Personnel` and they want access to be restricted to personnel team members only. This is easily done by creating a Personnel group in Windows, ensuring that its membership consists of the members of the personnel team, and setting the appropriate permissions on the `Personnel` directory.

However, there may be some files within the directory that the personnel team members need to access using a custom-built ASP.NET application. To enable them to do this, you would make sure that the ASP.NET application has the appropriate `<identity impersonate="true" />` tag set in `Web.config`. You then ensure that Integrated Windows Authentication has been set for the `Personnel` virtual directory in IIS (assuming that this is an all-Windows 2000/XP environment!) and check that the authentication mode in `Web.config` is also set to Windows (which it should because Windows is the default). Then try out the security settings. Impersonation is a very simple process and requires almost no code.

## Using URL Authorization

URL authorization enables you to determine which resources individual users and groups have access to.

The `<authorization>` tags can be found within the `<system.web>` section of `Web.config`. The tags are where you define the users and groups that do (or do not) have access to your application. The default form of these tags is shown in the following snippet:

```
<authorization>
      <allow users="*" />
</authorization>
```

This approach gives all users access. If you wish to force an authentication process, you alter the tags as follows:

```
<authorization>
        <deny users="?" />
</authorization>
```

For example, if you are applying Forms authentication to your application, you need to set the deny tag as shown above.

Additionally you can grant and deny access to particular users as follows:

```
<authorization>
    <allow VERB="POST" users="Mary,Bill,Chris" />
    <allow VERB="GET" roles="Staff" />
    <allow roles="Administrators,Sales" />
    <deny users="Frank" />
    <deny users="?" />
<authorization />
```

In this example, we allow Mary, Bill, and Chris to post to the resources. Members of the Staff group are allowed to use GET to access the resources. Members of the Administrators and Sales groups are granted access, Frank is explicitly denied (poor Frank!), and any anonymous users are also denied, forcing an authentication process.

When URL authorization is used, the rules are read sequentially down until a match is found.

## Setting Up SSL in IIS

The purpose of SSL is to set up a secure and encrypted exchange between your server and the client's browser. Even if some of the transmission is intercepted, the packets will be indecipherable. In the following scenario, we will look at a common situation in which a client needs to know that the information they are sending will be secure and that you are in fact who you say you are (such as when a client submits credit card details).

SSL works because a certificate is installed on both the browser and the server. The major browsers come preinstalled with a range of certificates from various certificate authorities and have existing support for SSL. In order to create an SSL connection, you need to obtain a server certificate for your website from a certificate authority (preferably one of the authorities whose certificates are widely distributed on browsers) and set up SSL on your server.

When you have obtained and installed your certificate, you enable the secure channel port (443) and then enforce SSL for your website. Once this is established, users can access only those portions of your website covered by SSL using the https:// protocol. To set up SSL, carry out the following steps:

1. You begin by creating a Client Certificate Request (CCR). Open up the IIS Management Console and expand the nodes in the left pane to expose the website you wish to encrypt. Right-click the website and select the Properties option.

2. Click the Directory Security tab and locate the Secure Communications section. Click the Server Certificate button to start the Web Server Certificate Wizard, as shown in Figure 21.4. Click Next.

3. Select the Create a New Certificate option and click Next.

4. At this screen, you have the option of preparing the certificate to be sent immediately (assuming you have an active connection) or preparing the request and sending it later. Make an appropriate choice and click Next.

5. At the Name and Security Settings screen, give the certificate a meaningful name (you can leave it as the default, which is the name of your website, if that is appropriate). Choose your level of encryption from the drop-down box. The minimum is normally 1024-bit encryption but the higher the value, the stronger the encryption. However, you may take more of a performance hit with the higher encryption levels. (The Name and Security Settings screen is shown in Figure 21.5.) Click Next.

**FIGURE 21.4:**

Starting the Web Server
Certificate Wizard

**FIGURE 21.5:**

Choosing your
encryption level

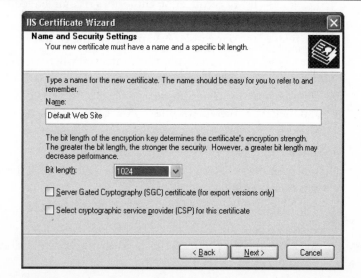

6. Fill out the appropriate information about your organization's name. Work through the next two screens, completing all relevant details about your organization. Click Next.

7. If you have chosen to send the request later, you will be prompted to save the file as a text file. Choose a convenient location and a meaningful filename and click Next. You will be presented with a summary screen, shown in Figure 21.6. Review the information and click Next.

**FIGURE 21.6:**

Summary details for
certificate request

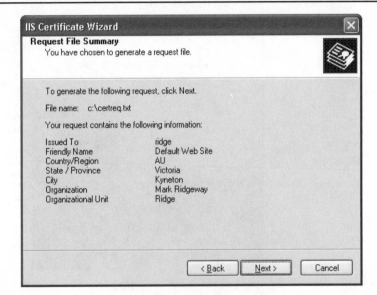

8. The final screen gives you some details on contacting a potential CA with your request, including a list of certification authorities recommended by Microsoft. You will need to send the request to one of these authorities to obtain your certificate. Click Finish. Send the request to your chosen CA and obtain the certificate.

9. Once you have received your certificate, you will need to install it on your server. Place it somewhere convenient on your machine. Open up the IIS Management Console, right-click the node for your website, and choose Properties. Select the Directory Security tab and click the Server Certificate button. Click Next at the opening screen. The next screen gives you the option to process the pending request and install the certificate, as shown in Figure 21.7. Select this option and click Next.

10. Use the Browse button to locate your certificate, click through to the end of the wizard, and click Finish.

11. The next part of the process is to make sure that port 443 is enabled and to enforce the SSL security. From the IIS Management Console, open the property pages for your website and select the Web Site tab. In the Web Site Identification section, make sure the SSL Port field contains the value 443.

FIGURE 21.7:

Processing the
pending request

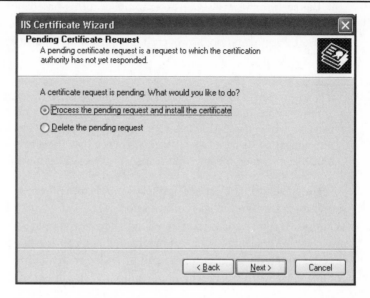

**12.** Click the Advanced button. Make sure that port 443 is listed under Multiple SSL Identities for This Web Site. Select the server's IP address and add the value 443 into the SSL Port field. Click OK and return to the property pages.

**13.** The final step is to enforce SSL. Select the Directory Security tab and click Edit in the Secure Communications section. Select Require Secure Channel (SSL). Exit the property pages.

SSL should now be configured for the site. You can check this by trying to access the site using http://*your site address* and https://*your site address*. You should be able to get in using the secure connection only.

## Building an Example of Forms-Based Security

Forms-based security is a robust and relatively easily configured mechanism that you can use for your authentication. It has the advantage that it is not platform dependant for your clients, and if used with SSL, it can be very secure. Its main drawback is that in its default form, it relies on cookies, which can be an issue in a cookieless environment.

However, you can configure forms-based security to run in cookieless mode (you'll see an example of this in Chapter 22).

Additionally, forms-based security enables you to manage your client's authentication details, which requires extra work and overhead in setting up and maintaining, but it can also provide you with a number of advantages.

In this section, we will set up an example of forms-based authentication using cookies. As our data store, we will use an XML document. This example is derived from one given in the Microsoft documentation; however, it has been simplified and translated from its original C# into Visual Basic.

SecurityDemo1, the sample application that we will create, will consist of two forms: a simple login form and a login confirmation page (WebForm1). Users access the application via WebForm1. If they are not authenticated, they are redirected to the login form, where they can provide some credentials. Once authenticated, the user is redirected back to WebForm1, where they are greeted with their name and provided with a logout option. Once the project is complete, we will also take the opportunity to experiment with URL authorization.

Open a new ASP.NET Web application in Visual Studio .NET and name it SecurityDemo1. The first step will be to create the XML file that contains the authentication data.

## Creating the XML-Based User Details File

From the Project menu, select Add New Item and choose the XML File template. Name the document users.xml and click the Open button.

Add the code from Listing 21.1 to the designer for users.xml and save the project.

---

**Listing 21.1**     *users.xml*

```xml
<?xml version="1.0" encoding="utf-8" ?>
<Users>
    <User>
        <UserName>fred</UserName>
        <Password>fred</Password>
    </User>
    <User>
        <UserName>mary</UserName>
        <Password>mary</Password>
    </User>
    <User>
        <UserName>chris</UserName>
        <Password>chris</Password>
    </User>
</Users>
```

---

## Setting Up WebForm1

Click the tab for WebForm1.aspx and add two Label controls and a Button. Set their properties as follows:

| Control | Property | Value |
|---------|----------|-------|
| Label1 | Font: Size | X-Large |
| | Text | Security Demo |
| | ID | LabelHeading |
| Label2 | Text | <empty> |
| | ID | LabelGreeting |
| Button1 | Text | Log Out |
| | ID | ButtonLogout |

Arrange the controls appropriately on the WebForm. The final layout should look something like Figure 21.8.

**FIGURE 21.8:**

Control layout for
WebForm1.aspx

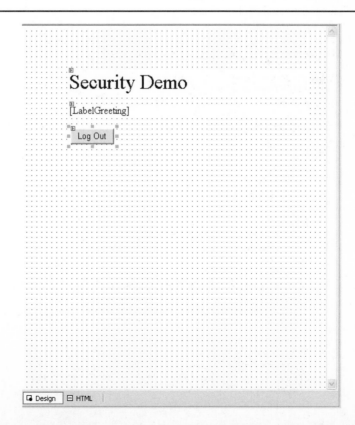

Double-click the form to enter Code Behind and add the code from Listing 21.2 to the Page_Load event handler. The purpose of this code is to populate the LabelGreeting control with a personalized greeting once the user is authenticated.

**Listing 21.2    Page_Load for *WebForm1.aspx***

```
Private Sub Page_Load(ByVal sender As System.Object, _
 ByVal e As System.EventArgs) Handles MyBase.Load

        LabelGreeting.Text = "Hello " & _
 Context.User.Identity.Name

End Sub
```

You now need to add some code directly onto WebForm1.aspx from HTML view. Switch back to WebForm1.aspx and choose HTML view.

Add the System.Web.Security namespace to the document and create a handler for the Logout button's Click event. Listing 21.3 gives the full ASPX code for this page once the additions have been made.

**Listing 21.3    ASPX Code for WebForm1**

```
<%@ Page Language="vb" AutoEventWireup="false" _
 Codebehind="WebForm1.aspx.vb" _
 Inherits="SecurityDemo1.WebForm1"%>
<%@ Import namespace ="System.Web.Security" %>
<!DOCTYPE HTML PUBLIC "-//W3C//DTD HTML 4.0 _
 Transitional//EN">
<HTML>
    <HEAD>
        <title>WebForm1</title>
        <script runat="server">
            Private Sub Logout_Click(sender As _
System.Object, e As System.EventArgs)
            FormsAuthentication.SignOut
            Response.Redirect("login.aspx")
            End Sub
        </script>
        <meta name="GENERATOR" content="Microsoft Visual _
Studio.NET 7.0">
        <meta name="CODE_LANGUAGE" content="Visual Basic _
7.0">
        <meta name="vs_defaultClientScript" _
content="JavaScript">
        <meta name="vs_targetSchema" _
content="http://schemas.microsoft.com/intellisense/ie5">
    </HEAD>
    <body MS_POSITIONING="GridLayout">
```

```
<form id="Form1" method="post" runat="server">
    <asp:Label id="LabelHeading" style="Z-INDEX:_
101; LEFT: 76px; POSITION: absolute; TOP: 70px" _
runat="server" Width="387px" _
Font-Size="X-Large">Security Demo</asp:Label>
    <asp:Label id="LabelGreeting" _
style="Z-INDEX: 102; LEFT: 77px; POSITION: absolute; _
TOP: 122px" runat="server" Width="382px"></asp:Label>
    <asp:Button id="ButtonLogout" _
style="Z-INDEX: 103; LEFT: 79px; POSITION: absolute; _
TOP: 160px" runat="server" Text="Log Out" _
OnClick="Logout_Click"></asp:Button>
    </form>
  </body>
</HTML>
```

The additions that are made consist of a handler to manage the Click event for the Logout button and a call to the Click event in the ButtonLogout tag. You also need to add a directive to import the System.Web.Security namespace. This is in the form <%@ Import namespace="System .Web.Security" %> and is added to the top of the page immediately under the Page directive.

The handler is placed in the Head area and consists of the following code:

```
<script runat="server">
        Private Sub Logout_Click(sender As _
  System.Object, e As System.EventArgs)
        FormsAuthentication.SignOut
        Response.Redirect("login.aspx")
        End Sub
</script>
```

The code signs out the user and redirects back to the Login page. (Cookie persistence may cause some problems if the user then tries to log in right away using a different account.)

To access the handler, you add OnClick="Logout_Click" to the ButtonLogout tag.

## Creating the Login Page

The next step is to create the actual Login page. From the Project menu, choose Add WebForm and name the new form login.aspx.

Place four Labels, two TextBoxes, and a Button control on the page. Set the properties for the controls as follows:

| Control | Property | Value |
| --- | --- | --- |
| Label1 | Font: Size | X-Large |
| | Text | Login Page |
| | ID | LabelTitle |

| Control | Property | Value |
|---------|----------|-------|
| Label2 | Text | UserName |
|  | ID | LabelUsername |
| TextBox1 | Text | <empty> |
|  | ID | TextBoxUsername |
| Label3 | Text | Password |
|  | ID | LabelPassword |
| TextBox2 | Text | <empty> |
|  | TextMode | Password |
|  | ID | TextBoxPassword |
| Button1 | Text | Login |
|  | ID | ButtonLogin |
| Label4 | ForeColor | Red |
|  | Text | <empty> |
|  | ID | LabelWarning |

Figure 21.9 shows the control layout for login.aspx.

**FIGURE 21.9:**

Control layout for
login.aspx

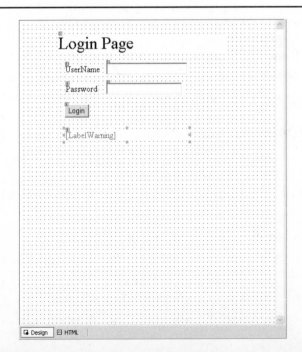

All of the code for this page is written directly onto the ASPX page in HTML view. Shift to HTML view and add the following directives to the top of your page:

```
<%@ Import namespace ="System.Web.Security" %>
<%@ Import namespace ="System.Data" %>
<%@ Import namespace ="System.Data.SqlClient" %>
<%@ Import namespace ="System.IO" %>
```

In the Head area, add the following code:

```
<script runat="server">

   Private Sub Login_Click(sender As System.Object, e _
 As  System.EventArgs)

      Dim checkUsername as string = "UserName='" &  TextBoxUsername.Text & "'"
      Dim Dataset1 as new DataSet
      Dim userList as new _
 Filestream(Server.MapPath("users.xml"), FileMode.Open, _
 FileAccess.Read)
      Dim reader as new StreamReader(userList)

      Dataset1.ReadXML(reader)
      userList.close

      dim users as DataTable = Dataset1.Tables(0)
      dim findUser as DataRow()

      findUser = users.select(checkUsername)

      If findUser.length > 0
        Dim foundUser as DataRow = findUser(0)

        If TextBoxPassword.Text = foundUser("Password") _
   then

            FormsAuthentication.RedirectFromLoginPage _
 (TextBoxUsername.text, false)
          Else
            LabelWarning.Text = "Please try your password again"
        End if

      Else
        LabelWarning.text = "Please enter a valid user name"
      End If
   End Sub
</script>
```

This code creates a search string from the contents of the TextBoxUsername text box. It then sets up a DatSet (Dataset1) that will be used to hold the contents of the XML data file. You then load the contents of the XML file into the userList filestream. This is read into the reader StreamReader, which is then used to populate Dataset1.

From there you can drill-down through the DataSet, first by table and then by row, until you locate a match for the checkUsername string that you created earlier. If a match is found, the password entered in TextBoxPassword is verified and the user is authenticated and redirected back to the original page using these lines:

```
FormsAuthentication.RedirectFromLoginPage _
(TextBoxUsername.text, false)
```

The parameters for FormsAuthentication.RedirectFromLoginPage are employed to identify the user for URL authorization purposes (TextBoxUsername.text) and to determine whether a persistent cookie needs to be created (true for yes and false for no). If you have decided to create a persistent cookie, you can also add a second string as a parameter to describe a path for the cookie.

You then finish with a couple of appropriate prompts if either the username or password is incorrect.

Further down in the ASPX page, you add the event handler to the tag for the ButtonLogin control in the form OnClick="Login_Click".

The complete code listing for the login.aspx page is given in Listing 21.4.

**Listing 21.4     Complete ASPX Code for *login.aspx* Page**

```
<%@ Import namespace ="System.Web.Security" %>
<%@ Import namespace ="System.Data" %>
<%@ Import namespace ="System.Data.SqlClient" %>
<%@ Import namespace ="System.IO" %>
<%@ Page Language="vb" Debug=true _
 AutoEventWireup="false" Codebehind="login.aspx.vb" _
 Inherits="SecurityDemo1.login"%>
<!DOCTYPE HTML PUBLIC "-//W3C//DTD HTML 4.0 _
 Transitional//EN">
<HTML>
   <HEAD>
      <title>login</title>
      <script runat="server">
         Private Sub Login_Click(sender As _
System.Object, e As System.EventArgs)
            Dim checkUsername as string = _
"UserName='" & TextBoxUsername.Text & "'"
            Dim Dataset1 as new DataSet
            Dim userList as new _
```

```
Filestream(Server.MapPath("users.xml"), _
FileMode.Open, FileAccess.Read)
          Dim reader as new _
StreamReader(userList)
          Dataset1.ReadXML(reader)
          userList.close

          dim users as DataTable = _
Dataset1.Tables(0)
          dim findUser as DataRow()
          findUser = users.select(checkUsername)

          If findUser.length > 0
          Dim foundUser as DataRow = findUser(0)

      If TextBoxPassword.Text = _
foundUser("Password") then

   FormsAuthentication.RedirectFromLoginPage _
(TextBoxUsername.text, false)
          Else
      LabelWarning.Text = _
"Please try your password again"
          End if

          Else
          LabelWarning.text = "Please enter a valid user name"
          End If
      End Sub
    </script>
    <meta name="GENERATOR" content="Microsoft Visual _
Studio.NET 7.0">
    <meta name="CODE_LANGUAGE" content="Visual Basic _
7.0">
    <meta name="vs_defaultClientScript" _
content="JavaScript">
    <meta name="vs_targetSchema" _
content="http://schemas.microsoft.com/intellisense/ie5">
  </HEAD>
  <body MS_POSITIONING="GridLayout">
    <form id="Form1" method="post" runat="server">
      <asp:TextBox id="TextBoxUsername" _
style="Z-INDEX: 101; LEFT: 167px; POSITION: absolute; _
TOP: 78px" runat="server"></asp:TextBox>
      <asp:TextBox id="TextBoxPassword" _
style="Z-INDEX: 102; LEFT: 167px; POSITION: absolute; _
TOP: 115px" runat="server" TextMode="Password"> _
</asp:TextBox>
      <asp:Label id="LabelTitle" _
```

```
style="Z-INDEX: 103; LEFT: 76px; POSITION: absolute; _
TOP: 25px" runat="server" Width="316px" _
Font-Size="X-Large">Login Page</asp:Label>
        <asp:Label id="LabelUsername" _
style="Z-INDEX: 104; LEFT: 89px; POSITION: absolute; _
TOP: 81px" runat="server">UserName</asp:Label>
        <asp:Label id="LabelPassword" _
style="Z-INDEX: 105; LEFT: 90px; POSITION: absolute; _
TOP: 117px" runat="server">Password</asp:Label>
        <asp:Button id="ButtonLogin" _
style="Z-INDEX: 106; LEFT: 88px; POSITION: absolute; _
TOP: 156px" runat="server" Text="Login" _
OnClick="Login_Click"></asp:Button>
        <asp:Label id="LabelWarning" _
style="Z-INDEX: 107; LEFT: 90px; POSITION: absolute; _
TOP: 203px" runat="server" Width="232px" _
ForeColor="Red"></asp:Label>
    </form>
  </body>
</HTML>
```

## Configuring *Web.config*

Once you have set up the Web Forms and the appropriate code, the last step is to set the <authentication> and <authorization> tags in the Web.config file.

From the Solution Explorer, open Web.config and locate the <authentication> tag. Set the tag as follows (note that case is important):

```
<authentication mode="Forms" />
```

Identify the <authorization> tag and edit the section to appear as it does in the following code snippet:

```
<authorization>
        <deny users="?" />
</authorization>
```

The purpose of this code is to deny access to the site to any unauthenticated users and to ensure that they are redirected to the Login page.

This completes the process. Compile and run the project. It should open to the Login screen, into which you can enter one of the sets of user details as shown in Figure 21.10.

Once you enter correct details and click the Login button, the site redirects you to WebForm1 and displays the appropriate details, as shown in Figure 21.11. Clicking the Log Out button returns you to the Login screen.

**FIGURE 21.10:**

The Login page in
Internet Explorer

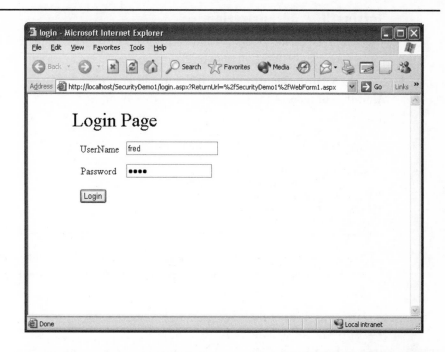

**FIGURE 21.11:**

Login confirmation in
Internet Explorer

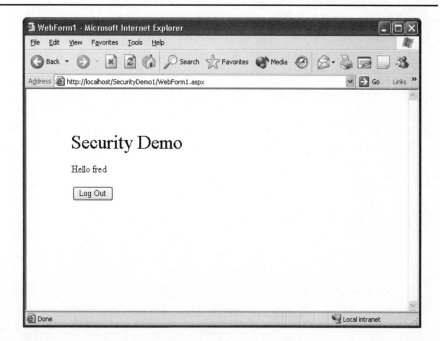

## Setting URL Authorization

We will finish this section by briefly looking at how you can exploit URL authorization with forms-based authentication to determine who has access to certain site resources.

In the SecurityDemo1 project, open up `Web.config` and locate the `<authorization>` tags. Alter the contents of the tags to appear as they do in Listing 21.5.

---

**Listing 21.5**      **URL Authorization Code**

```
<authorization>
        <allow users="fred,mary"/>
        <deny users="chris"/>
        <deny users="?" />
</authorization>
```

---

Compile and run the project. Logging in as Fred or Mary should produce a successful login. However, if you attempt to log in as Chris, you shouldn't go any further than the Login screen.

## Summary

As you can see, there are a number of different options when it comes to setting security for your ASP.NET application. The particular combination of methods that you use depends on the exact nature and requirements of your site and users. It is important to include security considerations as part of your planning process and to make them integral to your development process as much as possible.

However, although security is important when you are dealing with sensitive information, it can also have an impact on site performance and place a burden on your users in terms of remembering passwords, going through the actual authentication process, and possibly being required to change the type of browser they are using. Thus it is important that you don't overdo security to the point that it becomes counterproductive to the purpose of your site.

The other point to be aware of is that nothing replaces ongoing monitoring and maintenance. Good security is not a set-and-forget thing. To protect your site and its users, you need to be prepared to closely monitor its activity and keep up-to-date with relevant patches and updates. One important area of security that we haven't covered in this chapter is the issue of the physical security of your web servers and associated equipment. Proper backup regimes and simple procedures such as keeping the door locked can either solve a lot of potential problems before they occur or provide peace of mind in the event of a major disaster.

In the next chapter, we will be examining the process using ASP.NET and the Microsoft Mobile Internet Toolkit to create sites and applications that target mobile users.

# CHAPTER 22

# Targeting Mobile Devices

- Introducing the Mobile Internet Toolkit (MIT)

- Obtaining the tools of the trade

- Getting started with the MIT

- Exploring the MIT controls

- Building a simple application

- Working with Code Behind

- Using the mobile controls

- Deploying with the MIT

- Building a mobile application for accessing the corporate database

Increasingly, developers are being asked to cater to the growing market of small and portable computing devices that have appeared over the last few years. We have also seen the appearance of new standards—such as WAP (Wireless Application Protocol), i-mode, and SMS (Short Message Service)—that specifically target these devices and the growth of languages—such as HDML (Handheld Device Markup Language), WML (Wireless Markup Language), and cHTML—designed to support these standards. Developers are also faced with the choice of creating embedded applications that are designed for and run on a given device or developing online applications that can be accessed via some form of web browser (commonly referred to as a *microbrowser* in the mobile world).

To assist developers in building sophisticated applications that can be used across a wide range of devices, Microsoft has produced a range of tools in line with its .NET strategy and compatible with Visual Studio .NET. For the developer seeking to create websites and online applications accessible to mobile devices, Microsoft has released the Mobile Internet Toolkit (MIT). Although not discussed in this chapter, Microsoft has also released the .NET Compact Framework and Smart Device Extensions for building rich client-based applications.

The Mobile Internet Toolkit provides a range of controls that can dynamically render themselves in an appropriate format according to the individual device that accesses them. This enables developers to take a "build once and run on anything" approach to their mobile site development. It avoids the problems and work overhead associated with building multiple versions of a site coupled with sophisticated device and protocol detection for the range of devices that may be used to access the site. With the Mobile Internet Toolkit, you can build a site secure in the knowledge that it can be correctly accessed by a WAP-enabled cell phone, a Pocket PC with an HTML browser, or a cHTML-enabled i-mode device. You can afford to focus on the design and functionality of the site rather than being consumed by the need to address compatibility issues.

In this chapter, we will take a brief look at the Mobile Internet Toolkit and see how it can be used together with Visual Studio .NET and other third-party tools to build online applications accessible to a wide range of devices. We will also briefly explore some of the more advanced features of the MIT that enable developers to optimize their sites for particular devices and extend support to newly emerging devices.

## Introducing the Mobile Internet Toolkit

The Mobile Internet Toolkit provides a special set of controls for use in ASP.NET. The controls are added to an ASP.NET Web Form known as a Mobile Web Form and can have additional functionality developed for them using the "code behind" approach in the language (.NET compatible, of course) of the developer's choice.

Although it is possible to create applications with the MIT employing only a standard text editor and the command-line compiler, the preferred method is to use the Visual Studio .NET graphical (and standardized) IDE, shown in Figure 22.1. Mobile Web Forms are saved with the same `.aspx` file extension used now for all ASP.NET Web Forms.

**FIGURE 22.1:**

Visual Studio .NET
running the MIT

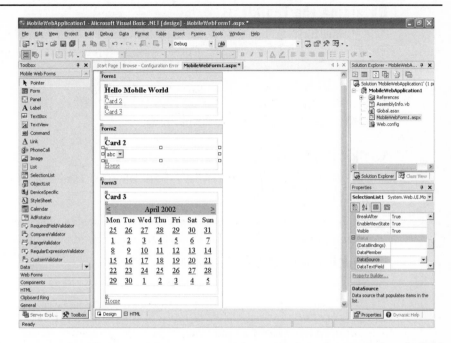

Applications and sites built with the MIT can be tested using real devices or emulators such as the Openwave or Nokia emulators. (Figure 22.2 shows the Openwave generic simulator.)

**FIGURE 22.2:**

The Openwave Generic
Simulator (image
courtesy Openwave
Systems Inc.)

## Obtaining the Toolkit

The Mobile Internet Toolkit may be obtained from the Microsoft download site at `http://msdn.microsoft.com/downloads`. Enter "Mobile Internet Toolkit" into the search box. The download size is a little over 4MB. If the toolkit has been included with your copy of Visual Studio .NET, then use Windows Explorer to navigate to `Program Files\Microsoft Visual Studio .NET\Visual Studio SDKs\Mobile Internet Toolkit`. Install by double-clicking the `MobileIT.exe` file and following the prompts.

## Toolkit Contents

The Mobile Internet Toolkit consists of the following items, which are installed when you run the `MobileIT.exe` file:

**Mobile Internet Controls Runtime**    A set of controls that can be dropped onto a Mobile Web Form and can dynamically render themselves according to the device accessing them

**Mobile Internet Designer**    Development interface that integrates into Visual Studio .NET for building mobile applications

**Device Capabilities**    Capabilities for the range of mobile devices

**Device Adapter Code**    Code that enables support for new devices to be added through the extensibility model

**QuickStart Tutorial**    Introductory tutorial on the MIT

**Documentation**    Language and technical reference

# Obtaining the Tools of the Trade

There is a range of additional tools that are extremely useful for building mobile applications with the MIT. These include the individual device and browser emulators available from Microsoft and other third-party vendors.

One of the requirements of building mobile applications is extensive testing across a wide range of devices. This is necessary even when using a tool such as the MIT. Although it takes a lot of the pain out of device-compatibility issues, in the real world, problems still happen and it is best to try to forestall them. Because it is practically impossible for the normal developer to have on hand a complete set of real devices that are likely to access the site, the next best thing is to use software emulators. Most device manufacturers and browser developers freely provide emulators that can run on the developers' computers and simulate the real device or browser.

It is important to realize that you won't always get perfect results when you use emulators for testing. Not all emulators fully simulate the real product (in fact, nearly all don't), nor do emulators provide the individual device/browser/gateway combinations that exist in the "wild" and throw up their own unique set of circumstances.

Nevertheless, emulators are vital tools in the development and testing phases of mobile applications. Typically, mobile developers would have copies of the Nokia and Openwave software development kits (SDKs) because they cover two of the major browser types for WAP-enabled mobile phones. (See Figure 22.3 for an example of the Openwave SDK).

**FIGURE 22.3:**

The Openwave SDK (image courtesy Openwave Systems Inc.)

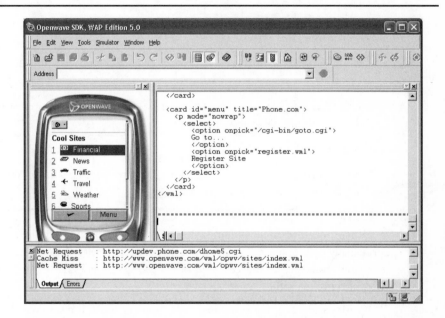

The Openwave SDK can be obtained from www.openwave.com (and select the link to the developer site) and the Nokia SDK can be obtained from http://forum.nokia.com. You may need to register with the sites to obtain the SDKs. The Openwave SDK features an extremely informative compiler window, and the Nokia SDK features a tool for creating WBMP images. (WBMP images are optimized for the mobile environment.)

Naturally, you can use the default browser internal to Visual Studio .NET. Although not precisely a microbrowser, it remains a good method for quickly checking the state of your application. Figure 22.4 illustrates a simple mobile application being run in the integrated browser in Visual Studio .NET.

Simple mobile
application running in
the integrated browser
in Visual Studio .NET

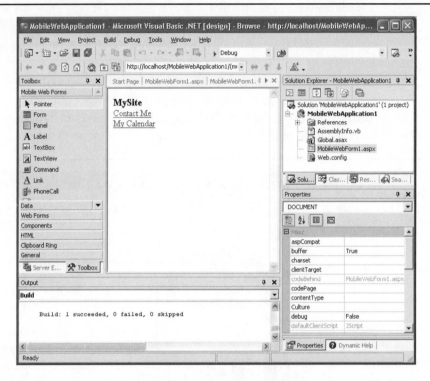

Other tools that can be obtained depend to a certain extent on the environment that you are principally developing for. Emulators exist for most platforms and a wide range of SDKs is also available from various sources. Additional tools such as WBMP image editors and converters may also prove useful.

Various sites exist that provide a wide range of tools, links, news, and tutorials relevant to the mobile world. One that is very useful is the mobile section of www.devx.com. The Microsoft mobile site at www.microsoft.com/mobile is an excellent source of the latest updates in the Microsoft mobile space, and Microsoft also provides an MIT newsgroup that is a valuable source of support for developers. The newsgroup can be accessed via http://msdn.microsoft .com/newsgroups.

## Getting Started with the MIT

Once you have installed the Mobile Internet Toolkit, open Visual Studio .NET in the usual fashion. When you click the New Project button, you will see that a Mobile Web Application option is now included in the New Project dialog box, as shown in Figure 22.5.

FIGURE 22.5:

**FIGURE 22.5:**

Mobile Web Application option in the New Project dialog box

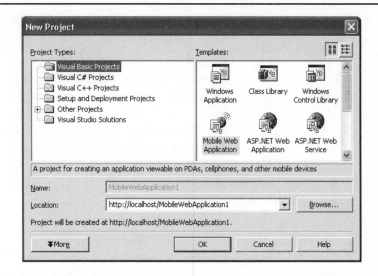

Select the Mobile Web Application option and accept the defaults to create Mobile WebApplication1. Your screen should appear as in Figure 22.6.

**FIGURE 22.6:**

Mobile Web Application1

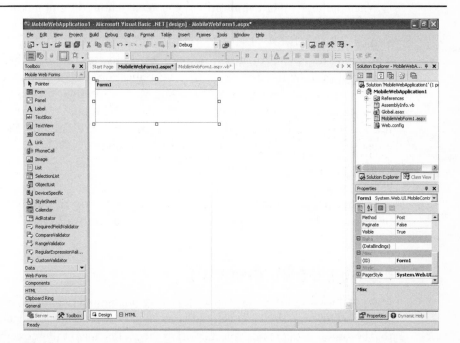

**TIP**    It is often easier to initially run and test mobile applications using Internet Explorer because you are less likely to have to deal with artifacts created by the browser. This is particularly useful when working on developing the business logic for the project.

Visual Studio .NET running the MIT should look familiar to those of you who have used the Visual Studio .NET IDE before. The mobile controls are available from the Toolbox on the left side of the screen under the Mobile Web Forms tab. Controls are dragged and dropped onto the individual Form controls in MobileWebForm1 in the center of the screen, and the various Properties windows and Solution Explorer are found on the right side of the screen. When the application is compiled, all the debugging information appears at the bottom of the screen, and you use the Start button or the various options available under the Debug menu to compile and run your projects.

As with ASP.NET, you can alternate between HTML and Design view. You can alter properties using the Properties window or directly by altering the code in HTML view. You can add functionality to your project by coding directly into HTML view or by using Code Behind (select the View Code option in Design view). Although some elements of using the MIT require coding within HTML view, some have a personal preference for separating the business logic from the design elements and using Code Behind.

When building mobile applications, you need to limit the amount of data being sent to the device at any one time. This is because of device limitations in terms of cache size, and it's also related to network speeds, which for wireless WAP devices can be as slow as 9600bps. The standard approach to this is to adopt a "card and deck" strategy that divides key elements of an application into separate cards. The application itself may consist of a single deck of cards or be split across multiple decks. The Mobile Internet Toolkit emulates this scenario by enabling the creation of multiple forms on each MobileWebForm (ASPX page). The forms can be found as one of the controls available in the Toolbox. Each MobileWebForm effectively becomes a deck within the mobile application. When a MobileWebForm is accessed by a mobile device, the first Form control on the page is automatically accessed by default.

Additional controls are then dropped onto the Form controls, with the exception of the StyleSheet control, which must be placed directly on the ASPX page.

## Exploring the MIT Controls

Many of the MIT controls are superficially very similar to the controls found in the Web Forms Toolbox. However, there are many differences in the execution and functionality of the controls that become apparent once you start using them. The main thing to remember is that the mobile tools tend to not be as powerful and versatile as their Web Forms counterparts. Some controls, such as the PhoneCall control, have no Web Forms counterpart. Table 22.1 includes a list and brief description of the available mobile controls. Note that it is possible to develop your own custom controls and third-party controls are beginning to appear on the Internet.

**TABLE 22.1:** Mobile Controls

| Category | Mobile Control | Description |
| --- | --- | --- |
| Container | Form | Acts as a container for other controls and models a card within the WAP environment |
| | Panel | Provides a mechanism for organizing controls in a form and assigning common properties |
| Standard | AdRotator | Rotates advertisements or images in an application |
| | Calendar | Provides calendar functions |
| | Command | Posts input from user input elements back to the server |
| | Image | Displays images |
| | Label | Presents text on a form |
| | Link | Provides in-site and offsite links |
| | PhoneCall | Automatically display or call phone numbers |
| | TextBox | Accepts data input for an application |
| | TextView | Displays large amounts of text with some additional manipulation with markup tags |
| List | List | Displays a list of items |
| | ObjectList | Interacts with data sources |
| | SelectionList | Extends basic List control |
| Validation | CompareValidator | Compares one control to another |
| | CustomValidator | Enables custom validation requirements to be developed |
| | RangeValidator | Checks that the values of a control are within a set range |
| | RegularExpression-Validator | Checks that the contents of a control match a particular expression |
| | RequiredField-Validator | Checks that the contents of a control have been updated or changed |
| | ValidationSummary | Displays a summary of validation errors that have occurred |
| Special | DeviceSpecific | Enables content to be targeted at a specific device type |
| | StyleSheet | Sets styles for application to other controls |

# Building a Simple Application

Return to MobileWebApplication1 in Visual Studio .NET and drag two additional Form controls to the MobileWebForm1.

Drag a Label control and two Link controls to Form1. Drag a Label, PhoneCall, and Link to Form2 and a Label, Calendar, and Link to Form3.

Notice that the controls only insert sequentially down the forms. The option does not exist to create some form of layout and locate the various controls at precise locations on the page.

**TIP**    It is possible to persuade some controls to render across the page (depending on the device) by setting the BreakAfter property of the individual controls to False.

Use the Properties window to set the individual properties of the various controls as follows (when the properties are set, your application should look like the one in Figure 22.7):

| Form | Control | Property | Value |
|------|---------|----------|-------|
| Form1 | Label1 | StyleReference | title |
| | | Text | MySite |
| | Link1 | Text | Contact Me |
| | | NavigateURL | #Form2 |
| | Link2 | Text | My Calendar |
| | | NavigateURL | #Form3 |
| Form2 | Label2 | StyleReference | title |
| | | Text | MySite—Contact Me |
| | PhoneCall1 | Text | Ring Me |
| | | AlternateURL | http://mysite.net |
| | | PhoneNumber | 555 555 555 |
| | Link3 | Text | Home |
| | | NavigateURL | #Form1 |
| Form3 | Label3 | StyleReference | title |
| | | Text | My Calendar |
| | Calendar1 | Defaults for all property settings | |
| | Link4 | Text | Home |
| | | NavigateURL | #Form1 |

FIGURE 22.7:

Completed Form
setup for MobileWeb-
Application1

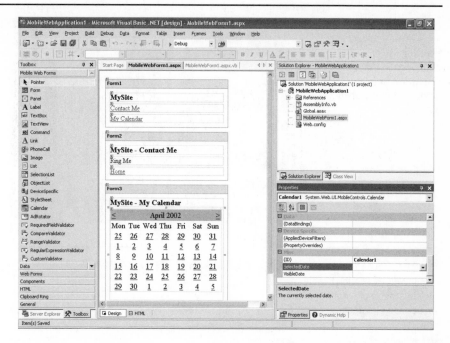

Save the project and run it in the Openwave emulator. Figures 22.8 and 22.9 demonstrate how the various screens should look in the emulator. Note that both the PhoneCall and Calendar controls are rendered initially as links that drill-down to more specific information. Figure 22.10 shows the same application running in Internet Explorer. In this instance, the Phone-Call control is rendered as a URL because IE is incapable of supporting a phone dialing facility.

FIGURE 22.8:

MobileWebApplication1
showing the phone
call sequence in the
Openwave emulator
(image courtesy Open-
wave Systems Inc.)

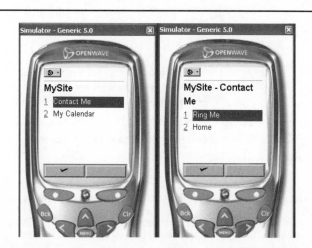

MobileWebApplication1 showing the calendar sequence in the Openwave emulator (image courtesy Openwave Systems Inc.)

MobileWebApplication1 showing the phone call sequence in Internet Explorer.

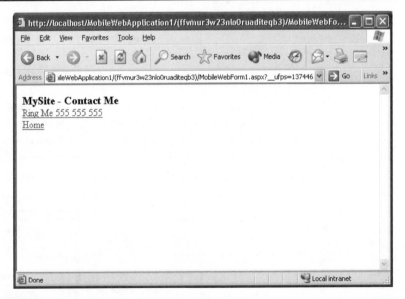

Select the HTML view (down the bottom of the Mobile Web Form designer) to display the ASPX code that has been generated to support this application. The code has been reproduced in Listing 22.1.

**Listing 22.1**     **Code from the HTML Source View for MobileWebApplication1**

```
<%@ Register TagPrefix="mobile" _ Namespace="System.Web.UI.MobileControls" _
Assembly="System.Web.Mobile, Version=1.0.3300.0, _
Culture=neutral, PublicKeyToken=b03f5f7f11d50a3a" %>
```

```
<%@ Page Language="vb" AutoEventWireup="false" _
 Codebehind="MobileWebForm1.aspx.vb" _
 Inherits="MobileWebApplication1.MobileWebForm1" %>
<meta name="GENERATOR" content="Microsoft Visual _
 Studio.NET 7.0">
<meta name="CODE_LANGUAGE" content="Visual Basic 7.0">
<meta name="vs_targetSchema" _
 content="http://schemas.microsoft.com/Mobile/Page">
<body Xmlns:mobile="http://schemas.microsoft.com/ _
Mobile/WebForm">
    <mobile:Form id="Form1" runat="server">
      <mobile:Label id="Label1" runat="server" _
StyleReference="title">MySite</mobile:Label>
      <mobile:Link id="Link1" runat="server" _
NavigateUrl="#Form2">Contact Me</mobile:Link>
      <mobile:Link id="Link2" runat="server" _
NavigateUrl="#Form3">My Calendar</mobile:Link>
    </mobile:Form>
    <mobile:Form id="Form2" runat="server">
      <mobile:Label id="Label2" runat="server" _
StyleReference="title">MySite - Contact Me _
</mobile:Label>
      <mobile:PhoneCall id="PhoneCall1" runat="server" _
AlternateUrl="http://mysite.com" _
PhoneNumber="555 555 555">Ring Me</mobile:PhoneCall>
      <mobile:Link id="Link3" runat="server" _
NavigateUrl="#Form1">Home</mobile:Link>
    </mobile:Form>
    <mobile:Form id="Form3" runat="server">
      <mobile:Label id="Label3" runat="server" _
StyleReference="title">MySite - My Calendar _
</mobile:Label>
      <mobile:Calendar id="Calendar1" runat="server"> _
</mobile:Calendar>
      <mobile:Link id="Link4" runat="server" _
NavigateUrl="#Form1">Home</mobile:Link>
    </mobile:Form>
</body>
```

Within the Body section of the code, you can see the tags that define each of the mobile controls that we have used. The properties that we have specified for these controls are now specified within these tags. You can edit these properties directly within this window. If you wished to change the telephone number in the PhoneCall control, you could edit the tag to read as follows (for example):

```
<mobile:PhoneCall id="PhoneCall1" runat="server" _
 AlternateUrl="http://mysite.com" _
 PhoneNumber="777 777 777">Ring Me</mobile:PhoneCall>
```

If you return to Design view, you'll find this change reflected in the property settings for PhoneCall1.

## Working with Code Behind

You can build extra functionality into your site by writing your business logic into Code Behind. In this example, we will add a button to adjust some of the calendar settings in Form3.

When you use the Calendar control, you have the option of allowing your users to select by date, week, or month. This option is set with the SelectionMode property.

Add a Command control (Command1) to Form3 immediately below Label3 and above Calendar1. Set the Text property to Calendar Settings. Double-click the control to enter Code Behind and add the code from Listing 22.2.

**Listing 22.2    Code to Add Functionality to Command1 in MobileWebApplication1**

```
Private Sub Command1_Click(ByVal sender As _
System.Object, ByVal e As System.EventArgs) _
Handles Command1.Click
        Select Case Calendar1.SelectionMode
            Case CalendarSelectionMode.Day
                Calendar1.SelectionMode = _
Calendar1.SelectionMode.DayWeek
                Command1.Text = "Day & Week"
            Case CalendarSelectionMode.DayWeek
                Calendar1.SelectionMode = _
Calendar1.SelectionMode.DayWeekMonth
                Command1.Text = "Day, Week & Month"
            Case CalendarSelectionMode.DayWeekMonth
                Calendar1.SelectionMode = _
Calendar1.SelectionMode.Day
                Command1.Text = "Day"
        End Select
    End Sub
```

This is a simple SELECT CASE statement that alters the SelectionMode property of the Calendar1 control depending on the existing value of the SelectionMode property. It also adjusts the Command1 text accordingly.

To test the application, click the Start button in Visual Studio .NET. The application should compile and appear in Internet Explorer. (Because you have added code into Code Behind, you must compile the project, whereas previously you only needed to save it.) You can also test the project in the Openwave emulator (or any of our other third-party emulators you may be using).

**TIP**    Make sure that Internet Explorer is not set to "Work Offline" because this can cause problems with the debug process when compiling.

Figure 22.11 illustrates choosing the Calendar settings when running this project in the Openwave browser.

**FIGURE 22.11:**

Choosing the Calendar settings when running MobileWebApplication1 in the Openwave browser (image courtesy Openwave Systems Inc.)

## Using the Mobile Controls

The following set of simple projects illustrates many of the mobile controls that ship with the Mobile Internet Toolkit. We are not able to cover these in a great deal of detail here, but considerable documentation ships with the MIT and the Microsoft QuickStart tutorials are also an excellent source of pointers for use with these tools.

### Creating MobileTestProject1

MobileTestProject1 is designed to illustrate the use of the Panel, TextView, StyleSheet, and DeviceSpecific controls and the various Validator controls.

Create a new project and give it the name MobileTestProject1.

---

**TIP**     Mobile projects are named by changing the URL in the New Project dialog box. For example, in this case we would use the URL `http://localhost/MobileTestProject1`.

---

Drop a Panel control onto Form1 and set its BackColor property to an appropriate shade (we chose pale mauve) and its ForeColor property to something else (we chose dark red).

Drag a StyleSheet control to the Mobile Web Form and locate it below the Form1 control. Right-click the control and choose the Edit Styles command. In the Styles Editor dialog box, double-click Style in the Style Types list. This creates Style1 in the Defined Styles list. Edit the properties of Style1 to set the Font property to Comic Sans MS, the Alignment property to Center, and the StyleReference property to title, as shown in Figure 22.12.

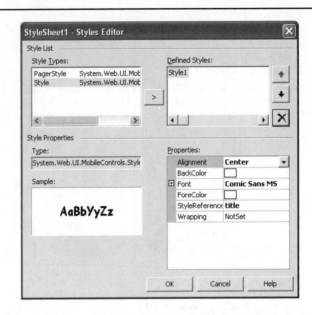

Drop a Label control onto the Panel1 control. Notice that its text color immediately adopts the value that you have chosen for the Panel's ForeColor property. In the StyleReference property for the Label control, you should now find the Style1 property specified in the StyleSheet control. Select this property. Set the Text property to Test Project 1.

**NOTE**    The Styles rendered by the Panel and StyleSheet controls will be displayed only on devices that are capable of supporting them. Compare the results of running the project in the Internet Explorer and Openwave browsers.

Drag another Label control to the Panel and set its Text property to Stylesheets and Validators.

Insert a TextView control underneath the Panel control on Form1. The style of this control should remain unaffected by the Panel control. Switch to HTML view and insert the following block of text into the TextView tag:

```
<mobile:TextView id="TextView1" runat="server">Rhubarb,
  Rhubarb, Rhubarb, Rhubarb, Rhubarb, Rhubarb, Rhubarb,
  Rhubarb, Rhubarb, Rhubarb, Rhubarb, Rhubarb, Rhubarb,
  Rhubarb, Rhubarb</mobile:TextView>
```

The text can be formatted using some simple HTML text formatting tags such as <b> and <i>. You can also add a hyperlink and a break <br/>. The following code snippet illustrates this:

```
<mobile:TextView id="TextView1" _
  runat="server"><b>Rhubarb,</b> Rhubarb,
  <i>Rhubarb,</i> Rhubarb, Rhubarb,
  <a href="http//mysite.net">My Site link</a>,
```

```
Rhubarb,<br/> Rhubarb, Rhubarb, Rhubarb, Rhubarb,
Rhubarb, Rhubarb, Rhubarb, Rhubarb</mobile:TextView>
```

Finally, switch back to Design view and add a second Form control to the MobileWebForm and add a Link control to Form1. Set the Link control's text property to Form 2 and its NavigateURL to #Form2. The project should appear as shown in Figure 22.13.

**FIGURE 22.13:**

MobileTestProject1

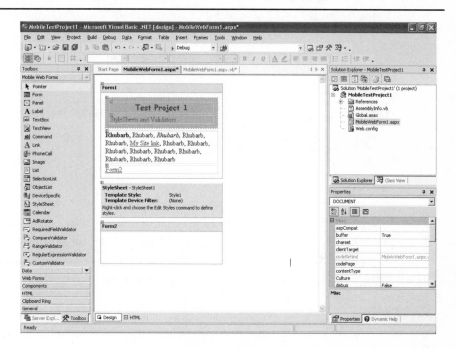

Note that the text in the TextView control has been formatted with the HTML tags that we added. We will return to this project and take a look at the validation controls.

## Pagination

One problem often faced by mobile developers is how to handle large quantities of text. It doesn't translate too well to a small screen or limited file sizes. The MIT offers a solution to this in the form of *pagination*. When the Pagination property of a form is set to True, large quantities of text will be automatically split over multiple forms. This is ideal in a situation in which you may have added a considerable amount of text to your TextView control. You can also alter the user interface (UI) of the paginated form by changing the link titles for navigating between the paginated forms (the defaults are Next and Previous).

Some controls, such as the List and ObjectList controls, offer additional pagination capabilities. The process is called *chunking*, and it limits the amount of processing of data to only the data required to populate the portion of a list being displayed on a paginated form. Refer to Microsoft documentation for more information on this technique.

## The Validation Controls

Return to MobileTestProject1 and add two TextBox controls to Form2. Add a Compare-Validator control and set its ErrorMessage property to **Values do not match**. Set the ControlToCompare property to TextBox1 and the ControlToValidate property to TextBox2.

Drop two more RequiredFieldValidators to Form2 and set their ErrorMessage properties to **Value in Field 1** and **Value in Field 2** respectively. Set their ControlToValidate properties to TextBox1 and TextBox2 respectively.

Add a Command control to the form. Set its Text property to Submit and double-click the control to enter Code Behind. Include the code contained in Listing 22.3.

---

**Listing 22.3**      **Code for the Command Control in MobileTestProject1**

```
Private Sub Command1_Click(ByVal sender As _
  System.Object, ByVal e As System.EventArgs) _
  Handles Command1.Click
        ActiveForm = Form2
  End Sub
```

---

Return to Design view and add a Link control to Form2. Set its text property to Form1 and its NavigateURL property to #Form1. The completed form will look like the form in Figure 22.14.

---

**FIGURE 22.14:**

The completed Form2 in MobileTestProject1

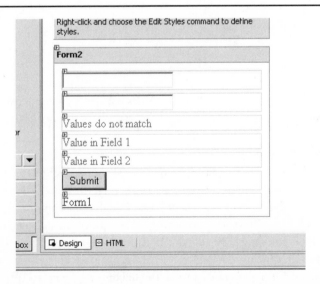

Compile and run the project. The Validator controls should throw up appropriate error messages when incorrect entries are made into the two TextBoxes and the Submit button/link is activated. Try by entering two different values into the fields or by leaving either of the two fields blank.

You can extend the power of the validation process by using a ValidationSummary control. Drop a copy of the control onto Form1 and set its FormToValidate property to Form2. Experiment with the project again but use the Link2 control on Form2 to process the validation. The ValidationSummary control provides a list of validation errors on Form1 and a back link to enable the user to continue trying until they get it right!

Additionally, you also have the RangeValidator, RegularExpressionValidator, and Custom-Validator controls to choose from and use where appropriate.

### Using the DeviceSpecific Control

Finally, we will add some simple device-specific rendering to the project. Add a DeviceSpecific control to Form1. Right-click the control and select Templating Options from the menu. In the Templating Options dialog box, click the Edit button. This opens the Applied Device Filters dialog box for DeviceSpecific1. Choose the is WML11 option from the drop-down list of available device filters. Click the Add to List button and click OK to return to the Templating Options dialog box. Choose is WML11 from the drop-down list of applied device filters and click the Close button, which closes all the dialog boxes.

Right-click the DeviceSpecific1 control again and choose the Edit Template ➢ Header and Footer Templates menu option. This opens a Header and Footer template area in Device-Specific1. Type **Hello WML User!** into the Header template as shown in Figure 22.15.

**FIGURE 22.15:**

Using the Device-Specific control

Save and compare the results in Openwave and Internet Explorer (as depicted in Figure 22.16). The "Hello WML User" message only appears in the Openwave emulator.

**FIGURE 22.16:**

The output of the
DeviceSpecific control
compared in Openwave
and IE (image courtesy
Openwave Systems Inc.)

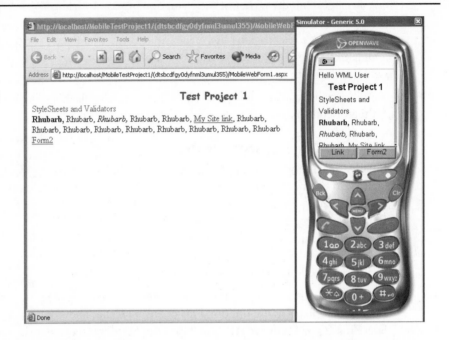

## Creating MobileTestProject2

In MobileTestProject2, we will experiment with the AdRotator and Image controls. Create a new mobile project in Visual Studio .NET and name it MobileTestProject2.

**TIP** In practice, the default naming option MobileWebApplication1, MobileWebApplication2, MobileWebApplication3, and so on, can be a little awkward. Visual Studio .NET simply continues to offer the next increment as an option (even if it is already used) until an available one is eventually found. This can become rather tedious. Using meaningful names for projects is a lot more effective.

Drag an instance of the Image and AdRotator controls to Form1. Before we set the properties of the controls, we will need to create an Images file (with the appropriate images) and an Advertisements file (XML) for the AdRotator.

Figure 22.17 illustrates the sequence of images that we have used for this project. They were all saved as GIF files in an Images subdirectory in the root web directory for the project. (C:\Inetpub\wwwroot\MobileTestProject2\Images if you have used the defaults.)

The feet images will form the AdRotator sequence and the letters are for the Image control. The feet images are saved as `foot1.gif`, `foot2.gif`, and so on, and the letters as `image.gif`. Note that we haven't allowed for devices that only support black-and-white images or WBMPs in this example. We will only use IE, which can support colored GIFs. (We used color images, although they appear in black-and-white in this book.)

To use the Image control, simply click the button with the ellipsis points in the ImageUrl property of the Image control to open the Select Image dialog box. Enter the relative path of the image file (`images/image.gif`) into the URL field and click OK. Additional properties such as AlternateText may also be set.

With the AdRotator control, you not only need to designate the images to be used, you also need to create an XML-based Advertisements file that lists various properties of the images, such as their location, relative weight, alternative images, and so on. A sample file listing the various criteria that can be used is provided in the Help documentation under the AdRotator heading. Listing 22.4 illustrates a simple rendition of this code applicable to this example.

**Listing 22.4**      **Ad1.xml for Use with the AdRotator Control**

```xml
<?xml version="1.0" ?>
<Advertisements>
    <Ad>
        <ImageUrl>Images/foot1.gif</ImageUrl>
        <NavigateUrl>The URL of the page to _
display</NavigateUrl>
        <AlternateText>Feet</AlternateText>
        <Keyword>Feet</Keyword>
        <Impressions>
            80
        </Impressions>
    </Ad>
    <Ad>
        <ImageUrl>Images/foot2.gif</ImageUrl>
        <NavigateUrl>The URL of the page to _
display</NavigateUrl>
        <AlternateText>Feet</AlternateText>
        <Keyword>Feet</Keyword>
        <Impressions>
            80
        </Impressions>
    </Ad>
    <Ad>
        <ImageUrl>Images/foot3.gif</ImageUrl>
```

```
        <NavigateUrl>The URL of the page to _
   display</NavigateUrl>
        <AlternateText>Feet</AlternateText>
        <Keyword>Feet</Keyword>
        <Impressions>
           80
        </Impressions>
      </Ad>
      <Ad>
        <ImageUrl>Images/foot4.gif</ImageUrl>
        <NavigateUrl>The URL of the page to _
   display</NavigateUrl>
        <AlternateText>Feet</AlternateText>
        <Keyword>Feet</Keyword>
        <Impressions>
           80
        </Impressions>
      </Ad>
      <Ad>
        <ImageUrl>Images/foot5.gif</ImageUrl>
        <NavigateUrl>The URL of the page to _
   display</NavigateUrl>
        <AlternateText>Feet</AlternateText>
        <Keyword>Feet</Keyword>
        <Impressions>
           80
        </Impressions>
      </Ad>
   </Advertisements>
```

Each set of Ad tags contains information relevant to one of the foot images. It includes the location of the image, the URL that the image is supposed to point to, a text option if the image cannot be displayed, a keyword for filtering advertisements, and weight index (Impressions tag) to determine which ads get greater exposure. (All the advertisements in this example have been given the equal weight of 80.) Not included in this example are options such as an alternative image to be shown on black-and-white-only browsers.

Copy the code to a text editor such as Notepad and save it as ad1.xml to the root of the project's web directory (C:\Inetpub\wwwroot\MobileTestProject2). Alternatively, select Add New Item from the Project menu in Visual Studio .NET. Select XML File from the Templates pane in the Add New Item dialog box, name the document ad1.xml, and click the Open button. A code window should now be opened for ad1.xml and the code from the listing can be added.

Once the advertisements file has been assembled, we can assign the AdvertisementFile property in the AdRotator control. Clicking the ellipsis points button for this property will open the Select XML File dialog box. Enter **ad1.xml** as a relative address into the URL field. There are other properties that we might also wish to set here, such as the KeyWordFilter. If we had a large range of images in the Advertisement file and only wished to show the feet, we could enter the keyword Feet into this property. We have used this keyword against all the foot images in ad1.xml.

Save and run the project in IE. If you continuously hit the Refresh button, the advertisement images should be cycled by the AdRotator control. The completed project is illustrated in Figure 22.18.

**FIGURE 22.18:**

MobileTestProject2 in
Visual Studio .NET
and IE

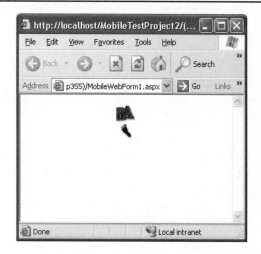

## Deploying with the MIT

Once projects have been assembled and completed using the Mobile Internet Toolkit, they can be deployed fairly easily on a web server running the latest version of the .NET Framework and with the MIT runtime controls installed.

If your site is also meant for larger-screen clients, it is quite simple to set up a redirect to pick up mobile clients and feed them the MIT-driven site. Microsoft provides an example of the type of script required in the documentation accompanying the MIT. We have reproduced this script in Listing 22.5.

**Listing 22.5**      **Redirection Code for Mobile clients (as supplied by Microsoft in MIT)**

```c#
<script runat="server" language="c#">

    public void Page_Load(Object sender, EventArgs e)
    {
        if (Request.Browser["IsMobileDevice"] == "true" )
        {
            Response.Redirect("MobileDefault.aspx");
        }
        else
        {
```

```
            Response.Redirect("DesktopDefault.aspx");
        }
    }

</script>
```

Note that there are some issues attached to using such a redirect. Many mobile devices (typically units using Nokia-based browsers) do not support cookies. By default, the `Web.config` file for mobile applications has cookie support turned off. (Session state is maintained by writing the session ID into the URL.) The <sessionState> tag is set to `cookieless="true"`. If you anticipate these types of devices accessing your site, you may have to consider setting the ASP.NET portions of the site to cookieless as well.

A second consideration is that many mobile devices (typically those using Openwave-based browsers) do not support relative addresses. URLs used in redirects and so forth need to have a full address. In mobile applications, the `Web.config` file has the following tag: `<httpRuntime useFullyQualifiedRedirectUrl="true" />`. This tag ensures that all URLs presented to the mobile device are fully qualified. Again, it may be necessary to set this tag in the ASP.NET application.

A performance issue that applies to all ASP.NET applications when deploying is the advantage to be gained from setting `debug="false"` in the <compilation> tag in `Web.config`.

It is important to remember that the MIT controls are all server-side controls and that all processing performed by applications created with the MIT occurs at the server. Essentially, mobile devices running these applications are operating as dumb terminals (although it is possible to include within your code client-side scripts that can be downloaded and executed on the client). When writing code at the ASPX page level, all the controls must have their `runat` attributes set to `server`.

It is also important to keep a close eye on file sizes generated by the application. (In particular, dynamically generated files can vary widely in size from one instance to the next.) File sizes can be checked using the compiler windows of emulators and SDKs such as Openwave or by using application tracing within ASP.NET.

Finally, Microsoft also produces two flavors of its Mobile Information Server that are optimized for delivering mobile applications and provide a mechanism for providing mobile support to Outlook and Exchange. The Mobile Information Server Enterprise Edition is for use within a corporate firewall, and the Carrier Edition is designed to be used by a wireless carrier outside the corporate firewall to provide a secure connection for customers running the Enterprise Edition.

## Building a Mobile Application for Accessing the Corporate Database

The purpose of this application is to demonstrate how we can access data using applications built with the MIT. We will also take a look at using forms-based security with this technology.

## Rationale

One of the areas in which mobile devices really shine is in providing instant access to the very latest information. This is particularly useful for consultants and sales representatives who need to spend considerable time outside the office and who have a considerable advantage if they have the very latest prices and availability of the items that they market.

Using the MIT, it is a relatively straightforward process to provide this level of connectivity for devices such as mobile phones or Pocket PCs that have access to the Internet. This type of application is very typical of the sort of development being undertaken by mobile developers today.

## Planning the Application

We will build the application using two mobile web pages. This is to accommodate the forms-based authentication, which requires a separate page to handle the authentication process.

We will use the Microsoft Access–based Northwind database as our data source. This gives us the opportunity to illustrate the use of a database management system (DBMS) other than SQL Server and the associated OleDbDataAdapters. For authentication, we can use the last name of the employee (LastName field) for user ID and their extension as a password (this saves us from redesigning the database, but it would hardly be an ideal setup for deployment in the wild).

**NOTE**    If you are using Windows XP and have kept up with all the security patches, you may find that IIS is no longer able to talk to the database (or any database for that matter). To fix this, you will need to alter the security permissions for Users (i.e., give them greater access rights than the default) on the `Samples` folder and the `Northwind.mdb` that holds the Northwind database (n `C:\Program Files\Microsoft Office\Office10\Samples`). If you are having difficulty altering security in Windows XP, refer to the tip about the Security tab in Windows XP.

**TIP**    The Security tab that we have all come to know and love in NT and 2000 is hidden by default in Windows XP. To make it visible, open a directory window and select Folder Options from the Tools menu. Select the View tab and uncheck the Use Simple File Sharing option at the bottom. This will restore the Security tab to the Properties dialog box for any file or directory.

## Building the Login Page

We will begin the project by creating the login page to which unauthorized users will be redirected to provide their login credentials. We create this page on a second MobileWebForm:

1. Open a new mobile web project and name it MyConnection.

2. Add a second MobileWebForm from the Project menu and name it `login.aspx`.

3. In Design view for `login.aspx`, expose the Data tools in the Toolbox.

4. Drag an OleDbDataAdapter to `login.aspx`. This opens the Data Adapter Configuration Wizard. Click Next.

5. From the Choose Your Data Connection screen, click the New Connection button.

6. In the Data Link Properties dialog box, establish a connection to the Northwind database with the following steps:

   **A.** Click the Provider tab and select the Microsoft Jet 4.0 OLE DB Provider option. Click Next.

   **B.** Under the Connection tab, enter the path to the Northwind database (typically `C:\Program Files\Microsoft Office\Office10\Samples\Northwind.mdb`).

   **C.** Check the connection with the Test Connection button and click OK to close the dialog box.

7. Back in the Data Adapter Configuration Wizard, the path for the connection should be visible. Click Next. Your Query Type should be limited to SQL statements. Click Next again.

8. Click the Query Builder button. Set up the SQL statement on the Employees table as illustrated in Figure 22.19. Click OK to close the Query Builder dialog box. It may also be worth opening Advanced Options and deselecting the two available items in there because we will not need them for this part of the project.

**FIGURE 22.19:**

Using the Query Builder

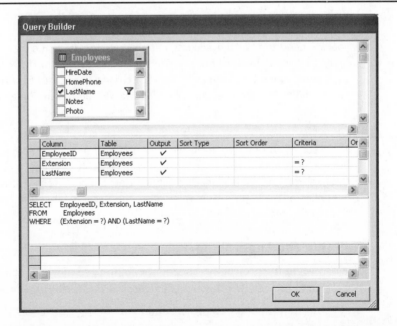

9. Click through the rest of the Data Adapter Configuration Wizard and exit it by clicking the Finish button.

10. In Design view, right-click the OleDbDataAdapter1 and select Generate Dataset from the menu. Create DataSet1, which should now appear as DataSet11 in the designer.

11. Drag a second Form control to login.aspx and set the two forms up with the controls and properties specified as follows:

| Form | Control | Property | Value |
|------|---------|----------|-------|
| Form1 | | Title | MyConnection—Login |
| | Label1 | StyleReference | title |
| | | Text | MyConnection |
| | Label2 | Text | Login Page |
| | Label3 | Text | Enter User Name: |
| | TextBox1 | Text | <empty> |
| | Label4 | Text | Enter Password: |
| | TextBox2 | Text | <empty> |
| | | MaxLength | 10 |
| | | Password | True |
| | | Size | 10 |
| | Command1 | Text | Login |
| | | SoftKeyLabel | Login |
| Form2 | | Title | MyConnection—Error |
| | Label5 | StyleReference | title |
| | | Text | MyConnection |
| | TextView1 | Text | <empty> |
| | Link1 | Text | Login |
| | | SoftKeyLabel | Login |
| | | NavigateURL | #Form1 |

The completed forms should look like the form in Figure 22.20.

Note that we have made use of the SoftKeyLabel and Title properties. These will be rendered only on the devices that support these attributes. For example, you will see the title of the Form controls in IE but not in the Openwave browser. However, mobile devices such as Openwave have buttons that can be dynamically allocated functionality, i.e., *soft* keys.

Layout of the `login`
`.aspx` page for the
MyConnection
application

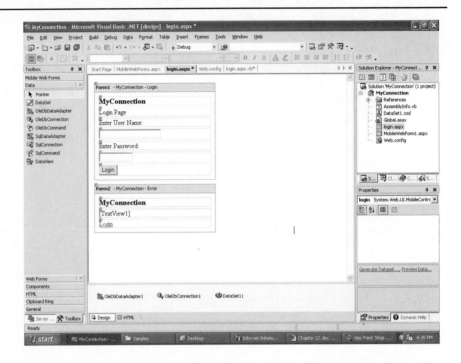

**WARNING**   The SoftKeyLabel property only renders the first five letters of whatever text it holds.

Code for this page will be entered directly into the ASPX page in HTML view. The Mobile-FormsAuthentication object that we will be using is only supported in HTML view. Switch to HTML view and complete the code as shown in Listing 22.6. Much of this code will be auto-generated, but you will need to add the code that appears between the opening and closing <script> tags and add onclick="Command1_Click" to the tag for the Command1 control. You also need to add the following two additional directives to the top of the page:

```
<%@ Import Namespace="System.Web.Mobile" %>
<%@ Import Namespace="System.Web.Security" %>
```

**Listing 22.6**   **Full ASPX Code for *login.aspx***

```
<%@ Page Language="vb" AutoEventWireup="false" _
  Codebehind="login.aspx.vb" _
  Inherits="MyConnection.login" debug="True"%>
<%@ Register TagPrefix="mobile" _
  Namespace="System.Web.UI.MobileControls" _
```

```
Assembly="System.Web.Mobile, Version=1.0.3300.0, _
Culture=neutral, PublicKeyToken=b03f5f7f11d50a3a" %>
<%@ Import Namespace="System.Web.Mobile" %>
<%@ Import Namespace="System.Web.Security" %>
<meta content="Microsoft Visual Studio.NET 7.0" _
name="GENERATOR">
<meta content="Visual Basic 7.0" name="CODE_LANGUAGE">
<meta content="http://schemas.microsoft.com/ _
Mobile/Page" name="vs_targetSchema">
<script id="Script1" runat="server">
   Private Sub Command1_Click(sender As System.Object, _
e As System.EventArgs)
      OleDbDataAdapter1.SelectCommand.Parameters _
("LastName").Value = TextBox1.Text
        OleDbDataAdapter1.SelectCommand.Parameters _
("Extension").Value = TextBox2.Text

      Try
       OleDbDataAdapter1.Fill(DataSet11, _
"Employees")
        If DataSet11.Tables("Employees").Rows.Count _
= 0 Then
          ActiveForm = Form2
          TextView1.Text = "Sorry, either your _
password or user name was incorrect. Please enter your _
details again."
        Else
          Dim user_id As String = _
DataSet11.Tables("Employees").Rows(0).Item("EmployeeID")
          MobileFormsAuthentication.RedirectFromLoginPage _
(user_id, False)
        End If
      Catch
       ActiveForm = Form2
       TextView1.Text = "Sorry, the server is _
temporarily unavailable. Please try again."
      End Try
   End Sub
</script>
<body Xmlns:mobile="http://schemas.microsoft.com/ _
Mobile/WebForm">
   <mobile:form id="Form1" title="MyConnection - Login" _
runat="server">
      <mobile:Label id="Label1" runat="server" _
StyleReference="title">MyConnection</mobile:Label>
      <mobile:Label id="Label2" runat="server">Login _
Page</mobile:Label>
      <mobile:Label id="Label3" runat="server"> _
Enter User Name:</mobile:Label>
      <mobile:TextBox id="TextBox1" _
runat="server"></mobile:TextBox>
      <mobile:Label id="Label4" runat="server"> _
```

```
Enter Password:</mobile:Label>
      <mobile:TextBox id="TextBox2" runat="server" _
Size="10" Password="True" MaxLength="10"></mobile:TextBox>
      <mobile:Command id="Command1" _
onclick="Command1_Click" runat="server" _
SoftkeyLabel="Login">Login</mobile:Command>
    </mobile:form>
    <mobile:form id="Form2" title="MyConnection - Error" _
runat="server">
      <mobile:Label id="Label5" runat="server" _
StyleReference="title">MyConnection</mobile:Label>
      <mobile:TextView id="TextView1" _
runat="server"></mobile:TextView>
      <mobile:Link id="Link1" runat="server" _
SoftkeyLabel="Login" _
NavigateUrl="#Form1">Login</mobile:Link>
    </mobile:form>
</body>
```

Quickly running through the mechanics of this code, we will look at our main addition in Script1. This script sets the parameters we identified in our SQL statement in OleDbData-Adapter1 with the values entered in the two TextBoxes. We then make use of the new structured exception handling capabilities of Visual Basic .NET to introduce a Try...Catch statement that directs the user to an error message if for any reason our server is unable to process their request.

We then fill the DataSet with information returned by our parameterized SQL statement. (Note that we could have used a DataReader here and gained a bit of a performance boost.) If the response is null, then the user is directed to a request to resubmit their credentials by the first part of the If...Then...Else statement. If their credentials are confirmed, the Mobile-FormsAuthentication object redirects them back to MobileWebForm1. We have also included the EmployeeID in this redirect so that we can easily identify the user later in the application.

Once this code has been completed, we will also need to make some adjustments to the Web.config file. The purpose of these changes is to automatically direct an unauthorized user to the login page. We need to set the authentication mode to Forms and deny access to unauthorized users.

Open the Web.config file (double-click the file in the Solution Explorer) and locate the <authorization> and <authentication> tags. Change them to match the tags in Listing 22.7.

**Listing 22.7    Changes to the *Web.config* file for the MyConnection Application**

```
<authentication mode="Forms" />

<authorization>
      <deny users="?" />
</authorization>
```

Finally, right-click on the `MobileWebForm1.aspx` listing in the Solution Explorer and click the Set as Start Page option. This identifies `MobileWebForm1.aspx` as `Default.aspx`, the default ASPX page in the application. This is important because MobileFormsAuthentication redirects back to `Default.aspx` once the user has been authenticated.

---

**TIP**    When testing the login process in IE, be aware that IE will cache user credentials for a period of time, which can be a bit of a hassle when you're trying to repeatedly test the login process after a user has been authorized. There are various ways around this; the simplest is to make a minor change (such as add or delete an additional Label control) between each test.

## Building the MobileWebForm1

We will need to set up MobileWebForm1 with five OleDbDataAdapters and two DataSets. Set up the DataAdapters connected to the Northwind database with SQL statements as follows (by using DataSets, we keep the code very simple and leave the option open for some point in the future when we might make the application more interactive by adding update and delete facilities to it):

| OleDbDataAdapter | Table(s) | SQL Statement |
| --- | --- | --- |
| OleDbDataAdapter1 | Products, Categories | `SELECT Products.ProductID, Products.ProductName, Products.QuantityPerUnit, Products.UnitPrice, Products.UnitsInStock, Products.UnitsOnOrder, Products.CategoryID, Products.Discontinued, Categories.CategoryID AS Expr1, Categories.CategoryName, Categories.Description FROM Products INNER JOIN Categories ON Products.CategoryID = Categories.CategoryID` |
| OleDbDataAdapter2 | Employees | `SELECT EmployeeID, FirstName FROM Employees WHERE (EmployeeID = ?)` |
| OleDbDataAdapter3 | Categories | `SELECT DISTINCT CategoryID, CategoryName FROM Categories` |

| OleDbDataAdapter | Table(s) | SQL Statement |
| --- | --- | --- |
| OleDbDataAdapter4 | Products, Categories | `SELECT Products.CategoryID, Products.ProductID, Products.Discontinued, Products.ProductName, Products.QuantityPerUnit, Products.UnitPrice, Products.UnitsInStock, Products.UnitsOnOrder, Categories.CategoryID AS Expr1, Categories.CategoryName, Categories.Description FROM Products INNER JOIN Categories ON Products.CategoryID = Categories.CategoryID WHERE (Products.CategoryID = ?)` |
| OleDbDataAdapter5 | Products, Categories | `SELECT Products.CategoryID, Products.Discontinued, Products.ProductID, Products.ProductName, Products.QuantityPerUnit, Products.UnitPrice, Products.UnitsInStock, Products.UnitsOnOrder, Categories.CategoryID AS Expr1, Categories.CategoryName, Categories.Description FROM Products INNER JOIN Categories ON Products.CategoryID = Categories.CategoryID WHERE (Products.ProductName LIKE ?)` |

OleDbDataAdapter1 locates all the products for use with the All Products Command control. OleDbDataAdapter4 identifies products by the categories (for use with the categories list). OleDbDataAdpter5 provides a search facility based on all or part of a word. OleDbData-Adpter2 identifies the employee's first name based on their ID, and OleDbDataAdapter3 identifies the individual product categories.

For each DataAdapter, generate a table in DataSet21 or DataSet31 by following the defaults, according to the following list of OleDbDataAdapter settings:

- OleDbDataAdapter1 (Products, DataSet31)
- OleDbDataAdapter2 (Employees, DataSet21)
- OleDbDataAdapter3 (Categories, DataSet21)

- OleDbDataAdapter4 (Products, DataSet31)
- OleDbDataAdapter5 (Products, DataSet31)

Set up MobileWebForm1 with the controls and properties listed here (you will need three Form controls):

| Form | Control | Property | Value |
| --- | --- | --- | --- |
| Form1 | | Title | MyConnection |
| | Label1 | StyleReference | title |
| | | Text | MyConnection |
| | Label2 | Text | <empty> |
| | Label3 | Text | Available categories are: |
| | List1 | DataMember | Categories |
| | | DataSource | DataSet21 |
| | | DataTextField | CategoryName |
| | | DataValueField | CategoryID |
| | Label4 | Text | Search for a product: |
| | TextBox1 | Text | <empty> |
| | Command1 | Text | Click to Search |
| | | SoftKeyLabel | Look |
| | Command2 | Text | All Products |
| | | SoftKeyLabel | Items |
| | Command3 | Text | Logout |
| | | SoftKeyLabel | Exit |
| Form2 | | Title | Logout Confirm |
| | Label5 | StyleReference | title |
| | | Text | MyConnection—Logout |
| | Label6 | Text | Logout confirmed |
| | Label7 | Text | <empty> |
| Form3 | | Title | MyConnection—Products |
| | | Pagination | True |
| | Label8 | StyleReference | title |
| | | Text | MyConnection—Products |

| Form | Control | Property | Value |
|------|---------|----------|-------|
| | Link1 | Text | Home |
| | | SoftKeyLabel | Home |
| | | NavigateURL | #Form1 |
| | Label9 | Text | <empty> |
| | ObjectList1 | DataMember | Products |
| | | DataSource | DataSet31 |
| | | LabelField | ProductName |
| | | TableFields | ProductName;UnitPrice; QuantityPerUnit;UnitsInStock; |
| | Link2 | Text | Home |
| | | SoftKeyLabel | Home |
| | | NavigateURL | #Form1 |

The completed forms are shown in Figures 22.21 and 22.22.

**FIGURE 22.21:**

Search form in the MyConnection application

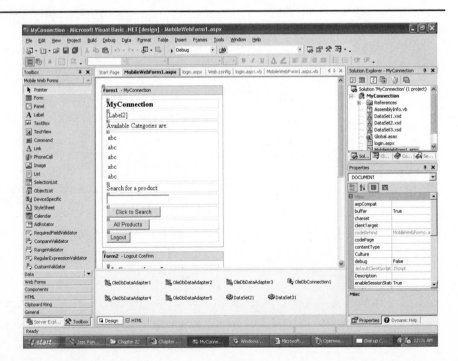

**FIGURE 22.22:**

Logout and search
results forms in the
MyConnection
application

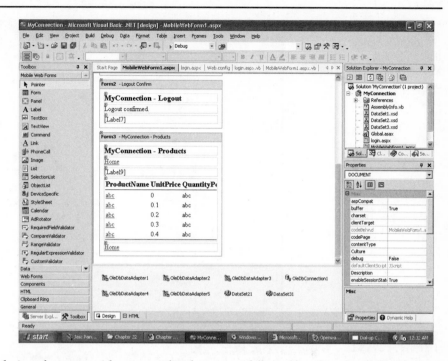

Form1 is designed to open with a personalized greeting, followed by a list of available product categories. Clicking any of the categories within the list will open Form3 and expose the products attached to that category. The user also has a search option based on all or part of a word and can also identify all products if necessary.

Once the products are listed in Form3, the user can select a product for a greater range of information. In browsers capable of supporting it (such as IE), we also have a tabular presentation based on the options chosen in the TableFields property of the ObjectList control.

When setting up the TableFields property for the ObjectList, the chosen fields may be typed directly in or more easily added from the ObjectList Properties dialog box opened by clicking the button with ellipsis points in the TableFields property. This dialog box is shown in Figure 22.23. Choose from the Available Fields box, use the arrows to move them into the Selected Fields box, and then click OK.

We have used pagination on Form3 to help display the ObjectList when returning large numbers of products. We have also placed two return links on this form, one at the top and the other at the bottom to assist with navigation options when paginating a long list. Once a user chooses to log out, they are directed to Form2, which gives a personalized message.

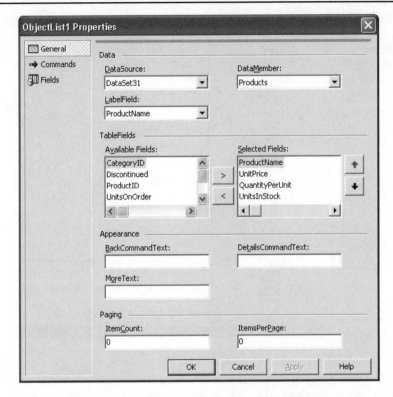

Some additional code will need to be added into HTML view of the ASPX page. The purpose of this code is to provide a logout facility. We will need to add the following script to the page:

```
<script id="Script1" runat="Server">
    Sub Command3_Click(o as Object, e as EventArgs)
        MobileFormsAuthentication.SignOut
        ActiveForm = Form2
    End Sub
</script>
```

Within the tag for the Command3 control, add the onclick attribute to read as follows:

```
<mobile:Command id="Command3" onclick="Command3_Click" _
  runat="server" _
  SoftkeyLabel="Logout">Logout</mobile:Command>
```

As with login.aspx, we also need to add the following two additional directives to the top of the page:

```
<%@ Import Namespace="System.Web.Mobile" %>
<%@ Import Namespace="System.Web.Security" %>
```

The full code for the ASPX page is reproduced in Listing 22.8.

---

○→ **Listing 22.8**    **Full ASPX Code for MobileWebForm1 in the MyConnection Application**

```
<%@ Register TagPrefix="mobile" _
Namespace="System.Web.UI.MobileControls" _
Assembly="System.Web.Mobile, Version=1.0.3300.0, _
Culture=neutral, PublicKeyToken=b03f5f7f11d50a3a" %>
<%@ Import Namespace="System.Web.Mobile" %>
<%@ Import Namespace="System.Web.Security" %>
<meta content="Microsoft Visual Studio.NET 7.0" _
 name="GENERATOR">
<meta content="Visual Basic 7.0" name="CODE_LANGUAGE">
<meta content="http://schemas.microsoft.com/ _
Mobile/Page" name="vs_targetSchema">
<script id="Script1" runat="Server">
    Sub Command3_Click(o as Object, e as EventArgs)
        MobileFormsAuthentication.SignOut
        ActiveForm = Form2
    End Sub
</script>
<body Xmlns:mobile="http://schemas.microsoft.com/ _
Mobile/WebForm">
    <mobile:form id="Form1" title="MyConnection" _
 runat="server">
        <mobile:Label id="Label1" runat="server" _
 StyleReference="title">MyConnection</mobile:Label>
        <mobile:Label id="Label2" _
runat="server"></mobile:Label>
        <mobile:Label id="Label3" runat="server"> _
Available Categories are:</mobile:Label>
        <mobile:List id=List1 runat="server" _
 DataSource="<%# DataSet21 %>" DataMember="Categories" _
 DataTextField="CategoryName" _
 DataValueField="CategoryID">
        </mobile:List>
        <mobile:Label id="Label4" runat="server"> _
Search for a product:</mobile:Label>
        <mobile:TextBox id="TextBox1" _
runat="server"></mobile:TextBox>
        <mobile:Command id="Command1" runat="server" _
SoftkeyLabel="Look">Click to Search</mobile:Command>
        <mobile:Command id="Command2" runat="server" _
SoftkeyLabel="Items">All Products</mobile:Command>
        <mobile:Command id="Command3" _
onclick="Command3_Click" runat="server" _
SoftkeyLabel="Logout">Logout</mobile:Command>
    </mobile:form>
    <mobile:form id="Form2" title="Logout Confirm" _
runat="server">
        <mobile:Label id="Label5" runat="server" _
 StyleReference="title"> _
MyConnection - Logout</mobile:Label>
        <mobile:Label id="Label6" runat="server"> _
```

```
Logout confirmed.</mobile:Label>
      <mobile:Label id="Label7" runat="server"> _
</mobile:Label>
   </mobile:form>
   <mobile:form id="Form3" title="MyConnection - _
 Products" runat="server" Paginate="True">
      <mobile:Label id="Label8" runat="server" _
 StyleReference="title"> _
MyConnection - Products</mobile:Label>
      <mobile:Link id="Link1" runat="server" _
 SoftkeyLabel="Home" _
 NavigateUrl="#Form1">Home</mobile:Link>
      <mobile:Label id="Label9" runat="server"> _
</mobile:Label>
      <mobile:ObjectList id=ObjectList1 runat="server" _
 CommandStyle-StyleReference="subcommand" LabelStyle-
StyleReference="title" DataSource="<%# DataSet31 %>" _
 DataMember="Products" LabelField="ProductName" _
 TableFields="ProductName;UnitPrice;QuantityPerUnit; _
UnitsInStock;">
      </mobile:ObjectList>
      <mobile:Link id="Link2" runat="server" _
 SoftkeyLabel="Home" _
 NavigateUrl="#Form1">Home</mobile:Link>
   </mobile:form>
</body>
```

Once the ASPX page has been set up and the additional code added, switch to Code Behind and add the code from Listing 22.9.

## Listing 22.9     The Code Behind for the MyConnection Application

```
Private Sub Page_Load(ByVal sender As System.Object, _
  ByVal e As System.EventArgs) Handles MyBase.Load
      OleDbDataAdapter2.SelectCommand.Parameters _
("EmployeeID").Value = User.Identity.Name
      OleDbDataAdapter2.Fill(DataSet21, "Employees")
      Session("user_name") = _
DataSet21.Tables("Employees").Rows(0).Item("FirstName")
      Label2.Text = "Hello " & Session("user_name")
   End Sub

   Private Sub Form1_Activate(ByVal sender As _
System.Object, ByVal e As System.EventArgs) _
Handles Form1.Activate
      OleDbDataAdapter3.Fill(DataSet21)
      List1.DataBind()
   End Sub

   Private Sub Form2_Activate(ByVal sender As _
System.Object, ByVal e As System.EventArgs) _
```

```
Handles Form2.Activate
        Label7.Text = "Goodbye " & Session("user_name")
    End Sub

    Private Sub Command1_Click(ByVal sender As _
System.Object, ByVal e As System.EventArgs) Handles _
Command1.Click
        OleDbDataAdapter5.SelectCommand.Parameters _
("ProductName").Value = TextBox1.Text & "%"
        OleDbDataAdapter5.Fill(DataSet31, "Products")
        If DataSet31.Tables("Products").Rows.Count > 0 Then
            ObjectList1.DataBind()
            Label9.Visible = True
            Label9.Text = "Search Criteria was: " & _
TextBox1.Text
        Else
            ObjectList1.Fields.Clear()
            Label9.Visible = True
            Label9.Text = "Sorry, no products matching _
your criteria are listed."
        End If
        ActiveForm = Form3

    End Sub

    Private Sub Command2_Click(ByVal sender As _
System.Object, ByVal e As System.EventArgs) Handles _
Command2.Click
        OleDbDataAdapter1.Fill(DataSet31, "Products")
        ObjectList1.DataBind()
        Label9.Text = ""
        Label9.Visible = False
        ActiveForm = Form3
    End Sub

    Private Sub List1_ItemCommand(ByVal sender As _
System.Object, ByVal e As _
System.Web.UI.MobileControls.ListCommandEventArgs) _
Handles List1.ItemCommand
        Session("Category") = e.ListItem.Value
        OleDbDataAdapter4.SelectCommand.Parameters _
("CategoryID").Value = Session("Category")
        OleDbDataAdapter4.Fill(DataSet31, "Products")
        ObjectList1.DataBind()
        Label9.Visible = True
        Label9.Text = "Category: " & e.ListItem.Text
        ActiveForm = Form3
    End Sub
End Class
```

In the Page_Load subroutine, we identify the user from their EmployeeID contained in user.identity.name and use it to retrieve their first name from the database. This allows us to personalize the application. A session variable is created to hold the user's name. We could take this further and structure the application to provide services that are directly relevant to their employment profile within the organization.

When Form1 is activated, the List1 control is loaded with the current list of product categories. The Form2_Activate code simply personalizes the logout message as the user quits the application.

The code in Command1_Click is designed to return the TextBox1 entry as the search criteria in the SQL statement for OleDbDataAdapter5. The If…Then statement determines whether there were any products matching the request and produces an appropriate message if not. Any messages (including the search criteria itself) are reported in Label9.

Command2_Click returns the full list of products in the database. It also disables any previous search criteria messages that might still be hanging around in Label9.

The code in List1_ItemCommand sets up the List1 items as links that forward the user to Form3. It also inserts an appropriate message concerning the category chosen in Label9 and returns the products belonging to the chosen category from the database.

Once the coding is complete, compile and run the application. Compare the different renderings of the ObjectList in IE as opposed to Openwave. Figure 22.24 illustrates how the application should look running in Openwave.

**FIGURE 22.24:**

MyConnection running in Openwave (image courtesy Openwave Systems Inc.)

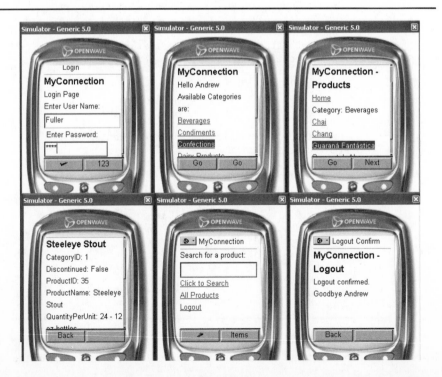

# Summary

The MyConnection project is a simple demonstration of the power and flexibility of designing mobile applications with the MIT. There are many ways you could easily extend this project, some of which we have touched on in the text. We have explored only some of the more obvious features of the MIT in this chapter. Features of the MIT such as Device Capabilities enable developers to have an extraordinary amount of granular control over content and presentation with their applications and sites.

The sheer advantage of using the MIT is that it allows developers to focus on the job of developing and building elegant solutions without getting bogged down in all the compatibility issues that plague the mobile world. It also enables developers to work mainly within their language of choice.

The extensibility of the MIT enables it to keep pace with the constant change occurring in the mobile space. New device adapters can be easily incorporated into its framework and additional features can be included to cater to existing devices as they are upgraded.

However, the MIT does not remove the necessity of having a sound understanding of the medium. Good design principles are still paramount when designing for the mobile world, and a sound understanding of the various devices likely to be accessing a site can assist in optimizing user experience and avoiding any pitfalls.

# Getting Started with SQL Server 2000

**S** QL Server 2000 offers a wide range of features that make it attractive as an enterprise-level database management system. It combines performance with ease of use. It is widely used on Microsoft-based systems, and from a developer's perspective, it is important to understand it. This is particularly true if you are developing with .NET because the specific optimizations included in the .NET Framework for SQL Server 2000 make the two technologies a powerful combination.

As a developer, it is most likely that you will be installing and using the Developer Edition of the product. However, it also pays to be familiar with the other releases because they may be required for the production versions of your software. The purpose of this appendix is to introduce the range of features available with SQL Server 2000 and to assist you in choosing an appropriate edition to meet your needs. We will also cover areas such as licensing and system requirements.

## SQL Server 2000 Editions

SQL Server 2000 ships in a number of different flavors:

- SQL Server 2000 Enterprise Edition
- SQL Server 2000 Standard Edition
- SQL Server 2000 Personal Edition
- SQL Server 2000 Developer Edition
- SQL Server 2000 Desktop Engine Edition
- SQL Server 2000 Windows CE Edition
- SQL Server 2000 Evaluation Edition

The Enterprise Edition includes everything available for SQL Server. Not only does it ship with all the bells and whistles, it provides a greater degree of scalability than the other versions do. It can support up to 64GB of memory and up to 32 processors when it is installed on a Windows 2000 Datacenter Server. Its memory and processor support diminishes for other Windows versions (4GB and 4 processors on NT Server) and it is capable of being run only on server versions of NT and 2000.

The Standard Edition has most of the features the Enterprise Edition has but lacks its scalability. Its maximum support is for 2GB of memory and 4 processors. As with the Enterprise Edition, it can run only on server versions of NT and 2000.

The Personal Edition will run on any Windows OS from 98 up. It contains nearly all the features of the Standard Edition with the following exceptions: support for a maximum of 2 processors, reduced performance when handling multiple simultaneous T-SQL commands, and limited replication capabilities. Further limitations apply when running the Personal

Edition in the Windows 98 and Windows ME environments (single processor only and Analysis Services are not available). The Personal Edition is designed for installation on computers such as laptops, on which a user may need access to a local and disconnected copy of a database. It ships as part of the Standard and Enterprise Editions of SQL Server 2000 and cannot be purchased separately.

The Developer Edition has all the features and functionality of the Enterprise Edition but is also capable of being run on Windows 2000 Professional and NT Workstation. However, you are not licensed to distribute production databases from the Developer Edition.

The Desktop Engine Edition is a redistributable version of the database engine designed for distribution with applications that require built-in database support. It has the same features as the Personal Edition (with the exception of any administrative capability). It ships with the Enterprise and Developer versions of SQL Server 2000.

The Windows CE Edition is a scaled-down, small-footprint version designed to provide SQL Server 2000 support for Windows CE–based devices. It can replicate with full versions of SQL Server 2000 to support data synchronization between server versions of the database and CE devices.

SQL Server Evaluation Edition is a full-featured version of SQL Server 2000 that has a 120-day operational life before it ceases to function. It is freely available as a download from the Microsoft website (and appears quite regularly on CD in trade show bags at Microsoft-sponsored events).

Upgrade paths exist between the various editions of SQL Server 2000. Essentially, you can go from Standard to Enterprise or Personal/Desktop Engine to Standard or Enterprise (given that you have paid the upgrade price, of course).

Choosing the appropriate version of SQL Server 2000 will obviously depend on the circumstances under which it will be run. From a developer's perspective, the Developer Edition is a logical choice. It is significantly cheaper than Enterprise but has the same feature set. However, when deploying databases built with SQL Server, you will need to choose the appropriate versions based on the environment in which the database will be run, the design of the database, and cost. There is a significant cost difference between the Standard Edition and the Enterprise Edition (the most likely choices for a commercial distribution), and you will need to weigh carefully the justification and necessity of going with the more expensive product. This in turn has to be considered before development commences because you don't want to be stuck with an Enterprise-level application that has to run on the Standard Edition. Additionally, most modern enterprises will likely need to run multiple editions of the product. In particular, as many organizations begin to look to mobile solutions on handheld devices, the Windows CE Edition becomes an important part of the package.

Another consideration to make when deploying a solution is what type of licensing model to follow. In the next section, we will look briefly at the licensing options available.

## SQL Server 2000 Licensing

Two forms of licensing are available for SQL Server 2000: the familiar CAL (Client Access License) approach and Processor licensing. These apply to the Enterprise and Standard editions of the product. They may also apply indirectly to the Personal, CE, and Desktop Engine versions in circumstances in which they are connected to a server version of SQL Server 2000. It's worth checking the licensing agreements for these products because their licensing can depend on the circumstances under which they are being used.

The CAL form of licensing involves the purchase of a server license for the machine running SQL Server plus a separate CAL for each client accessing the program. Normally, a set number of CALs are purchased as part of the server license and additional CALs can be purchased separately.

Processor licensing is useful (or applicable) when the number of clients is particularly large or unknown. This includes large enterprise and web server situations. A single license is purchased for each CPU running on the machine on which SQL Server 2000 is installed. This covers all forms of access and no additional licensing is required.

Pricing obviously varies, depending on what country you are in and Microsoft's current pricing policy. Generally, however, in small to medium concerns in which the number of clients is known and database access is limited to the corporate side of the firewall, the CAL approach is the most economical. However, if you're a larger concern with hundreds or thousands of clients and/or you make your database available over the Internet, then the per-processor option becomes attractive.

Before making the decision, it is worth obtaining quotes for both options and doing the math to determine when the per-processor option becomes more economical. Remember that this value will also depend on whether you are running the Enterprise Edition or the Standard Edition of SQL Server 2000. Licensing can also vary if you are running cluster servers. Again, it is worth checking the fine print because there are some circumstances in which you will not have to license every processor in a cluster setup.

## System Requirements

Hardware and software requirements vary according to the version of SQL Server 2000 you are using. Essentially, for the Enterprise and Standard editions, if your machine is capable of running Windows 2000 Server with any level of respectability, it can also run SQL Server 2000. This is particularly true for the CPU (the minimum SQL Server requirement is a P166 processor). However, there are some things that you may need to consider, particularly if you are installing on to a system that is not exactly brand-new.

## RAM

Databases like lots of memory, so it is always worth investing in extra RAM if you are planning a SQL Server 2000 installation. Having your server equipped with at least a gigabyte of RAM is not an expensive option these days and is well worth the investment in terms of performance and peace of mind. (The minimum specification recommended by Microsoft is 64MB of RAM for the Standard Edition, and for the Enterprise Edition, we recommend nothing less than 512MB on a Windows 2000 Server equipped with SQL Server.) Requirements for other versions are considerably less (particularly the CE version), but if you are planning on running the Developer Edition in conjunction with Visual Studio .NET, we think 512MB RAM is a comfortable amount to work with.

## Hard Drive

In terms of hard drive requirements, a full installation of SQL Server won't leave much change out of 500MB. This can vary according to individual system specifications, and it is possible to pare the install down to less than half of this by only installing absolute essentials. (The desktop engine itself is only 44MB.) On top of your installation, you will need whatever space that actual data component of your database contributes.

Additionally, you might consider a Redundant Array of Independent Disks (RAID array) for improved performance and reliability of your database. A hardware-based RAID controller coupled with fast Small Computer System Interface (SCSI) drives may add significant dollars to the cost of your server, but they also add considerable performance and peace of mind. When looking at this solution, it is also worth investing in hot swappable drives, particularly if downtime has to be kept to an absolute minimum. With this sort of setup, it takes as long to fix a machine with a failed hard drive as it does to pull the failed drive out of the slot in the front of the machine and put the new one in. If you are running a RAID-5 setup, the new disk simply picks up where the old one left off without any further intervention on your part. The only disadvantage of this setup (apart from expense) is that SCSI drives tend to be smaller (storage-wise) than their IDE counterparts and the redundancy aspects of a RAID array mean that you lose even more of your total memory space (around a third for RAID-5). Other RAID configurations exist, configurations that offer better overall performance and greater or lesser fault tolerance. RAID-10 is probably the best overall but is expensive in terms of hard drives. Generally, for every situation there is a RAID configuration that is best suited to it, and these are not always the most expensive options.

## Software

Earlier in this appendix we covered the various OS requirements for the individual editions of SQL Server 2000. SQL Server 2000 is not supported on NT Terminal Server, and you must be running at least Service Pack 5 on any NT machines on which the product is installed.

Additionally, if you are running the Personal Edition on a Windows 98 machine without a network card, you will need to be running Windows 98 SE. Internet Explorer 5.0 or above is required for all installations, and TCP/IP must be enabled.

From a client perspective, SQL Server 2000 supports any Microsoft operating system from Windows 95 up. Additionally, Apple Macintosh, OS2, and Unix clients are supported as long as they are compliant with the Open Database Connectivity standard. (Apple Macintosh, OS2, and Unix clients do not, however, support SQL Server graphical tools.)

## SQL Server 2000 Components

SQL Server 2000 is not a single application, nor is it even just a database with a few administration tools. It is designed to be a full enterprise-level database management system, and consequently, it is made up of a number of distinct components. The nature and design of the system that you are running will determine which components you will run. The two principal components for an enterprise environment are the SQL Server 2000 Database Engine and the SQL Server 2000 Analysis Services. However, there are a number of other key components and services provided by the package.

### Database Engine

The SQL Server Database Engine is the core of the SQL Server package. It provides the level of functionality that one would expect for a modern enterprise-level, industrial-strength database. It is a relational database engine that stores data in a table structure. Table columns represent database fields and rows are used to hold data. Physically, data is stored in 8KB *pages*. A collection of eight pages is called an *extent*. Transactions are managed using a form of Structured Query Language (SQL) known as Transact-SQL (or T-SQL). Additionally, SQL Server 2000 can read, write, and store data in XML format.

The database engine itself is highly scalable and very fast. The Enterprise Edition supports server clusters that provide the scope for extremely large databases and bulletproof failsafe mechanisms (if one server goes down, the others can pick up the slack). Further performance enhancements can be introduced with careful management of indexing. Most administrative tasks can now be carried out without having to stop and restart service.

Login security can be managed at the database level or through Windows authentication. Secure Sockets Layer (SSL) encryption can be employed to secure data as it transfers between client applications and the database.

Data integrity can be enforced at the database end using defined rules and other data integrity constraints. A collection of GUI tools and wizards make for relatively easy administration of the database.

## Analysis Services

The sheer volume and breadth of data stored by many organizations these days has resulted in a change in the way data is stored and accessed. This has given rise to so-called data warehousing. Online Analytical Processing (OLAP) systems are used to analyze information stored in these warehouses to target important information and identify trends. The process of identifying key factors and trends from a data collection is known as *data mining*.

SQL Server 2000 provides the tools for building and maintaining data warehouses. It also provides the tools for carrying out various levels of analysis using OLAP technology provided by SQL Server 2000 Analysis Services. Analysis Services require a separate install in the SQL Server 2000 installation procedure. They are not installed by default.

Once installed, they can be accessed via the `Analysis Services` subfolder in the Microsoft SQL Server Start menu items. Using the Analysis Manager out of Analysis Services, you can connect to a SQL Server 2000 database containing a data warehouse. *Data cubes* can be defined on this data to enable data mining. Queries are handled using Multidimensional Expressions (MDX), which is a query language similar in syntax to SQL. Figure A.1 shows the MDX Sample Application running a sample MDX query.

**FIGURE A.1:**

The MDX Sample Application running a sample MDX query

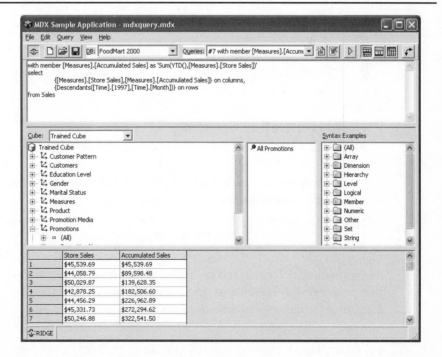

A detailed discussion of Analysis Services is beyond the scope of this book, but it offers a powerful set of tools for analyzing data and identifying and summarizing trends. Figure A.2 shows the Analysis Manager snap-in with the sample FoodMart database that ships with it.

**FIGURE A.2:**

The Analysis Services Manager

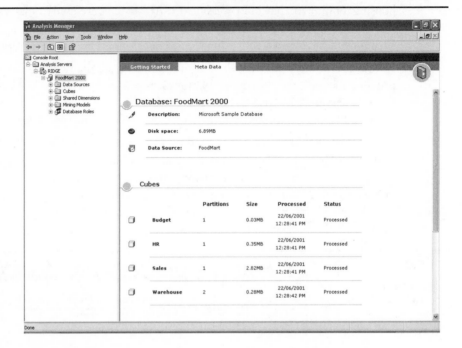

## Data Transformation Services

The Data Transformation Services (DTS) component is used to import and export data to and from SQL Server 2000. It can be accessed via the Data Transformation Services Import/Export Wizard, which in turn in accessed from the Microsoft SQL Server Start menu options. The opening screen of the wizard is shown in Figure A.3.

DTS can also be accessed by opening the DTS Designer in SQL Server Enterprise Manager. To do so, double-click the Data Transformation Services folder in SQL Server Enterprise Manager, right-click the Local Packages node, and choose New Package. Elements for the transformation can be dragged and dropped into the designer window, graphically building your transformation process from the connections required (between your data source and destination) to the range of tasks required. Figure A.4 shows the designer begin used to import data from an Excel spreadsheet into a SQL Server database.

FIGURE A.3:

The Data Transformation
Services Import/Export
Wizard

FIGURE A.3:

The Data Transformation
Services Import/Export
Wizard

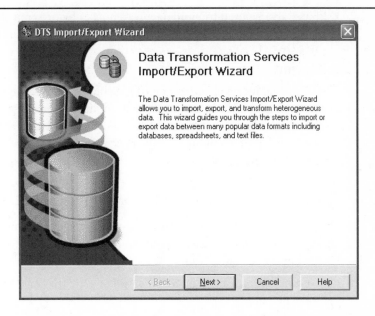

FIGURE A.4:

Using the DTS Designer

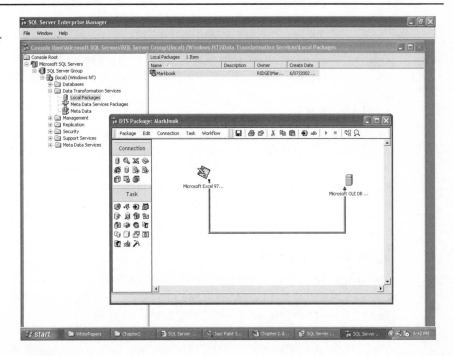

DTS can also be used to build data warehouses by extracting and processing data from multiple Online Transaction Processing (OLTP) sources such as other SQL Server databases.

## Replication

Replication enables synchronization of data between multiple databases. This might be a group of SQL Server 2000 databases or it might include any other ODBC- or OLEDB-compliant databases such as Oracle. It enables offline databases (such as those used on Windows CE devices or laptop computers) to be synchronized at intervals with the main corporate database, and it enables a database to be run from multiple computers to increase performance and reliability.

There are three main types of replication supported by SQL Server 2000:

- Transactional replication is for use in cluster situations. Transactions are carried out on one machine and then propagated downstream to additional copies of the database. The process is fast but not instantaneous.

- Snapshot replication produces a complete copy (or snapshot) of the data is taken at a particular time.

- Merge replication is used for offline machines (such as laptops) to synchronize their databases with the central database at irregular (or regular) intervals.

SQL Server 2000 replication relies on a Publisher/Subscription model to replicate data. The *Publisher* is the server that contains the data to be replicated. The *Subscriber* is the server that receives the replicated data. Replication is set up from Enterprise Manager.

## English Query

As with Analysis Services, the SQL Server 2000 English Query service also needs to be explicitly installed and is not a default installation under SQL Server 2000. It enables natural language queries to be handled by the database. It translates questions (such as "How many green widgets are in stock?") into SQL statements that can then be processed by the database. It can also be used as a front end for Analysis Services to generate MDX statements for use by OLAP.

## Meta Data Services

Meta Data Services provides a service for managing descriptions of the objects in a database system. It is highly flexible in terms of the information and objects that you choose to store in it. This includes packages created with the DTS system. These can be saved in the Metadata store by using the Save As option in the DTS Designer. (Choose Meta Data Services from the Location drop-down box.) Additionally, you can include logging and information about data lineage by choosing these items in the Properties dialog box (under the Package menu in the DTS Designer). Figure A.5 illustrates the Metadata view of the DTS package previously shown in Figure A.4.

DTS package saved in the Metadata Store

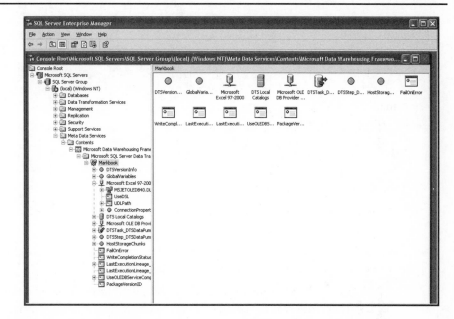

You can also use the Distributed Transaction Coordinator service in conjunction with the Metadata repository to run distributed transactions across the Windows 2000 environment.

## Graphical Tools

SQL Server 2000 includes a range of graphical tools for carrying out specified tasks. We have previously looked at some of these tools when exploring the SQL Server 2000 components. This section is devoted to some of the other key tools available for the developer and the administrator.

### SQL Server Enterprise Manager

Enterprise Manager is the main entry point for administering and working with SQL Server databases. It operates from an MMC console and is illustrated in Figure A.6. The left pane provides access to all the relevant tools and the right pane reflects the contents of the chosen option. In Figure A.6, the list of available databases has been opened.

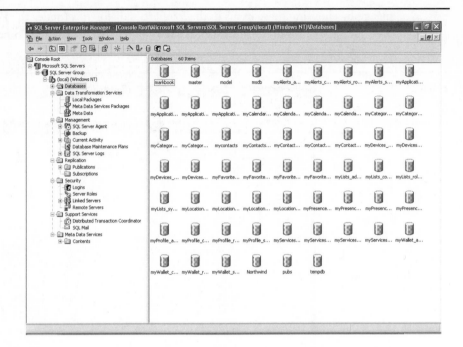

## SQL Query Analyzer

The Query Analyzer is the main place to build and run T-SQL scripts. It can be accessed directly from its shortcut in the Microsoft SQL Server section of the Start menu. A number of improvements have been made to the tool in SQL Server 2000, such as the inclusion of a debugger for stored procedures.

Figure A.7 shows the Query Analyzer with the Object Browser (left pane) open to Templates and a simple Create Database template open in the right pane. The Object Browser can also be tabbed to view available databases and other objects such as the various available functions.

## SQL Server Service Manager

The Service Manager is a handy little tool that sits in the Taskbar tray and can be used to start, pause, and stop a number of SQL Server 2000 services such as SQL Server itself, the Distributed Transaction Coordinator, OLAP services, and SQL Server Agent. It displays a green arrow for an active service, a black pause symbol for a paused service, and a red box for a stopped service. Because it is normally set to SQL Server, it gives a quick indication of the relevant health and status of the server from the desktop. It can also be accessed via the SQL Server section of the Start menu.

FIGURE A.7:

The SQL Query Analyzer

FIGURE A.7:

The SQL Query Analyzer

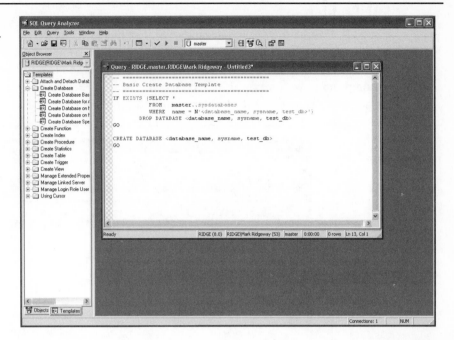

The Service Manager is shown in Figure A.8, and Figure A.9 shows the Manager running in the Taskbar tray.

FIGURE A.8:

SQL Server Service Manager

FIGURE A.9:

Service Manager running in the Taskbar tray

## SQL Profiler

The SQL Profiler can be used to capture SQL statements and queries sent to the server. It is a very useful tool for diagnosing various problems and confirming that everything is happening as it should. It can be used to resolve performance issues and identify any malicious attempts to compromise your server. It is accessed via the SQL Server portion of the Start menu. Figure A.10 shows the SQL Profiler running a simple trace.

**FIGURE A.10:**

The SQL Profiler

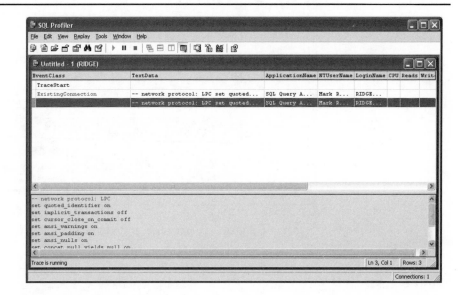

## SQL Server Agent

The Server Agent is a scheduling tool that can be accessed from Enterprise Manager. It can be used to handle alerts, run scripts, and complete assorted tasks.

## Configure SQL XML Support in IIS

The IIS Configuration tool is used to manage virtual directories for SQL Server in Internet Information Server (IIS). It is necessary for configuring XML support and setting up XML Web services for use with SQL Server. The SQLXML 3 package ships with a more updated and advanced version of this tool, which is shown in Figure A.11.

## Additional Graphical Tools

A number of other tools are also available, including the Server Network and Client Network utilities, which are used to manage server and client Net-Libraries.

**FIGURE A.11:**

The IIS Configuration tool for SQLXML 3

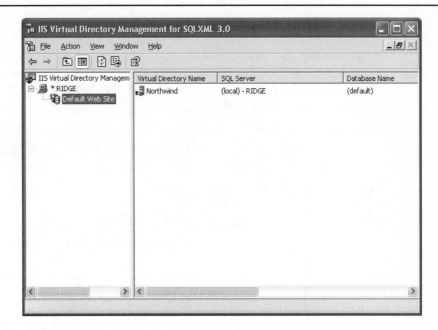

The SQL Server Upgrade Wizard is used to upgrade databases from SQL Server 6.5 to SQL Server 2000.

## Installing SQL Server 2000

The installation procedure for SQL Server 2000 is quite straightforward. There are a few configuration options to set as you go through the process, but most of them can be altered later if necessary. You will also need to install Analysis Services and English Query separately (if you wish to use them), although it all occurs from the same interface, as you can see in Figure A.12. Installation of the three main components (Database Engine, English Query, Analysis Services) occurs from the SQL Server 2000 Components screen. The SQL Server 2000 Prerequisites option has a control library update for Windows 95.

As a developer, your most likely choice of installation will be the Developer Edition, particularly if you do most of your development work on a non-server OS such as Windows XP Professional. However, deployment may mean making some choices regarding appropriate editions. Previously in this appendix, we briefly covered each of the editions of SQL Server 2000. The installation process for the other editions is very similar to that for Developer.

When setting up a production copy, you will need to consider such issues as the desirability of loading SQL Server onto a separate disk or partition of the operating system (many server setups keep a logical and/or physical separation between application and system software). It is also a good idea to set up the data files on a separate disk away from the OS and application software to help boost performance.

**FIGURE A.12:**

Installation screen for
SQL Server 2000,
Developer Edition

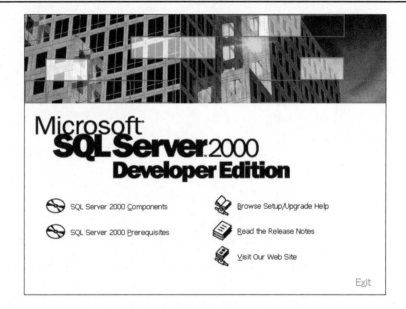

With SQL Server 2000, you can load multiple copies (*instances*) of the program onto a single server (up to 16 instances). These instances are entirely separate from each other and enable a single machine to host databases from separate clients.

Figure A.13 illustrates the Setup Type dialog box. This is where you can make some decisions about location of data and application files.

The next dialog box (Services Accounts) gives you the option to run the SQL Server and Server Agent services under a local account (which makes sense for stand-alone machines) or as a domain user (this is essential if you are on a network and plan to use network resources). The accounts can be individually customized for the two services or the services can both operate from the same account (which is quite satisfactory). If you are choosing the domain user option, make sure the account is one that has domain administrative privileges. It is normal practice to set up a specific domain account to handle this role rather than just assigning it to an existing one. The Services Accounts dialog box is shown in Figure A.14.

**FIGURE A.13:**

The Setup Type
dialog box

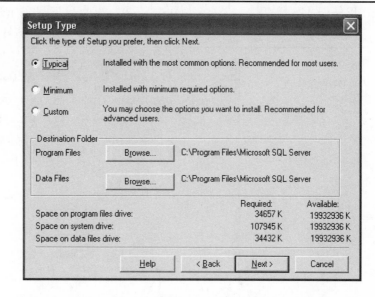

**FIGURE A.14:**

The Services Accounts
dialog box

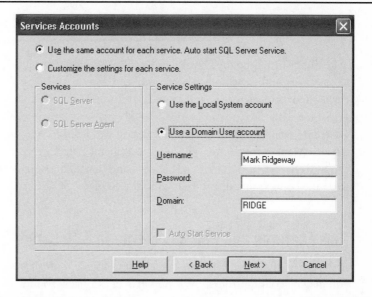

The Authentication Mode dialog box (Figure A.15) gives you a choice between Windows authentication and a combination of Windows authentication and SQL Server authentication. The second choice is probably the better option for development purposes. You will be asked to enter a password for the sa (SQL Server system administrator) account. This can be changed at any time from the security section of Enterprise Manager.

**FIGURE A.15:**

The Authentication Mode dialog box

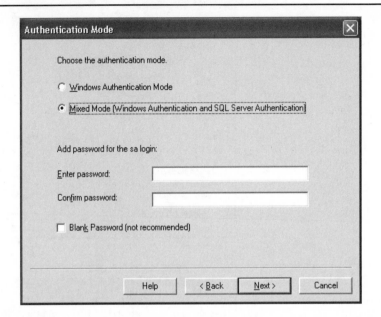

If you are installing the Developer Edition, you should now be presented with a message that all necessary information has been gathered and the installer will proceed on its merry way through to a satisfactory installation. In an Enterprise or Standard installation, you may also be presented with the Collation settings and Network Libraries dialog boxes. If you have installed a second instance of SQL Server 2000, you will need to start the new instance by using the Service Manager, and you will need to register it in Enterprise Manager by right-clicking the SQL Server Group icon in the left-hand pane, choosing New SQL Server Registration from the context menu, and following the Register SQL Server Wizard.

## New Features and Enhancements in SQL Server 2000

Although SQL Server 2000 has been with us for a couple of years now, it is quite possible that you may be coming from a SQL Server 7 or 6.5 backgrounds.

SQL Server 2000 introduced a number of new features and enhancements over previous versions. We will not cover them all here (some have been covered previously), but it is worth highlighting a few of the main ones.

From the perspective of working with Visual Studio .NET, probably the main change has been the inclusion of XML support. Additionally, other new features have included user-defined functions, indexed views, new data types (bigint, sql_variant, and table), text in row data, federated database servers (distributed partition views), Kerberos security, cascading referential integrity constraints, and INSTEAD OF and AFTER triggers.

Enhancements have included major revisions of OLAP services (now Analysis Services) and the Repository component (now Meta Data Services). Other enhancements include improvements to full-text search, 64GB memory support (Enterprise Edition on Windows 2000 Advanced Data Server), back up and restore, and indexing.

There is much more to SQL Server 2000 than can be covered in this appendix. If you require more information, then *Mastering SQL Server 2000* by Mike Gunderloy and Joseph L. Jorden (Sybex, 2000) and *SQL Server Developer's Guide to OLAP with Analysis Services* by Mike Gunderloy and Tim Sneath (Sybex, 2001) are two excellent professional references on the topic.

# Index

**Note to the reader:** Throughout this index **boldfaced** page numbers indicate primary discussions of a topic. *Italicized* page numbers indicate illustrations.

# B

# G

# O

# V

# Z

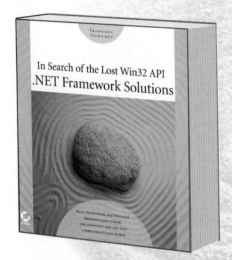

*The quotation at the bottom of the front cover is taken from Lao Tzu's* Tao Te Ching, *the classic work of Taoist philosophy. These particular verses are from the translation by D. C. Lau (copyright 1963) and are part of a larger exploration of the nature of the Tao, sometimes translated as "the way."*

*It is traditionally held that Lao Tzu lived in the fifth century* B.C. *in China, but it is unclear whether he was actually a historical figure. The concepts embodied in the* Tao Te Ching *influenced religious thinking in the Far East, including Zen Buddhism in Japan. Many in the West, however, have wrongly understood the* Tao Te Ching *to be primarily a mystical work; in fact, much of the advice in the book is grounded in a practical moral philosophy governing personal conduct.*